ASCENT
CENTER FOR TECHNICAL KNOWLEDGE

AutoCAD® 2018
Review for Professional Certification

Official Certification Preparation

Student Guide
Mixed Units - 1st Edition

AUTODESK
Authorized Publisher

ASCENT - Center for Technical Knowledge®
AutoCAD® 2018
Review for Professional Certification
Mixed Units - 1st Edition

Prepared and produced by:

ASCENT Center for Technical Knowledge
630 Peter Jefferson Parkway, Suite 175
Charlottesville, VA 22911

866-527-2368
www.ASCENTed.com

Lead Contributor: Renu Muthoo

ASCENT - Center for Technical Knowledge is a division of Rand Worldwide, Inc., providing custom developed knowledge products and services for leading engineering software applications. ASCENT is focused on specializing in the creation of education programs that incorporate the best of classroom learning and technology-based training offerings.

We welcome any comments you may have regarding this student guide, or any of our products. To contact us please email: feedback@ASCENTed.com.

© ASCENT - Center for Technical Knowledge, 2017

All rights reserved. No part of this guide may be reproduced in any form by any photographic, electronic, mechanical or other means or used in any information storage and retrieval system without the written permission of ASCENT, a division of Rand Worldwide, Inc.

The following are registered trademarks or trademarks of Autodesk, Inc., and/or its subsidiaries and/or affiliates in the USA and other countries: 123D, 3ds Max, Alias, ATC, AutoCAD LT, AutoCAD, Autodesk, the Autodesk logo, Autodesk 123D, Autodesk Homestyler, Autodesk Inventor, Autodesk MapGuide, Autodesk Streamline, AutoLISP, AutoSketch, AutoSnap, AutoTrack, Backburner, Backdraft, Beast, BIM 360, Burn, Buzzsaw, CADmep, CAiCE, CAMduct, Civil 3D, Combustion, Communication Specification, Configurator 360, Constructware, Content Explorer, Creative Bridge, Dancing Baby (image), DesignCenter, DesignKids, DesignStudio, Discreet, DWF, DWG, DWG (design/logo), DWG Extreme, DWG TrueConvert, DWG TrueView, DWGX, DXF, Ecotect, Ember, ESTmep, FABmep, Face Robot, FBX, Fempro, Fire, Flame, Flare, Flint, ForceEffect, FormIt 360, Freewheel, Fusion 360, Glue, Green Building Studio, Heidi, Homestyler, HumanIK, i-drop, ImageModeler, Incinerator, Inferno, InfraWorks, Instructables, Instructables (stylized robot design/logo), Inventor, Inventor HSM, Inventor LT, Lustre, Maya, Maya LT, MIMI, Mockup 360, Moldflow Plastics Advisers, Moldflow Plastics Insight, Moldflow, Moondust, MotionBuilder, Movimento, MPA (design/logo), MPA, MPI (design/logo), MPX (design/logo), MPX, Mudbox, Navisworks, ObjectARX, ObjectDBX, Opticore, P9, Pier 9, Pixlr, Pixlr-o-matic, Productstream, Publisher 360, RasterDWG, RealDWG, ReCap, ReCap 360, Remote, Revit LT, Revit, RiverCAD, Robot, Scaleform, Showcase, Showcase 360, SketchBook, Smoke, Socialcam, Softimage, Spark & Design, Spark Logo, Sparks, SteeringWheels, Stitcher, Stone, StormNET, TinkerBox, Tinkercad, Tinkerplay, ToolClip, Topobase, Toxik, TrustedDWG, T-Splines, ViewCube, Visual LISP, Visual, VRED, Wire, Wiretap, WiretapCentral, XSI.

NASTRAN is a registered trademark of the National Aeronautics Space Administration.

All other brand names, product names, or trademarks belong to their respective holders.

General Disclaimer:

Notwithstanding any language to the contrary, nothing contained herein constitutes nor is intended to constitute an offer, inducement, promise, or contract of any kind. The data contained herein is for informational purposes only and is not represented to be error free. ASCENT, its agents and employees, expressly disclaim any liability for any damages, losses or other expenses arising in connection with the use of its materials or in connection with any failure of performance, error, omission even if ASCENT, or its representatives, are advised of the possibility of such damages, losses or other expenses. No consequential damages can be sought against ASCENT or Rand Worldwide, Inc. for the use of these materials by any third parties or for any direct or indirect result of that use.

The information contained herein is intended to be of general interest to you and is provided "as is", and it does not address the circumstances of any particular individual or entity. Nothing herein constitutes professional advice, nor does it constitute a comprehensive or complete statement of the issues discussed thereto. ASCENT does not warrant that the document or information will be error free or will meet any particular criteria of performance or quality. In particular (but without limitation) information may be rendered inaccurate by changes made to the subject of the materials (i.e. applicable software). Rand Worldwide, Inc. specifically disclaims any warranty, either expressed or implied, including the warranty of fitness for a particular purpose.

Contents

Preface xi

In this Guide xv

Practice Files xvii

Chapter 1: Draw Objects 1-1

    1.1 Drawing Lines 1-2
          Specifying Length and Angle 1-2
          Line Command Options 1-3

    1.2 Drawing Vertical and Horizontal Lines 1-4
          Polar Tracking 1-4
          Ortho Mode 1-6

    1.3 Drawing Rectangles 1-7

    1.4 Drawing Circles 1-8

    Practice 1a Basic Drawing and Editing Commands 1-11

    Practice 1b Create Simple Shapes 1-17

    Practice 1c Create a Simple Drawing 1-18

    1.5 Drawing Arcs 1-19
          Arc Command Options 1-19
          Notes on Arcs 1-20

    Practice 1d Drawing an Arc 1-21

    1.6 Drawing Polygons 1-23

    Practice 1e Drawing Polygons 1-25

Chapter 2: Draw with Accuracy 2-1

    2.1 Polar Tracking at Angles 2-2

    Practice 2a Polar Tracking 2-4

    2.2 Object Snap Tracking 2-6

© 2017, ASCENT - Center for Technical Knowledge®

Practice 2b Object Snap Tracking I 2-8
Practice 2c Object Snap Tracking II 2-10
2.3 Locating Points with Tracking 2-12
    Object Snap Tracking Review 2-12
    Temporary Track Point 2-12
Practice 2d Locating Points with Tracking (Mechanical) 2-14
Practice 2e Locating Points with Tracking (Architectural) 2-16
2.4 Cartesian Workspace 2-18
    Locating Points 2-18
    Measuring Angles 2-19
    Drawings Created at Full Scale 2-19
2.5 Coordinate Entry 2-20
    Absolute Cartesian Coordinates (X,Y) 2-20
    Relative Cartesian Coordinates (@X,Y) 2-20
    Relative Polar Coordinates (@Distance< Angle) 2-22
    Notes on Coordinate Entry 2-23
Practice 2f Drawing Using Coordinate Entry 2-25
2.6 Isometric Drawing Environment 2-26

Chapter 3: Modify Objects 3-1

3.1 Moving Objects 3-2
3.2 Copying Objects 3-4
3.3 Copying and Pasting Between Drawings 3-6
    Match Properties Across Drawings 3-7
Practice 3a Working in Multiple Drawings 3-8
3.4 Rotating Objects 3-11
3.5 Scaling Objects 3-13
Practice 3b Modifying Objects 3-14
3.6 Creating Arrays of Objects 3-21
    Rectangular Array 3-21
    Polar Array 3-23
    Path Array 3-24
Practice 3c Rectangular Array 3-25
Practice 3d Polar Array 3-27
Practice 3e Path Array 3-29
3.7 Trimming and Extending Objects 3-31
    Trimming Objects 3-31
    Extending Objects 3-34

Contents

Practice 3f Extending and Trimming Objects 3-35
Practice 3g Trimming Objects on a Drawing 3-36
3.8 Mirroring Objects 3-38
3.9 Offsetting Objects 3-39
Practice 3h Offsetting Objects 3-41
3.10 Editing with Grips 3-43
    Working with Hot Grips 3-43
    Grips with Dynamic Dimensions 3-45
3.11 Using Grips Effectively 3-47
    Changing the Base Point 3-48
    Copying with Grips 3-48
    Rotate and Scale with the Reference Option 3-49
    Stretching Multiple Objects 3-50
    Grip Settings 3-50
Practice 3i Editing with Grips I 3-52
Practice 3j Editing with Grips II 3-54
Practice 3k Using Grips Effectively 3-55
3.12 Creating Fillets and Chamfers 3-56
    Filleting Objects 3-56
    Chamfering Objects 3-57
Practice 3l Filleting Objects 3-59
Practice 3m Chamfering Objects 3-60

Chapter 4: Use Additional Drawing Techniques **4-1**
4.1 Drawing Polylines 4-2
4.2 Editing Polylines 4-4
    Converting Lines and Arcs to Polylines 4-6
    Turning Polylines into Lines and Arcs 4-7
Practice 4a Drawing and Editing Polylines 4-8
4.3 Splines 4-12
4.4 Hatching 4-13
    Applying a Hatch: Tool Palettes 4-14
    Applying a Hatch: Hatch Command 4-15
    Hatch Pattern and Properties 4-16
    Hatch Options 4-20
4.5 Editing Hatches 4-23
    Hatch Editor Tab 4-23
    Edit Hatch Command 4-24
    Grip Editing Hatch Boundaries 4-25

Practice 4b Hatching Using the Tool Palettes 4-28

Practice 4c Hatching (Mechanical) 4-30

Practice 4d Hatching (Architectural) 4-34

Chapter 5: Organize Objects 5-1

   5.1 Working with Object Properties... 5-2
        Quick Properties.. 5-2
        Properties Palette.. 5-3
        Matching Properties 5-7
        Quick Select 5-8

   Practice 5a Working with Object Properties (Mechanical) 5-10

   Practice 5b Working with Object Properties (Architectural) 5-12

   5.2 Changing an Object's Layer.. 5-14
        Change with Layer Control.. 5-14
        Match Layer 5-15

   Practice 5c Changing an Object's Layer... 5-16

   5.3 Layer States 5-18
        On/Off... 5-18
        Thaw/Freeze 5-18
        Lock/ Unlock... 5-19

   Practice 5d Working with Layers and Layer States 5-20

   5.4 Setting Layer States.. 5-23

   Practice 5e Setting Up Layer States (Mechanical) 5-28

   5.5 What are Layers? 5-31
        Setting the Current Layer 5-32

   5.6 Additional Layer Tools 5-34
        Changing Object Layer States 5-34
        Isolating Layers 5-36
        Changing an Object's Layer 5-37
        Modifying Layers 5-38
        Layer Walk 5-39

   Practice 5f Layer Tools 5-42

   5.7 Creating New Layers... 5-44
        Layer Properties Manager.. 5-44
        Other Layer Options 5-49

   Practice 5g Saving a Template... 5-51

   5.8 Working in the Layer Properties Manager 5-57
        Displaying Columns in the Layer Properties Manager 5-57
        Layer Settings 5-60

   Practice 5h Working in the Layer Properties Manager 5-64

Chapter 6: Reuse Existing Content 6-1

6.1 What are Blocks? 6-2

6.2 Working with Dynamic Blocks 6-4
Manipulating Dynamic Blocks 6-4

6.3 Inserting Blocks 6-6

6.4 Inserting Blocks using the Tool Palettes 6-8
Controlling the Tool Palettes Window 6-9

6.5 Inserting Blocks using the DesignCenter 6-11
DesignCenter Content 6-12

Practice 6a Working with Blocks 6-14

6.6 Creating Blocks 6-19
Creating Single Named Objects 6-19
Block Settings 6-20
Creating Drawing Files from Objects (WBlock) 6-22

6.7 Editing Blocks 6-24

Practice 6b Create and Edit Blocks 6-27

6.8 Adding Blocks to Tool Palettes 6-31

6.9 Modifying Tool Properties in Tool Palettes 6-34
Modifying Tool Properties 6-34
Redefining Blocks in Tool Palettes 6-36

Practice 6c Modifying Tool Properties 6-37

6.10 Inserting Blocks with Attributes 6-40
What are Attributes? 6-40
How Attribute Values Are Entered 6-40
Retain Attribute Display 6-41

6.11 Editing Attribute Values 6-43
Editing Attributes One at a Time 6-43
Editing Multiple Attribute Values 6-45

Practice 6d Inserting and Editing Attribute Values 6-47

6.12 Defining Attributes 6-51
Attribute Definition 6-52
Associating Attributes with Blocks 6-54

Practice 6e Defining Attributes 6-55

6.13 Redefining Blocks with Attributes 6-58
Updating Blocks with New Attributes 6-60

Practice 6f Redefining Blocks with Attributes 6-62

6.14 Extracting Attributes 6-65

Practice 6g Extracting Object Data to a Table 6-73

Practice 6h Mechanical Attribute Project - Amplifier 6-76

6.15 Attaching External References 6-80
　External References Palette 6-82

6.16 Modifying External References 6-88
　Opening Reference Files 6-88
　Detaching and Unloading Reference Files 6-89
　Clipping Reference Files 6-91
　Modifying References 6-93
　Reference File Properties 6-94
　DWF Specific Adjustments 6-96

6.17 Xref Specific Information 6-98
　Attachments vs. Overlays 6-98
　Xref Layers 6-99
　Binding Drawing Reference Files 6-101
　Binding Drawing Reference File Components 6-102
　Demand Loading 6-103

Practice 6i Attaching External References 6-104

Chapter 7: Annotate Drawings 7-1

7.1 Adding Text in a Drawing 7-2
　Multiline Text 7-2
　Copying and Importing Text 7-4
　Spell Checking 7-5

Practice 7a Adding Text in a Drawing 7-7

7.2 Modifying Multiline Text 7-10
　Editing Multiline Text 7-10
　Changing Text Width and Length 7-10
　Changing Text Properties 7-11
　Spell Checking 7-12

Practice 7b Modifying Multiline Text 7-14

7.3 Formatting Multiline Text 7-17
　Formatting the Multiline Text Object 7-17
　Formatting Selected Text 7-19
　Formatting Paragraph Text 7-20
　Creating Columns 7-24

Practice 7c Formatting Multiline Text in a Drawing 7-26

7.4 Dimensioning Concepts 7-31
　General Dimensioning 7-32

7.5 Adding Linear Dimensions 7-33
　Individual Linear Dimensions 7-33
　Multiple Linear Dimensions 7-35
　Quick Dimensioning 7-36

Practice 7d Adding Linear Dimensions (Architectural)	**7-37**
7.6 Adding Radial and Angular Dimensions	**7-40**
Radius and Diameter Dimensions	7-40
Angular Dimensions	7-44
Practice 7e Adding Radial and Angular Dimensions (Architectural)	**7-46**
7.7 Editing Dimensions	**7-49**
Dimension Shortcut Menu	7-50
Editing Dimensions Using Grips	7-50
Dimension Grips Shortcut Options	7-51
Editing the Dimension Text	7-52
Adjusting Dimension Spacing	7-53
Dimension Breaks	7-54
Practice 7f Editing Dimensions (Mechanical)	**7-55**
7.8 Adding Notes with Leaders to Your Drawing	**7-57**
Modifying Multileaders	7-59
Practice 7g Adding Notes to Your Drawing	**7-64**
7.9 Working with Annotations	**7-67**
Working with Annotative Styles	7-68
7.10 Creating Text Styles	**7-70**
Practice 7h Creating and Using Text Styles	**7-73**
7.11 Creating Dimension Styles	**7-74**
Modifying Dimension Styles	7-76
Creating Dimension Sub-Styles	7-81
Practice 7i Dimension Styles (Mechanical)	**7-83**
7.12 Creating Multileader Styles	**7-86**
Practice 7j Creating Multileader Styles	**7-90**
7.13 Additional Annotative Scale Features	**7-92**
Modifying Annotative Object Scales	7-93
Practice 7k Additional Annotative Scale Features	**7-95**
7.14 Annotation Scale Overview	**7-98**
Working with Annotative Styles	7-99
Viewing Annotative Objects at Different Scales	7-101
Annotation Scale and Model Space	7-103
Modifying Annotative Object Scales	7-103
Practice 7l Annotation Scale	**7-106**
7.15 Creating Tables	**7-110**
Populating Table Cells	7-112
Calculations in Tables	7-114

Practice 7m Creating Tables 7-116

7.16 Modifying Tables 7-118
    Modifying Cells, Rows, and Columns 7-118
    Modifying the Entire Table 7-121

Practice 7n Modifying Tables 7-123

7.17 Working with Linked Tables 7-126
    Using the Data Link Manager 7-129
    Updating Table Links 7-131

7.18 Creating Table Styles 7-133
    Table Style Options 7-134
    Cell Style Options 7-135

Practice 7o Working with Tables 7-138

Chapter 8: Layouts and Printing 8-1

8.1 Working in Layouts 8-2
    Switch Between Paper Space & Model Space 8-4

8.2 Creating Layouts 8-6

8.3 Creating and Using Named Views 8-8

8.4 Advanced Viewport Options 8-11
    Creating Viewports from Named Views 8-11
    Clipping Viewports 8-15

8.5 Creating Layout Viewports 8-16
    Rectangular Viewports 8-16
    Polygonal Viewports 8-17
    Object Viewports 8-17
    Named Viewports 8-17
    Modifying Viewports with Grips 8-19
    Scaling Viewports 8-19
    Locking the Viewport 8-20

8.6 Layer Overrides in Viewports 8-21
    Overriding Layer Properties in Viewports 8-21
    Freezing Layers in Viewports 8-23

Practice 8a Working With Layouts 8-24

Practice 8b Viewports and Named Views 8-29

8.7 Printing Concepts 8-35
    Model Space Printing 8-36
    Paper Space Layout Printing 8-37

8.8 Printing Layouts 8-38
    Previewing the Plot 8-40

Contents

8.9 Print and Plot Settings	8-41
Practice 8c Printing Layouts and Check Plots	8-45
8.10 Output For Electronic Review	8-48
Plotting Electronic Files	8-49
Exporting DWF or PDF Files	8-50
8.11 Publishing Drawing Sets	8-53
Practice 8d Reviewing and Publishing Drawing Sets	8-56
Appendix A: Review Questions	**A-1**
A.1 Draw Objects	A-2
A.2 Draw with Accuracy	A-4
A.3 Modify Objects	A-6
A.4 Use Additional Drawing Techniques	A-9
A.5 Organize Objects	A-11
A.6 Reuse Existing Content	A-13
A.7 Annotate Drawings	A-18
A.8 Layouts and Printing	A-24
Index	**Index-1**

Preface

AutoCAD® 2018: Review for Professional Certification is a comprehensive review guide to assist in preparing for the AutoCAD Certified Professional exam. It enables experienced users to review learning content from ASCENT that is related to the exam objectives.

New users of the AutoCAD® 2018 software should refer to the following ASCENT student guides:

- *AutoCAD®/AutoCAD LT® 2018: Fundamentals*
- *AutoCAD®/AutoCAD LT® 2018: Essentials*
- *AutoCAD®/AutoCAD LT® 2018: Beyond the Basics*
- *AutoCAD® 2018: Advanced*

Autodesk Certification Exam Objectives

Exam Topic	Exam Objective	Chapter(s)
Draw Objects	Draw lines and rectangles	• 1.1 to 1.3
	Draw circles, arcs, and polygons	• 1.4 to 1.6
Draw with Accuracy	Use object-snap tracking	• 2.1 to 2.3
	Use Coordinate Systems	• 2.4 & 2.5
	Make isometric drawings	• 2.6
Modify Objects	Move and copy objects	• 3.1 to 3.3
	Rotate and scale objects	• 3.4 & 3.5
	Create and use arrays	• 3.6
	Trim and extend objects	• 3.7
	Offset and mirror objects	• 3.8 & 3.9
	Use grip editing	• 3.10 & 3.11
	Fillet and chamfer objects	• 3.12

Exam Topic	Exam Objective	Chapter(s)
Use Additional Drawing Techniques	Draw and edit polylines	• 4.1 & 4.2
	Blend between objects with splines	• 4.3
	Apply hatches and gradients	• 4.4 & 4.5
Organize Objects	Change object properties	• 5.1
	Alter layer assignments for objects	• 5.2
	Control layer visibility	• 5.3 & 5.4
	Assign properties by object or layer	• 5.5
	Manage layer properties	• 5.3, 5.6 to 5.8
Reuse Existing Content	Work with blocks	• 6.1 to 6.7
	Manage block attributes	• 6.8 to 6.12
	Reference external drawings and images	• 6.13 to 6.15
Annotate Drawings	Add and modify text	• 7.1 to 7.3
	Use dimensions	• 7.4 to 7.7
	Add and modify multileaders	• 7.8
	Create and assign annotative styles	• 7.9 to 7.14
	Use tables	• 7.15 to 7.18
Layouts and Printing	Create layouts	• 8.1 to 8.3
	Use viewports	• 8.4 to 8.6
	Set printing and plotting options	• 8.7 to 8.10

Note on Software Setup

This review guide assumes a standard installation of the software using the default preferences during installation. Lectures and practices use the standard software templates and default options for the Content Libraries.

Students and Educators can Access Free Autodesk Software and Resources

Autodesk challenges you to get started with free educational licenses for professional software and creativity apps used by millions of architects, engineers, designers, and hobbyists today. Bring Autodesk software into your classroom, studio, or workshop to learn, teach, and explore real-world design challenges the way professionals do.

Get started today - register at the Autodesk Education Community and download one of the many Autodesk software applications available.

Visit www.autodesk.com/joinedu/

Note: Free products are subject to the terms and conditions of the end-user license and services agreement that accompanies the software. The software is for personal use for education purposes and is not intended for classroom or lab use.

Lead Contributor: Renu Muthoo

Renu uses her instructional design training to develop courseware for AutoCAD and AutoCAD vertical products, Autodesk 3ds Max, Autodesk Showcase and various other Autodesk software products. She has worked with Autodesk products for the past 20 years with a main focus on design visualization software.

Renu holds a bachelor's degree in Computer Engineering and started her career as a Instructional Designer/Author where she co-authored a number of Autodesk 3ds Max and AutoCAD books, some of which were translated into other languages for a wide audience reach. In her next role as a Technical Specialist at a 3D visualization company, Renu used 3ds Max in real-world scenarios on a daily basis. There, she developed customized 3D web planner solutions to create specialized 3D models with photorealistic texturing and lighting to produce high quality renderings.

Renu Muthoo has been the lead contributor for the *AutoCAD Review for Professional Certification* since 2015.

In this Guide

The following images highlight some of the features that can be found in this Student Guide.

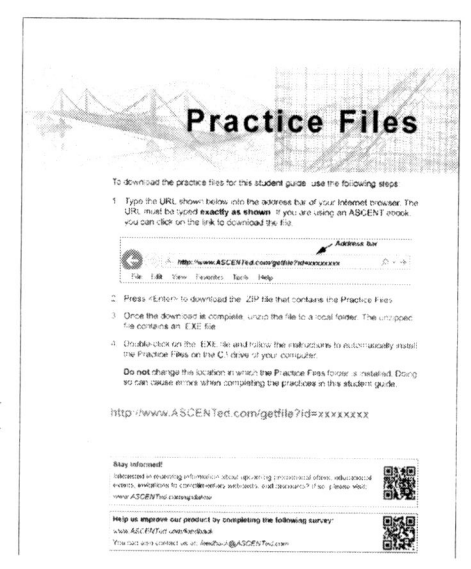

Link for practice files

Practice Files

The Practice Files page tells you how to download and install the practice files that are provided with this student guide.

Exam Topics and Objectives in the chapter

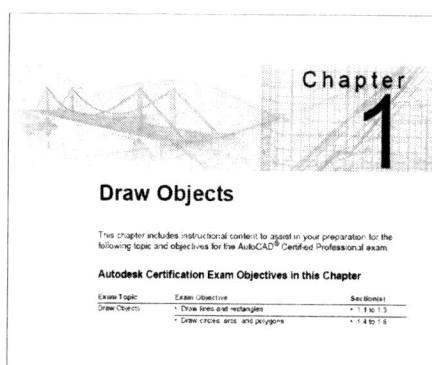

Chapters

Each chapter begins with a list of the exam topics and objectives covered in the chapter.

Side notes
Side notes are hints or additional information for the current topic.

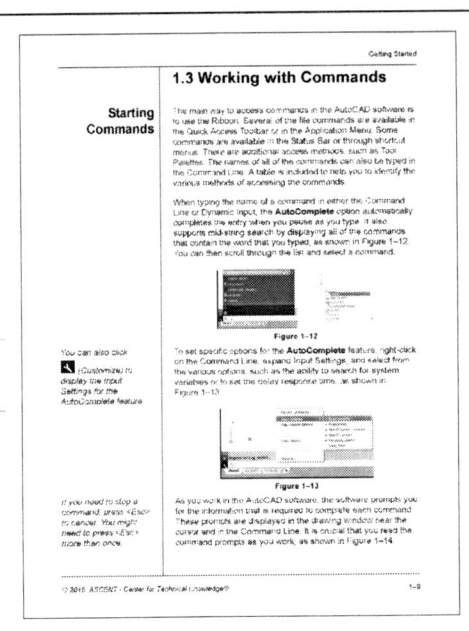

Instructional Content
Each chapter is split into a series of sections of instructional content on specific topics. These lectures include the descriptions, step-by-step procedures, figures, hints, and information you need to achieve the chapter's exam objectives.

Practice Objectives

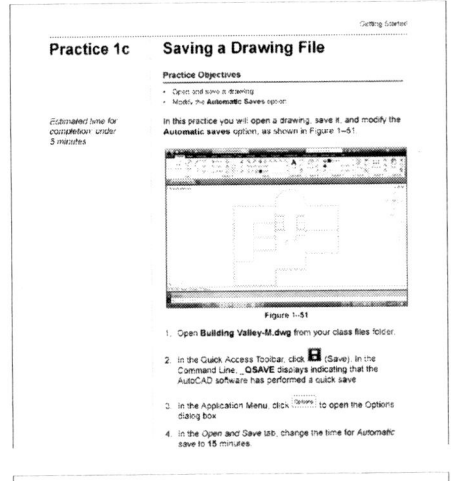

Practices
Practices enable you to use the software to perform a hands-on review of a topic.

Some practices require you to use prepared practice files, which can be downloaded from the link found on the Practice Files page.

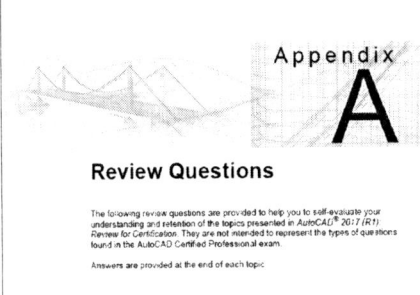

Review Questions
Review questions, located at the end of this guide, enable you to self-evaluate your understanding of the key topics and objectives in this guide.

Practice Files

To download the practice files for this student guide, use the following steps:

1. Type the URL shown below into the address bar of your Internet browser. The URL must be typed **exactly as shown**. If you are using an ASCENT ebook, you can click on the link to download the file.

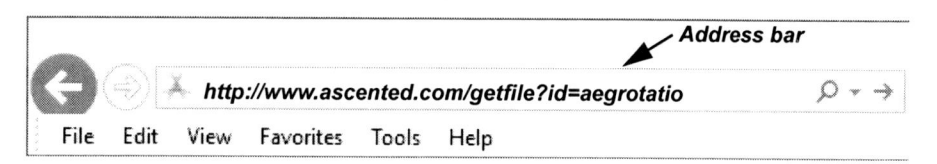

   Address bar
   http://www.ascented.com/getfile?id=aegrotatio

2. Press <Enter> to download the .ZIP file that contains the Practice Files.

3. Once the download is complete, unzip the file to a local folder. The unzipped file contains an .EXE file.

4. Double-click on the .EXE file and follow the instructions to automatically install the Practice Files on the C:\ drive of your computer.

   Do not change the location in which the Practice Files folder is installed. Doing so can cause errors when completing the practices in this student guide.

http://www.ascented.com/getfile?id=aegrotatio

Stay Informed!
Interested in receiving information about upcoming promotional offers, educational events, invitations to complimentary webcasts, and discounts? If so, please visit:
www.ASCENTed.com/updates/

Help us improve our product by completing the following survey:
www.ASCENTed.com/feedback
You can also contact us at: *feedback@ASCENTed.com*

© 2017, ASCENT - Center for Technical Knowledge®

Chapter 1

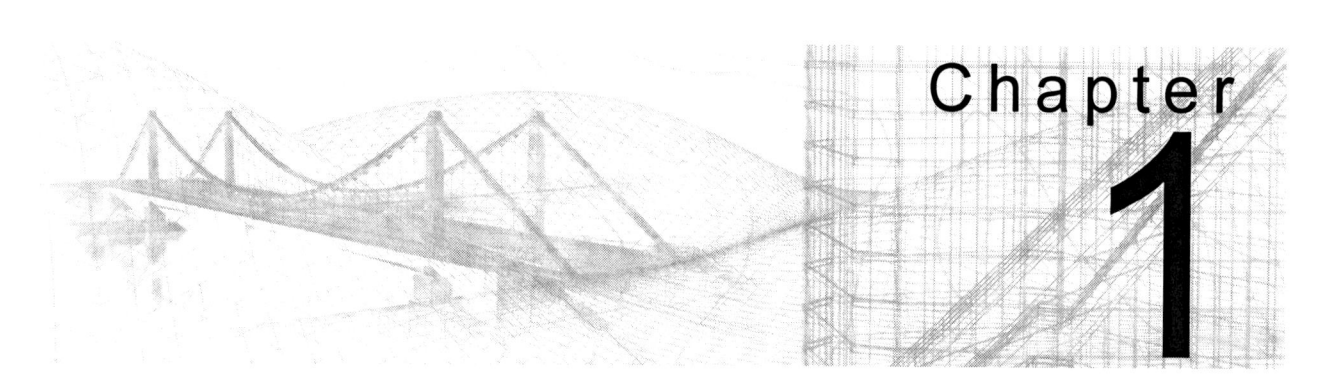

Draw Objects

This chapter includes instructional content to assist in your preparation for the following topic and objectives for the AutoCAD® Certified Professional exam.

Autodesk Certification Exam Objectives in this Chapter

Exam Topic	Exam Objective	Section(s)
Draw Objects	• Draw lines and rectangles	• 1.1 to 1.3
	• Draw circles, arcs, and polygons	• 1.4 to 1.6

1.1 Drawing Lines

The most fundamental drawing element is the line. Almost any drawing contains line segments. The **Line** command enables you to add straight-line segments to the drawing as required, as shown in Figure 1–1. Each segment created with the command is a separate object.

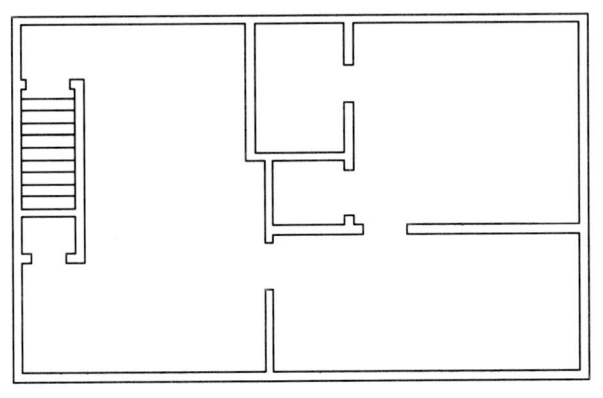

Figure 1–1

How To: Draw a Line

*You can also type **L** or **line** in the Command prompt.*

1. In the ribbon, in the *Home* tab>Draw panel, click (Line).
2. Select the first point.
3. Select the next point.
4. Continue to select points at the *Specify next point:* prompt to create a series of line segments as required or press <Enter> to complete the command.

Specifying Length and Angle

After you select the first point for the line and move the cursor, the AutoCAD® software displays its length and angle. The length value is highlighted, as shown in Figure 1–2. Enter the required length and press <Tab>, which highlights the angle value. Enter the required angle.

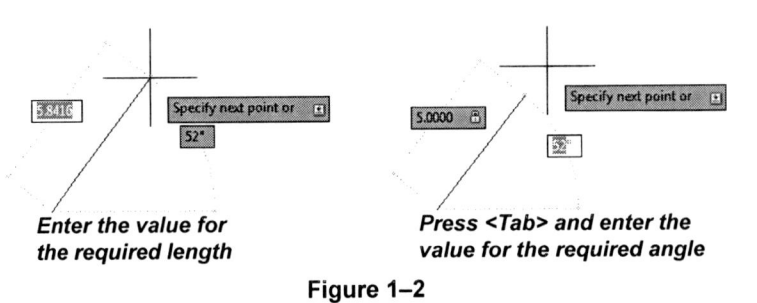

Enter the value for the required length

Press <Tab> and enter the value for the required angle

Figure 1–2

Draw Objects

- The angle depends on the direction in which the cursor is moved. For example, 90° can be either straight up or straight down, depending on where the cursor is located. Move the cursor in the approximate direction first.

- Note that 0° is the positive X-direction (straight and to the right).

- In the Status Bar, **Dynamic Input** must be toggled on for the length and angle to be displayed.

Line Command Options

At the *Specify next point:* prompt, press the <Down Arrow> to display the command options at the cursor prompt, as shown in Figure 1–3. Select an option or type the first letter (**C** or **U**) and press <Enter> to exit the command.

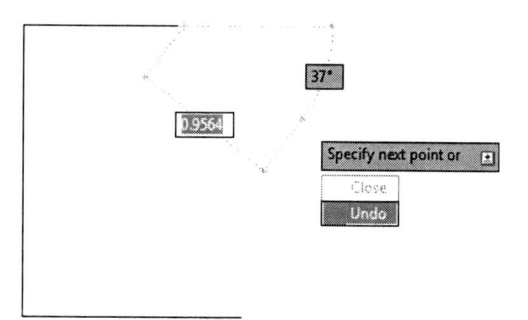

Figure 1–3

Close (C)	After two or more line segments are drawn, this option adds a final line segment between the first and last points entered.
Undo (U)	Removes the last segment drawn.

- You can also right-click at the *Specify next point:* prompt and select **Enter**, **Cancel**, **Close**, or **Undo**.

1.2 Drawing Vertical and Horizontal Lines

Polar Tracking

You can draw lines at specific lengths and angles by typing the numbers, as shown in Figure 1–4. The **Polar Tracking** command is helpful for reducing the amount of typing required as it restricts the movement of the cursor to the already specified (preset) angles.

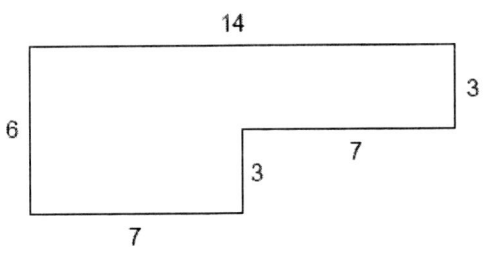

Figure 1–4

- Polar Tracking makes it easy to work with preset angles as you draw. Rather than typing the angle, you move the cursor to find the tracking line (dotted line) and then enter the distance.

- You can set the polar angles as required, but in this section you work with the standard 90° increments.

- To toggle Polar Tracking on and off, click (Polar Tracking) in the Status Bar, as shown in Figure 1–5, or press <F10>.

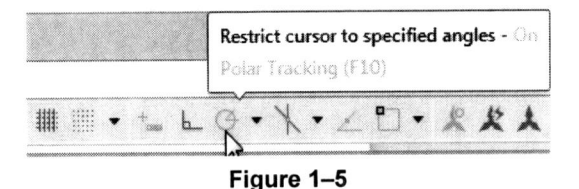

Figure 1–5

Draw Objects

How To: Use Polar Tracking to draw Vertical and Horizontal Lines

1. In the Status Bar, click the arrow in ▼ (Polar Tracking) to display the angles list. Select **90,180,270,360**, as shown in Figure 1–6.

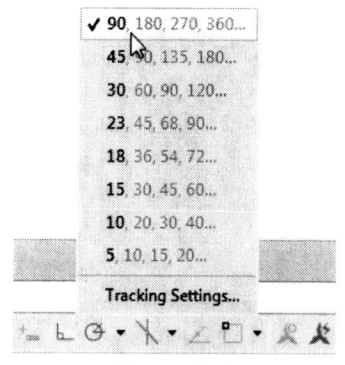

Figure 1–6

The tool highlights in blue when it is toggled on.

2. Click ▼ (Polar Tracking) or press <F10> to toggle it on, if required.
3. In the *Home* tab>Draw panel, click (Line) to start the **Line** command.
4. At the *Specify first point:* prompt, select a starting point for the line.
5. At the *Specify next point:* prompt, move the crosshairs in the direction in which you want the line to extend.
6. When the correct Polar Tracking line displays, enter a distance.
7. Press <Enter>. The line is drawn that length in the direction in which you pick.
8. Repeat for another line segment or press <Enter> to end the **Line** command.

- When the cursor approaches one of the polar angles, the dotted Polar Tracking line displays with a tooltip specifying *Polar:*, followed by the distance and angle from the last point (distance<angle), as shown in Figure 1–7.

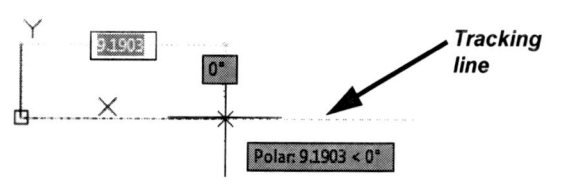

Figure 1–7

- You can use Polar Tracking with or without Dynamic Input.

© 2017, ASCENT - Center for Technical Knowledge®

Ortho Mode

Another way to draw horizontal and vertical straight lines is to use Ortho Mode. It always forces lines to use 90° angles only. To toggle Ortho Mode on or off, click ⌐ (Ortho Mode) in the Status Bar, as shown in Figure 1–8, or press <F8>.

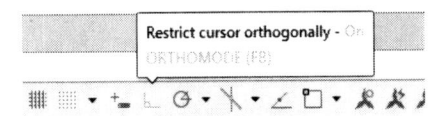

Figure 1–8

- Polar Tracking is the preferred method because it permits other angles to be used and displays the tracking lines.

- ⌐ (Ortho Mode) and ⊙ ▼ (Polar Tracking) cannot be toggled on at the same time.

1.3 Drawing Rectangles

Like lines, rectangles are fundamental building blocks in most drawings, as shown in Figure 1–9. A rectangle can be created from a series of lines or you can create it as a single object using the **Rectangle** command.

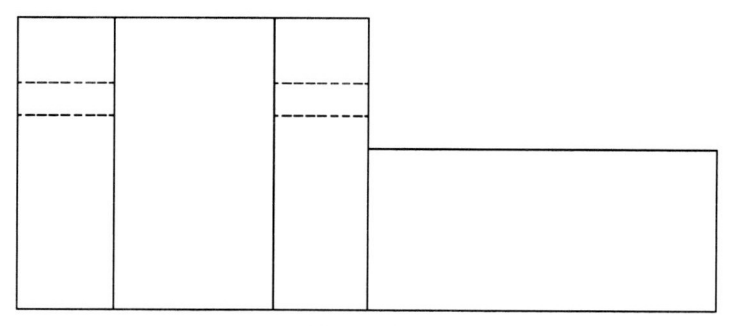

Figure 1–9

How To: Draw a Rectangle

1. In the *Home* tab>Draw panel, click ▢ (Rectangle).
2. Select the first corner of the rectangle.
3. Select the opposite diagonal corner of the box.

- You can also specify the exact length and width of a rectangle as you create it, using either:

  - **Dynamic Input:** At the *Specify other corner point:* prompt, enter a distance for the X axis (length) and Y axis (width), separated by a comma (e.g., **3,4**). The values (positive or negative) specify the direction in which the rectangle is created. Note that the ✛ (Dynamic Input) should be toggled **On** in the Status bar.
  - **Command Line:** At the *Specify other corner point:* prompt, select the **Dimensions** option. At the *Specify length for rectangles* prompt, enter a distance for the length and press <Enter>. At the *Specify width for rectangles* prompt, enter a distance for the width and press <Enter>. A preview of the rectangle displays, which you can reposition using the cursor. Click in the direction in which you want the rectangle.

- The numbers you enter for the length and width are X,Y coordinates that are measured relative to the first corner of the rectangle.

1.4 Drawing Circles

The **Circle** command enables you to place circles in the drawing as stand-alone objects or as parts of a more complex construction, as shown in Figure 1–10.

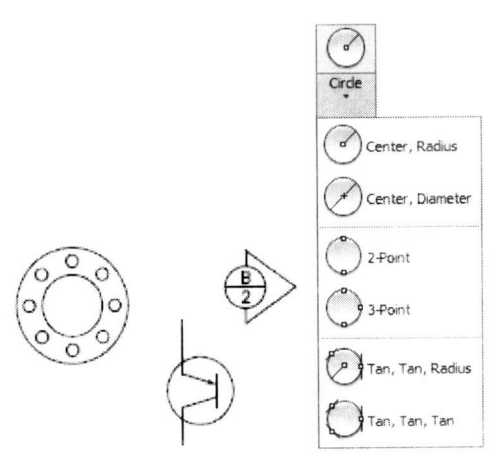

Figure 1–10

- In the *Home* tab>Draw panel, expand (Circle) to open the flyout (shown in Figure 1–10) to access the various options in the **Circle** command.

How To: Draw a Center, Radius Circle

1. In the *Home* tab>Draw panel, in the Circle flyout, click (Center, Radius).
2. Select the center point of the circle.
3. Specify the radius. The value can be entered or specified by selecting a point on the screen.

- The *Radius* is the distance from the center to the edge of the circle. The *Diameter* is the distance across the circle through the center point, as shown in Figure 1–11.

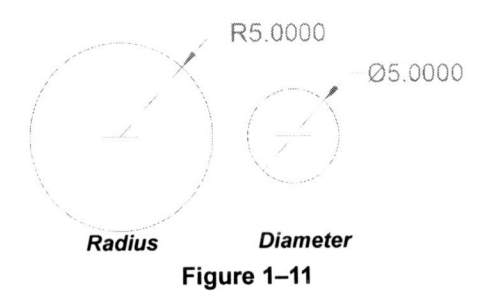

Radius *Diameter*
Figure 1–11

Draw Objects

How To: Draw a Center, Diameter Circle

1. In the *Home* tab>Draw panel, expand the **Circle** flyout and click ⌀ (Center, Diameter).
2. Select the center point of the circle.
3. Specify the diameter. The value can be entered or specified by selecting a point on the screen.

*Type **D** for **Diameter** option if you are using the typed command.*

- If you need to add circles with the same radius or diameter, you can restart the **Circle** command, select the center point, and press <Enter> to use the default value for the radius or diameter. You can also select the value in the Dynamic Input Prompt drop-down list (press <Down Arrow>), as shown in Figure 1–12.

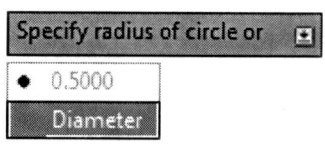

Specify radius of circle or
● 0.5000
Diameter

Figure 1–12

- The default value at the prompt is the same value as the last specified distance and is saved as the radius value. For example, if you specified a *Diameter* of **5.0**, the default value of the *Radius* is **2.5** the next time you start the command.

How To: Draw a 2 Point or 3 Point Circle

1. In the *Home* tab>Draw panel, expand the Circle flyout and click ◯ (2-Point) or ◯ (3-Point).
2. Select the two or three points that you want to use to draw the outside of the circle.

How To: Draw a Circle Tangent to Objects

A *tangent* is a point on a circle where another circle or object only touches it at one point, as shown in Figure 1–13. When you use these commands, an icon displays when you hover over a potential tangent point.

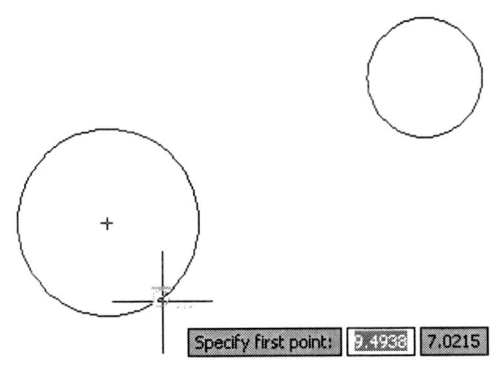

Figure 1–13

1. In the *Home* tab>Draw panel, expand the Circle flyout and click (Tan, Tan, Radius).
2. Hover the cursor over an object to which a circle can be tangent and click when the icon displays in the correct location.
3. Hover the cursor over another object to which the circle can be tangent and click to set its location.
4. Enter a radius for the circle or select an additional tangent point for **Tan, Tan, Tan**.

- If the radius is not big enough for the circle to be created in relationship to the tangent points, the circle is not created with a *Circle does not exist:* prompt displayed in the Command Line. This indicates that you need to use a larger radius.

The (Tan, Tan, Tan) option is only available in the Draw panel.

Draw Objects

Practice 1a

Basic Drawing and Editing Commands

Practice Objectives

- Draw lines using Dynamic Input.
- Delete objects from a drawing using the **Erase** command.
- Draw an object using the **Line** command with Polar Tracking.
- Draw rectangles and circles using various **Circle** command options.

Estimated time for completion: 20 minutes

In this practice, you will use drawing and editing commands. You will draw lines using Dynamic Input and then erase them, as shown on Figure 1–14. In Tasks 3 - 5, you will use Polar Tracking to draw an object. You will also draw rectangles and circles, as shown in Figure 1–15.

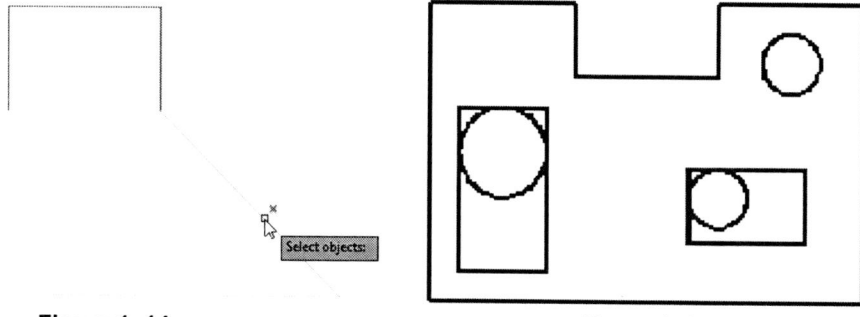

Figure 1–14

Figure 1–15

Task 1 - Draw lines with Dynamic Input.

In this task you will draw lines using Dynamic Input, as shown in Figure 1–16.

The dimensions are for reference only.

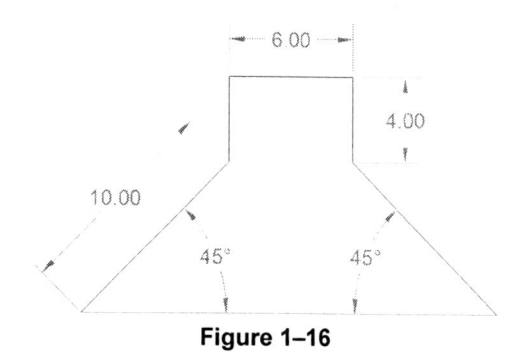

Figure 1–16

1. Open **Object.dwg** from your practice files folder. It is an empty drawing.

© 2017, ASCENT - Center for Technical Knowledge®

1–11

When the tool is toggled on, it should be highlighted in blue.

2. In the Status Bar, verify that (Dynamic Input) is toggled on.

3. In the *Home* tab>Draw panel, click (Line).

4. At the dynamic input, *Specify first point:* prompt, enter **5,5** (as shown in Figure 1–17) and press <Enter>.

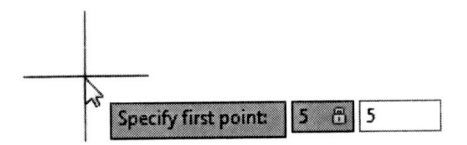

Figure 1–17

5. Move the crosshairs up and to the right from the first point, and enter **10** for the distance. Press <Tab>, enter **45** for the angle (as shown in Figure 1–18), and press <Enter>.

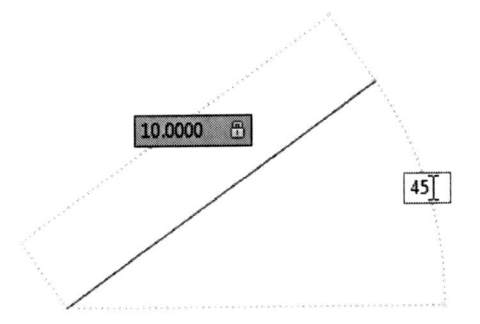

Figure 1–18

6. Move the crosshairs above the last point. Enter **4** for the distance, press <Tab>, enter **90**, and press <Enter> for the angle. This draws the next segment straight up.

7. Move the crosshairs to the right and draw the next segment **6 units** straight to the right (**0°**).

8. Move the crosshairs down and draw the next segment **4 units** straight down (**90°**).

9. Move the crosshairs down and draw the next segment **10 units** at **45°** down and to the right.

10. For the last segment across the bottom of the shape, press <Down Arrow> to display the command options. Select **Close** (as shown in Figure 1–19) to close the figure.

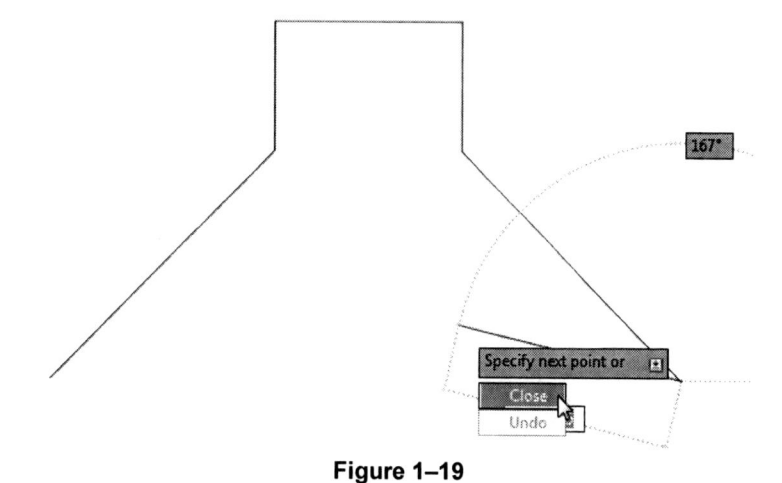

Figure 1–19

Task 2 - Erasing objects.

1. In the *Home* tab>Modify panel, click (Erase). Hover the cursor over a line segment. It turns light gray. Click on it to confirm selection. Similarly, select several other lines, which turn light gray indicating that they are selected for erasing, as shown in Figure 1–20. Press <Enter>.

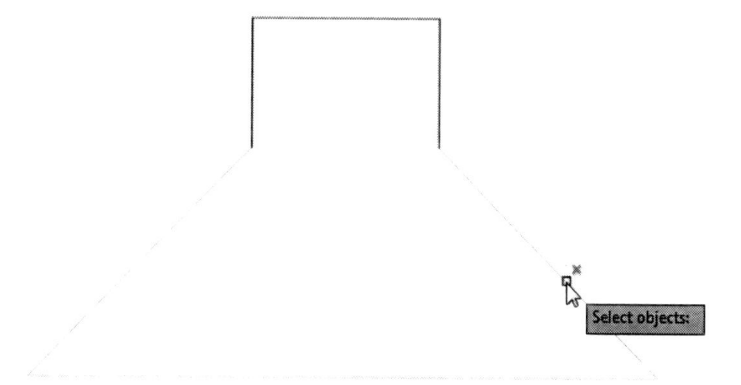

Figure 1–20

2. Without being in a command, select any remaining lines, which are highlighted with grips. Press <Delete>.

Task 3 - Use Polar Tracking.

In this task you will use the **Line** command with Polar Tracking to draw a precise object, as shown in Figure 1–21.

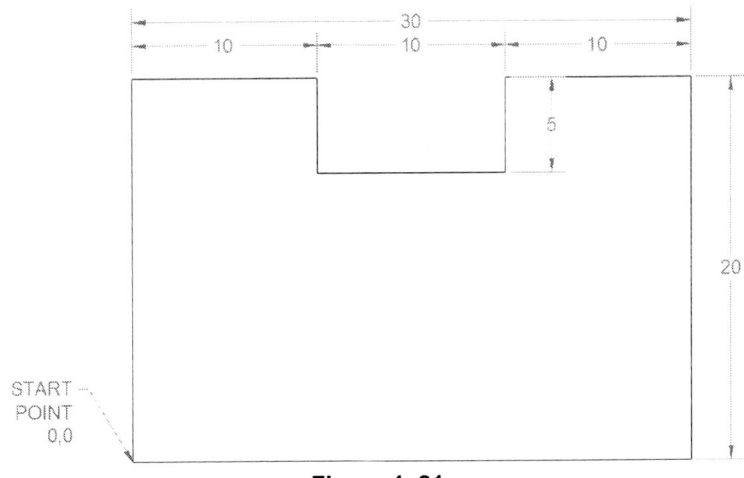

Figure 1–21

1. In the Status Bar, toggle on (Polar Tracking), if it is not already on.

2. Start the **Line** command. At the *Specify first point:* prompt, enter **0,0**, and press <Enter>.

3. Move the crosshairs straight to the right from the start point (you might need to first pan down in the drawing). When the tracking line displays with *Polar: distance < 0* (as shown on the left in Figure 1–22), enter **30**, which automatically overwrites the value in the length edit box, (as shown on the right in Figure 1–22). Press <Enter>.

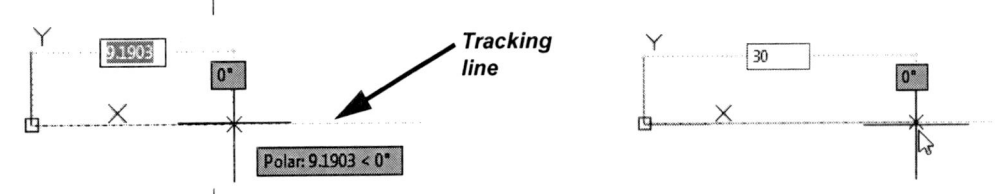

Figure 1–22

Draw Objects

4. Move the crosshairs straight up from the new point. When the tracking line displays with *Polar: distance < 90*, enter **20** and press <Enter>.

5. Continue to draw the shape shown in Figure 1–21, moving the crosshairs and typing the distance for each segment.

6. For the last segment, type **C** and press <Enter> to close the figure and exit the **Line** command.

Task 4 - Draw rectangles.

In this task you will draw rectangles and locate them precisely using coordinates and Dynamic Input, as shown in Figure 1–23.

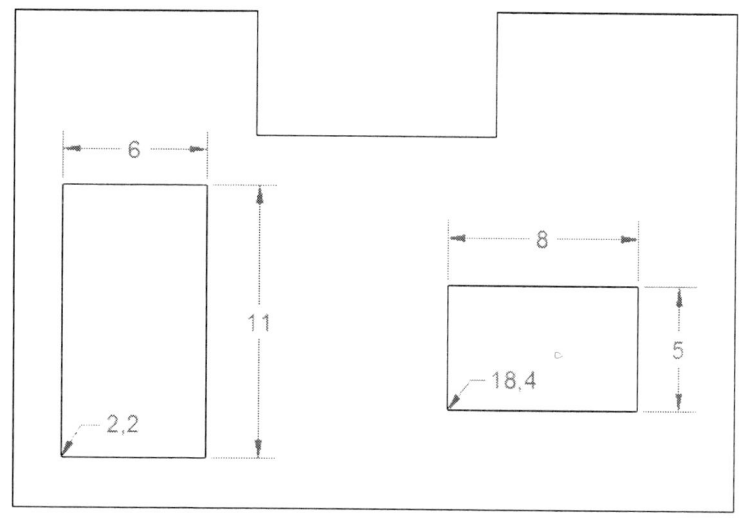

Figure 1–23

In the Status Bar, verify that (Dynamic Input) is toggled on.

1. In the *Home* tab>Draw panel, click (Rectangle).

2. For the first corner point, enter the coordinates **2,2** and press <Enter>.

3. For the other corner, enter **6,11** and press <Enter> to create a 6 x 11 rectangle.

4. Draw a second rectangle with the first corner at point **18,4** and the dimensions shown in Figure 1–23.

5. Save the drawing.

Task 5 - Draw circles.

In this task you will draw circles using the **Center, Diameter**, **Tan, Tan, Radius**, and **Tan, Tan, Tan** options, as shown in Figure 1–24.

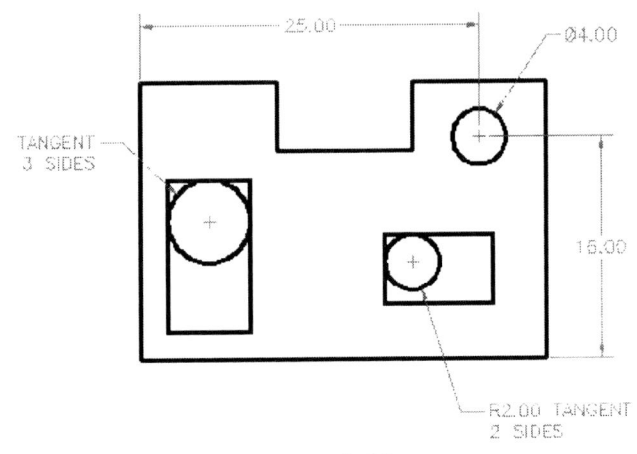

Figure 1–24

1. In the *Home* tab>Draw panel>Circle flyout> click (Center, Diameter). To create the circle in the upper right corner, enter **25,16** to place the center point and enter **4** for the diameter.

2. To draw a circle inside the rectangle on the right side, in the Circle flyout, click (Tan, Tan, Radius). Select the top line of the rectangle as the first deferred tangent point and the left one as the second tangent point. Press <Enter> to accept the default radius of **2**.

3. Draw a circle touching the three sides of the rectangle shown on the left side using the **Tan, Tan, Tan** option.

4. Save and close the drawing.

Draw Objects

Practice 1b

Estimated time for completion: 5 minutes

Create Simple Shapes

In this project you will create several simple shapes using the **Line** command, as shown in Figure 1–25.

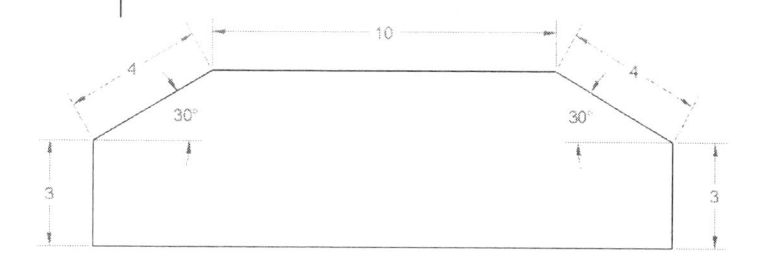

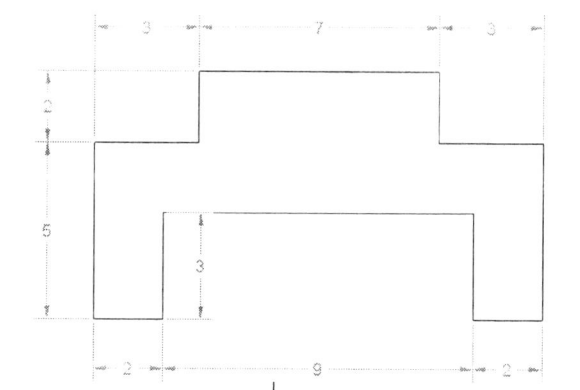

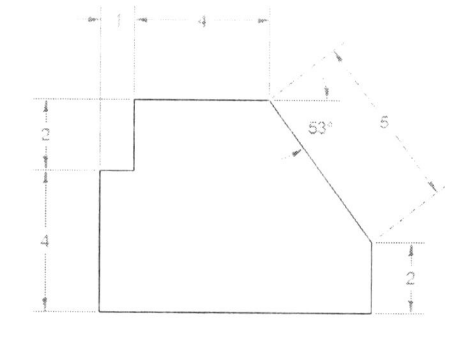

Figure 1–25

1. Open **Simple2.dwg** from your practice files folder. It is an empty drawing file.

2. Use the **Line** command to draw the shapes shown in Figure 1–25.

    - Use the lower left corner of each shape as the starting point and draw the shape clockwise.
    - Use the **Close** option for the last line segment.
    - You can select any point on the screen as the starting point, the exact coordinate location does not matter.
    - If you make a mistake on one segment, use the **Undo** option.

3. Save and close the drawing.

Practice 1c

Estimated time for completion: 5 minutes

Create a Simple Drawing

In this project you will create a simple drawing using the commands **Open**, **Line**, **Circle**, **Rectangle**, **Save**, **Erase**, and **Undo**, as shown in Figure 1–26.

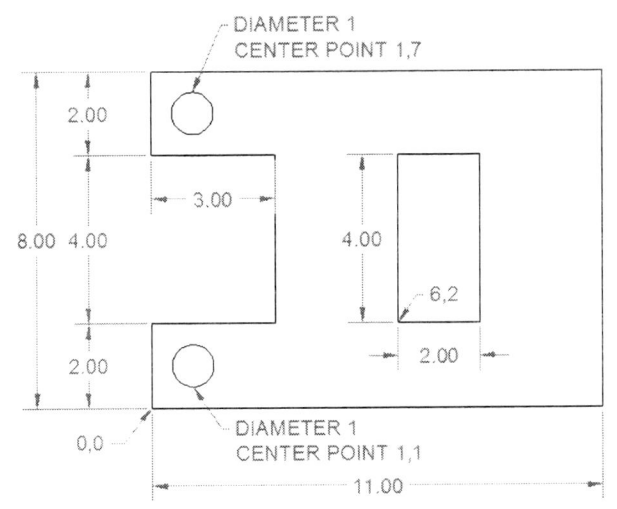

Figure 1–26

1. Open **Simple1.dwg** from your practice files folder. It is an empty drawing file.

2. Draw the object shown in Figure 1–26. Start with the lower left corner of the figure at point 0,0. Use exact coordinates to locate the centers of the circles and the first corner of the rectangle. Draw only the object, not the dimensions as they are for reference only.

3. Save and close the drawing.

Draw Objects

1.5 Drawing Arcs

The **Arc** command is used to add curved segments to a drawing, as shown in Figure 1–27. The information or geometry you have originally determines the option you use.

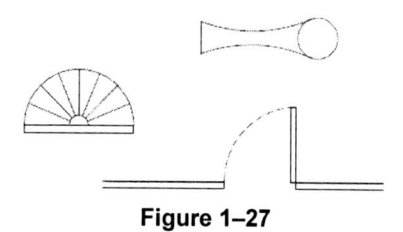

Figure 1–27

Arc Command Options

The **Arc** command has many options that enable you to create arcs. In the *Home* tab>Draw panel, expand (Arc) to access the different arc construction options available in the software, as shown on the left in Figure 1–28. The geometric definitions used for drawing arcs is shown on the right in Figure 1–28.

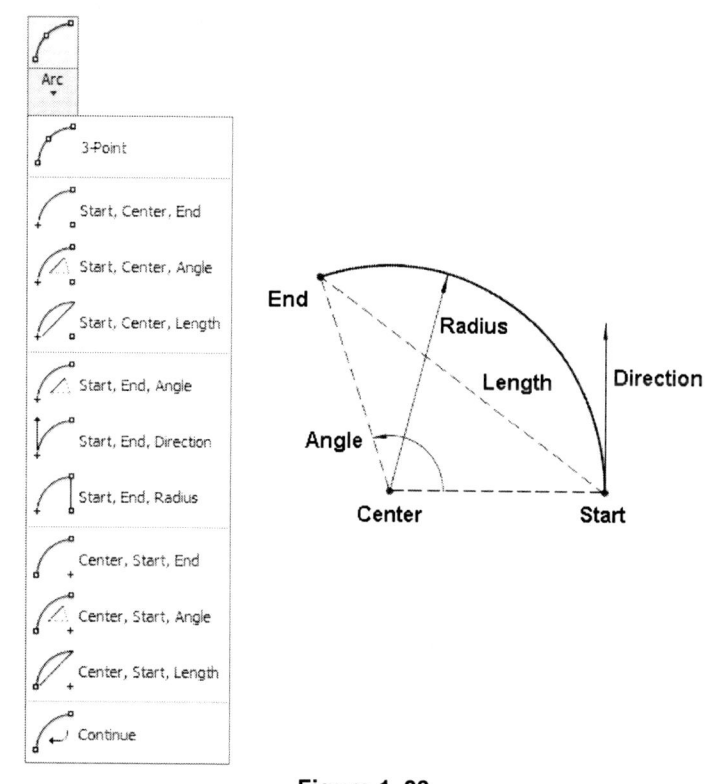

Figure 1–28

Start	Starting point of an arc.
Center	Center (or focal) point of an arc.
End	Ending point of an arc.
Radius	Radius of an arc.
Angle	Included angle turned by an arc.
Direction	Starting direction of an arc.
Chord (Length)	Chord length of an arc. (Distance between arc start and end points.)

Notes on Arcs

- Most arcs in the AutoCAD software are drawn in a counter-clockwise direction from the starting point. You can hold <Ctrl> to reverse the direction when constructing an Arc.

- Pressing <Enter> at the *Specify start point:* prompt starts drawing the arc from the end point of the last line or arc segment drawn. (This feature is only available when the *Specify start point:* prompt is the first prompt for the type of arc being created.)

- You can also type, use the shortcut menu, or use the <Down Arrow> menu to access the arc options.

Draw Objects

Practice 1d

Estimated time for completion: 10 minutes

Drawing an Arc

Practice Objective

- Draw arcs using various options.

In this practice, you will draw door swings in a floorplan using the **Arc** command, as shown in Figure 1–29.

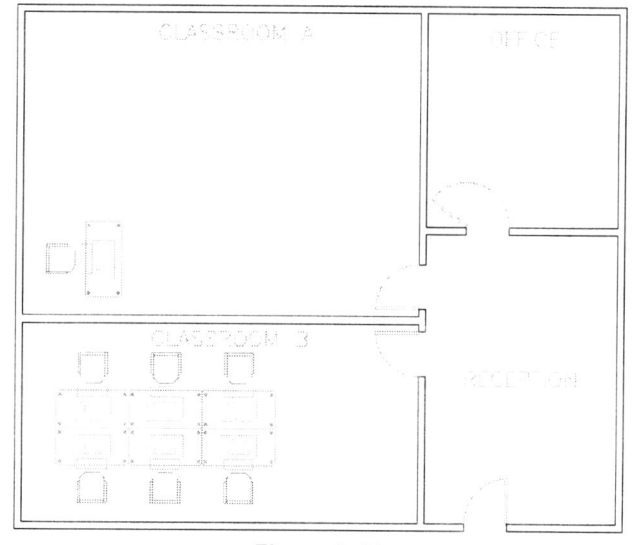

Figure 1–29

1. Open **Class-A.dwg** from your practice files folder.
2. In the Layer Control, set the current layer to **Doors**.
3. Verify that the **Endpoint** Object Snap is on.
4. Zoom in on the office door.
5. In the *Home* tab>Draw panel, expand (Arc) and click (Start, Center, End).
6. At the *Specify start point of arc:* prompt, select the upper right corner of the doorway wall, as shown in Figure 1–30.
7. At the *Specify center point of arc:* prompt, select the point where the door and wall meet, as shown in Figure 1–30.

© 2017, ASCENT - Center for Technical Knowledge® 1–21

8. At the *Specify end point of arc:* prompt, select the upper left corner of the door, as shown in Figure 1–30. The arc that indicates the door swing is created, as shown in Figure 1–30.

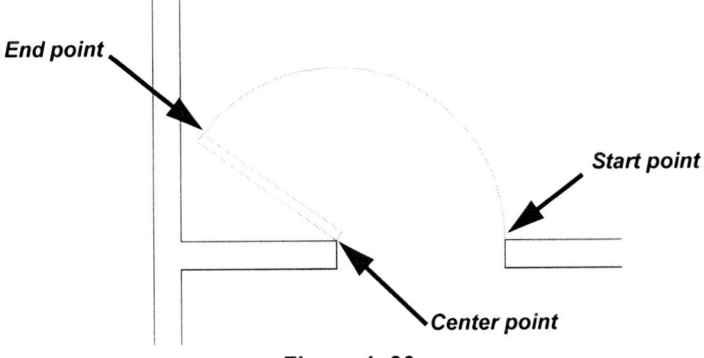

Figure 1–30

9. Pan over to Classroom A's door.

10. In the *Home* tab>Draw panel, expand (Arc) and click (Start, Center, Angle).

11. At the *Specify start point of arc:* prompt, select the upper left corner of Classroom A's doorway wall.

12. At the *Specify center point of arc:* prompt, select the point where the door and wall meet.

13. For the angle, enter **90** and press <Enter>.

14. Pan over to Classroom B's door.

15. In the *Home* tab>Draw panel, expand (Arc) and click (Start, Center, Angle).

16. For the start point, select the lower left corner of Classroom B's doorway wall. For the center point, select the point where the door and wall meet, and for the angle, enter **-90**. Press <Enter> to create the door swing and complete the command.

17. Pan over to the last door (Reception). Add the arc for the door swing using a **Start, Center, End**. **Tip:** To create the door arc in clockwise direction, press and hold <Ctrl> before selecting the end point of the arc.

18. Save and close the drawing.

1.6 Drawing Polygons

The **Polygon** command generates closed geometric figures with three or more equal sides, such as triangles, hexagons, and diamonds, as shown in Figure 1–31.

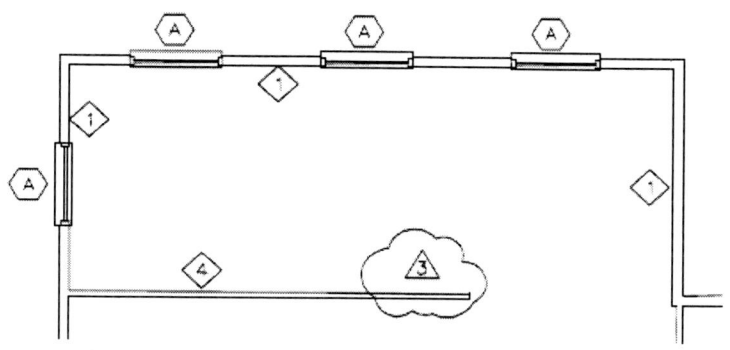

Figure 1–31

- The AutoCAD software builds these objects from polylines. Therefore, all of the sides form one unified object.

- Since polygons are made from polylines, you can use the **Edit Polyline** command to assign a width, explode them to create separate segments, or edit the vertices.

How To: Draw an Inscribed or Circumscribed Polygon

1. In the *Home* tab>Draw panel, expand the Rectangle drop-down list and click (Polygon).
2. Enter the number of sides for the polygon, and press <Enter>.
3. Locate the center point anywhere in the drawing window.

4. Select **Inscribed in circle** or **Circumscribed about circle**, as shown in Figure 1–32.
   - An *inscribed* polygon is defined by the distance from the specified center to one of its vertices (inscribed in the imaginary circle).
   - A *circumscribed* polygon is defined by the distance from the specified center to one of the edges (circumscribed about the imaginary circle).

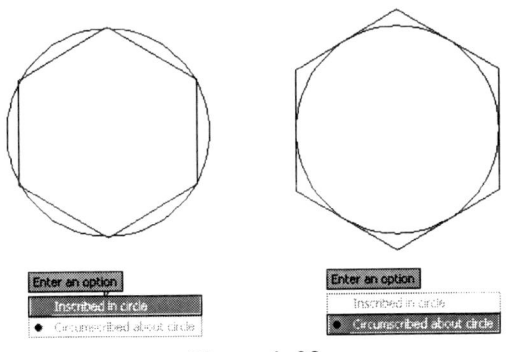

Figure 1–32

5. Enter the radius of the circle.

How To: Draw a Polygon by Edge

1. In the *Home* tab>Draw panel, expand the Rectangle drop-down list and click (Polygon).
2. Enter the number of sides for the polygon, and press <Enter>.
3. At the *Specify center of polygon:*, type **E** for the **Edge** option.
4. At the *Specify first endpoint of edge:*, select a point to locate an endpoint of one of the sides of the polygon.
5. At the *Specify second endpoint of edge:* prompt, select a point to locate the other endpoint of the side of the polygon. This input defines the length of all of the sides (edges) and the angle at which the polygon is rotated, as shown in Figure 1–33.

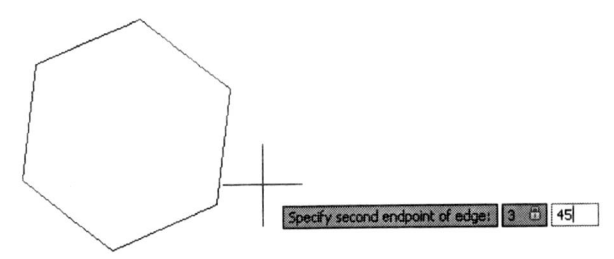

Figure 1–33

Practice 1e

Drawing Polygons

Practice Objective

- Create polygons.

In this practice, you will create symbols using the **Polygon** and **Rectangle** commands, as shown in Figure 1–34.

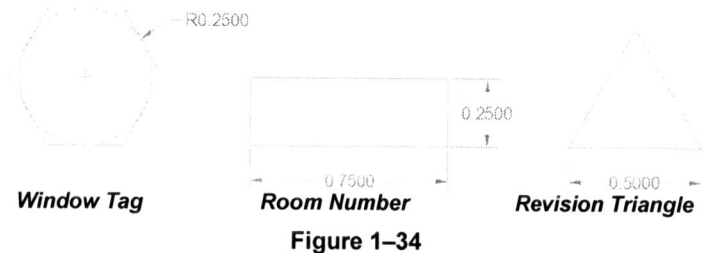

Estimated time for completion: 5 minutes

Window Tag   **Room Number**   **Revision Triangle**
Figure 1–34

Draw only the objects, not the text or dimensions.

1. Start a new drawing based on **AEC-Imperial.dwt**, which is located in your practice files folder, and save it as **Symbols.dwg**.

2. Draw the symbols shown in Figure 1–34. For the Window Tag, start the **Polygon** command (In the *Home* tab>Draw panel, expand the Rectangle drop-down list and click (Polygon)). For the number of sides, enter **6** and press <Enter>. Select anywhere in the drawing window as its center. Select **Circumscribed about circle** and enter **0.25** as the radius. Press <Enter> to complete the command. To zoom in closely, use **Zoom Extents**.

3. Draw the Room Number using the **Rectangle** command and the Revision Triangle using 3 sided **Polygon** command.

4. Save and close the drawing.

Chapter 2

Draw with Accuracy

This chapter includes instructional content to assist in your preparation for the following topic and objectives for the AutoCAD® Certified Professional exam.

Autodesk Certification Exam Objectives in this Chapter

Exam Topic	Exam Objective	Section(s)
Draw with Accuracy	• Use object-snap tracking	• 2.1 to 2.3
	• Use Coordinate Systems	• 2.4 & 2.5
	• Make isometric drawings	• 2.6

2.1 Polar Tracking at Angles

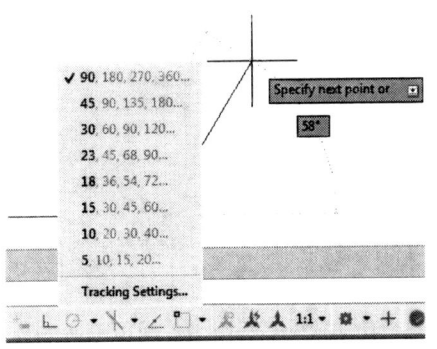

You can use Polar Tracking to draw horizontal lines, vertical lines, and lines at specific increment angles. (Polar Tracking) can be toggled on or off in the Status Bar. Right-click on (Polar Tracking) to select from the list of standard angles (as shown in Figure 2–1) to set the increment angles. You can also set the increment angle while working in a command.

Figure 2–1

Polar Tracking Settings

*You can also right-click on (Polar Tracking) and select **Tracking Settings...***

For more Polar Tracking options, expand (Polar Tracking) and select **Tracking Settings...** to open the Drafting Settings dialog box, as shown in Figure 2–2. In this dialog box you can specify additional angles and modify other settings.

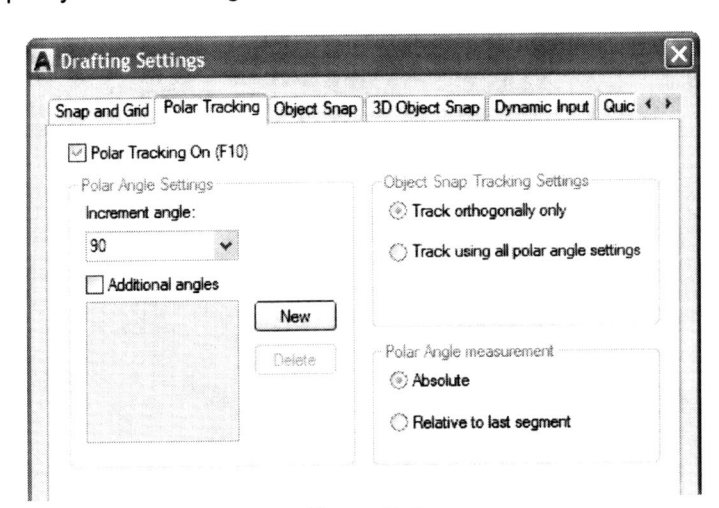

Figure 2–2

Increment angle:	Select an angle in the Increment angle list. All these angles are listed in the Polar Tracking list, which is available in the Status Bar.
Additional angles 35	Select this option to use angles other than the one specified in the Increment angle list. You can only snap to this angle (not to its multiples) and to multiples from the Increment angle list. The angle gets added to the Polar Tracking list.
New	Click to add an additional angle. You can add up to ten additional polar tracking alignment angles.
Delete	Deletes selected additional angles.

- When the **Absolute** option is selected, Polar Tracking is relative to the current X- and Y-axes. For example, if the *Increment Angle* is set to **90** and you draw a diagonal line at 40 degrees for the first segment, the subsequent line is still drawn in increments of 90 degrees relative to the X- and Y-axes (to the right, left, up, or down), as shown on the left in Figure 2–3.

- When the **Relative to last segment** option is selected, Polar Tracking is relative to the last segment drawn or to a segment to which you snap using OSNAP. This means that you can draw the subsequent line in 90 degree increments from the diagonal line drawn, as shown on the right in Figure 2–3.

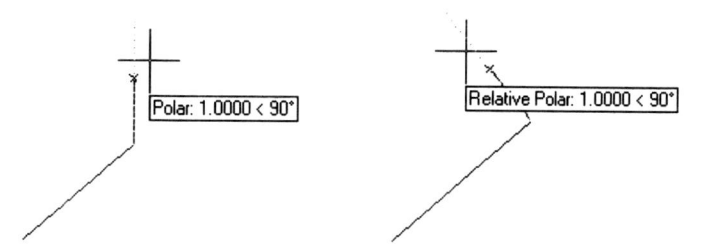

Figure 2–3

- In the Polar Tracking settings, you can select **Track orthogonally only** (i.e., horizontally and vertically) or **Track using all polar angle settings**.

Practice 2a

Polar Tracking

Estimated time for completion: 5 minutes

Practice Objective

- Draw an outline of a part using Polar Tracking and by setting the Polar Tracking options.

In this practice, you will adjust the Polar Tracking settings and then use **Polar Tracking** to draw the outline of the part, as shown in Figure 2–4.

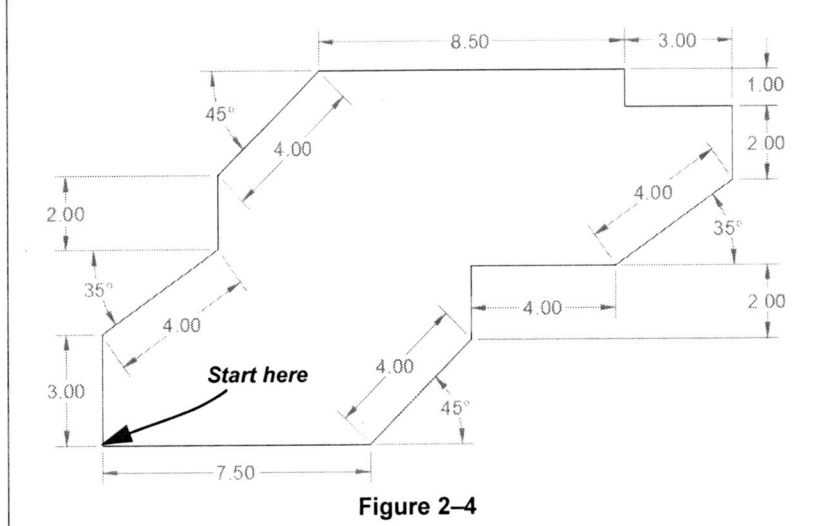

Figure 2–4

1. Open **Pattern.dwg** from your practice files folder. It is an empty drawing file.

2. In the Status Bar, expand ⌕ ▼ (Polar Tracking) and select **Tracking Settings...**.

3. In the Drafting Settings dialog box, select **Additional angles** and click **New.** In the edit box that is highlighted, enter **35** to add an additional angle. Click **OK**.

4. In the Status Bar, expand ⌕ ▼ (Polar Tracking) and select **45,90,135,180...**. Ensure that **Polar Tracking** is toggled **On**.

5. Start the **Line** command and select a point in the lower left corner of the screen (shown as "Start here" in Figure 2–4). Move the cursor straight to the right so that the tracking line at 0 degrees displays. Enter **7.5** and press <Enter>.

Draw with Accuracy

The opposite (or complementary) angle for 45 degrees is 135 degrees.

6. Move the cursor up and to the right until the 45 degree tracking line displays. Enter **4** and press <Enter>.

7. Continue to draw the outline (as shown in Figure 2–4) finding the appropriate tracking angle and typing the distance for each segment.

8. For the last angled segment, the 35 degree tracking does not work (because it is the opposite or complementary angle of 145 degrees, which is not set). Enter a distance of **4.00** (do not press <Enter>) and then use <Tab> to enter the angle as **145**.

9. Save and close the drawing.

2.2 Object Snap Tracking

Object Snap Tracking enables you to locate new points in relation to one or two existing points, as shown in Figure 2–5. Using Object Snaps and Object Snap Tracking together can speed up your work.

Object Snaps must be toggled on to use Object Snap Tracking.

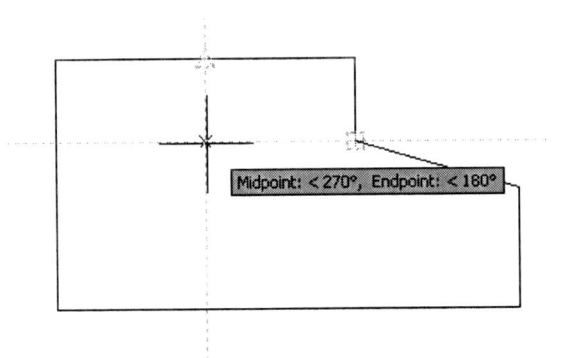

Figure 2–5

- Tracking builds a new point based on coordinates taken from two other points. The new X-coordinate is from one point and the new Y-coordinate from another point.

- When a point is selected for Object Snap Tracking, a small plus displays at the point. The point is said to be *acquired*. A dotted line displays from that point to indicate tracking.

- To clear an acquired point, move the cursor over the point again. Ensure that the small plus disappears.

- You can use Object Snap Tracking with Polar Tracking toggled on or off. However, in some cases Polar Tracking can interfere with the effects of Object Snap Tracking.

How To: Use Object Snap Tracking With One Point

1. In the Status Bar, toggle on both (Object Snap) and (Object Snap Tracking) and set the Object Snap options that you want to use.
2. Start a command, such as **Line**.

You can also use <F11> to toggle object snap tracking on and off.

3. Hover the cursor over the point from which you want to track (do not click on it). A small plus marks the point, as shown in Figure 2–6.

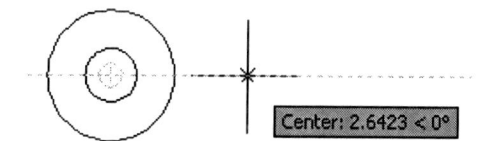

Figure 2–6

4. Move the cursor away from the point. A dotted line and tooltip display when the cursor locks into a tracking angle.
5. Enter the distance that you want to use and press <Enter>.

How To: Use Object Snap Tracking With Two Points

1. In the Status Bar, toggle on both (Object Snap) and (Object Snap Tracking) and set the Object Snap options that you want to use.
2. Start a command, such as **Line**.
3. Hover the cursor over the points from which you want to track (do not click on them). Small plusses mark each point.
4. Two dotted lines display, each passing through an acquired point. Move the cursor to the point at which the lines intersect. A description of each dotted line displays in the tooltip, as shown in Figure 2–7.

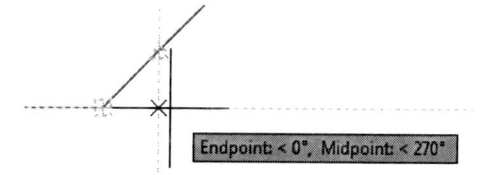

Figure 2–7

5. Select the point at the intersection of the tracking lines.

Practice 2b

Estimated time for completion: 5 minutes

Object Snap Tracking I

Practice Objective

- Create a top view of a part by using Object Snap Tracking.

In this practice, you will create a top view of a part by tracking the locations from the existing front and side views, as shown in Figure 2–8. Construction lines have been provided from the side view, and the other construction lines do not need to be drawn.

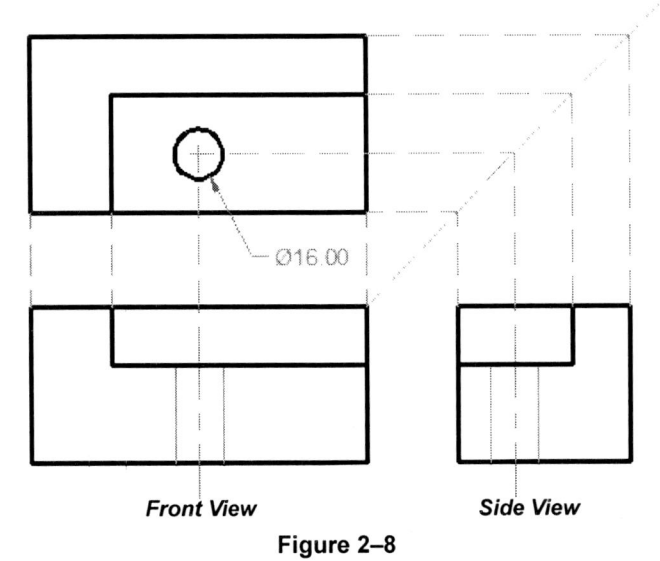

Front View   *Side View*

Figure 2–8

1. Open **Missing View.dwg** from your practice files folder.

2. Set the current Object Snaps as **Endpoint**, **Midpoint**, **Center**, **Quadrant**, and **Intersection**.

3. Toggle on ▢ ▼ (Object Snap) and ∠ (Object Snap Tracking), if required.

4. Start the **Line** command. At the *Specify first point:* prompt, hover the cursor over the top left corner of the front view, which displays the **Endpoint** object snap icon. Then, without clicking, move the cursor. Note that a small green plus mark displays at the top left corner of the front view. Hover the cursor over the top end point of the shortest construction line coming from the side view.

5. Move the cursor to where the two tracking lines intersect at a point, as shown in Figure 2–9. Select that point as the first point for the line.

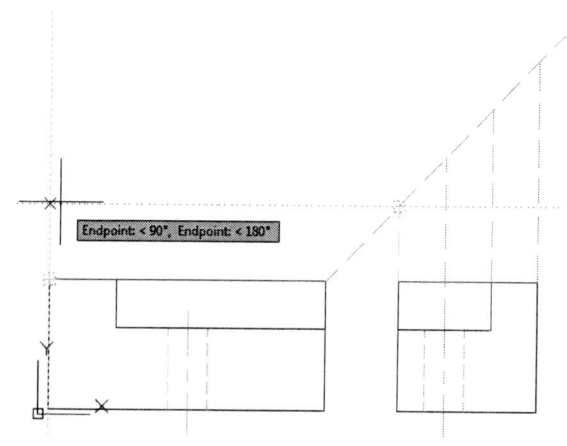

Figure 2–9

6. Continue to draw the rectangular outline of the top view, tracking from the appropriate points.

7. Draw the two interior lines on the top view (as shown in Figure 2–8) using tracking points.

8. Draw a circle (diameter=**16**) whose center point is established by tracking points.

9. Save and close the drawing.

Practice 2c

Object Snap Tracking II

Practice Objective

- Draw lines in a schematic diagram using Object Snap Tracking.

Estimated time for completion: 10 minutes

In this practice, you will use Object Snap Tracking to draw lines in a schematic diagram.

1. Open **Process.dwg** from your practice files folder.

2. Set the Object Snaps to **Midpoint** and **Quadrant**. Ensure that ▢▼ (Object Snap) and ✏ (Object Snap Tracking) are toggled on.

3. Use Object Snap Tracking to add lines between the Bleed Storage and Pump.

   - Zoom in on the two parts.
   - Start the **Line** command.
   - Select the midpoint on the bottom line of the Bleed Storage as the first point. Doing so also acquires the midpoint as a tracking point.
   - Hover the cursor over the left quadrant osnap of the Pump and then move the cursor away from that point (do not click). A small cross displays at the point.
   - Move the cursor to the left of the Pump. A snap tip and dotted tracking lines display from the Bleed Storage and Pump. When both tracking lines display (as shown on the left in Figure 2–10) click to place the second point of the line.
   - For the next point, select the left quadrant of the Pump, as shown on the right in Figure 2–10.

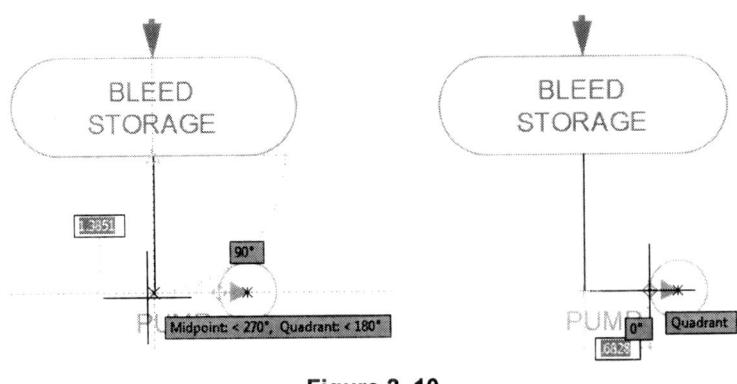

Figure 2–10

4. Draw additional lines between the components, as shown in Figure 2–11.

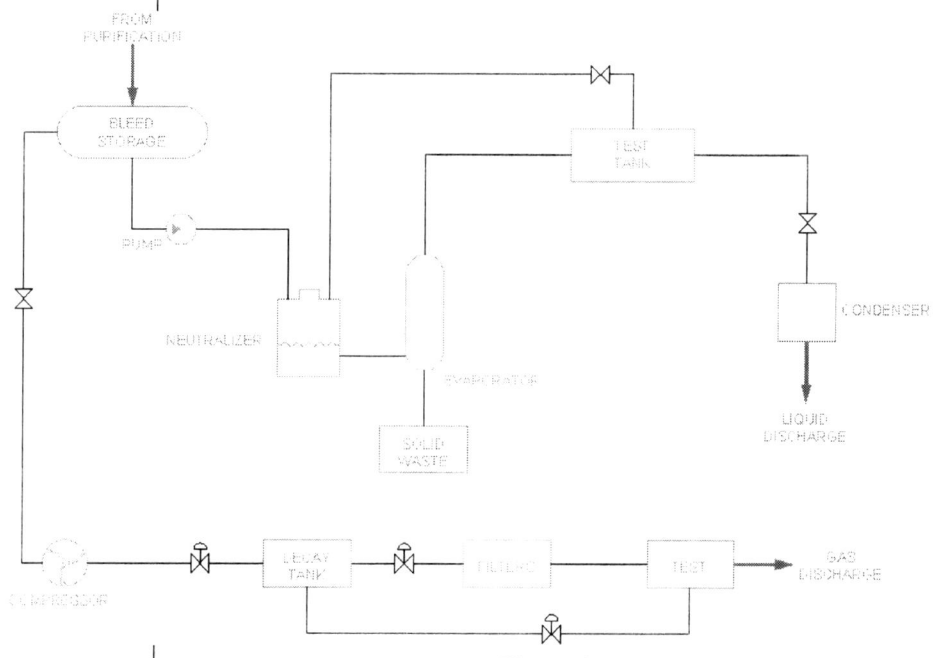

Figure 2–11

5. Save and close the drawing.

2.3 Locating Points with Tracking

Object Snap Tracking Review

You can track from two points to find the intersection point of their tracking lines.

You can use the technique of Object Snap Tracking to locate a new point based on existing object snap points. For example, you can find the precise center of an object in your drawing by tracking from the midpoints of two sides, as shown in Figure 2–12.

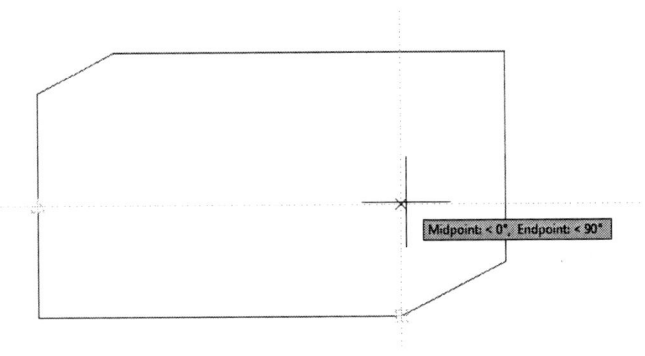

Figure 2–12

- (Object Snap) and (Object Snap Tracking) must both be toggled on to use Object Snap Tracking.

- Hover the cursor over the object snap point and then move it away vertically or horizontally to display the tracking line.

- You can select one point and type a distance to move in one direction along a tracking line from that point.

Temporary Track Point

(Temporary Track Point) can create additional tracking points, which can be useful when you are using Object Snap Tracking and need to have more than two tracking points. It enables you to find a location based on two distances from another point. For example, if you need to position a circle with its center five units to the left and three units up from an endpoint, you need to use Temporary Track Point to add the additional point.

- (Object Snap) and (Object Snap Tracking) must both be toggled on to use Temporary Track Point.

- You can start a Temporary Track Point by right-clicking and selecting **Snap Overrides>Temporary track point** in the shortcut menu or by typing **TT** in the Command Line, after invoking a draw command.

How To: Use a Temporary Track Point

1. In the Status Bar, toggle on (Object Snap) and (Object Snap Tracking).
2. Start a command, such as **Line** or **Circle**.
3. When prompted for a point, start (Temporary Track Point) by typing **tt**.
4. Hover the cursor over an existing point, which is then marked with a small plus mark.
5. Move the cursor to lock the required tracking angle from the temporary point, and then type a distance to move in relation to the temporary point, as shown in Figure 2–13.

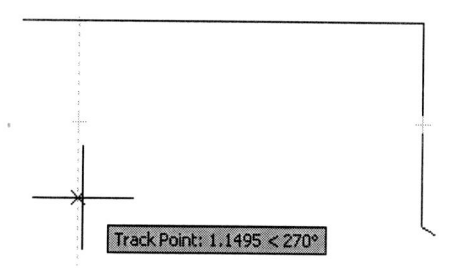

Figure 2–13

- Tracking lines display when you have locked a tracking angle from the temporary point.

- **IMPORTANT:** Do not move the cursor directly over the cross that marks the temporary point. Doing so clears the point.

Practice 2d

Locating Points with Tracking (Mechanical)

Practice Objective

- Place holes at certain locations.

Estimated time for completion: 5 minutes

In this practice, you will use Object Snap Tracking and Temporary Track Point to place holes on a machine part, as shown in Figure 2–14.

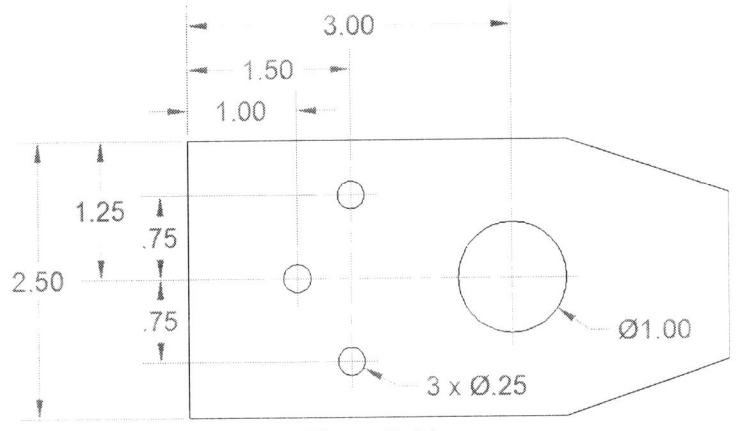

Figure 2–14

1. Open **Track-l.dwg** from your practice files folder.

2. Set the Object Snap Settings to **Midpoint**, and verify that (Object Snap) and (Object Snap Tracking) are toggled on.

3. To draw a circle using the **Circle** command, hover the cursor over the midpoint of the left line as a tracking point, and then pull the cursor to the right. Type **3,** press <Enter>, and set the *diameter* (using the <Down arrow>) to **1**.

4. Repeat this process to place the **0.25 diameter** circle, **1 unit** from the midpoint on the left, as shown in Figure 2–14.

5. Start the **Circle** command again and start the **Temporary Track Point** override, by right-clicking anywhere and selecting **Snap Overrides>Temporary track point**.

6. Hover the cursor over the midpoint of the left line, and pull the cursor to the right. Type **1.5** (as shown on the left in Figure 2–15) and press <Enter>. A small plus mark displays at the temporary track point. Move the cursor directly below the plus mark. A tracking line displays. Type **0.75** (as shown on the right in Figure 2–15) and press <Enter> to select another point 0.75 units down from the temporary point.

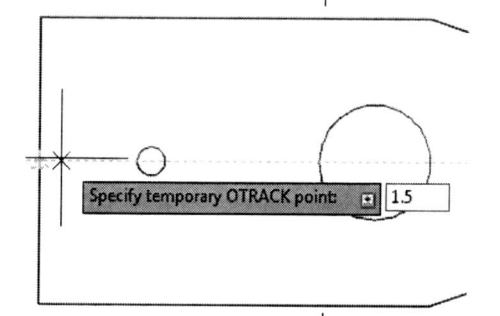

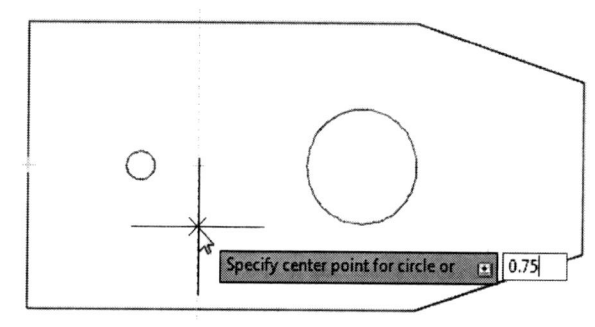

Figure 2–15

7. Place a **0.25 diameter** circle at this temporary track point location.

8. Repeat this process to place the last circle (**0.25 diameter**), but move the cursor directly above the cross as shown in Figure 2–14.

9. Save and close the drawing.

Practice 2e

Locating Points with Tracking (Architectural)

Estimated time for completion: 10 minutes

Practice Objectives

- Draw the walls of a building.
- Position additional wall lines using tracking methods.

In this practice, you will create walls for a simple building outline using the Polyline command and then use Object Snap Tracking and Temporary Track Point methods to help position interior partitions, as shown in Figure 2–16.

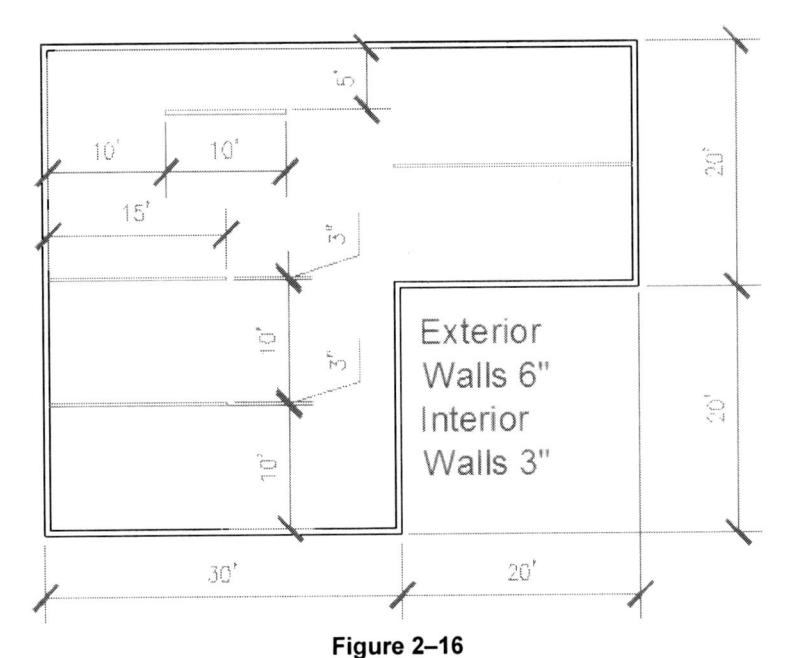

Figure 2–16

1. Start a new drawing based on **AEC-Imperial.dwt,** which is found in your practice files folder.

2. Make the layer **Walls** current and draw the outside of the building as shown in Figure 2–16, using the **Polyline** command (verify that the **Width** option is set to **0**). Start from the lower left corner and draw counter-clockwise.

    - (Object Snap Tracking) can help to position the point for the top left corner.

Note: Ignore the undimensioned partition wall.

3. Offset the exterior walls **6"** to the inside.

4. Make the layer **Partitions** current and draw the interior partitions as shown in Figure 2–16. Use ∠ (Object Snap Tracking) and **Temporary Track Point** to help position the lines precisely. Make all of the interior partitions **3"** wide.

5. Save the drawing as **Open Office.dwg** and close the drawing.

2.4 Cartesian Workspace

Locating Points

The AutoCAD software uses Cartesian (X,Y) coordinates to indicate locations in a drawing. Points are located by designating a horizontal (X) and vertical (Y) distance as measured from the origin (0,0), as shown in Figure 2–17. There is also a third coordinate (Z), which is only used in 3D drawings.

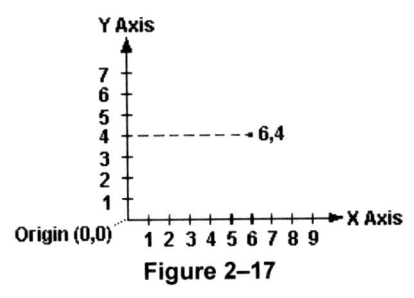

Figure 2–17

The current coordinate location of the cursor can be displayed in the Status Bar, as shown in Figure 2–18. By default, this display is toggled off. If you want to display the coordinates, click ≡ (Customization) in the Status Bar and select **Coordinates**.

Figure 2–18

When you start a drawing command that requires you to select a point, the current coordinates also display near the crosshair in the Dynamic Input prompt (When **Dynamic Input** option is toggled **On**). For example, to draw a line, you must indicate where to begin and end the line. You can specify the point using one of two methods:

- Selecting a point on the screen with the cursor.

- Typing coordinates (when it is requesting point entry) in the form X,Y as shown in Figure 2–19. For example, the point (6,4) would be typed as **6,4**.

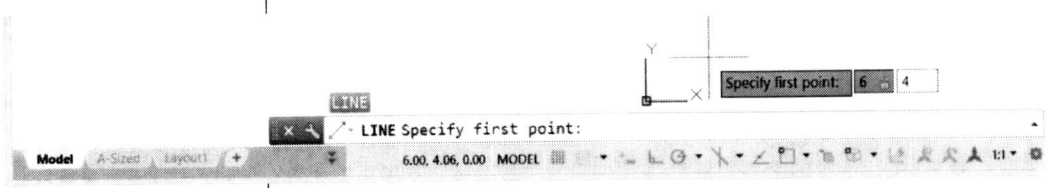

Figure 2–19

Draw with Accuracy

Measuring Angles

With the Cartesian coordinate system, you also need to understand how angles work in the AutoCAD software, as shown in Figure 2–20. This becomes important for coordinate entry, rotating objects, and working with arcs.

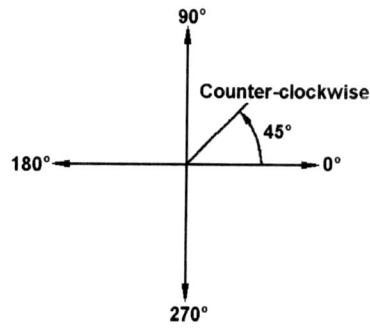

Figure 2–20

- By default, the AutoCAD software measures angles in a counter-clockwise direction relative to the positive X-axis.

Drawings Created at Full Scale

The AutoCAD Cartesian workspace is essentially unlimited in size. Whatever object you are creating, you typically draw it in the software at full scale, as shown in Figure 2–21. Whether you are drawing a building that is 100 x 200 meters or feet, a city that is 10 square kilometers or miles, or an IC chip that is 0.1" x 0.1", you always draw in the real units of the object. Your drawing area is as big as you need it to be. If needed, the entire solar system could be drawn at full scale in the software.

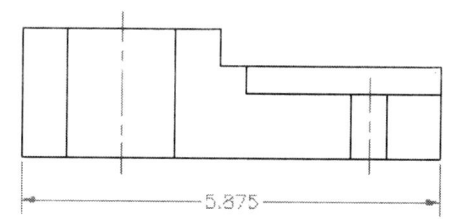

Figure 2–21

- Scaling the drawing only becomes necessary when the drawing is printed.

> **Hint: Drawing Accuracy**
>
> In addition to being potentially enormous, the AutoCAD drawing plane is also remarkably precise. Each point you enter in the software has an accuracy of at least 14 significant digits (e.g., 1.0000000000000).

2.5 Coordinate Entry

The AutoCAD® software has several ways of locating positions in a drawing by typing coordinates, or by coordinate entry, as shown in Figure 2–22:

- Absolute Cartesian Coordinates (X,Y)
- Relative Cartesian Coordinates (@X,Y)
- Relative Polar Coordinates (@Distance<Angle)

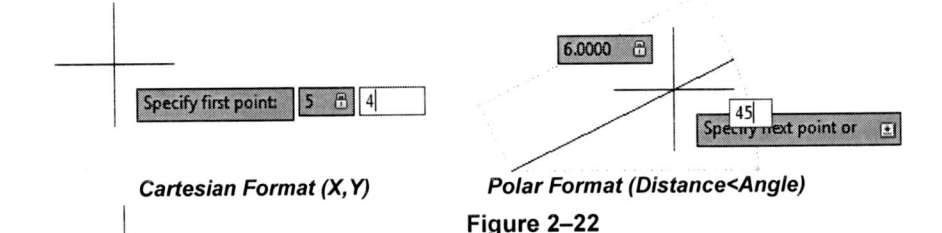

Cartesian Format (X,Y)   *Polar Format (Distance<Angle)*

Figure 2–22

Absolute Cartesian Coordinates (X,Y)

Absolute Cartesian coordinates (X,Y) specify a point's absolute location based on the origin (0,0). You can use absolute coordinates to specify the first point of a line or the center point of a circle. For example, typing **8,2** locates a point eight units in the X-direction and two units in the Y-direction from the origin, as shown in Figure 2–23.

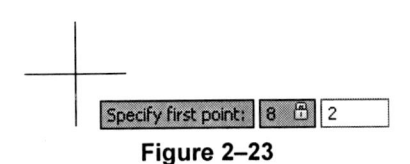

Figure 2–23

- Absolute Cartesian Coordinates are useful when you are given the coordinates to use, such as in some mapping applications or drawings for numeric control machinery.

Relative Cartesian Coordinates (@X,Y)

Relative Cartesian coordinates specify a point's distance away from the last point entered using X- and Y-values.

- Relative Cartesian coordinates are useful when you are given an X- and Y-distance rather than a distance and angle.
- When using (Dynamic Input), the coordinates you type for the *next point* or *second point* in a command are automatically relative by default.

- If ✛ (Dynamic Input) is toggled off, you have to force coordinates to be relative by putting @ in front of them (@X,Y). @ is a shorthand way of identifying the last point entered.

- When you type coordinates in the X,Y format, it overrides the default distance and angle format.

How To: Draw Using Relative Coordinates

In the example shown in Figure 2–24 the angled line is drawn using the specified dimensions and relative coordinates. The drawing requires X- and Y-values, rather than distance and angle values.

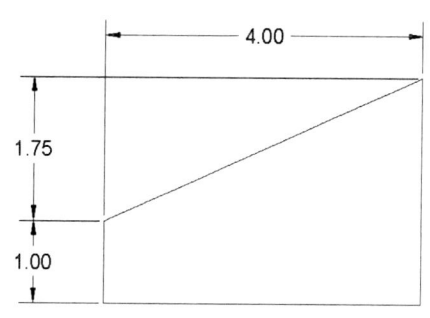

Figure 2–24

When ✛ (Dynamic Input) is toggled on, the coordinates you type for the next point or second point in a command are automatically relative by default. Therefore, @ is not required.

1. Verify that ✛ (Dynamic Input) is toggled on.
2. Start the **Line** command.
3. Draw the short vertical segment **1 unit** straight up.
4. At the *Specify next point:* prompt, type **4,1.75** and press <Enter>. This places the endpoint of the segment **4 units** to the right (X-value) and **1.75 units** up (Y-value) from the last point.
5. At the *Specify next point:* prompt, type **0,-2.75** and press <Enter>. This places the endpoint of the segment **0 units** to the right (X-value) and **2.75 units** down (Y-value) from the last point.
6. Type **C** to close the object and complete the drawing.

- The X- or Y-values can be either positive or negative. For example, @6,0 is a point 6 units straight to the right of the last point, but @-6,0 is a point 6 units to the left (back along the X-axis).

Relative Polar Coordinates (@Distance< Angle)

When you are selecting the *next point* for a line, dynamic dimensions display the distance from the last point and angle, as shown in Figure 2–25. Specifying the distance and angle is another form of coordinates, known as polar coordinates.

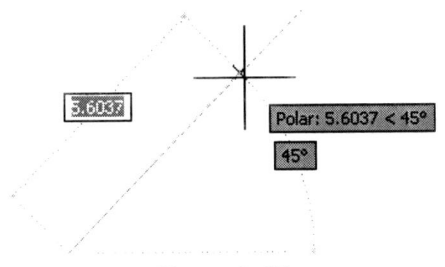

Figure 2–25

- Relative polar coordinates identify a point at a specific distance and angle from the last point selected.

- When drawing with (Dynamic Input) toggled on, you can enter the distance, press <Tab>, and enter the angle.

- You can also type polar coordinates in the form of **distance <angle**. For example, **@10<45** identifies a point ten units away, up, and to the right at a 45-degree angle from the last point entered (with (Dynamic Input) toggled off).

- You can use the AutoCAD angle scheme (shown in Figure 2–26) to help type the polar coordinates as **distance<angle** without needing to move the cursor to display the angle on the screen.

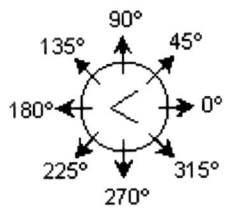

Figure 2–26

Draw with Accuracy

Notes on Coordinate Entry

- You can use coordinate entry with or without using (Dynamic Input). If (Dynamic Input) is toggled off, you must use **@** to make points relative to the last point.

- You can use **@** alone to indicate the last point.

- You can force coordinates to be absolute, rather than relative, by typing **#** in front of the X,Y value. For example, #1,1 always goes to the absolute point 1,1.

*Right-click on (Dynamic Input) and select **Dynamic Input Settings**.*

- The Dynamic Input settings can be changed so that the default for the second or next point is absolute instead of relative. In the Drafting Settings dialog box, in the *Dynamic Input* tab>*Pointer Input* area, click **Settings...** and modify the settings in the Pointer Input Settings dialog box.

- Relative coordinates can be useful in commands (such as **Move** and **Copy**), and in drawing commands. For example, you can use relative coordinates to copy an object at precise X- and Y- distances from the original. To copy the circle on the lower left (as shown in Figure 2–27), use the coordinates **5,3** as the second point.

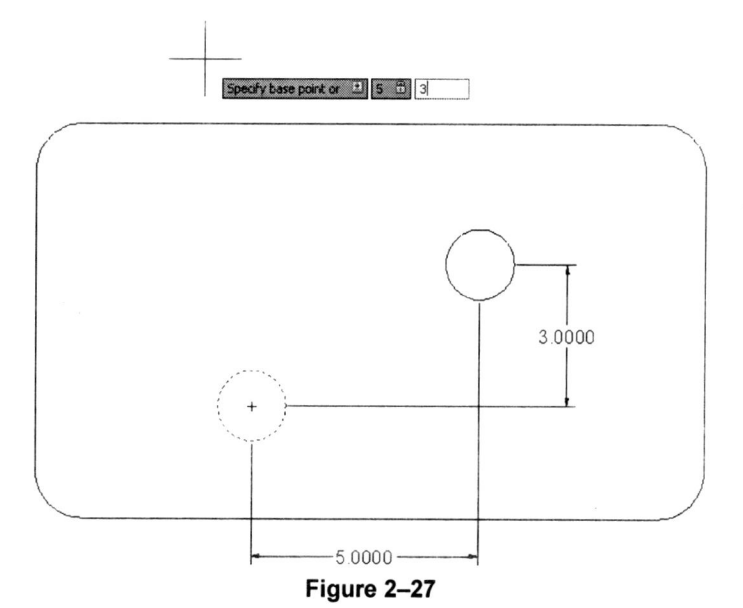

Figure 2–27

Hint: The User Coordinate System

The *User Coordinate System* (UCS) refers to the system of X-, Y-, and Z-coordinates, which define the AutoCAD Cartesian workspace. In the lower left corner of the window, a horizontal line labeled **X** and a vertical line labeled **Y** display. This is called the *UCS icon*, as shown in Figure 2–28.

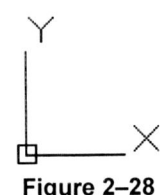

Figure 2–28

To hide the UCS icon, click (Hide UCS Icon) in the *View* tab>Coordinates panel, as shown in Figure 2–29. You might need to toggle on the Coordinates panel, as it is off by default. To have the UCS icon remain in the lower left corner of the screen (rather than moving with the 0,0 point), click (Show UCS Icon). By default, (Show UCS Icon at Origin) is selected.

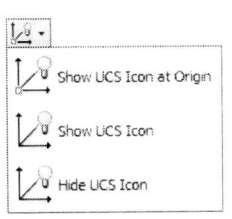

Figure 2–29

Typically, you work with a fixed coordinate system called the *World Coordinate System* or WCS. The UCS can also be changed to adjust the orientation of the drawing plane, which is primarily used in for 3D models.

- To return to the standard World Coordinate System at any time, click (World) in the *View* tab>Coordinates panel.

*If the Coordinates panel is not displayed, right-click in any panel of the View tab and select **Show Panels> Coordinates**.*

Practice 2f

Drawing Using Coordinate Entry

Estimated time for completion: 5 minutes

Practice Objective

- Draw an object using typed coordinates.

In this practice, you will draw using typed coordinates, as shown in Figure 2–30.

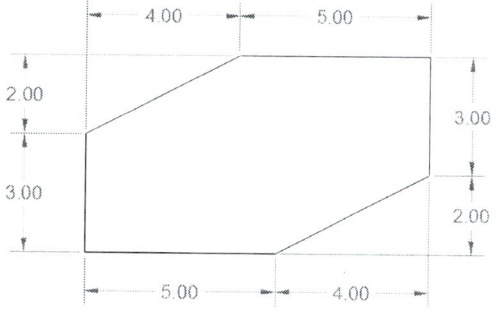

Figure 2–30

1. Start a new drawing based on **Mech-Inches.dwt**, which is located in your practice files folder. Save it as **New Plate.dwg**.

2. Toggle on (Dynamic Input) if it is not already on.

3. Start the **Line** command.

4. For the first point, type the absolute coordinates **5,5** and press <Enter>.

5. For the next point, type **5<0** and press <Enter>. This draws the first segment 5 units straight to the right (angle 0) from the last point.

6. For the next point, type **4,2** and press <Enter>. This places the endpoint 4 units to the right (X-value) and 2 units up (Y-value) from the last point.

7. For the next point, type **3<90** and press <Enter>.

8. For the next point, type **5<180** and press <Enter>.

9. For the next point, type **−4,−2** and press <Enter> to draw the angled segment down and to the left.

10. Type **C** and press <Enter> to close the figure.

11. Save and close the drawing.

2.6 Isometric Drawing Environment

In the Drafting settings dialog box>*Snap and Grid* tab, when the *Snap type* is set to **Isometric snap** (as shown in Figure 2–31), the grid and cursor become angled. This makes it much easier to draw a 2D isometric part, as shown in Figure 2–32.

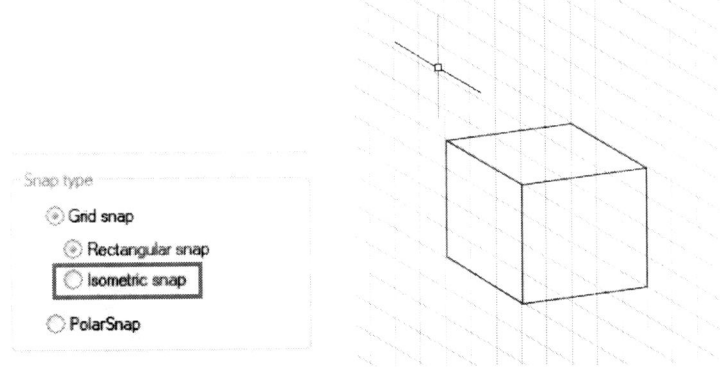

Figure 2–31   Figure 2–32

When the *Snap type* is set to **Isometric snap**, the rotation of the grid can be controlled using the **Isometric Drafting** tool in the Status Bar.

- Click (Isometric Drafting) in the Status Bar to toggle the Isometric Drawing environment on or off.

- Expand (Isometric Drafting) and click on one of the following options to select the environment in which you want to draw.

    - (Isoplane Left)
    - (Isoplane Top)
    - (Isoplane Right)

When the Isometric Drafting is toggled on, the icon displays the cursor lines in red and green.

The cursor and grid display is oriented to suit the selected option, as shown for **Isoplane Top** in Figure 2–33.

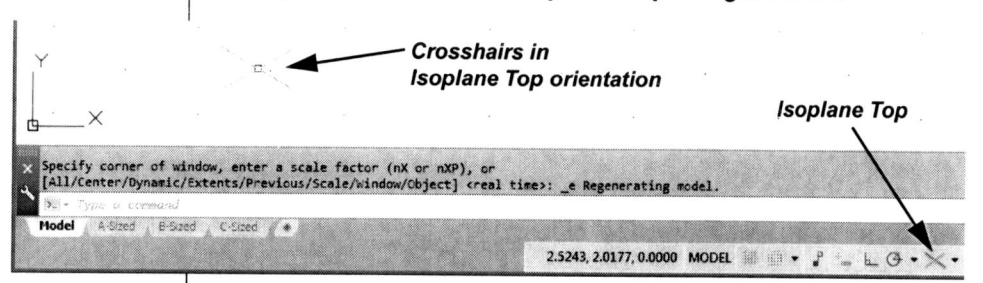

Figure 2–33

Chapter 3

Modify Objects

This chapter includes instructional content to assist in your preparation for the following topic and objectives for the AutoCAD® Certified Professional exam.

Autodesk Certification Exam Objectives in this Chapter

Exam Topic	Exam Objective	Section(s)
Modify Objects	• Move and copy objects	• 3.1 to 3.3
	• Rotate and scale objects	• 3.4 & 3.5
	• Create and use arrays	• 3.6
	• Trim and extend objects	• 3.7
	• Offset and mirror objects	• 3.8 & 3.9
	• Use grip editing	• 3.10 & 3.11
	• Fillet and chamfer objects	• 3.12

3.1 Moving Objects

The **Move** command enables you to relocate a selected object or group of objects from one place in the drawing to another.

How To: Move an Object

1. In *Home* tab>Modify panel, click ✥ (Move).
2. Select the objects that you want to move.
3. Press <Enter> or right-click to end the object selection.
4. Specify the base point, which is the *handle* by which you hold the objects.
5. Move the cursor. ✥ displays at the cursor and the selected objects get attached to the cursor. A temporary rubber-band (dashed) line extends from the original location to the new location of the objects, as shown in Figure 3–1. A paler (light gray) version of the selected object(s) displays at its original location.

Figure 3–1

Modify Objects

6. Specify a second point at which to place the objects. The original objects are moved to the new location.

- You can select the objects first and then start the **Move** command.

- You can also select the objects first (highlighted in blue with a thicker line weight and contains *grips)* and then click and drag them to a new location. Ensure that you do not select one of the grips. This method does not permit you to move precisely.

- You can also select the objects first, press and hold <Ctrl>, and use the appropriate arrow key to **Nudge** the selected objects a few pixels in the specified direction.

> **Hint: Drawing Aids for Moving Objects**
>
> Several drawing aids can help you to move objects precisely including Object Snaps, Coordinate Entry, and Object Snap Tracking.
>
> - **Object Snaps:** Start the **Move** command and select an object to move. Use Object Snaps to select a base point on the object, such as an end point. Then use Object Snaps to select the new location for the object, such as the center of a circle.
>
> - **Coordinate Entry:** Start the **Move** command and select an object to move. Enter coordinates for the base point and press <Enter> when prompted for the second point. The coordinates determine the distances and directions in which the object is moved. For example, entering **2,5** for the base point moves the object 2 units in the X-direction and 5 units in the Y-direction.
>
> - **Object Snap Tracking:** Start the **Move** command and select an object to move. With Osnap Tracking toggled on, hover the cursor over objects where the selected object is going to be placed and select two tracking points. Place the selected object at the intersection of the tracking points.
>
> You can also combine these methods to move an object. For example, you can use Object Snaps to select the base point and then enter coordinates for the second point.

3.2 Copying Objects

The **Copy** command is used to make additional copies of selected objects. The prompts for this command are similar to those used for **Move**.

How To: Copy an Object

1. In the *Home* tab>Modify panel, click (Copy).
2. Select the objects that you want to copy.
3. Press <Enter> or right-click to end the object selection.
4. Select the base point.
5. Move the cursor to copy the objects to a new location.

    displays at the cursor and the selected object(s) get attached to it. A temporary rubber-band (dashed) line extends from the original location to the new location of the objects, as shown in Figure 3–2. A highlighted version of the selected object(s) displays at the original location.

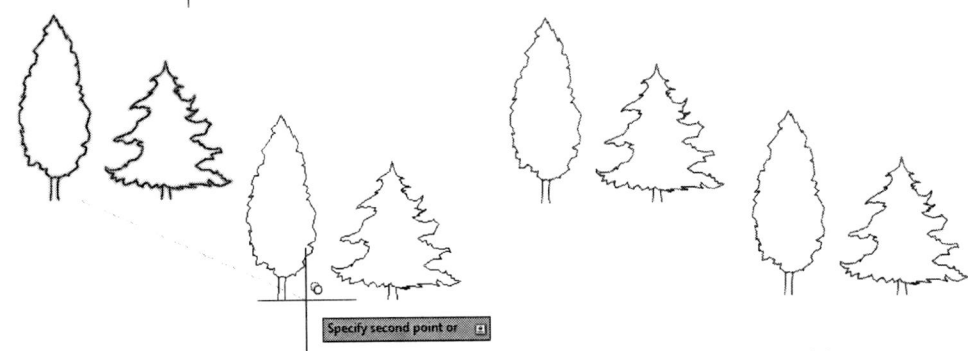

Select second point   *Original and copied objects*

Figure 3–2

6. Continue selecting points to create more copies, or press <Enter> or <Esc> to finish.

- Copied objects have the same color, linetype, and layer properties as the original. This rule also applies to other commands that make duplicates of objects.

- The **Undo** option enables you to undo the placing of a copy while remaining in the command.

- You can select the objects first and then start the **Copy** command.

- Similar to the **Move** command, you can use Object Snaps, Coordinate Entry, and Object Snap Tracking to select points for the **Copy** command.

Modify Objects

- You can also select the objects first, select a point on an object that does not touch a grip, drag the objects to a new location, and press <Ctrl> to make a copy. Do not press <Ctrl> until after you have started dragging, as it has a different purpose when you are selecting objects in 3D.

> **Hint: Editing Commands in the Shortcut Menu**
>
> If you select objects when a command is not active and then right-click, the shortcut menu displays some basic editing commands, as shown in Figure 3–3. This is another way of starting these commands.
>
> Figure 3–3
>
> You can also **Cut**, **Copy**, and **Paste** to the Clipboard from the shortcut menu by expanding the **Clipboard** option. The objects you select can then be pasted into other AutoCAD drawings and programs, such as spreadsheets and documents.
>
> The **Clipboard>Copy** command in the shortcut menu is actually **Copy to Clipboard**. The **Copy Selection** command is the same as the standard AutoCAD **Copy** command.

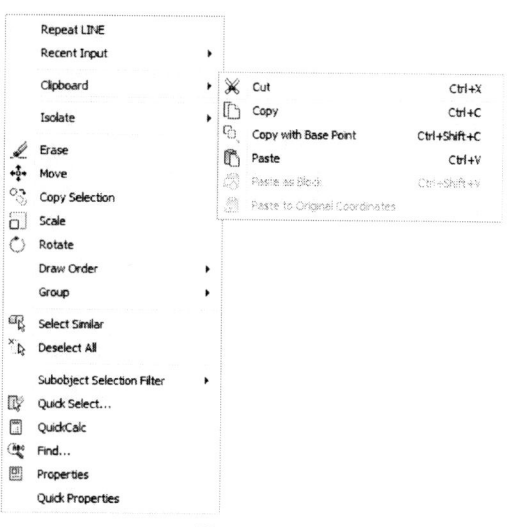

Enhanced in 2018

> **Hint: Rubber-band line color**
>
> By default, the rubber-band line that you get after selecting and moving the cursor in the **Move** and **Copy** commands, is a light orange color. You can control its color in the *Interface element* list in the Drawing Window Colors dialog box, which can be opened from Options dialog box>*Display* tab>**Colors**.

3.3 Copying and Pasting Between Drawings

*The AutoCAD **Copy** command does not work between drawings.*

You can place information on the clipboard by copying or cutting it from a document. You can then paste the information from the clipboard into the same document or into a different one, even in a different application. To copy, move and paste information between drawings you must use the Windows **Copy** command.

- **Cut**, **Copy**, and **Paste** are available in the *Home* tab> Clipboard panel and in the shortcut menu.

Cut to the Clipboard

As with other Windows applications, ✂ (Cut Clip) removes the selected objects from their file and places them on the clipboard.

Copy to the Clipboard

When using the Windows **Copy** command, you have the following options:

	Copy Clip	Copies the selected objects to the clipboard, using the lower left corner of the bounding box of all of the objects as the base point. <Ctrl>+<C> starts the command.
	Copy with Base Point	In the shortcut menu, expand **Clipboard** and select **Copy with Base Point**. It enables you to select the base point after the objects have been selected. This option provides more control over the location of the objects when they are placed. The base point is only significant when the objects are pasted into the AutoCAD software.
NA	**Copy Link**	Type **copylink** at the Command Line. It copies the contents of the current view to the clipboard.

Paste from the Clipboard

When using the Windows **Paste** command, you have the following options:

	Paste	Prompts you to select a location for the base point at which it then places the objects. <Ctrl>+<V> starts the command.

Modify Objects

	Paste as Block	The copied objects are placed as a block. The AutoCAD software gives the block an arbitrary name. This option is only available if the objects on the clipboard are AutoCAD objects.
	Paste to Original Coordinates	Places the objects at the same coordinates as in the drawing from which they were taken. This option is only available if the objects on the clipboard are AutoCAD objects.
	Paste as Hyperlink	Creates a hyperlink of an object, text or file already copied to clipboard, and then associates it with another object.
	Paste Special	Enables you to control the format of an already copied data while pasting it into the active drawing.

Drag-and-Drop Copying

When two drawing windows are open, you can also *drag-and-drop* objects to copy them from one drawing into another.

How To: Copy using Drag-and-Drop

1. Without a command running, select the objects that you want to copy.
2. Hold the mouse button with the cursor on the objects (do not select a grip).
3. Drag the objects into the other drawing window and release the mouse button.

Match Properties Across Drawings

(Match Properties) works across drawings. You can select an object in one drawing and apply its properties to objects in another drawing.

Match Properties works for general object properties, such as color, linetype, and lineweight, and for the formatting of some specific object types, including text, dimensions, hatching, and tables.

© 2017, ASCENT - Center for Technical Knowledge®

Practice 3a

Working in Multiple Drawings

Practice Objectives

- Switch between drawings and display them side by side.
- Copy and paste objects between drawings.

Estimated time for completion: 5 minutes

In this practice, you will switch between multiple drawings using *File* tabs and Open Documents. You will display drawings side by side using the Tile Vertical command. You will then copy and paste objects between the drawings, as shown in Figure 3–4.

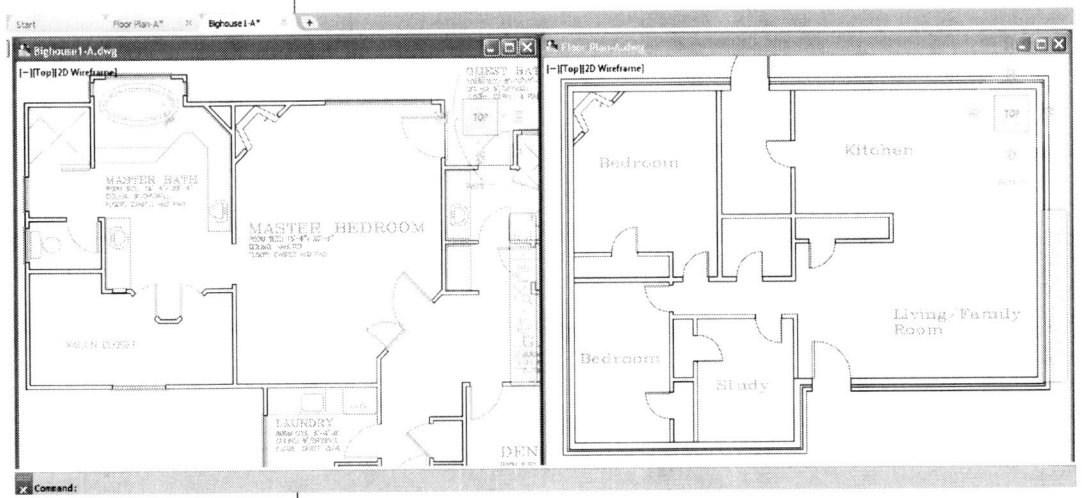

Figure 3–4

*Use <Ctrl> to select both files in the Select File dialog box and click **Open**.*

1. Open **Floor Plan-A.dwg** and **Bighouse1-A.dwg** from your practice files folder. Close any other open drawings.

2. If not already active, in the *Files* tab bar, select the **Bighouse1-A.dwg** tab. Then, hover the cursor over the **Floor Plan-A.dwg** tab to display its preview images, as shown in Figure 3–5. Select the **Model** preview to switch to **Floor Plan-A.dwg** with its *Model* tab active.

Modify Objects

Depending on the selection of the filenames in the Select File dialog box, your drawing tabs might be reversed.

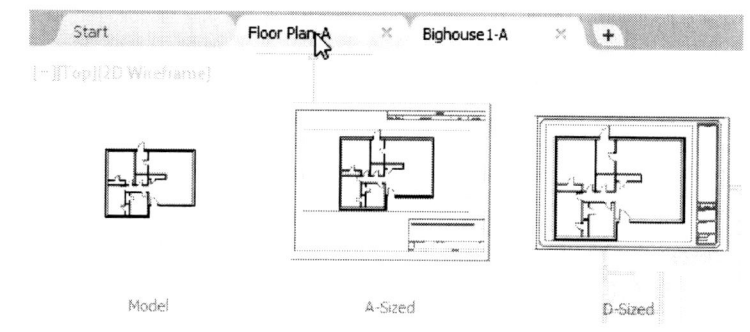

Figure 3–5

3. Thaw the layer **Text**.

4. In the Application Menu, click (Open Documents) and display the thumbnails of the two floor plans by hovering the cursor over them, as shown in Figure 3–6. Select **Bighouse1-A.dwg** to make that drawing current.

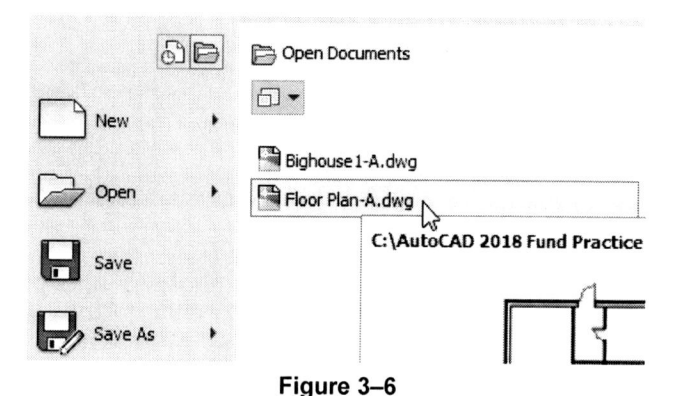

Figure 3–6

5. In the *View* tab>Interface panel, click (Tile Vertically) to display the drawings side-by-side. Minimize the *Start* tab display and click (Tile Vertically) again so that only the two drawings fill the drawing window.

6. In **Bighouse1-A.dwg**, in the *Model* tab, zoom in on the Master Bedroom (upper left corner of floorplan) and start the **Match Properties** command (*Home* tab>Properties panel). Select the text **MASTER BEDROOM** as the source object. Click inside **Floor Plan-A.dwg** once to activate it and then select each of the text labels in **Floor Plan-A.dwg** as the destination object, as shown in Figure 3–7. Press <Enter> to exit the command. The text properties are matched in both drawings.

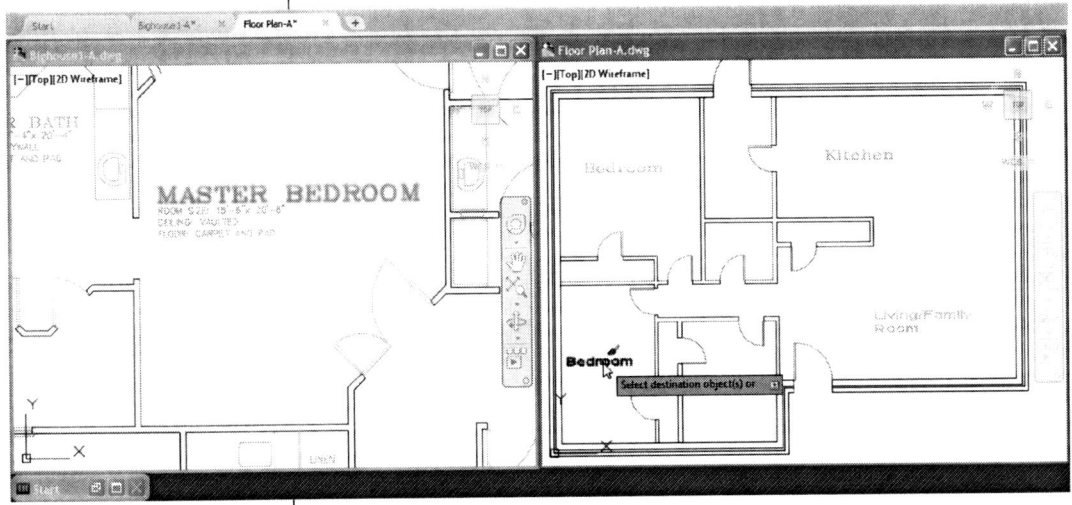

Figure 3–7

7. Make **Bighouse1-A.dwg** the active window. Right-click and select **Clipboard>Copy with Base Point**. For the basepoint, select the corner of the walls behind the fireplace (in the master bedroom). Select the fireplace (they might be separate objects) and the short diagonal walls that frame it and press <Enter>.

8. In the *File Tabs* bar, select the *Floor Plan-A* tab to switch to it and make it active. Right-click and select **Clipboard>Paste**. For the insertion point, select the top left corner of the larger bedroom to paste the fireplace there.

9. Close both drawings. Do not save changes.

10. Maximize the Start window.

3.4 Rotating Objects

Design changes sometimes require modifying the placement angle of an object. The **Rotate** command rotates selected objects around a defined pivot point.

How To: Rotate an Object

1. In the *Home* tab>Modify panel, click ⟳ (Rotate).
2. Select the objects to rotate.
3. Press <Enter> to end the object selection.
4. Select the base point around which the objects are going to rotate.
5. Move the cursor to rotate the objects. A dashed line indicates the location of the base point. ⟳ displays at the cursor, indicating that the **Rotate** command is active, as shown in Figure 3–8. It also indicates the direction in which typed values are going to be rotated, in this case, counter-clockwise (default). The original objects fade to gray while the new objects maintain their original properties.

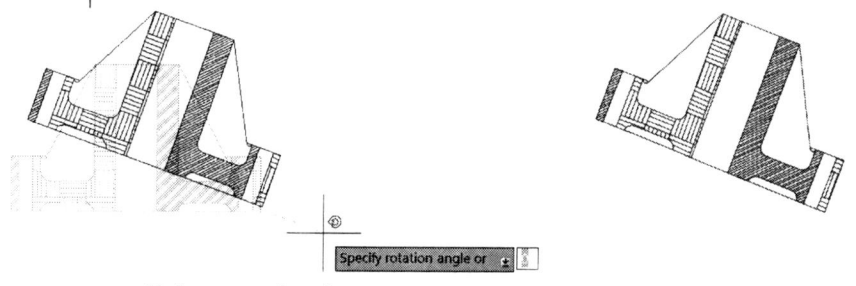

Enter an angle value   *Rotated object*

Figure 3–8

6. Enter a *Rotation Angle* or select a point to specify the rotation.

- A negative rotation angle enables you to turn the object clockwise.

- Polar Tracking can be used to constrain the rotation to a precise angle.

- At Specify rotation angle prompt, you can access the **Copy** option, which leaves the original object in place and rotates a copy of it.

- You can select the objects first and then start the **Rotate** command.

- You can change the default rotation direction used by the **Rotate** command by selecting or clearing the **Clockwise** option in the Drawing Units dialog box, as shown in Figure 3–9. (Application Menu> **Drawing Utilities>Units**)

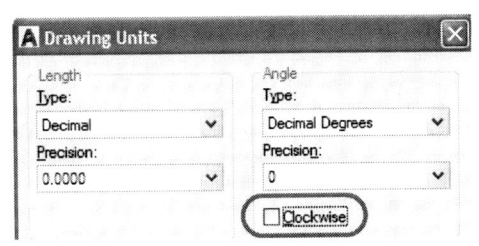

Figure 3–9

3.5 Scaling Objects

The **Scale** command enlarges or reduces the size of selected objects around a defined reference point.

How To: Scale an Object

1. In *Home* tab>Modify panel, click ☐ (Scale).
2. Select the objects to scale.
3. Press <Enter> or right-click to end the object selection.
4. Select the base point to be used for scaling.
5. Move the cursor to scale the objects. ☐ displays at the cursor, indicating that the **Scale** command is active, as shown in Figure 3–10. The original objects fade to gray while the new objects maintain their original properties.

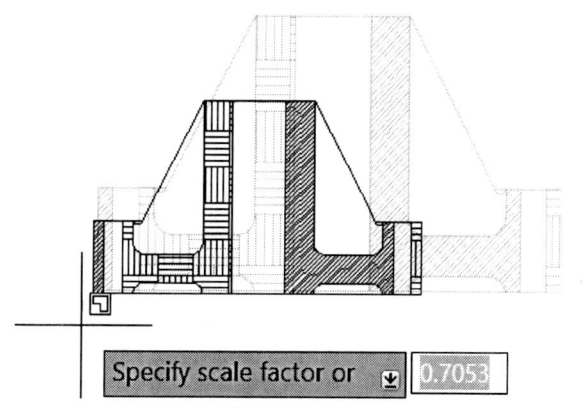

Figure 3–10

6. Enter a value for the scale factor.

- The **scale factor** enables you to set the required level of enlargement or reduction in size. Scale factors smaller than 1 decrease the size and scale factors larger than 1 increase the size.

- The **Copy** option in the **Scale** command leaves the original object unscaled and creates a scaled copy.

Practice 3b

Estimated time for completion: 25 minutes

Modifying Objects

Practice Objective

- Modify the location, quantity, and size of objects.

In this practice, you will use the **Move**, **Copy**, **Rotate**, **Scale**, and **Mirror** commands to place furniture in a floorplan, as shown in Figure 3–11. Some of the objects in the drawing are locked in place so that you do not move them by mistake.

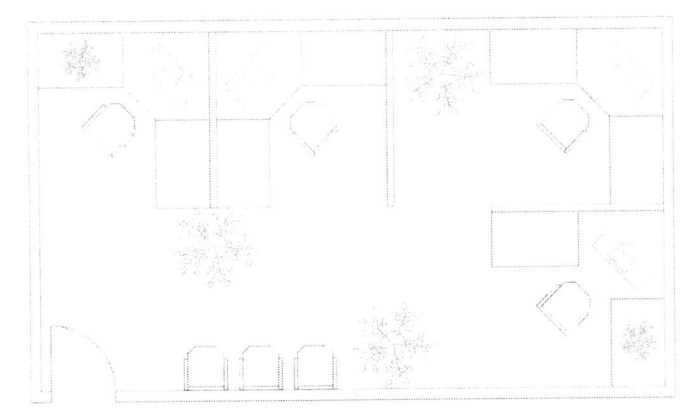

Figure 3–11

Task 1 - Move an object.

In this task you will use the **Move** command to place furniture in a floorplan, as shown in Figure 3–12.

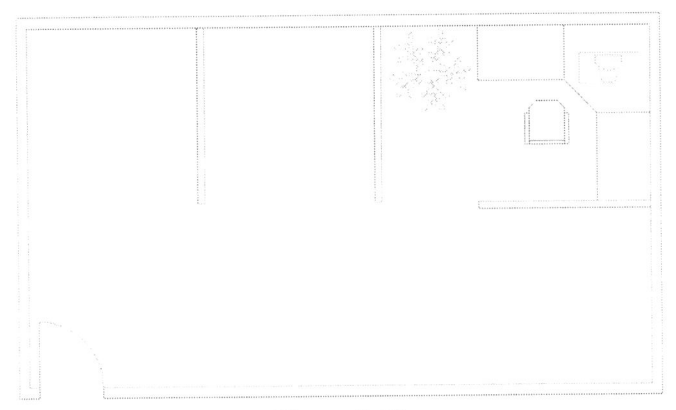

Figure 3–12

Modify Objects

1. Open **Arrange-A.dwg** from your practice files folder.

2. In the Status Bar, toggle off (Polar Tracking) and (Object Snap Tracking). Toggle on (Object Snap) and verify that **Endpoint** is selected.

3. In the *Home* tab>Modify panel, click (Move).

4. Select the desk and press <Enter> to end the object selection.

5. For the base point, snap to the end point at the back corner (upper right) of the desk.

6. Hover the cursor and snap it (without clicking) to the inside corner of the top right cubicle, as shown in Figure 3–13. The original objects fade to gray while the new objects maintain their original properties.

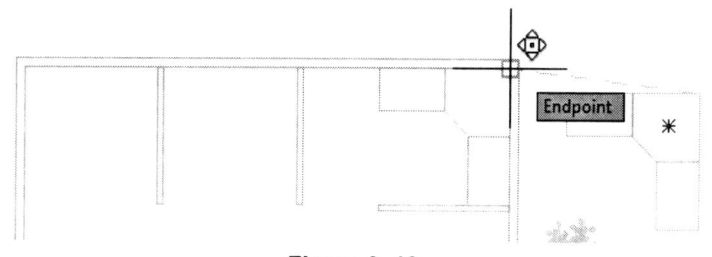

Figure 3–13

7. Click at that point to confirm the move.

8. Toggle off (Object Snap).

9. Move the chair to place it in front of the desk (use approximate location) and move the PC onto the desk, as shown in Figure 3–12. Do not rotate them now.

10. Move the plant to the open space next to the desk, as shown in Figure 3–12.

Task 2 - Copy an object.

In this task you will use the **Copy** command to copy several chairs and plants in the floorplan, as shown in Figure 3–14.

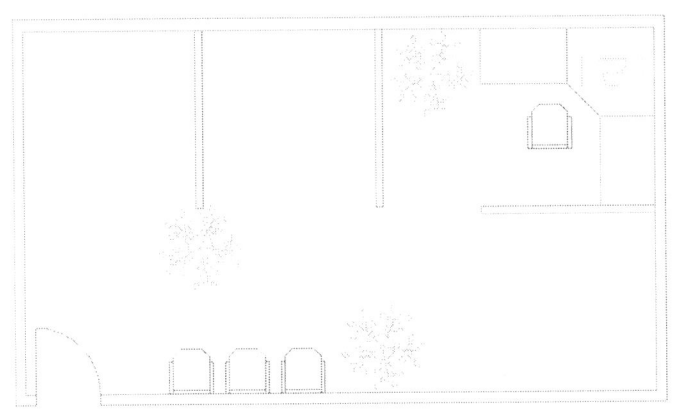

Figure 3–14

1. In the *Home* tab>Modify panel, click (Copy).

2. Select the plant and press <Enter> to end the object selection.

3. For the base point, click near the center of the plant.

4. Move the cursor near the bottom of the left most inner wall, as shown in Figure 3–15. Note that a copy of the plant is attached with the cursor. A dashed line connects with the cursor indicating the new location with the original object highlighted, as shown in Figure 3–15. Once you locate the required location for the copy (bottom of the leftmost inner wall), click to place the plant.

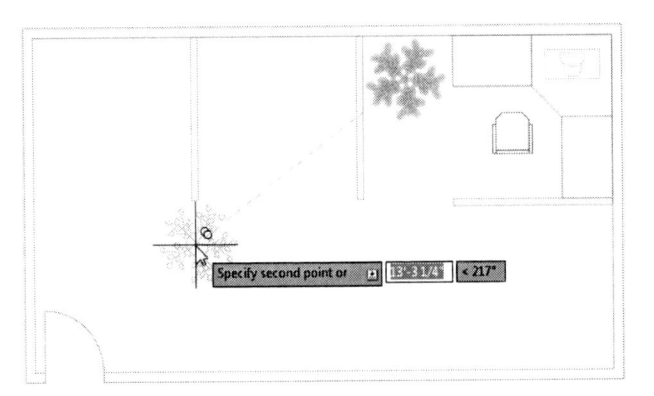

Figure 3–15

5. With the plant and the dashed line still attached to the cursor, move the cursor again and click to place another copy along the bottom wall. Press <Enter> to exit the command.

6. Copy the chair to the locations shown in Figure 3–14. (**Tip:** To position the chairs flush along the wall, use the **Midpoint** or **Endpoint** object snap to select the base point at the back of the chair. Then, select the **Nearest** object snap override (<Shift>+ right-click) to select points along the wall.)

Task 3 - Rotate an object.

In this task, you will rotate the chair and PC and then copy the entire set of furniture to other locations, as shown in Figure 3–16.

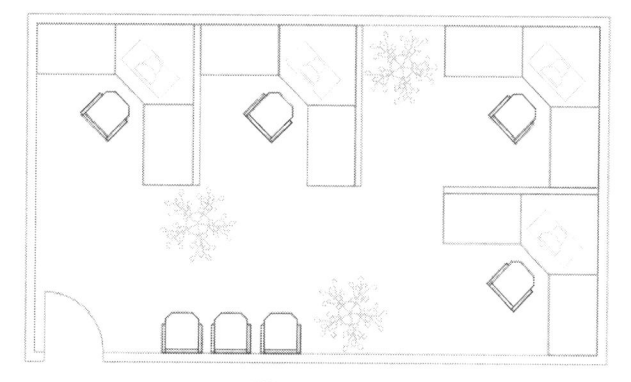

Figure 3–16

1. In the Status Bar, expand ⟲ ▼ (Polar Tracking) and select **45,90,135,180...**, if required. Toggle on ⟲ ▼ (Polar Tracking) and toggle off ▢ ▼ (Object Snap).

2. In the *Home* tab>Modify panel, click ↻ (Rotate) and select the chair near the desk. Press <Enter> and select the base point near the middle of the chair. Pull the cursor away from the chair until you see the 315 degree angle (multiple of 45) and the seat is facing the desk, as shown in Figure 3–17. Note that the original objects fade to gray while the new objects maintain their original properties. Click to accept the angle.

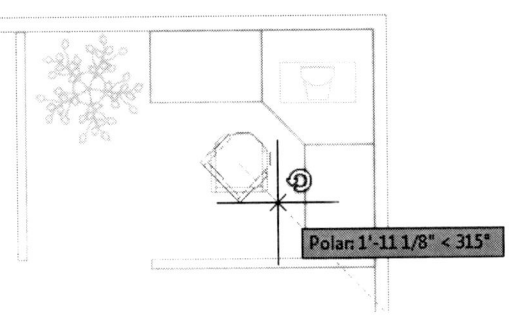

Figure 3–17

3. Repeat the process to rotate the PC using 135 degree angle such that the monitor is facing the chair, as shown in Figure 3–16.

4. Move the chair as required, to place it correctly in front of the desk. Do the same for the PC to center it on the desk.

Select the object and use <Ctrl> and the required arrow key to nudge the objects in place.

5. Toggle on ▭▼ (Object Snap) and verify that it is set to **Endpoint**.

6. Start the **Copy** command. Select the chair, desk, and PC, and then press <Enter>. For the base point, select the back corner (top right) of the desk. Copy the objects to the other three cubicles, as shown in Figure 3–16.

7. Save the drawing.

Task 4 - Scale an object.

In this task you will copy and scale some of the plants, as shown in Figure 3–18.

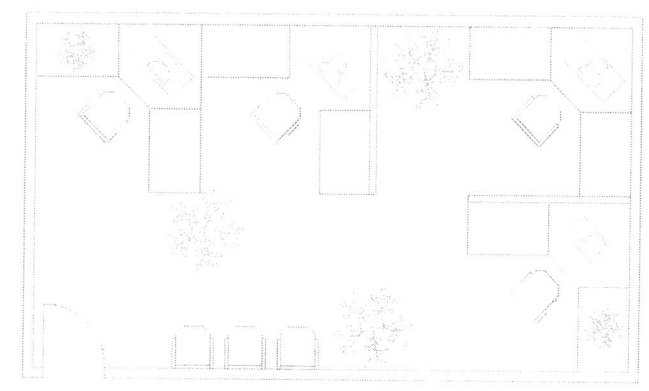

Figure 3–18

1. Copy one of the plants to the desk in the upper left cubicle.

2. In the *Home* tab>Modify panel, click ▢ (Scale). Select the plant, press <Enter>, and select the center of the plant as the base point. Enter **0.5** for the scale factor and press <Enter> to make it half of the original plant.

3. Copy the scaled plant to the desk in the lower right cubicle.

Task 5 - Mirror objects.

In this task you will use the **Mirror** command to mirror the contents of a cubicle, as shown in Figure 3–19.

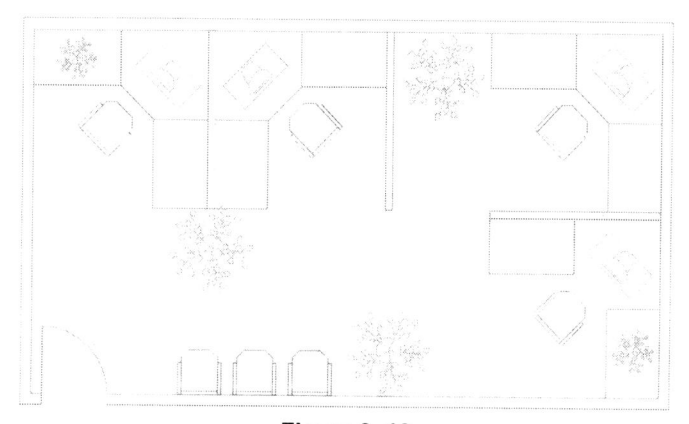

Figure 3–19

1. In the *Home* tab>Modify panel, click (Mirror).

2. At the *Select objects:* prompt, select the desk, PC, and chair in the middle cubicle, and press <Enter>.

3. At the *Specify first point of mirror line:* prompt, select the end point of the line that separates the corner desk section from the straight desk section at the top of the cubicle, as shown on the left in Figure 3–20.

4. At the *Specify second point of mirror line:* prompt, select a bottom end point, as shown on the right in Figure 3–20. At the *Erase source objects?* select **Yes** from the drop-down list. The contents of the middle cubicle are mirrored and the original objects are deleted.

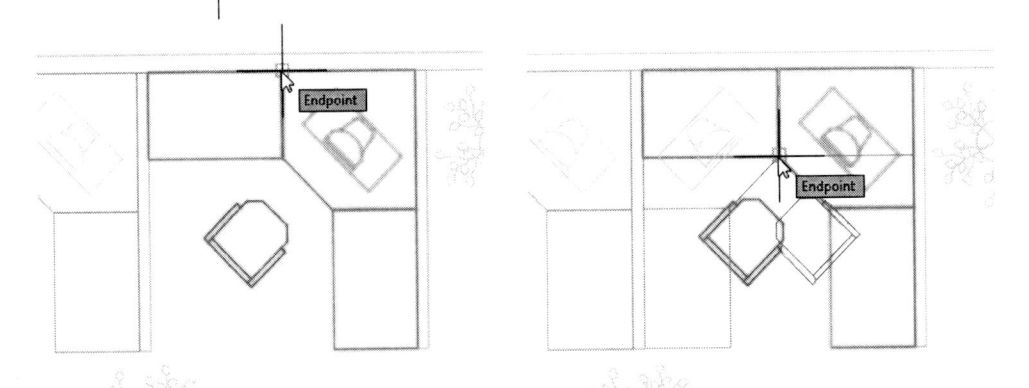

Figure 3–20

5. Save and close the drawing.

Modify Objects

3.6 Creating Arrays of Objects

The **Array** commands generate copies of selected objects at fixed intervals of rows and columns, around a center point, or along a path, as shown in Figure 3–21. For example, a rectangular array can be used to create light fixtures in a ceiling grid. Holes around a circular gasket or radial wings of a building are examples of a polar array. A path array can be used for lights along a walkway or the edge of an irregular shaped pool.

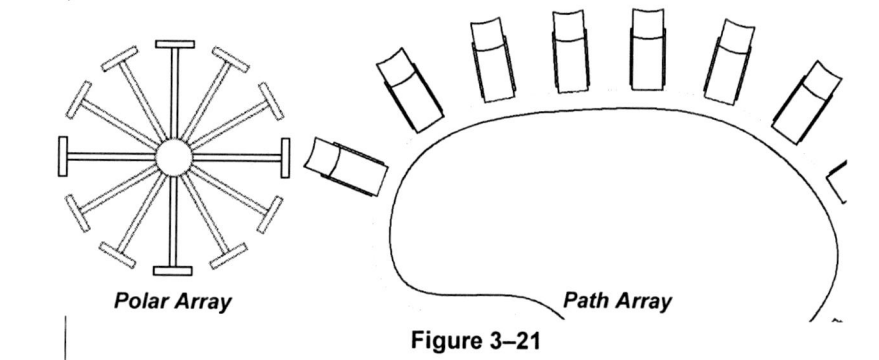

Rectangular Array   *Polar Array*   *Path Array*

Figure 3–21

Rectangular Array

A rectangular array consists of a pattern of objects that are divided into rows and columns.

- While creating rectangular arrays, you can use the **Angle** option to control the orientation angle of the array.

How To: Create a Rectangular Array

1. In the *Home* tab>Modify panel, expand the Array drop-down list and click (Rectangular Array).
2. At the *Select objects:* prompt, select the object(s) that you want to array and press <Enter>.

You can use windows or crossing selection to select objects.

3. A preview of the array displays a default number of objects in rows and columns, as shown in Figure 3–22. It also displays grips that enable you to modify the array.

Specify number of rows

Specify distance between rows

Specify destination point

Specify distance between columns

Specify number of rows and columns

Specify number of columns

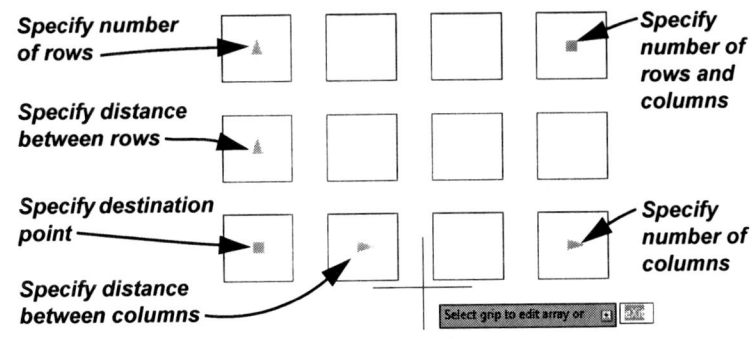

Figure 3–22

4. To specify the number of items to be in the array, use one of the following methods:
   - Use the *Specify number of rows*, *Specify number of columns*, and *Specify number of rows and columns* grips to change the number of columns and rows.
   - At the *Select grip to edit array or:* prompt, type **COU** and press <Enter> to use the **Count** option. You are prompted to enter a value for the number of columns, and then for the number of rows. Press <Enter> after you enter each value.

5. Specify the spacing between the arrayed items, using one of the following methods:
   - Use the *row* spacing and *column spacing* grips to change the number of columns and rows.
   - At the *Select grip to edit array or:* prompt, type **S** and press <Enter> to use the **Spacing** option. You are then prompted to enter a value for the distance between the columns and then for the rows. Press <Enter> after you enter each value.

6. If required, you can modify the location of the array by selecting the *Specify destination point* grip and then picking a destination point in the drawing window.

7. Press <Enter> to complete the command.

Polar Array

A polar array consists of a pattern of objects that are copied about a central radius.

- When creating polar arrays you can use the **ROWs** option to add additional offset rows around the center point, and the **ROTate items** option to set the arrayed items to be rotated in their orientation (or not) as they are placed around the center point.

How To: Create a Polar Array

1. In the *Home* tab>Modify panel, expand the Array drop-down list and click (Polar Array).
2. At the *Select objects:* prompt, select the object(s) that you want to array. Press <Enter> to end the selection of objects.
3. At the *Specify center point of array:* prompt, select a point on the screen to be the center of the polar array.
4. A preview of the array displays a default number of objects in a radial pattern, as shown in Figure 3–23. Additionally, it displays grips and an *Array Creation* contextual tab in the ribbon that enable you to modify the array.

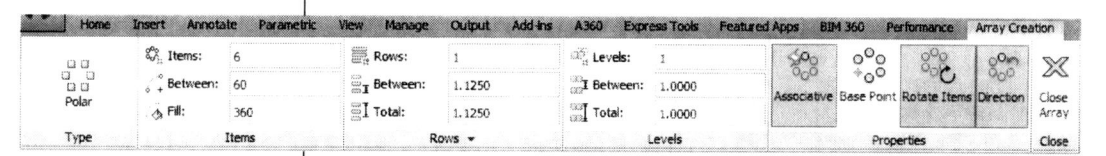

Figure 3–23

5. Specify the number of items in the Items panel.
6. Depending on the number of items and the *Fill* angle, the *Between* angle value changes to fit the specified number.
   - Using the **Fill** option, enter the angle that you want the arrayed items to fill.
7. If required, you can modify the rotation of the items and the direction of the array using the **Rotation Items** and **Direction** buttons is the contextual tab.
8. Press <Enter> to complete the command.

Path Array

A path array consists of a pattern of objects that are copied along a straight, curved, or irregular linear path.

- When using the path array, you might want to place the arrayed object in its final orientation and position. You need to place it near the start end point of the path for simplicity. Otherwise, you need to use the **Orientation** option to indicate how the object is to be oriented and positioned along the path.

- You can use the **Method** option, with its **Divide** option to evenly space the objects along the path.

How To: Create a Path Array

1. In the *Home* tab>Modify panel, expand the Array drop-down list and click (Path Array).
2. At the *Select objects:* prompt, select the object(s) that you want to array. Press <Enter> to end the selection of objects.
3. At the *Select path curve:* prompt, select the object that you want to use as the path.
4. A preview of the array displays a default number of objects copied along a path, as shown in Figure 3–24. It also displays grips that enable you to modify the array.

Specify distance between items

Specify number of rows

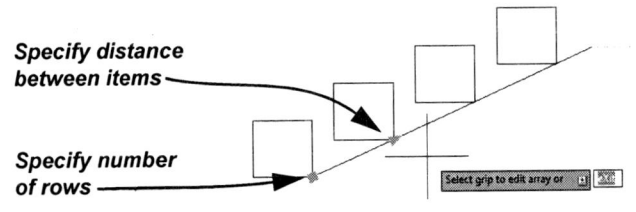

Figure 3–24

5. Specify the number of items in the array by selecting the square grip (as shown in Figure 3–24), typing a value, and pressing <Enter>.
6. Specify the distance between the items along the path by selecting the arrow grip (as shown in Figure 3–24), typing a value, and pressing <Enter>. You can also select the grip and drag the cursor to change the value.
7. Press <Enter> to complete the command.

> **Hint: Array Contextual Tabs**
>
> Once the required objects have been selected to be arrayed in any array style, you can use the *Array Creation* contextual tab in the ribbon to set the number of items, rows, columns, levels, or other properties.

Modify Objects

Practice 3c

Estimated time for completion: 5 minutes

Rectangular Array

Practice Objective

- Make copies of objects at fixed intervals of rows and columns.

In this practice, you will use a **Rectangular Array** to make copies of a workstation in a classroom, as shown in Figure 3–25.

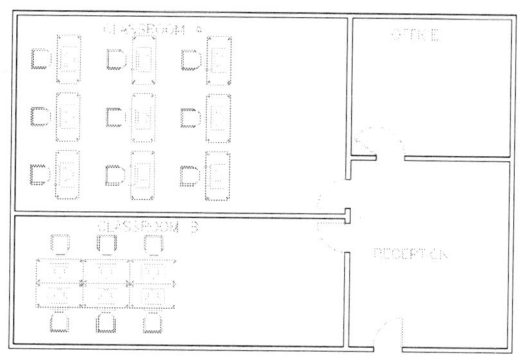

Figure 3–25

1. Open **Class3-A.dwg** from your practice files folder.

2. In the *Home* tab>Modify panel, expand the Array drop-down list and select (Rectangular Array).

You can use the window or crossing selection to select the three objects.

3. At the *Select objects:* prompt, select the desk, chair, and computer in Classroom A and press <Enter>.

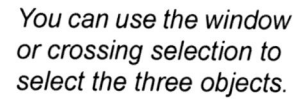

The top right square grip specifies the number of rows and columns.

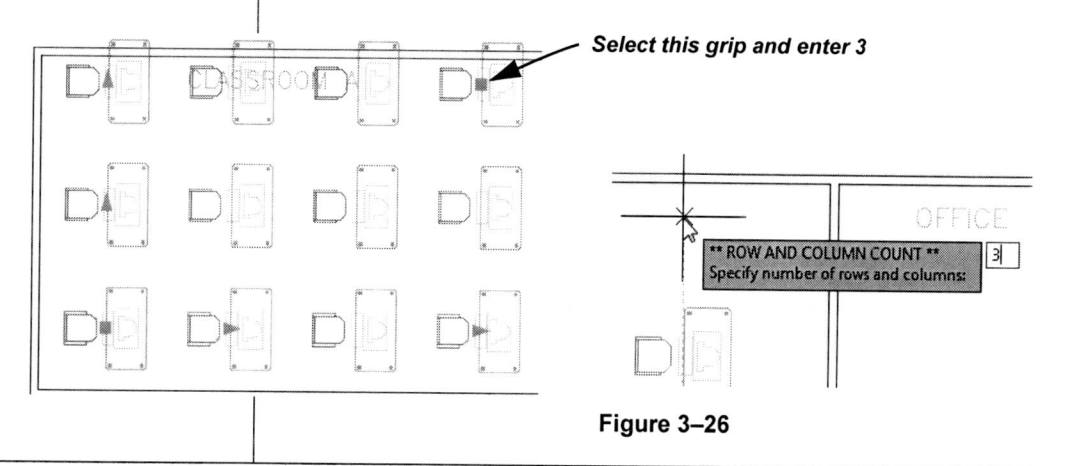

4. At the *Select grip to edit array*, select the top-right corner grip (square grip) and enter **3**, as shown in Figure 3–26. Press <Enter>.

Figure 3–26

© 2017, ASCENT - Center for Technical Knowledge®

The middle left arrow grip specifies the row spacing.

The middle bottom arrow grip specifies the column spacing.

5. Select the middle grip along the left side (upward facing arrow grip) and verify that **ROW SPACING** displays at the cursor prompt. Enter **6'**, as shown on the left in Figure 3–27. Press <Enter>.

6. Select the middle grip along the bottom (right facing arrow grip) and verify that **COLUMN SPACING** displays at the cursor prompt. Enter **8'**, as shown on the right in Figure 3–27. Press <Enter>.

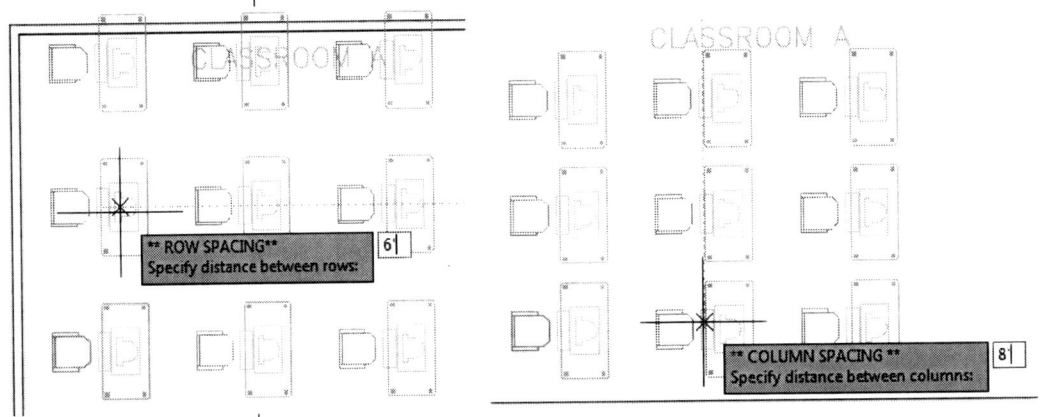

Figure 3–27

7. Press <Enter> to exit the command.

8. Save and close the file.

Practice 3d

Estimated time for completion: 5 minutes

Polar Array

Practice Objective

- Make copies of an object around a center point.

In this practice, you will use **Polar Array** to make copies of the nut around the flange, as shown in Figure 3–28.

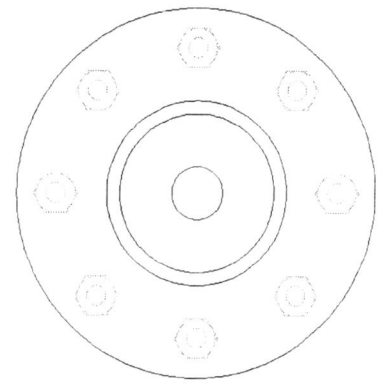

Figure 3–28

1. Open **Flange-I.dwg** from your practice files folder.

2. Select the **Center** object snap option and verify that **Object Snap** is active in the Status Bar.

3. In the *Home* tab>Modify panel, expand the Array drop-down list and click (Polar Array).

4. At the *Select objects:* prompt, select the nut. Press <Enter> to finish selecting objects.

5. At the *Specify center point of array:* prompt, select the center of any circle.

6. Note that the *Array Creation* contextual tab displays in the ribbon. In the Items panel, for *Items* enter **8** and press <Enter>. Note that the *Between* angle value changes to accommodate the specified number of items, as shown in Figure 3–29.

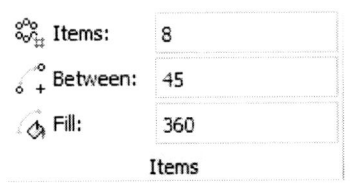

Items:	8
Between:	45
Fill:	360

Items

Figure 3–29

7. In the preview of the array, note that the nuts are rotated. In the *Array Creation* tab>Properties panel, click (Rotate Items) to clear it. Note that the nut is correctly arrayed around the flange.

8. Press <Enter> to complete the command.

9. Save and close the file.

Practice 3e

Estimated time for completion: 5 minutes

Path Array

Practice Objective

- Make copies of an object along a selected path.

In this practice, you will use a **Path Array** to make copies of a deck chair around the edge of a pool, as shown in Figure 3–30.

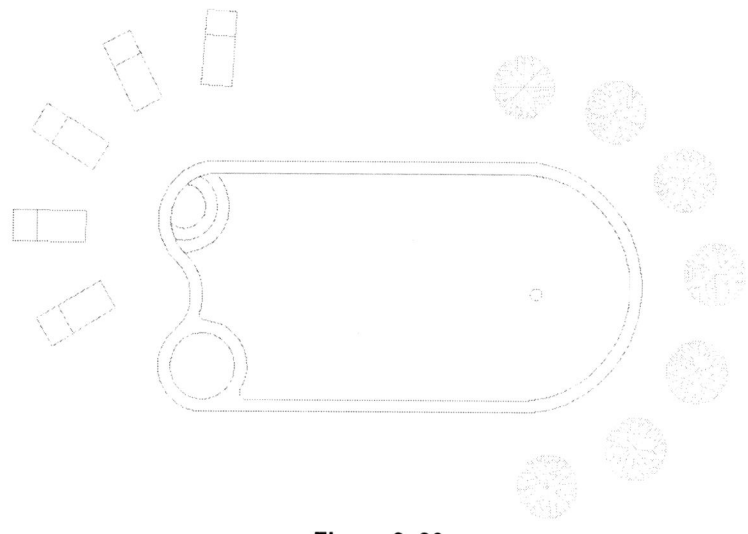

Figure 3–30

1. Open **Deckchair-I.dwg** from your practice files folder.

2. In the *Home* tab>Modify panel, expand the Array drop-down list and click (Path Array).

3. At the *Select objects:* prompt, select the tree to the right of the pool. Press <Enter> to finish selecting objects.

4. At the *Select path curve:* prompt, select the magenta arc that starts at the tree.

5. Select the arrow grip (located on the second tree) and enter **8'**, as shown in Figure 3–31. Press <Enter>.

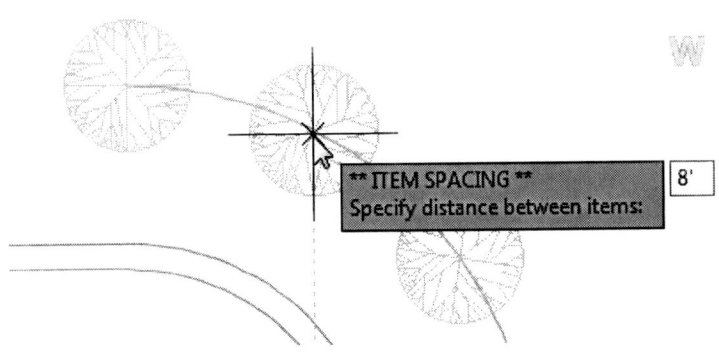

Figure 3–31

6. Press <Enter> again to exit the command.
7. Start the **Path Array** command again.

Select both rectangle and a line that makes up the chair.

8. At the *Select objects:* prompt, select the chair to the left of the pool. Press <Enter> to finish selecting objects.
9. At the *Select path curve:* prompt, select the magenta arc that starts at the chair.
10. In the *Array Creation* contextual tab, in the Properties panel, expand the Measure drop-down list and click (Divide). The chairs are now evenly spaced along the path.
11. In the *Array Creation* contextual tab, in the Items panel, for *Items* enter **5** and press <Enter>.
12. Press <Enter> to end the command.
13. Toggle off the layer **Path** to hide the paths that were used to create the arrays.
14. Save and close the file.

3.7 Trimming and Extending Objects

Trim and **Extend** commands can be used to modify already existing objects to ensure that they have the correct size and length, as shown in Figure 3–32.

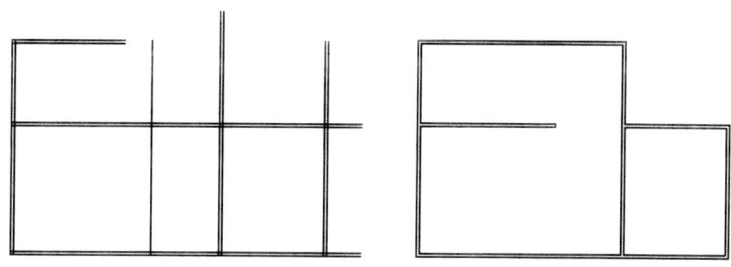

Figure 3–32

Trimming Objects

The **Trim** command erases any part of an object that extends past a user-defined cutting edge. It simplifies many drawing tasks. For example, an easy way to create an arc is to draw and then trim a circle.

How To: Trim Objects

1. In the *Home* tab>Modify panel, click ⁄ (Trim).
2. Select the cutting edges (they highlight in blue with a thicker line weight) or press <Enter> to select all of the edges (these edges do not highlight).
3. If you selected specific edges, press <Enter> to end the selection of cutting edges.

*You can also use the **Trim** command to extend an object. At the Select object to trim or Shift-select to extend prompt, you can hold <Shift> and select to extend an object.*

4. Hover the cursor over the part of the object that you want to trim. The portion is faded in a light gray line weight, providing a preview of the part that is going to be removed, as shown in Figure 3–33.

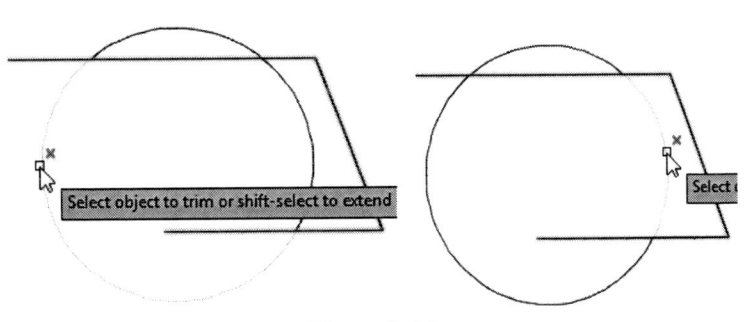

Figure 3–33

5. Select the part to be removed.
6. Press <Enter> to complete the command.

- If you select something by mistake, you can use the **Undo** option in the command (<Down Arrow> menu) to restore the last object trimmed. You can also click in the Quick Access Toolbar for the **Trim** and **Extend** commands. However, doing so causes you to lose all of the trimming you have done to that point.

Hint: Selecting Objects to Trim or Extend

Any method of object selection can be used to select the cutting or boundary edge(s). Objects to be trimmed or extended can be selected using the point-and-pick, Crossing, or Fence methods of object selection.

When you select the **Crossing** option, you are prompted to select two opposite corners, as shown in Figure 3–34. Everything touching or in the box is previewed (faded light gray) and is then trimmed or extended when you select the second corner. You remain in the command so that you can select more objects as required.

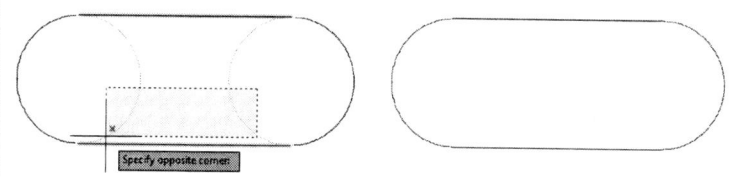

Figure 3–34

When you select the **Fence** option, you are prompted to select fence points. Everything touching these line segments is selected to be trimmed and displays a preview (faded light gray), as shown in Figure 3–35. Press <Enter> to trim the object. You remain in the command so that you can select more objects as required.

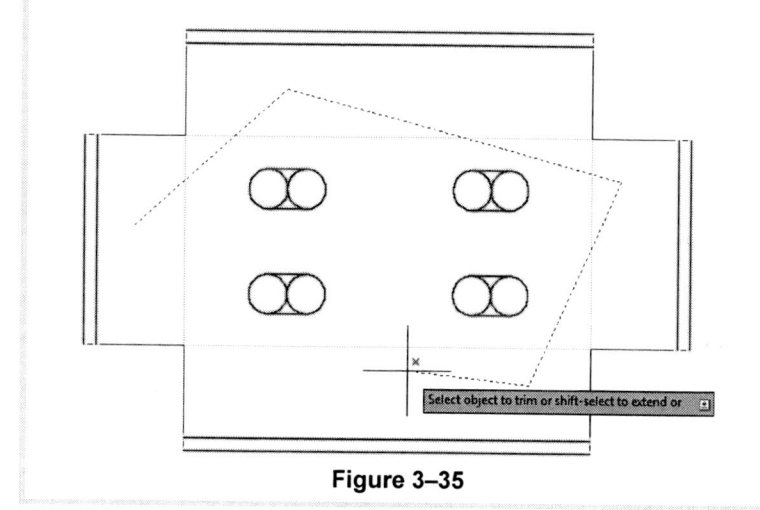

Figure 3–35

Extending Objects

*You can also use the **Extend** command to trim an object, At the Select object to extend or Shift-select to trim prompt, you can hold <Shift> and select to trim an object.*

Hint: Trimming Objects without Cutting Edges

The **Break** command can be used to cut an object without any overlapping edges. Two different options of the command are available in the *Home* tab>expanded Modify panel:

- **(Break):** Removes a portion of an object between two user-defined points, leaving a gap. This has the same effect as trimming between two cutting edges.

- **(Break at Point):** Breaks an object at one point so that it becomes two pieces, but does not have a gap. This option is useful if you need to change a portion of a line into a different linetype.

Using the **Extend** command, any object that does not reach a boundary edge is lengthened until it meets the boundary, as shown in Figure 3–36.

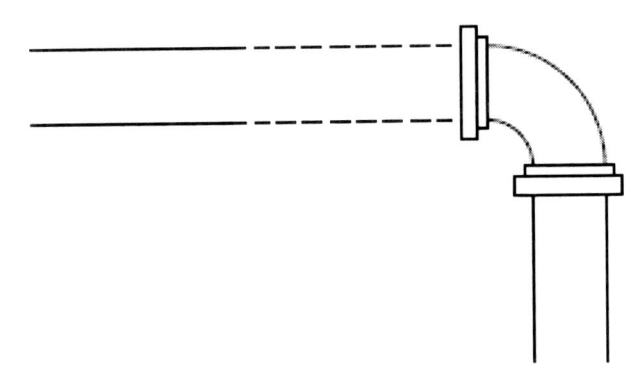

Figure 3–36

How To: Extend Objects

1. In the *Home* tab>Modify panel, click (Extend).
2. Select the boundary edges (they highlight in blue with a thicker line weight) or press <Enter> to select all of the edges (these edges do not highlight). If you selected specific edges, press <Enter> to end the selection of boundary edges.
3. Hover the cursor over the object that you want to extend (closer to the boundary edge), and a preview of the part that is going to be added displays.
4. Select to extend the object.
5. Press <Enter> to complete the command.

You can also draw a crossing or fence across multiple objects. Press <Enter> to select the object.

Practice 3f

Estimated time for completion: 10 minutes

Extending and Trimming Objects

Practice Objective

- Remove and extend objects.

In this practice, you will extend and trim lines to complete a drawing, as shown in Figure 3–37.

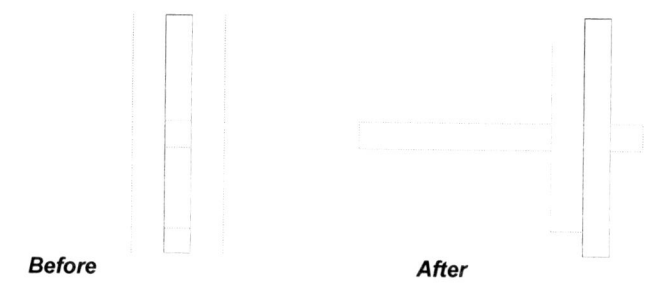

Before *After*

Figure 3–37

1. Open **Shaft-M.dwg** from your practice files folder.

2. In the *Home* tab>Modify panel, click ⁻⁻/ (Extend).

3. Select the two vertical red lines as the boundary edges, and press <Enter>. Note that they are highlighted in blue and a thicker line weight.

4. Select the pair of short horizontal red lines to extend them to the vertical red lines. You will need to select each short red line twice, closer to either end, to extend it on both sides. Press <Enter> to complete the command.

5. Start the **Extend** command again. Select the vertical blue line as the boundary edge. Extend the pair of short horizontal blue lines to the vertical blue line.

6. In the *Home* tab>Modify panel, click ⁻/⁻ (Trim). Select the two horizontal red lines as the boundary objects and press <Enter>. Select the top and bottom portions of both vertical red lines and press <Enter>.

7. Start the **Trim** command again to clean up the object, as shown on the right in Figure 3–37.

8. Save and close the drawing.

Practice 3g

Trimming Objects on a Drawing

Practice Objective

- Remove parts of objects.

Estimated time for completion: 5 minutes

In this practice, you will use the **Trim** command to remove parts of lines and to trim circles to create slots, as shown in Figure 3–38.

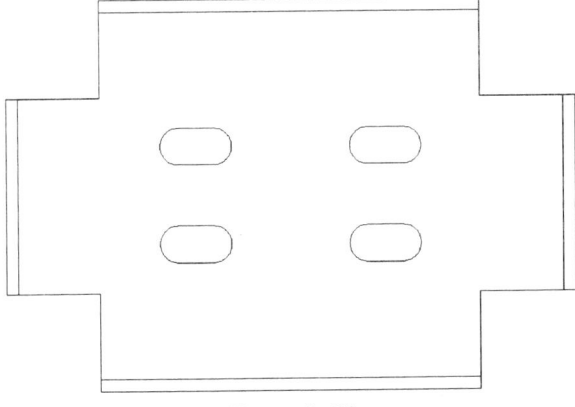

Figure 3–38

1. Open **Bracket-I.dwg** from your practice files folder.

2. Start the **Trim** command. At the *Select objects or <select all>:* prompt, select the two long horizontal and two long vertical lines in the middle of the drawing. Press <Enter>.

3. At the *Select object to trim:* prompt, select the four lines again, in the middle of each line. Press <Enter> to complete the command.

Select the four lines to trim individually, without using a fence or crossing window.

4. Zoom in closer to the four sets of circles and lines.

5. Start the **Trim** command again. At the *Select objects or <select all>:* prompt, press <Enter> to select all of the objects.

Modify Objects

Note that it might work differently than how it is shown in the Figure. Depending on which portions got trimmed, click and remove the inner parts to have the hollow shapes.

6. At the *Select object to trim:* prompt, select near the center part of the circles, as shown in Figure 3–39. You might have to select the middle portion twice until a gap is created. Select the arcs in both circles, on the sides where they touch, as shown in Figure 3–39.

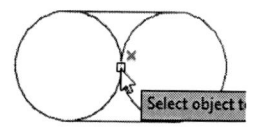

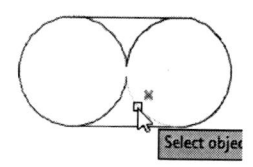

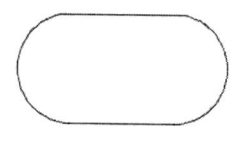

Before   **Gap created and select arcs**   **After**

Figure 3–39

7. Without leaving the command, select and trim the same parts in the other three circle pairs.

8. Press <Enter> to exit the command.

9. Save and close the drawing.

© 2017, ASCENT - Center for Technical Knowledge®

3–37

3.8 Mirroring Objects

The **Mirror** command creates reversed or symmetrical copies of objects across a user-specified mirror line.

How To: Mirror an Object

1. In the *Home* tab>Modify panel, click (Mirror).
2. Select the object(s) you want to mirror.
3. Press <Enter> to end the selection set.
4. Select the first point of the mirror line. The mirror line is the axis of symmetry or hinge about which the object(s) are mirrored.
5. Move the cursor to mirror the objects. A preview displays the mirror line and the potential location of the new mirrored object, as shown in Figure 3–40.

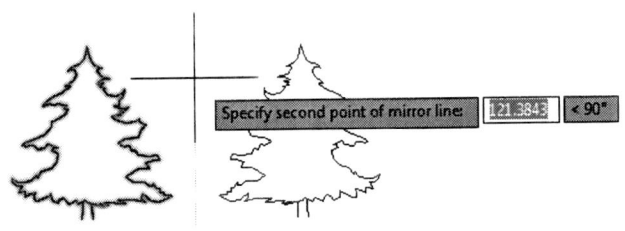

Figure 3–40

6. Select the second point of the mirror line.
7. At the *Erase source objects?* prompt, select **No** (default) to keep the original objects or **Yes** to delete them.

- Polar Tracking is useful for controlling the angle of the mirror line.

3.9 Offsetting Objects

The AutoCAD software enables you to create parallel shapes with a single editing command called **Offset,** as shown in Figure 3–41.

Offset distance set to 6"

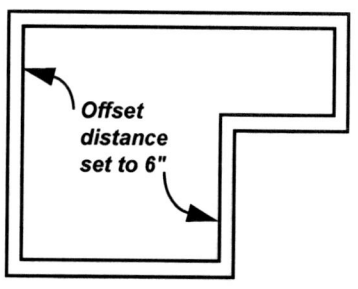

Figure 3–41

- The **Offset** command works with lines, circles, arcs, and polylines.

- You can specify a distance between the original object and the offset copy, or select a point through which the copy is going to pass.

How To: Offset Objects Using a Distance

1. In the *Home* tab>Modify panel, click (Offset).
2. Enter the offset distance and press <Enter>.
3. Select the object to offset.
4. Hover the cursor on either side of the object to display a preview of the offset copy.

- You can change the offset distance before selecting the side to place the offset copy.

5. Select a point on either side of the object to place the offset copy on that side.
6. Select another object to offset by the same distance, or press <Enter> to complete the command.

- If you want to offset one object multiple times, select the **Multiple** option before you select the side you want to offset. The new objects are placed at the same distance from the last object that was offset.

- The **Through** option enables you to select a point through which the offset object must pass. You can drag the cursor on either side of the object to display a preview of the offset copy before placing the offset.

- The **Erase** and **Layer** options are settings that remain active until you change them. By default, objects from which you offset are not erased, and the layer of the new object matches the layer of the source object rather than the current layer.

- If you offset a polyline, all of the sides are offset equally, as shown in Figure 3–42. To only offset one side of a polyline, you need to explode it first.

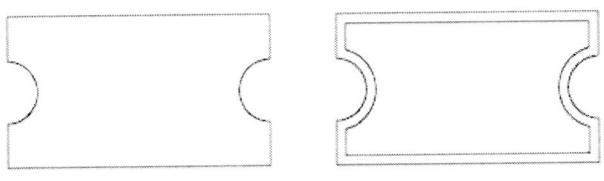

Figure 3–42

Practice 3h

Offsetting Objects

Estimated time for completion: 10 minutes

Practice Objective

- Offset polylines, lines, and arcs.

In this practice, you will use the **Offset** command on polylines, lines, and arcs to create walls and steps, as shown in Figure 3–43.

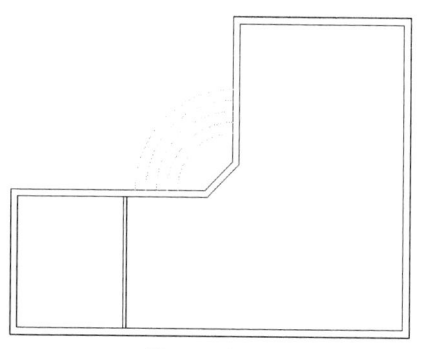

Figure 3–43

1. Open **Offset-A.dwg** from your practice files folder. Distances in the drawing are in feet and inches.

2. In the *Home* tab>Modify panel, click (Offset). Enter the *offset distance* as **1'** and press <Enter>. Select the large polyline as the object to offset. Drag the cursor inside the polyline to display the preview of the offset copy.

3. Select a point inside the polyline to create the offset copy on the inside. Press <Enter> to complete the command.

4. Start the **Offset** command. Enter the *offset distance* as **1'6"** and press <Enter>. Select the yellow arc as the object to offset. Drag the cursor outside (above) the arc to display the preview and select a point outside (above) the arc to create the offset copy.

5. Note that you are still in the **Offset** command and at the *Select object to offset:* prompt, select the arc you just created. At the *Specify point on side to offset:* prompt, press <Down Arrow> and select the **Multiple** option to make the command repeating. Select three points outside (above) the arcs to have a total of five arcs. Press <Enter> twice to complete the command.

6. Use the **Explode** command to turn the inner polyline you created into multiple single line objects.

7. Start the **Offset** command again, and set the *offset distance* to **15'**. Select the inside vertical line on the left bottom as the object to offset. Move the cursor to right of the line to preview the offset line (as shown on the left in Figure 3–44). Select a point to place the offset line.

*Since you had previously selected the **Multiple** option, the setting remains active.*

8. Note that you are still in the **Offset** command. At the *Select object to offset:* prompt, select the line you just created. Note that an offset line is previewed at 15'. In the offset distance edit box, enter **6"**, (as shown on the right in Figure 3–44) to change the offset distance. Press <Enter> to place the offset line to make an interior wall. Press <Enter> again to exit the command.

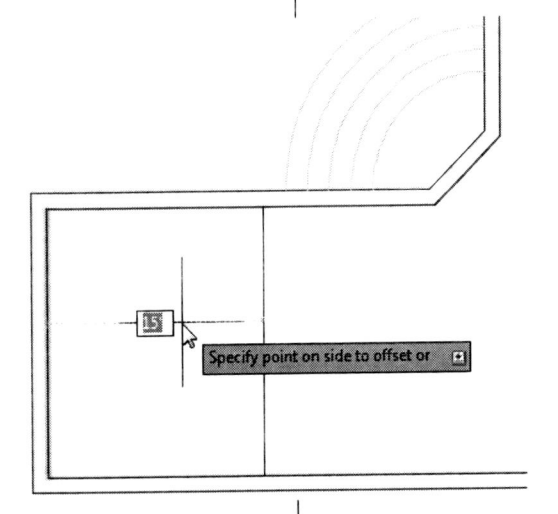

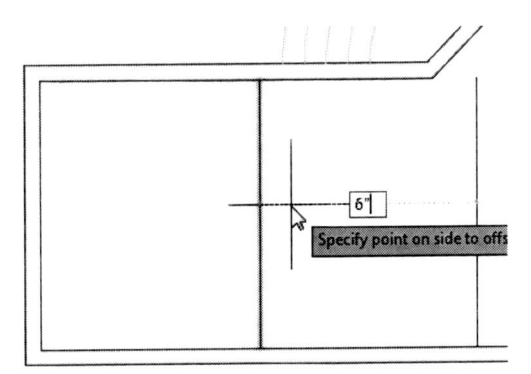

Figure 3–44

9. Save and close the drawing.

3.10 Editing with Grips

You can modify objects by using their grips without using an editing command. The AutoCAD software stores information about objects as geometric formulas. Therefore, lines are defined by their end points, circles by their center and radius, etc. The software can easily compute additional points, such as the midpoint of a line or quadrants of a circle, and enable you to modify them, as shown in Figure 3–45.

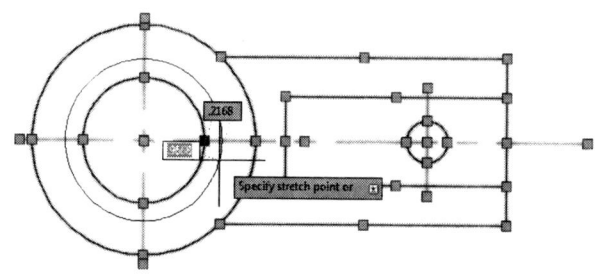

Figure 3–45

- By default, grips display as blue boxes on an object when it is selected without starting a command.

- If you hover the cursor over a grip but do not select it, the color changes to pink.

Working with Hot Grips

When you click directly on a grip, it changes to a selected or *hot grip* (red by default), as shown in Figure 3–46.

- Depending on the grip you make hot, the default mode is automatically enabled. For example, the quadrant grip of a circle stretches it, but the center grip moves the circle, as shown in Figure 3–46.

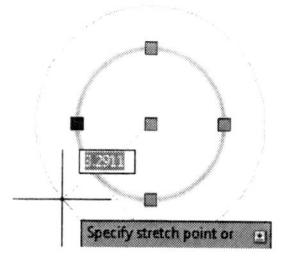

Hot grip selected on quadrant and used as Stretch   **Hot grip selected in center and used as Move**

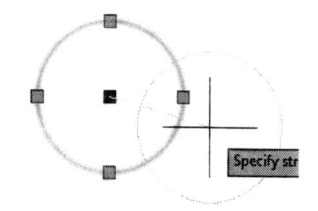

Figure 3–46

- If you hover the cursor over certain multi-functional grips, additional options display, as shown in Figure 3–47. The options for the endpoint grips of line segments and arcs include **Stretch** and **Lengthen**, and for the middle grip of arcs include **Stretch** and **Radius**.

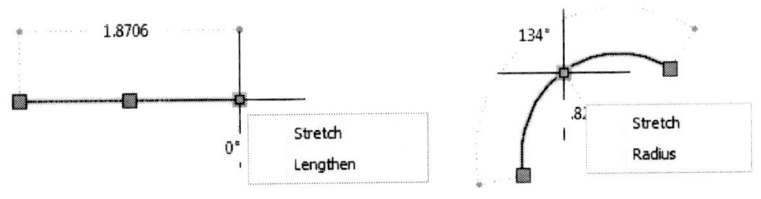

Figure 3–47

- To select a different option after you make a grip hot, you can right-click to display the various editing commands in the shortcut menu, as shown in Figure 3–48.

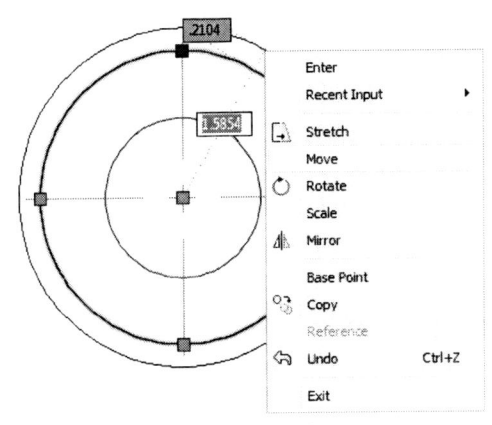

Figure 3–48

You can also press <Spacebar> to cycle through the available commands.

- Once a grip and an editing command have been selected, various advanced options (for the selected command) display by pressing <Down Arrow>, as shown in Figure 3–49.

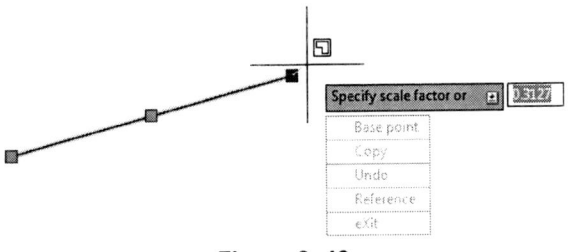

Figure 3–49

Modify Objects

- To clear objects and their grips, press <Esc>.
- When using grips, their default mode and multi-functional mode only apply to the object with the hot grip. However, **Move**, **Mirror**, **Scale**, and **Rotate** affect all of the selected objects.
- You can hold <Shift> to activate multiple modes of grips.
- When using grips on a block, **Stretch** has the same effect as **Move**. This is because you cannot stretch a standard block object.
- You can change the display of grips (size and color) and other settings in the *Selection* tab in the Options dialog box (Application Menu>**Options**).

Grips with Dynamic Dimensions

Grips enable you to quickly check the dimensions of an object. For example, when you hover the cursor over the end point grip of a line, dynamic dimensions display the line's length and angle and the quadrant grip on a circle displays the circle's radius, as shown in Figure 3–50.

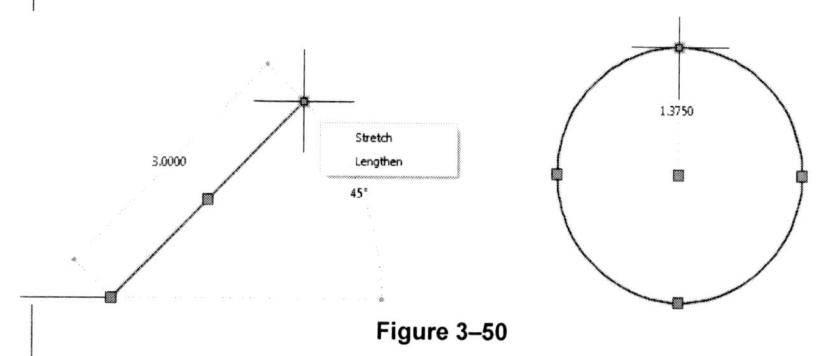

Figure 3–50

- (Dynamic Input) must be toggled on for the dimensions to be displayed.
- When you select the stretch grip of an object, you can edit the dimension instead of dragging the hot grip.

How To: Stretch a Line by 5 Units Using Grips

1. Select the line to display the grips.
2. Select the endpoint grip of the line, as shown in Figure 3–51.

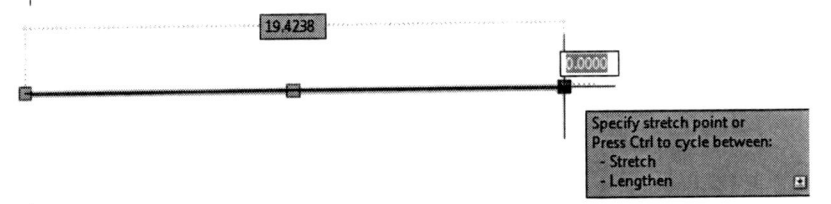

Figure 3–51

3. Two dimensions display for the length: one with the current overall length and one with the change in length (which is 0 unless you move the cursor). The change in length can be edited.

4. Enter **5** (as shown in Figure 3–52), and press <Enter> to change the length. The line length increases by 5 units and the angle does not change.

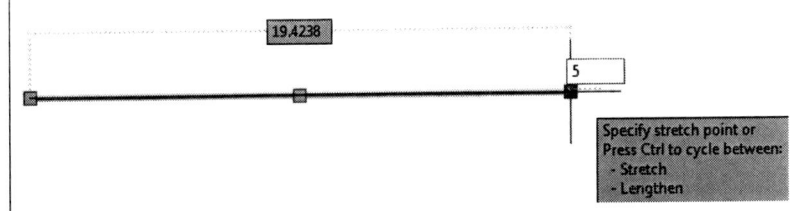

Figure 3–52

- If you press <Tab> when the change in length is highlighted, you can enter a new total length instead. Press <Tab> again to change the angle.

3.11 Using Grips Effectively

Grips are a very powerful tool and using them helps you to quickly and easily modify drawings. You can increase the effectiveness of using grips by changing the base point, copying with grips, using the reference option, stretching multiple objects (as shown in Figure 3–53), and modifying grip settings.

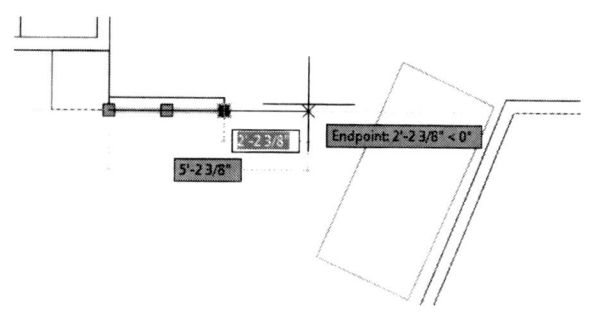

Figure 3–53

- If (Dynamic Input) is on, dynamic dimensions (and if it is a multifunctional grip, a dynamic list of options) display when you hover the cursor over a grip. Select one of the optional commands, such as **Stretch**, **Lengthen**, or **Add Vertex**.

- When you select a grip you can edit the dimensions to stretch the object. Use <Tab> to highlight the dimension that you want to change.

- Depending on which grip is selected, the Stretch mode either stretches or moves the object. Centers of circles and midpoints of lines move the objects. Standard blocks move because they cannot be stretched. Dynamic blocks have special grips.

- Pressing <Enter> while a grip is hot, sequentially toggles through **Move**, **Rotate**, **Scale**, **Mirror**, and then back to **Stretch**.

- To clear grips from objects, press <Esc> or right-click and select **Exit**.

Changing the Base Point

The hot grip becomes the default base point for moving, rotating, etc. To use a different base point, right-click and select **Base Point** as shown in Figure 3–54 (or type **B** in the Command Line). Select the new base point and continue with the command.

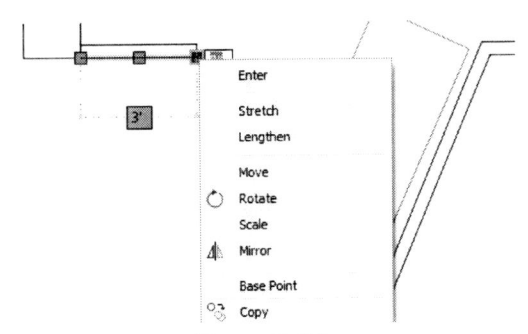

Figure 3–54

Copying with Grips

Use the **Copy** option with any of the grip editing modes to create multiple copies while you move, rotate, etc.

How To: Copy with Grips

1. Select the objects and make one grip hot.
2. Right-click and select the editing mode (**Stretch**, **Move**, **Rotate**, etc.).
3. Select the **Copy** option in the shortcut menu or Command Line.
4. Select (or type) the second point, rotation angle, mirror line, or scale factor.

- If you hold <Ctrl> while selecting the location for additional copies, the new objects snap to the same spacing as the first copy, as shown in Figure 3–55.

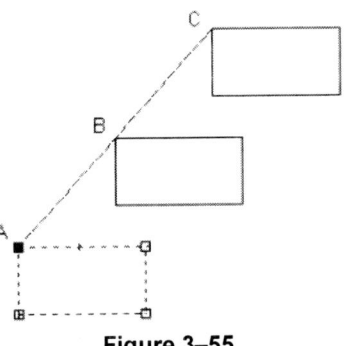

Figure 3–55

Holding <Ctrl> while selecting the point for stretching, moving, rotating, etc., also starts the multiple copy mode.

Rotate and Scale with the Reference Option

The **Reference** option enables you to select reference points in your drawing to describe the rotation angle or scale factor.

How To: Rotate and Scale with Grips and Reference

1. Select the objects that you want to rotate or scale.
2. Select the grip to be the base point for rotating or scaling.
3. Right-click and select **Rotate** or **Scale**.
4. Right-click and select **Reference**.
   - **For Rotate:** Specify the reference angle by typing the angle or selecting two points. Specify the new angle by typing the angle or selecting a second point. The first point of the new angle is the base point.
   - **For Scale:** Specify the reference length by typing the length or selecting two points. Specify the new length by typing the length or selecting a second point. The first point of the new length is the base point.

For example, you might want to straighten a rectangle that is rotated at an unknown angle, as shown in Figure 3–56. Select the rectangle and then select the grip at point 1 as the base point for rotation. Right-click and select **Rotate** and **Reference**. For the *Reference angle*, select the end points at **1** and **2** (this is the current angle of the object). For the *New angle*, type **0**.

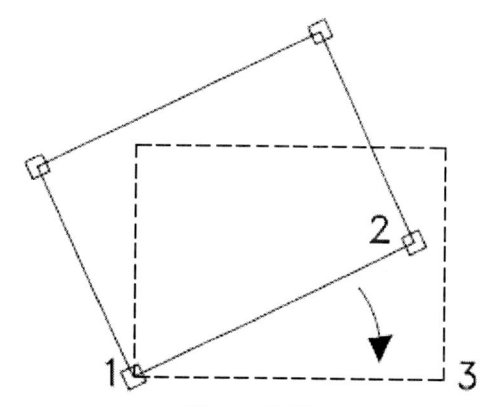

Figure 3–56

- The **Reference** option is also available with the regular **Rotate** and **Scale** commands.

Stretching Multiple Objects

In the Stretch mode, only hot grips or objects that contain hot grips are stretched. You can make multiple grips hot by holding <Shift> when selecting each grip, as shown in Figure 3–57.

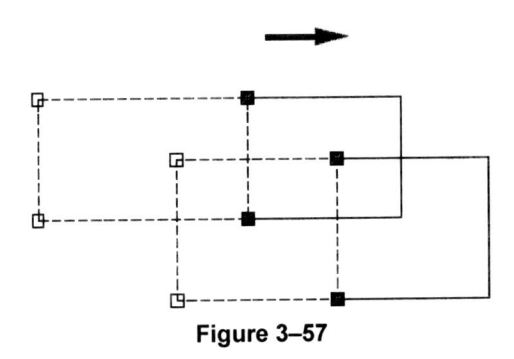

Figure 3–57

How To: Stretch with Grips

1. Select the objects that you want to stretch.
2. Hold <Shift> and select all of the grips that you want to move using **Stretch**.
3. Release <Shift>.
4. Select the grip that you want to use as a base point.
5. Select the point that you want to use as the second point of displacement.

Grip Settings

In the Options dialog box (expand the Application Menu and click **Options**), in the *Selection* tab, there are several settings related to grips, as shown in Figure 3–58.

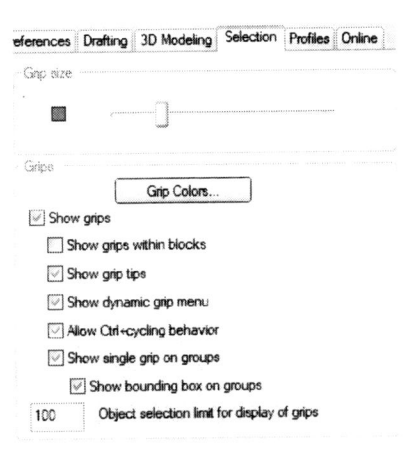

Figure 3–58

- *Grip size* enables you to control the size of the grip as it displays in the drawing window.

Modify Objects

- You can also change the grip colors by clicking **Grip Colors...** and adjusting the values in the Grip Colors dialog box, as shown in Figure 3–59.

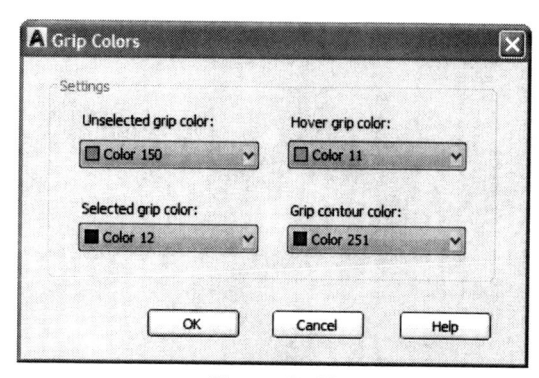

Figure 3–59

In addition to grip size and color, you can set the following:

Show grips	Turns grips on or off globally.
Show grips in blocks	Controls whether grips only display on a block's insertion point (off) or on all nested objects in the block (on). Normally it is easier to work with this option off. This only applies to standard blocks. Dynamic blocks still display grips.
Show grip tips	Grip tips are not available in the basic AutoCAD software, but can display for objects from software such as the AutoCAD® Architecture software.
Show dynamic grip menu	Controls whether a menu displays next to a dynamic grip.
Allow Ctrl+cycling behavior	Controls whether you can use <Ctrl> to cycle through the grip's options.
Show single grip on groups	Displays a single grip for an object group.
Show bounding box on groups	Displays a bounding box around the extents of grouped objects.
Object selection limit for display of grips	If you select more objects than the number set here, grips do not display on them.

Practice 3i

Estimated time for completion: 10 minutes

Editing with Grips I

Practice Objective

- Modify objects using grips.

In this practice, you will use grips to move, copy, rotate, mirror, and scale objects on the façade of a building. You will also use <Shift> to copy and specify a new base point, as shown in Figure 3–60.

Figure 3–60

1. Open **Facade-A.dwg** from your practice files folder.

2. Set the object snaps to **Endpoint**, **Midpoint**, and **Intersection**, and toggle (Object Snap) on. Toggle (Polar Tracking) off. Toggle on (Dynamic Input) if it is not already on.

3. With no command active, select the double door. Select the grip to make it hot (red by default). Move the door to the midpoint of the bottom line on the building. Press <Esc> to clear the object.

4. Repeat Step 3 with the arched window and place the grip at the midpoint of the top of the door.

5. Select the square window and select the grip. Right-click and select **Copy**. Select the intersections of the blue center lines to place windows at each intersection (9 in total). Press <Esc> twice to finish.

6. Erase the light blue center lines.

7. Select the four angled lines of the roof. Select the grip at the right end of one of the lines. Right-click and select **Mirror**, then right-click again and select **Copy** to keep the original objects. Select the midpoint of the roofline as the second point for the mirror line. Press <Esc> twice to finish.

8. Select the center top window in the top row and select the grip. Right-click and select **Base Point**. For the base point, select the intersection of the mullions at the center of the window.

9. Right-click again and select **Rotate**. For the rotation angle, enter **45** and press <Enter>.

10. Select the window grip again and change the base point to the center of the mullions. Right-click and select **Scale**. For the scale factor, enter **0.7** and press <Enter>. Press <Esc> to finish.

11. Select the arched window above the door and select the grip. Right-click and select **Scale**. For the scale factor, enter **0.65** and press <Enter>. Press <Esc> to finish.

12. Select the bottom line along the base of the building. Hover the cursor over the grip at either end point to display the dimension. What is the length of the line?

13. Select the top roofline on the left side of the building, and hover the cursor over the end point at the top. What is the length and angle of the line?

14. Save and close the drawing.

Practice 3j

Estimated time for completion: 10 minutes

Editing with Grips II

Practice Objective

- Modify objects using grips.

In this practice, you will use grips to move, copy, rotate, and scale objects as shown in Figure 3–61.

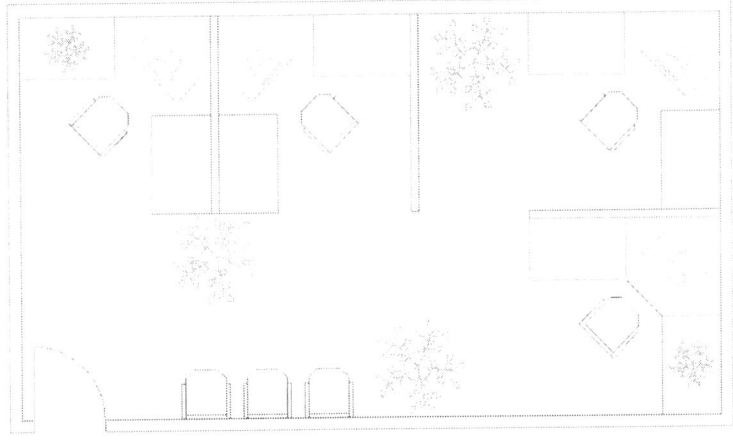

Figure 3–61

1. Open **Arrange-Grips-A.dwg** from your practice files folder.

2. Use grips to move, copy, rotate, and scale objects (as shown in Figure 3–62) so that they are placed as shown in Figure 3–61.

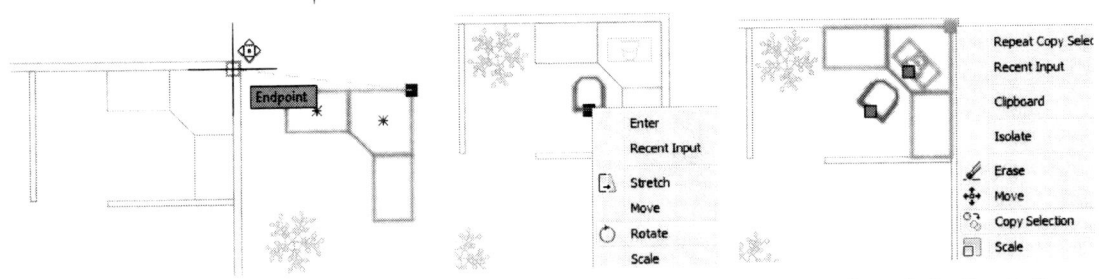

Hot grip used as Move   **Using Rotate in the hot grip Shortcut menu**   **Using Copy Selection in the hover grip Shortcut menu**

Figure 3–62

Practice 3k

Estimated time for completion: 10 minutes

Using Grips Effectively

Practice Objective

- Modify a drawing using grips.

In this practice, you will use grips to edit the schematic drawing, as shown in Figure 3–63.

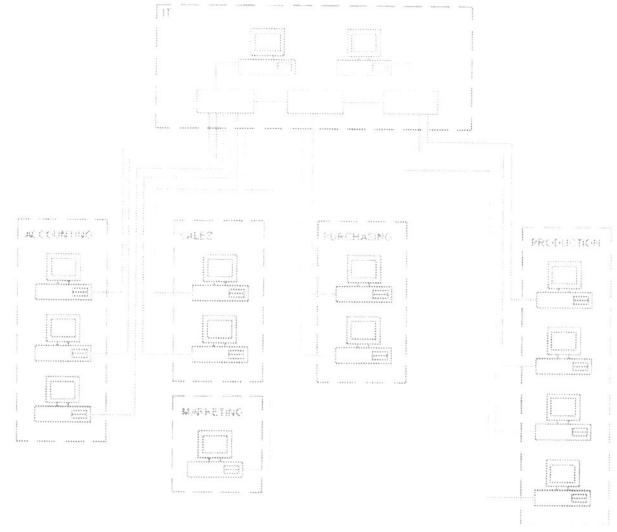

Figure 3–63

1. Open **Computer-I.dwg** from your practice files folder.

2. Use grips to add three, evenly spaced computers to **PRODUCTION**. Use <Ctrl> when selecting the locations for the copies, to place them at even intervals.

3. Use grips to stretch the red rectangle to include the new computers. Use <Shift> to select more than one hot grip.

4. Select the three, yellow polylines connecting the **ACCOUNTING** computers to the hubs. Use grips to **Mirror** and **Copy** the three polylines over to the **PRODUCTION** computers, using a base point at the midpoint of the middle hub. (After selecting one grip, use the shortcut menu to select **Mirror**, and then select **Base Point** before drawing the mirror line.)

5. Use grips to manipulate the new lines so they match up with the new computers.

6. Save and close the drawing.

3.12 Creating Fillets and Chamfers

Fillets and chamfers are used to create rounded corners and beveled edges respectively, as shown in Figure 3–64.

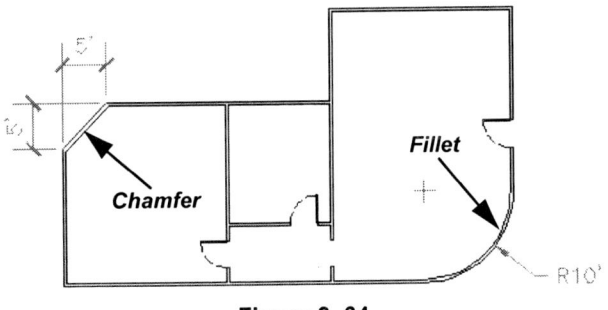

Figure 3–64

Filleting Objects

The **Fillet** command modifies the intersection of two objects and can be used to create inside and outside rounded corners, as shown in Figure 3–65. It can also be helpful in cleaning up a drawing by forcing lines to meet at an exact intersection.

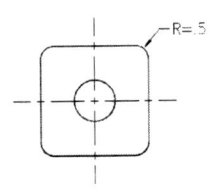

Figure 3–65

*The **Radius** option enables you to specify the fillet radius. This value should be selected and set before you pick the objects to fillet.*

How To: Fillet Objects

1. In the *Home* tab>Modify panel, click ⌐ (**Fillet**).
2. Select the **Radius** option (<Down Arrow> menu), enter the new radius, and press <Enter>.
3. If you are filleting several sets of objects, select the **Multiple** option (<Down Arrow> menu).
4. Select the first line that you want to fillet.

5. Hover the cursor over the second line that you want to fillet. A preview displays the fillet being highlighted in blue and the original object faded in light gray, as shown in Figure 3–66.

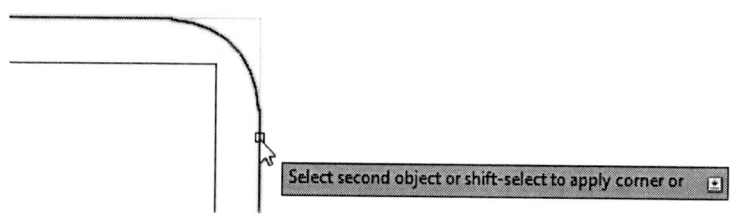

Figure 3–66

6. Select the second line to confirm the fillet.
7. If you have selected the **Multiple** option, you can continue selecting two lines to fillet until you press <Enter> to complete the command.

- A fillet with the **Radius** option set to **0** can be used to make lines meet at a square corner. You can also hold <Shift> as you select the two lines without having to change the radius.

- You can fillet two parallel lines. In this case, the radius is automatically calculated so that the arc is tangent to both lines.

- The **Undo** option undoes the last fillet without exiting the command.

- The **Polyline** option fillets all of the vertices of a selected polyline. You can still fillet one vertex by selecting segments to fillet.

- The **Trim/NoTrim** option determines whether selected lines are trimmed after the arc is added.

- You can fillet both the lines and arcs in a polyline.

Chamfering Objects

The **Chamfer** command angles or bevels the intersection of two lines to create an angled corner, as shown in Figure 3–67.

Figure 3–67

How To: Chamfer Objects

1. In the *Home* tab>Modify panel, click (Chamfer).
2. Select the **Distance** option and enter two distances.
3. If you are chamfering several sets of objects, select the **Multiple** option.
4. Select the first line that you want to chamfer, which is highlighted in blue.
5. Hover the cursor over the second line that you want to chamfer. A preview displays the chamfer being highlighted in blue and the chamfered portion being faded in light gray, as shown in Figure 3–68.

The first chamfer distance is used on the first line that you select and the second chamfer distance is used on the second line that you select. Distances are measured from the intersection of the two lines.

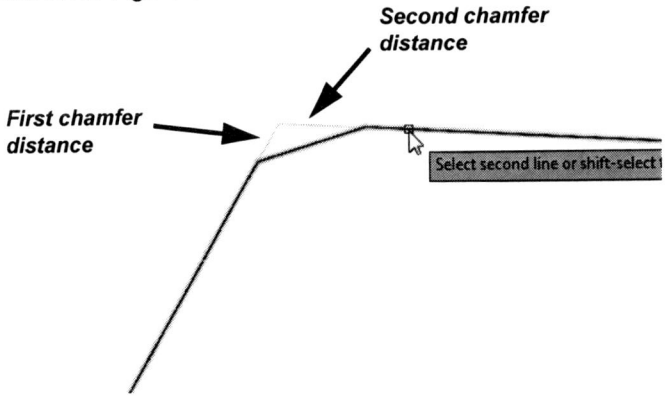

Figure 3–68

6. Select the second line.
7. If you selected the **Multiple** option, you can continue selecting two lines to chamfer until you press <Enter> to complete the command.

- Another way to specify the chamfer is to set the **Angle** option, which sets the chamfer length of the first line you select and then the angle between the original line and the chamfered edge.

- The distance and angle information are stored separately. Therefore, you can use the **Method** option to change between the two options in the same command. The last method you selected is used when a new command is started.

- The **Undo**, **Trim/NoTrim**, and **Polyline** options work the same way as when using the **Fillet** command.

Practice 3l

Filleting Objects

Practice Objective
- Create rounded corners and fillet parallel lines.

In this practice, you will use the **Fillet** command to round the outer corners of a part with two different radius sizes, as shown in Figure 3–69. You will also fillet parallel lines to create slots.

Estimated time for completion: 5 minutes

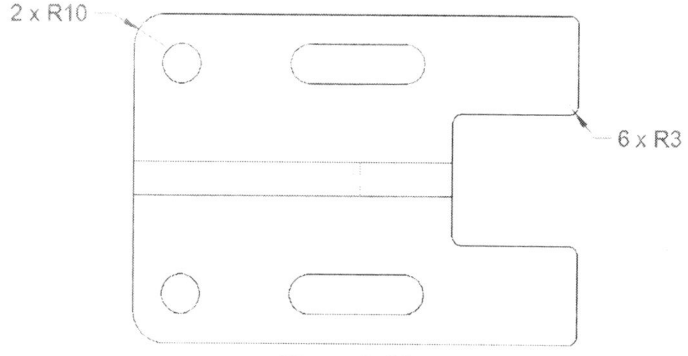

Figure 3–69

1. Open **Visebase-M.dwg** from your practice files folder.

2. In the *Home* tab>Modify panel, click (**Fillet**). Set the **Radius** option (<Down Arrow> menu or enter **R**). Set *Radius* to **10**.

3. Select the two upper lines that create the upper left corner to fillet that corner.

4. Repeat the command to fillet the lower left corner with the same radius. Select the lines without entering the **Radius** option.

You are not required to re-enter the radius. It has been set in Step 2.

5. Start the **Fillet** command again. Select the **Radius** option and enter the radius as **3**. Select the **Multiple** option to make the command repeating. Fillet the six corners on the right side of the object. Press <Enter> to complete the command.

6. Start the **Fillet** command again. Select the two horizontal lines in the rectangle near the top of the part, selecting near the left end of the lines. Repeat for the right end of the lines. Erase the short vertical lines to clear out the slot.

7. Repeat Step 6 for the other rectangle.

8. Save and close the drawing.

Practice 3m

Chamfering Objects

Practice Objective

- Create different sizes of angled edges.

In this practice, you will use the **Chamfer** command with several different distances to create the angled edges on a part, as shown in Figure 3–70.

Estimated time for completion: 5 minutes

Chamfer length 0.75
Chamfer angle 5

Chamfer distances 0.1

Chamfer distances 0.02

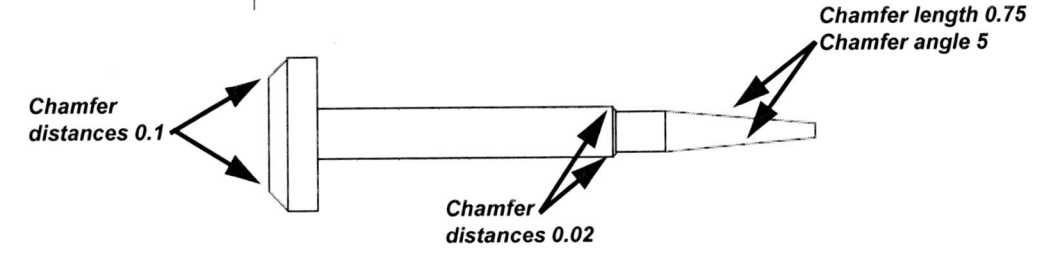

Figure 3–70

1. Open **Punch-I.dwg** from your practice files folder.

2. In the *Home* tab>Modify panel, click (Chamfer). Select the **Distance** option. Set both *Chamfer distances* to **0.1**.

*Select **Distance** in the <Down Arrow> menu or enter **D**.*

3. Select the two lines in the top left corner of the part to apply the chamfer.

4. Repeat the command to chamfer the bottom left corner using the same distances.

5. Start the **Chamfer** command and select the **Distance** option. Set both *Chamfer distances* to **0.02**. Select the **Multiple** option to make the command repeating. Chamfer both corners where the shaft changes size.

6. Start the **Chamfer** command and select the **Angle** option. Set the *Chamfer length* on first line to **0.75**. Set the *chamfer angle* to **5**. Apply the chamfer to the right end of the part, selecting the top horizontal line first, and then the short vertical line. Repeat for the bottom corner of the right end.

7. Add vertical lines to indicate the edges of the three chamfers, as shown in Figure 3–70.

8. Save and close the drawing.

Chapter 4

Use Additional Drawing Techniques

This chapter includes instructional content to assist in your preparation for the following topic and objectives for the AutoCAD® Certified Professional exam.

Autodesk Certification Exam Objectives in this Chapter

Exam Topic	Exam Objective	Section(s)
Use Additional Drawing Techniques	• Draw and edit polylines	• 4.1 & 4.2
	• Blend between objects with splines	• 4.3
	• Apply hatches and gradients	• 4.4 & 4.5

4.1 Drawing Polylines

Polylines are complex objects consisting of lines and arcs. Each segment in a polyline sequence is considered to be part of a single object. In addition, polylines can be assigned a width that can vary for each segment.

Polylines are ideal for drawing complex single objects, such as walls, transmission lines, ductwork, and schematic traces or area outlines, as shown in Figure 4–1.

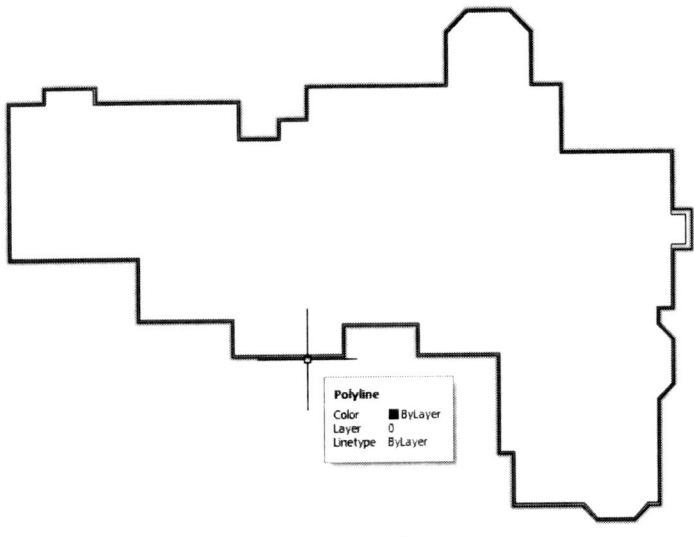

Figure 4–1

- Polylines can be used anywhere a regular line or arc can be used.

- When creating one continuous object, you cannot leave and restart the **Polyline** command.

- A polyline can be either open or closed. An open polyline can only have one start point and one end point.

How To: Draw a Polyline with Width and Arcs

1. In the *Home* tab>Draw panel, click (Polyline).
2. Select a start point. A cross displays, indicating that it is the start point. This is useful when creating complex polylines. The cross disappears when the polyline creation is completed.

Use Additional Drawing Techniques

In the Polyline arc, use <Down Arrow> to display the Arc options.

3. (Optional) Select the **Width** option in the <Down Arrow> menu (as shown on the left in Figure 4–2), or type **W** and press <Enter>.
4. Enter a starting width or select two points to define the width.
5. Enter an ending width. If you want it to be the same as the starting width, you can press <Enter> to accept the default.
6. Select the next point(s).
7. (Optional) When you want to create an arc segment, do not end the **Polyline** command. Instead, select the **Arc** option in the <Down Arrow> menu or type **A** and press <Enter>.
8. Follow the prompts to create the required type of arc. The prompts are similar to those in the **Arc** command. When drawing an arc, you can press <Ctrl> to draw in the opposite direction.
9. To switch back to line segments, type **L** and press <Enter> or select the **Line** option from the <Down Arrow> menu, or the shortcut menu, as shown on the right in Figure 4–2.

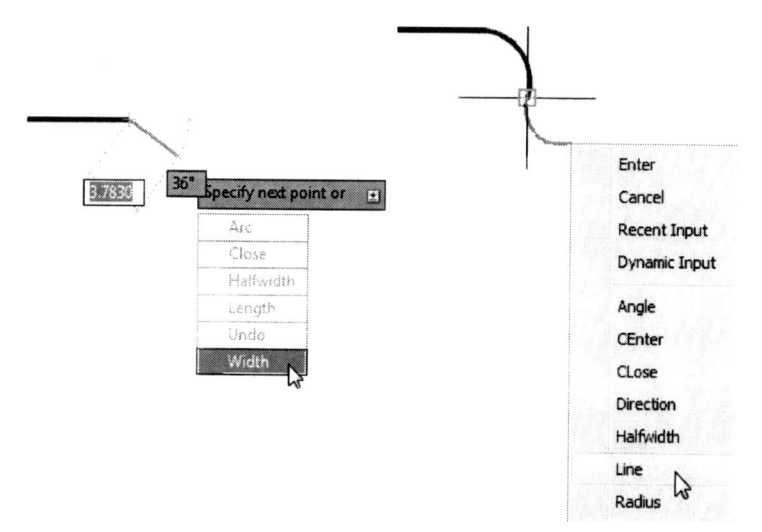

Figure 4–2

10. If you want to create a closed polyline, use the **Close** option (CL). It attaches the last segment back to the start point.

- You can use the **Undo** option to remove the last segment drawn without ending the command.

- Other options include **Halfwidth**, which specifies the distance from the center of a wide polyline to one of its edges, and **Length**, which draws a segment of the specified length at the same angle as the previous segment.

4.2 Editing Polylines

You can edit polylines by moving a vertex, changing its width, joining polylines or lines and arcs together, and converting polylines into individual segments. You can also add and remove vertices from existing polylines and convert arcs to lines and vice-versa.

How To: Change the Width of an Existing Polyline

1. In the *Home* tab>expanded Modify panel, click ✎ (Edit Polyline).
2. At the *Select polyline:* prompt, select the polyline. An options menu displays, as shown in Figure 4–3.

You can also double-click on a polyline to display the options menu.

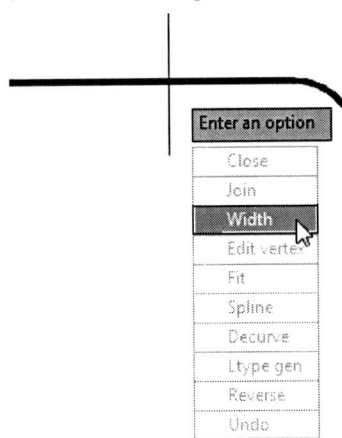

Figure 4–3

3. Select the **Width** option.
4. At the *Specify new width for all segments:* prompt, enter the new width and press <Enter>.
5. Press <Enter> to end the command.

How To: Modify Vertices in Polylines using Edit Polyline

1. In the *Home* tab>expanded Modify panel, click ✎ (Edit Polyline).
2. Select the polyline that you want to edit. You can also double-click on a polyline to display the options menu.
3. Select the **Edit vertex** option.
4. An icon displays on the polyline, indicating the vertex that is currently being edited. To select a different vertex, select the **Next** option until the one you want to edit displays.

Use Additional Drawing Techniques

5. Select one of the following options to modify the current vertex:

Break	Breaks the polyline at the selected vertex, separating it from the rest of the polyline. If you break a polyline in more than one place, the separated objects remain polylines.
Insert	Inserts a new vertex at the selected point on the polyline. You can place the new vertex anywhere on the polyline.
Move	Moves a vertex to a new position on the polyline. You can move the current vertex to a new location, anywhere on the polyline.
Straighten	Deletes segments and vertices between two selected vertices, and replaces them with a single straight line segment.
Tangent	Attaches a tangent direction to the selected vertex to be used for curve fitting later.
Width	Modifies the width of the selected line or arc between two adjacent vertices.

6. Use the **Next** and **Previous** options to continue modifying vertices. Select **eXit** to return to the **Edit Polyline** command options, or press <Esc> to end the command.

Modifying Polyline Vertices using Grips

If you select a polyline when you are not in a command, the vertex grips and midpoint grips display. You can modify them by adding or deleting vertices, stretching them, and converting them from a line to an arc and vice-versa. You can access these options by hovering the cursor over a multifunctional vertex grip and selecting an option in the list, as shown in Figure 4–4.

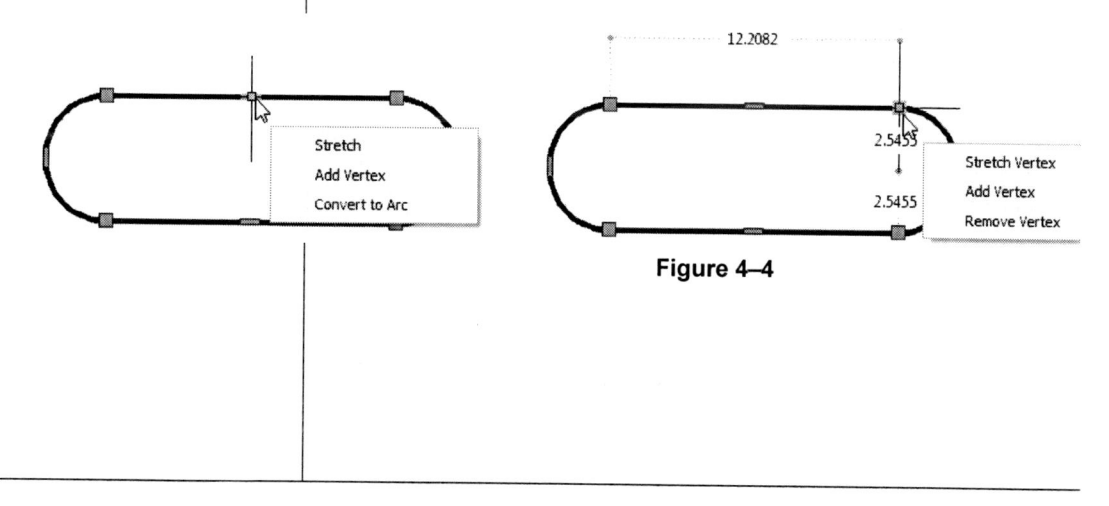

Figure 4–4

Converting Lines and Arcs to Polylines

How To: Use Vertices to Convert a Line to an Arc

1. When not in a command, select a polyline to display its vertices.
2. On the object, hover on a vertex that you want to change. For example, if you want to change a line into an arc, hover on the midpoint vertex on the line.
3. Select **Convert to Arc**.
4. Drag the arc to the required size or enter the required dimension.
5. Continue selecting vertices and modifying them or press <Esc> to end the command.

In some cases, creating lines and arcs and then turning them into a polyline is easier than using the **Polyline** command from the start. While separate lines and arcs work in most cases, having them work together as a polyline can be useful. For instance, selecting one object to move is easier than selecting all of the pieces from which it has been created, as shown in Figure 4–5.

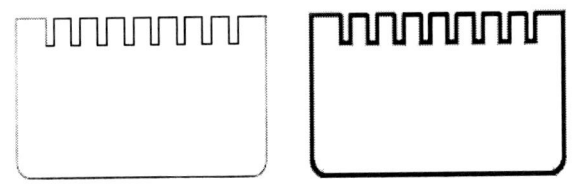

Figure 4–5

How To: Convert Lines and Arcs into a Single Polyline

1. In the *Home* tab>expanded Modify panel, click ✏ (Edit Polyline).
2. At the *Select polyline or:* prompt, select a line or arc.
3. At the *Do you want to turn it into one?:* prompt, press <Enter> to select the Y option.
4. Select **Join** in the options menu that displays.
5. Select the other objects that you want to join to the polyline, which get highlighted.
6. Press <Enter> once to end the *Select objects:* prompt.
7. Press <Enter> again to end the command.

- The **Multiple** option (at the *Select Polyline:* prompt) enables you to edit several polylines at once, or to convert multiple line segments into polylines at the same time.

- To be joined, each line segment or arc must be attached to the end point of the next.

- For open polylines, **Edit Polyline** displays the **Close** option; for closed polylines, it displays the **Open** option.

> **Hint: Joining Objects**
>
> ╶╫╴ (Join) (in the *Home* tab>expanded Modify panel) joins broken polylines, lines, arcs, elliptical arcs, and splines, as shown in Figure 4–6. Polylines that can be joined can overlap, gap, or touch end points. If you select two lines, they need to be touching each other end to end.
>
> Figure 4–6
>
> You can join objects of different types (e.g., lines, polylines, and splines). The final joined object becomes the most complex of the selected objects. Therefore, if you select a line and a polyline, the final joined object is a polyline.
>
> - With arcs, the **Close** option can be used to close arcs (e.g., to form circles).
>
> - The source object determines the properties (e.g., layer, color, etc.) of the new object.

Turning Polylines into Lines and Arcs

When a polyline has been created, you might want to break it into all of its separate component parts, so that you can remove individual segments or make other changes.

- In the *Home* tab>Modify panel, click (Explode) to convert a polyline into individual arcs and lines.

- Exploding a wide polyline causes it to lose its width information.

- The **Explode** command works on other object types that are made from polylines, such as rectangles or polygons. It also works on blocks.

Practice 4a

Drawing and Editing Polylines

Practice Objectives

- Draw polylines and convert a polyline into separate lines and arcs.
- Convert lines and arcs into a polyline.
- Change the width of a polyline.

Estimated time for completion: 15 minutes

In this practice, you will draw polylines. You will edit several polylines and change their width so that they will be used as symbols in a flowchart.

Task 1 - Draw polylines for a flowchart.

In this task you will create several polylines as symbols to be used in a flowchart, as shown in Figure 4–7.

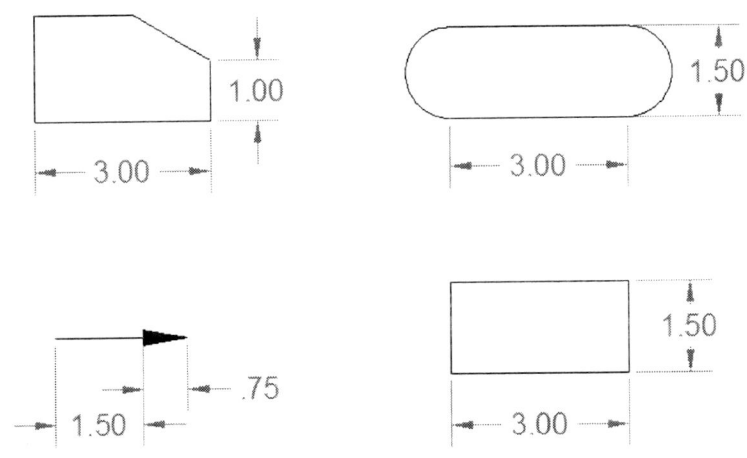

Figure 4–7

1. Start a new drawing based on **Mech-Inches.dwt**, which is located in your practice files folder, and save it as **Flowchart.dwg**.

2. Verify that ▢ ▼ (Object Snap) and ∠ (Object Snap Tracking) are both toggled on. The Object Snaps should be set to **Endpoint, Midpoint**, and **Extension**.

3. Expand ⟲ ▼ (Polar Tracking) and select **30,60,90,120....** Ensure that it is toggled on.

Use Additional Drawing Techniques

4. In the *Home* tab> Draw panel, click (Polyline) and draw the top left symbol, as shown in Figure 4–7.
   - Specify the start point anywhere.
   - Move the cursor right, enter **3**, and press <Enter>.
   - Move the cursor straight up, enter **1**, and press <Enter>.
   - Move the cursor at an angle of **150** degrees, enter **1.5**, and press <Enter>.
   - Make the next point straight to the left, but track it to make it directly above (even with) the start point.
   - Type **C** and press <Enter> to close the figure and finish the command.

5. Start the **Polyline** command again and draw the top right symbol, as shown in Figure 4–7.
   - Specify the start point anywhere.
   - Move the cursor right, enter **3**, and press <Enter>.
   - Type **A** and press <Enter> to switch to the **Arc** option.
   - Move the cursor straight up, enter **1.5**, and press <Enter>.
   - Type **L** and press <Enter> to switch to the **Line** option.
   - Move the cursor left, enter **3**, and press <Enter>.
   - Switch to the **Arc** option and type **CL** to close the figure and finish the command.

A rectangle is also a polyline.

6. The bottom right symbol shown in Figure 4–7 can be drawn using the **Rectangle** command or **Polyline** command.

7. Start the **Polyline** command and draw the arrow, as shown in Figure 4–7.
   - Specify the start point anywhere.
   - Move the cursor right, enter **1.5**, and press <Enter>.
   - Type **W** and press <Enter> to switch to the **Width** option.
   - For the starting width, enter **0.25** and press <Enter>.
   - For the ending width, enter **0** and press <Enter>.
   - Move the cursor straight to the right, enter **0.75**, and press <Enter>.
   - Press <Enter> to finish the command.

8. Arrange the objects to create the simple flowchart shown in Figure 4–8. Move, copy, and rotate the objects as required.

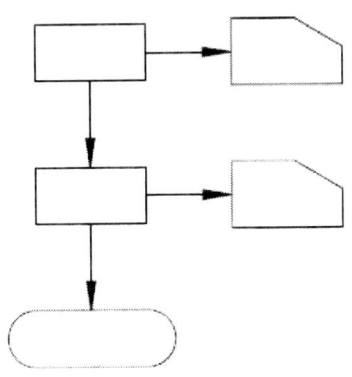

Figure 4–8

9. Save the drawing.

Task 2 - Edit polylines.

In this task you will explode a polyline, and then use the **Edit Polyline** command to join arcs and lines into a polyline and change the width, as shown in Figure 4–9.

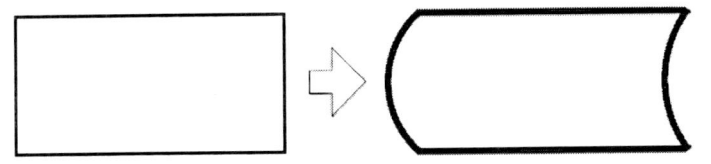

Figure 4–9

1. Make a copy of the rectangle.

2. Select the copied rectangle and explode it (in the *Home* tab>Modify panel, click (Explode)). Erase the vertical lines. You can select the lines individually because the object is no longer a polyline.

3. Draw a 3-point arc at each end of the two lines remaining from the rectangle that you exploded in Step 2. Use the **Endpoint** object snap to connect the arcs to the lines. (**Tip:** Draw it at one end and then copy it to the other end).

4. In the *Home* tab>expanded Modify panel, click (Edit Polyline) and select one of the lines. At the *Do you want to turn it into one?:* prompt, press <Enter> to select **Yes**.

5. In the options menu, select **Join**.

6. At the *Select objects:* prompt, select the other line and the arcs and press <Enter>.

7. Select the **Width** option. Set the *width* to **0.05** and press <Enter>. Press <Enter> again to exit the command.

8. Use the **Move** command to move the shape. It is now all one object.

9. Verify that you are not in a command and select the polyline.

10. Hover the cursor over one of the midpoint grip vertices on one of the arcs and select **Convert to Line**.

11. Repeat the previous step for the other arc. The shape is now a rectangle.

12. Save and close the drawing.

4.3 Splines

The **Edit Polyline** command has a **Spline** option that converts a polyline into an approximation of a smooth curve, called a *spline curve*, as shown in Figure 4–10. (The **Fit** option is similar but the curve is not as smooth.)

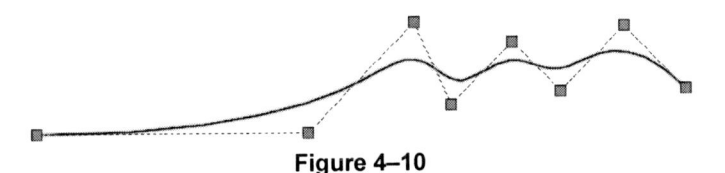

Figure 4–10

You can also use (Spline Fit) or (Spline CV) in the *Home* tab>expanded Draw panel for creating true spline curves. These are mathematically more exact and easier to control than splined polylines. After a spline has been created, its shape can be further refined using (Edit Spline) in the *Home* tab>expanded Modify panel.

Splines are important in special drawing applications that use curves extensively (such as contour maps), or that require exact control of complex curves (such as the shape of a hull in shipbuilding, or the aerodynamic surfaces of airplanes and cars.)

4.4 Hatching

Hatching is a pattern of lines or shapes that is used to distinguish certain areas of a drawing from other areas. For example, hatching might be used to indicate which rooms on a floor plan are occupied by a specific department, as shown in Figure 4–11. In mechanical design, hatching is typically used to indicate section views. The AutoCAD® software contains many predefined hatch patterns.

*There are two ways to apply hatching: Tool Palettes and the **Hatch** command.*

Many patterns for specific applications can be purchased from commercial third-party developers.

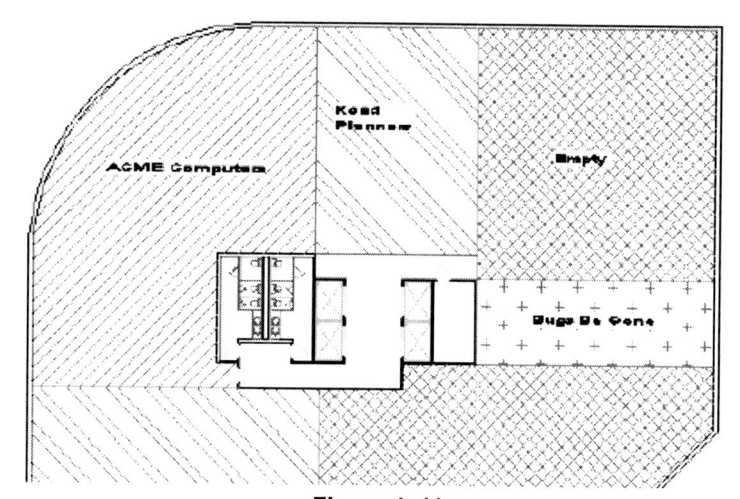

Figure 4–11

- Hatching should be placed on a separate hatch layer so that it can be easily toggled off or frozen.

- Hatching can be annotative, so you should apply it after a viewport has been prepared and scaled.

Applying a Hatch: Tool Palettes

Tool Palettes (*Hatches and Fills* tab) contains several hatch patterns that can be used for hatching a closed area in a drawing.

- Click on a pattern. It is attached to the cursor, as shown in Figure 4–12. Move the cursor inside the closed area that you want to hatch. A preview of the hatch in the area displays. Click to hatch the area.

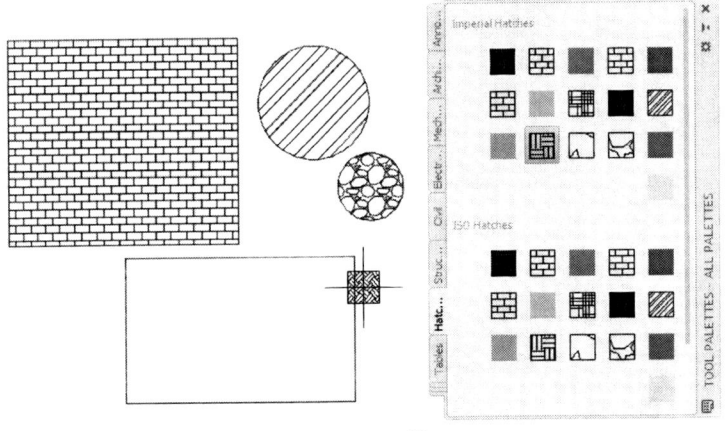

Figure 4–12

- The area for hatching should be completely bounded, with no gaps.

- Closed objects and text inside the bounded area (known as *islands*) are not normally hatched.

- The default *Hatches and Fills* tab in Tool Palettes comes with hatches that are scaled for Imperial and ISO (Metric) drawings, and several gradient hatches, as shown in Figure 4–12.

- By default, the hatch patterns provided are not annotative. You can change that after the hatch has been applied to the object by opening its Properties palette, and changing *Annotative* to **Yes**, as shown in Figure 4–13.

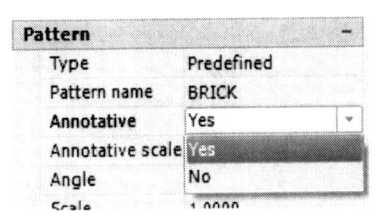

Figure 4–13

In the Tool Palettes, if the tab is hidden, click on the area just below the bottom tab and select **Hatches and Fills***.*

Use Additional Drawing Techniques

Applying a Hatch: Hatch Command

The **Hatch** command provides more control and options than hatching using Tool Palettes. Using this command, you can select from many different patterns and adjust the scale or angle of the hatch as you apply it, as shown in Figure 4–14.

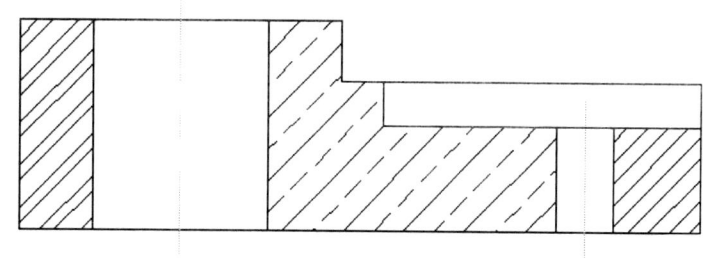

Figure 4–14

How To: Hatch Objects

1. In the *Home* tab>Draw panel, click (Hatch).
2. In the *Hatch Creation* contextual tab, set the *Pattern*, *Scale*, *Angle*, and *Transparency*, as shown in Figure 4–15.

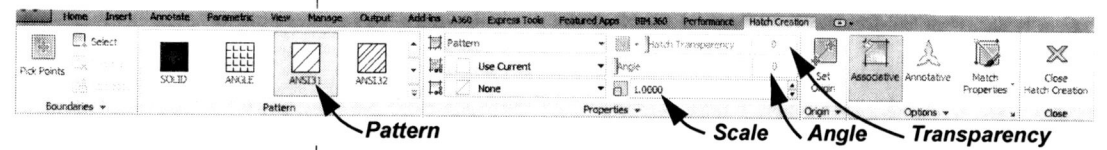

Figure 4–15

3. Click (Pick Points) and hover the cursor inside the bounded area to preview the hatch. Click to add the hatch or modify the settings until the correct results display in the preview.

   - You can also click (Select Boundary Objects) and select a closed object or group of objects that form a closed boundary.

© 2017, ASCENT - Center for Technical Knowledge®

- If the hatch cannot be created due to invalid hatch boundaries, an alert box opens, as shown in Figure 4–16.

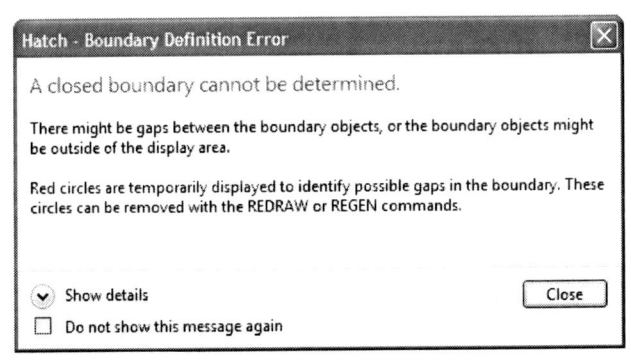

Figure 4–16

4. Press <Enter> or click ✕ (Close Hatch Creation) to end the command.

- Click (Remove Boundaries) to select objects in the drawing to remove them from the selection.

In the *Hatch Creation* contextual tab, you can set the *Pattern*, *Scale*, *Angle*, and *Transparency* of the hatch.

Pattern Panel

In the Pattern panel, select a pattern from the list. You can expand the list by clicking , as shown in Figure 4–17.

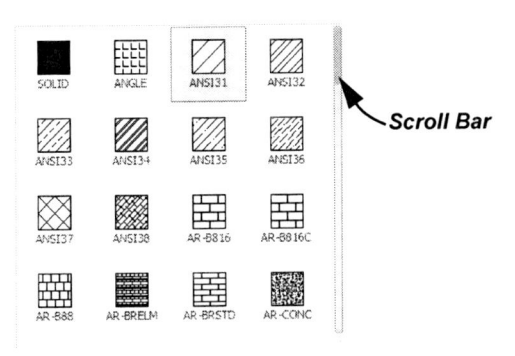

Figure 4–17

Hatch Pattern and Properties

If your ribbon is reduced in size due to the size of the interface, you might need to expand (Hatch Pattern) in the Pattern panel first.

Properties Panel

In the Properties panel, you can set the *Hatch Type*, *Hatch Color*, *Background Color*, *Hatch Transparency*, *Hatch Angle*, *Hatch Pattern Scale*, and *Hatch Layer Override*. These enable you to customize how the hatch displays in the drawing.

Hatch Type

The type of hatch can be **Solid**, **Gradient**, **Pattern**, or **User defined**, as shown in Figure 4–18. Select the hatch type, and then select a pattern in the Pattern list.

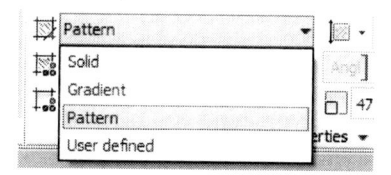

Figure 4–18

- User-defined patterns are parallel lines with a spacing and angle that you specify. You can create a cross-hatch by expanding the Properties panel and clicking ▦ (Double).

- To create a solid fill, set the *Hatch Type* to **Solid** and the *Hatch Color* to **ByLayer** or a color.

- To create a gradient fill, set the *Hatch Type* to **Gradient** and set the colors for *Gradient Color 1* and *Gradient Color 2*.

Hatch Color

Use this option to set the color of the hatch. You can select a specific color, use the current color, or set the color to **ByLayer**, where the color of the hatch is controlled by the color of the layer.

Background Color

Use this option to add a background color to the hatch. For example, if you have two hatches of the same pattern, you can set a different background color for each one.

Hatch Transparency

Use this option to control the level of transparency for the hatch. This is useful for displaying objects below the hatch, such as furniture, walls, or annotations. You can use the slider or enter the value, as shown in Figure 4–19. You can also expand

▨ ▾ (Transparency Values) and set the transparency to **ByLayer Transparency** or **ByBlock Transparency**.

Figure 4–19

Hatch Angle

The *Hatch Angle* sets the rotation angle of the hatch pattern. An angle of **0** creates the pattern at its original angle. Increase the value to get an angled pattern, as shown in Figure 4–20.

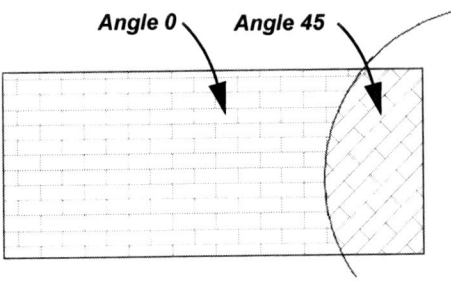

Figure 4–20

Hatch Pattern Scale

The *Hatch Pattern Scale* controls the space between the lines in the pattern (which are normally based on the drawing's plot scale factor). Enter the scale required to correctly display the hatch pattern so that its lines and spaces display clearly.

Use Additional Drawing Techniques

- If you are working in a viewport and using Annotative scaling, you should expand the Properties panel and click ▦ (Relative to Paper Space). It calculates the scale based on the viewport scale. **Annotative** maintains the hatch scale relative to Paper Space if the viewport scale is changed.

Hatch Layer Override

You can set the layer on which the hatch is placed, overriding the current layer.

- You can use the **HPLAYER** system variable to set the layer on which the hatch is placed, overriding the current layer.

- If the layer you want to use does not exist in the drawing, type the new layer name. The next time you start the **Hatch** command, the layer is created and the hatch is placed on it.

Hatch Origin

The hatch origin determines how the hatch fits into the selected area. If you are using a pattern (such as brick hatching), the hatch origin enables you to start and end the pattern appropriately inside the boundary.

- Click ▦ (Set Origin), select the point at which the pattern is going to start, and then select an internal point to set the boundary. You can use the preset options to set the origin to the **Bottom Left**, **Bottom Right**, **Top Left**, **Top Right**, or **Center**, as shown in Figure 4–21.

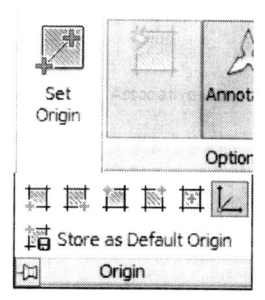

Figure 4–21

- You can select **Use Current Origin** to return to the default origin point.

- You can select **Store as Default Origin** to save the current location as the default origin.

Hatch Options

You can set the hatch to be **Annotative**, so that it uses the annotative scale of the viewport in which it displays, as shown in Figure 4–22.

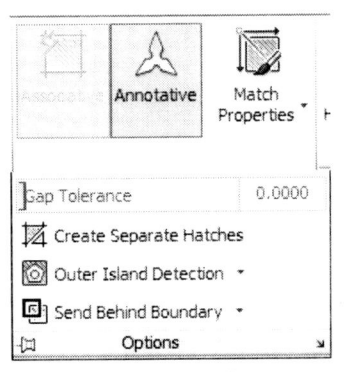

Figure 4–22

- Hatches are typically set to **Associative** (the default if **Annotative** is selected). This means that the hatch is associated with the boundary. If the boundary is changed (i.e., moved, stretched, etc.), the hatch pattern area changes to fill the new boundary.

- Click (Create Separate Hatches) if you want each boundary selected during one command to be created as individual hatches. Otherwise, they are all one hatch object no matter how many boundaries you select.

- (Send Behind Boundary) controls whether the hatch is behind or in front of overlapping objects. You can specify the relationship for any overlapping objects or just the boundary.

- Click (Match Properties) to select an existing hatch object in the drawing and use it to hatch other areas.

Use Additional Drawing Techniques

- ⬚ (Island Detection) sets whether or not the areas in overlapping or complex objects are hatched. Expand the drop-down list and select the required type of detection, as shown in Figure 4–23.

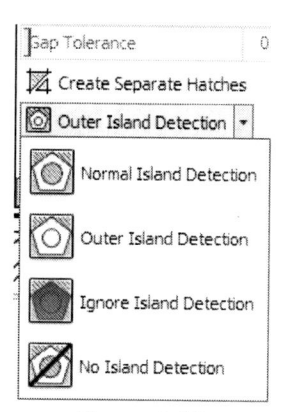

Figure 4–23

- **Gap Tolerance** sets the largest gap permitted in the boundary of an area to be hatched. If set to **0** (the default), no gaps are permitted.

Hint: Finding the Area of a Hatch

The *Area* of a hatch displays in the Properties palette, as shown in Figure 4–24. It can be used as a quick way to find the area of an object with holes.

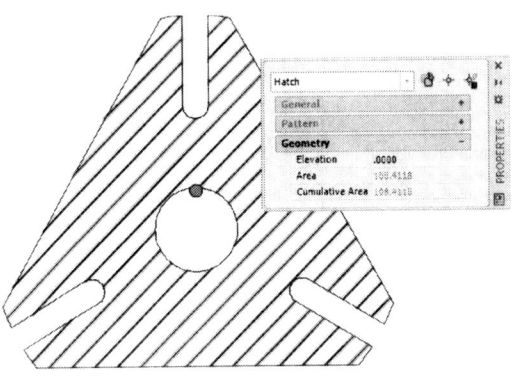

Figure 4–24

If more than one hatch is selected, it provides the cumulative area. For example, you might want to know the area of several rooms in a building. Hatch the rooms, select the hatches, and note the *Cumulative Area* in the Properties palette, as shown in Figure 4–25.

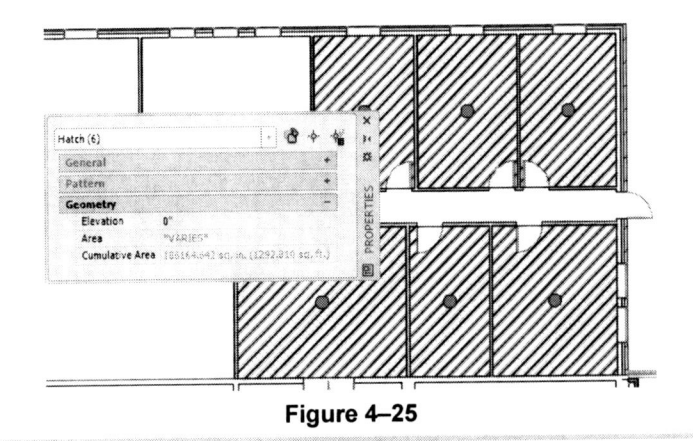

Figure 4–25

4.5 Editing Hatches

Instead of erasing and reapplying hatching to change the pattern or scale, you can adjust the hatch using:

- The *Hatch Editor* contextual tab in the ribbon.
- The **Edit Hatch** command.
- Grips.

You can change the hatch pattern, scale, or angle, and add or remove areas from the existing hatch boundary.

When you modify the boundaries of associative hatches, the hatch automatically updates, as shown in Figure 4–26.

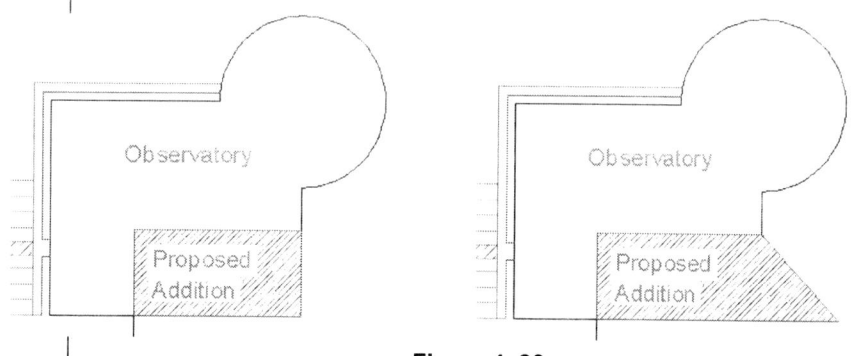

Figure 4–26

Hatch Editor Tab

To edit an existing hatch, select a hatch by clicking on it to display the *Hatch Editor* contextual tab.

How To: Edit a Hatch Using the *Hatch Editor* Tab

1. Select the hatch to be modified.
2. In the *Hatch Editor* contextual tab, change the properties as required.
   - The options in this contextual tab are the same as those available for placing the hatch.
3. If required, modify the boundaries using (Recreate Boundary) or (Display Boundary Objects).

▨	**Recreate Boundary:** Creates a new object around the hatch area, and associates the hatch with the new object separate from the original boundary.
▨	**Display Boundary Objects:** Displays the selected objects and their boundary with grips. Modifying the grips changes both the boundary and the hatch if the hatch is associative. If the hatch is not associative, different grips display and you can modify the hatch separately from the original boundary.

4. Press <Enter> to apply the changes.

Edit Hatch Command

To open the Hatch Edit dialog box (shown in Figure 4–27), in the *Home* tab>expanded Modify panel, click ▨ (Edit Hatch). The dialog box contains tools that are similar to the Hatch Editor.

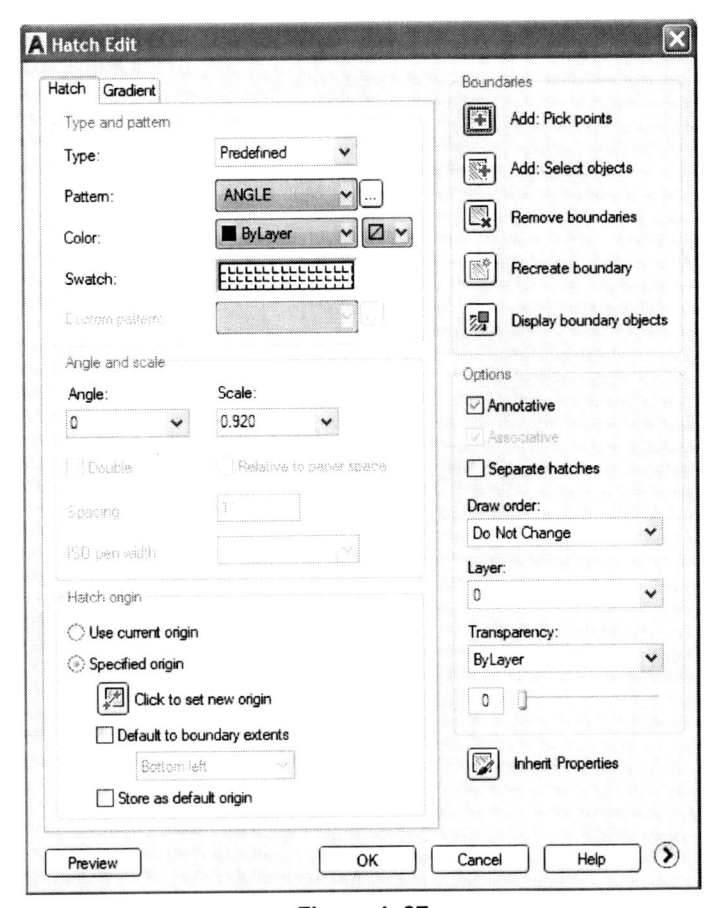

Figure 4–27

Grip Editing Hatch Boundaries

When associative hatches are selected, a single grip displays at the centroid of the hatch, as shown on the left in Figure 4–28. However, non-associative hatch boundaries display grips at each of their corners and at the midpoint of the edges, as shown on the right in Figure 4–28.

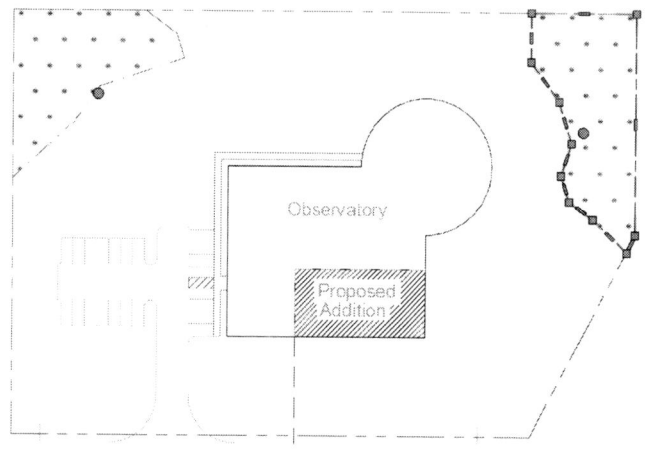

Figure 4–28

Non-associative Hatch Boundaries

Add Vertex: To add a vertex to the boundary, hover over a multifunctional edge grip at the required location and select **Add Vertex** in the dynamic list, as shown in Figure 4–29. Drag and place the new vertex point.

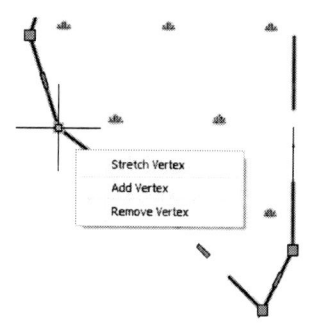

Figure 4–29

Convert to Arc: To change an edge to an arc, hover over the multifunctional edge grip and select the **Convert to Arc** option, as shown in Figure 4–30. Drag and place the midpoint of the arc.

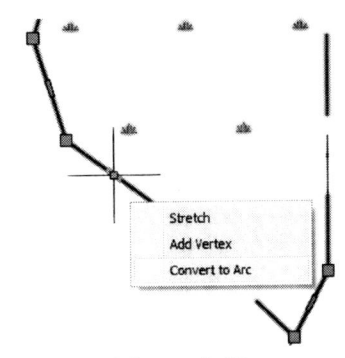

Figure 4–30

Arc Grip Options: When you hover over a multifunctional arc grip, the options enable you to stretch it, add a vertex, or convert the arc to a line.

Remove Vertex: To delete a vertex, hover over the multifunctional vertex grip, and select the **Remove Vertex** option.

Associative Hatch Boundaries

When you are editing associative hatches, you can use one multifunctional grip to access several options (**Stretch**, **Origin Point**, **Hatch Angle**, and **Hatch Scale**) using the dynamic list, as shown in Figure 4–31.

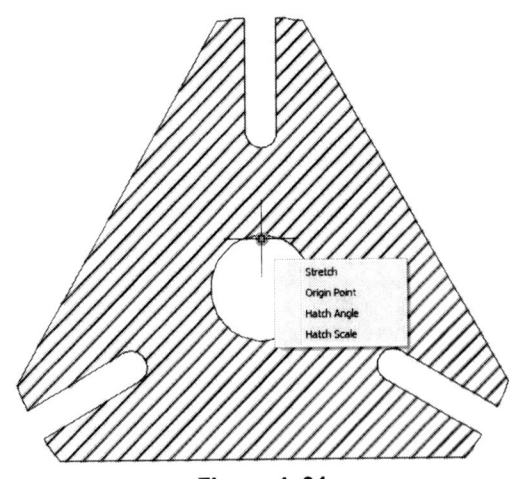

Figure 4–31

Hover the cursor over the grip and select one of the following options:

Stretch	Moves the entire hatch and makes it non-associative. This is the default when you select the grip.
Origin Point	Enables you to select a new point for the origin of the hatch.
Hatch Angle	Enables you to specify an angle at the Command Line or select a point to define the angle.
Hatch Scale	Enables you to specify a scale at the Command Line or select a point to define the scale.

Practice 4b

Hatching Using the Tool Palettes

Practice Objective

- Add hatching to a floor plan.

Estimated time for completion: 5 minutes

In this practice, you will add hatches to a floor plan using the Tool Palettes, as shown in Figure 4–32.

Figure 4–32

1. Open **Law Office-A.dwg** from your practice files folder.

2. Toggle off the layer **A-Door**. Toggle on the layer **A-Flor**, and make it active.

3. Open Tool Palettes (*View* tab>Palettes panel) if it is not already open.

*Click on the area just below the bottom tab and select **Hatches and Fills**.*

4. In Tool Palettes, in the *Hatches and Fills* tab, click on any of the solid colors. Click inside one of the *Office Carpet* areas.

5. Similarly, use the same solid color to fill all of the Office Carpet areas.

6. Use different solid colors for the Office Carpet Trim, Entry Carpet, and Mahogany Flooring.

7. Use the Properties palette to find the areas of the Office Carpet Trim and the Mahogany Flooring. Select the hatch, and open the Properties palette. The Area displays in the Geometry section, as shown for Mahogany Flooring in Figure 4–33.

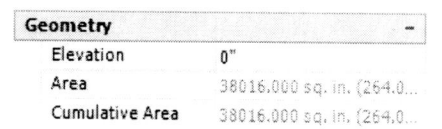

Geometry	
Elevation	0"
Area	38016.000 sq. in. (264.0...
Cumulative Area	38016.000 sq. in. (264.0...

Figure 4–33

8. Save and close the drawing.

Practice 4c

Hatching (Mechanical)

Estimated time for completion: 5 minutes

Practice Objectives

- Apply hatching to a section and modify it.
- Create a hatch with an annotative scale.

In this practice, you will apply hatching to a section and then modify it using the *Hatch Creation* contextual tab. You will also create a hatch with an annotative scale, as shown in Figure 4–34.

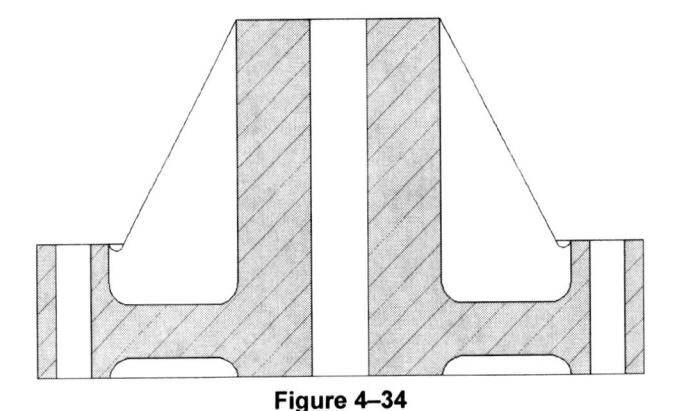

Figure 4–34

Task 1 - Apply a hatch.

1. Open **Wheel-Section-I.dwg** from your practice files folder.

2. Set the current layer to **Hatching**.

3. In the *Home* tab>Draw panel, click (Hatch).

4. In the *Hatch Creation* contextual tab>Properties panel, verify the following:
   - *Hatch Type* is set to **Pattern**.
   - *Scale* is set to **1.000**.
   - *Angle* is set to **0**.

5. In the Pattern panel, verify that *Hatch Pattern* is set to **ANSI31**.

6. In the Options panel, select **Annotative**. In the expanded Options panel, verify that (Create Separate Hatches) is NOT selected.

7. In the Boundaries panel, click ➕ (Pick Points). Select points inside the areas of the section view that display hatching, as shown in Figure 4–35.

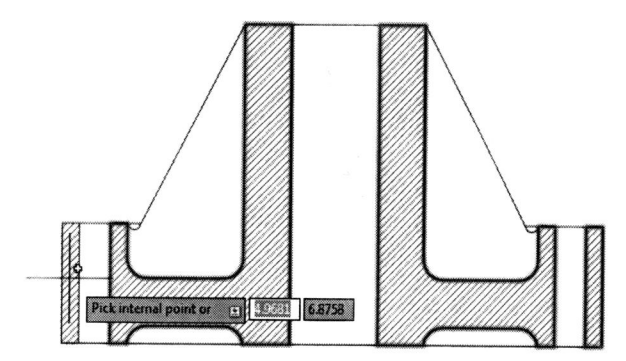

Figure 4–35

8. The hatch pattern lines are very close together. Change the *Scale* to **2.0**. Press <Enter> to apply the hatching. The hatch updates in the drawing.

9. Press <Esc> to exit the hatching selection.

10. Hover the cursor over the hatching and note that it is a single object.

Task 2 - Edit a hatch pattern.

1. Select the hatching. The *Hatch Editor* contextual tab opens.

2. Set the *Scale* to **4.0** and click ✕ (Close Hatch Editor).

3. Use the **Move** command to move each of the two vertical lines near the center of the part, **0.5** units closer to the center. The hatch pattern automatically adjusts, as shown in Figure 4–36.

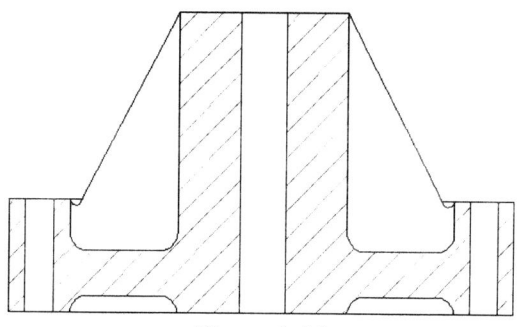

Figure 4–36

4. Save the drawing.

Task 3 - Change the background color, origin, and transparency of the hatch.

1. While not in a command, select the hatch object. The grip and the *Hatch Editor* contextual tab display.

2. Change the *Background Color* to **Cyan,** as shown in Figure 4–37.

3. Set the *Hatch Angle* value to **15,** as shown in Figure 4–37.

4. Set the *Hatch Transparency* value to **6,** as shown in Figure 4–37.

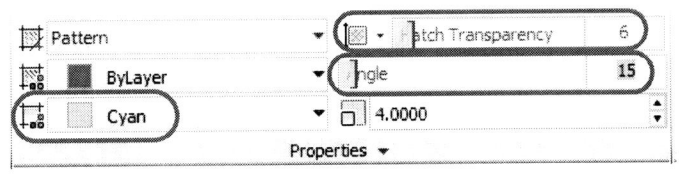

Figure 4–37

5. Click ✕ (Close Hatch Editor).

Task 4 - (Optional) Hatch with the Annotative Scale.

1. Switch to the **B-sized** layout. It contains two viewports that have been set to different scales. If **Annotative** was selected in the *Hatch Creation* contextual tab, hatching is not displayed in either viewport because the hatch in Model Space was set to 1:1.

2. Make the bottom the viewport active.

3. Start the **Hatch** command.

4. Use the **ANSI31** pattern and set the *Scale* to **1.**

5. In the expanded Properties panel, select **Relative to Paper Space**. In the Options panel, verify that **Annotative** is selected.

6. Select the points for hatching the appropriate areas and accept the hatch. No hatch displays in the top viewport.

7. With the bottom viewport still active, in the Status Bar, note that the scale is **1:2**.

Use Additional Drawing Techniques

8. Click in the top viewport to make it active. In the Status Bar, note that the scale is **1:4**.

9. Activate the bottom viewport. Select the hatch, right-click and then select **Properties**.

10. With the hatch still selected, in the Properties palette, click the button to the right of *Annotative scale*, as shown in Figure 4–38.

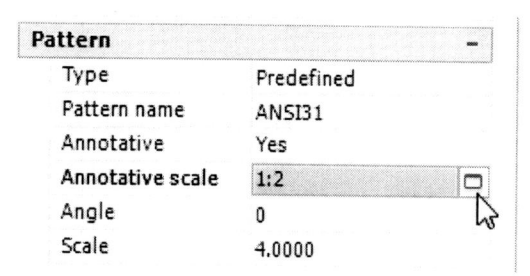

Pattern	
Type	Predefined
Pattern name	ANSI31
Annotative	Yes
Annotative scale	1:2
Angle	0
Scale	4.0000

Figure 4–38

11. In the Annotation Object Scale dialog box, click **Add**.

12. In the Add Scales to Object dialog box, select the **1:4** scale from the list.

13. Click **OK** in both the dialog boxes. The hatch displays in the top viewport automatically, as shown in Figure 4–39.

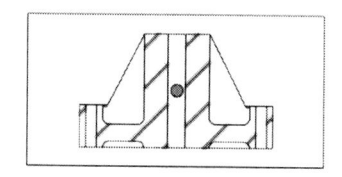

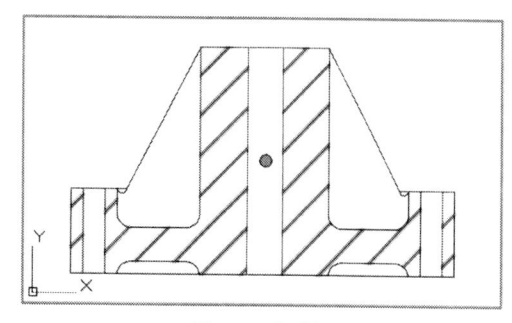

Figure 4–39

14. Press <Esc> to clear the hatch selection.

15. Save and close the drawing.

Practice 4d

Hatching (Architectural)

Practice Objective

- Apply hatching to a floor plan.

Estimated time for completion: 5 minutes

In this practice, you will apply hatching to a floor plan using the **Hatch** command, as shown in Figure 4–40.

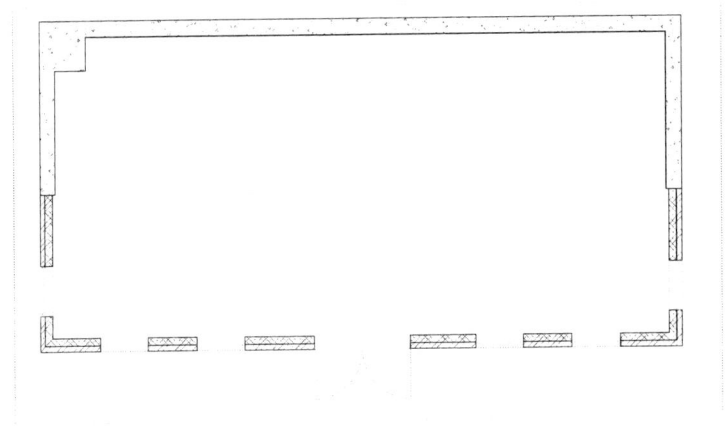

Figure 4–40

1. Open **Basement-A.dwg** from your practice files folder.

2. Set the layer to **Hatching**.

3. Switch to the **D-sized** layout tab. This layout has two viewports at different scales.

4. Double-click in the larger viewport to make it active.

5. Start the **Hatch** command. Set the *Hatch type* to **Pattern** and the *Pattern* to **AR-CONC** (used to show poured concrete). Leave the *Scale* at **1.000** and the *Angle* at **0**.

6. Click (Pick Points). At the *Pick internal point:* prompt, select a point inside the back wall.

7. Click (Close Hatch Creation) to close the *Hatch Creation* contextual tab.

Use Additional Drawing Techniques

8. Start the **Hatch** command again. Set the *Hatch Pattern* to **ANSI37** (a crosshatch that symbolizes a concrete block). Set the *Scale* to **1.000**, and select **Relative to Paper Space** and **Annotative**. Use ⊕ (Pick Points) to select internal points on the inside portions of the other walls, as shown in Figure 4–41. Zoom in as required to accurately select the areas to hatch. Ensure that the *Scale* is still at 1.0000. If it is not, reset it to 1.000.

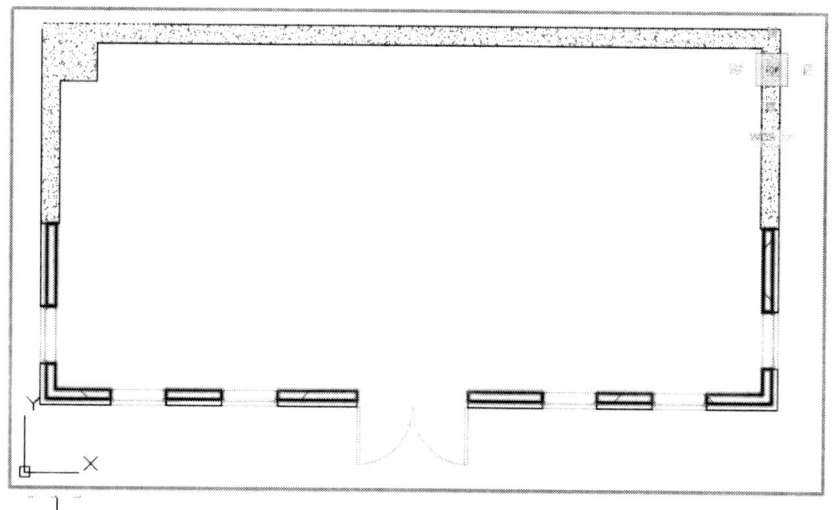

Figure 4–41

9. Press <Enter> to apply the hatch. If the hatch does not display correctly (i.e., as a cross hatch), you might have to select it and reset the *Scale* to **1.0000** in the *Hatch Editor* contextual tab. You might also need to click on **Relative to Paper Space** again and reset the scale to **1** until you get the correct crosshatch pattern. Press <Esc> to clear the hatch selection.

*If the hatch displays at the wrong scale, select the hatch and reset the Scale to **1.000** in the Hatch Editor contextual tab.*

10. Hatch the outside portions of the walls, as shown in Figure 4–40, using the *Hatch pattern* **ANSI31** (a hatch that symbolizes brick). Use a *Scale* of **1.000**, and select **Relative to Paper Space** and **Annotative**.

11. Click ✕ (Close Hatch Creation) to close the *Hatch Creation* contextual tab.

12. Zoom out to display both viewports. The first hatch pattern that you applied displays in both viewports, while the other two hatch patterns only display in the larger viewport. This is because they are annotative and only display in a viewport matching the scale 1/2"=1'0".

13. Hover the cursor over the **ANSI37** hatch. (Annotative) displays next to the cursor, indicating that it is annotative. Hover the cursor over the **AR-CONC** hatch. An icon is not displayed because it is not annotative.

14. Select the **AR-CONC** hatch pattern.

15. The *Hatch Editor* contextual tab opens. Change the *Scale* to **0.25** and select **Annotative**.

16. Click (Close Hatch Editor) to close the *Hatch Editor* contextual tab.

17. Save and close the drawing.

Chapter 5

Organize Objects

This chapter includes instructional content to assist in your preparation for the following topic and objectives for the AutoCAD® Certified Professional exam.

Autodesk Certification Exam Objectives in this Chapter

Exam Topic	Exam Objective	Section(s)
Organize Objects	• Change object properties	• 5.1
	• Alter layer assignments for objects	• 5.2
	• Control layer visibility	• 5.3 & 5.4
	• Assign properties by object or layer	• 5.5
	• Manage layer properties	• 5.3, 5.6 to 5.8

5.1 Working with Object Properties

Every object in the AutoCAD® software has properties, such as layer, color, and linetype, and geometric information (e.g., the end points of a line, center points of a circle or arc, etc.). Many properties can be changed using Quick Properties, the Properties palette, or **Match Properties**. You can also use properties to help you select objects when using **Quick Select**.

- Hover the cursor over an object to display a tooltip containing basic information about the object, as shown in Figure 5–1.

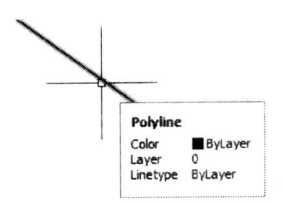

Figure 5–1

Quick Properties

When you select an object when not in a command and display its grips, the basic information about that object displays in the Quick Properties panel, as shown in Figure 5–2. These vary depending on the type of object selected.

Press <Esc> to clear a selected object.

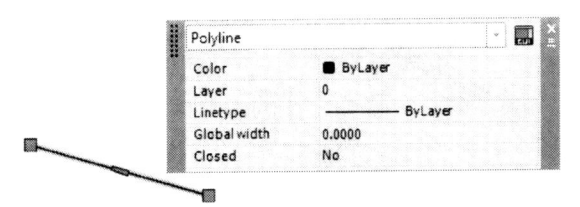

Figure 5–2

*To display (Quick Properties) in the Status Bar, expand (Customization) and select **Quick Properties**.*

- The Quick Properties panel displays along with a selected object (in grip mode) when (Quick Properties) is toggled **On** in the Status Bar.
- When (Quick Properties) is toggled **Off,** you can display the Quick Properties for individual objects by selecting them (in grip mode), right-clicking, and selecting **Quick Properties** in the shortcut menu.
- You can preview and change some properties in the Quick Properties panel. Click on a property and select a different option from the drop-down list, as shown in Figure 5–3.

Organize Objects

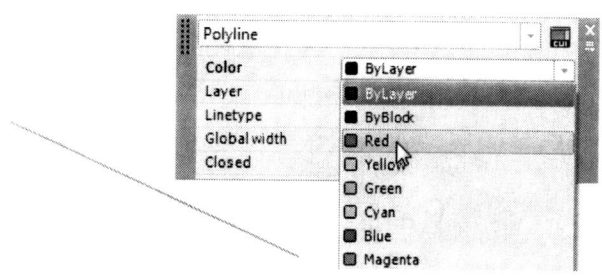

Figure 5–3

You can also display a list of the basic properties for an object using (List) in the *Home tab*>expanded Properties panel. The AutoCAD Text window opens, displaying some of the properties of the selected object. You cannot change any properties using the **List** command.

Properties Palette

The primary way to get detailed information about the objects in your drawing is to use the Properties palette, as shown in Figure 5–4. It reports all of the properties of the object and enables you to change many of them.

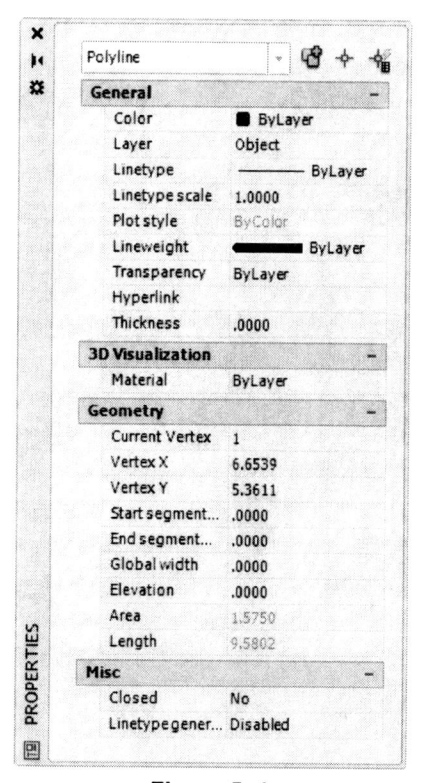

Figure 5–4

© 2017, ASCENT - Center for Technical Knowledge®

5–3

- You can toggle the Properties palette on or off using any of the following methods:
    - In the *View* tab>Palettes panel, click (Properties).
    - Press <Ctrl>+<1>.
    - In the *Home* tab>Properties panel, click.
    - In grip mode, right-click on an object and select **Properties** in the shortcut menu.
- You can have the Properties palette open even when an object is not selected. Once you select any object, its properties display in the open Properties palette.
- As with other palettes, you can dock the Properties palette to any side of the screen. Click, hold, and drag using its title bar and move it to either side of the screen. Once it shows the docking outline, leave the cursor as it automatically docks it in place. You can also hide the palette by clicking the icon located in the Properties title bar, as shown in Figure 5–5. Once hidden, it displays as a bar along the docked side and you can temporarily unhide it by hovering the cursor over the bar. You can also unhide it permanently by clicking in the title bar. Use **X** to close the palette.

Figure 5–5

How To: Modify Objects Using Properties

1. Open the Properties palette if it is not already open and select an object. The properties of the object display in the palette, as shown in Figure 5–6.

Organize Objects

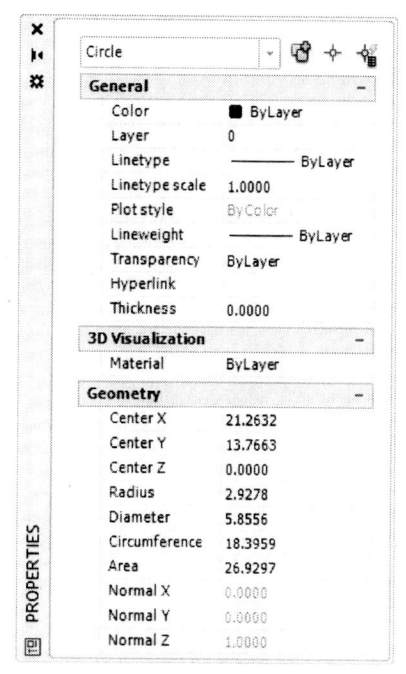

Figure 5–6

2. Change the properties as required by selecting the value you want to change and then typing or selecting a new value.

   - As you move the cursor over the options in the drop-down lists, the object in the Drawing window changes to provide a preview of the highlighted option.

3. To clear the object, move the cursor into the drawing window and press <Esc>.

- Some properties display a list of options, such as the *Layer* property shown on the left in Figure 5–7.

- Other options are numerical, as shown on the right in Figure 5–7. You can enter a number, click 🗔 to open the QuickCalc calculator dialog box, or click 🗔 to modify the location of a point on the screen.

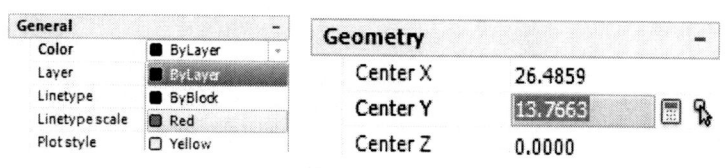

Figure 5–7

- Information in grayed-out cells cannot be changed.

Properties of Multiple Objects

- If you select more than one object of the same type (e.g., two circles), the AutoCAD software lists the types of properties that they have in common. If their values are different they are listed as ***VARIES***, as shown in Figure 5–8. You can change these properties for all of the selected objects at the same time (e.g., select several circles and change their radius to 2.25).

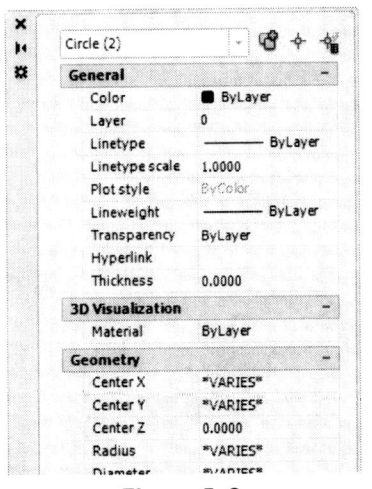

Figure 5–8

- If you select different types of objects (e.g., a circle and a line), the AutoCAD software displays the only types of properties that they have in common. If their values are different, they are listed as ***VARIES***. You can change the common properties of all of the selected objects at the same time. You can also switch between different types of objects using the drop-down list, as shown in Figure 5–9.

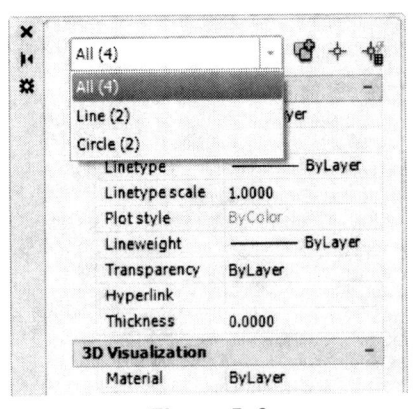

Figure 5–9

Matching Properties

To make objects in your drawing have the same properties as another object, use the **Match Properties** command. It enables you to select one object as a *model* and then copy its properties to any other object you select.

How To: Copy an Object's Properties

1. In the Home tab>Properties panel, click (Match Properties).
2. At the *Select source object:* prompt, select the object you want to use as a model. The cursor changes into a small square box with a paint brush.
3. As you move the cursor over the object that you are going to select, the object changes and displays a preview of the new properties. Select the objects to which you want the properties to be copied.
4. Press <Enter> to end the command.

- **Match Properties** works across drawings. Specify the source object in one drawing, and in the drawing tab bar click on another drawing to switch to it and select the destination objects. If the layer does not exist in the destination drawing, it is created. When you hover over the object in the second drawing, the object highlights but does not display a preview of the new properties.

- **Match Properties** enables you to match all or some of an object's properties. To control which properties are matched, use the **Settings** option (available in the shortcut menu or Command Line) when you have started the command and selected the source object. By default, all of the properties are selected, as shown in Figure 5–10.

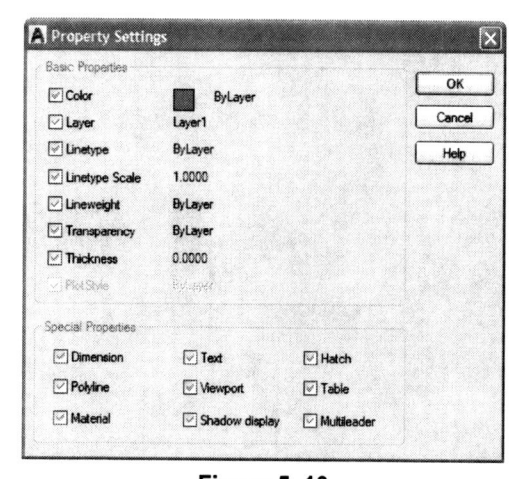

Figure 5–10

Quick Select

Quick Select can be used to select objects using their properties. It opens a dialog box in which you can specify a selection set by object type and/or properties (such as all of the circles with a radius of 0.25), as shown in Figure 5–11.

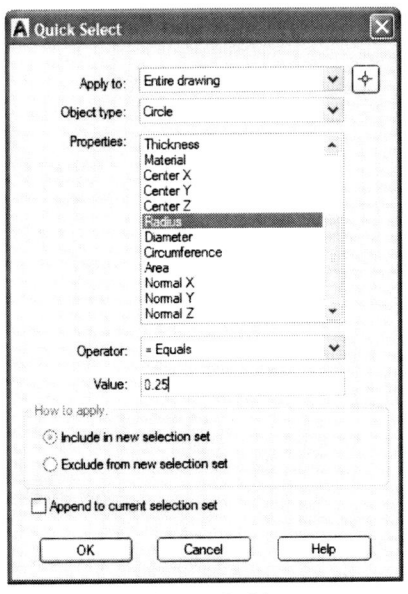

Figure 5–11

To select all of the objects in your drawing, in the Home tab>Utilities panel, click (Select All).

How To: Select Objects Using Quick Select

1. In the *Home* tab>Utilities panel or in the Properties palette, click (Quick Select).
2. In the Quick Select dialog box, in *Apply to*, use **Entire drawing** or click (Select objects) to create a selection set.
3. Select the required *Object type*. **Multiple** selects all of the object types. Only object types that are currently in the selection set display in the drop-down list.
4. In *Properties:*, select the property that you want to filter. This varies according to the selected object type.
5. Select an *Operator:*, as shown in Figure 5–12. The available operators vary depending on the selected property type.

*To select all of the objects of a specific type, regardless of their properties, use **Select All** for the Operator. For example, you can use this method to find all of the circle objects.*

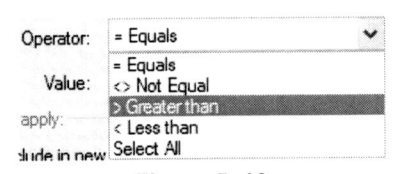

Figure 5–12

Organize Objects

6. Specify the value that you want to find for the selected property. The available values vary depending on the selected property type. For example, values for the property **Layer** include all of the layers defined in the drawing. For the Radius value (of a circle), you need to enter a number.
7. Select an option for how the filter is going to be applied:
    - **Include in new selection set:** Places all of the objects that meet the criteria in a new selection set.
    - **Exclude from new selection set:** Places all of the objects that DO NOT meet the criteria in a new selection set.
8. If you want to build a selection set from several filters, select the **Append to current selection set** option, which adds the results to the current selection, rather than creating a new selection set.
9. Click **OK** to close the Quick Select dialog box. Objects that match the criteria are selected.
10. Use an editing command on the selected objects (such as **Erase** or **Properties**) to modify them.

Practice 5a

Working with Object Properties (Mechanical)

Estimated time for completion: 5 minutes

Practice Objective

- Obtain information about objects.

In this practice, you will get information about some objects (as shown in Figure 5–13) and then make changes to them, using the Quick Properties panel and the Properties palette.

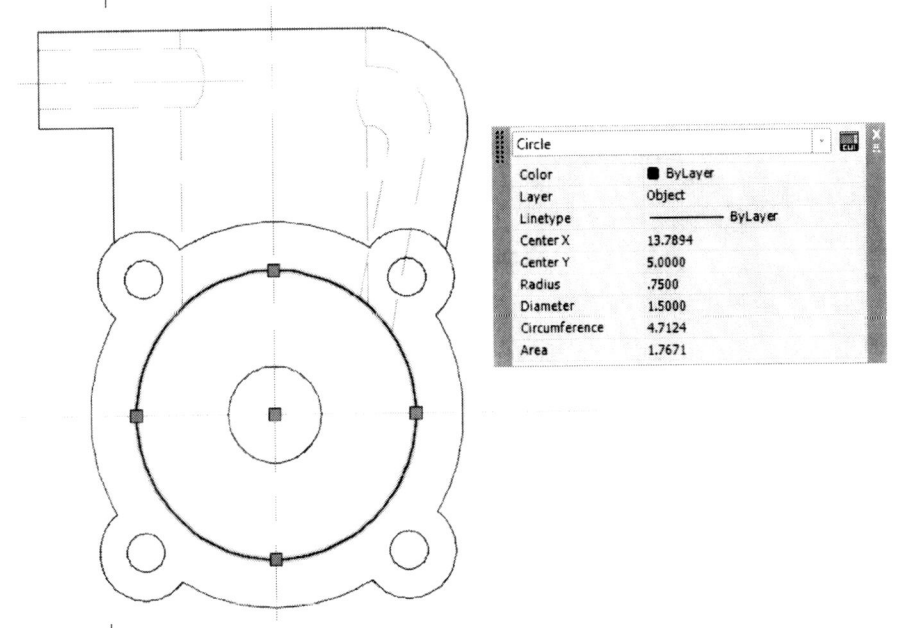

Figure 5–13

1. Open **Crank-I.dwg** from your practice files folder.

2. In the Status Bar, toggle on (Quick Properties).

3. Select the large full circle to display the Quick Properties panel, as shown in Figure 5–13. Press <Esc> to clear the selection.

4. Select the gray horizontal center line at the top left of the object. In its Quick Properties, note that it contains the *Layer* **CONSTRUCTION**. Click anywhere in the *CONSTRUCTION* row to open its edit box. Expand the Layer drop-down list. Hover the cursor over the layer Center and note how the gray line previews as orange, as shown in Figure 5–14. Select **Center** to change the layer.

Organize Objects

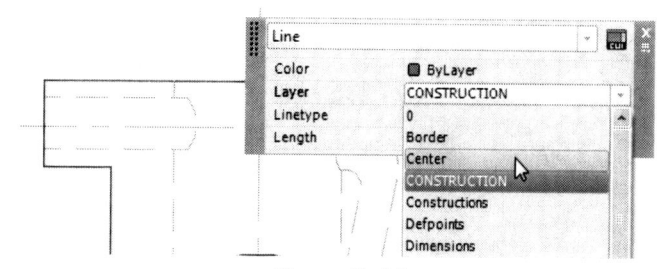

Figure 5–14

5. Clear your selection and toggle (Quick Properties) off in the Status bar.

6. In the *Home* tab>Utilities panel, click (Quick Select).

7. In the Quick Select dialog box, set the *Object type* to **Circle**, *Properties* to **Diameter**, and *Operator* to **= Equals**. In the, *Value* edit box, enter **0.2** and click **OK**. The objects with the above properties (four small circles with the diameter 0.2) are selected and highlighted in the drawing.

8. Click in the *Home* tab> Properties panel to open the Properties palette. To dock the palette to one side of the screen, click, hold, and drag using its title bar and move it to either side of the screen. Once it shows the docking outline, leave the cursor as it automatically docks it in place.

9. In the *Geometry* area, change the diameter to **0.2750**, as shown in Figure 5–15. As soon as you press <Enter>, note that the selected circles become bigger.

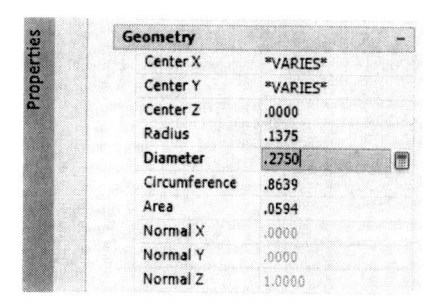

Figure 5–15

10. Clear the selection.

11. Hover the cursor on the Properties title bar and click **X** to close the Properties palette.

12. Save and close the drawing.

Practice 5b

Working with Object Properties (Architectural)

Practice Objective

- Locate objects based on their properties and change their values.

Estimated time for completion: 10 minutes

In this practice, you will use the Properties palette and Quick Select to find objects based on their layer, and then move them to the correct layer. You will also find text based on its height and change it to the correct height, as shown in Figure 5–16.

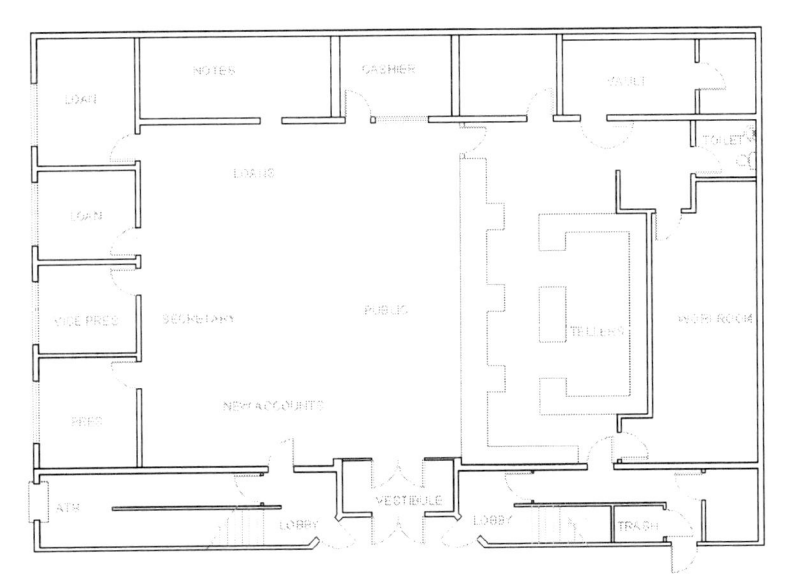

Figure 5–16

1. Open **Bank-Building-A.dwg** from your practice files folder.

2. In the *Home* tab>Layers panel, expand the Layer Control and scroll through the names. The Layer Control contains the layers **WALL** and **Walls**. You need to place all of the walls on the layer **Walls**.

3. Open the Properties palette, if it is not already open. Dock it to one side and hide it by clicking the ◄ icon located in the Properties title bar.

Click in the Home tab>Properties panel or use <Ctrl>+<1> to open the Properties palette.

Organize Objects

4. In the *Home* tab>Utilities panel, click (Quick Select). To select everything on the layer **WALL**, in the Quick Select dialog box, set the *Object type* to **Multiple**, *Properties* to **Layer**, *Operator* to **= Equals**, and *Value* to **WALL**, as shown in Figure 5–17. Click **OK**. The selected objects are highlighted in the drawing.

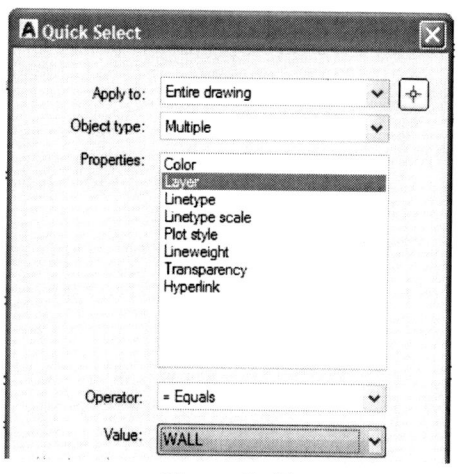

Figure 5–17

5. Hover the cursor over its title bar to unhide the Properties palette. In the *General* area, in the *Layer edit box,* change the WALL to **Walls** and press <Esc> to clear the objects.

6. In the *Home* tab>Utilities panel, click (Quick Select), and in the dialog box, set the *Object type* to **Text** and the *Operator* to **Select All**. Click **OK**. All of the text in the drawing is highlighted. What layer is the text on? In the Properties palette, change the text to layer **Text** and press <Esc> to clear the objects.

7. Use (Quick Select) and the Properties palette to select all of the text that is less than **11"** in height and change its *Height* to **1'-0"**.

8. Close the Properties palette.

9. Save and close the drawing.

© 2017, ASCENT - Center for Technical Knowledge®   5–13

5.2 Changing an Object's Layer

You can move objects from one layer to another so that they show differently in the drawing, as shown in Figure 5–18.

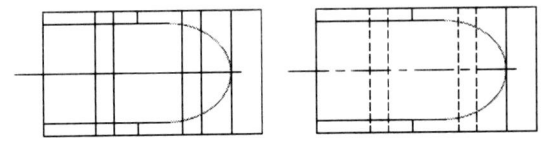

Figure 5–18

Change with Layer Control

You can change the layer of a selected object(s) using the Layer Control.

How To: Change Object Layers with the Layer Control

1. Select an object before you start a command. The Layer Control displays the layer of the object.
2. Expand the Layer Control, and hover the cursor on another layer. Note that the selected object previews with the new layer, as shown in Figure 5–19.

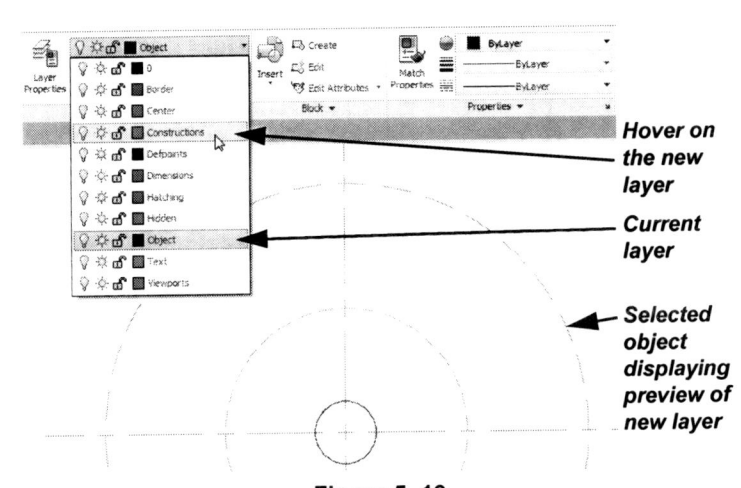

Figure 5–19

3. Select the layer to change it.
4. Press <Esc> to clear the selected object.

Organize Objects

- You can select multiple objects to change their layers. If the selected objects are on different layers, a layer name does not display in the Layer Control. You can still hover to preview and then select a layer to move all of the objects to that layer.

Match Layer

Another way to change the layer of an object is to use the **Match Layer** command. This command can be used when you have other objects on that layer in your drawing.

How To: Match Layers

1. In the *Home* tab>Layers panel, click (Match Layer).
2. Select the objects that you want to change.
3. Press <Enter> to finish the selection set.
4. Select an object on the destination layer.
5. Instead of selecting an object on the destination layer, you can press the <Down Arrow> which lists the **Name** option. Selecting **Name** opens the Change to Layer dialog box, in which you can select a layer name from a list, as shown in Figure 5–20.

Use this option if you do not know which object layer to select. Otherwise, it is faster to select the objects and then select the layer in the Layer Control.

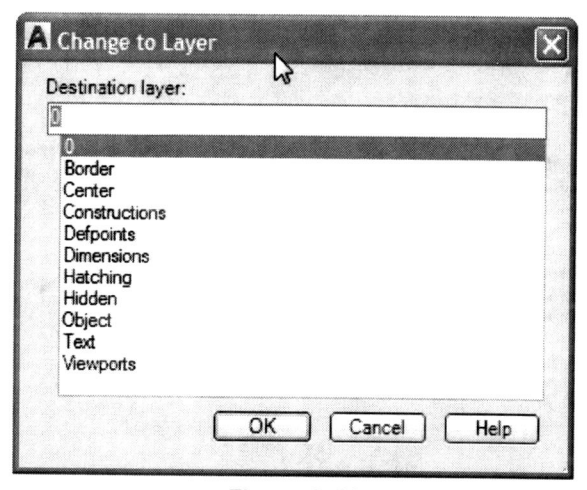

Figure 5–20

5–15

© 2017, ASCENT - Center for Technical Knowledge®

Practice 5c

Estimated time for completion: 5 minutes

Changing an Object's Layer

Practice Objective

- Move objects to different layers.

In this practice, you will use the Layer Control and the **Match Layer** command to move objects to different layers, as shown in Figure 5–21.

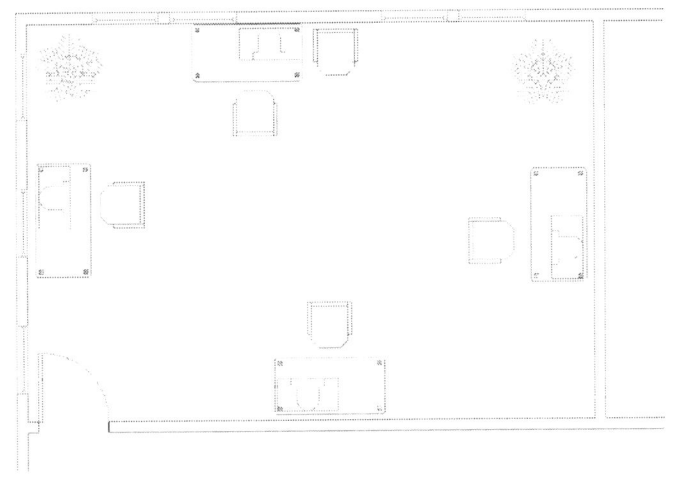

Figure 5–21

1. Open **Suite-A.dwg** from your practice files folder. Currently, all of the objects are on layer **0**.

2. With no command active, select any one line of the wall (blue grips display on the line and it highlights in blue with a thicker lineweight). The layer of that line (layer **0**) displays in the Layer Control.

3. Expand the Layer Control and hover the cursor over the layer **Walls**. The selected wall changes to blue color (the color of layer Wall). Click to change the layer to **Walls**. Press <Esc> to clear the line.

4. Select one of the desks and repeat Step 3 to change its layer to the layer **Furniture**.

5. In the *Home* tab>Layers panel, click (Match Layer). Select the other desks in the room as the objects to be changed, and then press <Enter> or right-click. Select the desk that you changed in Step 4 as the object on the destination layer. All of the desks change layers to match the destination desk.

6. Use (Match Layer) to change the remaining walls to the layer **Walls** using the changed wall as the destination layer.

7. With no command active, select the two plants. Use the Layer Control to change their layer to **Misc**.

8. Change the remaining objects (chairs, PCs, door, and windows) to the appropriate layers. Use layer **Furniture** for chairs and layer **Electrical** for PCs.

9. Save and close the drawing.

5.3 Layer States

The state of the layer determines how the objects on it are displayed and selected.

- The following three aspects of a layer's state can be changed in the Layer Control by selecting the appropriate symbol, as shown on the left in Figure 5–22.

- You can also use an object in the drawing to change its layer state by using the appropriate icon in the Layers panel, as shown on the right in Figure 5–22.

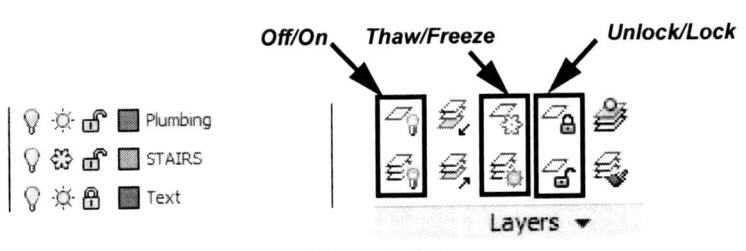

Figure 5–22

On/Off

A layer can be toggled on (displayed) or toggled off (hidden). Toggling a layer off is like temporarily removing it from the drawing. Layers that are toggled off are not displayed and are not plotted.

- The current layer can be toggled off, but the software warns you with an alert box. If the current layer is toggled off, you can draw but cannot see what you are drawing.

Thaw/Freeze

Layers that are not needed or displayed for a long time should be frozen. Freezing a layer is similar to toggling it off, except that the layer does not require calculation time when regeneration occurs.

- You cannot freeze the current layer and a frozen layer cannot be made current.

- If you thaw a layer, you might need to perform a regeneration operation to display the layer.

Lock/Unlock

Objects on layers that are locked can be viewed but not edited. When you hover the cursor over them, a small lock icon displays. By default, locked layers are also slightly grayed out.

- Locking a layer is useful when you do not want to accidentally edit the objects in the layer.

Returning a Layer to its Previous State

You sometimes need to change the state of layers to edit a drawing and then change them back to their previous state. After you have changed the current layer or state of layers, in the *Home* tab>expanded Layers panel, use (Layer Previous) to return to the previous layer settings.

Practice 5d

Working with Layers and Layer States

Practice Objectives

- Draw an object on specific layers.
- Change the state of a layer using Layer Control.

Estimated time for completion: 10 minutes

In this practice, you will draw an object on specific layers and then change the state of the layers.

Task 1 - Draw on and change layers.

In this task you will draw an object on specific layers, as shown in Figure 5–23.

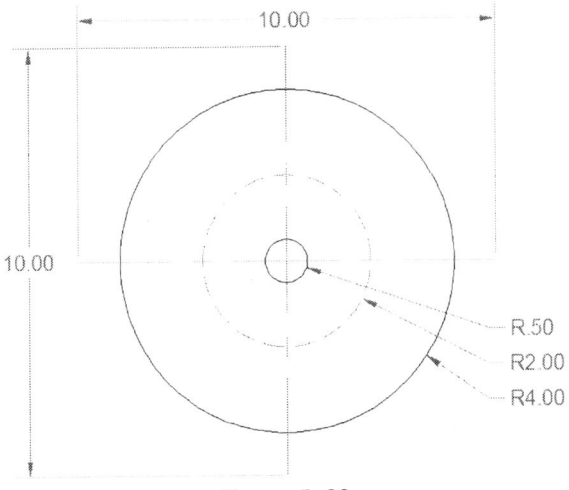

Figure 5–23

1. In the Application Menu, click **New**. Start a new drawing based on **Mech-Inches.dwt**, which is located in your practice files folder.

2. In the *Home* tab>Layers panel, expand the Layer Control and select **Center** to set it as the current layer.

3. Draw a horizontal line, **10 units** long near the center of the screen. The line should be gold with a centerline style.

You can also toggle on Layer Control in the Quick Access Toolbar and use the Layer tools there.

Organize Objects

4. Draw a vertical line, **10 units** long separate from the line you just drew. Move it so that its midpoint is on the midpoint of the other line.

5. Change the current layer to **Object** by selecting it in the Layer Control.

6. Draw a circle with a radius of **4** with its center point at the intersection of the gold lines. The circle should be white on a black background (or black if the background is white).

7. Change the current layer to **Hidden**.

8. Draw another circle with a radius of **2** at the same center point as the first circle. It should be blue/green with a hidden line style.

9. In the *Home* tab>Layers panel, click (Make Current) and select the large black circle. The current layer changes to **Object**.

10. Draw another circle with a **0.5** radius at the same center point. It should be white (or black) and continuous.

11. Save the drawing as **Wheel.dwg**.

Task 2 - Change the layer state.

In this task, you will change the state of layers.

1. Make layer **0** the current layer.

2. Use the Layer Control to toggle off the layer **Center**, as shown in Figure 5–24. The center lines should disappear.

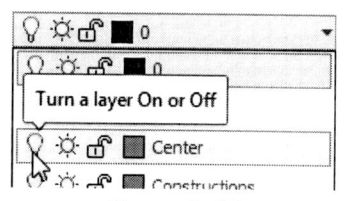

Figure 5–24

3. Use the Layer Control to freeze the layer **Hidden**, as shown in Figure 5–25. The blue/green circle should disappear.

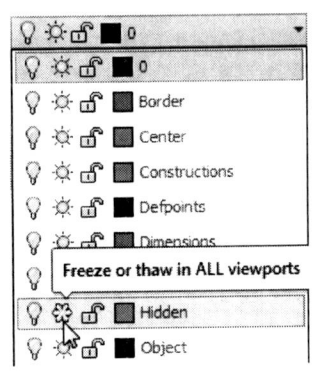

Figure 5–25

4. Use the Layer Control to lock the layer **Object**. The circles on that layer stay displayed, but are slightly grayed out.

5. Try to erase the largest circle and then try to move it. You cannot edit the circle because it is on the locked layer **Object**.

6. Use the Layer Control to unlock the layer **Object**.

7. Erase the largest circle. Use **Undo** to bring it back.

8. Save and close the drawing.

5.4 Setting Layer States

Layer States enable you to save a specific configuration of layers (their status of on/off, thawed/frozen, etc.) and later restore it. Layer States can be created, edited, saved, and renamed in the Layer States Manager, as shown in Figure 5–26. You can also import and export layer states to use in other drawings.

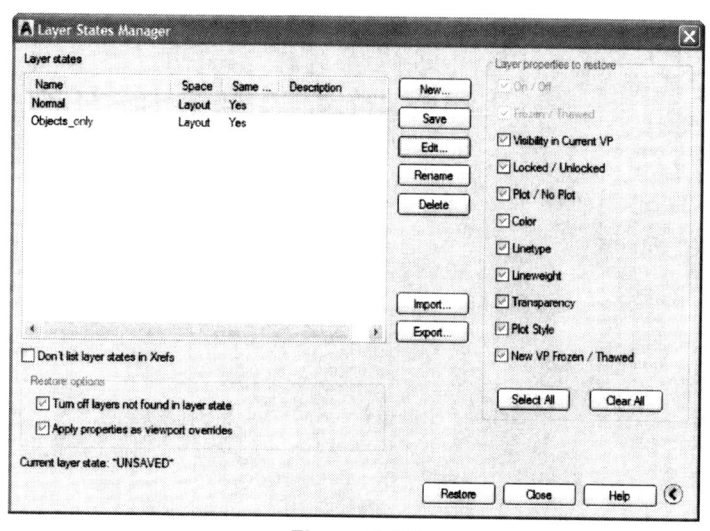

Figure 5–26

For example, in a floor plan drawing you could set up a layer state to display the appropriate layers for the Reflected Ceiling Plan, another state with the appropriate layers displayed for dimensions, etc. Restoring the saved state is easier than adjusting the individual layers each time you need to view or print the drawing in different ways.

How To: Create a New Layer State

1. Set the status of the layers in the drawing (on or off, thawed or frozen, etc.) as required.
2. In the *Home* tab>expanded Layers panel>Layer State drop-down list, select **Manage Layer States**.
3. In the Layer States Manager, click **New**.
4. Type a name and description for the Layer State and click **OK**.
5. You can create additional states and click **Edit** to modify them.
6. When you are finished, select the layer state that you want to use and click **Restore**. If you do not want to restore a layer state at this time, click **Close**.

The layer state also saves which layer is active.

You can also open the Layer States Manager by clicking (Layer States Manager) in the Layer Properties Manager.

Click ⓒ (Less Restore Options) to hide it again.

- Layer States can be saved and restored in the model or in a layout view.

- By default, all of the layer settings, such as on/off, color, and lineweight, are included in the layer state.

- You can modify the *Layer properties to restore* area in the Layer States Manager by expanding ⓢ (More Restore Options).

- The **Don't list layer states in Xrefs** option, filters the list of layer states to only display those in the current drawing.

- If you expect other layers to be added after you create a layer state and you do not want the new layers to be included in the layer state, select **Turn off layers not found in layer state**. When you restore the state, the new layers are toggled off.

- By default, the **Apply properties as viewport overrides** option is selected. After selecting a viewport, you can select this option and save a layer state that overrides the viewport's layer properties.

- To rename a Layer State, select it and click **Rename**. The layer state's name highlights in blue and you can type a new name.

- The *Same as Dwg* column displays **Yes** or **No** depending on whether the Layer State settings match those in the drawing.

Restoring a Layer State

Layer States can be restored from the Layer States Manager. Double-click on the Layer State name or select the name and click **Restore**.

You can also restore a layer state using the Layer State drop-down list in the *Home* tab>Layers panel, as shown in Figure 5–27.

Organize Objects

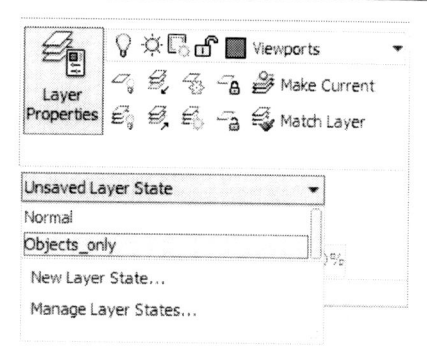

Figure 5–27

How To: Edit a Layer State

You can modify the information saved by a layer state including the current layer, layer status, layer properties, etc. For example, you might want the layer **Walls** in an electrical plan to be gray so that the walls fade into the background while the electrical layers have a heavier lineweight.

1. Open the Layer States Manager.
2. Select the Layer State that you want to modify and click **Edit**. The Edit Layer State dialog box opens, as shown in Figure 5–28.

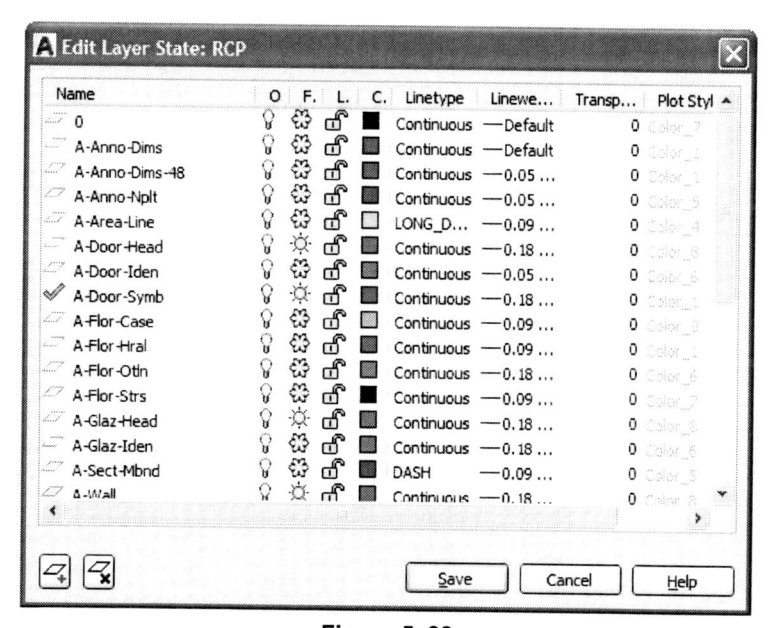

Figure 5–28

3. Modify the layers, as required.

4. If you want to add a layer that is not included in the state, click ![icon] (Add layer to layer state). The Select Layers to Add to Layer State dialog box opens, in which you can select the layers that you want to add.
5. To delete a layer from the layer state, select the layer(s) and click ![icon] (Remove layer from layer state).
6. When you are finished, click **Save** to save the changes and close the Edit Layer State dialog box. You can also click **Cancel** to exit without saving changes.

How To: Import a Layer State

Layer states can be imported from other drawing files, drawing template files, and drawing standards files, as well as from layer states files, as shown in Figure 5–29.

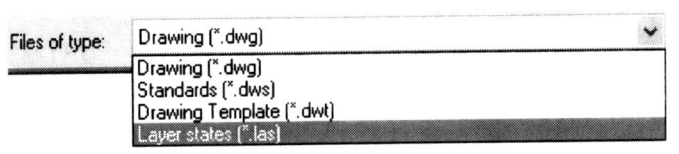

Figure 5–29

1. Open the Layers States Manager and click **Import**.
2. The Import Layer State dialog box opens. In the Files of Type drop-down list, select **Drawing (.dwg)**, **Standards (.dws)**, **Drawing Template (.dwt)**, or **Layer states (.las)**.
3. Browse to the location of the file that you want to import, select it, and click **Open**. The Select Layer States dialog box opens.
4. Select the Layer States that you want to import, as shown in Figure 5–30.

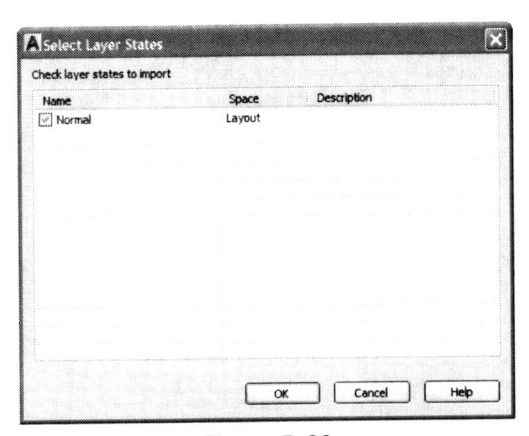

Figure 5–30

Organize Objects

5. Click **OK**.
6. If a Layer State of the same name exists in the drawing, a warning box opens. Click **Replace** to replace the existing Layer State and **Cancel** to cancel importing the new Layer State.

- You can click **Export** to export a Layer State to an .LAS file. It can then be imported into other drawings. If the layers are not defined in a drawing, they are automatically created when the Layer State is imported.

> **Hint: Layer Previous**
>
> If you make a quick, temporary change to the status of your layers and want to return to the previous status, use **Layer Previous**, as shown in Figure 5–31. Similar to **Zoom Previous**, this tool can step back repeatedly through a series of layer changes. The only layer changes that it does not affect are the renaming of layers and creating new ones.
>
> **Figure 5–31**

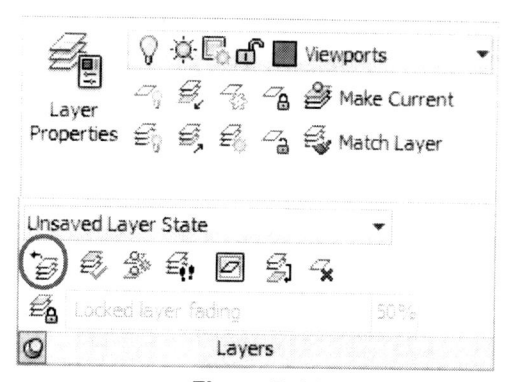

Practice 5e

Setting Up Layer States (Mechanical)

Estimated time for completion: 10 minutes

Practice Objective

- Set up layer states.

In this practice you will restore and edit layer states and then create a new layer state. Two of the layer states are shown in Figure 5–32.

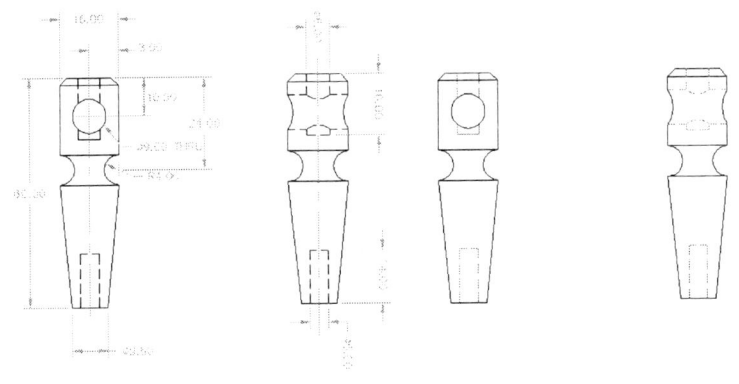

Figure 5–32

Task 1 - Work with layer states.

1. Open **Spindle Detail-M.dwg** from your practice files folder.

2. In the *Home* tab>Layers panel (shown in Figure 5–33), use the Layer State drop-down list to set the layer state to **Normal**, as shown in Figure 5–33.

*The current layer is **0** and the hidden lines are black/white.*

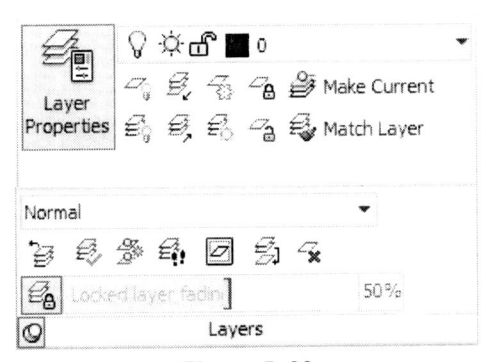

Figure 5–33

Organize Objects

*The layer **Object** is current and layers with hidden linetypes are blue with no dimensions.*

3. Switch the Layer State to **Objects only**, as shown in Figure 5–34.

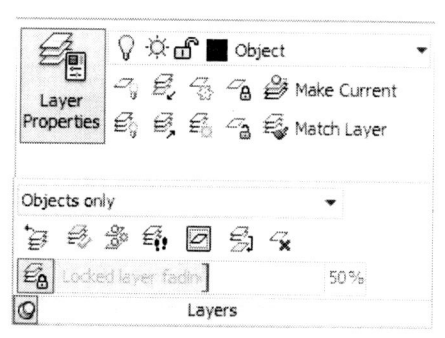

Figure 5–34

4. Open the Layer States Manager.
5. Click **New** to create a new layer state.
6. In the *New layer state name* field, type **Visible Objects only** and click **OK**.
7. In the Layer States Manager, select the layer state **Visible Objects only** and click **Edit**.
8. In the Edit Layer State dialog box, in addition to the default states, freeze the layers **Hidden-Front** and **Hidden-Side**, as shown in Figure 5–35.

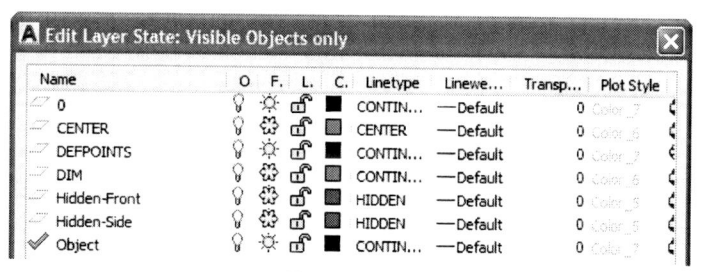

Figure 5–35

9. Click **Save** to close the Edit Layer State dialog box.
10. Click **Close** to close the Layer States Manager.
11. Check each layer state using the Layer State drop-down list to see the changes. You might need to use **REGEN** to refresh the screen after switching layer states.

Task 2 - Import layer states.

1. Open the Layer States Manager and click **Import**.

2. Browse to **Mech Part-M.dwg** in your practice files folder and click **Open**.

3. Select the layer state **heavy objects**, as shown in Figure 5–36. Click **OK**.

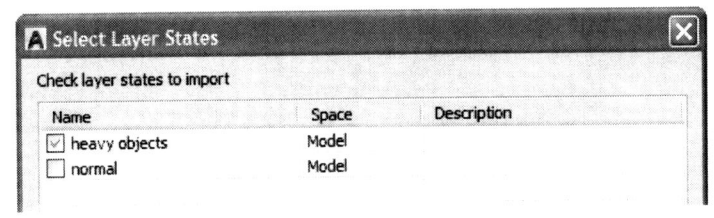

Figure 5–36

4. In the Layer States Manager, select the layer state **heavy objects** and click **Restore**. (You might need to toggle on (Show/Hide Lineweight) in the Status Bar.)

5. Switch the layer state to **Normal**.

6. Save and close the file.

5.5 What are Layers?

The AutoCAD software enables you to create an infinite number of layers in a drawing to organize the objects. Similar to overlays or transparencies, layers assist with editing, presentation, and system performance.

Layers organize a drawing into logical categories. For example, in mechanical drafting, views, hidden lines, sections, symbols, notes, and dimensions might be placed on separate layers. In an architectural drawing, there would be layers for walls, furniture, plumbing features, etc., as shown in Figure 5–37.

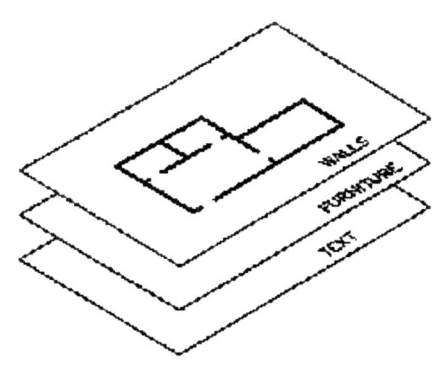

Figure 5–37

- The *current layer* is the layer on which newly drawn objects, such as lines, circles, and text, are placed.

- A color, linetype, and lineweight are assigned to each layer. When a layer is made current, you are automatically drawing in its assigned color, linetype, and lineweight.

- By toggling layers *on* or *off*, you can control which part of the drawing displays or plotted.

- The layer **0** is present in every drawing and cannot be removed or renamed. It is normally not used like the other layers and has special properties for blocks.

Setting the Current Layer

The current layer displays in the Layer Control in the *Home* tab>Layers panel, as shown on the left in Figure 5–38. Selecting the current layer name displays the drop-down list containing all of the existing layers in the current drawing, as shown on the right in Figure 5–38.

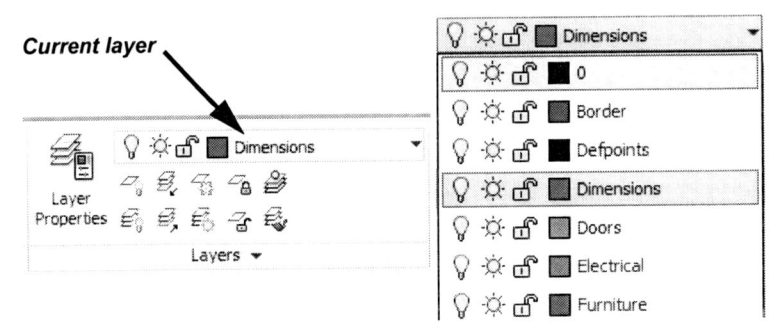

Figure 5–38

- To make a layer active, select its name in the Layer Control drop-down list.

- Another way to make a layer active is to select an object in the drawing and then in the *Home* tab>Layers panel, click (Make Current). This makes the selected objects' layer active. You can also click (Make Current) first and then select an object.

- For easy access to various Layer tools, you can display the Layer Control bar in the Quick Access Toolbar, as shown in Figure 5–39. By default, the Layer Control does not display in the Quick Access Toolbar, but you can display it by selecting **Layer** in the (Quick Access menu).

Figure 5–39

Using (Make Current) indicates the active layer name in the Command Line as well.

Enhanced in 2018

Organize Objects

Hint: Properties Panel

You can change the layer and *color*, *linetype*, *lineweight*, *plot style*, and *transparency* of individual objects. In the *Home* tab, the Properties panel enables you to set these characteristics for objects (as shown in Figure 5–40), just as the Layer Control enables you to set the layer.

Color
Lineweight
Linetype

Plot Style
Transparency
List

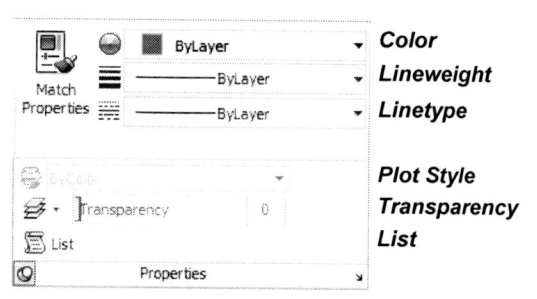

Figure 5–40

Normally, these properties are set to **ByLayer**, indicating that the objects do not have a specific color, linetype, lineweight, plot style, and transparency of their own. Instead, the layer that the objects are on defines their properties.

Although you can assign colors, linetypes, lineweights, plot style, and transparency to individual objects, it is usually best to let the object take its properties from its layer. This method ensures greater consistency and control over properties. You can easily change the color, lineweight, linetype, plot style, and transparency of all of the objects on a specific layer by changing the properties of the layer.

5.6 Additional Layer Tools

The additional layer commands in the *Home* tab>Layers panel, can help you to work quickly with layers. They include commands that enable you to select layers rather than their names, and to change their layer state or current status.

Changing Object Layer States

The commands to freeze, toggle off, lock, and unlock layers are the most basic of the additional layer commands. They can be accessed in the *Home* tab>Layers panel, as shown in Figure 5–41.

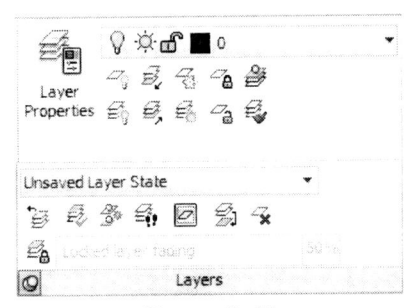

Figure 5–41

How To: Freeze or Turn Layers Off

1. Start (Layer Freeze) or (Layer Off).
2. Select an object on the layer that you want to change. It changes automatically.
3. You can continue selecting objects on other layers as required.
4. Press <Enter> to finish the command.

Two other commands are helpful with layer states:

- (Turn All Layers On)
- (Thaw All Layers)

Organize Objects

In the Home tab>extended Layers panel, use ▱ (VP Freeze in All Viewports except Current) to freeze a selected layer in all other viewports except the active one.

Settings

Layer Freeze and **Layer Off** have settings for how blocks, Xrefs, and Viewports respond to the commands. These settings remain in effect until you change them.

Block selection	Sets the nesting level of a block or Xref:
	Block (default): Freezes or turns off the layer on which the block was inserted. If it is part of an Xref, it freezes the layer of the object.
	Entity: Only freezes or turns off the layer in the block or Xref that you actually select.
	None: Freezes or turns off the layer on which the block or Xref was inserted.
Viewports	Sets the way the command responds when you are working in a Paper Space viewport.
	VPFreeze (default): Only freezes or turns off the layer in the current viewport.
	Freeze/Off: Freezes or turns off the layer across the entire drawing.

How To: Lock or Unlock Layers

1. Click ▱ (Layer Lock) or ▱ (Layer Unlock).
2. Select an object on the layer that you want to change. It changes automatically.

- A small padlock icon displays when you hover the cursor over a locked layer, as shown in Figure 5–42.

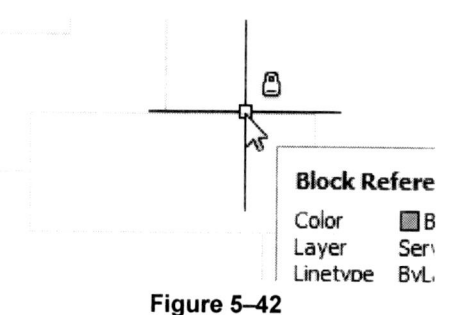

Figure 5–42

© 2017, ASCENT - Center for Technical Knowledge®

- Locked layers fade but are still displayed in the drawing. Use the **Locked layer fading** slider in the extended Layers panel to control how much the layers fade, as shown in Figure 5–43.

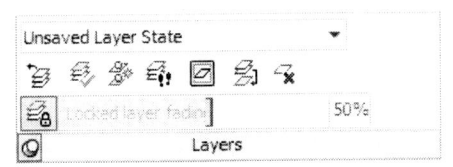

Figure 5–43

Isolating Layers

(Layer Isolate) is similar to changing the layer state, but it locks and fades (or turns off) all of the objects in a drawing EXCEPT those that are on the layers that you selected to isolate, as shown in Figure 5–44. When you have finished working with the isolated layers, you can return them to their original layer state.

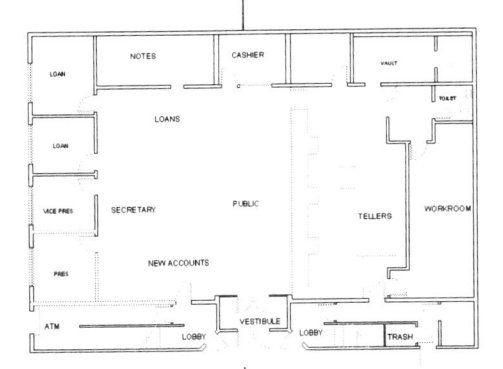

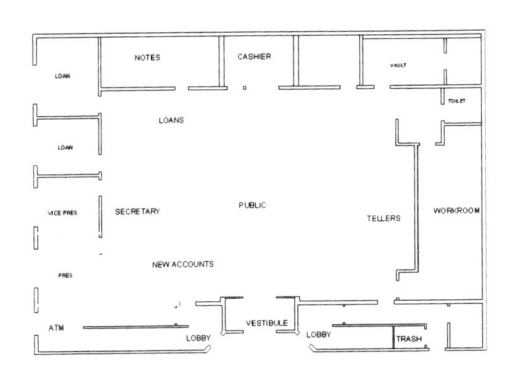

Figure 5–44

How To: Isolate Layers

1. Click (Layer Isolate).
2. Select objects on the layer(s) in which you want to work.
3. Press <Enter>. All of the other layers are locked and faded.

- If you only select one layer to isolate and it is not the current layer, it becomes current.

Organize Objects

- The layers that are not selected to be isolated are either locked and faded or toggled off. To change this, start the **Layer Isolate** command, select **Settings**, and select the required option, as shown in Figure 5–45.

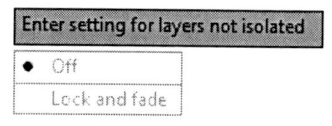

Figure 5–45

- When you select **Off** you are prompted to set the way it works in Paper Space viewports. The **Vpfreeze** option freezes the unisolated layers in the active viewport, and the **Off** option turns the unisolated layers off in all of the viewports.

How To: Unisolate Layers

1. Click (Layer Unisolate).
2. All of the isolated layers are restored.

- (Layer Previous) also restores layers that have been isolated and changes the current layer back to the original if **Layer Isolate** was last used to change it.

Changing an Object's Layer

There are other ways of changing the layers of objects in a drawing including: (Change to Current Layer) and (Copy Objects to New Layer). These commands change an object's layer by selecting other objects.

How To: Change to the Current Layer

1. Click (Change to Current Layer).
2. Select the objects that you want to place on the current layer.
3. Press <Enter> to finish the command and move the objects to the current layer.

How To: Copy an Object to a New Layer

This command creates new copies of selected objects and places them on a new layer. You can then move the copies to a new location while you are still in the command or leave them on top of existing objects.

1. Click (Copy Objects to New Layer).
2. Select the objects that you want to copy and press <Enter> to complete the selection set.
3. Select an object on the destination layer or use the **Name** option to open the Copy to Layer dialog box, in which you can select a layer name, as shown in Figure 5–46.

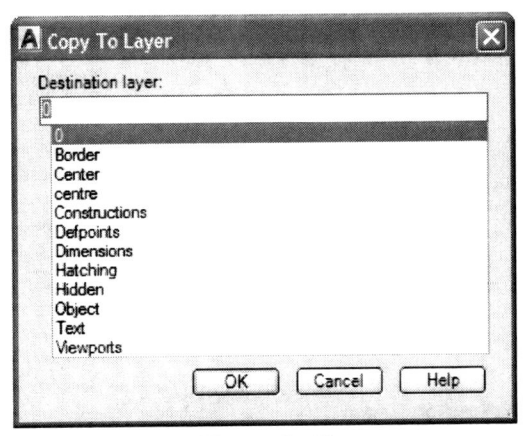

Figure 5–46

4. Select a base point from which to copy. If you want the new copies to be on top of the originals, you can press <Enter> to exit without moving the objects.
5. Select a second point to place the new objects on the selected layer.

- The new layer to which objects are going to be copied must exist for this command to be used.

Modifying Layers

In the *Home* tab>extended Layers panel use (Layer Merge) to move all of the objects on selected layers to a target layer and then delete the selected layers. (Layer Delete) removes a layer and any objects associated with that layer.

- The default response to the final prompt of *Do you wish to continue?* for each of these commands is **No**. You must specify **Yes** to complete the process.

Organize Objects

How To: Merge Layers

1. Click ![icon] (Layer Merge).
2. Select an object on the layer that you want to merge. You can select several layers before pressing <Enter> to continue.
3. Select an object on the target layer.
4. A warning box opens, listing the layers that you are going to merge into the target layer. If you type **Y** for **Yes**, the objects are moved to the target layer and the other layers are deleted from the drawing.

How To: Delete Layers

1. Click ![icon] (Layer Delete).
2. Select an object on the layer that you want to delete. You can select several layers before pressing <Enter> to continue. If you select multiple layers, the objects disappear from the drawing as you click them.
3. A warning box opens, listing the layers that you are going to delete. If you type **Y** for **Yes**, the objects and layers are deleted from the drawing.

- If blocks are associated with the layer, they are redefined with objects from the deleted layer.

Layer Walk

Use this command to find out which layers the objects display on and then use other commands to move them to the correct layer.

![icon] (Layer Walk) provides an interface in which you can quickly display objects on specified layers and then modify them in a dialog box, as shown in Figure 5–47.

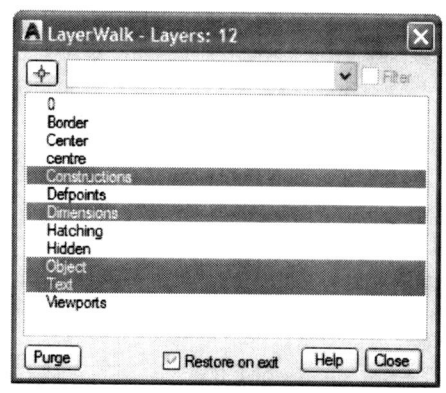

Figure 5–47

- You can either select from the list of layer names in the LayerWalk dialog box or use ⊕ (Select Objects) to select objects in the drawing window.

- Use <Ctrl> and <Shift> or drag to select multiple layers.

- Double-click on the name if you always want a layer to be displayed. An asterisk displays next to the name. You can also right-click and select **Hold Selection**. You can release the hold layers individually or as a group by right-clicking and selecting **Release Selection** and **Release All**.

- If a layer does not contain any objects, you can click **Purge** to remove it from the drawing.

- When you have finished working in the dialog box, you can display the layer setup in your drawing if you clear the **Restore on exit** option. If it is selected, the modifications you made in the dialog box are not displayed in the drawing window.

Filtering Layers

You can use filters to select layers more quickly. Type information including a wildcard character (such as *) and press <Enter> to only display the layer names that match the filter, as shown in Figure 5–48.

*All of the layers display if you clear the **Filter** option.*

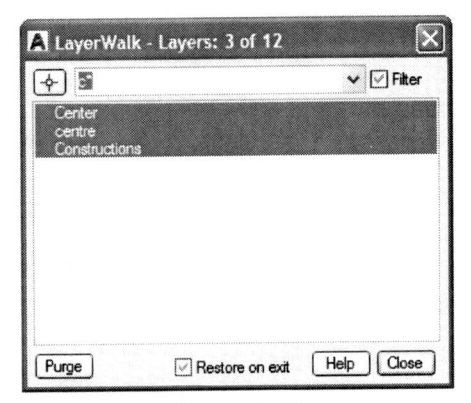

Figure 5–48

- To save a filter, right-click in the Layer list and select **Save Current Filter**. The filter is added to the drop-down list.

- In the LayerWalk dialog box, right-click and select **Save Layer State** to save the current selection of layers to be used later in the Layer State Manager.

- In the LayerWalk dialog box, right-click and select **Inspect...** to display the number of layers in the drawing, number of layers selected, and number of objects on the selected layers, as shown in Figure 5–49.

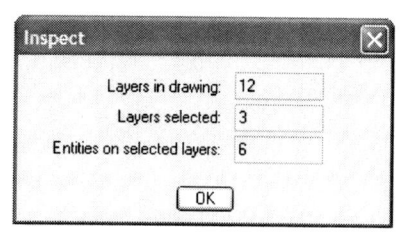

Figure 5–49

Practice 5f

Layer Tools

Practice Objective

- Modify the layers using the additional layer commands.

Estimated time for completion: 10 minutes

In this practice, you will freeze and toggle off layers, as shown in Figure 5–50, and then restore the layer states. You will isolate and unisolate layers. You will use the **Layer Walk** and **Layer Merge** commands to determine whether any layers are incorrect in the drawing and then fix them as required.

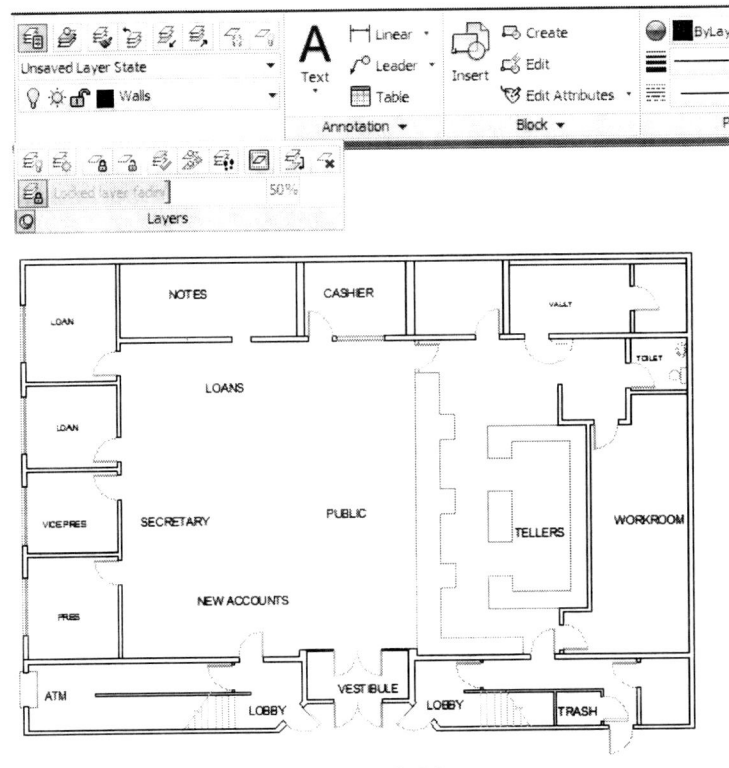

Figure 5–50

1. Open **Bank-A.dwg** from your practice files folder.

2. In the *Home* tab, expand and pin the Layers panel.

3. Practice freezing and toggling off layers using (Layer Freeze) and (Layer Off).

Organize Objects

4. Restore the layer states using ⛉ (Turn all Layers On) and ⛉ (Thaw All Layers).

5. You can also try isolating layers using ⛉ (Layer Isolate) and ⛉ (Layer Unisolate).

6. Set the current layer to **Electrical**.

7. Click ⛉ (Layer Freeze). At the *Select an object* prompt, press <Down Arrow> and select **Settings>Block selection>Block** from the down arrow menus. Select a door to freeze and note what happens.

8. Click ⛉ (Thaw All Layers).

9. Click ⛉ (Layer Freeze) again. At the *Select an object* prompt, press <Down Arrow> and select **Settings>Block selection>Entity** from the down arrow menus. Select a door to freeze and note what happens (All of the doors disappear).

10. Click ⛉ (Thaw All Layers).

11. Click ⛉ (Layer Walk). Select **Doors**, **Furniture**, **STAIRS** to display the objects on each layer. Select the layer **Walls** first and then select the layer **WALL**. Note that the walls in the drawing are on two different layers. Close the Layer Walk dialog box.

12. Set layer **0** to be active. Click ⛉ (Layer Merge) and select an object on the layer **WALL**. Press <Enter>. Select an object on the layer **Walls** and check the Layer Control in the Layers panel to verify that the one of the wall layers is deleted.

13. Save and close the drawing.

5.7 Creating New Layers

A layering scheme is the most important organizing tool in any drawing. A standard layer scheme should be included in your template drawings. Use the Layer Properties Manager to create new layers and change the properties or status of existing layers, as shown in Figure 5–51.

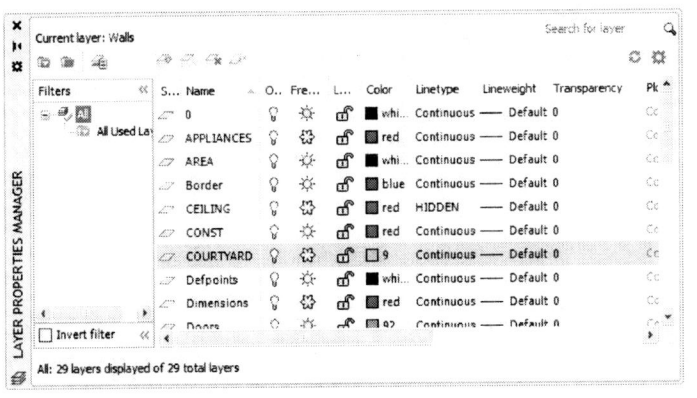

Figure 5–51

Layer Properties Manager

The Layer Properties Manager is a palette and can stay open while you are working in the drawing. It can also be docked and hidden to create space in the drawing area. When layers are modified in the Layer Properties Manager, the changes are automatically applied to the drawing and listed in the Layer Control list in the *Home* tab>Layers panel.

- When you create layers, you set their color, linetype, lineweight, and plot or no-plot status, and the plot style (if applicable).

- Layers defined in a template establish a consistent layer standard for all drawings based on that template.

- The icon in the *Status* column indicates whether the layer contains objects ( ), does not contain objects ( ), or is the current layer ( ).

Organize Objects

How To: Create a New Layer

1. in the *Home* tab>Layers panel, or in the View tab> Palettes panel, click ▦ (Layer Properties).
2. Click ▦ (New Layer). A new layer is added to the list with the default name, **Layer1**.
3. Type a name for the new layer. Layer names can have up to 255 characters and can include letters, numbers, spaces, and most other special characters (the following symbols are not permitted: < > / \ ? * | , = `.).
4. To set the **Color**, select the color swatch for that layer, select a color in the Select Color dialog box (as shown in Figure 5–52), and click **OK**.

To create several new layers quickly, click ▦ (New Layer) once and then type the layer names separated by a comma.

The Select Color dialog box has three tabs: Index Color, True Color, and Color Books. The Index Color list (256 colors) is adequate for most needs.

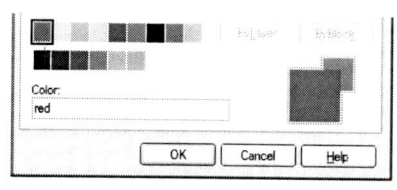

Figure 5–52

5. To set the **Linetype**, select the linetype name for that layer, select a different linetype in the Select Linetype dialog box (as shown in Figure 5–53), and click **OK**.

Linetypes are set by default to display in a Paper Space viewport according to the current viewport scale.

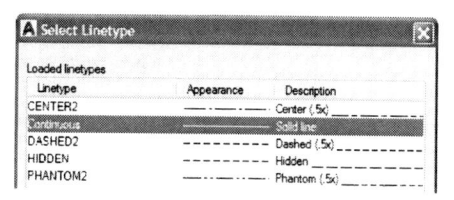

Figure 5–53

6. To set the **Lineweight**, select the lineweight setting for that layer, select a width in the Lineweight dialog box (as shown in Figure 5–54), and click **OK**.

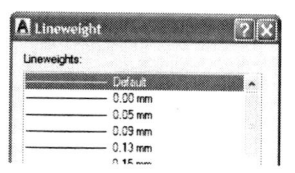

Figure 5–54

7. To make the layer non-plotting, click 🖶 (Plot) or 🖶⊘ (No Plot), as shown in Figure 5–55. No Plot layers are useful for construction lines, notes, viewports, and other information that is required for drawing construction, but not for the plotted output.
8. If you want to freeze a layer by default in a new viewport, click (New VP Freeze), as shown in Figure 5–55. For example, you might want to create a layer that is only displayed in one viewport.

Figure 5–55

9. To add a description, click in the *Description* column and type the description.

- The changes are automatically applied to the drawing.

- If a layer is selected in the Layer Properties Manager when you click (New Layer), the new layer copies the properties of the selected layer.

Sorting Layers by Properties

- You can sort layers in the list according to their properties by selecting any of the column headings at the top of the list. For example, selecting the *Name* column sorts the list alphabetically by name, and selecting the *Freeze* column separates the frozen from the thawed layers. Clicking on a heading again reverses the sort order.

- You can rearrange the display order of columns in the Layer Properties Manager by dragging the column header to a new location, as shown in Figure 5–56. The new location is saved by the AutoCAD software.

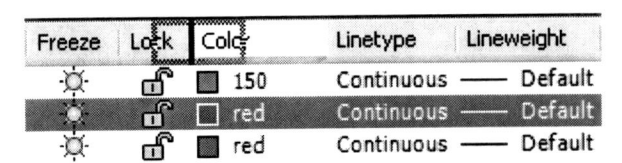

Figure 5–56

Organize Objects

- You can resize the width of the columns in the Layer Properties Manager by dragging the border between the column headings. You can also right-click on a column header and select **Maximize column** to maximize one column, or select **Maximize all columns** to resize all of the columns to the width of their largest cell.

- You can remove any columns that you do not want displayed. Right-click on any column header and select a column name to clear the checkmark and remove it from the display. **Name** is grayed out and cannot be removed, as shown in Figure 5–57.

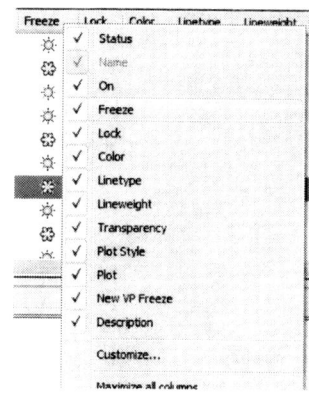

Figure 5–57

- Additional column names display if you are in a layout.

Lineweights

Lineweight refers to how heavy or wide the lines are in an object, as shown in Figure 5–58. Heavier lineweights are used to emphasize parts of the drawing. This becomes important when the drawing is plotted.

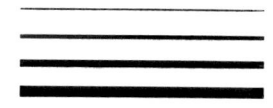

Figure 5–58

(Show/Hide Lineweight) in the Status Bar controls the visibility of lineweights on the screen.

- Depending on the resolution of your monitor, you might not be able to distinguish between similar lineweights in your drawing. When you print the drawing, the lineweights are easier to differentiate.

- Plotted lineweight in the AutoCAD software is often controlled by color.

Linetypes

Linetype refers to whether the objects are drawn with dashed, dotted, continuous, or other line styles, as shown in Figure 5–59. Usually, specific types of lines are used for specific types of objects. For example, hidden lines are usually dashed, while most objects are drawn with continuous linetypes.

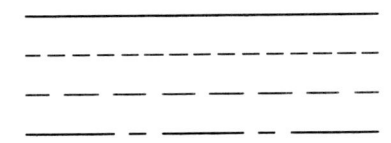

Figure 5–59

How To: Load a Linetype

The AutoCAD software comes with a wide selection of standard linetypes. If the required style does not display in the Select Linetype dialog box, you can load other linetypes into the drawing.

1. In the Layer Properties Manager, select the linetype name for the layer that you want to modify. The Select Linetype dialog box opens.
2. Click **Load...**.
3. In the Load or Reload Linetypes dialog box, select the Linetype(s) that you want to use. To select more than one, hold <Shift> or <Ctrl> while selecting.
4. Click **OK**. The linetypes are now available for use.

- The standard linetype definitions are stored in the file **Acad.lin**.

Hint: Linetype Scale

The Linetype Scale controls the length of segments and gaps for all of the linetypes in the drawing. A larger value for the linetype scale places longer segments and gaps. Depending on the size of your drawing, you might need to adjust the linetype scale so that linetypes display and plot at an appropriate size.

- By default, the linetype scale is set to display in Paper Space viewports so the linetypes are scaled correctly for each viewport.

- You can type **ltscale** in the Command Line to launch the command.

Organize Objects

Other Layer Options

The left panel in the Layer Properties Manager displays the layer filter tree. Layer filters are an advanced layer management tool that are used to control the layer list and to group layers.

- One layer filter, **All Used Layers**, is predefined. Selecting this filter only lists layers that contain objects. To return to the full list, select **All** in the Layer Filter tree.

- If you do not use layer filters, you can hide that portion of the Layer Properties Manager by clicking « (Collapses Layer filter tree), as shown in Figure 5–60.

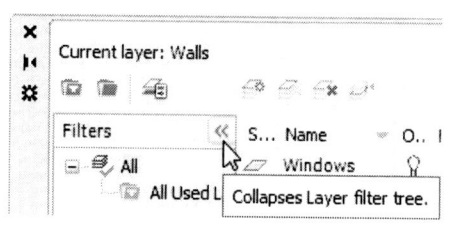

Figure 5–60

How To: Delete a Layer

1. Select a layer name in the list.
2. Click (Delete Layer). The layer is removed.

- You cannot delete layers that contain objects or certain special layers, such as layer **0**.

How To: Rename a Layer

1. In the list, click once on the layer name to select it and then click it again. An edit box displays around the highlighted name (you can also right-click on a Layer name and select **Rename Layer**).
2. Type a new name.

- You cannot rename layer **0** and should not rename the default layer **defpoints**.

© 2017, ASCENT - Center for Technical Knowledge®

5–49

How To: Merge Layers

You can select multiple layers in the Layer Properties Manager and merge their objects into one layer. All of the objects on the selected layers are moved to the merged layer and the selected layers are removed from the drawing.

1. In Layer Properties Manager, use <Shift> or <Ctrl> to select one or more layers to merge.
2. Right-click and select **Merge selected layer(s) to...**
3. In the Merge to Layer dialog box, select the layer to which you want to merge the other layers.
4. Click **OK**.
5. In the warning box, click **Yes**.
6. The AutoCAD Text window opens displaying the progress of the merge procedure. The selected layers are merged to the target layer. The selected layers are then deleted.

Organize Objects

Practice 5g

Saving a Template

Practice Objectives

- Set the units and limits in a drawing.
- Create a set of layers in a drawing.
- Create a page setup and apply it to a Layout tab.
- Add a title block to a Layout tab.
- Save the drawing as a template.

Estimated time for completion: 30 minutes

In this practice, you will create a drawing that you will turn into a template. You will set the units and test them by measuring distances using grips and use the Layer Properties Manager to create and modify new layers. You will also create a Page Setup and apply it to a standard layout, and then save the drawing as a template.

Task 1 - Control and test the units display.

In this task you will create a drawing that you will turn into a template. You will set the units and test them by measuring distances using grips, as shown in Figure 5–61.

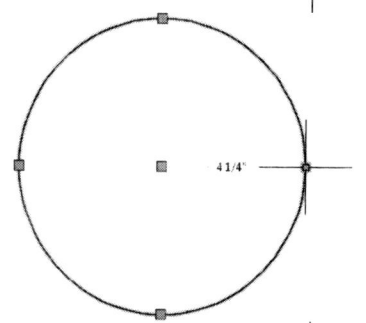

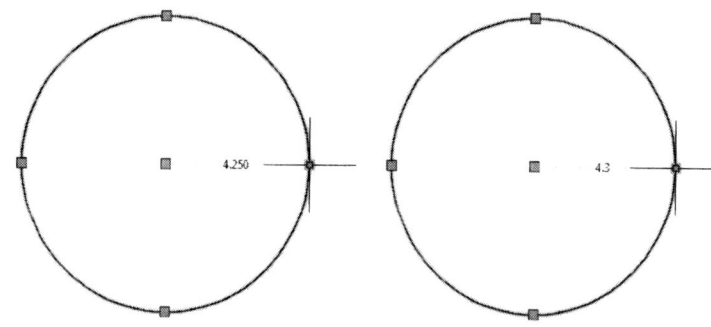

Figure 5–61

*In the AutoCAD LT software, select **acadlt.dwt**.*

1. Start the **New** command and select **acad.dwt** from the AutoCAD 2018 Template folder (default folder). Save the new drawing as **AEC-Facilities.dwg** in you practice files folder.

2. In the Application Menu, select **Drawing Utilities>Units**. In the Drawing Units dialog box, in the *Length* area, set the *Type* to **Architectural** and the *Precision* to **0'-0 1/16"**.

3. Verify that the *Insertion scale* is set to **Inches**. Click **OK**. Note that the coordinate display in the Status Bar changes to display in feet and inches.

© 2017, ASCENT - Center for Technical Knowledge®

5–51

4. Draw a **4 1/4"** radius circle (type **4-1/4** for the radius).

5. Select the circle and hover the cursor over one of the outer grips. The radius should be listed as 4 1/4".

6. Start the **Units** command again to open the Drawing Units dialog box. Change the *Length Type* to **Decimal** and the *Length Precision* to **0.000**, and click **OK**.

7. Select the circle again and hover the cursor on one of the grips. The radius is reported as **4.250**.

8. Start the **Units** command to open the Drawing Units dialog box. Change the *Length Precision* to **0.0**.

9. Select the circle and hover the cursor over one of the outer grips. The radius is reported as **4.3**.

10. Start the **Units** command to open the Drawing Units dialog box. Set the *Length Type* to **Architectural** with a **0'-0 1/8"** *Precision*.

11. In the Command Line, type **limits**. Set the lower left corner to **0,0** and the upper right corner to **100',75'**.

12. Use (Zoom All) to fit the drawing on the screen. The circle displays very small near the bottom of the drawing window.

13. (Optional) Set the *Scale List* to only display **Architectural** scales.

14. Save the drawing.

Task 2 - Create new layers.

In this task you will use the Layer Properties Manager to create new layers and change their properties, as shown in Figure 5–62.

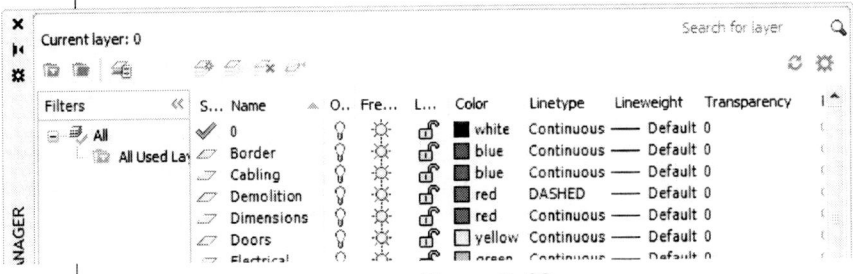

Figure 5–62

Organize Objects

1. Open the Layer Properties Manager and using ⛭ (New Layer), create the layers specified in the following table, as shown for few layers in Figure 5–63.

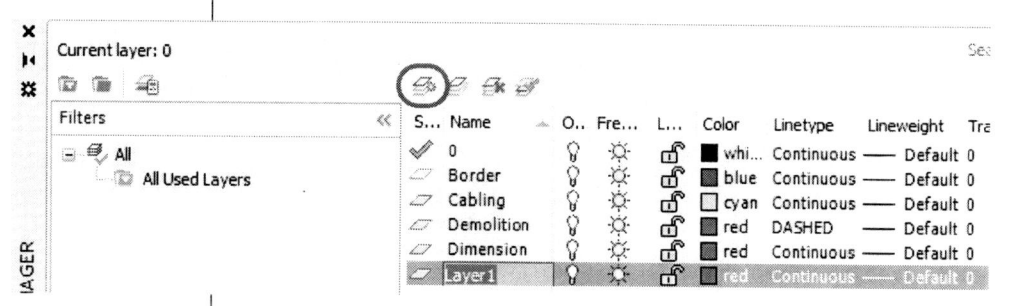

Figure 5–63

*The DASHED linetype is not listed in the Select Linetype dialog box. Select **Load...** and then **DASHED** in the list.*

If you have a white background then the white color will display as black in the Select Color dialog box.

Layer Name	Color	Linetype	Other
Border	blue	Continuous	
Cabling	cyan	Continuous	
Demolition	red	DASHED	
Dimensions	red	Continuous	
Doors	yellow	Continuous	
Electrical	green	Continuous	
Equipment	green	Continuous	
Furniture	green	Continuous	
HVAC	blue	Continuous	
Notes	cyan	Continuous	
Plumbing	magenta	Continuous	
Titles	blue	Continuous	
Viewports	gray (8)	Continuous	No plot
Walls	white	Continuous	
Windows	yellow	Continuous	

- You are using a color-to-lineweight scheme, in which red is the lightest color and white the heaviest. Gray is used to indicate a no plot layer.
- The layers are automatically added to the Layer Control.

2. Close the Layer Properties Manager and verify that all of the layers display in the Layer Control.

© 2017, ASCENT - Center for Technical Knowledge®   5–53

Task 3 - Create a page setup.

In this task, you will create a page setup and apply it to a standard layout for the template file, as shown in Figure 5–64.

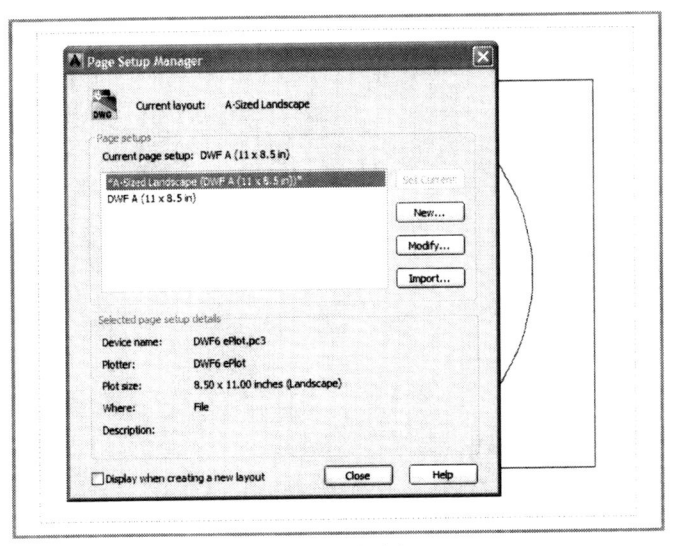

Figure 5–64

1. Switch to **Layout1**. In the Status bar, right-click on the *Layout* tab and select **Page Setup Manager...**.

2. In the Page Setup Manager, click **New**, enter the name as follows (**DWF A (11 x 8.5 in)**) and click **OK**. In the Page Setup dialog box set the remaining information from the table below and click **OK**.

Name:	DWF A (11 x 8.5 in)
Printer/plotter:	DWF6 ePlot.pc3
Paper size:	ANSI expand A (11.00 x 8.50 Inches)
Drawing Orientation:	Landscape

3. In the Page Setup Manager, click **Set Current** to apply the setup to **Layout1**. Close the Page Setup Manager.

4. Rename *Layout1* as **A-Sized Landscape**.

Organize Objects

Task 4 - Add a title block and border.

1. Make the layer **Border** current.

2. Using the **Insert** command, insert **Tblk-Ansi Expanded A (11.00 X 8.50).dwg** from the practice folder. Use **0,0,0** for the insertion point.

3. Select the viewport and change it to the layer **Viewports**.

4. Resize the viewport as required to fit title block inside the border.

5. Center the circle in the viewport.

6. In the Status Bar, set the *Viewport Scale* to **1/8"=1'-0"**, as shown in Figure 5–65. The circle is very small at this scale.

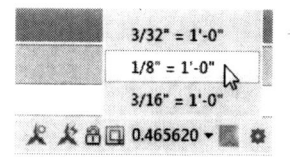

Figure 5–65

7. Save the drawing.

Task 5 - Save a template.

In this task you will save a drawing file as a template, as shown in Figure 5–66.

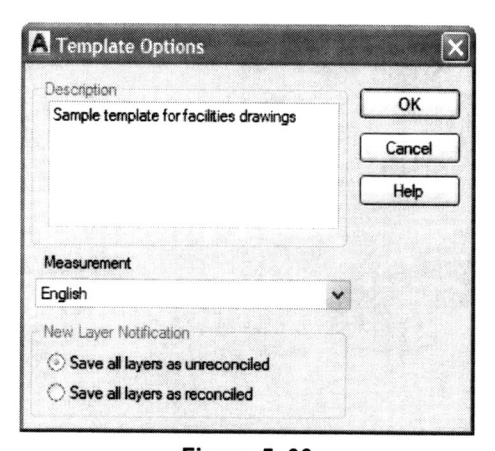

Figure 5–66

1. Switch to the **Model** layout.

2. Erase everything in the drawing, zoom all, and set the current layer to **Walls**.

3. In the Application Menu, select **Save As>Drawing Template**. In the Save Drawing As dialog box, navigate to your practice files folder. Verify that the *Files of type* is set to **AutoCAD Drawing Template (*.dwt)**. For the name, verify that **AEC-Facilities.dwt** is already displayed. Click **Save** to continue.

4. In the Template Options dialog box, enter the description **Sample template for facilities drawings** and verify that **English** is selected as the *Measurement*. Click **OK** to finish.

5. Close the template file.

6. Start a new drawing based on **AEC-Facilities.dwt**, which you saved in the practice files folder.

7. Verify that the settings you built into the template (units, layers, and layouts) work in the new drawing.

8. Close the file without saving changes.

Organize Objects

5.8 Working in the Layer Properties Manager

The Layer Properties Manager (shown in Figure 5–67) can be used to create new layers and to work with layer property overrides in viewports.

- The Layer Properties Manager contains other tools that can be use to manage layers, including controlling the properties columns and the layer settings.

- The Layer Properties Manager can be opened by clicking (Layer Properties Manager) in the *Home* tab>Layers panel or *View* tab>Palettes panel.

You can resize the Layer Properties Manager by dragging its edges.

Figure 5–67

Displaying Columns in the Layer Properties Manager

The Layer Properties Manager column display order can be rearranged to suit your needs. Select a column header and drag it to a new location, as shown in Figure 5–68. The AutoCAD® software retains the new location of the column.

Figure 5–68

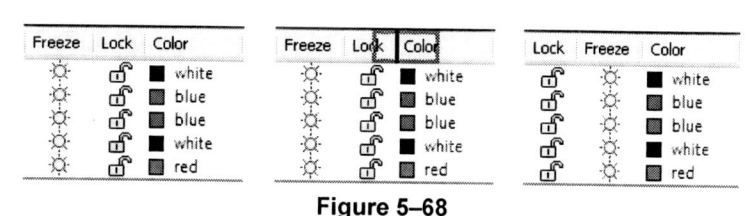

Columns that you do not want to display can also be removed. Right-click on a column header and select a column name to clear the check and remove it from the display, as shown in Figure 5–69.

Note that the name is grayed out and cannot be removed.

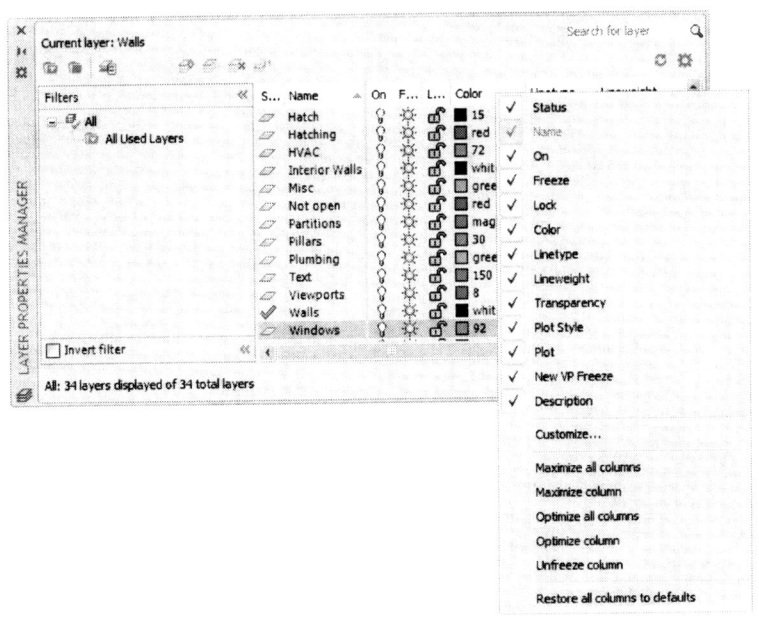

Figure 5–69

- Additional column names display if you are in a layout. These provide access to the viewport layer property overrides.

- Other selections in the shortcut menu include:
  - **Maximize column** and **Maximize all columns:** The maximize options change the column width so that the full header name displays.
  - **Optimize all column** and **Optimize column:** The optimize options change the column width based on the length of the column content
  - **Freeze/Unfreeze column:** The *Freeze* column acts like freeze panes do in Excel. It causes the selected column and columns to the left of it to constantly display. When scrolling to the right to show other columns, the frozen column remains visible.
  - **Restore all columns to defaults:** Sets the column display back to the default options.
  - **Customize...:** Enables you to modify more than one column at a time.

Organize Objects

- Selecting **Customize...** opens the Customize Layer Columns dialog box (shown in Figure 5–70), in which you can clear the checkmark from any columns that you do not want to display. Use **Move Up** and **Move Down** to change a selected column's position in the display.

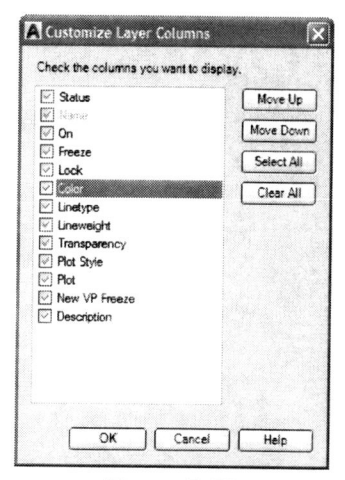

Figure 5–70

- Freezing keeps the column visible even if you scroll to the end of the options. For example, you might want to freeze the *Name* column (shown in Figure 5–71), so that it displays when you make changes to the plot columns.

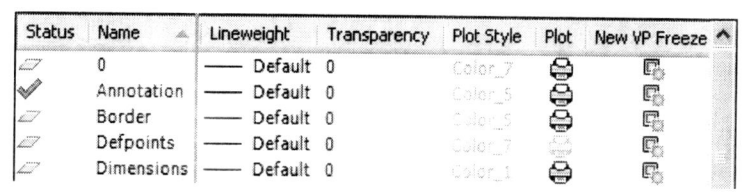

Figure 5–71

- The tooltips for the column headers display the column name and a description of the information displayed in the column, as shown in Figure 5–72.

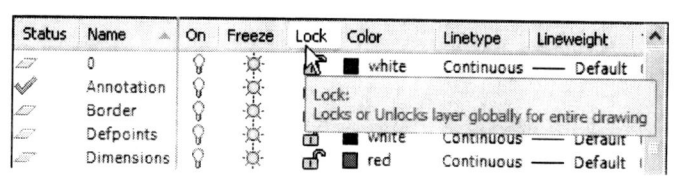

Figure 5–72

Layer Settings

Click ⚙ (Settings) to open the Layer Settings dialog box, as shown in Figure 5–73. These options are helpful when you use reference files that have different layer property overrides or might impact the created Layer States.

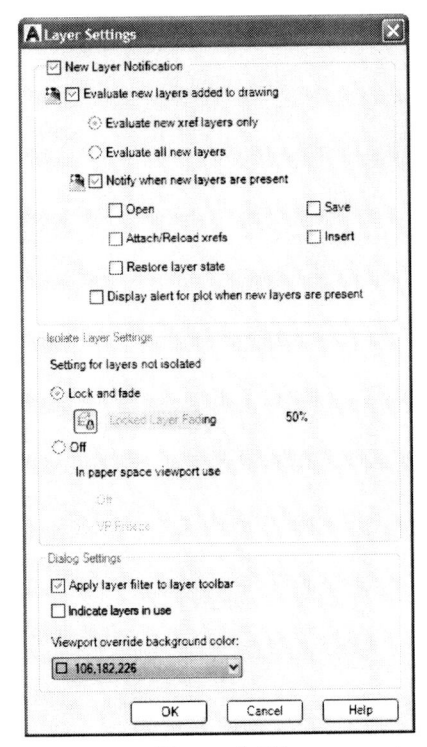

Figure 5–73

Layer Settings Options

Evaluate new layers added to drawing	If selected, evaluates and detects whether new XREF layers or new layers have been added to the drawing based on the setting.
Notify when new layers are present	Notifies you that new layers (or XREF layers) have been added to the drawing and enables you to customize the actions that trigger the display of the notification. Options include **Open**, **Attach/Reload xrefs**, **Restore layer state**, **Save**, and **Insert**.
Display alert for plot when new layers are present	Layer Notification Warning box opens when you use **Plot** in a drawing containing new layers.

Organize Objects

Settings for layers not isolated	Controls the behavior of layers that are not selected when using **Layer Isolate**.
Apply layer filter to layer toolbar	Layer filter set in Layer Properties Manager is also applied to Layer Control.
Indicate layers in use	Displays icon in list view to indicate layers that contain objects.
Viewport override background color	Sets color of highlight indicating that viewport settings override overall layer settings.

Reconciling New Layers

(Unreconciled New Layers) in the Status Bar, alerts you that there are unreconciled layers in a drawing. Click the icon to open the Layer Properties Manager. A new layer filter is automatically created displaying only those layers so that you can easily modify or reconcile.

- To reconcile layers, select the ones you want to accept into your main list of layers, right-click and select **Reconcile Layer**, as shown in Figure 5–74.

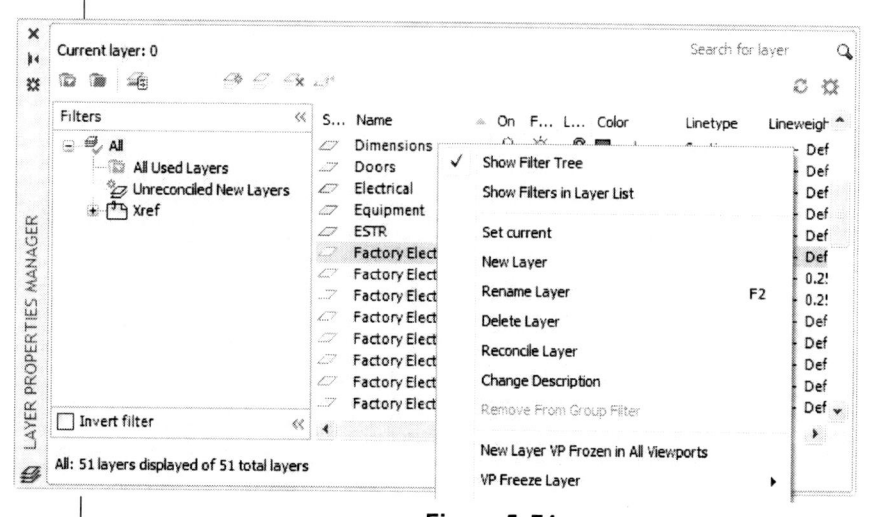

Figure 5–74

Freezing Layers in New Viewports

The *New VP Freeze* column displays whether or not the layer is frozen in new viewports, as shown in Figure 5–75. For example, you might want to create a layer that is only displayed in one viewport. Select **New VP Freeze** so that layer is not displayed in any additional viewports that you create.

Figure 5–75

Freezing Layers in All Viewports Except Current

You can freeze selected layers in all viewports except the current viewport. Activate the viewport in which you want to keep the layer(s) visible. In the Layer Properties Manager, select the layer(s), right-click and select **VP Freeze Layer>In All Viewports Except Current**, as shown in Figure 5–76. Select **VP Thaw Layer in All Viewports** to return the layer back to normal.

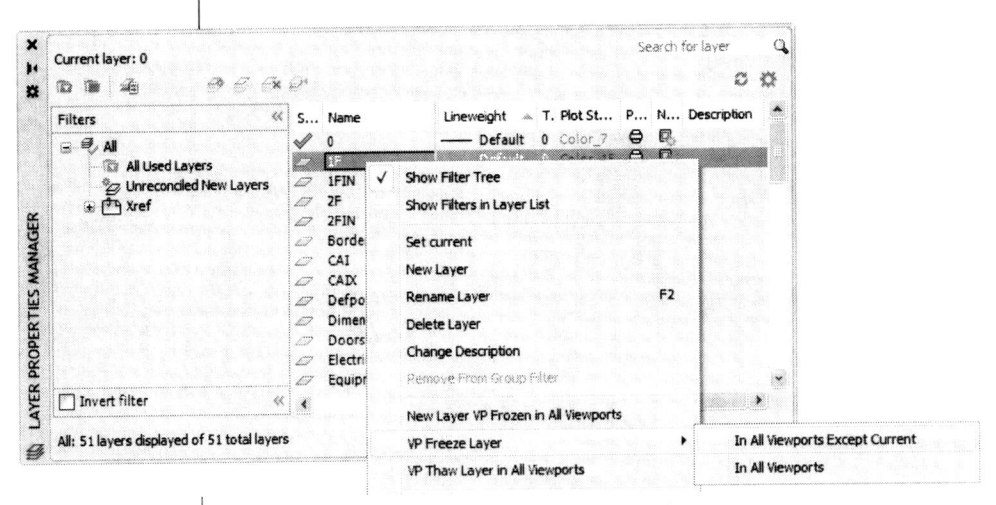

Figure 5–76

Overriding Layer Properties in Viewports

You can change layer properties (such as color, linetype, lineweight, and plot style) in a viewport without that change being made in other viewports. The changes only affect the current viewport and not the model or other viewports.

Organize Objects

- The viewport-specific options include:
  - New VP Freeze
  - VP Freeze
  - VP Color
  - VP Linetype
  - VP Lineweight
  - VP Transparency
  - VP Plot Style
- To create these changes, you must be in a layout tab (Status Bar) and working through a viewport.

How To: Modify Layer Properties in a Viewport

1. In a layout tab, double-click in a viewport to activate Model Space.
2. Open the Layer Properties Manager and modify the viewport properties as required. They are highlighted as they are modified.

- When you select a viewport with Layer property overrides, (Viewport has Layer property overrides) displays in the Status Bar. If a viewport does not have layer overrides, it does not display.

- The **Viewport Overrides** layer filter is automatically created when you have viewport overrides and you maximize a specific viewport, as shown in Figure 5–77.

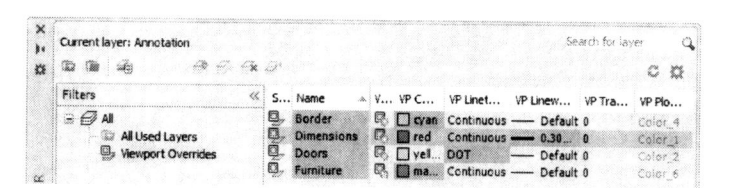

Figure 5–77

- The layer name and any viewport-specific modifications are highlighted in the Layer Properties Manager.

Practice 5h Working in the Layer Properties Manager

Practice Objective

- Modify the layer settings and the way in which columns display in the Layer Properties Manager.

Estimated time for completion: 10 minutes

In this practice you will change the way the columns display in the Layer Properties Manager, modify the Layer Settings, and reconcile new layers in a drawing. The Layer Properties Manager is shown in Figure 5–78.

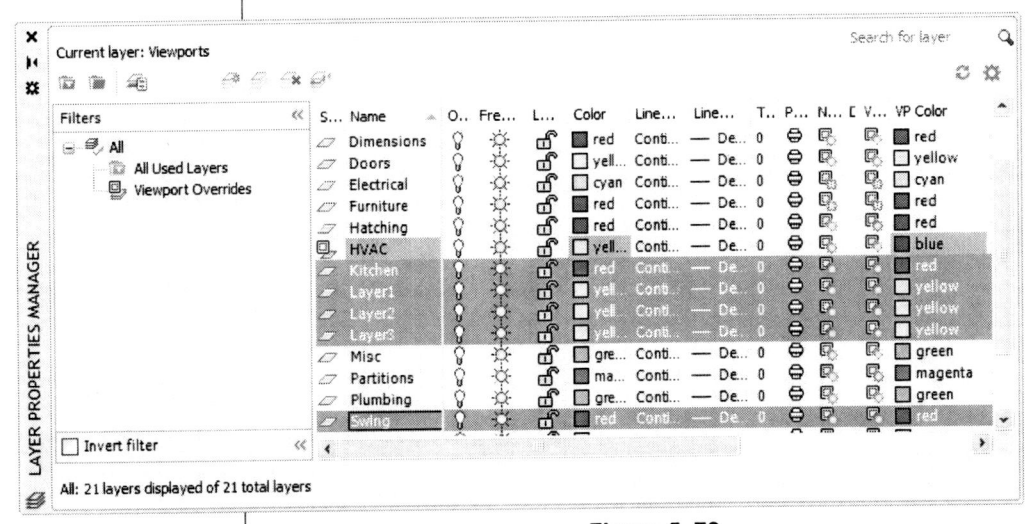

Figure 5–78

1. Open **Small House-A.dwg** from your practice files folder.

2. In the *Home* tab>Layers panel, click ▣ (Layer Properties). In the Layer Properties Manager, the layers and their properties are listed in the columns.

3. Right-click on any of the column titles and select **Maximize all columns**. The columns shift so that the information listed in each column is completely displayed.

This option maximizes to either the column's heading or its contents, whichever is larger.

4. Right-click on the *Plot Style* column and toggle it off by selecting it to clear the checkmark.

Organize Objects

5. For the layers **Electrical** and **Furniture**, click (New VP Freeze) to freeze them.

6. Auto-hide the Layer Properties Manager.

7. Switch to the **Proposal** layout. The existing viewport displays all of the layers as thawed.

8. Right-click on the **Viewports** layer and select **Set current**.

*The **Electrical** and **Furniture** layers are frozen in this viewport, but not in the existing viewport.*

9. Create a new viewport in the right half of layout.

10. Make the new viewport active and display the Layer Properties Manager.

11. More properties are now available for Layer Property Overrides. Override the layer **HVAC** by making the *VP Color blue*. Note that the change is highlighted in blue, as shown in Figure 5–79.

Figure 5–79

12. Click (Settings) to open the Layer Settings dialog box.

13. Select **Evaluate all new layers**, **Notify when new layers are present**, and **Save**, as shown in Figure 5–80.

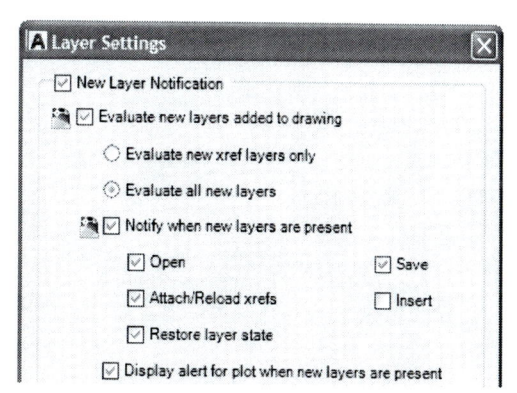

Figure 5–80

© 2017, ASCENT - Center for Technical Knowledge®

14. In the *Dialog Settings* area, change the *Viewport override background color* to **green**, as shown in Figure 5–81.

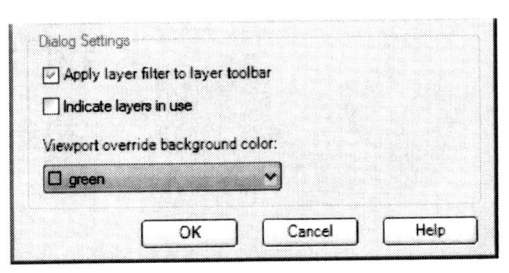

Figure 5–81

15. Click **OK** to return to the Layer Properties Manager and note that the changes are highlighted in green.

16. Create three new layers using the default layer settings.

17. Save the drawing.

18. The Unreconciled New Layers balloon alert displays, as shown in Figure 5–82. Click the **View unreconciled new layers in the Layer Properties Manager** link.

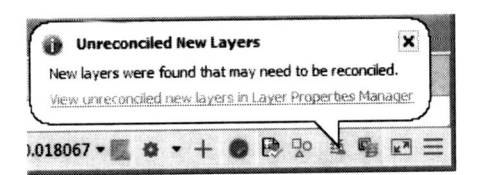

Figure 5–82

19. The Layer Properties Manager displays with the *Unreconciled New Layers* filter active, as shown in Figure 5–83.

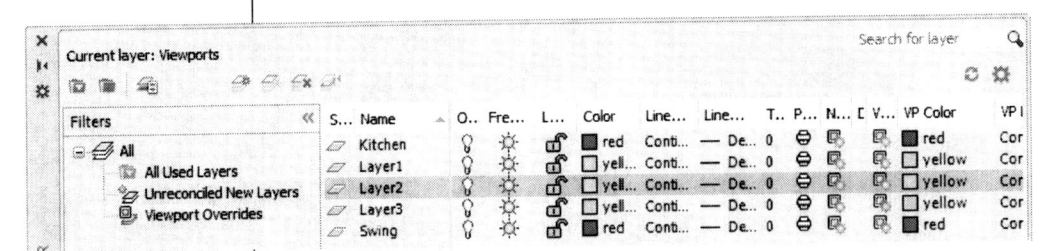

Figure 5–83

20. Select all of the layers, right-click and select **Reconcile Layer**. The layers are reconciled.

21. Save and close the drawing.

Chapter 6

Reuse Existing Content

This chapter includes instructional content to assist in your preparation for the following topic and objectives for the AutoCAD® Certified Professional exam.

Autodesk Certification Exam Objectives in this Chapter

Exam Topic	Exam Objective	Section(s)
Reuse Existing Content	• Work with blocks	• 6.1 to 6.9
	• Manage block attributes	• 6.10 to 6.14
	• Reference external drawings and images	• 6.15 to 6.17

6.1 What are Blocks?

A group of objects can be converted into a single symbol or block. Blocks can be anything from furniture (as shown in Figure 6–1) to schematic symbols, to entire drawings, such as a roof detail. Different types of drawings use different blocks. For example, architects need blocks, such as doors, windows, and roof sections. Mechanical designers would have a stock of nuts, bolts, and reusable parts.

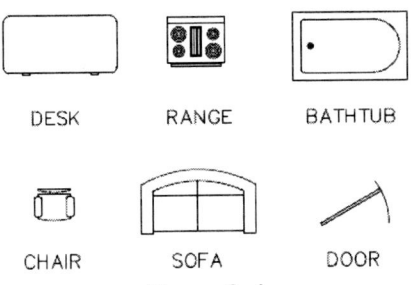

DESK RANGE BATHTUB

CHAIR SOFA DOOR

Figure 6–1

The benefits of using blocks in the AutoCAD software:

- Ease of manipulating the blocks in a drawing, since they are unified objects. Some blocks, called *dynamic blocks*, are designed so that you can adjust their size or other features after inserting them.

- Consistency of standard details or parts.

- Reduced file size, since each instance of the block in a drawing refers to a single block definition.

You can insert blocks into your drawings in several ways, including the **Insert** command, Tool Palettes, DesignCenter, and Autodesk Seek.

'Creating blocks' has been discussed in the AutoCAD/AutoCAD LT Fundamentals - Part 2 and in the Beyond the Basics student guides.

Hint: Blocks and Layers

When you insert a block, the insertion point is always placed on the current layer. The way the block was created determines whether the block objects use the properties of the current layer, or have a layer or layers that are already associated with objects in the block. Block objects created on layer **0** use the properties of the current layer. Block objects created on other layers use the properties of those layers, no matter which layer is current when the block is inserted. Ask your CAD Manager how blocks are handled in the drawings in which you work.

While there is no absolute standard for how blocks are created, you are most likely to use multilayer compound blocks. For example, you might create a detail that includes hatching, text and the objects, as shown in Figure 6–2. These blocks should be inserted on layer **0**.

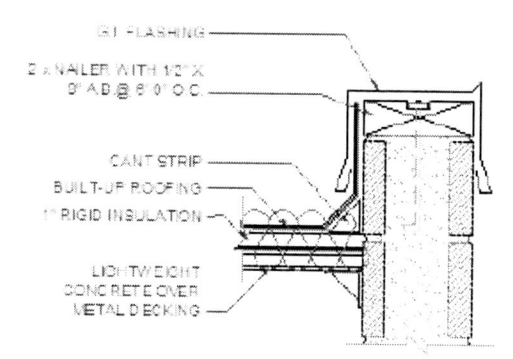

Figure 6–2

Simple blocks, such as a symbol or screw (as shown in Figure 6–3), are more likely to be created on layer **0** and inserted on the required layer.

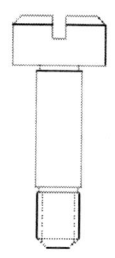

Figure 6–3

6.2 Working with Dynamic Blocks

Dynamic blocks are special kinds of blocks that can be changed dynamically. Once they are in your drawing, they can be manipulated in a variety of ways, including lengthening a side, flipping the direction, aligning to other objects, rotating, or selecting from a list of options, as shown in Figure 6–4. Dynamic blocks are powerful tools and in many cases, several standard blocks can be replaced by one dynamic block.

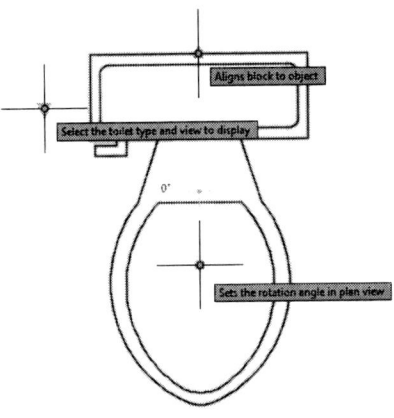

Figure 6–4

Manipulating Dynamic Blocks

When you select a dynamic block, special grips display the types of modifications that are available. Hover the cursor over one of the grips to display its tooltip. Click on the required grip to change the block, as shown in Figure 6–5.

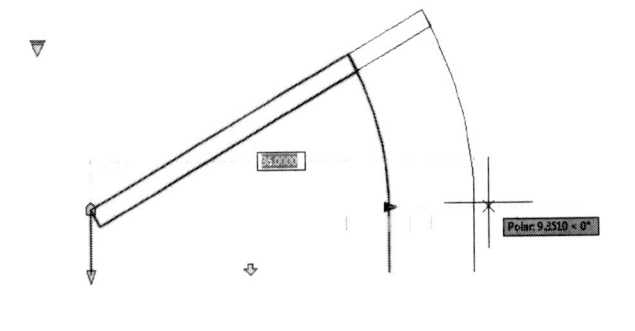

Figure 6–5

- The modification features in dynamic blocks can differ from one block to another. For example, one block might only have the Lengthen/Shorten grip, while another might have the Flip, List, and Rotate grips.

Dynamic Block Grips

The available block grips are described as follows.

▷	**Lengthen/ Shorten**	Enables you to scale, stretch, or array a block. The action depends on how the block was defined.
▽	**List**	Opens a list of options from which to select, such as size, number of items, view displayed, etc.
▪	**Insert/Move**	Indicates the insertion point of the block and other points that might have been assigned in the block. It can move the entire block or just one entity in the block.
⇩	**Flip**	Flips the entire block in the direction of the arrow.
△	**Align**	Aligns the entire block at the angle of an object when you move the block near that object.
○	**Rotate**	Enables you to rotate the block or specific objects in the block. The objects that rotate are preset in the block definition.

- Blocks that are not dynamic only have an Insert/Move grip, which you can use to drag the block to a new location.

- After you have finished modifying the dynamic block, press <Esc> to clear it and its grips from modification.

6.3 Inserting Blocks

Blocks can be placed in a drawing using the **Insert** command where you can either use the Insert dialog box or Insert drop-down list, as shown in Figure 6–6. You are prompted to select the block name, insertion point, scale, and rotation. It also enables you to insert other drawings into the current drawing.

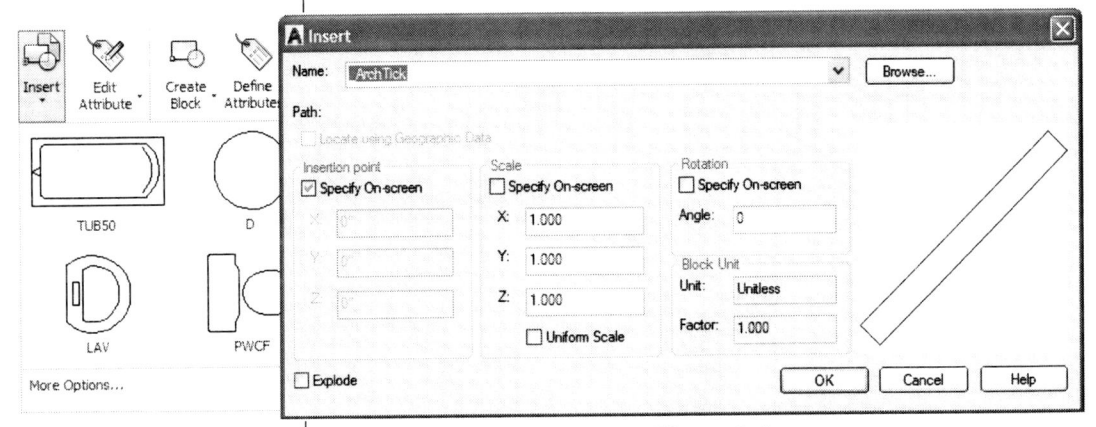

Figure 6–6

How To: Insert a Block from the Insert Dialog Box

1. In the *Home* tab>Block panel or *Insert* tab>Block panel, expand (Insert Block) and select **More Options...** to open the Insert dialog box.
2. In the Insert dialog box, expand the Name: drop-down list and select a block. The blocks must be available in the drawing.
3. Specify the *Insertion point*, *Scale*, and *Rotation*. You can set these in the dialog box or on-screen.
4. Click **OK**.

How To: Insert a Block from the Drop-down List

1. In the *Home* tab>Block panel or *Insert* tab>Block panel, expand (Insert Block) and select a block.
2. In the drawing, either click to place the block at the required location or select the **Basepoint**, **Scale**, **X**, **Y**, **Z**, or **Rotate** options and set their values.

Reuse Existing Content

- Since you do not usually know the precise X,Y coordinates of the *Insertion point*, you can specify them in the drawing rather than by entering them in the dialog box.

- You can insert any AutoCAD drawing as a block by clicking **Browse** in the Insert dialog box. The file becomes a block in the current drawing and is then listed with the other blocks in the Name: drop-down list in the dialog box and the Insert drop-down list in the ribbon.

- If you select the **Explode** option in the Insert dialog box, the block is converted into its component parts when it is inserted into the drawing. If you use this option, the block is hidden while you specify its insertion point, scale, and rotation on-screen (you can also explode a block after it has been inserted using the **Explode** command).

- The *Block Unit* area in the Insert dialog box displays the units (inches, millimeters, etc.) in which the block was drawn. If inserted into a drawing that uses different units, the block is scaled automatically.

- Blocks are normally created at the appropriate size for the drawing and the insertion scale should generally be set to **1**.

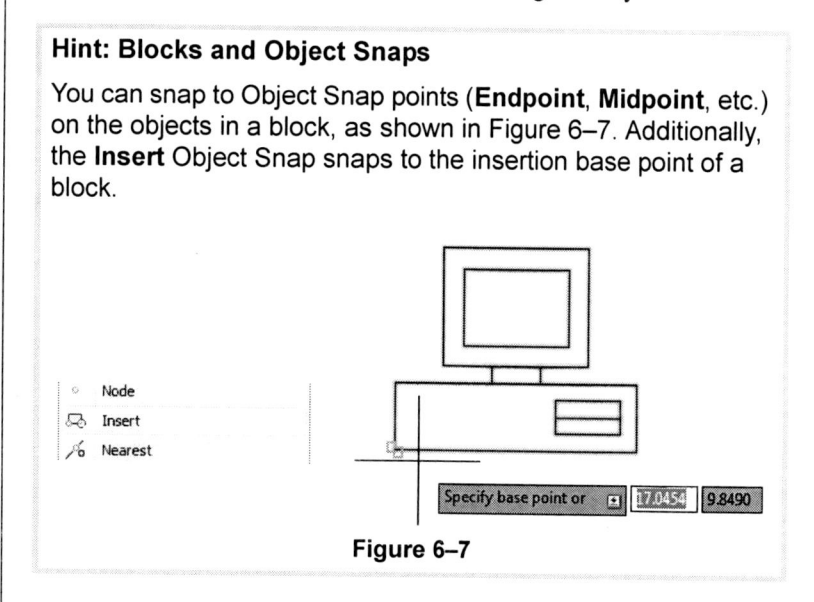

> **Hint: Blocks and Object Snaps**
>
> You can snap to Object Snap points (**Endpoint**, **Midpoint**, etc.) on the objects in a block, as shown in Figure 6–7. Additionally, the **Insert** Object Snap snaps to the insertion base point of a block.
>
> **Figure 6–7**

6.4 Inserting Blocks using the Tool Palettes

The AutoCAD software comes with many blocks, which are stored in the Tool Palettes window (*View* tab>Palettes panel> (Tool Palettes)). After you locate the required block in one of the Tool Palette tabs, you can drag and drop it from the palette into the drawing.

- The AutoCAD software comes with example blocks that are located on several tabs of the palette, as shown in Figure 6–8. You can also create custom palettes.

Press <Ctrl>+<3> to toggle the Tool Palettes open or closed.

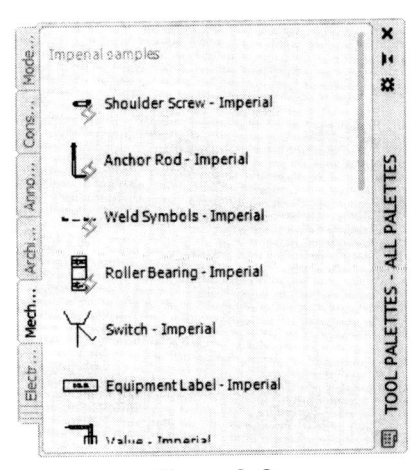

Figure 6–8

- In the Tool Palettes, dynamic blocks are indicated by a lightning bolt symbol.

- If there are more objects than can fit in the window, a scroll bar displays next to the title bar, enabling you to scroll through the list.

Insertion Options

The drag and drop method inserts the block without any options. The block is placed where you drop it. If you click on the block image in the palette instead, the block image gets attached to the cursor along with the *Specify insertion point:* prompt. You can either click to place the block at the required location or select one of the command options (<Down Arrow>), as shown in Figure 6–9.

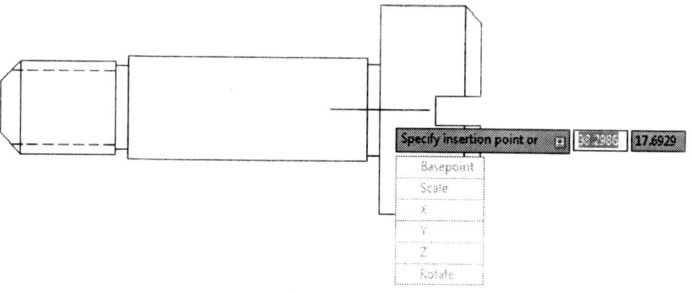

Figure 6–9

- If you want to rotate the object before you insert it, select the **Rotate** option, enter the rotation angle, and select the point at which to insert the rotated block.

- The **Basepoint** option enables you to select a different base point on the object from the one that was created with the block.

- Most blocks are correctly scaled for the drawing in which you are inserting them. However, the **Scale** (uniform), **X**, **Y**, and **Z** options enable you to change the scale.

Controlling the Tool Palettes Window

It is useful to display the Tool Palettes as you are working. For efficient use of screen space, you can dock and hide the palette to one side of the drawing window with either the icon or text displayed. When you need to display the full palette, move the cursor over the icon (or text depending on your setting), as shown in Figure 6–10.

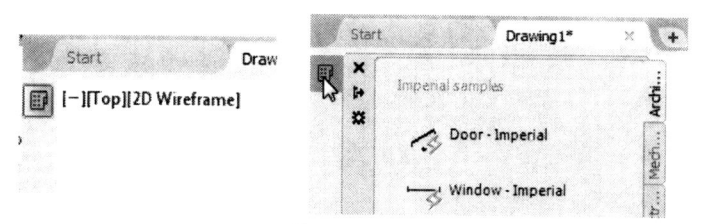

Figure 6–10

This process also applies to other palettes, such as Properties.

How To: Dock and Hide a Palette

1. Open the Tool Palettes.
2. Place the cursor over the title bar of the palette and drag it to one side of the screen. It should dock. If it does not, right-click on the title bar, select **Allow Docking**, and try again.
3. Minimize the palette by clicking ▌◀ (Auto-hide). The palettes stack if more than one is docked.
4. Move the cursor over the title bar or icon to display the full-size palette.

- To save more space, right-click on the palette title bar and set the docked view to **Icons only**, as shown in Figure 6–11.

*Right-click on the title bar of an undocked palette, and select **Anchor Left** or **Anchor Right** to dock and auto-hide the palette. (**Allow Docking** must be selected first for anchoring to work.)*

✓	Icons only
	Text only

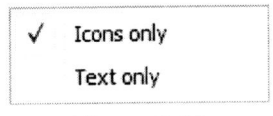

Figure 6–11

6.5 Inserting Blocks using the DesignCenter

DesignCenter is available to manage your standards. It enables you to access named objects in any drawing to copy them into the current drawing and is also used for inserting blocks. You can have a library of drawings that include typical blocks grouped in a useful order, as shown in Figure 6–12. From DesignCenter, you can open the drawing and then drag and drop the blocks into your current drawing.

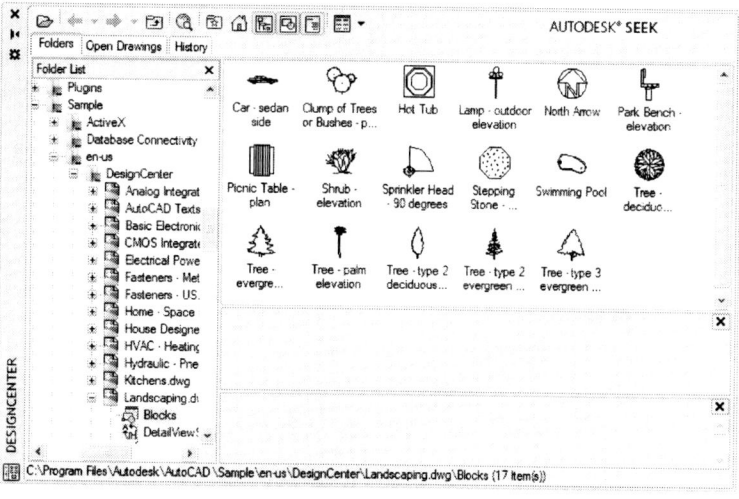

Figure 6–12

- In addition to blocks, you can copy other named objects using the DesignCenter, including layers, linetypes, layouts, reference files (xrefs), and text, table, or dimension styles. Open DesignCenter, locate the drawing containing the objects you want to use, and drag them into your current drawing.

- You can open the DesignCenter by clicking (DesignCenter) in the *View* tab>Palettes panel.

Press <Ctrl>+<2> to toggle DesignCenter open or closed. DesignCenter is a palette and can be docked and hidden in the same way as the Tool Palettes and Properties palette.

DesignCenter Content

Three tabs across the top of DesignCenter provide access to different parts of its content. These tabs are:

Folders	Enables you to use the *Folder List* to navigate to drawings on your computer or network drives.
Open Drawings	Provides access to drawing(s) that are open in the AutoCAD software. You can copy components from any of the open drawings into your current drawing window.
History	Lists several of the last drawings used in DesignCenter. Double-click on the filename to load the drawing in the *Folders* tab.

New in 2018

- Click **AUTODESK Seek** to launch the BIMobject® website. In the Welcome to BIMobject window, click **Browse BIM objects** to search for available content online, as shown in Figure 6–13. BIMobject is an online service that provides access to 2D drawings and 3D models, along with product information that has been made available directly by the product manufacturers and suppliers.

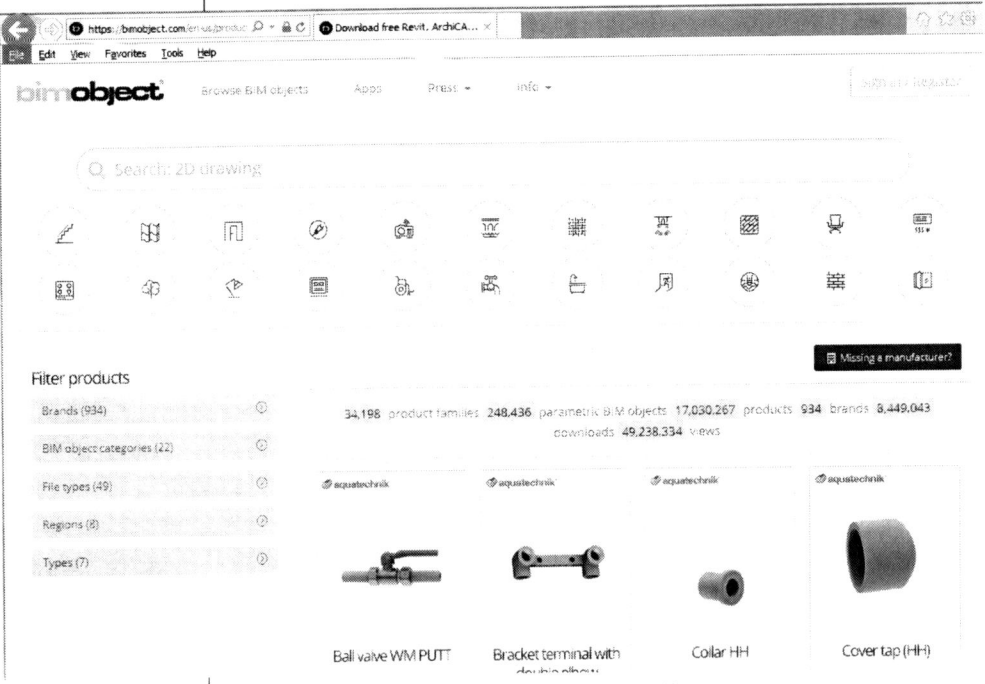

Figure 6–13

Navigation and Display Options

The DesignCenter palette contains tools for navigating to drawings and changing the display, as shown in Figure 6–14.

Figure 6–14

Icon	Description
	Load: Opens the Load dialog box. When you select a drawing, it opens in DesignCenter without opening in the AutoCAD software.
	Back/Forward: Returns to the previous drawing selected. Click ▼ to expand the list of the available drawings.
	Up: Backs up one folder level each time the button is clicked. Use this if you have toggled off the tree view.
	Search: Opens the Search dialog box in which you can search for drawings, blocks, layers, etc., by name.
	Favorites: Similar to other Windows programs, you can specify favorite places from which to get drawings or web sites. Right-click in DesignCenter to add items to your favorites list.
	Home: Switches to the *DesignCenter* folder.
	Tree View Toggle: Toggles the left side of DesignCenter off and on. If it is off, only the level to which you have expanded displays.
	Preview: Displays a preview of the selected block.
	Description: Displays a description of the selected block if one is available.
	Views: Toggles through the various types of views. Use the **Large Icons** option to display a thumbnail image of the blocks.

- Set the drawings or folders that you need to access most often as **Favorites**. Right-click on the file or folder in DesignCenter and select **Add to Favorites**. Click (Favorites) in the toolbar for quick access.

Practice 6a

Estimated time for completion: 25 minutes

Working with Blocks

Practice Objective

- Add blocks and dynamic blocks using the **Insert** command, Tool Palettes, and DesignCenter.

In this practice, you will add blocks and dynamic blocks using the **Insert** command and the Tool Palette. You will also add landscaping blocks using the Design Center, as shown in Figure 6–15.

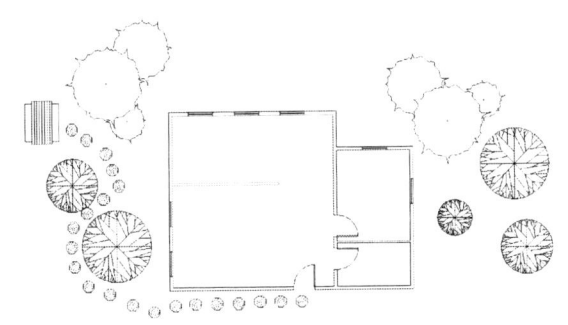

Figure 6–15

Task 1 - Insert blocks.

In this task you will insert blocks in a floor plan using the **Insert** command, as shown in Figure 6–16. The blocks in this drawing were created on their own layers. You will insert them all on layer **0**.

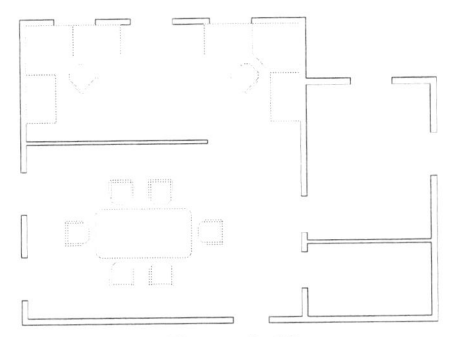

Figure 6–16

1. Open **Plan-A.dwg** from your practice files folder.

2. In the *Insert* tab>Block panel, expand (Insert) and select the block named **Desk Unit,** as shown in Figure 6–17.

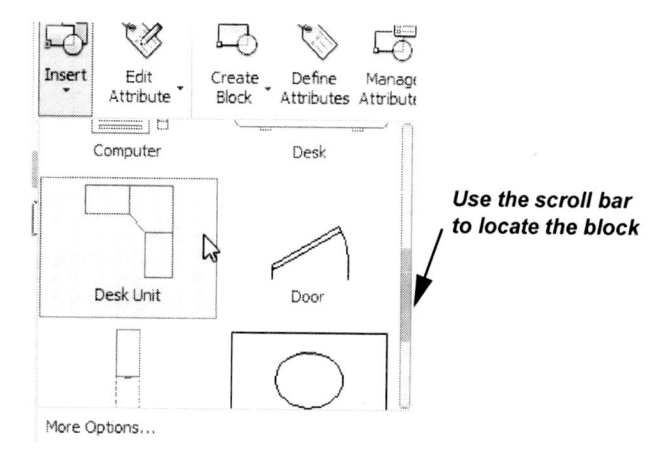

Use the scroll bar to locate the block

Figure 6–17

3. The desk is attached to the cursor. Type **R** and press <Enter> to select the **Rotate** option. Ensure that **0** is set for rotation angle, and press <Enter>.

4. Type **X** and press <Enter>. Ensure that **1** is set as the X scale factor, and press <Enter>.

5. Similarly, ensure that both for the Y and Z scale factors are set as **1**.

6. Place the desk in the top right corner of the office, as shown in Figure 6–16.

7. Insert another **Desk Unit** in the top left corner. Set the *Rotation Angle* to **90** degrees.

8. Insert **Chair** blocks facing each of the desks. Set the rotation angles to **45** and **-45**.

9. In the ribbon, expand **Insert** and select **More Options...** to open the Insert dialog box. Click **Browse** and select **Table-A.dwg** (in your practice files folder) and click **Open**. Click **OK** in the Insert dialog box and place the table in the largest room.

10. Insert chairs around the table. You might want to insert one chair and then use other commands, such as **Copy** and **Mirror** to place the additional ones.

Task 2 - Work with dynamic blocks.

In this task you will add dynamic blocks from the Tool Palettes to the floor plan and then manipulate them, as shown in Figure 6–18.

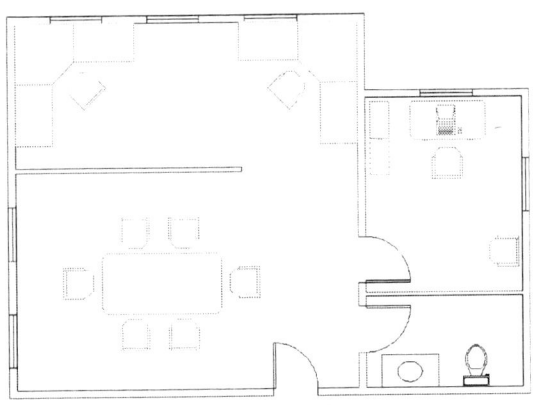

Figure 6–18

1. Zoom in on the opening along the bottom wall of the plan.

2. Ensure that ▢ ▼ (Object Snap) is toggled on and **Endpoint** is selected.

View tab>Palettes panel, ▦ *(Tool Palettes).*

3. Open Tool Palettes, if it is not already open. Note the types of blocks that are available in the different tabs.

4. In Tool Palettes, switch to the *Architectural* tab and insert a **Door-Imperial** into the opening by dragging and dropping it from the Tool Palettes. Snap to the upper end point on the left wall. If the door snaps vertically, rotate it such that it aligns horizontally along the wall, as shown in Figure 6–19. The door does not fit in the opening.

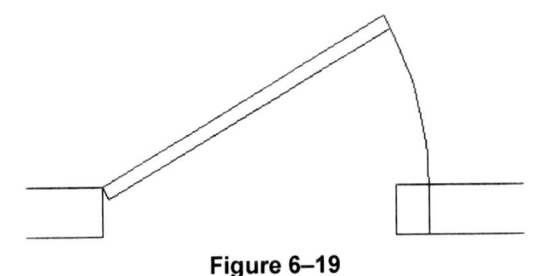

Figure 6–19

Reuse Existing Content

5. Select the inserted door to display the grips. Click ▷ (Lengthen) at the right end of the door and note the current length (3'-4"). Drag the cursor to the left to make the length **3'** (as shown in Figure 6–20), and click to place it at that location.

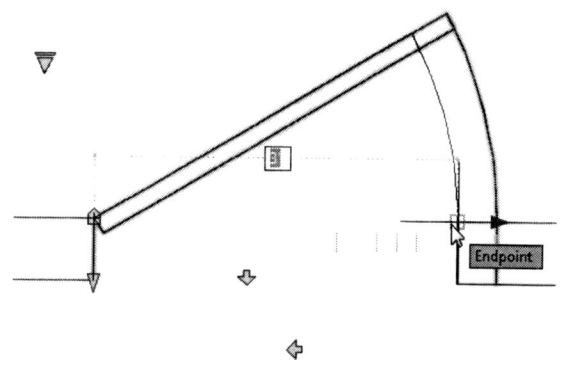

Figure 6–20

6. Click ▽ (List) and select **Open 90°**. The door swing changes to this angle. Press <Esc> to clear the door.

7. Pan to the smallest room, and then drag and drop a **Toilet-Imperial** into it. The toilet displays as a front view.

8. Select the **Toilet** to display the grips. Click ▽ (List) and select **Elongated (Plan)**. A plan (top) view of the toilet displays.

Move the toilet from inside the room and then toward the inside wall.

9. Click △ (Align) and move the cursor to place the toilet along the bottom wall. It aligns with the wall.

10. Use the **Insert** command to add a **Sink** along the wall on the left side of the toilet.

11. Move the sink and toilet to the layer **Plumbing**.

12. Add doors (**Door-Imperial** in Tools Palette) to the bathroom and the small office. (Place one door, rotate it, and adjust it with grips, as required. Then, copy it to create the other door and flip it using grips.)

13. Add windows using the **Window-Imperial** dynamic block in the Tool Palettes. You can also use the **Insert** command to add computers and file cabinets to the offices.

Task 3 - Insert blocks using DesignCenter.

In this task you will insert landscaping blocks using DesignCenter, as shown in Figure 6–21.

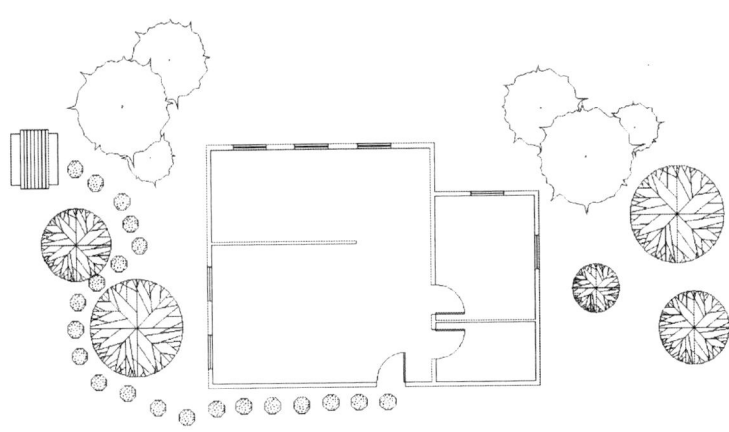

Figure 6–21

1. Toggle off the layers **Furniture** and **Plumbing**.

2. In the Layer Control, make the layer **Planting** as the current layer.

3. Zoom out so that there is room around the outside of the building.

4. Open DesignCenter.

5. In the *DesignCenter* folder supplied with the AutoCAD software (generally in *Sample>en-us* folder), find the file **Landscaping.dwg**. Expand it and select **Blocks** to open it.

6. Drag and drop several trees (in plan view) into the drawing. **Move**, **Rotate**, and **Scale** them as required.

7. Set the current layer to **Hardscape**.

8. Create a path of **Stepping Stone-Hexagonal** blocks around the trees.

9. Save and close the drawing.

*The blocks in DesignCenter are created on layer **0**. Therefore, you need to select the layer on which you want to place them.*

You can open the DesignCenter in the View tab>Palettes panel, and click (DesignCenter).

Reuse Existing Content

6.6 Creating Blocks

The objects that are reused frequently can be saved as a blocks. The blocks you need to use might already exist in your drawings, or you can buy block libraries for almost any type of drawing. You can also easily create your own blocks. A block can be locally defined in a drawing or saved as a file for use in other drawings.

Creating Single Named Objects

The **Create Block** command converts a group of selected objects into a single named object or *local block definition* that only belongs to the current drawing.

How To: Create a Block

1. Draw the objects that you want to include in a block.
2. In the *Insert* tab>Block Definition panel or *Home* tab>Block panel, click (Create Block).
3. In the Block Definition dialog box (as shown in Figure 6–22), specify the *Name*, *Base point*, *Objects*, *Behavior*, *Settings*, and *Description*.

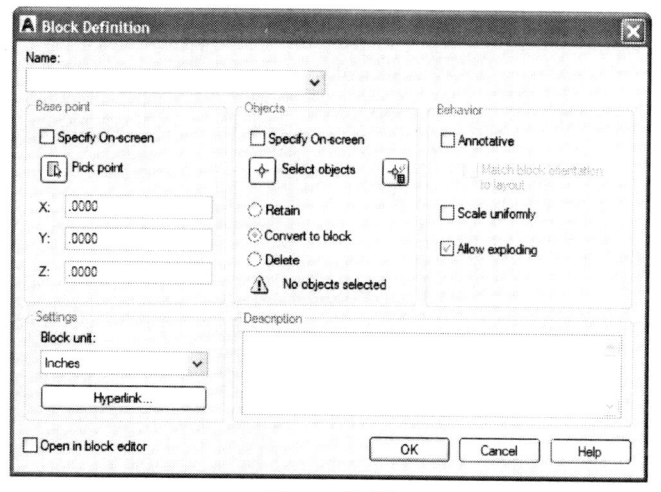

Figure 6–22

4. Click **OK**.

6–19

Block Settings

When you create a block, you need to specify various parameters in the Block Definition dialog box, as shown in Figure 6–23.

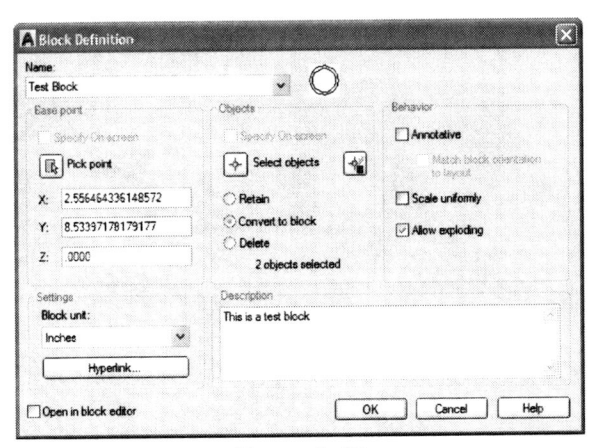

Figure 6–23

Base Point Area

The *Base point* is a critical setting, which controls the handle of the block when it is inserted. In the example shown in Figure 6–24, the block for a door has its base point at the hinge corner, where it attaches to the end of the wall and the block for the manhole cover has its base point at the center of the cover.

A good base point makes a block much easier to insert.

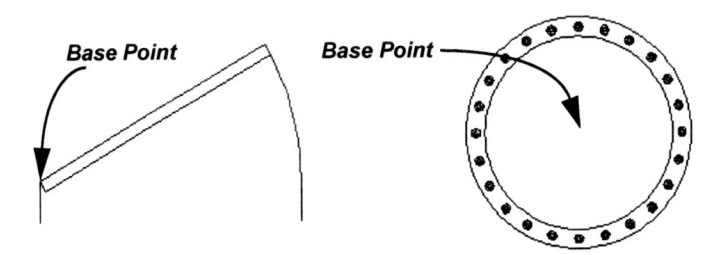

Figure 6–24

In the *Base point* area, you can specify the base point by doing one of the following:

- Select **Specify On-screen** to select the base point after you close the dialog box.

- Click (Pick point) to select a point on the screen and then return to the dialog box.

- Type an exact X,Y,Z coordinate.

Objects Area

- Select **Specify On-screen** to select the objects after you close the dialog box.

- Click ⊕ (Select objects) to select objects on the screen and then return to the dialog box.

- Define what you want to do with the objects after you select them. You can retain them, convert them to a block, or delete them.

- Click (Quick Select) to start the **Quick Select** command, which can be used to filter out objects in your selection as required.

Behavior Area

- Blocks can be annotative, which means they scale appropriately to the sheet of paper when they are plotted. This is used when you are creating annotation blocks, which often include text (such as a section callout bubble or room tags), as shown in Figure 6–25. Use **Annotative** to make the new block annotative.

Create annotative blocks at the correct size for plotting. The Annotation Scale factor of a viewport scales them when they are inserted through the viewport.

Figure 6–25

- When you insert an annotative block, an annotative icon displays in the preview in the Insert dialog box, as shown in Figure 6–26.

Annotative icon

Figure 6–26

- You can also use **Scale uniformly** to force the X- and Y-scaling of the block to be the same when the block is inserted into the drawing.

- Use **Allow exploding** to explode the block into its components when it is inserted into the drawing.

Settings Area

- Select a type of measurement in the Block unit drop-down list. This controls the scaling of the block when it is inserted into another drawing that uses a different type of unit. For example, if the unit in the block and the units in the drawing are different, the block is automatically scaled when it is inserted.

- Click **Hyperlink...** to add a link to another file or to a web address.

- Select **Open in block editor** to add dynamic features to the block.

- In the *Description* area, you can type a description of the block or any notes as required.

Creating Drawing Files from Objects (WBlock)

Blocks created with the **Create (Block)** command are stored in the drawing file in which they were created and are only available through that drawing. If you want to select objects and save them as a separate drawing file that can be used in other drawings, use the **Write Block (Wblock)** command.

- The **Write Block** command saves a copy of a block definition on your computer as a drawing file. Each use of **Write Block** creates a separate drawing file (.DWG).

- As with any .DWG file, the drawing files created with the **Write Block** command can be inserted into other drawings. Drawings to be used as blocks are often stored in a *block library*, which is a shared network folder containing drawings that are available to everyone in an office.

- You can use **Write Block** to break a large drawing into smaller components.

- To insert a file made with **Write Block** into another drawing, use **Browse...** in the Insert dialog box and select a file to insert.

Reuse Existing Content

- Once you have inserted the file, it creates a local block definition in the drawing. The local block definition is not linked to the DWG file that was made with **Write Block**.

How To: Create a Wblock

1. In the *Insert* tab>Block Definition panel, expand Create Block and click (Write Block). The Write Block dialog box opens, as shown in Figure 6–27.

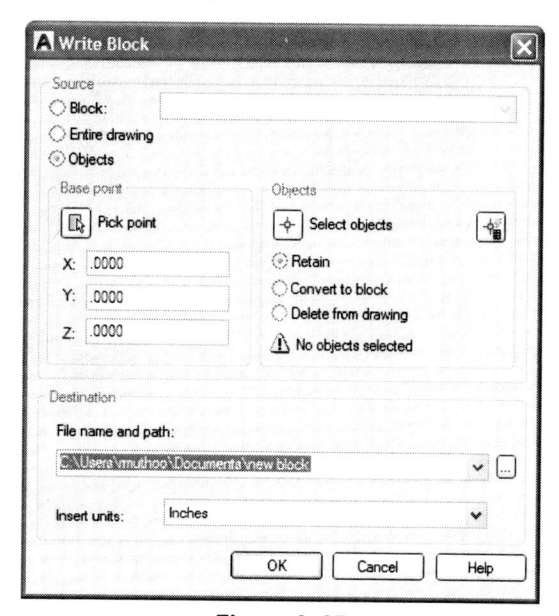

Figure 6–27

2. Select an option in the *Source* area:
    - **Block:** Select a block name from the drop-down list to create a Wblock from an existing block in the drawing.
    - **Entire Drawing:** Selects all of the objects in the drawing including any named objects (such as layers and dimension styles that are associated with the objects), and the current layer. Any unused named objects (such as empty layers) are not included. This is a quick way to clean up a file before it is stored.
    - **Objects:** Select the objects using the options in the *Base point* and *Objects* areas.
3. In the *Destination* area, specify the destination filename and path.
4. Also, specify the *Insert units* if they are to be different than the default units.
5. Click **OK**.

6.7 Editing Blocks

You might have a library of standard details, but need to change one of them for your current project. You can change a local block definition in a drawing using the **Block Editor**, as shown in Figure 6–28.

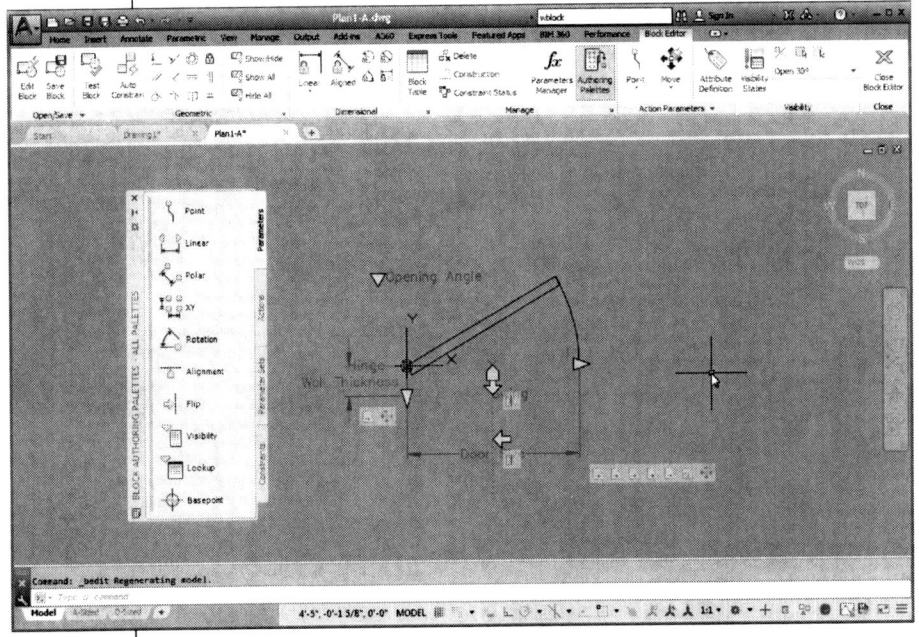

Figure 6–28

- When you open the Block Editor, the *Block Editor* contextual tab opens containing the tools that are required to create complex dynamic blocks, including constraints and special parameters. You can use the tools on any of the other tabs as well to create or modify block objects.

- Changing the block definition modifies all of the instances of the block in the drawing.

- The fastest way to start the Block Editor is to double-click on the block that you want to edit.

Reuse Existing Content

How To: Edit a Block in the Block Editor

1. Double-click on the block that you want to edit. Alternatively, in the *Insert* tab>Block Definition panel, click (Block Editor).
2. In the Edit Block Definition dialog box (as shown in Figure 6–29), select the block that you want to edit and click **OK**.

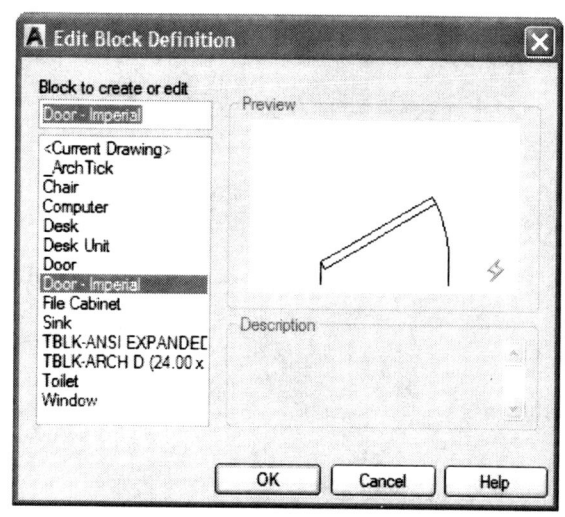

Figure 6–29

3. The *Block Editor* contextual tab opens, the drawing window background changes to gray, the Block Authoring Palette displays, and many of the constraint tools display with the selected block.
4. Modify the block.
5. When you are finished, click (Close Block Editor).

- The selected block displays in the Block Editor in its original position, even if you selected an instance that was rotated.

Remaking Blocks

- To modify a single instance of a block (rather than the block definition), you can **Explode** the block into its original raw components, provided that the **Allow Exploding** option was toggled on when the block was created. This command also converts polylines into lines and arcs.

- If the block objects were originally created on layer **0**, they revert to this layer when the block is exploded.

- If you have exploded a block and modified its components, you can use the **Create (Block)** command to make the components into a block again.

- If other instances of the block are in the drawing, select the insertion point that was used for the previous block.

- If you use the same name as the original block when you redefine it, all of the instances of that block in the drawing update to match the new block definition.

- If you make changes to a drawing file that you inserted as a block, you need to click **Browse...** in the **Insert** command to insert the updated drawing file. You are then prompted to redefine the existing local block definition.

Practice 6b

Estimated time for completion: 20 minutes

Create and Edit Blocks

Practice Objectives

- Define a block.
- Create a new drawing file from a local block.
- Create a new file and then redefine the block.

In this practice, you will define a block for a couch, first drawing the objects and then using the **Create Block** command. You will then use **Write Block** to create a new drawing file from your local block. You will also use **Write Block** to select part of a drawing and create a new file, and then use **Block Editor** to redefine a block.

Task 1 - Creating a local block.

In this task you will define a block for a couch, first drawing the objects and then using the **Create Block** command, as shown in Figure 6–30.

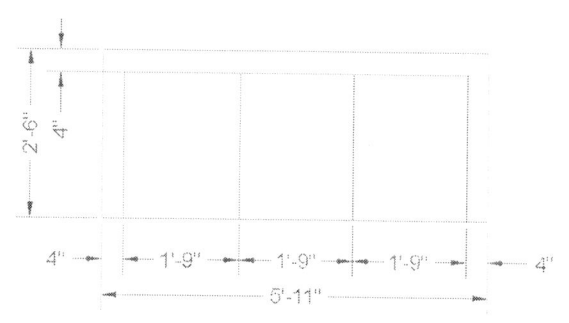

Figure 6–30

1. Open **California House-A.dwg** from your practice files folder.

2. Set the current layer to **Furniture**. (Hint: You will draw the block on this layer so that it retains the properties of the layer **Furniture** no matter what layer you insert it on.)

For quick access, you can display the Layer Control in the Quick Access Toolbar.

3. Zoom in on one of the rooms and draw a couch, as shown in Figure 6–30.

4. In the *Insert* tab>Block Definition panel, click (Create Block). In the Block Definition dialog box, name the block **Couch**.

5. In the *Base point* area, click (Pick point) and select the midpoint at the back of the couch as the base point.

6. In the *Objects* area, click ⊕ (Select objects), select the couch objects, and press <Enter>. Select the **Delete** option.

7. Verify that the *Block unit* is set to **Inches**.

8. Verify that **Open in block editor** is NOT selected.

9. Click **OK**. The couch is deleted from the active drawing.

10. Set the current layer to **0**.

11. Use the **Insert (Block)** command to insert a couch in several rooms (note that it is still the color of the layer **Furniture**).

12. Save the drawing with a few couches inserted.

Task 2 - Creating a drawing file from a block.

1. In the *Insert* tab>Block Definition panel, expand Create Block and click 🗎 (Write Block).

2. In the Write Block dialog box, for the *Source*, select **Block**, expand the drop-down list of local blocks in the drawing, and select **Couch**. You do not need to select the *Base point* or *Objects* because you are using an existing block definition.

3. In the *Destination* area, set the path to your practice folder and the filename to **Couch,** as shown in Figure 6–31. The *Insert units* should be set to **Inches**. Click **OK** to create the new drawing file.

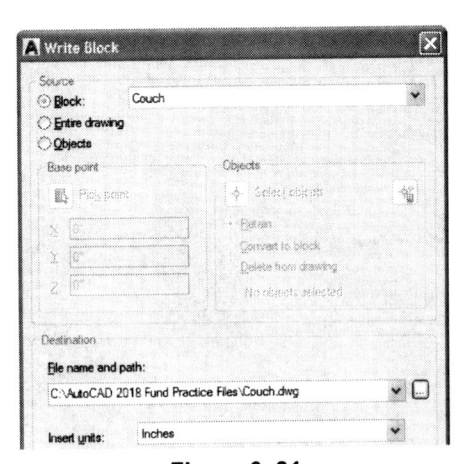

Figure 6–31

4. In the practice files folder, open the new drawing **Couch.dwg**.

Reuse Existing Content

5. Use the **Zoom Extents** command to display the couch. Save and close the drawing.

6. Open **Plan1-A.dwg** from your practice files folder.

7. Start the **Insert Block** command and note the list of blocks. The **Couch** block is not in the graphics list. Click **More Options...** to open the Insert dialog box. Click **Browse...** and select the **Couch.dwg** file in your practice folder. Insert a couch into one of the rooms. It becomes a local block in the drawing **Plan1-A.dwg**.

8. Save and close all of the drawings.

Task 3 - Create a new drawing from part of a drawing.

In this task you will toggle off most of the layers in a drawing and use **Write Block** to copy the remaining objects to a new file, as shown in Figure 6–32.

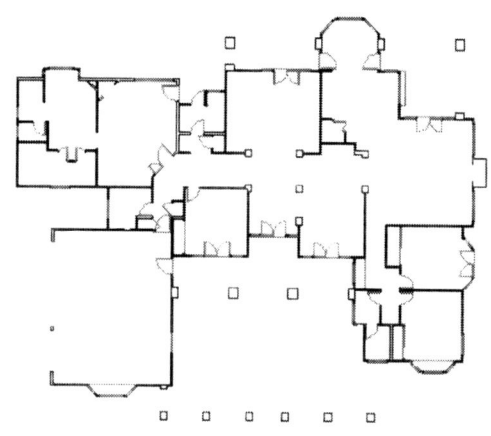

Figure 6–32

1. Open **California House-A.dwg** from your practice files folder.

2. Use the **Zoom Extents** command to display the entire plan.

3. Freeze all of the layers except **0**, **Doors**, **Walls**, and **Windows** (many layers are already frozen).

4. Start the **Write Block** command. In the Write Block dialog box, in the *Source* area, select **Objects**.

5. In the *Objects* area, click (Select objects) and select all of the visible objects. Right-click to return to the dialog box.

6. Leave the *Base point* at **0,0,0**. Set the path to your practice folder and name the file **Floorplan.dwg**.

7. Click **OK** to close the dialog box.

8. Close **California House-A.dwg**. Do not save changes.

9. Open **Floorplan.dwg**. Only the objects that you selected display along with the layers related to those objects.

10. Close the drawing. Do not save changes.

Task 4 - Edit a block.

In this task you will use the Block Editor to redefine a block with a new design, as shown in Figure 6–33.

Figure 6–33

1. Open **California House-A.dwg** from your practice files folder.

2. Toggle on the layer **Furniture** if the Couch is not displayed. Double-click on one of the **Couch** blocks.

3. In the Edit Block Definition dialog box, **Couch** is highlighted with its preview displayed. Click **OK** to continue.

4. The Block Editor opens with the block filling the drawing area. Also the background changed to gray and the Block Authoring Palette displays. Close or hide the Block Authoring Palette.

5. Fillet the back corners of the couch, as shown in Figure 6–33. Zoom in as required.

6. In the *Block Editor* contextual tab, click ✕ (Close Block Editor) and save the changes.

7. All of the instances of the **Couch** block in this drawing are automatically updated to the new style. Insert another **Couch** and note that it has also changed.

8. Save and close the drawing.

6.8 Adding Blocks to Tool Palettes

Tool palettes are the easiest way of inserting blocks into your drawing. You can create custom palettes in the Tool Palettes to organize your blocks into logical categories.

Once the palette has been created, drag and drop blocks into it to create tools for those blocks. Then use the palette tools to insert the blocks into the drawings in which you want to use them, whether or not the block has been defined in the drawing.

How To: Create a New Tool Palette

1. Right-click in the Tool Palettes title bar or tab and select **New Palette**.
2. In the *Edit* field, type a name for the palette (as shown in Figure 6–34), and press <Enter>. The new palette does not contain any tools.

Figure 6–34

- Although you can add tools to the default palettes supplied with the AutoCAD software, creating custom palettes enables you to better organize the tools as you want.

- You can also right-click on the tab and select **Delete Palette** or **Rename Palette** to delete or rename existing palettes.

How To: Add Blocks to a Palette

1. Select a block in the drawing area.
2. Drag and drop it onto the palette, as shown in Figure 6–35.

The file containing the blocks must be saved before you can add a block to a palette.

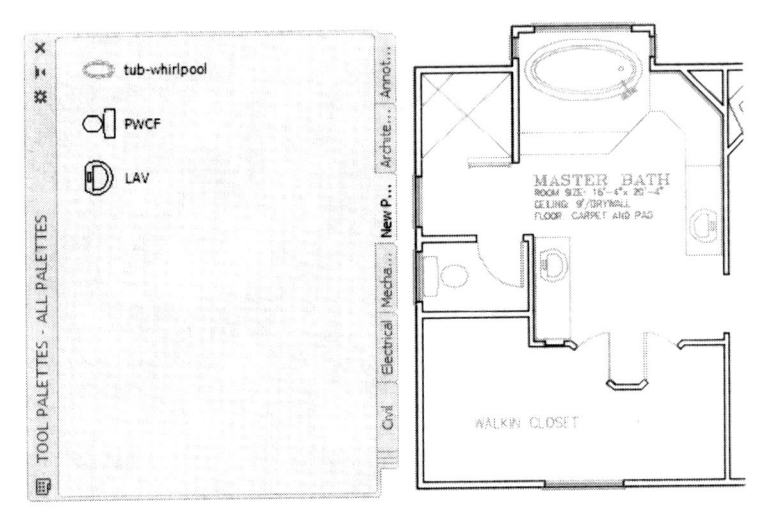

Figure 6–35

- Drag the block onto the palette by its *edge*, not by its blue grip. Dragging the grip moves the block in the drawing but does not enable you to drop it into the palette.

- The tool uses the layer, color, and other properties of the object used to create it. Therefore, blocks that you insert with the tool are automatically placed on the same layer as the original block, no matter which layer is current.

- You can rearrange the tools in the palette by dragging and dropping.

- You can also delete individual tools from the Tool Palettes. Select the tools that you want to delete (use <Shift> or <Ctrl> to select multiple icons), right-click, and select **Delete**.

- You must add blocks to the palette one at a time using this method.

Preparing Blocks for a Tool Palette

- The drawing from which you add the block to a palette becomes the source file for the block tool in the palette. If you move or delete this source drawing file, the palette tool no longer works.

- Create and store your blocks in a library drawing, or several such drawings for different categories of blocks. For example, you can define your furniture blocks in a drawing called *Furniture Library* and then add the blocks to a palette from that drawing.

- Keep your block library drawings in a location from which they cannot be moved or deleted. Make it a network location if everyone needs to access these blocks.

> **Hint: Creating a Tool Palette from DesignCenter**
>
> DesignCenter offers a quick way of creating a tool palette using the entire set of blocks in a drawing. Right-click on the drawing name in DesignCenter and select **Create Tool Palette**, as shown in Figure 6–36. A palette is created with the same name as the drawing, containing tool icons for all of the blocks defined in that drawing.
>
> **Figure 6–36**

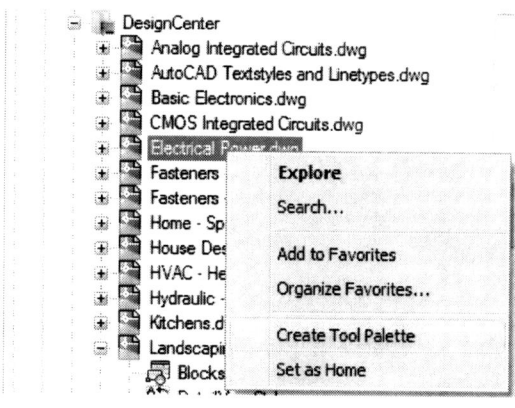

6.9 Modifying Tool Properties in Tool Palettes

Each tool in a palette can be modified to insert the object using specific properties, such as layer, scale, or rotation. For example, you might need to place a block at two different angles.

- You can create two tools in the palette for inserting the block, each preset to be inserted at the required angle.

- Once a tool has been added to a palette, you can drag and drop it to different places in the palette or to other tabs as required.

Modifying Tool Properties

To modify a tool's properties, right-click on a tool in the palette and select **Properties...** The Tool Properties for a block tool are shown in Figure 6–37. Other types of tools (e.g., for hatching or commands) have different properties.

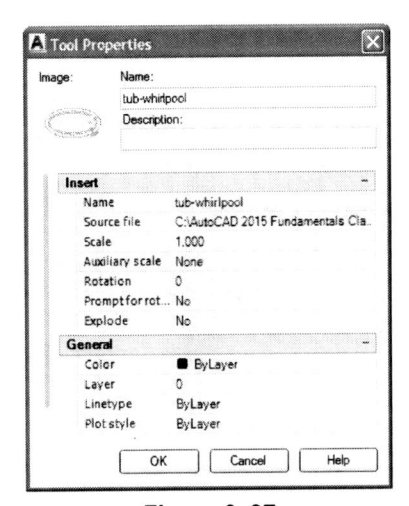

Figure 6–37

Command Options

Image	The preview image that displays for the tool.
Name	The name that displays with the tool in Tool Palettes. By default, this is set to the name of the block.
Description	An optional description for the tool, taken from the block description.

Insert Options

Name	The name of the block in the source file.
Source file	The drawing file used to create this tool in the palette and where the block definition is stored.
Scale	Insertion scale for the block. You can preset a value here. **Auxiliary scale** enables you to scale based on the current dimension scale factor or plot scale factor.
Rotation	Sets the rotation angle for the block when inserted.
Prompt for Rotation	If set to **Yes**, you are prompted for the rotation angle in the Command Line when you insert using the click and pick point method. This has no effect when you insert using the drag-and-drop method.
Explode	If set to **Yes**, the block is inserted as its component pieces, not as a single block object.

General Options

Layer	Sets the layer on which the block is inserted.
Other Options	The other General options (**Color**, **Linetype**, etc.) are normally set to **ByLayer** so that their properties are controlled by the layer.

- If the layer specified in the Tool Properties does not exist in the current drawing, it is automatically created when you insert the block.

- If the specified layer is toggled off or frozen, the block is still placed on that layer. However, it does not display until you toggle on or thaw the layer.

Redefining Blocks in Tool Palettes

If the block definition in the source file changes, it does not automatically update in the palette. Open the Tool Properties dialog box and select the source file again.

- You can update a block definition in the current drawing to match a block in the tool palettes by right-clicking and selecting **Redefine**, as shown in Figure 6–38.

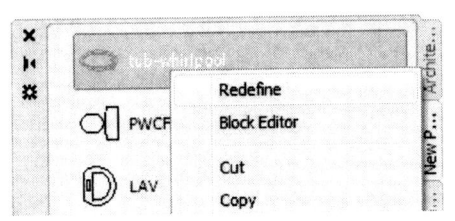

Figure 6–38

- If you open a block in the Tool Palettes in the **Block Editor**, any changes are saved to the block in the palette and automatically update in the active drawing.

- You can specify an image for a tool palette icon. Right-click on the tool and select **Specify image...**, as shown in Figure 6–39. In the Select Image File dialog box, you can select the file you want to use. BMP, JPG, PNG, GIF, and TIF files are all supported image types.

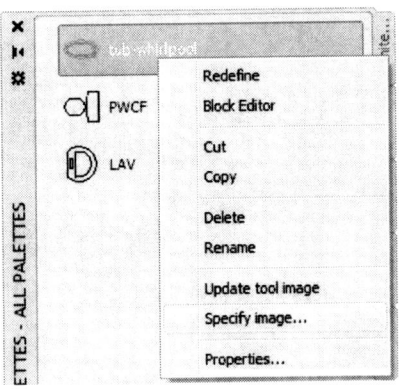

Figure 6–39

Practice 6c

Estimated time for completion: 10 minutes

Modifying Tool Properties

Practice Objectives

- Create a custom tool palette and add blocks to the palette.
- Copy and modify a block tool.

In this practice, you will create a custom tool palette with blocks and use the palette to insert the blocks. You will then add blocks to the custom tool palette using the drag and drop method. You will also modify the properties of the blocks in the tool palette.

Task 1 - Add blocks to a custom tool palette.

In this task you will create a custom tool palette with blocks and use the palette to insert the blocks, as shown in Figure 6–40.

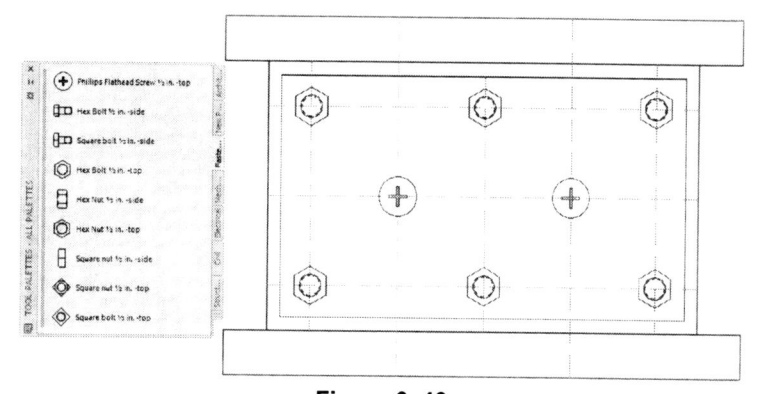

Figure 6–40

1. Open **Fasteners-I.dwg** from your practice files folder. The objects are all defined as blocks in this drawing.

2. In the *View* tab>Palettes panel, click (Tool Palettes) to open Tool Palettes if it is not already open.

3. Right-click in the palette title bar or the tab bar and select **New Palette**. In the *New Palette* edit field, type **Fasteners** and press <Enter>. A new blank palette is created with the *Fasteners* tab active.

Do not select the object by its grip. Select any other highlighted part instead.

4. In the Drawing window, select the round Phillips screw and drag and drop it onto the palette. An icon and description for the block should be added automatically as shown in Figure 6–41.

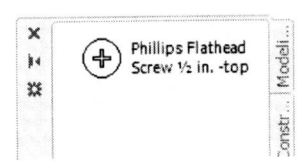

Figure 6–41

5. Repeat Step 4 to add the other bolt and nut blocks to the palette. You must add them one at a time.

6. Close **Fasteners-I.dwg**. Do not save changes.

7. Open **Assembly-I.dwg** from your practice files folder.

8. Set *OSNAP* to **Endpoint** and **Intersection**.

9. Drag and drop the block **Phillips Flathead Screw 1/2 in. -top** to the intersections of the construction lines as shown in Figure 6–40.

10. Drag and drop the **Hex Bolt 1/2 in. -top** blocks into the drawing, as shown in Figure 6–40.

Task 2 - Modify the tool properties.

In this task you will copy a block tool in the new tool palette and modify the tool properties, as shown in Figure 6–42.

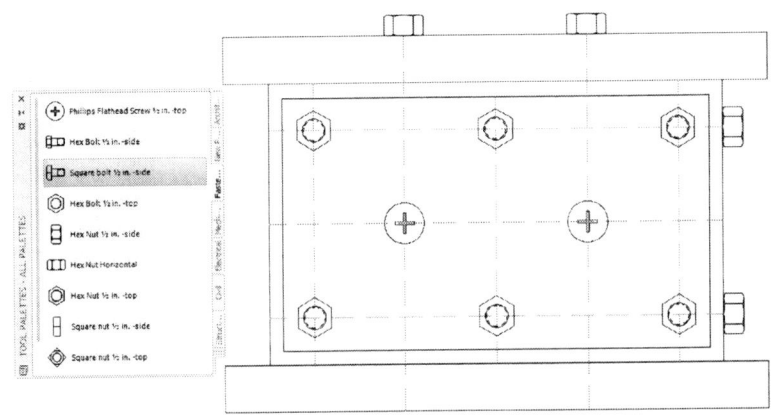

Figure 6–42

Reuse Existing Content

1. To make a copy of the **Hex Nut 1/2 in -side** tool, hold <Ctrl> and drag and drop the tool directly below the original one in the palette. The copy of the tool has the same name.

2. Right-click on the new tool icon and select **Properties,** as shown in Figure 6–43.

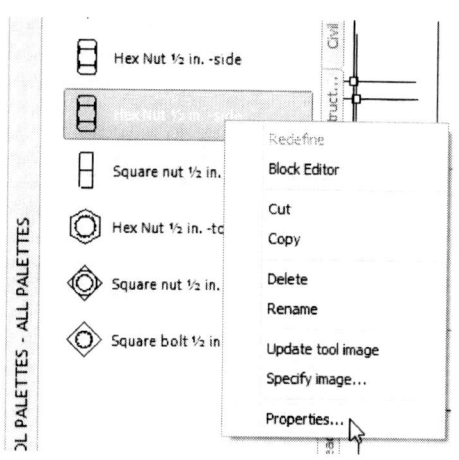

Figure 6–43

3. In the Tool Properties dialog box, change the *Name* next to the image to **Hex Nut – Horizontal**. (Do not change the name under the Insert properties. Doing so breaks the link to the block definition.)

4. In the Insert properties, change the *Rotation* to **90**. As you press <Enter> to accept the values, note that the image in the dialog box displays horizontally.

5. In the General properties, verify that the *Layer* is set to **Object**, so that the block is always inserted on this layer. Click **OK**.

6. Insert the Hex nut- Horizontal and the Hex Nut 1/2 in. -side along the top and side respectively, as shown in Figure 6–42.

7. Save and close the drawing.

6.10 Inserting Blocks with Attributes

What are Attributes?

Attributes are data elements that are associated with blocks. Each time a block with attributes is inserted into a drawing, a new data record is inserted into the master database of the drawing.

From these records in the drawing database, the AutoCAD® software can extract information for creating parts lists and bills of materials, estimating takeoffs, doing inventory counts, and creating schedules. Attributes also enable you to create graphic standards for tasks, such as reference and location numbering. Attributes are also used to assign tag labels on blocks and store information, such as part numbers in a drawing.

How Attribute Values Are Entered

A block that contains attributes inserts them into the drawing database each time the block is inserted. The AutoCAD software prompts you to provide values for each of the attributes that are associated with the block. Figure 6–44 shows an example of attribute tags in a block definition and populated attribute values in a block reference.

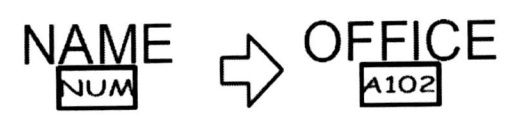

Attribute Tags   *Inserted Attribute*

Figure 6–44

The **attdia** system variable controls how attribute values are entered.

- **attdia** = **0** causes attributes to be entered at the Command Prompt, as shown in Figure 6–45.

- **attdia** = **1** (the default value) causes attributes to be entered in a dialog box, as shown in Figure 6–46.

- Entering the values using a dialog box enables all of the categories of information to be displayed at the same time and enables you to edit a value before closing the dialog box.

- Some blocks with attributes are set to enter the information automatically. You can modify them when they are in the drawing.

Reuse Existing Content

Attdia set to 0

```
Command: _insert
Specify insertion point or [Basepoint/Scale/Rotate]:
Enter attribute values
Voltage <120>: 120/240
KVA <75>:
# of Taps: 4
Coil: Auto
```

Figure 6–45

Attdia set to 1

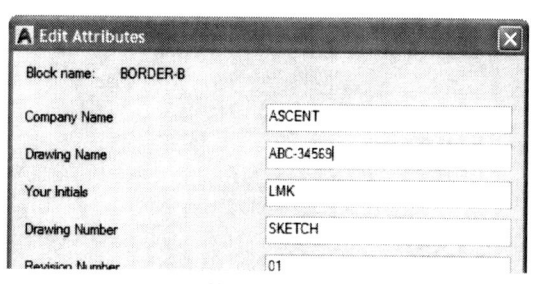

Figure 6–46

Retain Attribute Display

When inserted as part of a block, some attributes can be visible and some not. The visibility of an attribute is determined when the attribute is created, before it is associated with a block. If you want to display the invisible attributes, you can make them visible temporarily, as shown in Figure 6–47.

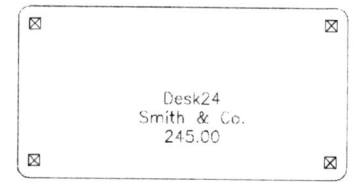

Attribute Display set to Normal *Attribute Display set to On*

Figure 6–47

- The **Retain Attribute Display** command enables you to toggle the visibility of attributes on or off.

- In the ribbon, in the *Home* tab>expanded Block panel, or in the *Insert* tab>expanded Block panel, click (Retain Attribute Display).

Command Options

Retain Display (Normal): Displays attributes according to their defined modes. Invisible attributes do not display, while visible attributes display.

Display All (ON): Displays all of the attributes, regardless of their defined visibility modes, making them all temporarily visible.

Hide All (OFF): Hides all of the attributes, regardless of their defined visibility modes, making them all temporarily invisible.

6.11 Editing Attribute Values

When attributes have been inserted into a drawing, you might need to change their values. For example, the cost of a part might change, or one with a different model number might replace the part number that you originally specified. Attribute values in multiple blocks can be replaced using **Find and Replace**.

Editing Attributes One at a Time

The Enhanced Attribute Editor dialog box (shown in Figure 6–48), enables you to change the attribute values in individual blocks. It also enables you to change the text appearance and properties (layer, color, etc.) for each attribute in a block. The quickest way to start this command is to double-click on the block containing the attributes you want to edit.

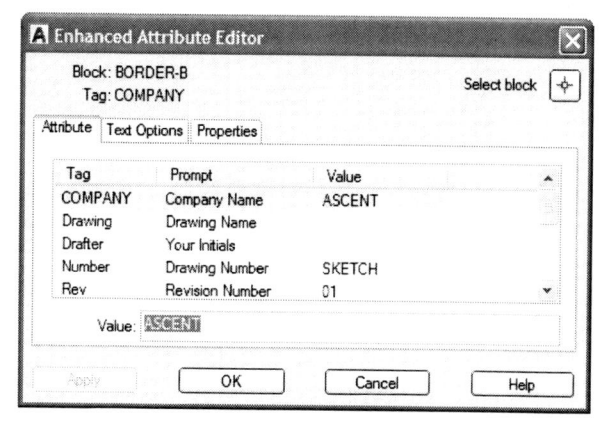

Figure 6–48

How To: Edit an Individual Attribute

1. In the *Home* tab>Block panel or *Insert* tab>Block panel, click (Edit Attribute) and select the block.
2. In the Enhanced Attribute Editor dialog box, in the *Attribute* tab, select the tag you want to modify from the list, if it is not already selected.

You can also double-click on the attribute that you want to modify.

3. In the *Value* field, change the information as required, as shown in Figure 6–49.

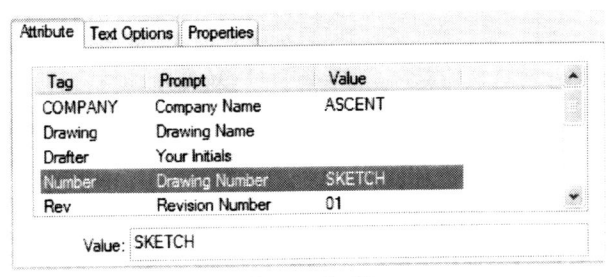

Figure 6–49

4. In the *Text Options* tab (shown in Figure 6–50), you can modify the *Text Style*, *Justification*, *Height*, and other text options that are typically set in the text style.

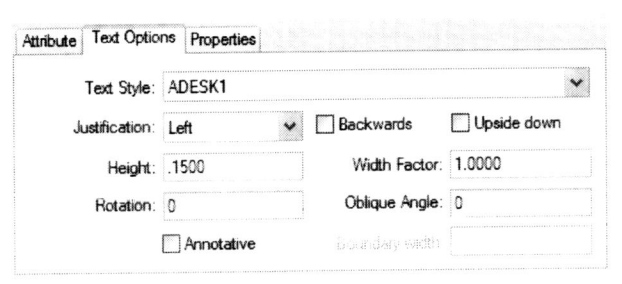

Figure 6–50

5. In the *Properties* tab (shown in Figure 6–51), you can modify the *Layer*, *Linetype*, *Color*, *Lineweight*, and *Plot style* of the attribute.

*Note that it is recommended that you leave these as **ByLayer** in most cases.*

Figure 6–51

- You can only edit the attributes one block at a time, but you can switch to another block in the Enhanced Attribute Editor using ⊕ (Select block). It displays the drawing window and enables you to select another block with attributes to edit. If you changed the previous attribute, a warning box opens prompting you to save the changes.

- When you edit a multiline attribute, the *Value* field is grayed out. Click ⌷ (Browse) to open a simplified version of the Text Formatting toolbar in which you can modify the attribute content, as shown in Figure 6–52.

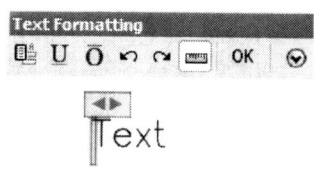

Figure 6–52

- Tag names and prompts cannot be changed in the Enhanced Attribute Editor dialog box, you must edit the block that contains the attributes to update this information.

- The *Text Options* and *Properties* tabs apply to the attribute that is selected in the list in the *Attribute* tab.

Editing Multiple Attribute Values

To change multiple attribute values, the easiest tool to use is **Find and Replace**, as shown in Figure 6–53. It works on attributes and regular text.

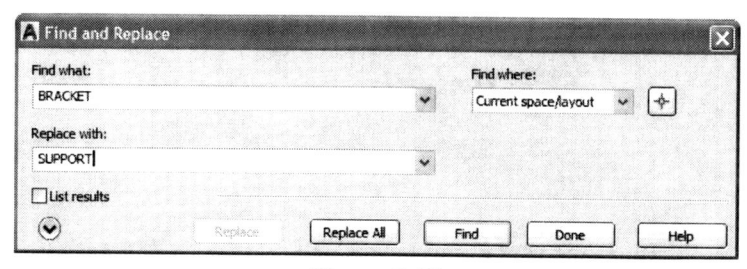

Figure 6–53

For example, you might want to change a department name in all of the related attributes in a drawing or you might want to change a part number. If you know the original information, it is easy for the AutoCAD software to find and replace it for you.

How To: Edit Multiple Attribute Values

1. In the *Annotate* tab>Text panel, type the string you want to find in the *Find Text* field and click (Find). The Find and Replace dialog box opens.
2. In the *Replace with:* field, type the string you want to use to replace the existing text.
3. Specify how you want to select the objects to be modified in the Find where: drop-down list. This can be **Entire drawing**, **Current space/layout**, or **Selected objects**.
4. Click (Select objects) to specify a selection set.
5. Click **Find** to find the first instance of the text in the drawing and display it in the context box on the left. The button changes to **Find Next**.
6. Click **Replace** to replace the instance of the word highlighted in the drawing window or click **Replace All** to replace all of the instances of the word in the drawing.
7. When you are finished, click **Done**.

- Click to expand the Find and Replace dialog box and modify the type of objects to be included in the search, as shown in Figure 6–54. You can also set the command to match the case of the letters or to only find whole words.

*You can also right-click in the drawing window and select **Find** in the shortcut menu.*

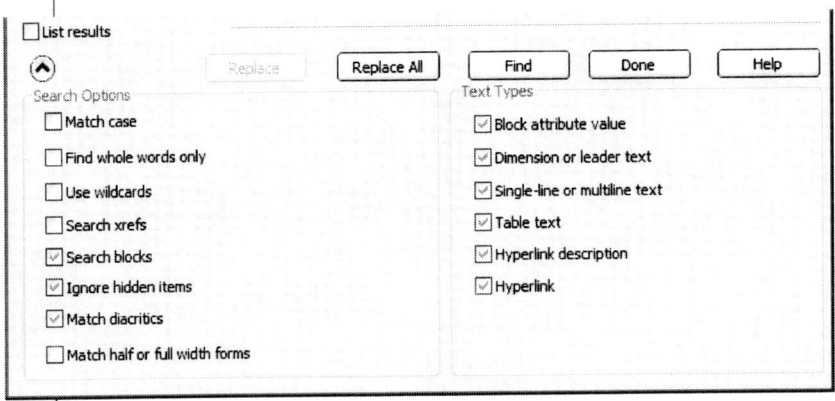

Figure 6–54

Reuse Existing Content

Practice 6d

Inserting and Editing Attribute Values

Practice Objectives

- Insert blocks with attributes.
- Modify both the value and properties of attributes in a titleblock.

Estimated time for completion: 10 minutes

In this practice you will insert several blocks with attributes. You will also use **Find and Replace** and the Enhanced Attribute Editor to change the value and properties of attributes in a titleblock.

Task 1 - Insert attributes.

In this task you will insert several blocks with attributes. The completed drawing is shown in Figure 6–55.

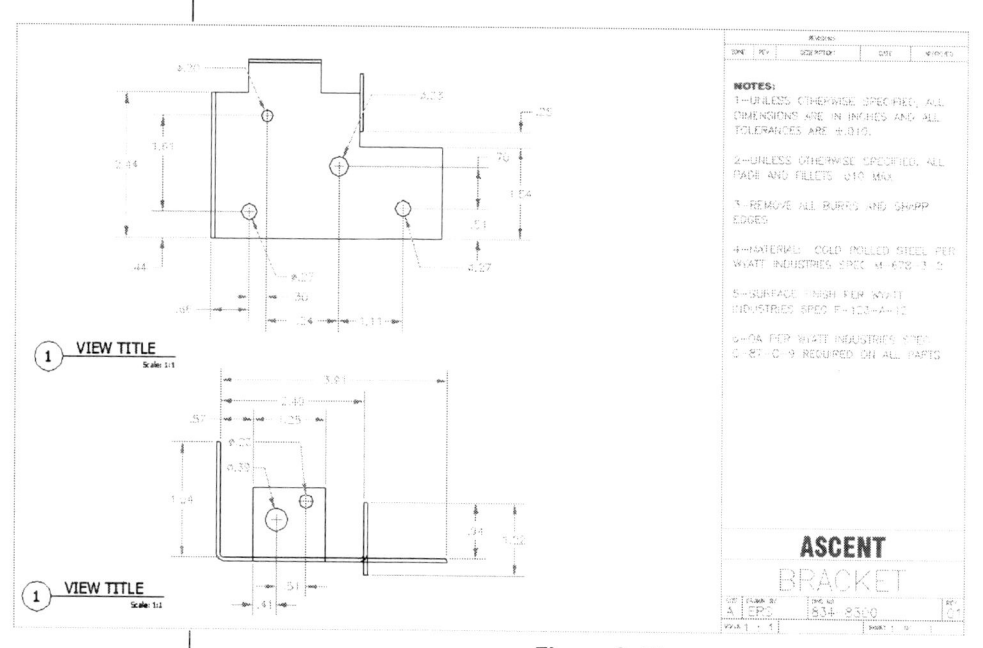

Figure 6–55

1. Open **Bracket-Ad-I.dwg** from your practice files folder.
2. Insert the block **BORDER-B** at **0,0**.

*If the Edit Attribute dialog box does not open, set attdia to **1** and repeat Step 3.*

3. In the Edit Attributes dialog box, fill out the fields as shown in Figure 6–56, and click **OK**.

Edit Attributes

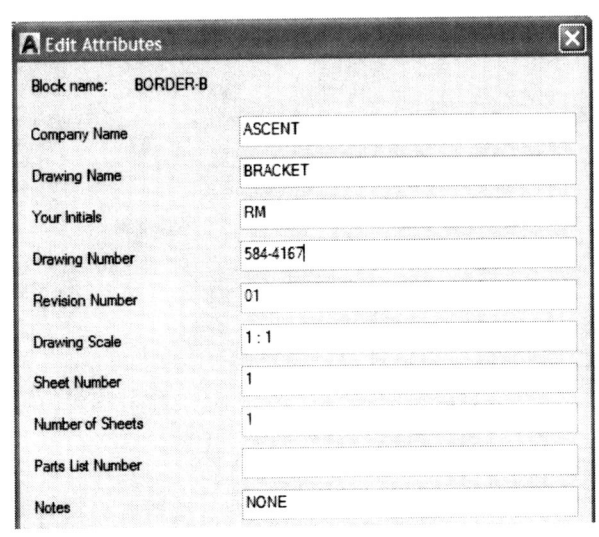

Block name: BORDER-B

Company Name	ASCENT
Drawing Name	BRACKET
Your Initials	RM
Drawing Number	584-4167
Revision Number	01
Drawing Scale	1 : 1
Sheet Number	1
Number of Sheets	1
Parts List Number	
Notes	NONE

Figure 6–56

4. Open the Tool Palette and select the *Annotation* tab, if required.

5. Insert a copy of **Drawing Title-Imperial** under each of the drawing views. It is inserted without prompting for the values. All of the attribute values in this block have been preset, as shown in Figure 6–57.

(1) VIEW TITLE
      Scale: 1:1

Figure 6–57

6. Insert an additional copy of the **Drawing Title-Imperial** block to one side.

7. Explode it. The information is lost and the attribute tag information displays instead, as shown in Figure 6–58.

(#) VIEWNAME
      VPSCALE

Figure 6–58

Reuse Existing Content

8. Erase all the components of the exploded block.

9. Zoom in to the lower right corner of the titleblock.

10. In the *Insert* tab>expanded Block panel, expand ![icon] (Retain Attribute Display) and click ![icon] (Hide All Attributes). All of the attributes become invisible.

11. In the *Insert* tab>Block panel, expand ![icon] (Retain Attribute Visibility) and click ![icon] (Retain Attribute Display). All of the attributes return to their normal visibility status.

12. Save the drawing.

Task 2 - Edit attributes.

In this task you will use **Find and Replace** and the Enhanced Attribute Editor to change the value and properties of attributes in a titleblock, as shown in Figure 6–59.

Figure 6–59

1. In the *Annotate* tab > Text panel, type **ASCENT** in the *Find text* field and click ![icon] (Find).

2. In the Find and Replace dialog box, click ![icon] and verify that **Block attribute value** is selected to be included in the search. Ensure the *Find what* string is set to **ASCENT** and in the *Replace with* string, enter **ASCENT - RAND Worldwide**. Click **Replace All** to replace all of the strings.

3. A smaller Find and Replace dialog box opens indicating the number of matches that were found and changed. Click **OK**, and then click **Done** to close the Find and Replace dialog box.

4. The new company name in the titleblock is too long. Double-click anywhere on the titleblock to start the **Edit Attribute** command that opens the Enhanced Attribute Editor dialog box.

5. In the *Attribute* tab, in the list of attributes, select **Company**. In the *Text Options* tab, change the *Width Factor* to **0.7**, as shown in Figure 6–60.

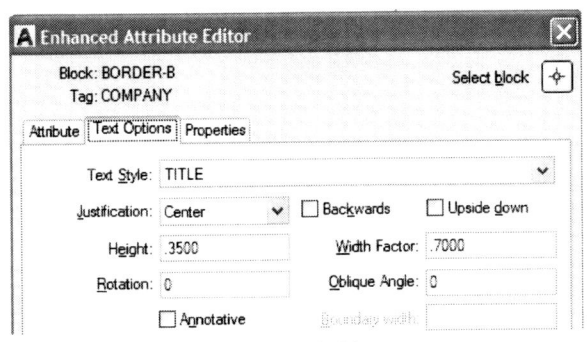

Figure 6–60

6. In the *Attribute* tab, select the **Drawing** attribute. In the *Text Options* tab, change the *Text Style* to **TITLE**. In the *Properties* tab, change the *Color* to **Green**.

7. Click **OK** to close the Enhanced Attribute Editor dialog box. Note the affected changes in the title block, as shown in Figure 6–59.

8. Save and close the drawing.

6.12 Defining Attributes

Attribute definitions are special objects that you include with a block when the block is defined. The **Define Attribute** command creates an attribute definition using a dialog box.

How To: Create a Block with Attributes

1. Draw the objects that you want to include in the block.
2. In the *Home* tab>expanded Block panel or *Insert* tab>Block Definition panel, click (Define Attributes) to create the attributes.
3. Using the **Block** command, select the attributes and other objects that make up the block.
4. Insert the block and fill in the attribute information.

- Attributes can be annotative.

- A block can contain other objects in addition to the attributes, or just attributes without other objects.

- You can also add attributes using (Attribute Definition) in the *Block Editor* contextual tab>Action Parameters panel.

- Block attribute information can contain multiple lines of text while remaining a single attribute. This is very useful for title block information, such as addresses or information that varies in length, but needs to remain in one area in a block.

Attribute Definition

The Attribute Definition dialog box (shown in Figure 6–61) is used to configure attributes before they are associated with a block.

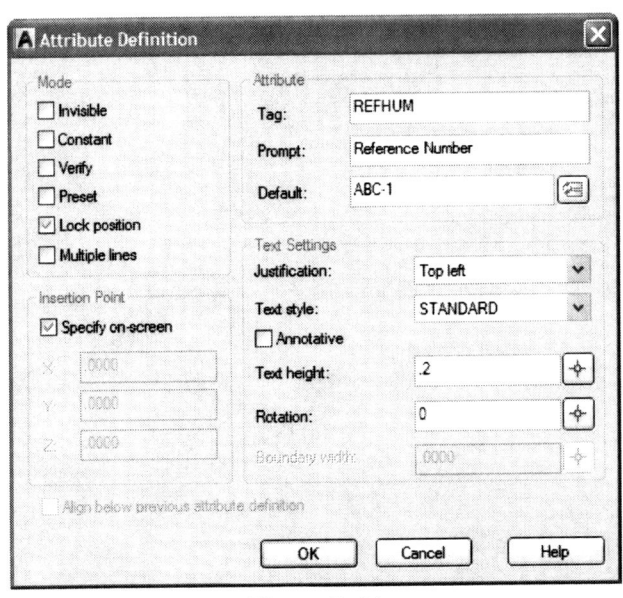

Figure 6–61

Attribute Components

Tag	A label for the category of information that is stored in a particular attribute. Attribute tags in the software are similar to the *field names* or *column labels* in other data systems. Some common tags are *type*, *cost*, *rating*, *manufacturer*, *reference_number*, and *material*. This label cannot be blank or have spaces.
Prompt	The prompt that displays in the Command Line or dialog box when a block with this attribute is inserted. If empty, the Tags name is used for the prompt. Phrase your prompt to help users to enter the correct information. For example, you could write a question for the prompt.
Default	The initial contents or actual data value of a specific block instance. This value is used as a default value and can be blank in the dialog box. You can click (Insert field) to insert a field as the value.

Attribute Modes

The Attribute Mode controls how an attribute value displays in a drawing and how much control you have over the value.

Invisible	Controls whether an attribute value normally displays in the drawing, or is just stored in the database. For example, reference numbers and part locations WOULD NOT typically be invisible, while costs, remarks, and manufacturers would be invisible.
Constant	Controls whether the attribute is defined ahead of time or is entered by the operator when the block is inserted. The part number of a specific part can be constant, while a reference number or detail sheet number would not be constant. Constant attributes CANNOT be edited.
Verify	Use for some non-constant attributes, such as serial numbers and costs, which are so important that they need to be confirmed by the operator. The Verify mode causes the software to prompt for the value twice when the block is inserted. If dialog boxes are used, verify does not have an effect.
Preset	Similar to **Constant**, except that values can be edited after insertion. Preset values are not requested at the Command Line when the block is inserted. However, the value displays in the dialog box for editing.
Lock position	Select if you do not want the attributes to move separately from the rest of the block.
Multiple lines	Select if you want to create a multiline attribute. The *Default* field is grayed out. Click ⋯ (Browse) to specify the location and default text.

Insertion Point and Text Settings

Use these options to determine the attribute text placement and properties. You can specify the *Justification*, *Text style*, *Text height*, and *Rotation* of the text, or make the text *Annotative*. The **Specify On-screen** option is the most common method that is used to place the attribute definition text.

- Once you have placed one attribute, you might want to speed up the process by using the same text options. To do so, select **Align below previous attribute definition**.

- The *Boundary width* setting is only available for multiline attributes.

Associating Attributes with Blocks

Once the attributes have been defined, they must be associated with a block. This is done by including attributes as part of the block while in the **Block** or **Wblock** command or in the Block Editor authoring mode.

Select the attributes individually, rather than with a window or crossing box. The order in which the attribute information displays during block insertion depends on the order in which the attributes were selected for inclusion in the block.

- To edit an attribute before it is associated with a block, double-click on the attribute. This opens the Edit Attribute Definition dialog box (shown in Figure 6–62), which enables you to change the *Tag*, *Prompt*, or *Default* value.

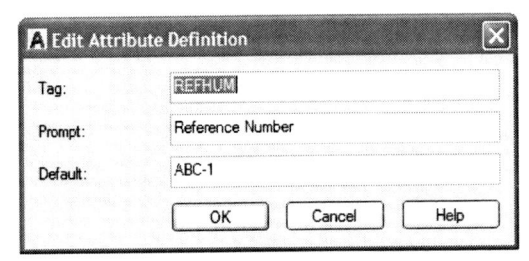

Figure 6–62

Practice 6e

Estimated time for completion: 10 minutes

Defining Attributes

Practice Objective

- Define multiple attributes using given values and use them to create a block for use in a drawing.

In this practice you will create attributes in a block that you will then use in another drawing. The block with attribute definitions is shown in Figure 6–63.

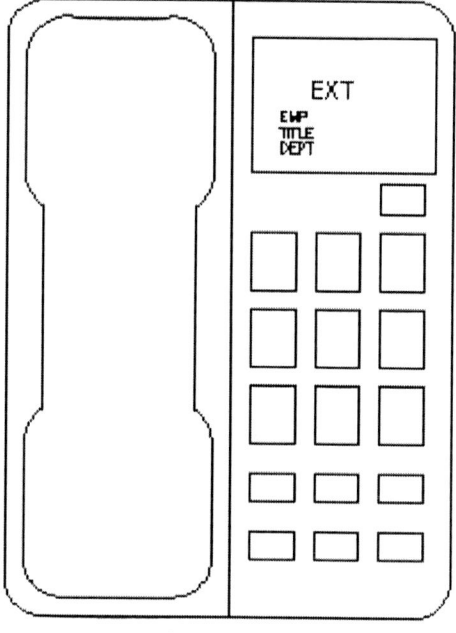

Figure 6–63

1. Open **Attributes-A.dwg** from your practice files folder.

*You need to create each of the attributes separately. Enter the settings for each attribute and click **OK** to place it in the drawing.*

Start (Define Attributes) again to create each remaining attribute.

2. In the *Insert* tab>Block Definition panel, click (Define Attributes) to create four attributes using the values given in the table below. In the Attribute Definition dialog box, enter the values in the appropriate fields and select the specified *Mode* options, as shown in Figure 6–64 for the EXT tag.

Tag:	EXT	EMP	TITLE	DEPT
Prompt:	Extension	Employee Name	Title	Department
Default:	(none)	(none)	(none)	Design
Mode:	(none)	Invisible and Multiple lines	Invisible	Invisible and Preset
Justification:	Center	Middle left	Click **Align below previous attribute definition** near the bottom of the dialog box.	Click **Align below previous attribute definition** near the bottom of the dialog box.
Text style:	BLOCK	Standard	---	---
Annotative	Yes	No	---	---
Text height:	1/4"	1/8"	---	---
Insertion Point:	6,7,0	5.25,6.75,0	---	---

Reuse Existing Content

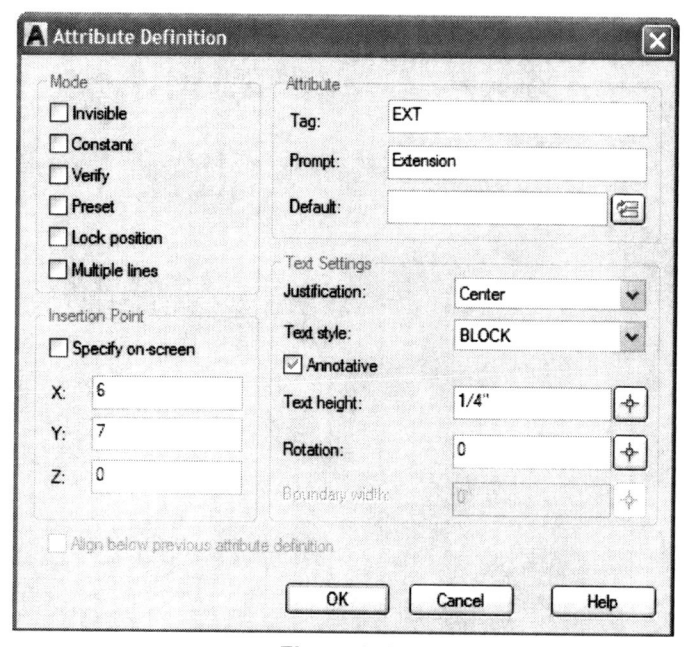

Figure 6–64

3. Use **Wblock** to create a new drawing called **Phone.dwg** containing the drawing of the phone and the attributes. Set the *Source* to **Objects**. Set the *Base point* to the middle of the top of the phone. Select the attributes in the order in which you want to enter the information. Set the file path to your practice files folder and *Insert units* to **Inches**.

4. Save and close the drawing.

5. Open **Office-A.dwg** from your practice files folder.

6. Insert the block **Phone** on each of the four desks to test the attributes.

7. Save and close the drawing.

6.13 Redefining Blocks with Attributes

The Block Attribute Manager (shown in Figure 6–65) simplifies the process of modifying attributes in blocks and updating the blocks.

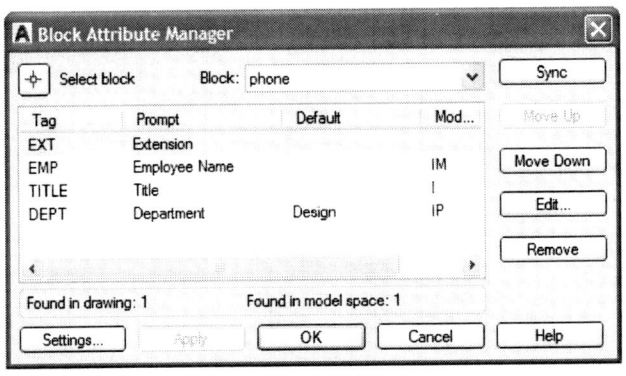

Figure 6–65

- The Block Attribute Manager does not affect (or enable you to modify) the attribute values in blocks. To modify those values, use the **Edit Attribute** command.

- You cannot add attributes to a block using the Block Attribute Manager. You need to explode the block, add the new attribute, and redefine the block. Then use the **Synchronize Attributes** command to update the blocks and their attributes.

How To: Use the Block Attribute Manager

1. In the *Home* tab>expanded Block panel, or in the *Insert* tab>Block Definition panel, click (Manage Attributes) to open the Block Attribute Manager dialog box.
2. Expand the Block drop-down list and select a block.

   - You can also use (Select block) to select a block in the drawing window.

3. The block's attributes display. To modify an attribute, select it in the list and click **Edit**.
4. In the Edit Attribute dialog box, make the required changes.

Only blocks with attributes are listed

5. In the Block Attribute Manager, click **Apply** to apply the changes and stay in the dialog box, or click **OK** to apply the changes and close the dialog box.

- Use **Move Up** and **Move Down** to change an attribute's position in the list. The location in the list determines the order in which the prompts display when you insert the block and fill in the attribute values. It does not change the physical order of the attributes.

- **Sync** updates existing blocks that were not updated automatically when you made a change using the Block Attribute Manager.

- You can remove an attribute from a block definition by selecting it in the list and clicking **Remove**.

Editing Options

When an attribute is edited, the Edit Attribute dialog box is used as it was when the attribute was defined, as shown in Figure 6–66.

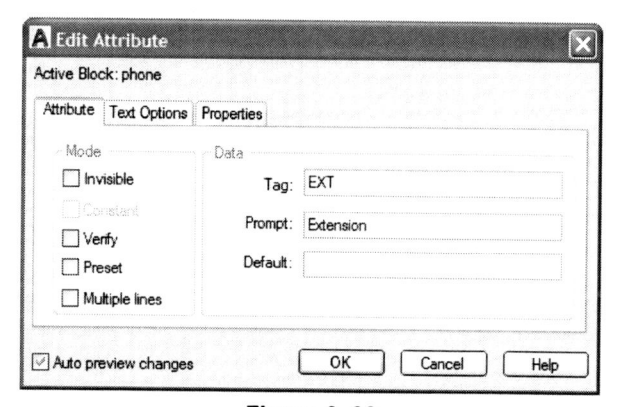

Figure 6–66

- The *Text Options* and *Properties* tabs apply to the attribute selected in the list in the *Attribute* tab.

- **Auto preview changes** makes the changes visible in the drawing immediately. Toggling this off provides a slightly faster performance.

Settings

The Settings control the properties that display in the Block Attribute Manager. By default, only the **Tag**, **Prompt**, **Default**, **Modes**, and **Annotative** properties display, as shown in Figure 6–67.

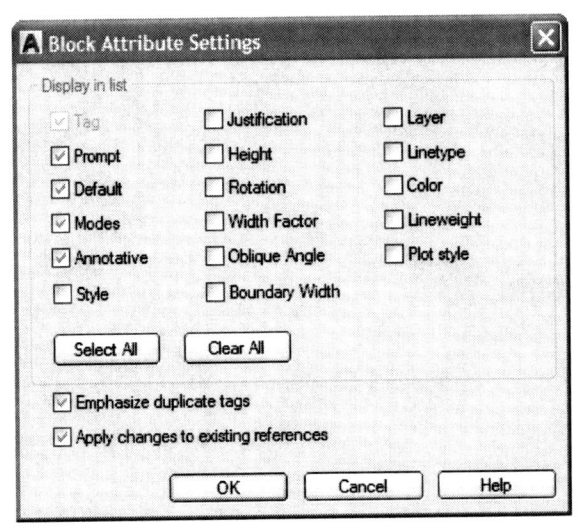

Figure 6–67

Emphasize duplicate tags	If selected, duplicate tag names display in red in the Block Attribute Manager.
Apply changes to existing references	If selected, all of the existing and new instances of the block reference are updated with the changes specified in the Block Attribute Manager. If not selected, only new instances of the block display the changes. You can use the **Synchronize Attributes** command if this option has been toggled off.

Updating Blocks with New Attributes

To add an attribute to a block, open the block definition in the Block Editor authoring environment and add the attribute. Alternatively, you can explode a copy of the block, add the attribute, and redefine the block. New instances of the redefined block include the new attribute, but existing instances of the block do not. You can use **Synchronize Attributes** to update all of the blocks and their attributes.

How To: Synchronize Attributes

1. Open the block in the Block Editor authoring environment, add the required attribute(s), and save the block.
2. In the *Home* tab>expanded Block panel, or in the *Insert* tab>expanded Block Definition panel, click (Synchronize Attributes).
3. Press <Enter> to select a block (type **?** to display a list or **N** to type a name).
4. Select the block.
5. At the *Resync Process* prompt, enter **yes** or **no**.

- This command also works on existing blocks that were not automatically updated when you made a change using the Block Attribute Manager.

- At least one attribute must already be in the block that you are trying to update with other attributes.

Practice 6f

Redefining Blocks with Attributes

Estimated time for completion: 10 minutes

Practice Objectives

- Modify block attribute values and block attribute settings using the Block Attribute Manager.
- Redefine a block and then synchronize all of the existing instances of that block in the drawing to be updated.

In this practice you will use **Edit Attribute**, make changes to existing attributes in the Block Attribute Manager, and use **Synchronize Attributes**. The completed drawing is shown in Figure 6–68.

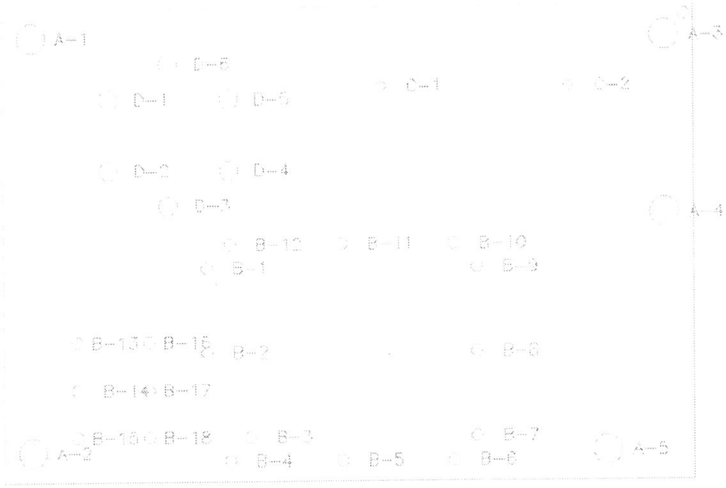

Figure 6–68

1. Open **PCB-I.dwg** from your practice files folder.

2. Double-click on the **A-3** attribute in the bottom right corner of the part to open the Enhanced Attribute Editor.

3. In the *Value* edit box, change the *NUMBER* value to **A-5**, and note that *USE* is listed above *NUMBER*, as shown in Figure 6–69. Click **OK** to close the Enhanced Attribute Editor dialog box.

Reuse Existing Content

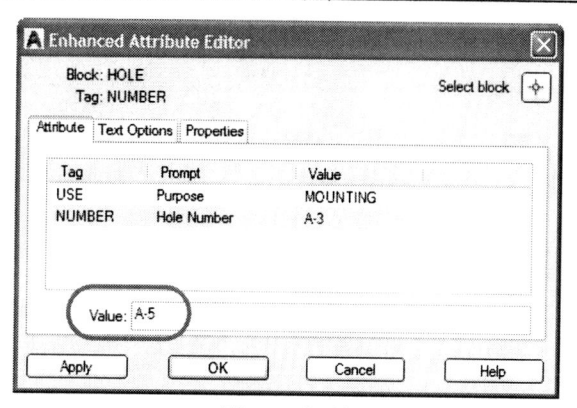

Figure 6–69

4. In the *Insert* tab>Block Definition panel, click (Manage Attributes) to open the Block Attribute Manager. **HOLE** is the selected block, and its attributes are listed. The *USE* attribute has the **I** (Invisible) mode set.

5. Select the *NUMBER* attribute in the list and click **Move Up** to move it above *USE*.

6. With *NUMBER* selected, click **Edit**. In the *Properties* tab, change the *Color* to **Cyan**. Click **OK** to close the Edit Attribute dialog box.

You might need to select a different Block first and then reselect the original Block before you click Sync.

7. If any of the blocks have not updated automatically, click **Sync** to update all of the instances of the block. Click **OK** to close the Block Attribute Manager. The *NUMBER* attribute now displays in cyan.

8. Double-click on any attribute to edit it. *NUMBER* is now at the top of the list. Click **Cancel** to close the Enhanced Attribute Editor.

9. Insert the block **Hole Plus** to one side of the part, using the default values for the attributes, and explode it. It contains three attributes: *NUMBER*, *LOCATION*, and *USE*.

10. In the *Insert* tab>Block Definition Panel, click **Create Block** to start the **Create Block** command. Set the following:
    - In the Block Definition dialog box, name the block **HOLE**.
    - In the *Objects* area, use **Select objects** to select the three attributes (from the Hole Plus block that was exploded) to be used for the block object.
    - In the *Base Point* area, select **Specify On-screen**.
    - In the *Objects* area, select **Delete**, and then clear the **Open in block editor** option.

11. Click **OK** to close the Block Definition dialog box.

12. When prompted, select **Redefine block** to redefine the block **HOLE**.

13. Select a point just to the left of *NUMBER* to specify the insertion base point.

14. Insert a copy of the redefined block **HOLE** to one side, using the default values for the attributes. It includes the *LOCATION* attribute with the default value of **Unknown**. The attributes for the existing blocks named **HOLE** in the part have not changed.

15. In the *Insert* tab>expanded Block Definition panel, click (Synchronize Attributes). Press <Enter> and select the new block **HOLE**.

16. At the *ATTSYNC block HOLE?* prompt, select **Yes**. Note that the existing blocks update to include the new attribute with the default value **Unknown**.

17. In the *Insert* tab>Block Definition panel, click (Manage Attributes) to open the Block Attribute Manager dialog box.

18. For the block **HOLE**, select the *Tag* named **LOCATION** in the list, and click **Edit**. The Edit Attribute dialog box opens.

*If the **Auto preview changes** option is toggled on, the drawing changes immediately. If this option is off, the change displays after you exit the Block Attribute Manager.*

19. In the *Attribute* tab, in the *Mode* area, toggle on **Invisible** and then click **OK** to return to the Block Attribute Manager dialog box.

20. Click **OK** to apply the changes and exit the Block Attribute Manager dialog box. The *LOCATION* attribute with the default value **Unknown**, to which all of the other blocks were updated, is now invisible.

21. Save the drawing.

6.14 Extracting Attributes

Attributes can be used in a drawing for labels, tags, etc. They can also be used to extract information into a database or table format, as shown in Figure 6–70. The extracted information can then be used for parts lists, inventories, etc.

```
1084X
Steelcase
Fabric
Red
```

Furniture Schedule					
Quantity	TYPE	STYLE	MANUFACTURER	MATERIAL	COLOR
2	chair	1084X	Steelcase	Fabric	Blue
6	chair	1084X	Steelcase	Fabric	Red
2	chair	1084X	Steelcase	Fabric	Green
4	chair	1084X	Steelcase	Wood	Cherry

Figure 6–70

- In the *Annotate* tab>Tables panel, or in the *Insert* tab>Linking & Extraction panel, click (Extract Data) to start data extraction.

- The **Extract Data** command uses a wizard that automates the process. The major steps in the process are to select the drawing(s) from which to extract the attributes that you want in a table, and select the format to use for the extracted data.

- You can also extract attributes and other data using the **Table** command.

- You can extract information from multiple drawings at the same time.

- Once you have set up the extraction information, you can save it to a *template* so that you do not have to go through the entire wizard again. The template is a text file (Block Template File, .BLK) that specifies the parameters for extraction.

- Data can be exported to a file or made into an AutoCAD table object.

You can create a table by extracting data from objects in the current drawing or from other drawings. In the **Table** command, in the Insert Table dialog box, select **From object data in the drawing (Data Extraction)**, as shown in Figure 6–71. The Data Extraction Wizard opens. It guides you through the selection of objects, whether you want to extract data from the current drawing or another one, and how the data displays in the table.

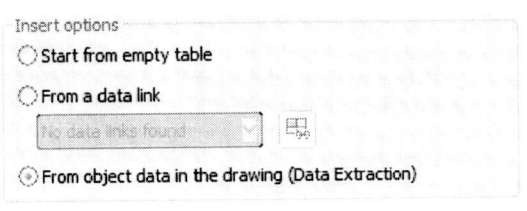

Figure 6–71

How To: Extract Attributes to a Table or File

1. In the *Annotate* tab>Tables panel, or in the *Insert* tab>Linking & Extraction panel, click (Extract Data). Alternatively, you can use the **Table** command.
    - If you are using the **Table** command, select **From object data in the drawing (Data Extraction)** and click **OK**. The Data Extraction Wizard opens.
2. On the *Begin* page, select **Create a new data extraction**, as shown in Figure 6–72.
    - If you have an existing template that was made from another data extraction file (.DXE) or a block template file (.BLK), select the box and then select the template file.

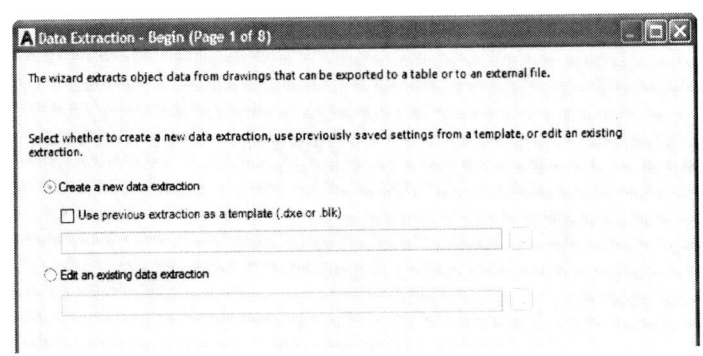

Figure 6–72

3. Click **Next >**.

Reuse Existing Content

4. Select a location. In the Save Data Extraction As dialog box, type a name for the new data extraction files (.DXE) as shown in Figure 6–73, and click **Save**.

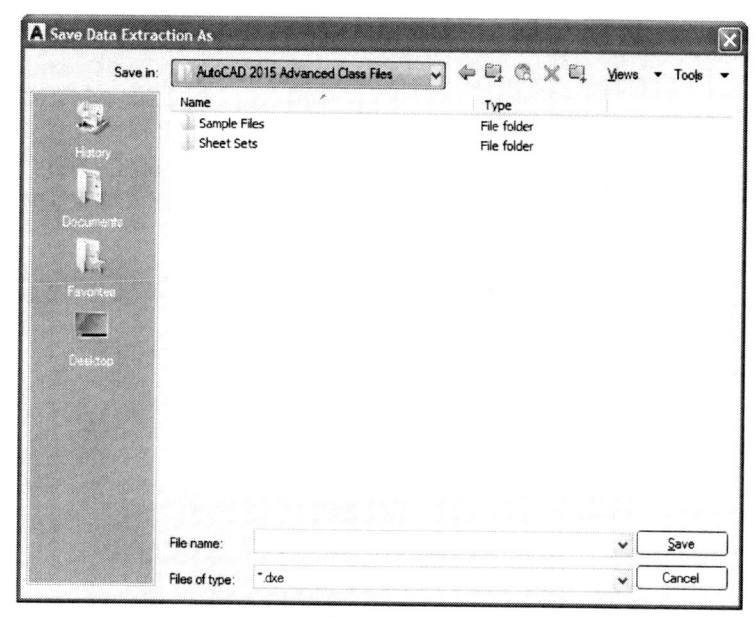

Figure 6–73

5. On the *Define Data Source* page, you can select the file(s) or objects in a drawing from which you want to extract information, as shown in Figure 6–74.

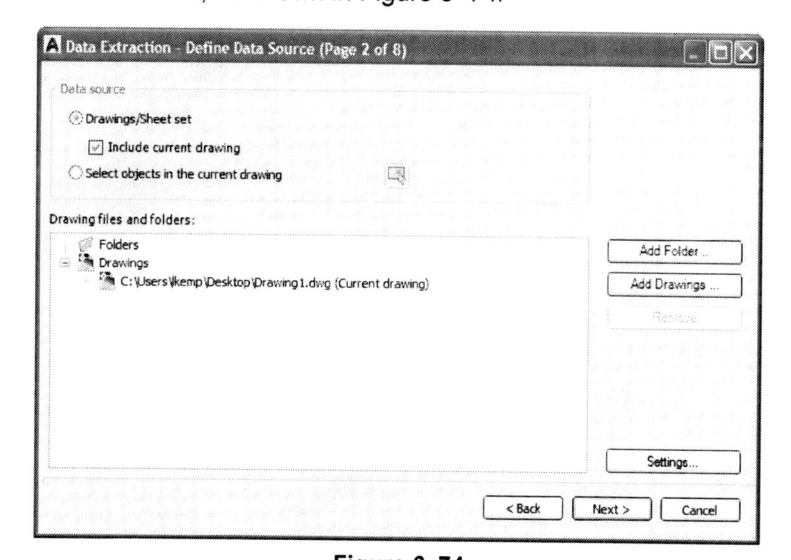

Figure 6–74

- If you select **Select object in the current drawing**, click ▣ (Select Objects) and select the required objects.
- If you select **Drawings/Sheet set**, you can select **Include current drawing** and add other folders or drawings. Click **Add Drawings** to add one or more drawings to the selection or click **Add Folder** to include all of the drawings in a specified folder.
- In the Add Folder Options dialog box, you can specify the folder and how drawings are added to the list, as shown in Figure 6–75.

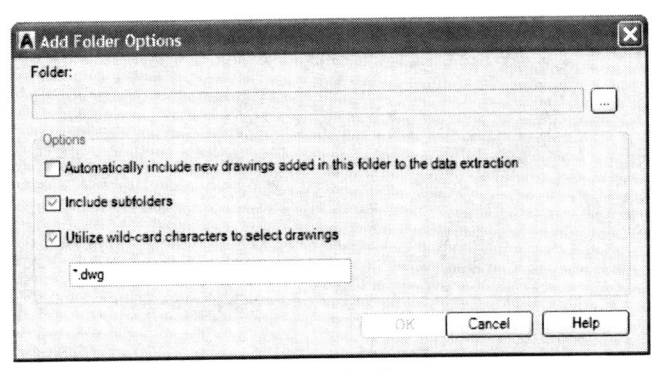

Figure 6–75

6. In the Define Data Source dialog box, you should also click **Settings** to verify that you are extracting the correct information, as shown in Figure 6–76.

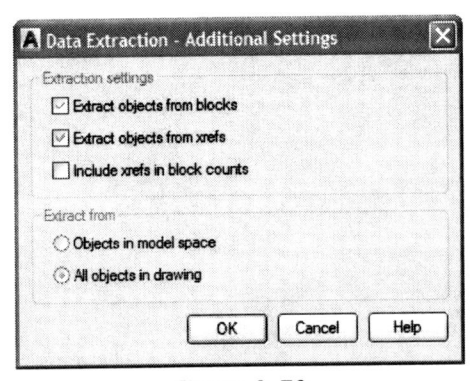

Figure 6–76

7. Click **Next >** when you have finished adding drawings or objects.

Reuse Existing Content

8. On the *Select Objects* page, select the objects that you want to include in the data extraction, as shown in Figure 6–77.
    - These include attributes and other objects, such as blocks, lines, and polylines.
    - Use the **Display** options as selection aids.
    - You can also right-click in the *Objects* area and select **Check All**, **Uncheck All**, **Invert Selection**, and **Edit Display Name**.

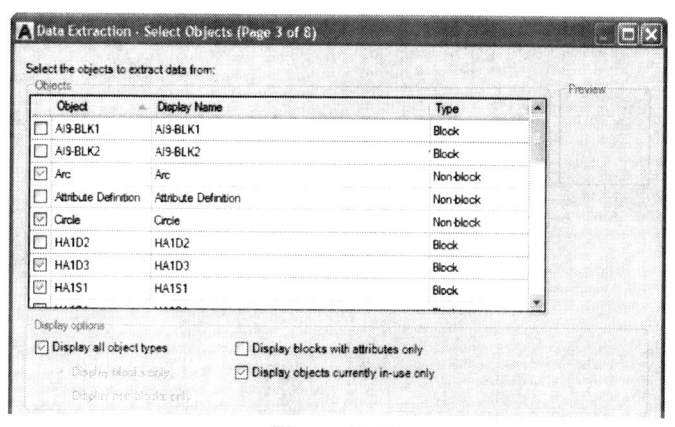

Figure 6–77

9. Click **Next >**.
10. On the *Select Properties* page, all of the properties are selected by default. Select or clear them as required (as shown in Figure 6–78), to select the options you want to use.
    - Right-click to clear everything to more easily select only the objects you want to use.
    - You can also modify the *Display Name*, which controls the name that displays in the table.

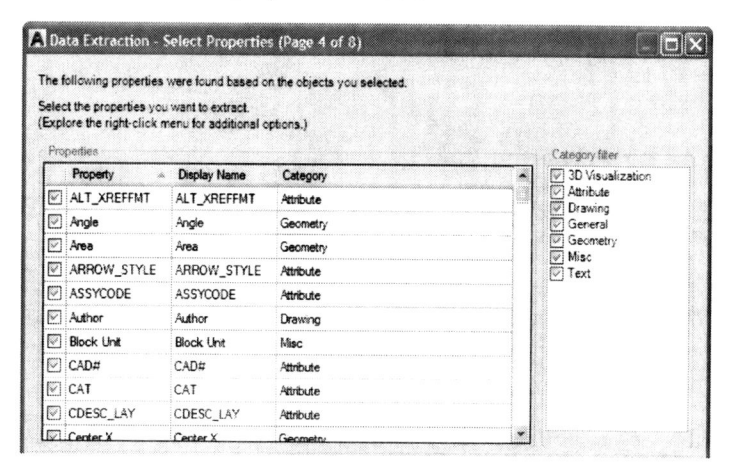

Figure 6–78

11. Click **Next >**.
12. The data is extracted from the drawings and the results display on the *Refine Data* page, as shown in Figure 6–79.
    - You can modify the appearance of the columns. Select the options that you want to display. Reorder the column locations by dragging the headers to new locations.
    - To reorder the column information alphabetically, click once on the column name.
    - To rename a column, right-click on the header.
    - If you have additional information stored in a spreadsheet, click **Link External Data** to select the data link.
    - Click **Sort Columns Options** to open the Sort Columns dialog box, in which you can also modify the column information.

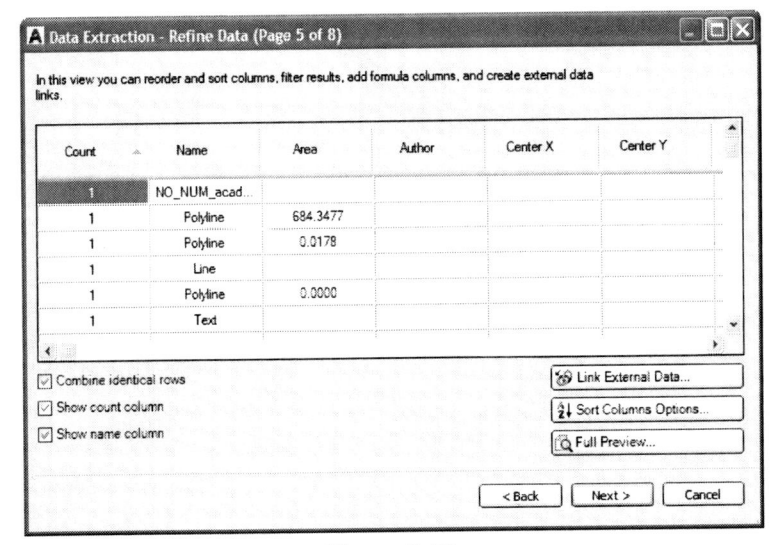

Figure 6–79

13. Click **Full Preview** to display the results.
14. Click **Next >**.
15. On the *Choose Output* page, in the *Output options* area (shown in Figure 6–80), select **Insert data extraction table into drawing** and/or **Output data to external file**.
    - The external files that you can create include XLS, CSV, MDB, and TXT.

Reuse Existing Content

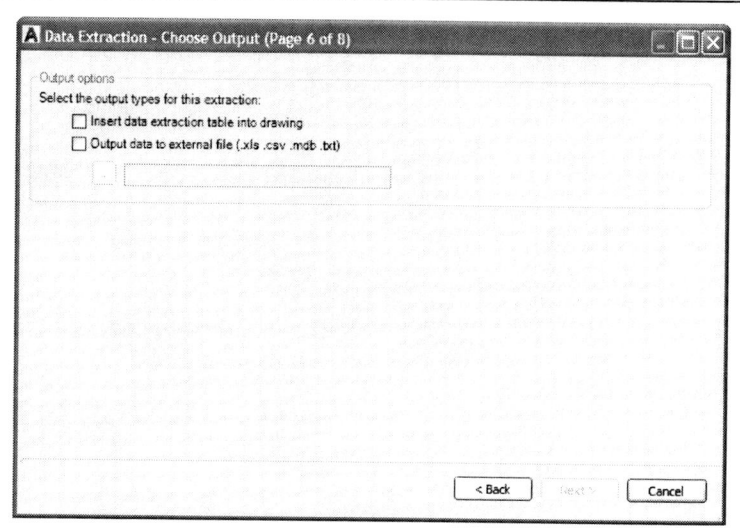

Figure 6–80

16. Click **Next >**.

17. If you select the AutoCAD table option, the *Table Style* page opens, in which you can set up the Table Style information and add a title for the table, as shown in Figure 6–81.

- By default, the Headers are the attribute tag names, unless you modified them in the previous step.

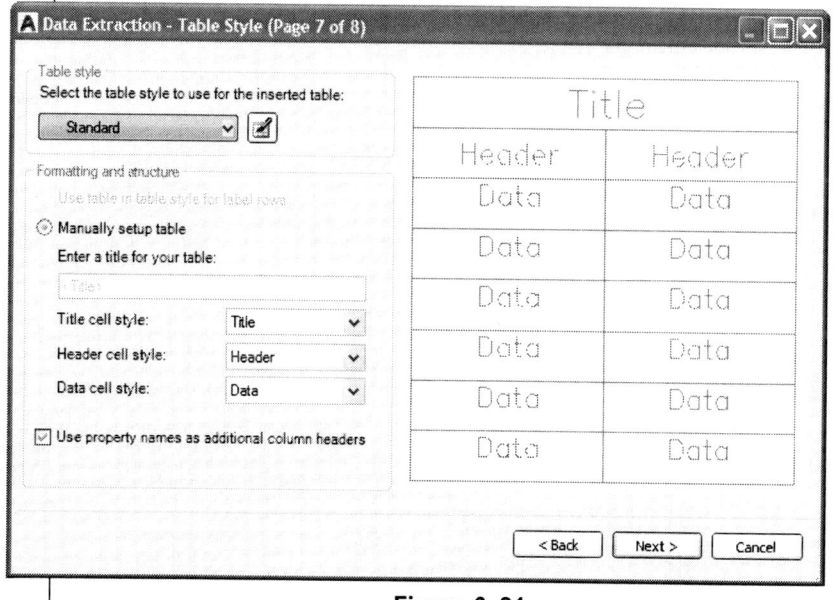

Figure 6–81

18. Click **Next >**.
19. Click **Finish** to close the Data Extraction Wizard. Pick a point in the drawing to insert the table.
20. Use grips to adjust the table to fit in the available space.

- The text in the resulting table is linked to the attribute data. Any manual changes that you make in the table are lost if you refresh the table data. A warning box opens when you place the table.

- You can add data columns from external sources next to those containing the data extracted from the objects.

- To update the table to include any modifications you have made to the data in the drawing, right-click on the table and select **Update Table Data Links** or right-click on (Data Link) in the Status Bar.

Practice 6g

Extracting Object Data to a Table

Practice Objective

- Extract attribute information from blocks and insert that information into a table.

Estimated time for completion: 10 minutes

In this practice you will extract attribute information from blocks in a drawing and insert the information into a table, as shown in Figure 6–82.

Count	Name	Catalog	Manufacturer
	Bill of Materials		
1	HTS12	9025-GXW2	SQD
1	HPS12		
1	HLS12	CR115B201	GE
1	HA1S1		
1	HA1D3		
1	PLCIO_9EE	1771-OA	AB
1	PLCIO_7E9	1771-IA	AB
1	AI9-BLK2		
1	AI9-BLK1		
2	HA1S4		
2	HCR1	700-R220A1	AB
2	HPB12	800H-BR6D2	AB
3	HMS1	AN16DNOAB	EATON
3	HLT1G	800T-P16H	AB
3	HCR1	700-P400A1	AB
3	HPB11	800H-BR6D1	AB
4	HA1D2		
5	HCR21		
6	HCR22		

Figure 6–82

1. Open **Control-I.dwg** from your practice files folder.

2. In the *Annotate* tab>Tables panel, click (Extract Data). The Data Extraction Wizard opens.

*You can also start the **Table** command, select **From object data in the drawing (Data Extraction)**, and then click **OK***

3. Select **Create a new data extraction** (if required) and click **Next >**.

4. In the Save Data Extraction As dialog box, navigate to your practice files folder, set the *File name* to **BOM**, and click **Save**.

5. In the Data Extraction Wizard, in the *Data source* area, select **Drawings/Sheet Set** and **Include current drawing**, and click **Next >**.

6. On the *Select Objects* page, clear the **Display all object types** option and select **Display blocks only**, as shown in Figure 6–83.

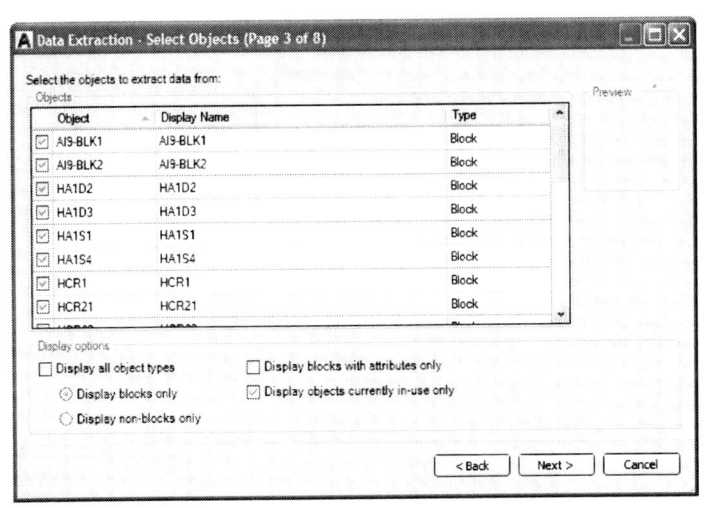

Figure 6–83

7. Scroll through the list of blocks and clear **LOGO**, **NO_NUM_acade_title**, and all the blocks starting with **WD**.

8. Click **Next >**.

9. In the *Category filter* area, clear all of the options except **Attribute**.

10. In the *Properties* area, all of the properties are selected by default. Right-click and select **Uncheck all**. Then select **CAT** and **MFG**.

11. Change the display name of CAT to **Catalog** (as shown in Figure 6–84) and display name of MFG to **Manufacturer**.

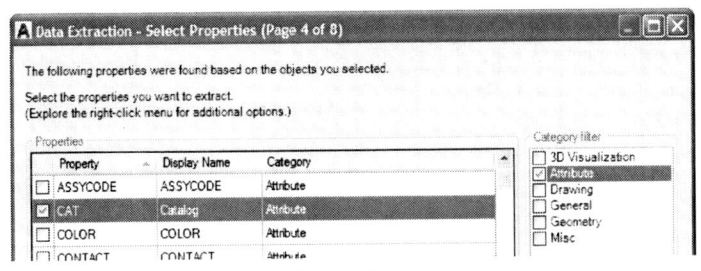

Figure 6–84

12. Click **Next >**.

13. The data is extracted from the drawings and the results display on the *Refine Data* page. Click **Next >**.

14. In the *Choose Output* page, in the *Output options* area, select **Insert data extraction table into drawing**.

15. Click **Next >**.

16. In the *Table Style* page, in the *Formatting and structure* area, type **Bill of Materials** for the title of the table, as shown in Figure 6–85.

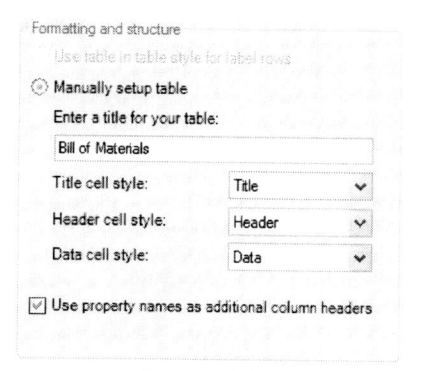

Figure 6–85

17. Click **Next >**.

18. Click **Finish** to close the Data Extraction Wizard.

19. Pick a point in the drawing inside the title block at which to insert the table. Note that the table contains only the Catalog and Manufacturer information, as shown in Figure 6–85.

20. Save and close the drawing.

Practice 6h — Mechanical Attribute Project - Amplifier

Estimated time for completion: 60+ minutes

In this practice, you will create and insert blocks with attributes (as shown in Figure 6–86), to store information about components in a drawing and then extract the attributes to a table. The commands to be used include: **Insert**, **Attribute Define**, **Attribute Edit**, **Synchronize Attributes**, and **Extract Attributes**.

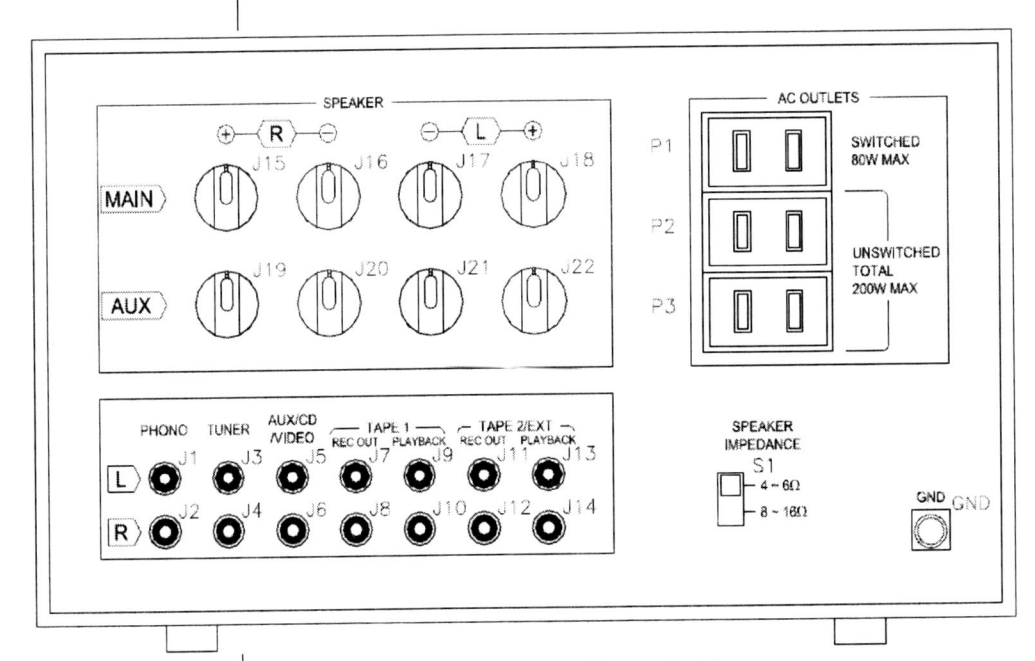

Figure 6–86

1. Open **Amplifier-I.dwg** from your practice files folder.

2. Insert the blocks **Speaker-Pos**, **Speaker-Neg**, **Phono-L**, and **Phono-R**, as shown in Figure 6–86. Each of these blocks has an attribute that you designate using the numbers J1 through J22.

3. Create the blocks with the attributes shown in Figure 6–87 for **Ground**, **Switch**, and **AC-Outlet**. Use the following parameters:
   - Draw the objects on layer **0**
   - Draw the attributes on layer **Text**
   - Set the *Text height* to **0.125**
   - Place the *DESIG* attribute over and above the upper right corner of the object and make it visible (leave all of the other Modes cleared).
   - The other attributes should be aligned below the first one and be invisible. They are the same for all four items but with different defaults. Therefore, you can make one set and copy it to the other two objects before creating the blocks.

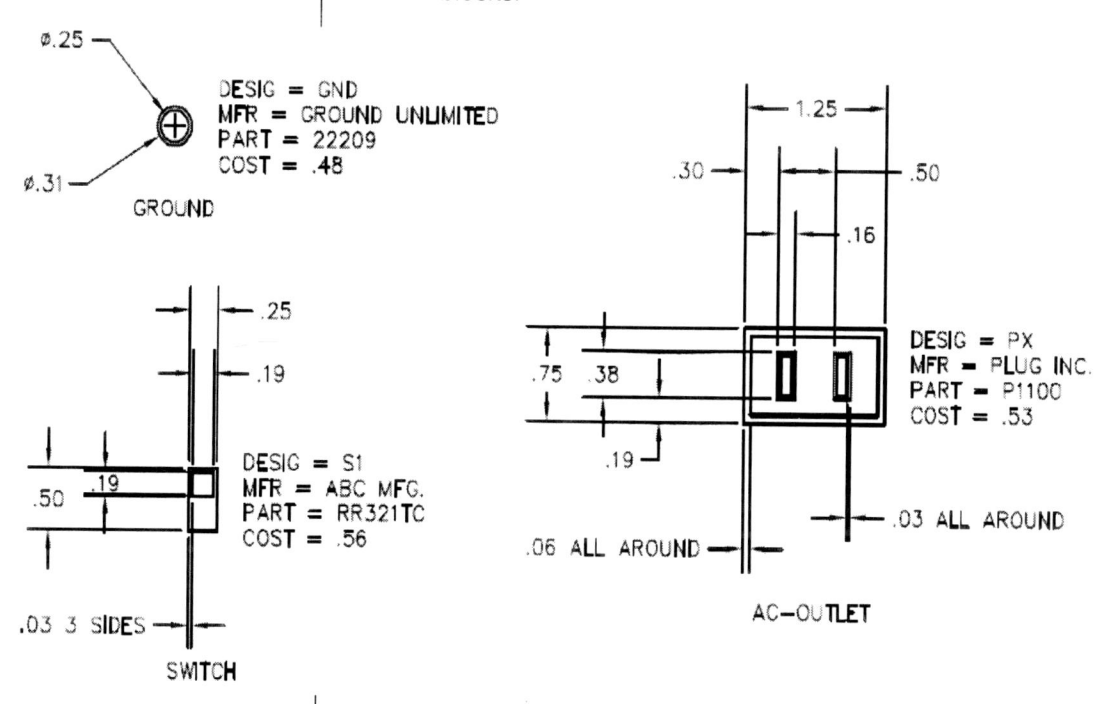

Figure 6–87

4. Insert the blocks on layer **Components** and fill in the attribute information, as shown in Figure 6–88.

5. Use grips to move the visible plug attributes (P1, P2, and P3) to the left side of the plugs, as shown in Figure 6–88.

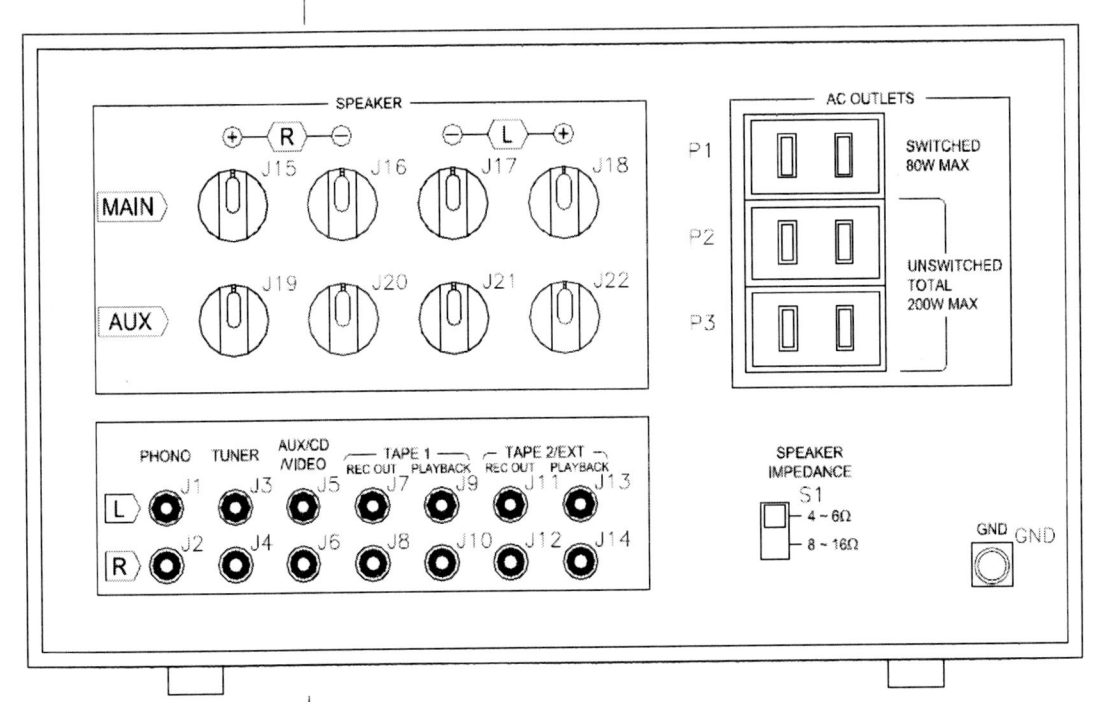

Figure 6–88

6. If time permits, create the **Speaker-Pos**, **Speaker-Neg**, **Phono-L**, and **Phono-R** blocks again that you inserted earlier with the added attributes shown in Figure 6–89. The *DESIG* attribute already exists.

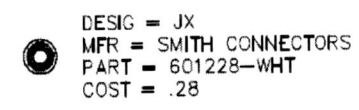

PHONO-L
DESIG = JX
MFR = SMITH CONNECTORS
PART = 601228–WHT
COST = .28

PHONO-R
DESIG = JX
MFR = SMITH CONNECTORS
PART = 601228–RED
COST = .28

SPEAKER-POS
DESIG = JX
MFR = H.R. JONES CO.
PART = 2819ORG
COST = .32

SPEAKER-NEG
DESIG = JX
MFR = H.R. JONES CO.
PART = 2819BLK
COST = .32

Figure 6–89

7. Use **Synchronize Attributes** to update the existing blocks with the new block definitions so that they include the new attributes.

8. Use **Edit Attributes** to fill in the attribute values for the blocks where they have already been inserted.

9. Use the **Data Extraction** command to create an AutoCAD® table for a parts list of the components, as shown in Figure 6–90. When selecting the attributes, include all of the blocks, except the *DESIG* attribute. Use the Standard table style and place the table in the layout.

Quantity	PART	Name	COST	MFR
\multicolumn{5}{c}{PART LIST}
1	22209	GROUND	.48	GROUND UNLIMITED
1	RR321TC	SWITCH	.56	ABC MFG.
3	P1100	AC–OUTLET	.53	PLUG INC.
4	2819ORG	SPEAKER–POS	.32	H.R. JONES CO.
4	2819BLK	SPEAKER–NEG	.32	H.R. JONES CO.
7	601228–WHT	PHONO–L	.28	SMITH CONNECTORS
7	601228–RED	PHONO–R	.28	SMITH CONNECTORS

Figure 6–90

10. Save the drawing.

6.15 Attaching External References

When you insert one drawing into another as a block, the graphics are merged and no link remains between the two files. External References enable you to combine files and retain the link, as shown in Figure 6–91. This serves two main purposes: it controls the file size because objects in the referenced drawing do not become part of the host drawing, and objects modified in the reference file are automatically updated in the host drawing because the files are linked.

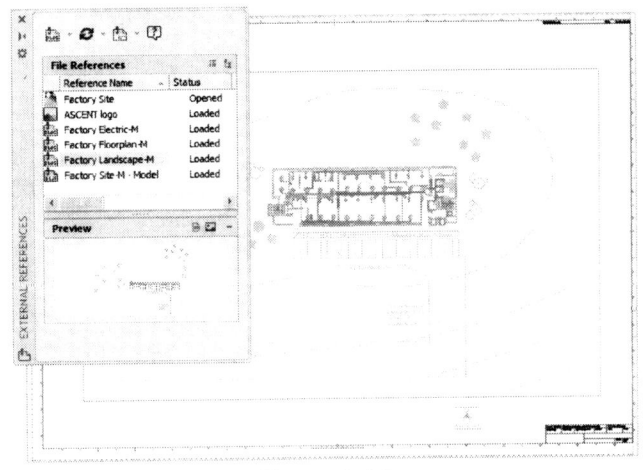

Figure 6–91

- Reference files enable members of a design team to share common source files and still have the most current information.

- External reference files can be managed through the External References palette.

Reuse Existing Content

Enhanced in 2018

- When you open a drawing that contains an external reference file that cannot be found, a References - Not Found Files warning box opens, as shown in Figure 6–92. These files also displays the ![warning] warning symbol with their file icon and an **!** (exclamation mark) besides the file in the External Reference palette.

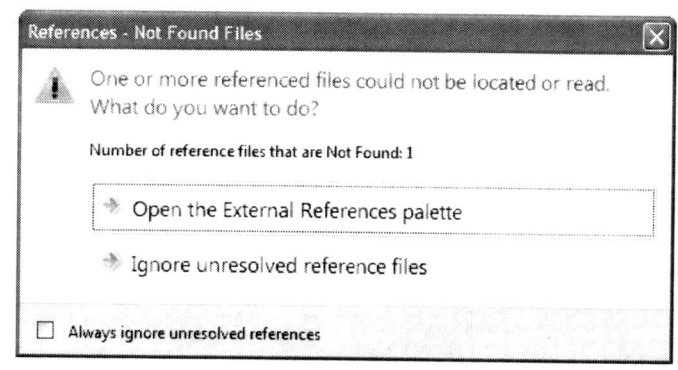

Figure 6–92

Several file formats can be used as external references:

AutoCAD® drawing files	Also known as Xrefs, they are connections to other drawings that you can edit in-place or externally, while retaining the link. You can turn layers on and off in the host drawing.
Raster image files	Various types of graphic files, such as GIF, JPG, and PNG. They can be renderings or scanned images that can be used as a reference as you trace over existing drawings.
DWF underlays	Non-editable files that include vector information that can be displayed in the DWF viewer and incorporated as an underlay in any drawing file.
DGN underlays	Files that come from the MicroStation platform. You can also import and export to DGN files.
PDF Underlays	Attach PDF files as underlays one page at a time.

External References Palette

You can use the External References palette (shown in Figure 6–93) to attach, unload, reload, and detach reference files. You can open a reference file in an appropriate software to make modifications to the original file and can also change the location in which the original file is saved if it is moved.

- You can open the External References palette by clicking in the *Insert* tab>Reference panel or by typing **Xref** in the Command Line.

- If you have a reference file in the drawing, you can right-click on it and select **External References** to open the palette.

- When you have external references in a drawing, (Manage Xrefs) displays near the right end of the Status Bar. Click it to open the External References palette.

(Manage Xrefs) does not display in the Status Bar until the drawing contains at least one xref.

The External References palette is similar to other palettes in that it can be either floating or docked and hidden.

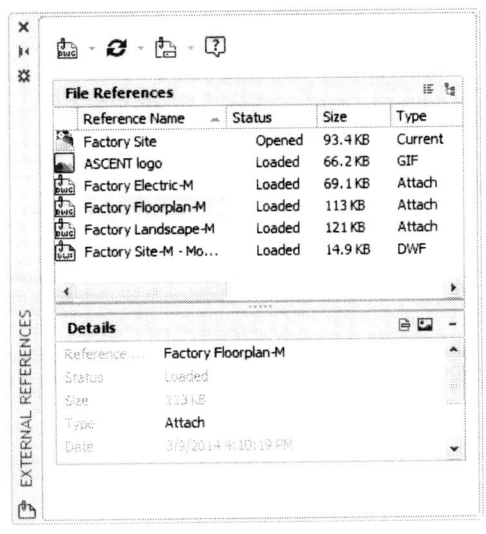

Figure 6–93

The External References palette is divided into two panes.

Top Pane

In the top pane, a list of file references displays as shown in Figure 6–94.

- By selecting the appropriate column heading, you can sort the files in the list according to name, status, size, date, and saved path.

Reuse Existing Content

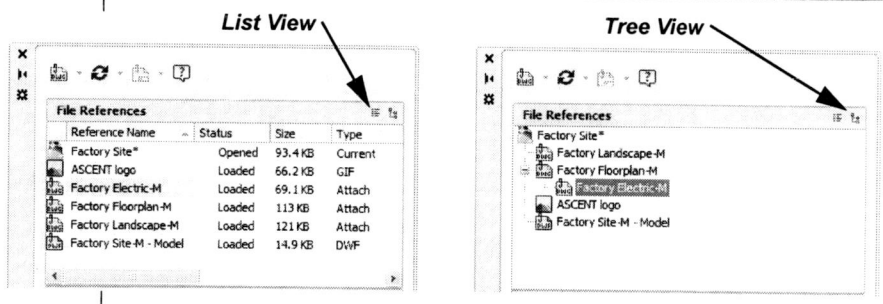

Figure 6–94

- ![List View icon] (List View) displays all of the attached external references and detailed information including: size, date, and saved path.

- ![Tree View icon] (Tree View) switches to an hierarchical view that displays nested reference files (i.e., drawings that are attached to referenced drawings). Double-click on a reference filename in Tree View to display or hide the nested reference files below it.

Bottom Pane

In the bottom pane, a list of details about a selected file or a preview of the file displays as shown in Figure 6–95.

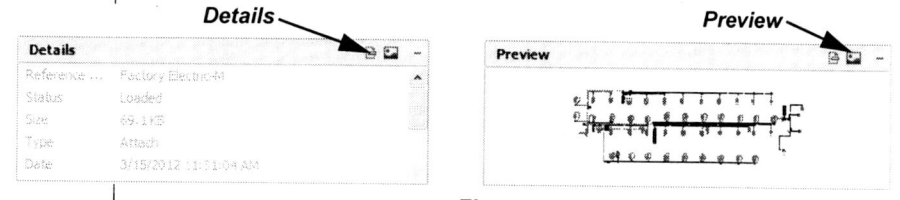

Figure 6–95

- ![Details icon] (Details) displays information about a selected file and enables you to modify the name of the reference. If the file is a drawing file, it enables you to modify the type of attachment.

- ![Preview icon] (Preview) displays a small image of the selected file.

How To: Attach a Reference File

You can also open the External References Palette by clicking the Reference panel arrow in the Insert tab.

1. In the *View* tab>Palettes panel, click (External References Palette).
2. In the External References palette, expand (Attach DWG) as shown in Figure 6–96, and select a file format to attach.

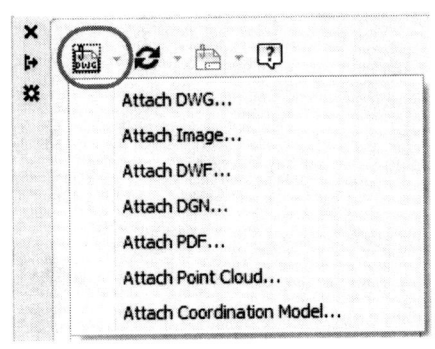

Figure 6–96

3. In the Select Reference File dialog box, select the file that you want to attach and click **Open**.
4. In the Attach External Reference dialog box, set the options as required, as shown in Figure 6–97.

The options and title of the dialog box (External Reference, Image, or Attach DWF Underlay) vary depending on the type of file selected. Several options are used in every situation.

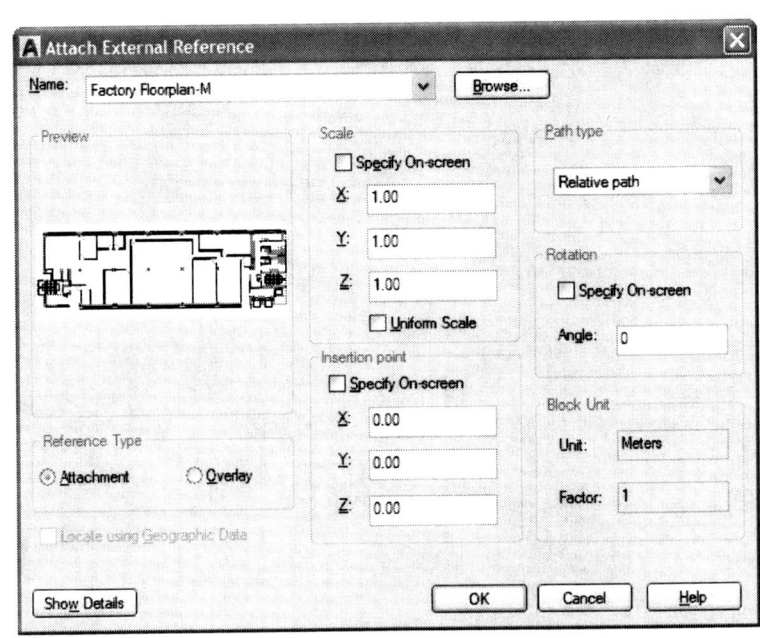

Figure 6–97

5. Click **OK**.
6. If you used the **Specify On-screen** option for *Insertion Point*, *Scale*, and *Rotation* in the dialog box, then specify them in the drawing window.

- You can use the Reference tools in the *Insert* tab> Reference panel to attach or modify various types of externally referenced files, as shown in Figure 6–98.

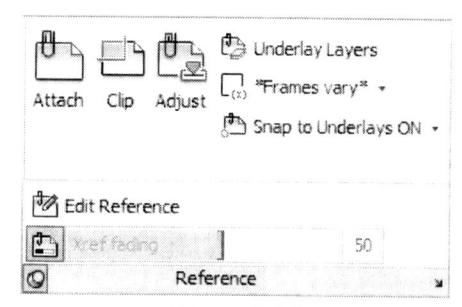

Figure 6–98

General Attachment Options

Enhanced in 2018

Name	Select a name from the list or click **Browse...** and select a different file to attach.
Path type	Controls how the AutoCAD software searches for the reference file to load it. By default, the Path type is set to **Relative Path**. It starts from the folder of the host drawing. **Full path** uses the entire path. With **No path**, the AutoCAD software searches in the current folder of the host drawing, and in the project paths, support paths, and *Start-in* folder.
Insertion Point, Scale, and Rotation Angle	These options are similar to the selections for block insertions. The values can be entered in the Attach External Reference dialog box or in the Command Line.

New in 2018

- When a drawing has an external reference that has been moved and cannot be found, the shortcut menu offers you options to find the file, as shown in Figure 6–99. The **Select New Path** option enables you to fix the missing path by selecting the file from the new location. Once the reference file's new location has been selected, the software prompts you to use the new path for the other missing references or leave the rest of the paths as is. The **Find and Replace** option opens the Find and Replace dialog box, which enables you to find the current path and replace all of its instances with the new path, all at once.

Enhanced in 2018

- The shortcut menu also provides you with the option of changing the path type by selecting **Change Path Type**. If the path type option of the selected reference file is grayed out and cannot be selected, it indicates that it is the one currently used. Figure 6–100 shows an example of the referenced file using the Relative Path type, which is grayed out to indicate that the path type is currently used.

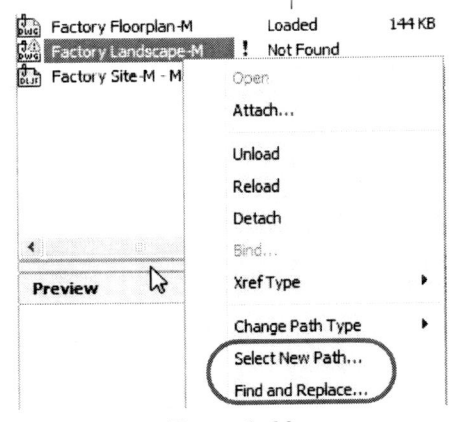

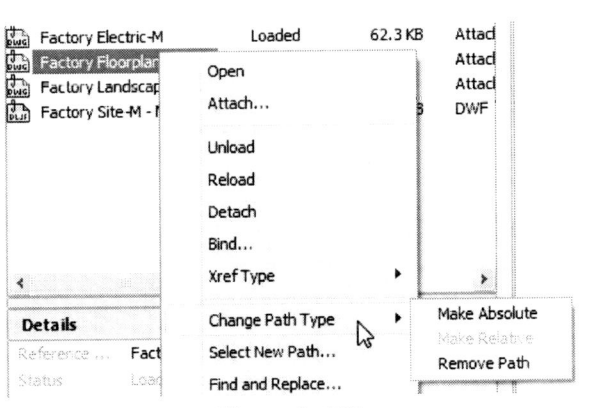

Figure 6–99   Figure 6–100

Xref Specific Attachment Options

Reference Type	Two types of references are available when one AutoCAD drawing is inserted into another: **Attachment** and **Overlay**.
Block Unit	The Insertion Scale units of the reference file and host drawings (expand Application Menu, expand Drawing Utilities, click ![0.0] (Units)) control the automatic scale factor that displays in the *Block Units* area.

Reuse Existing Content

Image Specific Attachment Options

You can attach an image as many times as required in the same drawing file. If a raster image by that name already exists in the drawing (even if the extension type is different) a Substitute Image Name dialog box opens in which you can type a new name. This is the name that displays in the External References palette.

DWF Specific Attachment Options

Select one or more sheets	If you are using a multi-sheet DWF file you can select any of the sheets to insert into the host drawing.

- If you set the *scale factor* to **Specify on Screen** then, at the *Specify Scale Factor or [Unit]:* prompt, you have the option to select the units of the existing drawing and have the software automatically scale the DWF file to those units. For example, if you are working in a drawing whose insertion scale units are set to **Meters** and the DWF file is in Architectural units, it automatically scales the DWF file by 0.0254. The default insertion scale unit is set to the current drawing units.

- You can insert multiple copies of a DWF file using the same sheet or different sheets in a multiple sheet file.

DGN Specific Attachment Options

MicroStation DGN file units are set up in *Master units* and *Sub units*. When you insert a DGN as an underlay, you need to specify the units that you want to convert. For example, if you attach a mechanical drawing that is created with *Master units* of millimeters and *Sub units* of thousandths of millimeters you would convert the *Master units*. However, if you are working with a file that has *Master units* of feet and *Sub units* of inches and you want to insert it into an AutoCAD Architectural unit file (which uses inches as its default units) you would convert the *Sub units*.

PDF Specific Attachment Options

Select one or more pages	If you are using a multi-sheet PDF file, you can select any sheet(s) to insert into the host drawing.

- All the supported objects in the PDF file are converted into 2D geometry, raster images, and TrueType text.

- If the PDF file contains SHX fonts, these are converted to separate geometric representations, which can be converted to multiline text objects using the **Recognize SHX Text** tool in the *Insert* tab>Import panel (**PDFSHXTEXT** command).

6.16 Modifying External References

When you have attached external references to your drawing, you can modify the way they function in the drawing.

- You can **Open**, **Unload**, **Reload**, and **Detach** individual references, as shown in Figure 6–101.

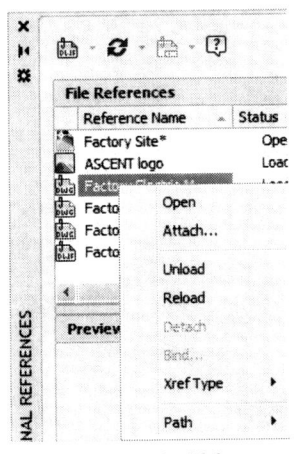

Figure 6–101

- All of the reference file formats can be clipped to display part of the reference. You can make changes to a selected reference in the Properties palette.

- You can use standard AutoCAD® commands, such as **Move**, **Rotate**, and **Scale** on references. Raster images can also be used to trim or extend to another object.

Opening Reference Files

You can modify a reference file in the software in which it was created and then reload it into the drawing. You can open a reference file from within the host drawing. Select the file in the External References palette, right-click, and select **Open**.

- A drawing reference file opens the drawing in the AutoCAD software.

- Image files open the image in the software with which the file format is associated.

- A360 Viewer is a free online file viewer provided by Autodesk® to help you view DWF files. To open it, use https://a360.autodesk.com/viewer/.

Reuse Existing Content

- DWF files also open in the Autodesk® Design Review software, if it is installed. DGN files cannot be opened with the AutoCAD software.

- You can also open drawing reference files by picking the reference in the drawing window, right-clicking and selecting **Open Xref**, as shown in Figure 6–102.

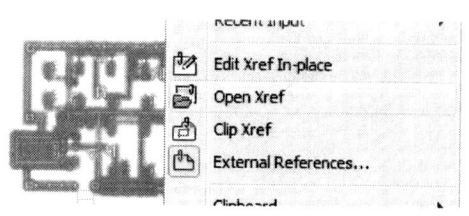

Figure 6–102

- When you return to the host file, an alert balloon opens in the Status Bar indicating that an external reference has changed, as shown in Figure 6–103. Select the link in the balloon to reload the reference. This message also displays when someone else changes a reference while you have the host file open.

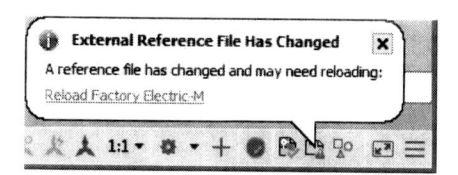

Figure 6–103

Detaching and Unloading Reference Files

There are two ways of removing a reference file from your drawing: **Unload** and **Detach** (as shown in Figure 6–104).

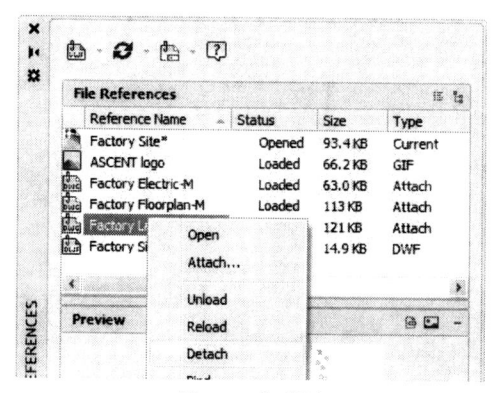

Figure 6–104

Detaching Files

Use **Detach** to permanently remove a reference file from your drawing.

- It severs the link between the current drawing and the external reference drawing.

- To get the reference back after detaching it, you need to re-attach it.

- If you have attached multiple copies of a DWF file, **Detach** removes all of them.

Unloading and Reloading Files

Enhanced in 2018

Use **Unload** to temporarily remove a reference file.

- When you unload a reference file, the AutoCAD software hides the reference geometry. However, it keeps the file in the External References palette list and remembers its insertion point, scale, and other attachment information.

- Unloading references that are not currently required causes a drawing to open and perform faster.

- To display an unloaded reference again, it must be reloaded using the **Reload** option.

- You can use the **Open** option in the shortcut menu to quickly open the unloaded reference file.

- Reloading loads the most recently saved version of the reference.

- All of the references reload automatically when you open the host drawing.

- Renaming the unloaded reference file in the External Reference palette does not automatically reload the renamed file. You have to explicitly reload it, as it remains unloaded till then.

Reuse Existing Content

- **Refresh** synchronizes information stored in memory when used with the Autodesk® Vault software.

- **Reload All References** (shown in Figure 6–105) updates all of the references in a drawing so that you are using the most up-to-date versions that have been saved.

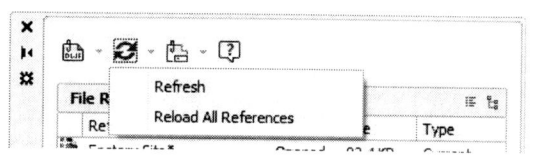

Figure 6–105

Clipping Reference Files

When you attach an external reference to your drawing, the entire reference file displays. However, you might not want the entire file to display, even in Model Space. You can control which part of the referenced file is visible by clipping it, as shown in Figure 6–106.

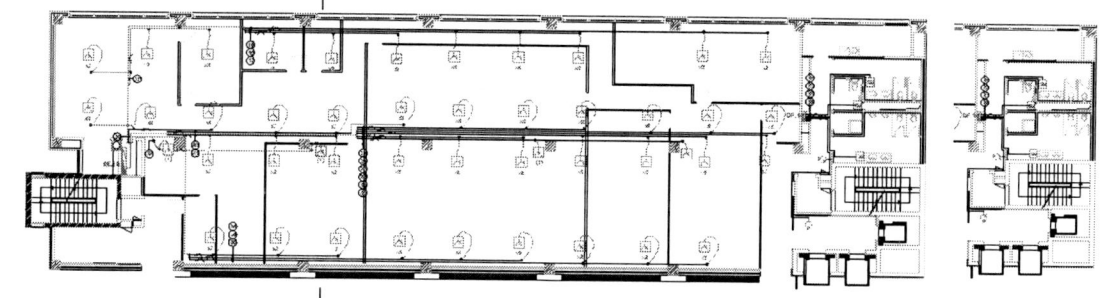

Figure 6–106

How To: Clip a Reference File

1. In the drawing, select the reference that you want to clip, right-click and select the appropriate **Clip** command for the type of reference selected. (Drawings: **Clip Xref**; Images: **Image>Clip**; DWF files: **DWF Clip**; DGN files: **DGN Clip**.)
2. Enter a **Clipping** option. Press <Enter> to accept the default **New boundary** option.
3. Select the **Rectangular** or **Polygonal** boundary option and draw a boundary.
4. Specify the points or existing polyline. The reference is clipped so the reference information outside the boundary is invisible.

If you have selected a drawing file, you have the additional option of selecting an existing polyline as the boundary.

© 2017, ASCENT - Center for Technical Knowledge®

- You can only clip one image, .DWF, or .DGN file at a time but you can clip multiple drawing files.

- Drawing reference files have an additional clip option: **Invert Clip**. Instead of masking everything outside the boundary it covers everything within the boundary. This can be very useful if you are working on a renovation project in which you are moving interior walls but not changing other parts of the building.

Other Clip Options

On/Off	Turns the clip boundary on or off without removing it from the reference. If the boundary is off the entire reference displays.
Clipdepth	Controls the front and back clipping planes in the Z-direction of the clip. Drawing reference files only.
Delete	Removes the clipping boundary from the reference files. You cannot use the **Erase** command to remove the clipping boundary.
Generate Polyline	Creates a polyline at the location of an existing clip boundary. This is a separate entity from the boundary. Drawing reference files only.

- If you run the command on a file that already has a boundary, the AutoCAD software prompts you to delete the current boundary first.

- To modify the clip boundary, start the associated **Clip** command. You can toggle the **Clip Boundary** on or off or delete it.

Clip Frames

The lines around clipped references are called *Clip Frames*. They can be toggled on or off for all of the references in a drawing using system variables that are related to each reference type: **xclipframe** for drawing references, **imageframe**, **dwfframe**, **pdfframe**, and **dgnframe**, as shown in Figure 6–107.

Frame ON   *Frame OFF*

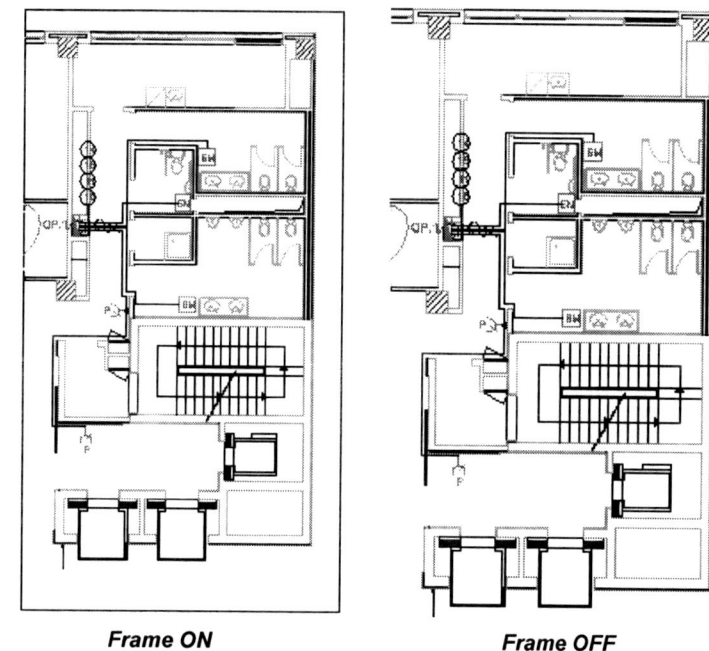

Figure 6–107

- **Frame Boundaries** have three options. When set to **0**, the boundary is invisible. When set to **1**, the boundary is visible. When set to **2**, the boundary is visible but does not plot.

- When the boundary is visible, you can select the external reference by selecting the boundary or any visible part of the reference file.

Modifying References

When you select the border of a reference file, a contextual tab displays according to the type of reference file that was selected. A DWF underlay has panels for Adjust, Clipping, Options, and DWF Layers, as shown in Figure 6–108. PDF and DGN underlays are the same.

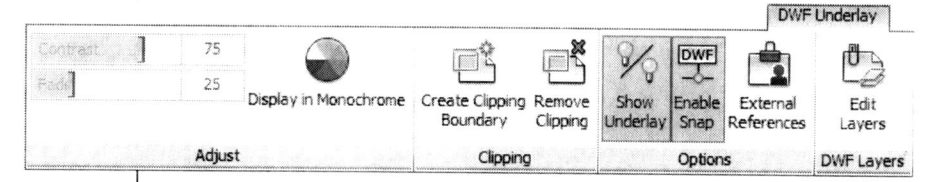

Figure 6–108

Modification options for drawing reference files include editing the reference, clipping, and access to the External References palette, as shown in Figure 6–109.

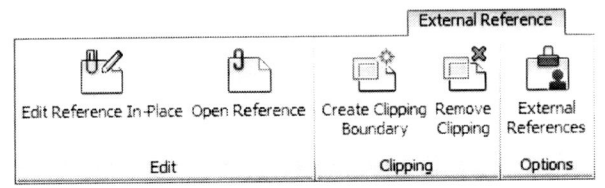

Figure 6–109

Image panels include Adjust and Clipping, and an additional **Transparency** option, as shown in Figure 6–110.

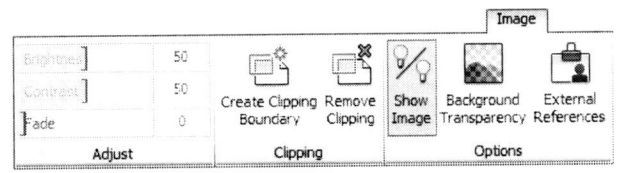

Figure 6–110

- Underlays and image references can only be selected when the frame surrounding them is on. You can change the state of the frames in the *Insert* tab>Reference panel, as shown in Figure 6–111.

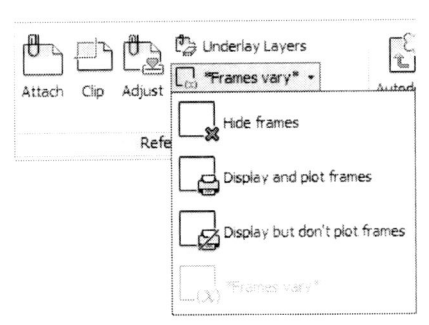

Figure 6–111

Reference File Properties

DWF, DGN, and Image references have several properties that can be modified, including how and what they display in the drawing.

These options can be modified in the Properties palette.

Reuse Existing Content

Miscellaneous Options

In the *Misc* area in the Properties palette, you can toggle off DWF or DGN underlays or Images without unloading the files. Set *Show image* to **No**, as shown in Figure 6–112.

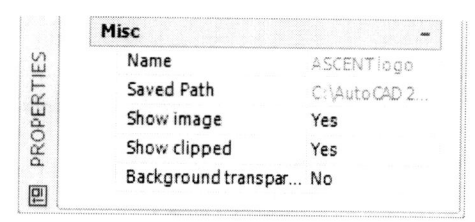

Figure 6–112

- The **Show clipped** option changes the status of displaying whether the object is clipped or not clipped. This is different than displaying the clipping frame.

- Images have the additional **Background Transparency** option. This permits the background of the image to become transparent, so that it matches the general background. However, not all of the file formats enable transparency. You can also access this option in the ribbon and in the shortcut menu under **Image**.

Adjusting Underlays and Images

DWF and DGN underlays and image reference properties can be adjusted.

- With a reference file selected, in the Properties palette, in the *Underlay Adjust* or *Image Adjust* areas, you can specify the amount of *Contrast* and *Fade*, as shown in Figure 6–113. DWF and DGN files can be set to **Monochrome** and Image files have an additional **Brightness** adjustment.

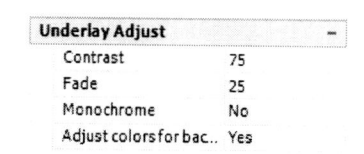

Figure 6–113

- DWF underlays have an option to adjust the colors for the background.

© 2017, ASCENT - Center for Technical Knowledge®   6–95

- Click (Adjust) in the *Insert* tab>Reference panel to adjust the *Fade*, *Contrast*, or *Monochrome* settings for underlay and image files.

- Image references can also be adjusted in the *Image Adjust* contextual tab as shown in Figure 6–114. A preview of the changes displays in the drawing window as the modifications are made. The contextual tab is opened by selecting the underlay or image.

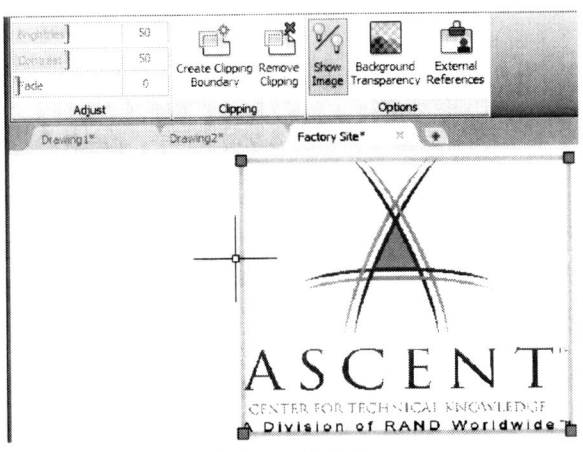

Figure 6–114

- The quality of an image can be set to **High** or **Draft** by typing **imagequality** at the Command Line.

> **Hint: Creating an Image File**
>
> In the AutoCAD software, there are several ways of creating a raster file, which can then be used as an image:
>
> - You can copy the contents of the current viewport using **saveimg** at the Command Line. The image can be saved in the .BMP, .PCX, .TGA, .TIF, .JPEG, or .PNG file formats.
>
> - You can render the display to a file (usually done with 3D objects). Rendering can create several different raster formats.

DWF Specific Adjustments

DWF reference files have two additional options because they are created from drawing files: toggling layers on and off and snapping to objects in the DWF underlay.

Reuse Existing Content

- Layer visibility can be controlled in DWF underlays (as shown in Figure 6–115), if the DWF file was created with the layers toggled on. When you have selected a DWF underlay, right-click and select **DWF Layers**. Select the layers you want to toggle on or off and click **OK**.

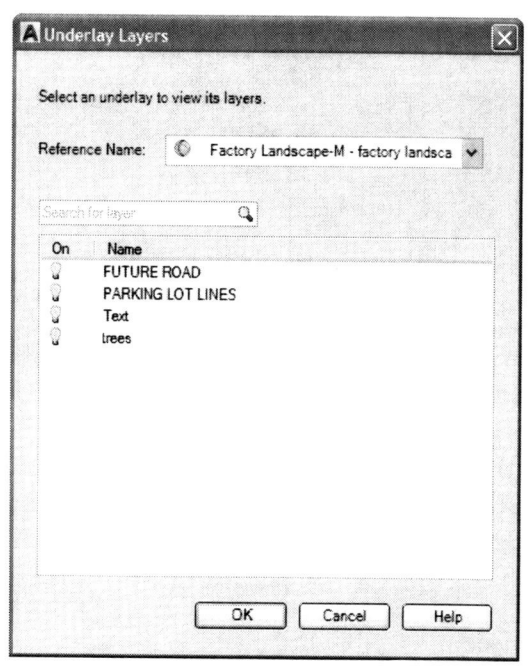

Figure 6–115

- To adjust another reference file's layers, select it in the Reference Name drop-down list.

- If a reference file does not contain layers, this is indicated in the Underlay Layers dialog box. By default, layers are not saved in the **DWF6ePlot.pc3** file supplied with the software.

- You can snap to objects in a DWF underlay. If you do not want object snaps to work with DWF files, select the DWF underlay, right-click and clear **DWF Object Snap**, as shown in Figure 6–116. This impacts all of the DWF underlays in a drawing.

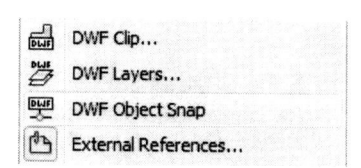

Figure 6–116

6.17 Xref Specific Information

The reference file tools works slightly differently with drawing references (also known as Xrefs). Because drawing reference files contain the same components as the host files, you can manipulate them using methods that cannot be applied to raster images, .DWF, and .DGN files. You can set drawing reference files to be attachments or overlays and can modify Xref layer states in the host drawing without impacting the original file. You can also import (bind) layers and block components of the drawing reference file into your drawing.

Attachments vs. Overlays

You can specify whether a drawing reference file should be an attachment or an overlay when it is originally referenced. Attachments and overlays work in the same way in the host file. You only notice the difference if you reference that host file in another file, as shown in Figure 6–117.

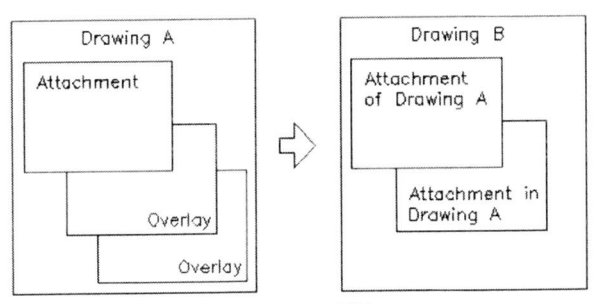

Figure 6–117

Attachment	When a file is referenced as an attachment, it displays with the host file if the host file itself is then referenced in another drawing. Using attachments enables a file to travel along the path with its host. A typical use for this option would be if there were a part referenced inside a subassembly, which is then referenced into a larger assembly.
Overlay	When a file is referenced as an overlay, it does not display in the host file if the host file itself is referenced in another drawing. Using overlays helps to avoid problems of circular references. (Circular references occur when a file references itself, usually indirectly. For example, drawing A references drawing B, which references drawing C, which references drawing A.)

Reuse Existing Content

- To change a drawing reference file from an attachment to an overlay, select the reference in the External References palette and modify it in the **Details** pane, as shown in Figure 6–118.

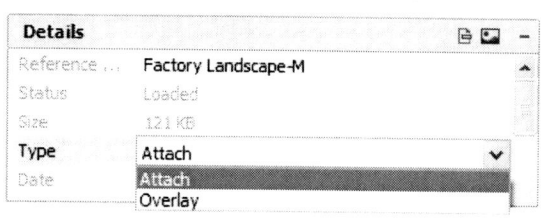

Figure 6–118

- You can also right-click on a filename(s) in the External References palette, expand Xref Type, and select **Overlay**.

Xref Layers

When you attach or overlay a drawing reference file, it brings the drawing objects and its named objects, such as layers and blocks, into the host drawing.

- A special prefix is added to any named objects from the referenced drawing when the names display in the host drawing, as shown in Figure 6–119. It consists of the name of the referenced drawing and a "¦". For example, a layer **Walls** in a reference file named **House5** would display as **House5¦Walls**.

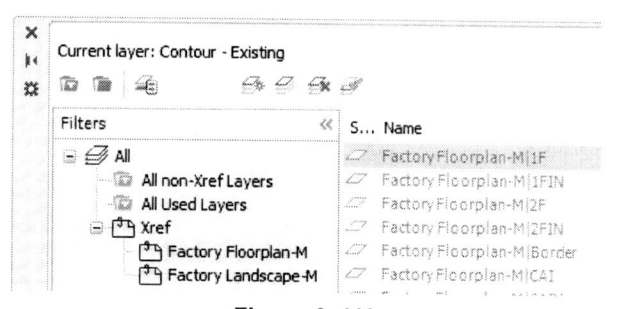

Figure 6–119

- In order to clearly distinguish which layers come from referenced drawings and which layer reside in the active drawing, xref layers are now shown in gray text in the *Home tab>Layers panel>Layers drop-down list*, as shown in Figure 6–120. Additionally, you can only change the visibility of xref layers in the layer panel drop-down.

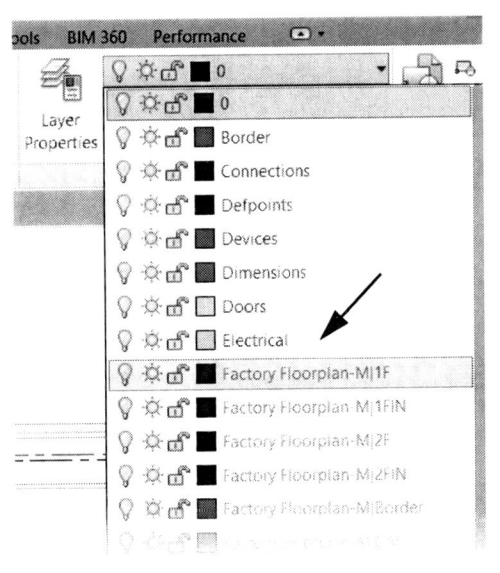

Figure 6–120

- If the Xref layers display in the Layer Control, you can change their state or properties (**Freeze/Thaw**, **Color**, etc.). However, you cannot make an Xref layer current in the host drawing.

- The layer on which the drawing reference file is inserted controls the visibility of the drawing reference file. The drawing reference file is hidden when that layer is frozen.

- If you change the properties of an Xref layer, the change does not affect the referenced drawing. However, the change is retained in the host drawing by default. The default is controlled by the **visretain** system variable. You can also modify it in the Options dialog box, in the *Open and Save* tab, by toggling the **Retain changes to Xref layers** option on or off.

- In Layer Properties Manager you can quickly display all of the layers in a specific drawing reference file by selecting the filter that is automatically created when the drawing reference file is attached. You can then use **Select All** and modify the layers as required.

- You can now control the display of layers for objects in an xref drawing that were not set to "ByLayer" for the layer property updates in the original xref. The new **XREFOVERRIDE** variable enables objects in the reference file to override properties set in the drawing file it is referenced into (host file). Setting the **XREFOVERRIDE** to **1** enables the original file to set the properties. Setting the **XREFOVERRIDE** to **0** enables the drawing in which it is referenced to control the properties.

Binding Drawing Reference Files

The **Bind** option in a drawing reference file copies all of the referenced drawing's data into the current drawing and then detaches the reference. The referenced drawing becomes an inserted block.

How To: Bind a Drawing Reference File

1. Open the External References palette.
2. Right-click on the drawing reference file that you want to bind in the list and select **Bind**.
3. In the *Bind Type* area, select **Bind** or **Insert** (as shown in Figure 6–121) and click **OK**.

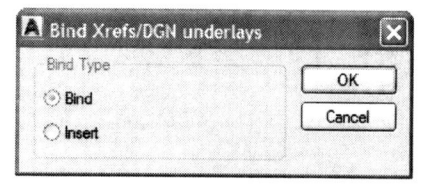

Figure 6–121

When a drawing reference file is bound, it brings all of its layers, blocks, and other named objects into the host drawing. The **Bind Type** controls how these named objects are named in the host drawing.

- When you use the *Bind Type* **Bind**, the object names are prefixed with the name of the reference file (filename0layername). For example, if the layer **Ref¦Floor** (from the drawing **Ref.dwg**) was bound to the current drawing, its name would become **Ref0Floor**. This can result in long names, but keeps the layers that were originally in the drawing reference file separate from the layers that were originally in the host file.

Binding Drawing Reference File Components

- When a drawing reference file is bound as an **Insert**, the block and layer names are added to the current file without change. For example, the Xref layer **Ref¦Floor** would become **Floor**. If the current file contains a block or layer with the same name, the drawing reference file object is updated to match the definition already in the current drawing.

- Binding a drawing reference file as an **Insert** is equivalent to detaching the reference file and inserting it as a block.

Instead of binding the entire drawing reference file, you can bind one or more blocks, layers, linetypes, text styles, and dimension styles. Binding any of these named objects adds their definition to the host drawing so that you can use them in the drawing.

- The **Xbind** command, accessed in the Command Line, enables you to bind specific named objects from a drawing reference file (such as layers or blocks).

- **Xbind** opens the Xbind dialog box (shown in Figure 6–122), in which you can select the drawing reference file from which to bind, the type of object (layer, block, etc.), and the specific named object to bind. Click the **+** sign to display the listings under each category. Select the object and click **Add** to add it for binding.

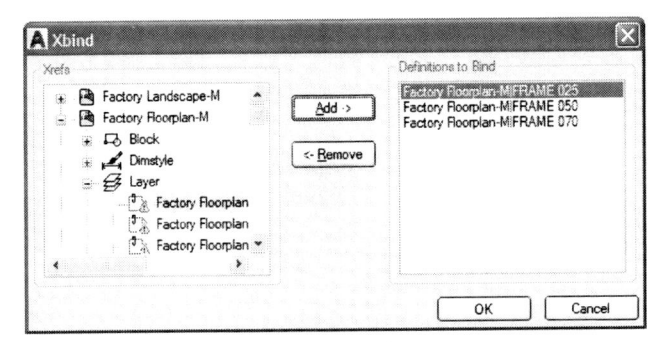

Figure 6–122

- When named objects are bound with **Xbind**, the "¦" in the name is replaced with "0". For example, the block **Office3¦Lamp** becomes **Office3$0$Lamp**. There is no option, such as **Insert**, to add the name without a change. However, you can rename the resulting objects using **Rename**.

- You can use DesignCenter to copy these components into your current drawing without using the long names.

Demand Loading

Demand Loading controls how much of a drawing reference file is loaded. With **Demand Loading** enabled, only the visible parts of the drawing reference file (that are not clipped or on layers that are off or frozen) are loaded. Since it does not have to load the entire drawing reference file, the AutoCAD software responds more quickly.

- **Demand Loading** can be set in the Options dialog box, in the *Open and Save* tab, by selecting the **Demand load Xrefs** options, as shown in Figure 6–123.

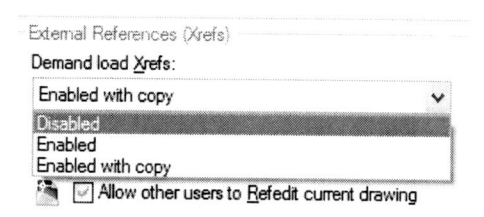

Figure 6–123

- When **Demand Loading** is enabled, others cannot edit the file that is being referenced. To enable others to use the file that is being referenced and take advantage of the improved performance, set *Demand Loading* to **Enabled with copy**. A copy of the file is used in place of the drawing reference file, so that others can use the file.

Practice 6i

Estimated time for completion: 35 minutes

Attaching External References

Practice Objectives

- Attach and modify external references and overlay drawing references.
- Adjust the layers in a referenced file.
- Bind a reference to a file.

In this practice, you will attach and modify external references using the External References palette. You will also attach and overlay drawing references and note how they function in another file. You will then adjust layers in a referenced file and bind a reference to a file, as shown in Figure 6–124.

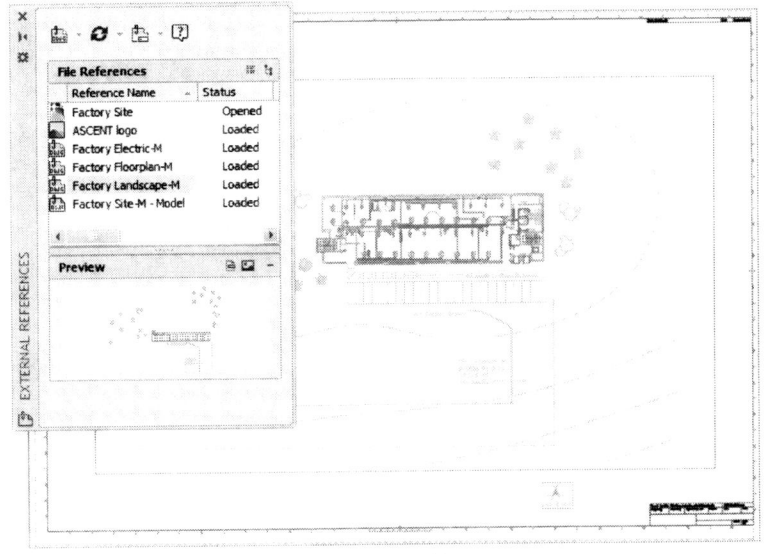

Figure 6–124

Task 1 - Attach external references.

In this task you will explore the features of the External References palette. You will attach a Reference File DWG, Raster Image, and DWF Underlay.

1. Start a new drawing based on **Civil-Meters.dwt**, which is located in your practice files folder and save the drawing as **Factory Site.dwg**.

2. In the *View* tab>Palettes panel, click (External References Palette) to open the External References palette.

Reuse Existing Content

3. Near the top of the External References palette, expand ![icon] (Attach DWG) and select **Attach DWF...**.

4. In the Select Reference File dialog box, open **Factory Site-M.dwf** from your practice files folder.

5. In the Attach DWF Underlay dialog box, for *Insertion point*, clear Specify on-screen and verify X,Y,Z values are set as **0,0,0**. Select **Specify on-screen** for the *Scale*. Click **OK** to continue.

6. Right-click and select **Unit**. Verify that **Meter** is selected and press <Enter> to accept the default selection.

7. Press <Enter> to finish placing the DWF underlay.

8. Using the above steps, and using **Attach DWG**, attach **Factory Floorplan-M.dwg** from your practice files folder at **0,0,0** *Insertion point* with the default scale and rotation. Verify that the *Reference Type* is set to **Attachment**.

9. **Zoom Extents** to display **Factory Site-M.dwf** and **Factory Floorplan-M.dwg**.

10. Attach **Factory Landscape-M.dwg** from your practice files folder at any location (*Insertion point*: **Specify On-screen**) at one side of the drawing (you will move it later).

11. Close the External References palette.

12. In the Status Bar, click ![icon] (Manage Xrefs) to open the External References palette.

13. Select **Factory Landscape-M.dwg** and in the Details pane, click ![icon] (Preview) to display an image of the landscape reference file.

14. Switch to the **ISO A0** layout. Activate the viewport and **Zoom Extents**.

15. Activate the Paper Space (double-click outside the viewport) and using **Attach Image**, attach **ASCENT logo.gif** from your practice files folder at a scale of **50**. Place it near the left of the title block.

16. Save the file.

Task 2 - Modify external references.

In this task you will move a reference file to a new location, clip a DWF file, open a reference file and make a change to that drawing, close and reload it, and detach and unload it. The completed drawing is shown in Figure 6–125.

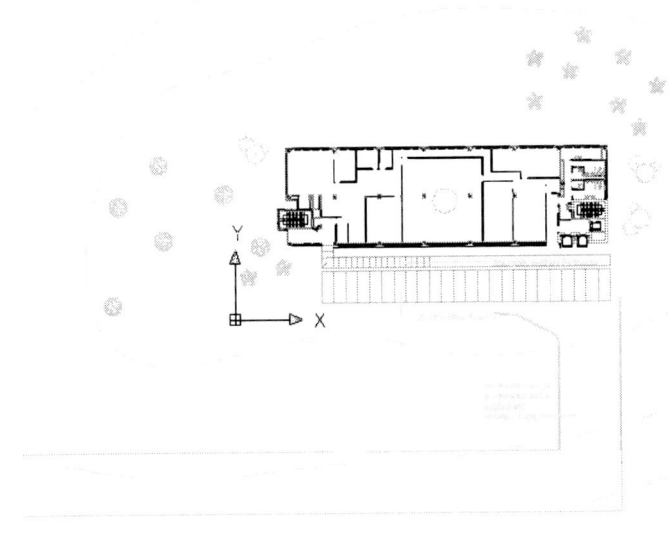

Figure 6–125

1. Switch to the *Model* tab and select **Factory Site-M.dwf** (outer rectangle). Right-click and verify that **DWF Object Snap** is enabled, as shown in Figure 6–126. Press <ESC> to exit selection.

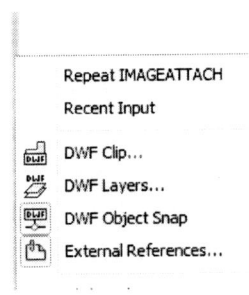

Figure 6–126

2. Move **Factory Landscape-M.dwg** (file with trees) so that the existing road in the DWF file is at the end of the new entrance to the parking lot, as shown in Figure 6–127.

Hint: In the landscape drawing, use the bottom left endpoint of the vertical portion of the road as your base point and move it to the right endpoint of the top horizontal line of the road in the site dwf.

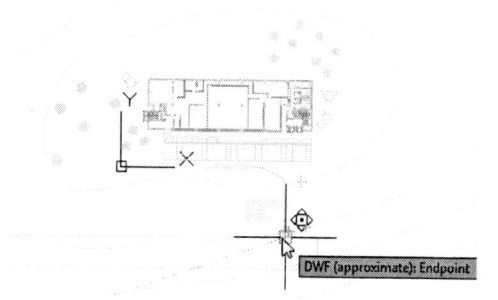

Figure 6–127

3. Select **Factory Site-M.dwf** (outer rectangle), right-click and select **DWF Clip...**. Press <Enter> to accept the **New boundary** option and create a new rectangular boundary close to the landscape elements, building, and road, similar to the area shown in Figure 6–125.

4. Type **dwfframe** and set the *system variable* to **0** to hide the boundary frame.

5. Check the Layer Control, and note that the layers associated with **Factory Floorplan-M.dwg** are listed but they are grayed out.

6. In the External References palette, detach **Factory Floorplan-M.dwg** (Right-click and select **Detach**). The building is removed from the drawing window and the file is removed from the External References palette.

7. Save the drawing.

8. Attach **Factory Floorplan-M.dwg** from your practice files folder to your file at an *Insertion point* of **0,0,0** and a *Rotation* of **0**.

9. In the External References palette, unload **Factory Floorplan-M.dwg** (right-click and select **Unload**). Note that the building is removed from the drawing window but the file is still listed in the palette with a red arrow displayed along with it, as shown in Figure 6–128.

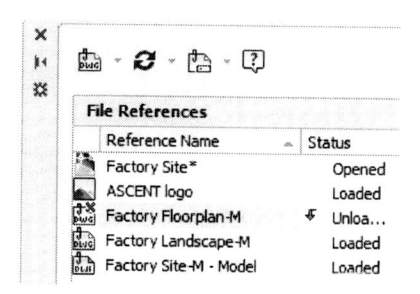

Figure 6–128

10. Reload **Factory Floorplan-M.dwg**. (Right-click and select **Reload**).

11. In the External References palette, select **Factory Floorplan-M.dwg**. Right-click and select **Open**.

12. Set the layer **Equipment** to be current and draw a circle with a *radius* of **2** near the middle of the floorplan.

13. Save and close **Factory Floorplan-M.dwg**.

14. In **Factory Site.dwg**, note that the new circle is not displayed. In the External References palette, reload **Factory Floorplan-M.dwg**. Note that the new circle displays.

15. Save and close the drawing.

Task 3 - Attach and overlay drawing references in another file.

In this task you will attach and overlay drawing references and note how they function in another file. You will then adjust layers in a referenced file and finally bind a reference to a file. The completed drawing is shown in Figure 6–129.

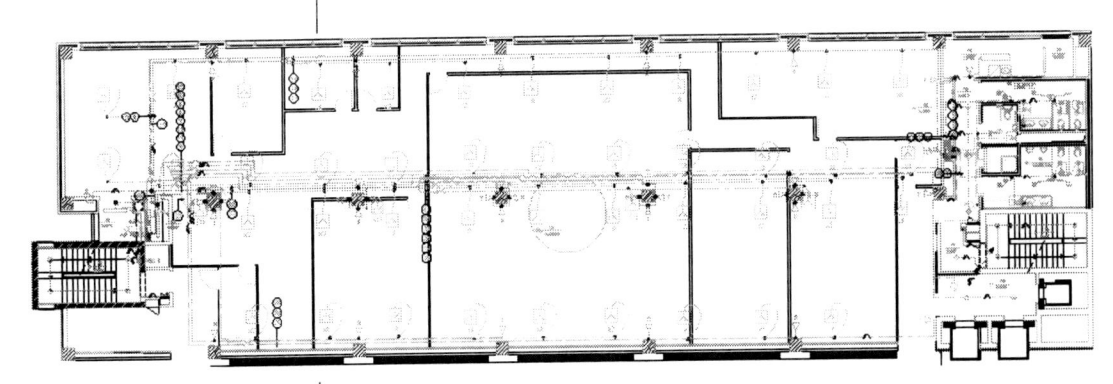

Figure 6–129

1. Open **Factory Floorplan-M.dwg** from your practice files folder.

2. Set layer **0** to be current and attach **Factory Electric-M.dwg** from your practice files folder to the current drawing at **0,0,0** as an attachment. Accept the defaults for the *Scale*, *Rotation*, and other options.

Reuse Existing Content

You can also change it in the Details pane.

3. Attach **Factory Lighting-M.dwg** from your practice files folder to the current drawing at **0,0,0**. Accept the defaults for the other options.

4. In the External References palette, right-click on **Factory Lighting-M.dwg**, expand **Xref Type**, and select **Overlay**. Close the palette. The overlay file remains visible in the drawing.

5. Save and close the drawing.

6. Open **Factory Site.dwg** if it is not already open. Note that the attached reference **Factory Electric-M.dwg** displays but the overlaid lighting reference is not.

7. Save and close the drawing.

Task 4 - Work with drawing reference file layers.

1. Open **Factory Floorplan-M.dwg** from your practice files folder.

2. Make a layer other than **0** current (it must be a layer found in the host drawing such as 2FIN) and freeze layer **0**. The other reference files, which were inserted on layer **0**, are hidden, as shown in Figure 6–130.

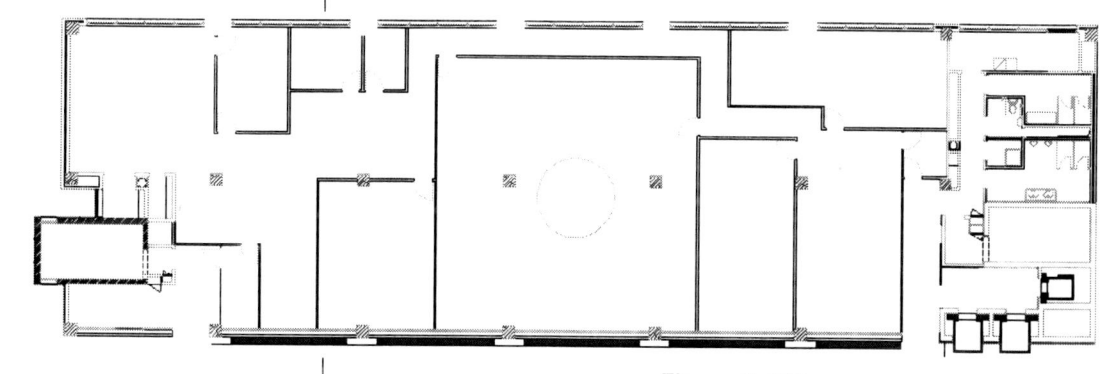

Figure 6–130

3. Thaw layer **0** and make it current again.

4. Expand the Layer Control and note the layers that begin with **Factory Electric-M** and **Factory Lighting-M** are all gray. All of these layers belong to the drawing reference files.

5. Open the Layer Properties Manager.

6. In the left pane, expand the Xref file group and select **Factory Electric-M**. All of the layers in the drawing reference file display in the right pane.

7. In the right pane, right-click and select **Select All**.

8. Select one of the color blocks and change the *color* to **light gray**. The selected layers display in that color in the current drawing. Change the *Layer Filter* back to **All**.

9. Save and close the file.

10. Open **Factory Electric-M.dwg** and verify that the layers retain their original colors. Close the file.

11. Open **Factory Floorplan-M.dwg**. The layers from the **Factory Electric-M.dwg** referenced drawing are still gray.

Task 5 - Bind drawing reference files.

1. Continue working in **Factory Floorplan-M.dwg**.

2. In the External References palette, right-click on **Factory Lighting-M.dwg** and select **Bind...** to bind it to the host file. In the dialog box click **OK**.

3. In the Layer Properties Manager, note that all of the Factory Lighting M layers contain 0 and have turned black, as shown in Figure 6–131. (Tip: Set the *Layer Filter* to **All**.)

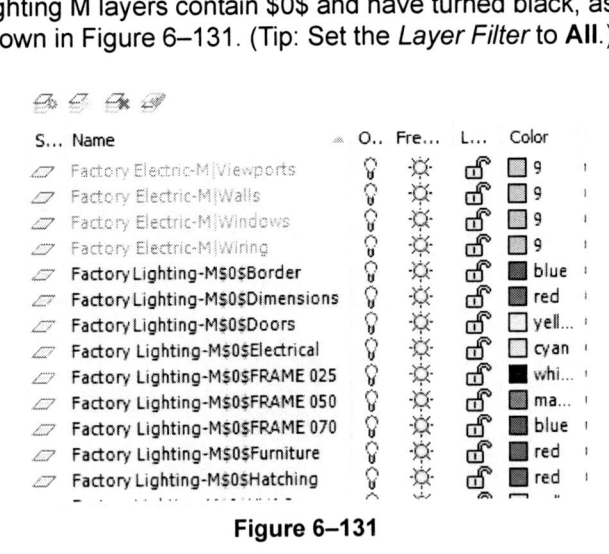

Figure 6–131

4. Undo the **Bind** process.
5. **Bind** the same file again, but this time as an **Insert**.
6. Look at the layers. They are now integrated into the main layer names.
7. Save and close the drawing.
8. Reopen **Factory Site.dwg** and update the change to the reference as required. The Lighting objects now display in the current drawing because they are no longer just an overlay in the referenced file.
9. Save the drawing.

Chapter 7

Annotate Drawings

This chapter includes instructional content to assist in your preparation for the following topic and objectives for the AutoCAD® Certified Professional exam.

Autodesk Certification Exam Objectives in this Chapter

Exam Topic	Exam Objective	Section(s)
Annotate Drawings	• Add and modify text	• 7.1 to 7.3
	• Use dimensions	• 7.4 to 7.7
	• Add and modify multileaders	• 7.8
	• Create and assign annotative styles	• 7.9 to 7.14
	• Use tables	• 7.15 to 7.18

7.1 Adding Text in a Drawing

Many drawings include notes about the objects and about the project, as shown in Figure 7–1. This might be a set of general notes in the titleblock or notes specific to a particular view.

Multiline Text

You can use the **Multiline Text** command to create, edit, and format paragraphs of text.

Text should be placed on its own layer.

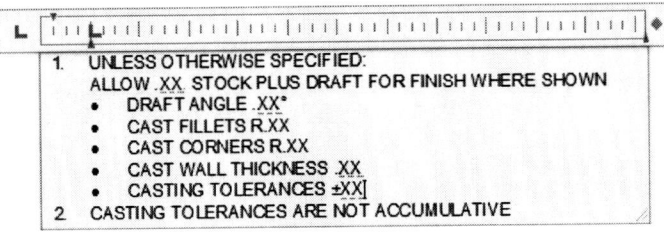

Figure 7–1

- Any text created in the Text Editor becomes one object, no matter how many lines it contains. Because you type it in a Text Editor, the text automatically wraps at the end of the line.

- Set the layer and the text style before you start the **Multiline Text** command. The text style sets the default font and height of the text.

How To: Add Multiline Text

1. In the *Annotate* tab>Text panel or in the *Home* tab> Annotation panel, click A (Multiline Text).
   - An example text string (abc) displays near the cursor as shown in Figure 7–2. This preview indicates the current text height and font.

If you are creating an annotative object, you might be prompted to set the annotation scale.

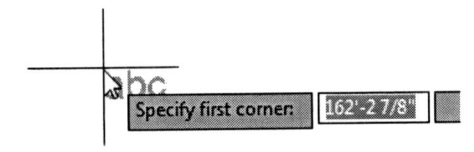

Figure 7–2

2. Select two points in the drawing to define a boundary box for the text. The Text Editor opens, as shown in Figure 7–3.

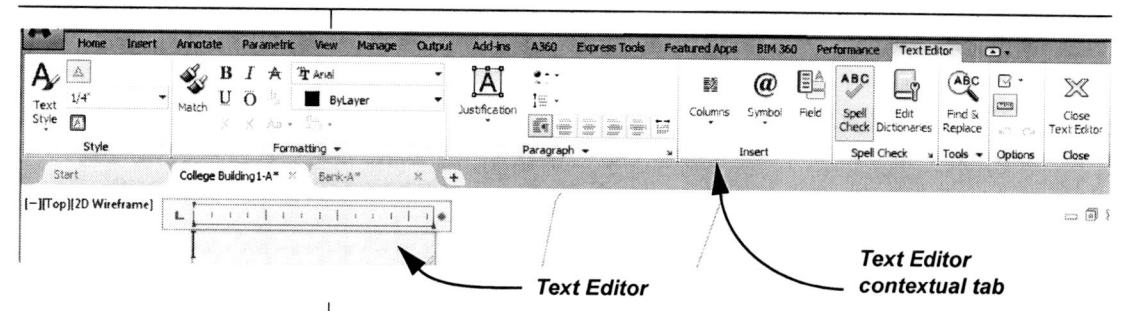

Annotate Drawings

Figure 7–3 — Text Editor / Text Editor contextual tab

- When creating the boundary box for the text, an arrow displays indicating the direction in which the text is going to flow, based on the current vertical justification. The boundary determines the position of the text and its width (i.e., the length of a line before words wrap to the next line), but does not limit the number of lines you can type.

3. Type the text in the Text Editor and apply formatting options from the contextual tab.
4. Click ✕ (Close Text Editor) or click in the drawing window to finish creating the text. The text is inserted in the drawing as one object.

- The background of the text editor is transparent. This enables any drawing objects that are covered by the text box to be displayed.

How To: Set the Text Height

1. In the *Annotate* tab>Text panel or in the *Home* tab>Annotation panel, click **A** (Multiline Text).
2. Select the first point of the boundary box.
3. Select **Height** from the Command Line or shortcut menu (<Down Arrow>), as shown in Figure 7–4.

*The text height specified with the **Height** option becomes the default text height for that text style. If you change the text height in the Text Editor, it is not saved.*

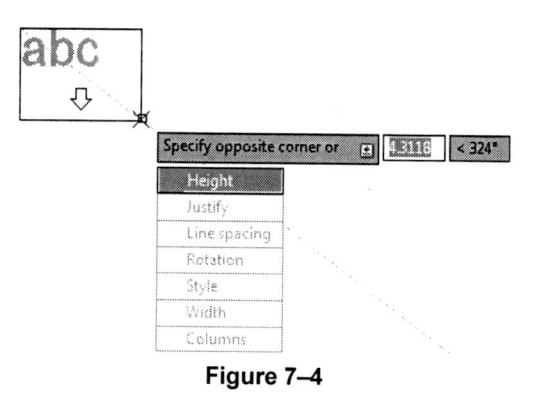

Figure 7–4

© 2017, ASCENT - Center for Technical Knowledge®

4. Enter the text height and press <Enter>.
5. Select the other point of the boundary box.

- Text can be placed in Paper Space or Model Space. In most cases, and especially if you are using an annotative text style, you should specify the height of the text to be the final plotted size.

Copying and Importing Text

You can copy text from a word processing software or other text editor and paste it directly into the Text Editor, as shown in Figure 7–5. You can also import text files that are saved in the ASCII or RTF format.

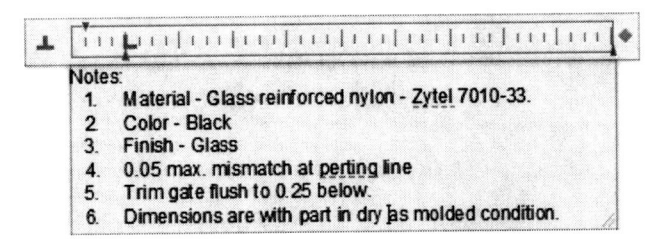

Figure 7–5

How To: Copy and Paste Text into the Text Editor

1. In a document file, copy the text to the Windows Clipboard.
2. In the AutoCAD software, in the *Annotate* tab>Text panel or in the *Home* tab>Annotation panel, click A (Multiline Text).
3. Select points for the boundary box.
4. In the Text Editor, right-click and select **Paste**. The text you copied is pasted into the Text Editor.

- If you use **Paste Special**, you can set the copied text to be pasted without character or paragraph formatting, as shown in Figure 7–6.

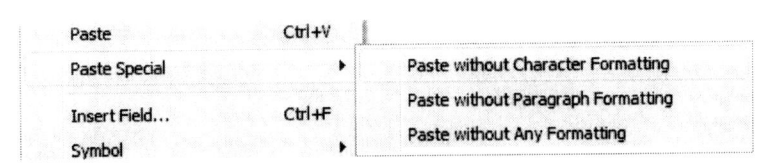

Figure 7–6

If you are creating an annotative object, you might be prompted to set the annotation scale.

When you copy and paste text created with Microsoft Word, it keeps the formatting from the document, including numbering or bullets and specific headings.

How To: Import Text

1. In the *Annotate* tab>Text panel or in the *Home* tab>Annotation panel, click **A** (Multiline Text).
2. Select points for the boundary box.
3. In the *Text Editor* contextual tab>expanded Tools panel, click **Import Text**. You can also right-click in the Text Editor and select **Import Text**.
4. In the Select File dialog box, select the file that you want to use and click **Open** to import the text.

- Imported text does not include formatting.

Hint: Text Symbols

You can add symbols to your text. In the *Text Editor* contextual tab>Insert panel, expand @ (Symbol) and select a symbol in the list. You can select **Other...** at the end of the list to open the Character Map dialog box to access specialty symbols in different fonts.

In the *Text Editor* contextual tab>Insert panel, click (Field) to add text objects that gather their information from objects or system variables, such as the date or drawing name in the AutoCAD software.

Spell Checking

The spellings are checked by default when you are in the Text Editor. It can be toggled on and off in the *Text Editor* contextual tab>Spell Check panel, as shown in Figure 7–7.

Figure 7–7

- Any misspellings are underlined with a dashed red line, but only in the Text Editor. Right-click on the word to display a list of suggestions, as shown in Figure 7–8. You can also add words to the dictionary or ignore the misspelled words.

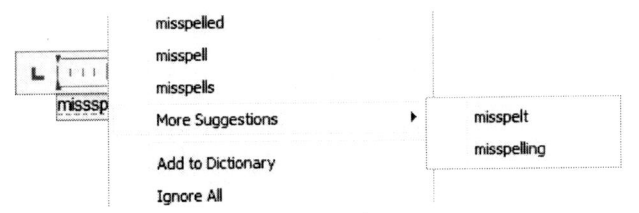

Figure 7–8

- Click ⌄ in the Spell Check panel title to open the Check Spelling Settings dialog box.

Annotate Drawings

Practice 7a

Adding Text in a Drawing

Practice Objectives

- Add text to a cover sheet with different text styles and sizes.
- Import text into the Text Editor.

In this practice, you will use the **Multiline Text** command to place text on a cover sheet using two different text styles and sizes, as shown in Figure 7–9. You will also import text into the Text Editor.

Estimated time for completion: 10 minutes

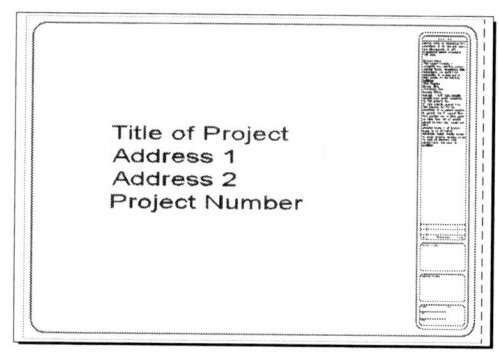

Figure 7–9

Task 1 - Add General Notes to the Cover Sheet.

1. Open **Cover Sheet-A.dwg** from your practice files folder.
2. Ensure that you are in the **Cover Sheet** layout tab.
3. Set the current layer to **Notes**. In the *Home* tab>expanded Annotation panel, set the current text style to **Standard**, as shown in Figure 7–10.

The text style can also be set in the Annotate tab>Text panel.

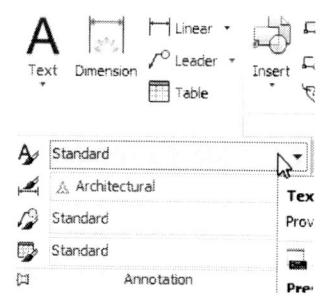

Figure 7–10

4. Zoom in on the top right corner of the layout, where it says General Notes.

© 2017, ASCENT - Center for Technical Knowledge®

7–7

*The **Multiline Text** command can also be accessed in the Annotate tab>Text panel.*

5. In the *Home* tab>Annotation panel, click **A** (Text), which is the **Multiline Text** command. The alphabet is attached to the cursor indicating the height of the text.

6. If ▢ ▼ (Object Snap) is on, toggle it off to avoid snapping to the lines in the titleblock.

7. In the *General Notes* area of the titleblock, select near the upper left corner under the General Notes line as the first point of the boundary box. Right-click, select **Height**, enter **1/8"**, and press <Enter>. Select the second point near the bottom right corner in the *General Notes* area, as shown in Figure 7–11. The Text Editor displays and the *Text Editor* contextual tab opens.

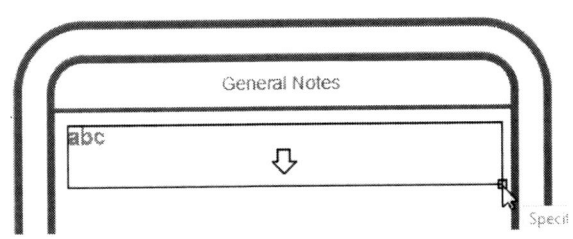

Figure 7–11

8. Type the text shown in Figure 7–12 and remain in the Text Editor.

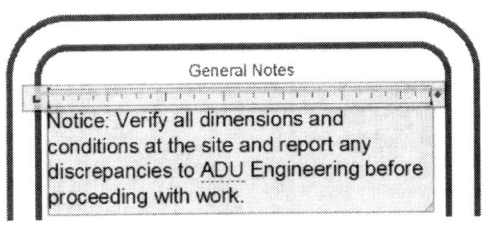

Figure 7–12

*For the words to be underlined, in the Text Editor tab, in the Spell Check panel, **Spell Check** must be toggled on.*

9. Note that **ADU** is underlined in red because the word is not recognized by the spell checker. Highlight it, right-click, and select **Add to Dictionary**.

10. Ensure that the cursor is at the end of the text, and press <Enter> twice to create a new line and a space.

11. Right-click in the Text Editor and select **Import Text**.

12. In the Select File dialog box, select the **General Notes.txt** file from your practice files folder and click **Open**. The text from the file is added.

Annotate Drawings

Your word wrap might be different because the size of your text boundary box might be different.

13. Select a point anywhere on the screen, outside of the Text Editor, to close it. The text displays as shown in Figure 7–13.

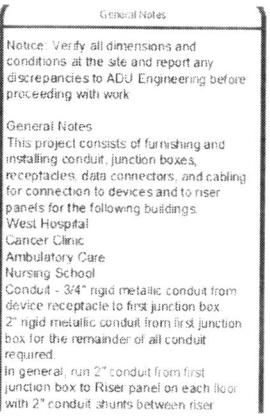

Figure 7–13

Task 2 - Add Project Information to the Cover Sheet.

1. Zoom out to display the entire cover sheet.

2. In the *Annotate* tab>Text panel, select the **Title** text style. Then, click **A** (Multiline Text).

The text style can also be set in the Home tab> expanded Annotation panel.

3. For the first corner, select the top left corner of the green rectangle at the center of the layout. (Use **Object Snap**.) Right-click, select **Height**, enter **1"**, and press <Enter>. Then, select the bottom right corner of the green rectangle.

4. Type the text shown in Figure 7–14.

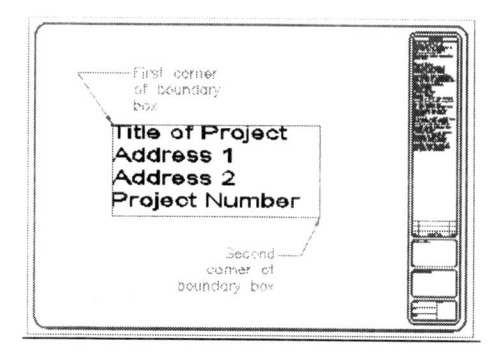

Figure 7–14

5. In the *Text Editor* contextual tab, click ✕ (Close Text Editor) to close the Text Editor.

6. Save and close the drawing.

7.2 Modifying Multiline Text

You can manipulate Multiline text with grips and adjust its various settings in the Properties palette. However, changing the text's layer, and copying, moving, and rotating the text can be achieved by using standard AutoCAD commands and processes.

Editing Multiline Text

*You can also right-click on the selected text and select **Mtext Edit**.*

You can edit the already existing multiline text in the Text Editor.

How To: Edit Multiline Text

1. Double-click on a text object to open the Text Editor. The *Text Editor* contextual tab also opens.
2. Edit the text, as shown in Figure 7–15.

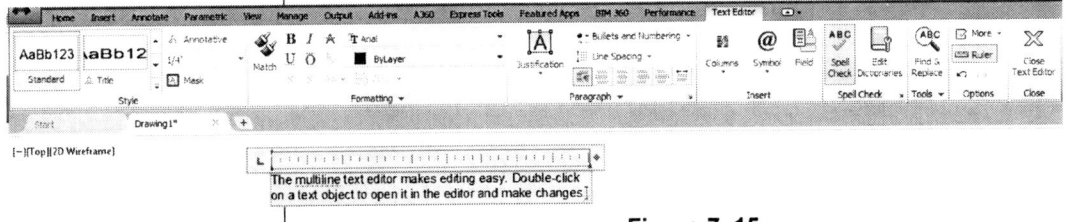

Figure 7–15

3. In the *Text Editor* contextual tab, click ✕ (Close Text Editor) or click in the drawing window to finish editing the text.

- If you press <Esc> to close the Text Editor, you are prompted to save your text changes.

Changing Text Width and Length

After you have placed Multiline text in your drawing, you can control the text boundary box width and length using grips or the Text Editor.

- Select some Multiline text without any commands running. Grips display at the location point and at the column width and height, as shown in Figure 7–16. Click on a grip to select it (it turns red), and then move the cursor and select another point to stretch the column width or height to a different size. To clear the grips, press <Esc>.

Figure 7–16

Annotate Drawings

- The location grip (square grip box) moves the entire Multiline text. It also designates the justification of the object.

- You can modify the text width and length in the Text Editor by hovering the cursor over the edges or the corner of the Text Editor and then dragging the double-arrows. You can also use the horizontal diamond on the right end of the ruler to modify the text box *Width*, as shown in Figure 7–17.

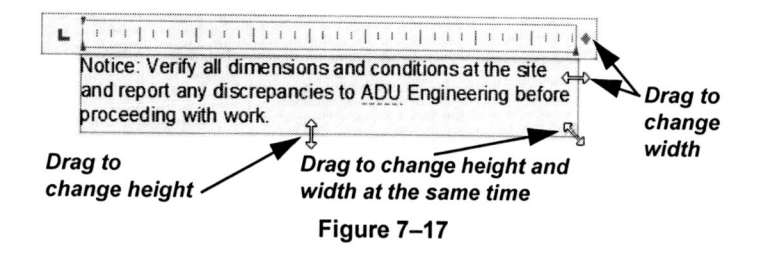

Figure 7–17

Changing Text Properties

The Properties palette is useful for changing multiple instances of text. You can change general properties (such as the layer) or specific properties (such as style, height, or justification).

- You can also add a Text Frame around multi-line text, as shown in Figure 7–18.

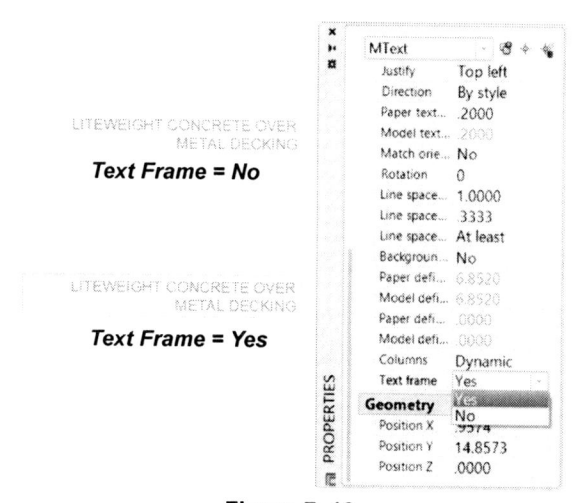

Figure 7–18

How To: Add a Text Frame

1. Select the multi-line text.
2. Right-click and select **Properties**.
3. In the Properties palette, change the *Text Frame* field to **Yes**.

Hint: Frame Offset Value

The Text Frame is offset from the text by the value specified in the Background mask, Border offset factor, as shown in Figure 7–19.

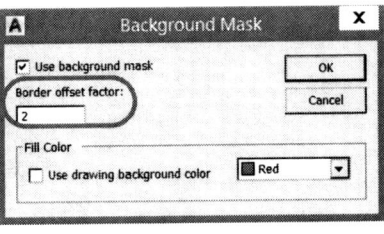

Figure 7–19

Spell Checking

While you are in the Text Editor you can have spell checking on and fix spelling errors on the fly. You can also check the spelling in an entire drawing or part of a drawing.

How To: Check the Spelling in a Drawing

1. In the Annotate tab>Text panel, click ABC (Check Spelling).
2. In the Check Spelling dialog box (shown in Figure 7–20), expand the Where to check drop-down list and select **Entire drawing, Current space/layout,** or **Selected objects**.

You can also click (Select Objects) to specify which objects to check.

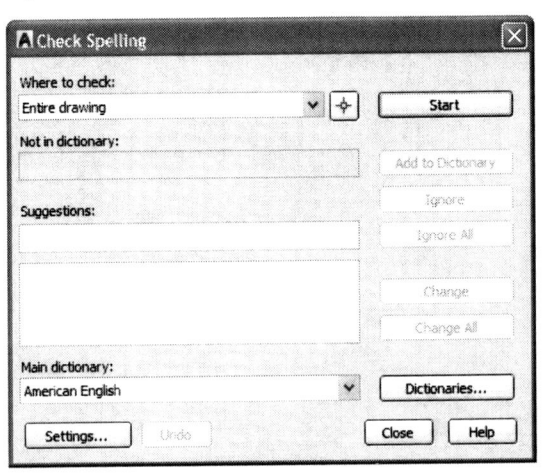

Figure 7–20

3. Click **Start**.
4. The AutoCAD software zooms to the text being checked and highlights any misspelled words. As with other spell checkers, you can:
   - Click **Change** or **Change All** to change the word to the selected suggestion.
   - Click **Ignore** or **Ignore All** to maintain the spellings.
   - Click **Add to Dictionary** to add a word to your custom dictionary.
   - Click **Undo** if you modify a spelling error by mistake.
5. When the spelling check is complete, a message box opens. Click **OK** and then **Close** in the Check Spelling dialog box.

- Click **Dictionaries...** to specify the Main and Custom dictionaries, and add words to your custom dictionary.

- Click **Settings...** to specify the types of items you want to check and how you want the checker to deal with specific variations of words.

Practice 7b

Modifying Multiline Text

Practice Objectives

- Modify Multiline text objects.
- Check the spelling in the drawing.

Estimated time for completion: 10 minutes

In this practice, you will modify text using grips, the Text Editor, and the Properties palette to clean up a redlined detail, as shown in Figure 7–21. You will also check the spelling in the drawing file.

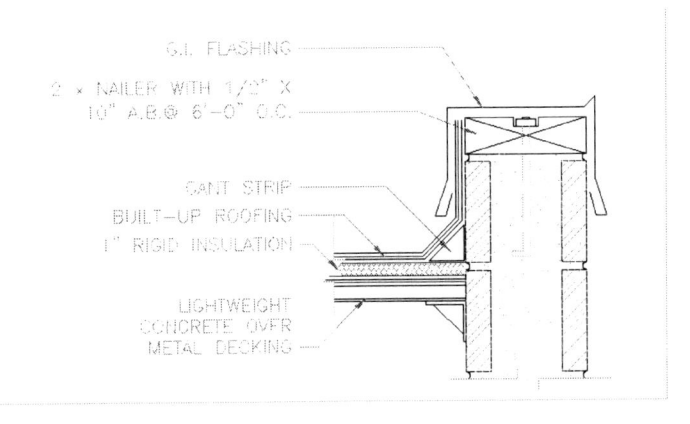

Figure 7–21

Task 1 - Edit multiline text in a drawing.

1. Open **Detail Sheet-A.dwg** from your practice files folder.

2. Ensure that you are in the **Detail Sheet** layout.

3. Zoom in on the Roof Detail in the upper left corner of the layout.

4. Double-click inside the viewport to make it active.

5. Click once on the text that ends in **O.C.** Select the top left grip and select a point farther to the left to make the text fit in two lines. Press <Esc> to clear the grips, as shown in Figure 7–21.

6. Double-click on the same piece of text. In the Text Editor, change *8"* to **10"**, as shown in Figure 7–22. Verify that the complete text is still in two lines, and use the left double-arrows to adjust the width as required. Press <ESC> and then click **Yes** to save the text changes.

Figure 7–22

7. Select the two pieces of text for the lower two leaders (starting with 1" and Liteweight), right-click and select **Properties**.

8. In the Properties palette, in the *Text* area, the *Paper text height* is **1/16"**. Click on it, change it to **1/8"** (as shown in Figure 7–23), and press <Enter>.

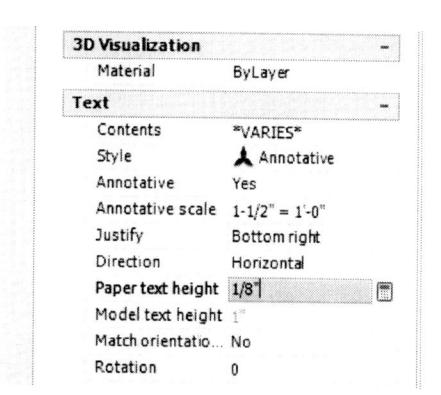

Figure 7–23

9. Close the Properties palette. Note that the selected text has become larger. Press <Esc> to clear the text.

10. Select the text **1" RIGID INSSULATION**. Use grips to stretch the text to the left so that it fits on one line. Press <Esc> to clear the text.

Task 2 - Check the spelling.

1. Remain in the Roof Detail viewport.

2. In the *Annotate* tab>Text panel, click (Check Spelling).

3. In the Check Spelling dialog box, in the Where to check drop-down list, select **Current space/layout**. Click **Start**.

4. Work through each of the spelling errors, correcting them as required and ignoring proper names. Note that the word **NAILER** is highlighted although it is spelled correctly. It is a technical term that is not found in the standard dictionary. Click **Ignore**.

5. Next, *INSSULATION* is highlighted. Correct it by clicking **Change** to use the spelling in the *Suggestions* area as shown in Figure 7–24.

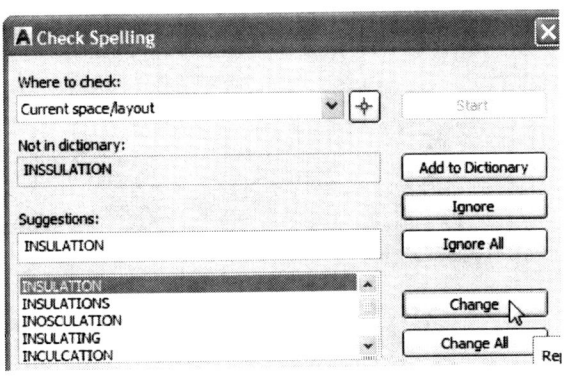

Figure 7–24

6. Similarly, the word **liteweight** should be corrected.

7. In the message box, click **OK** to finish checking the spelling.

8. Click **Close** to close the Check Spelling dialog box.

9. Two of the misspelled words are not modified by the Spell Checker because they are actual words. You need to modify these directly.

10. Double-click on the text *CHANT* and in the Text Editor, correct the spelling to **CANT** and then save the change.

11. Similarly, change the text *BUILD-UP* to **BUILT-UP**.

12. Toggle the layer **redline** off.

13. Double-click outside the viewport to return to Paper Space.

14. Save the drawing.

Annotate Drawings

7.3 Formatting Multiline Text

Multiline text offers formatting features similar to those found in word processing software. For example, you can bold, underline, or strikeout specific text, use bullets or numbered lists, and create columns of information, as shown in Figure 7–25.

Figure 7–25

- Some options affect the entire Multiline text object, some modify specific paragraphs in the text, and some only change selected text.

Formatting the Multiline Text Object

Changing the *Text Style* and *Justification* affects the entire Multiline text object. If you need to change these features, do so before you make any other modifications to the formatting.

Changing the Text Style

You can change the *Text Style* of the overall text object once you are in the Text Editor.

- Changing the style overrides any other formatting you have done. A warning box opens if you select a different style, as shown in Figure 7–26.

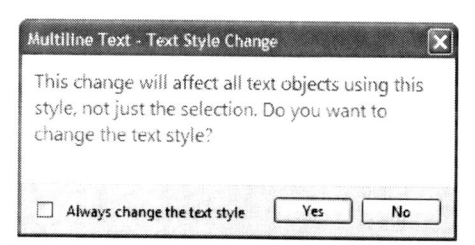

Figure 7–26

- If you are not using an annotative text style, you can click (Annotative) in the *Text Editor* contextual tab to make that instance of the text annotative without changing the text style.

Changing the Justification

The *Justification* sets the overall justification for the entire text object. In this case, the width and height of the boundary box are considered. For example, if you set the *Justification* to **Middle Center**, the text is centered in the middle of the boundary box, as shown in Figure 7–27. To change the Multiline text object, use the Justification tools located in the *Text Editor* contextual tab>Paragraph panel in the ribbon.

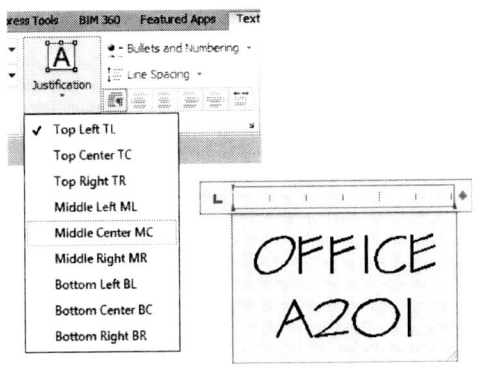

Figure 7–27

- (Background Mask) in the Style panel places a masking element behind the text so that other objects do not show through. You can use the drawing background color or a specific color, as shown in Figure 7–28.

Setting a background mask applies it to the entire Multiline text object.

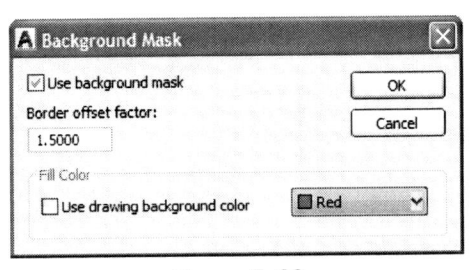

Figure 7–28

Annotate Drawings

Formatting Selected Text

In hand drafting, most text was placed on a drawing using all uppercase letters. However, as computers have taken over much of the text work, many people are using the sentence case format.

The Formatting panel in the *Text Editor* contextual tab enables you to change the font of individual text that you have selected, as well as bold, italicize, underline, overline, strikethrough, and change the case of the text, as shown in Figure 7–29.

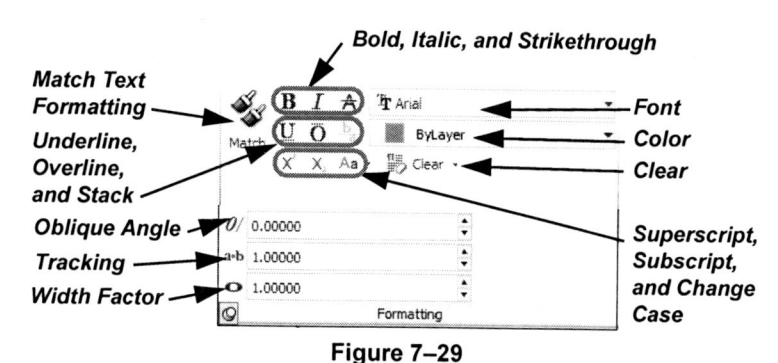

Figure 7–29

Labels: Match Text Formatting; Underline, Overline, and Stack; Oblique Angle; Tracking; Width Factor; Bold, Italic, and Strikethrough; Font; Color; Clear; Superscript, Subscript, and Change Case.

- Buttons are grayed out if the text is not selected or if the font does not support an option, such as **Bold** or *Italic*.

- In many cases, setting the color impacts the printed weight of the text, because colors are often used to control plotted line width.

- Three other text modification tools in the expanded area in the Formatting panel enable you to modify the text angle or spacing: **Oblique Angle**, **Tracking**, and **Width Factor**.

- You can use **Match Text Formatting** to copy the formatting from one set of text to another while using the Text Editor. You can also use this option to modify dimensions and tables.

- To remove the formatting from an mtext object, expand (Clear) and select the required option, You can remove the formatting from selected characters, from selected paragraphs, or from all of the text in a text object, as shown in Figure 7–30.

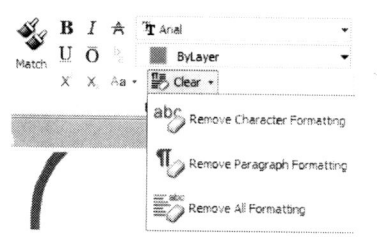

Figure 7–30

© 2017, ASCENT - Center for Technical Knowledge®

7–19

Fractions in Multiline Text

When you first enter a fraction in the Text Editor, it is automatically displayed as stacked, as shown in Figure 7–31.

Click ⚡ to display the **Stack** options.

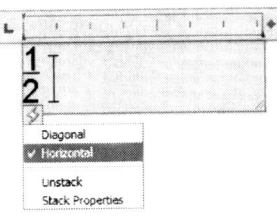

Figure 7–31

Select a fraction in the Text Editor, click ⚡ to use the basic **Stack** options or double-click on it to open the Stack Properties dialog box where you can modify the more advanced settings, as shown in Figure 7–32.

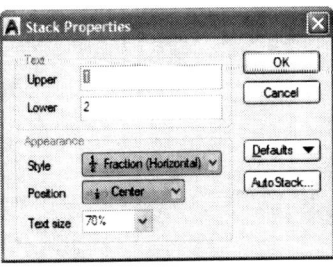

Figure 7–32

Formatting Paragraph Text

Paragraph settings also affect the next paragraph typed.

You can modify entire paragraphs of text including changing paragraph level justifications, line spacing, indents, bullets, and numbering, as shown in Figure 7–33.

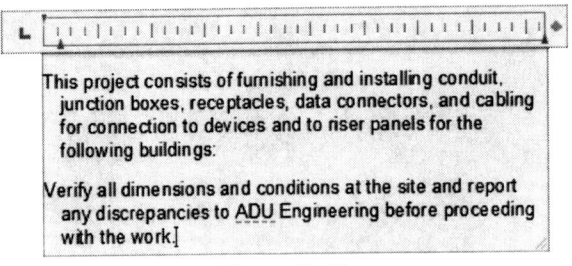

Figure 7–33

Annotate Drawings

- The paragraph formatting tools are located in the *Text Editor* contextual tab>Paragraph panel, as shown in Figure 7–34.

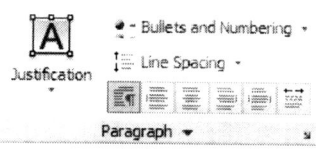

Figure 7–34

- A paragraph is any text that is typed before you press <Enter> to create a new line.

- To modify paragraphs, you can either select the entire paragraph or place the cursor somewhere in the paragraph.

Justifications

You can set justifications for individual paragraphs in a Multiline text object, as shown in Figure 7–35. The options are as follows:

- (Default)

- (Left)

- (Center)

- (Right)

- (Justify (Fit))

- (Distribute)

Figure 7–35

- **Justify (Fit)** spreads out the text so that the sentences are left- and right-justified. **Distribute** justifies to the left and right sides and spreads out whole words and individual letters across the space.

Line Spacing

You can set the line spacing using the supplied multiples of the text height, as shown in Figure 7–36, or select **More...** to create custom line spacing in the Paragraph dialog box. **Clear Line Spacing** returns the distance to the default setting.

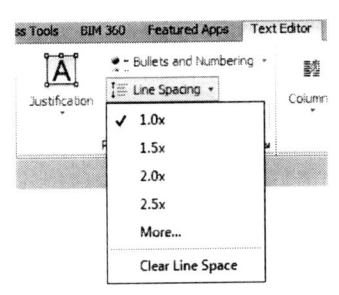

Figure 7–36

Bullets and Numbers

You can add bullets, numbers, or letters to text as you are typing, or add them to paragraphs that are already in the text object.

Select the type of list from the **Bullets and Numbering** list in the *Text Editor* contextual tab, as shown in Figure 7–37.

To create a sub-list of a list, press <Tab> at the beginning of the line. Press <Shift>+<Tab> to back up.

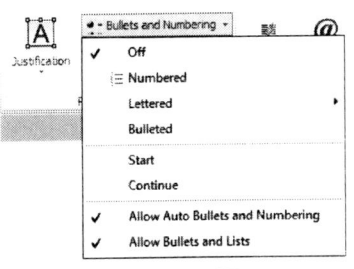

Figure 7–37

- The list can be in upper or lowercase letters, numbers, or bullets. Each time you press <Enter>, a new paragraph is created and numbered appropriately.

- You can **Restart** or **Continue** a numbered list and modify the default methods of using lists in the menu.

- Modify the indent and tab settings to set the locations of the numbers and text.

- Bullets and numbering are automatically applied to the text as you type if the line begins with a symbol or number followed by a space or <Tab>.

Setting Indents and Tabs

You can set the indents and tabs by using the ruler at the top of the Text Editor.

- Select the text that you want to indent and slide the markers to locate the indent. The top marker controls the first line of a paragraph and the bottom marker controls subsequent lines in the paragraph, as shown in Figure 7–38.

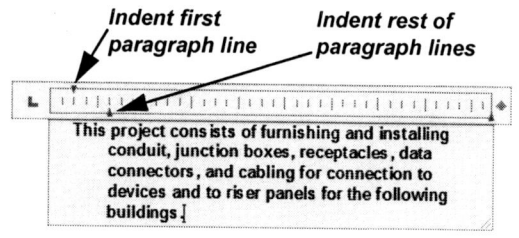

Figure 7–38

- The heavy **L** in the ruler marks preset tab stops, as shown in Figure 7–39. To add a manual tab, click on the ruler at the required location. You can drag the tab marker along the ruler to move it, or drag it off the ruler to delete it.

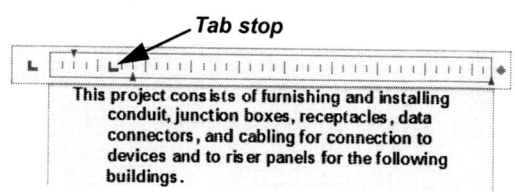

Figure 7–39

- There are tabs for (Left), (Center), (Right), and (Decimal). Click the tab box on the left side of the ruler to switch between the different types of tabs.

- You can also modify the tab settings in the Paragraph dialog box.

Creating Paragraph Formats

To modify the Paragraph settings, click ˟ in the Paragraph panel title. You can set the paragraph format options at any time using the Paragraph dialog box, as shown in Figure 7–40.

- You can only set the *Paragraph Spacing* in the Paragraph dialog box. It controls the distance before or after any paragraph.

If you do not select items in the dialog box, they do not affect the selected paragraph.

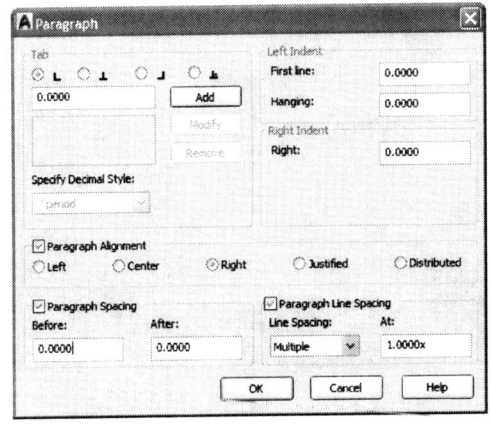

Figure 7–40

Creating Columns

You can place the text in a column format, as shown in Figure 7–41, using the column options in the Text Editor. There are two methods of column creation: **Dynamic** and **Static**.

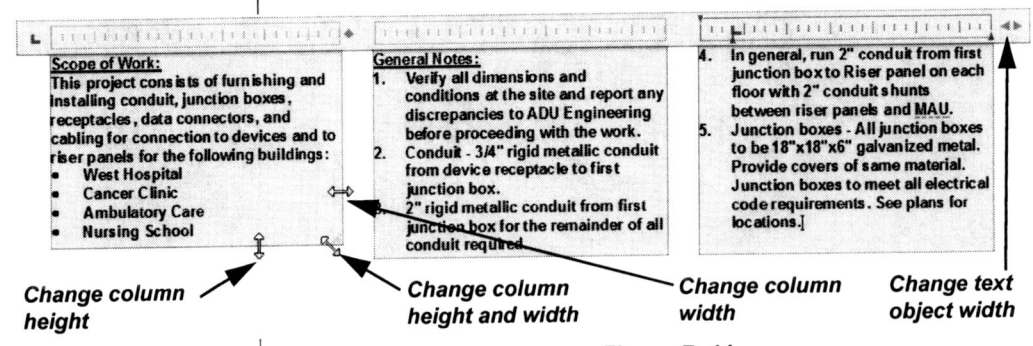

Change column height — Change column height and width — Change column width — Change text object width

Figure 7–41

Column settings affect the entire Multiline text object.

- By default, all of the Multiline text is set up to display dynamic columns with a manual height. This can be adjusted with grips or by dragging the edges of the first column to adjust the height and width separately, or both at the same time, as shown in Figure 7–41.

Annotate Drawings

Static Columns

With **Static Columns**, you can specify the number of columns in the list, as shown in Figure 7–42. The columns are evenly divided in the text box.

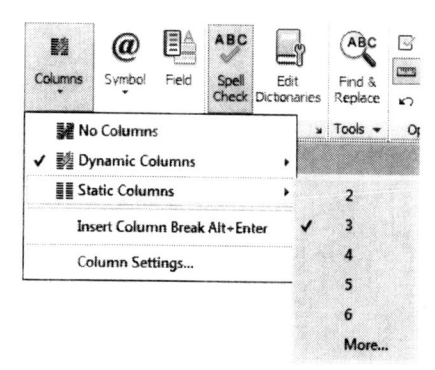

Figure 7–42

- If you need more than six columns, select **More…** or **Column Settings…** In the Column Settings dialog box, you can set the number of Static Columns, their height and width, and the gutter width.

Dynamic Columns

With **Dynamic Columns**, you can specify an automatic or manual height, as shown in Figure 7–43. The number of columns varies depending on the amount of text.

You can also set the height and width of columns in the Column Settings dialog box and modify them with grips.

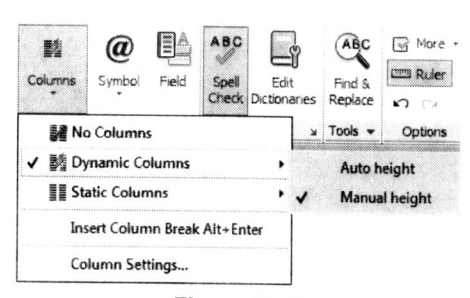

Figure 7–43

- After you start typing column information in the Mtext boundary, you can select **Insert Column Break** or type <Alt>+<Enter> to add a break before the end of the column. This enables you to control the flow of text in the Mtext object.

- When you have columns in your drawing, you can control the spacing with grips, depending on the type of columns and their settings.

Practice 7c

Formatting Multiline Text in a Drawing

Practice Objectives

- Change the formatting options of text objects.
- Add text and create columns.

Estimated time for completion: 10 minutes

In this practice, you will use formatting options in the Text Editor to set the style, modify individual objects, add numbering and indents, and set the justification of the text, as shown in Figure 7–44. If you have time, you can also add text and create columns.

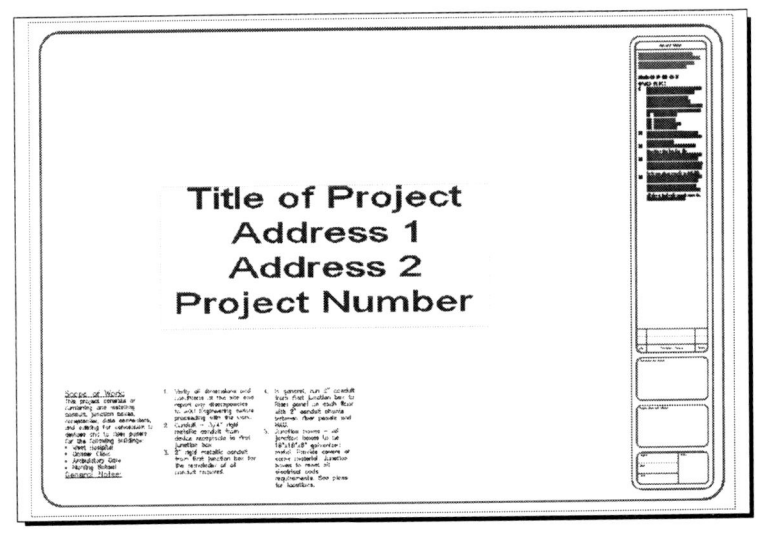

Figure 7–44

Task 1 - Format multiline text in a drawing.

1. Open **Cover Sheet2-A.dwg** from your practice files folder.

2. Zoom in on the *General Notes* area in the upper right corner of the titleblock.

3. Double-click on the text below the General Notes to open it in the Text Editor.

4. In the *Text Editor* contextual tab>Style panel, click ⬇ and select the style **Hand**. In the alert box, click **Yes**. The entire text object updates to the new style.

5. Highlight the first sentence (four lines), which starts with **Notice**. In the *Text Editor* contextual tab>Formatting panel, click U̲ to make the sentence underlined and in the Color list, select **Red**, as shown in Figure 7–45.

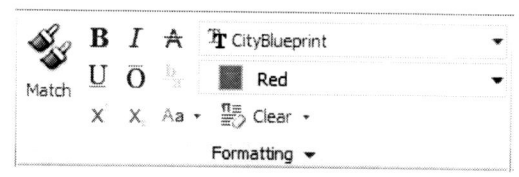

Figure 7–45

6. In the next paragraph of the text, highlight the text **General Notes** and change it to read **Scope of Work**. Change its *Font* to **Arial Unicode MS**, *Text Height* to **3/16"** and make all of the words **Uppercase**, as shown in Figure 7–46.

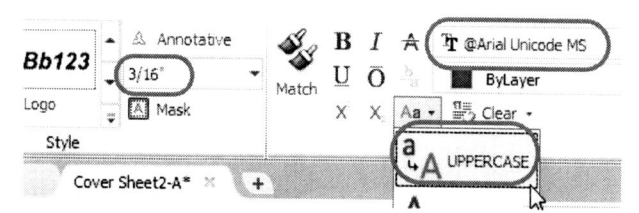

Figure 7–46

7. Select all of the text below SCOPE OF WORK. In the *Text Editor* contextual tab>Paragraph panel, expand **Bullets and Numbering** and select **Numbered** to apply autonumbering. Each paragraph becomes numbered.

8. Items 2-5 in the list should be sub-items under the first note. Select the insertion point in front of the text *West Hospital* and press <Tab>. The line becomes a sub-item. Repeat for the next three lines.

9. To adjust the indent for the sub-items, highlight those four lines. In the ruler, drag the first line indent marker to the **3/8" mark**, as shown in Figure 7–47.

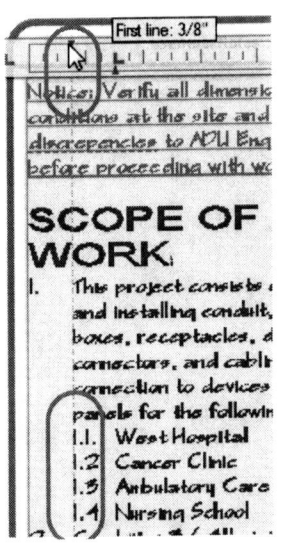

Figure 7–47

10. Click ✖ (Close Text Editor) to close the Text Editor.

11. Zoom out to display the entire layout.

12. Double-click anywhere on the four lines of Title text in the center of the cover sheet.

13. In the *Text Editor* contextual tab>Paragraph panel, change the *Justification* to **Middle Center MC**, as shown in Figure 7–48.

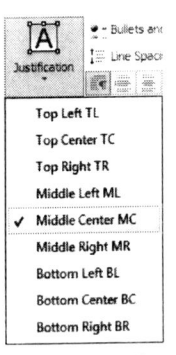

Figure 7–48

14. Exit the Text Editor.

15. Save the drawing.

Task 2 - (Optional) Create columns.

In this task, you will import a text file, apply formatting, and divide the text into columns, as shown in Figure 7–49.

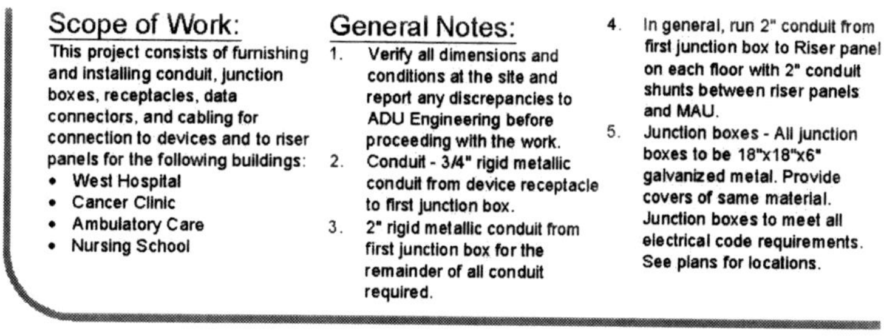

Scope of Work:
This project consists of furnishing and installing conduit, junction boxes, receptacles, data connectors, and cabling for connection to devices and to riser panels for the following buildings:
- West Hospital
- Cancer Clinic
- Ambulatory Care
- Nursing School

General Notes:
1. Verify all dimensions and conditions at the site and report any discrepancies to ADU Engineering before proceeding with the work.
2. Conduit - 3/4" rigid metallic conduit from device receptacle to first junction box.
3. 2" rigid metallic conduit from first junction box for the remainder of all conduit required.
4. In general, run 2" conduit from first junction box to Riser panel on each floor with 2" conduit shunts between riser panels and MAU.
5. Junction boxes - All junction boxes to be 18"x18"x6" galvanized metal. Provide covers of same material. Junction boxes to meet all electrical code requirements. See plans for locations.

Figure 7–49

1. In the lower left corner of the cover sheet, create a new Multiline Text object. Set the current text style to **Standard** with a *Height* of **3/16"**.

2. From the practice files folder, import the text file **Scope of Work.txt**. (This is similar to the text you placed under General Notes.)

3. Modify the formatting so that the items are bulleted and numbered (as shown in Figure 7–49), and the titles are larger and underlined.

4. In the *Text Editor* contextual tab>Insert panel, expand (Columns) and select **Static Columns>2**. The text is divided into two columns.

5. Click (Columns) and select **Column Settings**. The Column Settings dialog box opens.

The right pointing arrow increases the width. Drag and drop the bottom arrow to create columns and modify the column height.

6. In the *Width* area, set the *Column* to **3"** and *Gutter* to **1/2"**, as shown in Figure 7–50.

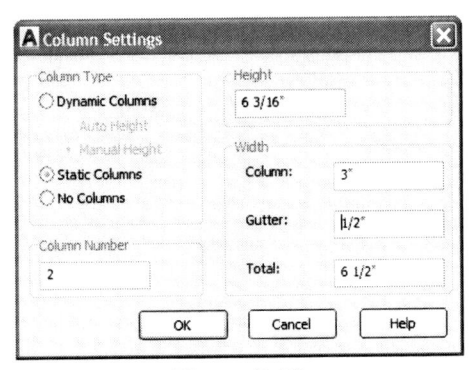

Figure 7–50

7. Click **OK** to close the Column Settings dialog box. The columns adjust to match the new values.

8. Close the Text Editor. The text is still not completely on the sheet.

9. Open the Text Editor again, expand (Columns), and select **Dynamic Columns>Manual height**. Close the Text Editor.

10. Use grips (i.e, the right pointing arrow and bottom arrow) to modify the columns so that the headings are on separate lines and the notes do not run over from column to column, as shown in Figure 7–51.

Figure 7–51

11. Save and close the drawing.

7.4 Dimensioning Concepts

The AutoCAD® dimensioning commands create dimensions based on points that you specify or by selecting the object for dimensioning. The AutoCAD software automatically draws the dimension with the appropriate extension lines, arrowheads, dimension lines, and text, as shown in Figure 7–52.

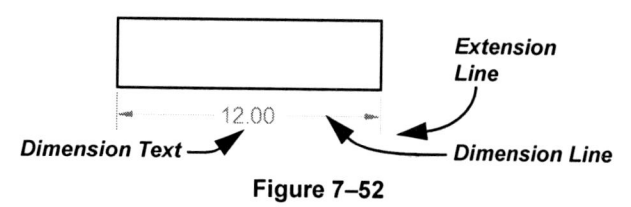

Figure 7–52

- Dimensions recalculate automatically when the objects that they refer to are modified. For example, when you stretch a wall 2'-0" to the right, the associated dimensions update.

As you prepare to dimension, you should:

- Set up a viewport in a layout that displays the part of the model that you want to dimension. You should set the Viewport Scale before you start dimensioning.

- Select the layer for dimensioning.

- Select a Dimension Style to be used for dimensioning.

- Use the *Annotate* tab>Dimensions panel, as shown in Figure 7–53, to access the dimensioning commands and set up the layer and dimension style.

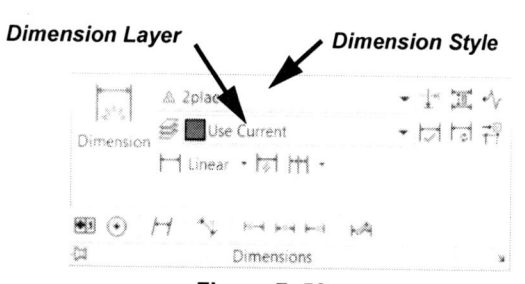

Figure 7–53

Lock the viewport to make it easier to zoom around the drawing without changing the scale by mistake.

Dimension styles can be annotative.

Some dimensioning commands can also be accessed in the Home tab>Annotation panel.

General Dimensioning

Dimensions can be added using a general dimension command or using commands specific to the type of dimension being added. The general dimension command automatically determines the type of dimension required based on the object or point selected.

- You can use a single **Dimension** command to add various dimensions, such as linear (horizontal, vertical), aligned, angular, radial etc. After placing a required dimension, the **Dimension** command remains active, enabling you to add other dimensions as required, without re-launching the command.

How To: Add Dimensions

Instead of selecting an object for dimension, you can use object snaps to snap to points to be dimensioned.

1. In the *Annotate* tab>Dimensions panel, click ▦ (Dimension) or in the *Home* tab>Annotation panel, click ▦ (Dimension).
2. Hover the cursor on the object that you want to dimension. Depending on the object that touches the cursor, a preview of a relevant dimension displays, as shown in Figure 7–54.

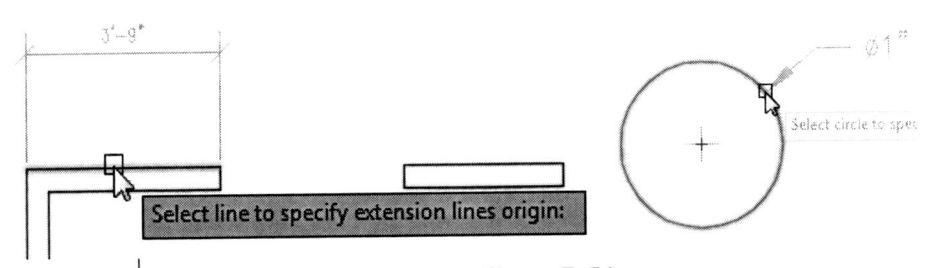

Figure 7–54

3. If the preview dimension is the correct one, click to save the dimension.
4. Drag the cursor to the location where you want the dimension to be located. Click to place the dimension or select an option from the Command Line (or use the <Down Arrow> menu).
5. Dimension another object in the drawing or press <Esc> to exit the command.

7.5 Adding Linear Dimensions

Linear dimensions measure a distance from one point to another, as shown in Figure 7–55.

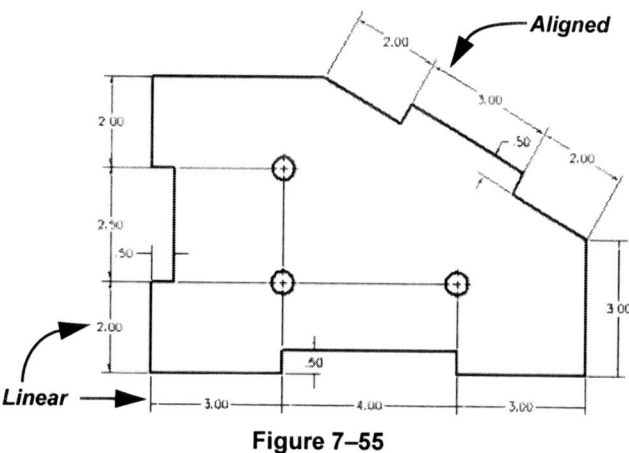

Figure 7–55

Individual Linear Dimensions

Linear dimensions can be horizontal or vertical, as shown in Figure 7–55. Aligned dimensions are also linear dimensions, however, they measure the linear distance parallel to the selected line or the selected points. The dimension line is placed parallel to the line between the points, as shown in Figure 7–55.

- The AutoCAD software determines the linear orientation (horizontal, vertical, or aligned) based on the selected object or where you select the point for the dimension line location.

How To: Add Linear and Aligned Dimensions

1. In the *Annotate* tab>Dimensions panel or the *Home* tab> Annotation panel, click (Dimension).
2. Select a line in the drawing.
3. Select a point to place the dimension line.

or

1. In the *Annotate* tab>Dimensions panel or the *Home* tab> Annotation panel, click (Dimension).
2. Select a point for the first extension line origin.
3. Select a point for the second extension line origin.
4. Select a point to place the dimension line.

Use Object Snaps to select the exact points for the extension line origins.

> **Hint: Oblique Extension Lines**
>
> If you want the extension lines of a linear dimension to be at an angle, you can click ⊬ (Oblique) in the *Annotate* tab> expanded Dimensions panel, to angle the lines.

Adding a Break in a Linear or Aligned Dimension

In some cases, you need to have a dimension with a break because the length of the dimension is too long to display on a sheet, as shown in Figure 7–56.

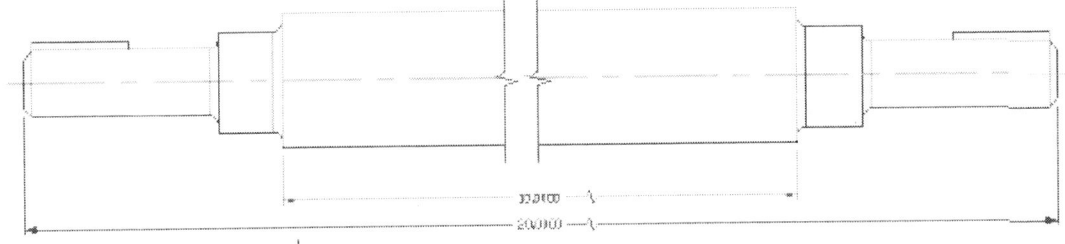

Figure 7–56

How To: Create a Jogged Linear Dimension

1. In the *Annotate* tab>Dimensions panel, click ⩘ (Dimjogline).
2. Select the dimension to which you want to add the jog.
3. Specify the jog location along the dimension or press <Enter> to accept the default location.

- To remove a jog line, use the command's **Remove** option.

Multiple Linear Dimensions

These commands can be used with Linear, Aligned, or Angular dimensions.

After you have placed a linear, aligned, or angular dimension, you can use that dimension as the beginning of a series of related dimensions by clicking ▯▯▯ (Continue) or ▭ (Baseline), as shown in Figure 7–57.

Continue Dimensions   **Baseline Dimensions**

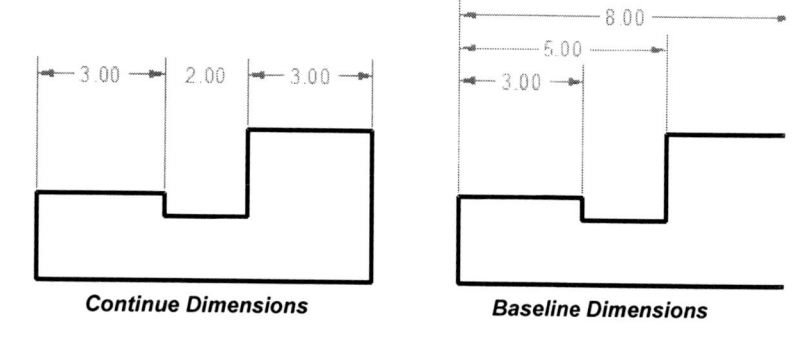

Figure 7–57

Continue dimensions use the last extension line placed as the first extension line for the next dimension. The dimension line remains at the same distance from the object.

Baseline dimensions use the first extension line as the base for all other dimensions. As you select additional extension line points, the new dimension is placed over the previous one. The distance between the dimension lines is set by the dimension style.

How To: Add Continue and Baseline Dimensions

1. Place a linear or aligned dimension.
2. In the *Annotate* tab>Dimensions panel, click ▯▯▯ (Continue) or ▭ (Baseline).
3. Select a point for the second extension line origin. The first extension line origin is automatically assumed to be from the last dimension you placed.
4. Continue selecting points for additional extension line origins.
5. Press <Enter> twice to finish the command.

- By default, the AutoCAD software uses the last dimension placed as the starting dimension. Use the **Select** option to select a different dimension to be referenced.

Quick Dimensioning

In some cases, you can place all of your dimensions along one edge of an object using one command, regardless of whether it is **Linear**, **Aligned**, **Baseline**, or **Continue**. As shown in Figure 7–58, the outside lines of the walls were selected using the **Quick Dimension** command and dimensioned at the same time.

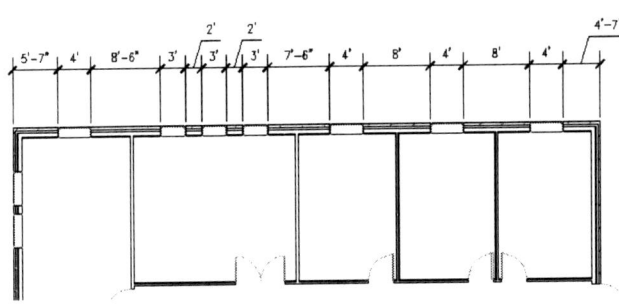

Figure 7–58

How To: Add Quick Dimensions

1. In the *Annotate* tab>Dimensions panel, click (Quick Dimension).
2. Select the objects that you want to dimension. When you have finished selecting objects, press <Enter>.
3. Specify the dimension line position.

- By default, the AutoCAD software creates continuous dimensions if you select linear objects or more than one object.

- You can switch between a number of other types of dimensions, including **Staggered**, **Baseline**, and **Ordinate**, in the Command Prompt, shortcut menu, or dynamic input drop-down list.

- Baseline and Ordinate dimensions start from a common point. You can set that point using the **datumPoint** option.

- There is also an **Edit** option that enables you to add or remove points. However, it is easier to do this using other commands.

Quick Dimension does not enable you to place a type of dimension that is not appropriate for the selection. For example, if you select a line, you cannot place a Radius or Diameter dimension on that line.

Practice 7d

Adding Linear Dimensions (Architectural)

Practice Objective

- Add dimensions using various dimensioning techniques.

In this practice, you will start to add dimensions using the general **Dimension** command. You will then dimension different portions of the architectural drawing using **Quick**, **Baseline**, and **Continue** dimensions, as shown in Figure 7–59.

Estimated time for completion: 10 minutes

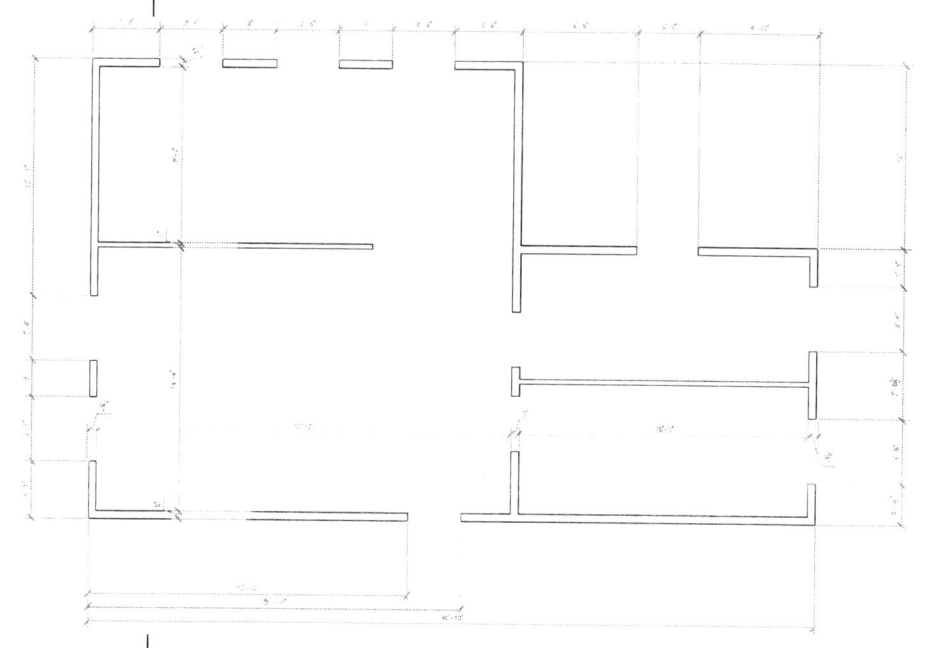

Figure 7–59

1. Open **Dimensioned Plan-A.dwg** from your practice files folder.

2. Switch to the **D-sized** layout. Make the existing viewport active and zoom extents.

3. In the Status Bar, set the *Viewport Scale* to **1/2"=1'-0"** and lock the viewport.

*Verify that the active Dimension Style is set as **Architectural**. This is an annotative style.*

4. In the *Annotate* tab>Dimensions panel, select the layer **Dimensions** in the drop-down list, as shown in Figure 7–60, to make it the active dimensioning layer.

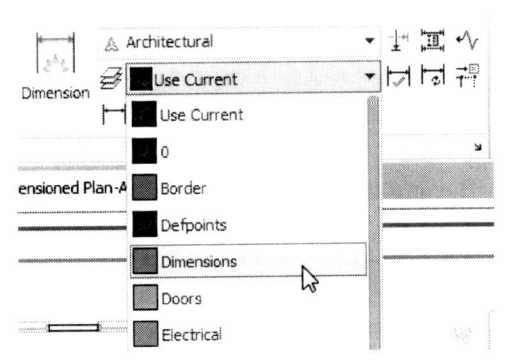

Figure 7–60

5. Freeze the layers **Doors** and **Windows** to make it easier to only select the walls to be dimensioned.

6. Verify that **Object Snap** is toggled off.

7. While still active in the viewport, in the *Annotate* tab> Dimensions panel, click (Dimension). Hover the cursor on the top left wall (outer line), as shown in Figure 7–61.

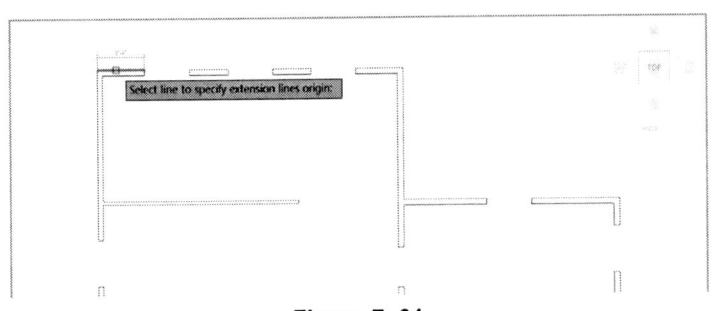

Figure 7–61

8. Select the object, drag the cursor up and click to place the dimension outside the building.

9. In the Status Bar, toggle on **Object Snap** and verify that **Endpoint** object snap is selected.

Annotate Drawings

10. Start the **Continue** command. Note that the cursor is attached with the last dimension you placed. Select the left endpoint of the second wall, as shown in Figure 7–62.

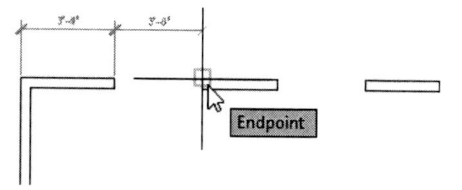

Figure 7–62

11. Select the rest of the dimension points along the same wall. Press <Enter> twice to complete the command.

12. Start the **Dimension** command. Select the two endpoints (first left and then right) of the bottom left wall. Place the dimension along the bottom side of the building.

13. Start the **Baseline** command and note that the cursor dimension is attached to the left extension line of the dimension.

The order of selection of points determines the start point of the baseline.

14. Select the right endpoint of the left side bottom wall to place the dimension.

15. Select the left endpoint of the right side bottom wall to place the third dimension. Press <Enter> twice to complete the command.

16. Start the **Quick Dimension** command.

17. Add dimensions to the left side of the building by selecting three outside wall objects, pressing <Enter>, and then clicking to place the dimensions.

18. Add dimensions to the right exterior of the building, and the interior.

19. Save and close the drawing.

7.6 Adding Radial and Angular Dimensions

Other types of dimensions include Radius, Diameter, and Angular dimensions. Radius/Diameter dimensions for arcs and circles are placed with a leader from the object. You can also create a Jogged Radial dimension for arcs whose center point would be outside the drawing and for dimensioning the length around the curve of an arc. Angular dimensions measure the angle of an arc or the angle between two objects.

Radius and Diameter Dimensions

Radius is typically used on arcs, while **Diameter** is normally used on full circles, as shown in Figure 7–63. You can also add a radius dimension for a circle.

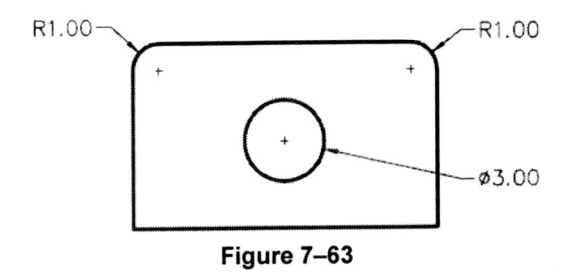

Figure 7–63

How To: Add Radius or Diameter Dimensions

1. In the *Annotate* tab>Dimensions panel, click (Dimension).
   You can also use (Radius) or (Diameter) individually.
2. Select a point on the rim of an arc or circle. (You do not need to use Object Snaps for this.)
3. Select a location along the arc or circle for the dimension line text.

- When you are dimensioning a radius, you can place the dimension beyond the arc. The AutoCAD software creates an additional arc extension line as required.

- **Quick Dimension** creates a radial dimension by default if you select an arc or circular object. However, you can select **Diameter** in the options.

Annotate Drawings

Associative Center Marks and Centerlines

There are two new tools which indicate the center of a arc or circle regardless of the objects' perspective. Both tools are on the *Annotate* tab>Centerlines panel.

- The Center Mark tool adds an associate center mark at the center of selected circles, arcs, or polygonal arcs, as shown in Figure 7–64.

- The Centerline tool creates centerline geometry that is associated with selected lines and polylines, as shown in Figure 7–65.

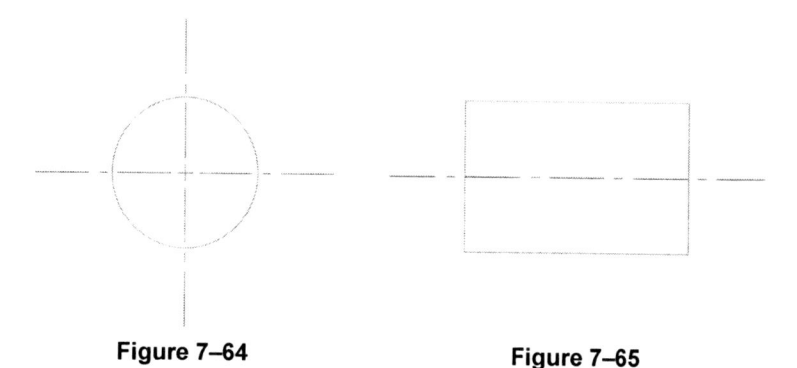

Figure 7–64   Figure 7–65

- If the associated objects move, the centerlines and center marks also update.

When a center mark or centerline is selected, grips display that enable you to control the extension line lengths, as shown in Figure 7–66. The appearance of center marks and centerlines is controlled by multiple system variables. Figure 7–66 and the table below lists the controlling variables and describes their effects.

CENTEREXE	• Sets the length of the extension line overshoots for centerlines and center marks.
CENTERMARKEXE	• Determines whether extension lines are created for center marks.
CENTERLAYER	• Sets the layer on which the centerlines and center marks are created.
CENTERLTYPE	• Sets the linetype used by centerlines and center marks.
CENTERLTSCALE	• Sets the linetype scale used by centerlines and center marks.
CENTERCROSSSIZE	• Sets the size of the central cross for center marks.
CENTERCROSSGAP	• Sets the extension line gap between the central cross and the extension lines in center marks.

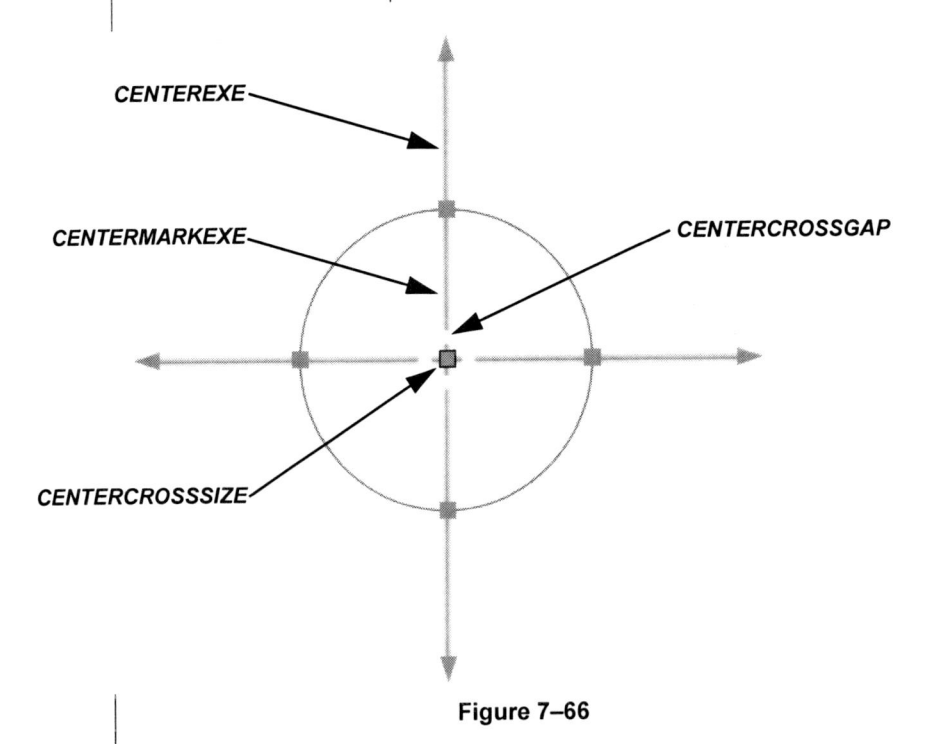

Figure 7–66

Annotate Drawings

- The system variables must be set prior to creating the center mark or centerline for the variable to take effect.

- The Properties palette can be used to modify select attributes, as shown in Figure 7–67.

- A multi-functional grip menu offers additional controls, as shown in Figure 7–68.

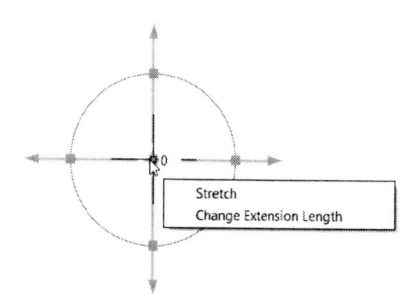

Figure 7–67

Figure 7–68

Jogged Radial Dimension

If the center mark of the circle or arc you are dimensioning does not display in the view, you can use the **Jogged** command to create an override for the center, as shown in Figure 7–69.

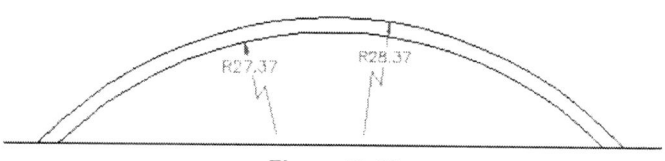

Figure 7–69

*You can also find the **Jogged** option (<Down Arrow>) in the **Dimension** command.*

How To: Create a Jogged Radial Dimension

1. In the *Annotate* tab>Dimensions panel, click (Jogged).
2. Select the arc or circle that you want to dimension.
3. Specify a point for the center location override.
4. Specify the dimension line location. This also sets the location of the text.
5. Specify the jog location.

Arc Length Dimension

The arc length describes the distance from one end point of an arc to the other end point along the curve of the arc, as shown in Figure 7–70. This command can be used to dimension individual arcs or arcs that are parts of polylines.

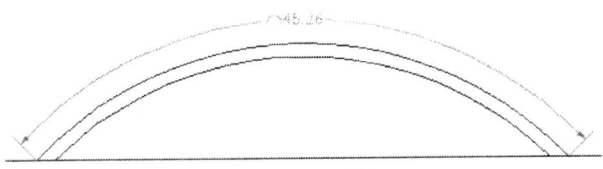

Figure 7–70

How To: Dimension the Arc Length

1. In the *Annotate* tab>Dimensions panel, click (Dimension).
2. Hover the cursor over the arc that you want to dimension.
3. Press <Down Arrow> and select **arc Length** from the list.
4. Specify the dimension location.

Angular Dimensions

You can add angular dimensions to lines, circles, and arcs and from a vertex, as shown in Figure 7–71.

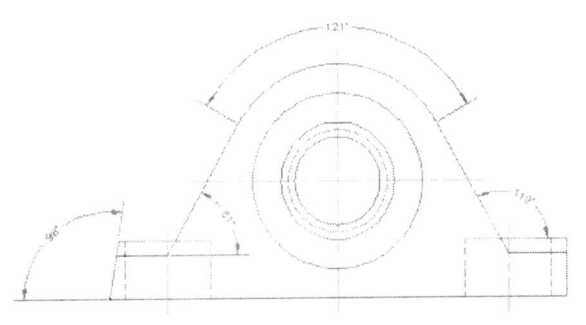

Figure 7–71

- When you are placing the Angular dimension, you can place it at any of the four quadrants of the angle.

Annotate Drawings

How To: Add Angular Dimensions

1. In the *Annotate* tab>Dimensions panel, click (Dimension).
2. Select a line, arc, or circle.
3. If you select a **line**, you are prompted to place a linear dimension. As you hover the cursor over another line, the preview changes to an angle dimension, as shown in Figure 7–72. Select the second line and specify the location of the dimension line.

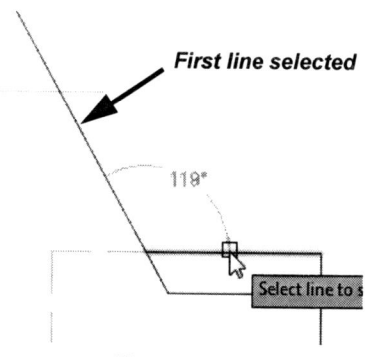

First line selected

Figure 7–72

4. If you hover over an **arc**, by default you can place a radial dimension. Press <Down Arrow> and select **Angular**. Then, click the arc to select it. Click again to set the location of the dimension line.
5. If you hover over a **circle**, by default you can place a diameter dimension. Press <Down Arrow> and select **Angular**. Then click the circle to select it. Click to specify the first side of the angle. Click again to set the second side of the angle. Click one more time to set the location of the dimension line.

- You can also dimension an angle from a vertex. Before selecting an object, press <Enter> and use Object Snaps to select an angle vertex. Specify the first and second angle end points and place the dimension line.

Practice 7e

Adding Radial and Angular Dimensions (Architectural)

Practice Objective

- Add dimensions including radial and angular to a drawing.

Estimated time for completion: 5 minutes

In this practice, you will add Angular, Radial, Diameter, Aligned, and Arc Length dimensions, as shown in Figure 7–73.

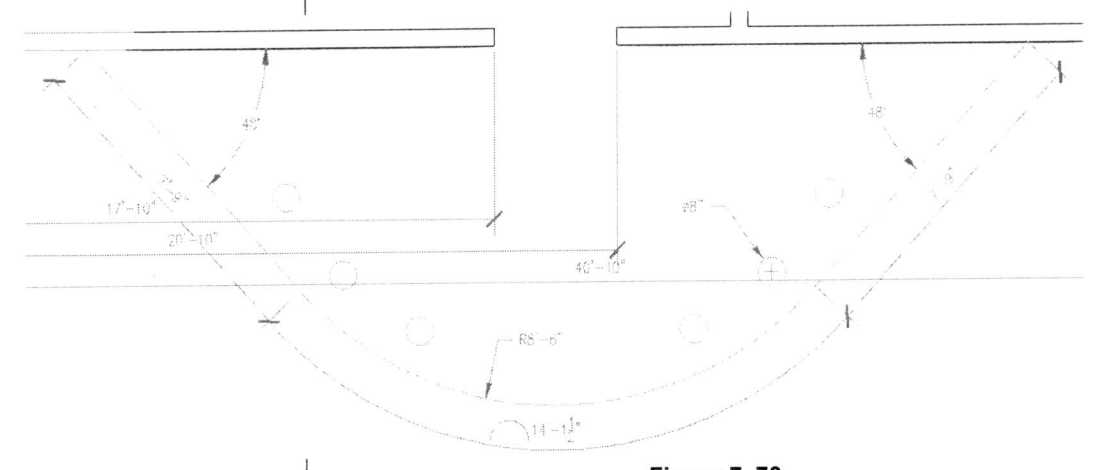

Figure 7–73

1. Open **Dimensioned Plan1-A.dwg** from your practice files folder.

2. In the Layer Control, toggle on the layer **Misc** to display the entrance portico.

3. Modify the viewport to display the entire entrance portico. If the viewport is locked, unlock it and pan the view until it fits. Zooming in and out of the view changes the viewport scale. Verify that the *Viewport Scale* is set at **1/2"=1'-0"**. Re-lock the viewport when you are finished. You can also change the size of the viewport if it is too small.

4. Activate the viewport. Verify that the layer **Dimensions** is active.

5. In the *Annotate* tab>Dimensions panel, verify that the dimension layer is set to **Use Current**.

Annotate Drawings

6. In the *Annotate* tab>Dimensions panel, click (Dimension).

7. Hover the cursor over one of the six circled columns. If the cursor does not display the diameter dimension (while hovering over the circle), toggle off **Object Snap** in the Status Bar. Select the circle to accept the diameter dimension and click again to place it at the required location.

8. Still in the **Dimension** command, hover the cursor over the arc of the portico. It displays the radial dimension.

9. Press <Down Arrow> and select **arc Length**, as shown in Figure 7–74.

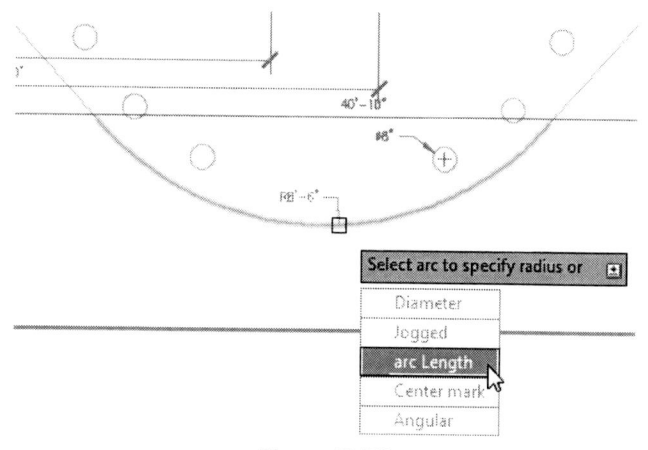

Figure 7–74

10. Select the arc and click again to place the dimension outside the arc, as shown in Figure 7–73.

11. Still in the **Dimension** command, hover the cursor over the arc of the portico again. Press <Down Arrow> and select **Radius**. Select the arc and click again to place the radius dimension on the inside of the portico arc.

12. Toggle on **Object Snap** in the Status Bar.

13. Still in the **Dimension** command, select the two endpoints of the angled line that joins the portico arc with the building wall. Add Aligned dimension to both the angled lines. (Use the end of the arc length dimension line to keep the connected dimensions in line.)

14. Still in the **Dimension** command, select one of the angled line again. Hover the cursor over the wall line that touches the selected angled line to display the angled dimension, as shown in Figure 7–75.

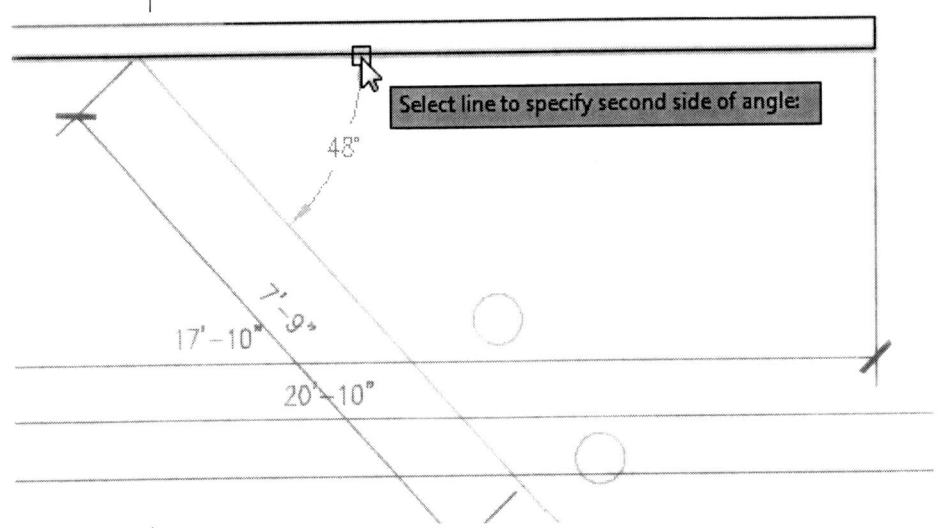

Figure 7–75

15. Select the line to accept the angled dimension and click again to place it, as shown in Figure 7–73.

16. Add **Angular** dimensions on the other side as well.

17. Exit the **Dimension** command.

18. Save and close the drawing.

7.7 Editing Dimensions

If the dimensions are interfering with other parts in a drawing, as shown in Figure 7–76, you can edit and modify them using grips and special tools in the shortcut menu. You can also edit the dimension text. Additional tools available to clean up dimensions include: aligning dimensions and breaking extension lines.

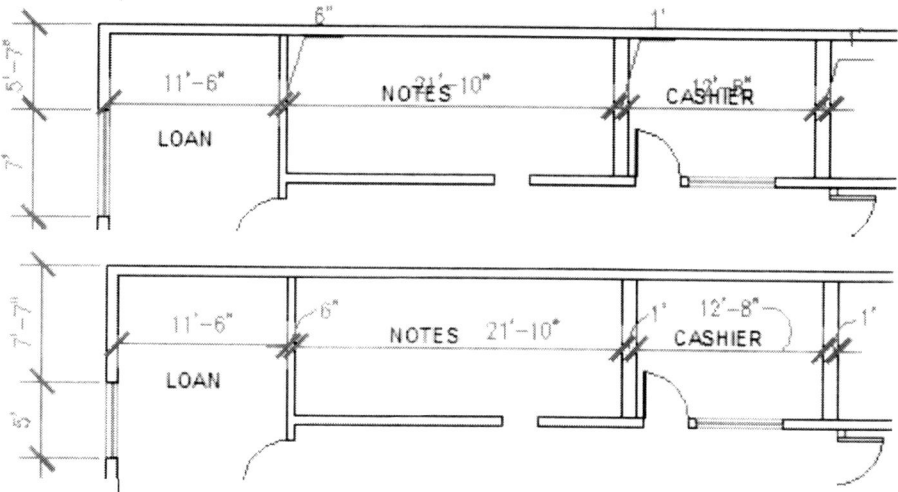

Figure 7–76

- The AutoCAD dimensions are associative. Therefore, when you change a dimensioned object, the dimensions update to reflect the change. If you move an object, the dimensions move as well. If you change the size of an object, the dimensions display the change.

- To change the dimension style of an existing dimension, select it and then set the appropriate dimension style in the Dimension Style drop-down list, in the *Annotate* tab> Dimensions panel.

Dimension Shortcut Menu

You can select a dimension or multiple dimensions, and then right-click to access additional options in the shortcut menu, as shown in Figure 7–77.

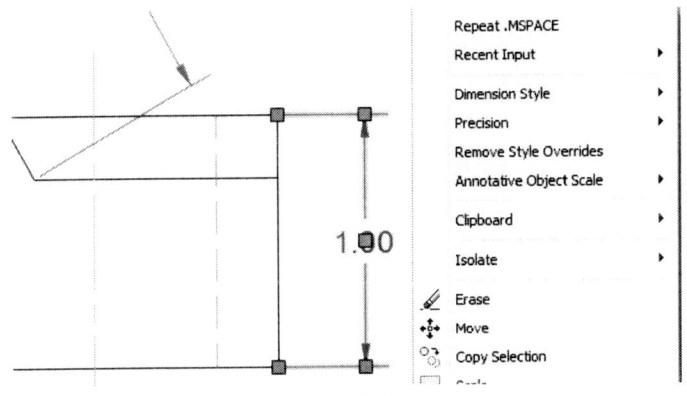

Figure 7–77

- You can change the Dimension Style of selected dimensions using the **Dimension Style** option. The dimension style controls the basic features of a dimension, such as the text location and number of decimal places.

- You can change the precision of selected dimensions using the **Precision** option. Precision helps you to display dimensions to a specific number of decimal places.

Editing Dimensions Using Grips

Grips can be used to relocate dimension elements. Without starting a command, select the following to display its grips at various parts of the dimension, as shown in Figure 7–78.

- Where extension lines touch the dimensioned object
- Where the extension line and dimension line meet
- On the dimension text

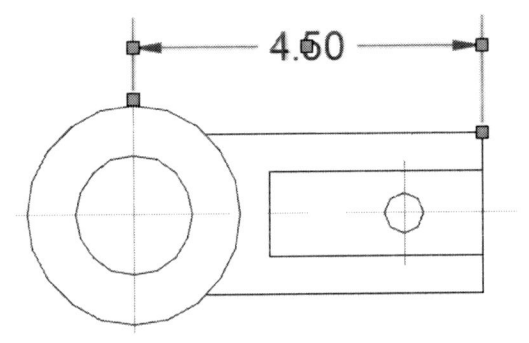

Figure 7–78

Annotate Drawings

Once the dimension grips display, you can edit the dimension as follows:

- Select the grip at the dimension line and move it to change the distance from the object.

- Select the grip on the text and move it to change the location of the text (and sometimes the dimension line).

- Select the grip at the extension line origin to change the length of the dimension. (This option might disconnect the associativity to the object it is dimensioning.)

- Press <Esc> to clear the grips.

Dimension Grips Shortcut Options

Additional options are available for editing dimensions using the multifunctional grips. Hover the cursor over a grip, and select an option in the dynamic input list. Depending on the specific grip you hover over, a different list of options displays, as shown in Figure 7–79.

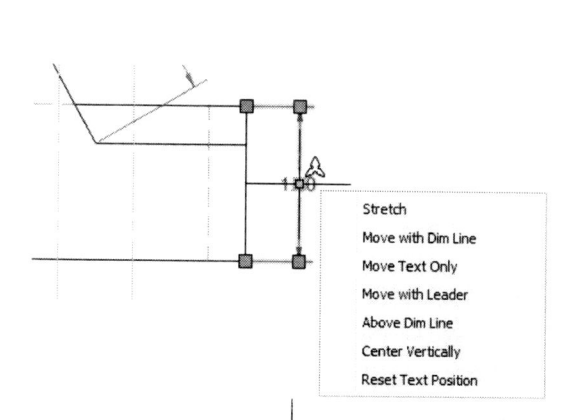

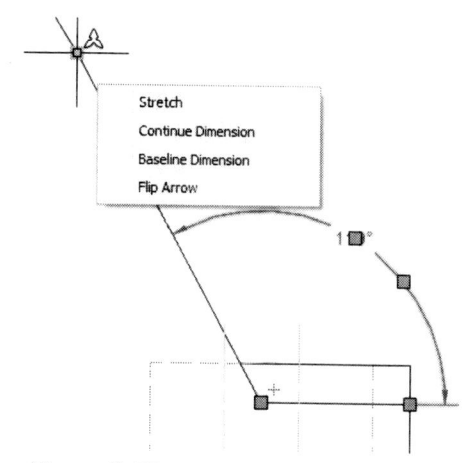

Figure 7–79

- Use the various text options, such as **Move Text Only** and **Above Dim Line** to move the text to a different position.

- **Reset Text Position** returns the moved text to its original location.

- You can use an existing dimension as the beginning of a series of related dimensions in either **Continue** or **Baseline**.

- Use **Flip Arrow** if the arrowheads on a dimension were pushed out and you want them to be inside the extension lines or on the opposite side.

- You can also access these options by selecting a grip (making it hot), and then using <Ctrl> to cycle through the options, or right-clicking and selecting one in the shortcut menu, as shown in Figure 7–80.

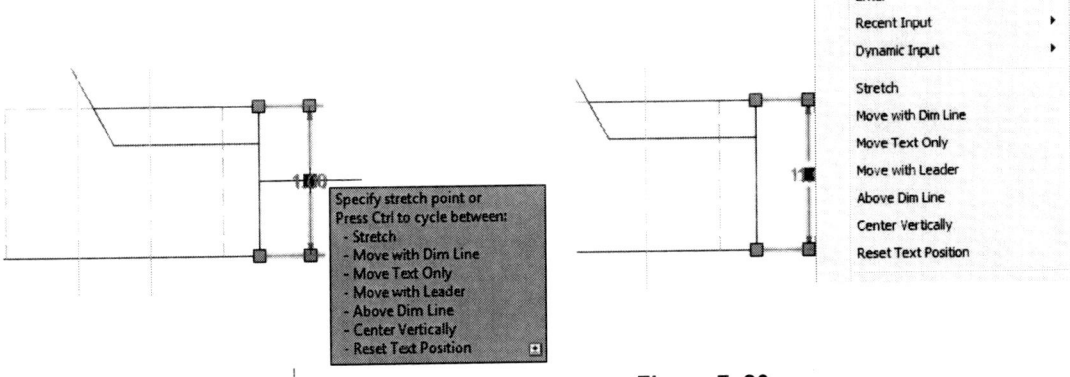

Figure 7–80

Editing the Dimension Text

Dimensions are associated with the objects they reference. However, sometimes you might need to add text to a dimension (such as +/- in renovation work), as shown in Figure 7–81.

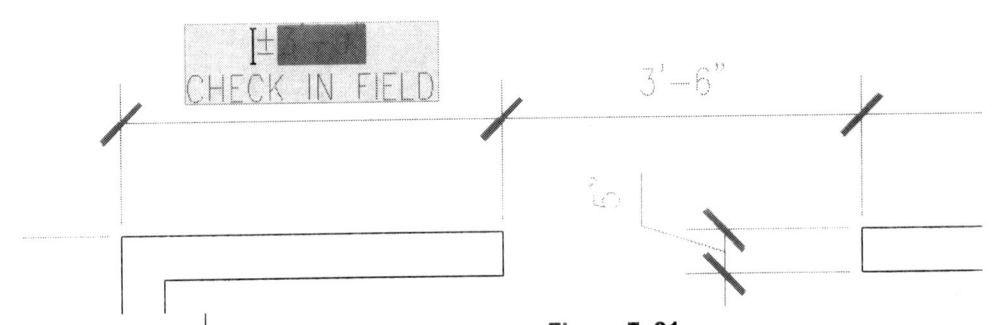

Figure 7–81

- To change the dimension text, double-click on the dimension text or type **ddedit**. The default dimension text or value is inserted as a special field in the Text Editor. You can add text before or after the field, or delete the field to completely replace the default text When editing dimension text, a width sizing control displays above the text. This enables you to adjust the text width for text wrapping, as shown in Figure 7–82.

Text Width Modifier

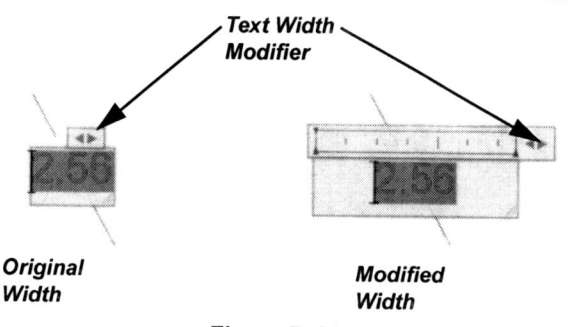

Original Width *Modified Width*

Figure 7–82

- If you remove the text associated with the dimension by mistake and want to get it back, type <> in the Text Editor.

Adjusting Dimension Spacing

When you create stacked angular or linear dimensions of any type, they might be too close together or unevenly spaced, as shown in Figure 7–83. Instead of moving each dimension, you can modify the space between sets of dimensions using the **Adjust Space** command.

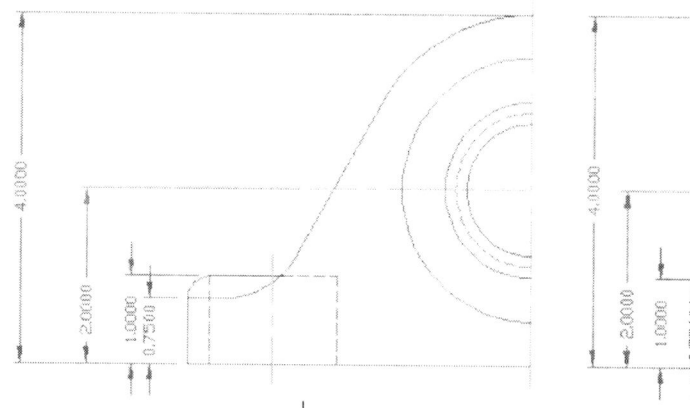

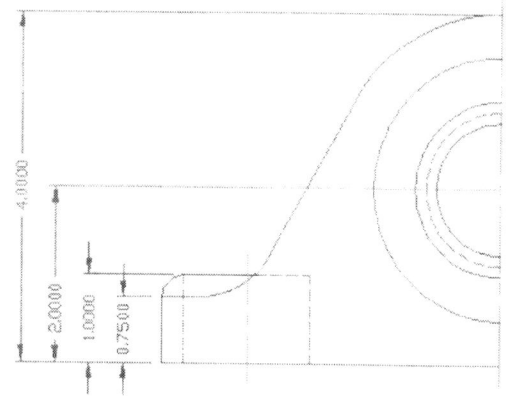

Figure 7–83

How To: Modify the Space Between Dimensions

1. In the *Annotate* tab>Dimensions panel, click (Adjust Space).
2. Select the base dimension (the one closest to the object) of the group you want to modify.
3. Select the rest of the dimensions in the group.
4. Enter the distance that you want to have between dimensions or press <Enter> to accept the automatic distance.

Dimension Breaks

When there are many dimensions in a drawing, the various extension lines and dimension lines can start to overlap. In that case, you can create dimension breaks without changing the associativity of the dimension object, as shown in Figure 7–84.

- When the object is stretched, the dimensions change and the breaks remain in place. This makes revising a drawing easier, as you no longer need to re-dimension a modified part.

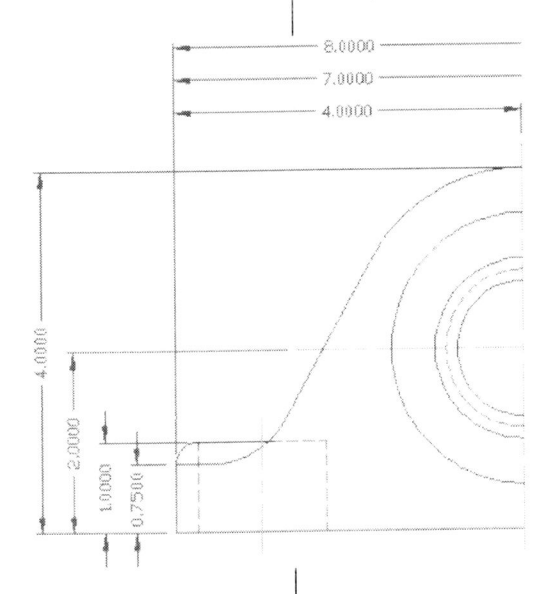

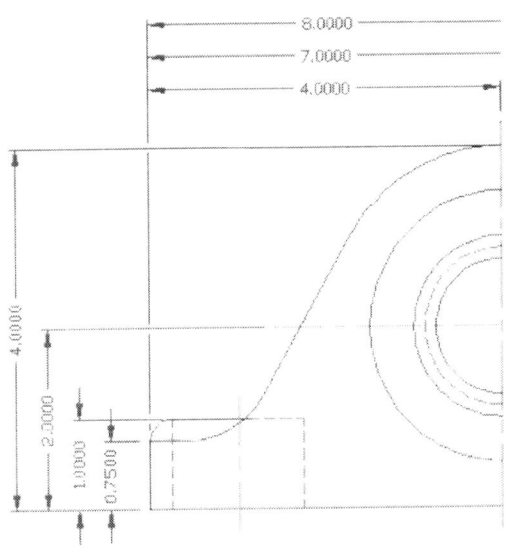

Figure 7–84

How To: Break One Dimension

1. In the *Annotate* tab>Dimensions panel, click (Dimension Break).
2. Select a dimension to break.
3. Select an object to break the dimension or select one of the options.
4. Continue to select other objects to break their dimensions as required.
5. Press <Enter> to complete the command.

- The **Multiple** option enables you to select more than one dimension to break. The selected dimensions are broken where they overlap other dimensions.

- To remove breaks from a dimension, start the **Break** command, select the dimension, and select the **Remove** option.

Practice 7f

Editing Dimensions (Mechanical)

Practice Objective

- Modify the text and move dimensions.

Estimated time for completion: 5 minutes

In this practice, you will modify the text of several dimensions and move the dimensions as required using grips, as shown in Figure 7–85.

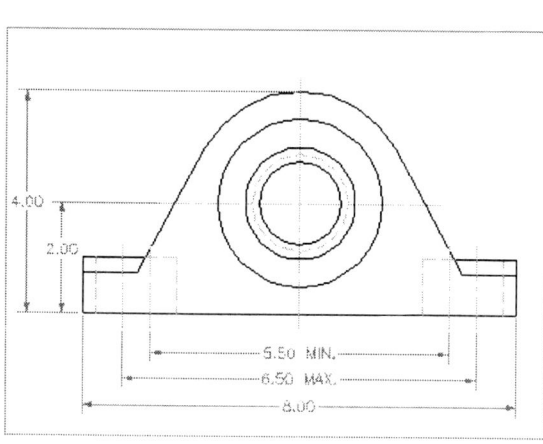

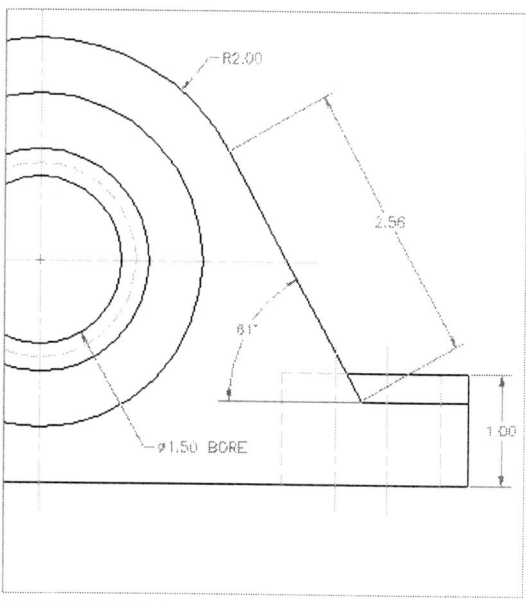

Figure 7–85

1. Open **Bearing Dimensions2-I.dwg** from your practice files folder.

2. Activate the **2:1** viewport (right side) and modify the text of the diameter dimension (of the innermost circle) so that it reads **Ø1.50 BORE**. Then change the width for text wrapping to display it in single line.

3. Using the grip, move the diameter dimension outside of the circles, as shown in Figure 7–86.

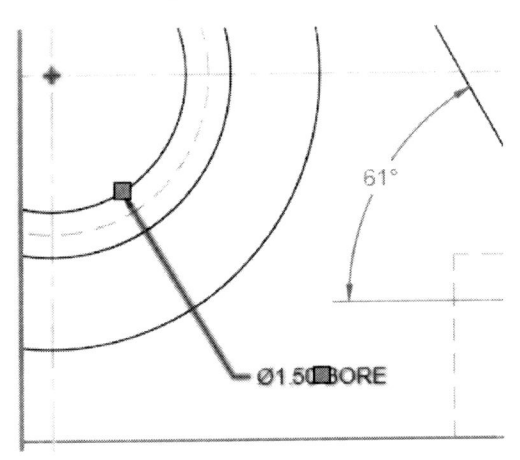

Figure 7–86

4. Activate the **1:1** viewport, modify the text of the two horizontal dimensions, as shown in Figure 7–87.

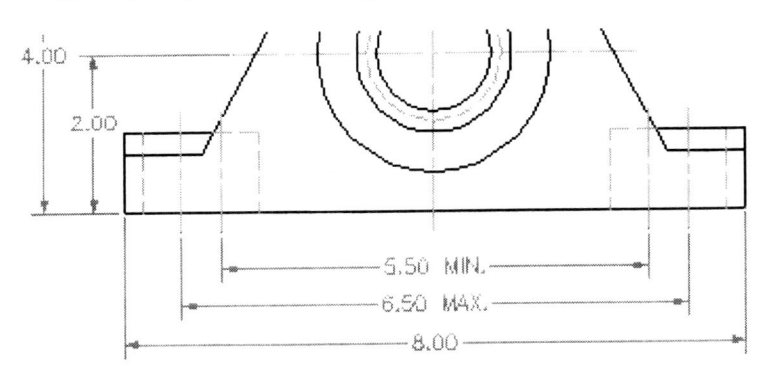

Figure 7–87

5. Use grips to move any of the other dimensions as required to a location where they are easier to read. You can also use the **Adjust Space** command to even out the bottom dimensions as required.

6. Save and close the drawing.

7.8 Adding Notes with Leaders to Your Drawing

In a drawing, you often need to use an arrow to point to objects in the drawing and add either text or keynotes. This can be done using the **Multileader** command. Multileaders consist of straight lines or splines can contain multiple leaders. You can use Multiline text or blocks for content, as shown in Figure 7–88.

The style of a multileader determines whether it uses text for the note or a block, such as a circle.

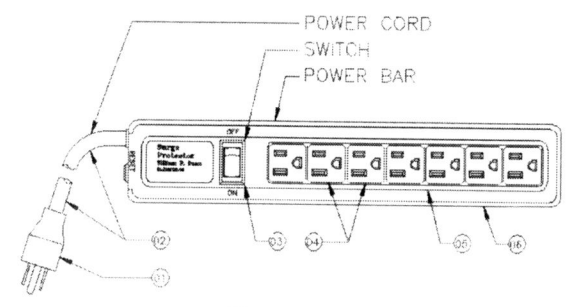

Figure 7–88

- As with other text and dimension objects, multileaders use a style and can be annotative.

How To: Add a Text Note

1. Select a Multileader style that uses text. Both the Standard and Annotative styles provided with the AutoCAD templates are designed this way.
2. In the *Annotate* tab>Leaders panel or in the *Home* tab>Annotation panel, click (Multileader)
3. Select a point for the leader arrowhead location.
4. Select a point for the leader landing. By default, a horizontal tag is attached to the end.
5. Type the text. To specify the text width so that it word-wraps, you can use the Text Width arrows in the Text Formatting ruler.

6. Click ✕ (Close Text Editor) in the *Text Editor* contextual tab or click away from the text in the drawing. The multileader displays as shown in Figure 7–89.

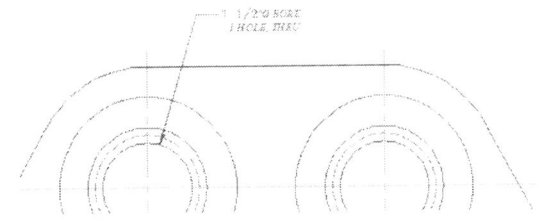

Figure 7–89

- The *Text Editor* contextual tab displays when you place multiline text using the **Multileader** command.

- You can change the order in which you place the leader using the **Leader Landing first** or **Content first** options, as shown in Figure 7–90. If you change the method of placing the leader, it becomes the default and is used the next time you start the command.

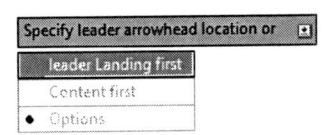

Figure 7–90

*You can use **Options** to modify the appearance of the leader, but creating Multileader Styles is recommended.*

Drawing Keynotes

You can draw Multileaders with numbers in a block that are related to a list of keynotes located elsewhere in the drawing, as shown in Figure 7–91. You need to use a multileader style that uses blocks.

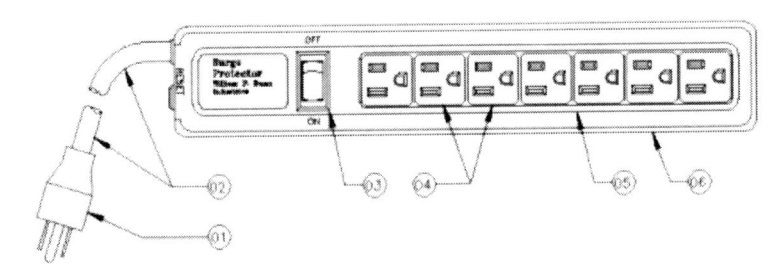

Figure 7–91

Modifying Multileaders

The leader and text (or block) of a multileader are one object. Multileaders can be modified using grips and text editing tools.

Grip Editing

You can use grips to modify the landing length (as shown in Figure 7–92), leader length and angle, and to move the multileader.

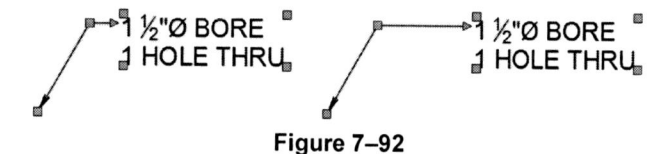

Figure 7–92

- The square grip at the end of the leader line changes the location at which the leader line is pointing.

- The square grip at the top left of the text moves the multileader.

- The arrow grip on the landing changes its length.

- If you hover over the square multi-functional grips on the leader line as shown in Figure 7–93, additional options display, such as **Add Vertex** and **Add/Remove Leader**.

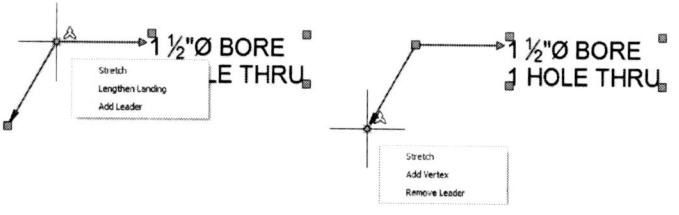

Figure 7–93

- If you are working with text leaders that have a specific text length, you can modify the text boundary using grips, as shown in Figure 7–94.

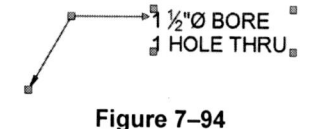

Figure 7–94

- If the text does not have a specified boundary, you can create one by clicking on the text again and modifying the boundary box using the Text Width ruler, as shown in Figure 7–95.

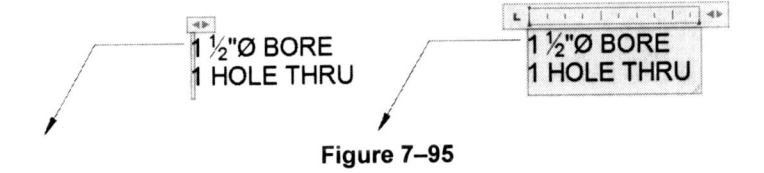

Figure 7–95

Adding and Removing Leaders

You can add or remove leader lines to create a single leader object, which points to multiple locations in the drawing, as shown in Figure 7–96.

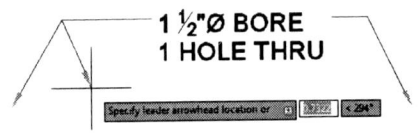

Figure 7–96

How To: Add Leaders

1. In the *Annotate* tab>Leaders panel, click (Add Leader).
2. Select an existing Multileader.
3. Select the location at which you want to add the new leader.
4. Continue adding leaders as required.
5. Press <Enter> to complete the command.

How To: Remove Leaders

1. In the *Annotate* tab>Leaders panel, click (Remove Leader).
2. Select an existing Multileader.
3. Select the leaders that you want to remove.
4. Press <Enter> to complete the command.

Annotate Drawings

Select Individual Leaders to Edit

You can select individual leaders and modify them. For example, in Figure 7–97, several leaders were modified to distinguish new plants from existing plants of the same type.

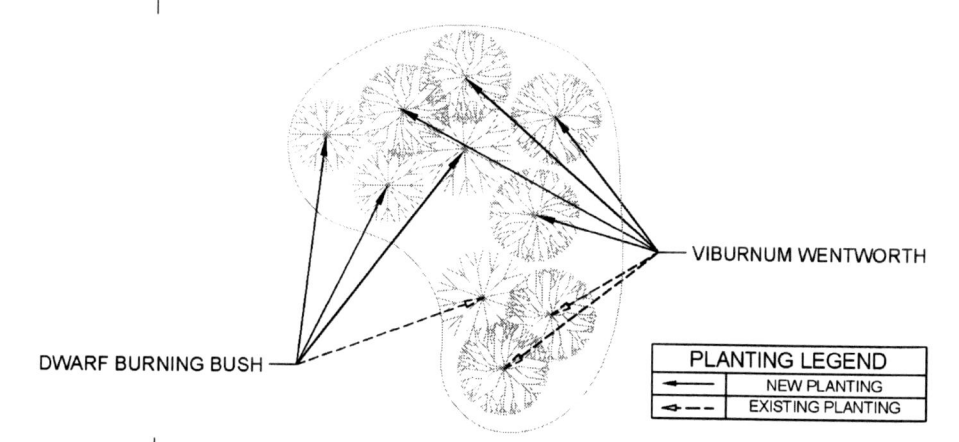

Figure 7–97

How To: Select and Edit Individual Leaders

1. Select an existing Multileader.
2. Hold <Ctrl> and click to select one or more leaders in a Multileader. The leaders display with red grips.
3. Once selected, right-click and select Properties. Use the Properties palette to change the properties of the selected leaders, such as their color, leader, or arrowhead size, as shown in Figure 7–98.

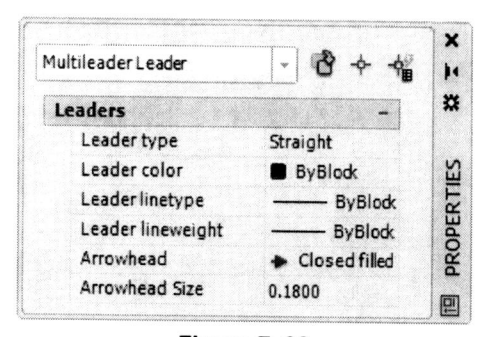

Figure 7–98

Aligning Multileaders

You can use the **Multileader Align** command to arrange multileaders so that they are evenly spaced and aligned, as shown in How To:Figure 7–99.

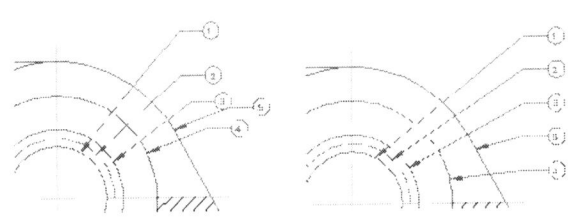

Figure 7–99

How To: Align Multileaders

1. In the *Annotate* tab>Leaders panel, click (Align, Multileader).
2. Select the multileaders that you want to align and press <Enter>.
3. You can change the current mode of aligning by pressing <Down Arrow>, selecting **Options**, and selecting an option.
4. Select the multileader or points to which you want to align.

The last option used becomes the default when you use the command again.

Distribute	Select two points. The multileaders are evenly spaced between them.
Make leader segments Parallel	Select a multileader to which to make the other leader segments parallel. The content remains in place and the leaders' angles are made parallel to the selected leader.
Specify Spacing	Select to type a distance for the spacing and then select a multileader to which to align and direction for alignment.
Use current spacing	Select to use the current spacing settings. The content is aligned and the spacing between the multileaders does not change.

Annotate Drawings

Collecting Multileaders

You can collect several multileaders together using one leader, as shown in Figure 7–100. This only works with multileaders that have block content, not those with text content. This enables you to combine multiple blocks into a string. The blocks can be displayed vertically, horizontally, or wrapped to fit into a selected space.

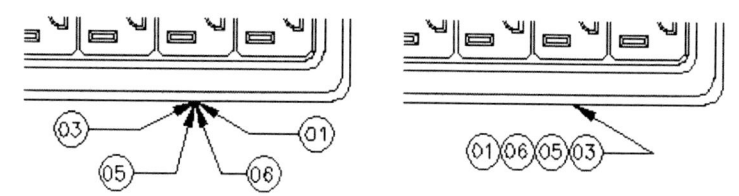

Figure 7–100

How To: Collect Multileader Blocks

1. In the *Annotate* tab>Leaders panel, click (Collect).
2. Select the leaders that you want to group together and press <Enter>
3. Select a location for the newly collected leaders.

- The default layout is **Horizontal**, but you can change it to **Vertical** using the shortcut menu. If there is a long line of bubbles, select the **Wrap** option and specify the wrap distance.

Practice 7g

Adding Notes to Your Drawing

Practice Objectives

- Add text and block-based multileaders to a drawing.
- Add leaders to multileaders, align and modify multileaders.

Estimated time for completion: 10 minutes

In this practice, you will add text and block-based multileaders. You will add leaders to multileaders and then align and modify leaders with grips as required, as shown in Figure 7–101.

- The multileader style **Keynotes** was created for this drawing.

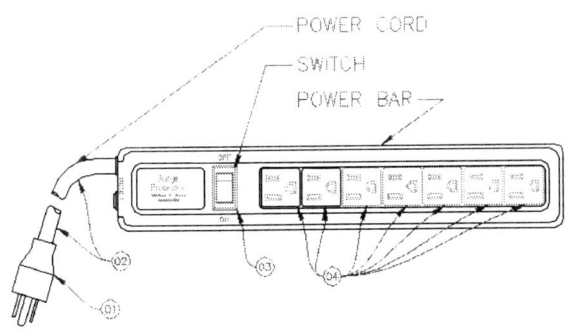

Figure 7–101

Task 1 - Draw multileaders.

1. Open **Power Protector-I.dwg** from your practice files folder.

2. Switch to the **A-Sized** layout and activate the viewport. You might have to use **Zoom Extents** to display the drawing in the viewport. Pan the model down so that more empty space is left at the top, and then lock the viewport.

3. Set the *current layer* to **Text**.

4. In the *Annotate* tab>Leaders panel, in the *Multileader style* list, click **Annotative**.

5. In the *Annotate* tab>Leaders panel, click (Multileader).

Annotate Drawings

6. Add multileaders as shown in Figure 7–102, to label the **POWER CORD**, **POWER BAR**, and **SWITCH**. Place the multileaders so they are not aligned.

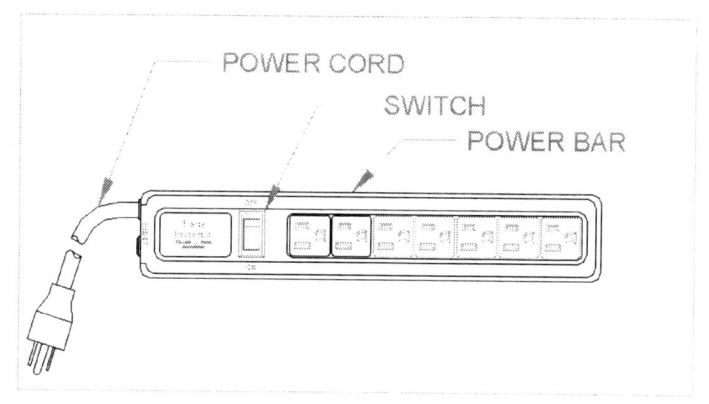

Figure 7–102

7. Set the current *Multileader style* to **Keynotes**.

8. Start the **Multileader** command. Add several multileaders and with each multileader, in the Edit Attributes dialog box, enter tag numbers to label the components as **01**, **02**, **03**, and **04**, as shown in Figure 7–103.

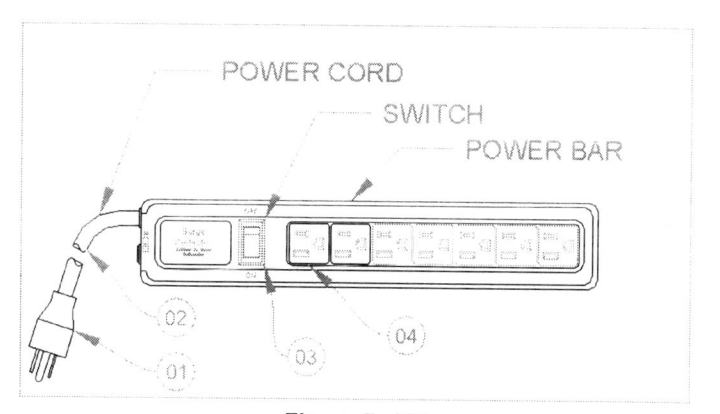

Figure 7–103

Task 2 - Modify multileaders.

1. Select the multileader with the label **02** and then in the *Annotate* tab>Leaders panel, click (Add Leader). A leader is attached to the cursor. Add a leader to the other half of the power cord (as shown in Figure 7–104) and press <Enter>.

2. Similarly, add leaders to the multileader labeled **04** to point to each of the remaining sockets.

3. In the *Annotate* tab>Leaders panel, click (Align, Multileader).

4. Select the multileaders **POWER BAR**, **POWER CORD**, and **SWITCH** and then press <Enter>. Align the multileaders to **SWITCH** by selecting it. To set the direction, move the cursor perpendicularly above the **SWITCH** multileader. Click to place the multileaders.

5. Modify the exact locations of the leaders and text as required using grips.

Task 3 - Add text.

1. Set the current *Text style* to **Annotative** (*Annotate* tab>Text panel).

2. Start the **Multiline Text** command.

3. Use a height of **.125** and then add a note above and to the left of the power bar, as shown in Figure 7–104. Use the grips to place the note in two lines.

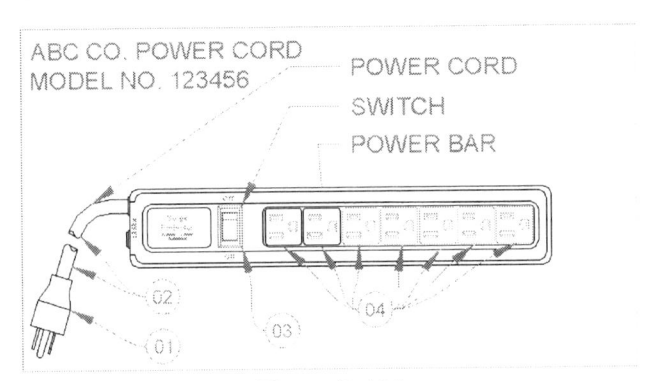

Figure 7–104

4. Save the drawing.

7.9 Working with Annotations

When you set up layouts with viewports at various scales, the parts of the model display at different sizes. However, the final printed sheet should have text and dimensions that are all of the same size when they are plotted, as shown in Figure 7–105. The *Annotation Scale* feature enables you to add text and dimensions to a drawing with views at many different scales. These annotation objects are scaled to suit and do not display in viewports with other annotation scales.

Annotation objects include: text, dimensions, hatches, and multileaders.

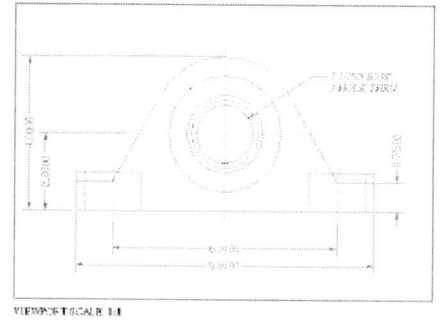

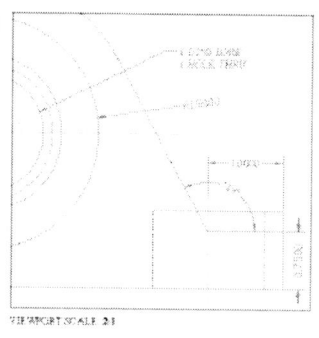

Figure 7–105

- When you create each viewport, set ▣ 1:2 ▾ (Viewport Scale) in the Status Bar, as shown in Figure 7–106. The Annotation Scale is automatically matched to the viewport scale.

Figure 7–106

- To add annotation objects, double-click inside the viewport to make it active and select the annotation tool. It is automatically scaled to match the viewport/annotation scale.

Click 🔒 (Lock/Viewport) to lock the viewport so that the scale and location are not changed by mistake.

- To understand the differences between annotations placed in Model Space and Paper Space, open the Properties palette and note the two parameters: **Paper text height** and **Model text height**.

For example, in the room shown in Figure 7–107, the text **Service Area** is placed in a viewport at a scale of *1/4"=1'-0"*, while the text for the title and scale is placed in Paper Space at a scale of 1:1. Note that the two text objects look the same size.

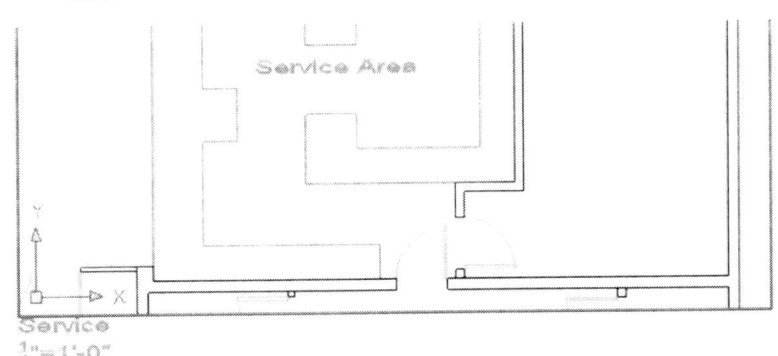

Figure 7–107

- If you select the text in Paper Space and then note the values of the parameters in the Properties palette, the **Paper text height** and **Model text height** are the same, as shown on the left in Figure 7–108. If you select the text inside the viewport and then note the values of the parameters in the Properties palette, the **Paper text height** and the **Model text height** are different, as shown on the right in Figure 7–108. The AutoCAD® software automatically scales the text inside the viewport so that it is 1/4".

Text	
Contents	\A1;{\W1;\LStairs\P\H0.7x\...
Style	Title
Annotative	Yes
Annotative scale	1:1
Justify	Top left
Direction	By style
Paper text height	1/4"
Model text height	1/4"

Text	
Contents	Service Area
Style	Title
Annotative	Yes
Annotative scale	1/4" = 1'-0"
Justify	Top left
Direction	By style
Paper text height	1/4"
Model text height	9 5/8"

Figure 7–108

Working with Annotative Styles

Many annotation objects are created using styles. The annotation styles (Text Styles, Dimension Styles, and Multileader Styles) can be made annotative. You should select a style that is designed to work with the Annotation Scale so that objects are correctly placed in each viewport.

- ⚞ (Annotation) displays next to annotative style names in the Text Style, Dimension Style, and Multileader Style Controls, as shown in Figure 7–109.

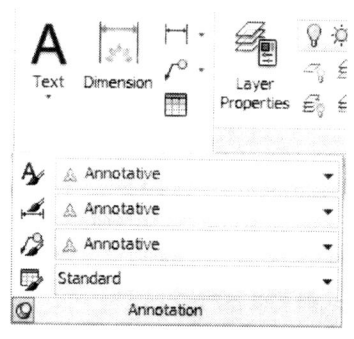

Figure 7–109

- When you have objects in your drawing that are annotative, ⚞ (Annotation) displays when you hover the cursor over them, as shown in Figure 7–110.

Figure 7–110

- You must change the Viewport Scale in the Status Bar for the annotative objects to change scale.

- You can annotate objects in Model Space by setting the ⚞ 1:1 ▼ (Annotation Scale) in the Status Bar, as shown in Figure 7–111. It is linked to the Viewport Scale and the annotation displays in viewports that have the same annotation scale.

Figure 7–111

- When you use annotation styles, the *Model text height* in the Properties palette is read-only.

7.10 Creating Text Styles

When you add text to your drawing, it uses the properties (e.g., height, font, etc.) of the current *text style,* as shown in Figure 7–112. Text styles should be created in the template file so that everyone on the same project uses the same styles. You can create a new style by assigning the height, width, and slant to a text font, or to a typeface design.

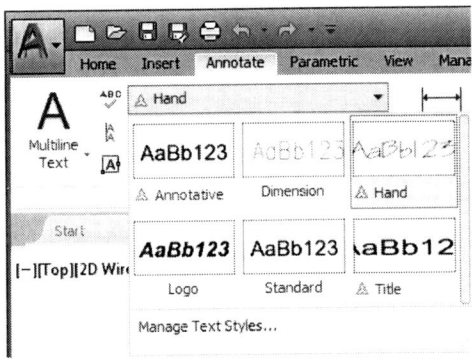

Figure 7–112

- There are two default styles: **Standard** and **Annotative**. You can create other styles as required.

- A variety of font files are available for creating different styles of text. There are two different types of fonts: Truetype fonts (used by most Microsoft Windows software) and AutoCAD® shape fonts. You can use the fonts that the AutoCAD software installs or the other Truetype fonts that were installed with Windows.

Annotate Drawings

You can also open the dialog box by clicking the panel arrow in the *Annotate tab>Text panel*.

How To: Create a Text Style

1. In the *Annotate* tab>Text panel>Text Style list, select **Manage Text Styles...**.
2. In the Text Style dialog box (shown in Figure 7–113), click **New...**. The new style takes on the attributes of the current text style.

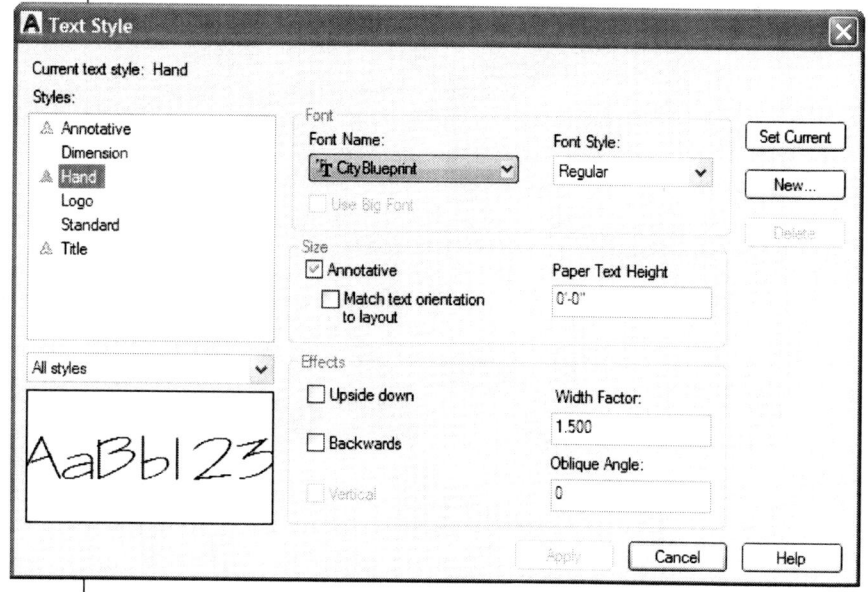

Figure 7–113

3. In the New Text Style dialog box, type a new name and click **OK**.
4. Expand the Font Name drop-down list, select a font (a preview of the font displays in the *Preview* area). For some fonts, you can also specify a Font Style (such as bold or italic).
5. Select the **Annotative** option if you want the text style to scale per viewport. You can also set a default height for the style, but this is typically left at **0** so that you can use one style for different sizes of text.
6. In the *Effects* area, set up the required properties.
7. Click **Apply** to continue working in the dialog box or **Close** to close the dialog box. The style that was created is now the current style.

- You can change the current style in the Text Style Control in the *Home* tab>expanded Annotation panel, the *Annotate* tab>Text panel, or the *Text Editor* contextual tab>Style panel when you have started the **Multiline Text** command.

- You can change the style of existing text by selecting the text object and then selecting a style in the *Home* tab>Annotation panel or *Annotate* tab>Text panel.

- If you modify an annotative style, you need to use **annoupdate** to update any existing objects to match the revised annotative style.

Style Effects

The style effects make a text style different from a standard font. You can define several text styles that use the same font but differ in width, oblique angle, etc.

Width Factor	Defines the character width relative to the height. A width factor of **1** is the default. Numbers greater than one increase the width and numbers less than one decrease the width. Typical width factors are in the range of 0.8 to 1.5.
Oblique Angle	Enables you to slant the lettering. Positive values incline the top of the text to the right and negative values slant it to the left. Typical obliquing angles range from +10 to -10. Angles of +30 and -30 are commonly used to label isometric drawings.

- Text is normally placed horizontally in a drawing. Vertical, upside-down, or backward text orientation can also be defined when creating text styles.

Notes on Text Styles

- The *Preview* displays an image of how your text style is going to be displayed when used in the drawing. All of the effects of a text style are previewed except the height.

- To rename a text style, double-click on the style name. In the Edit box, type the new name.

- To delete a text style, highlight it in the list and click **Delete**. It is only deleted if it is not in use.

- Some TrueType fonts can be filled or outlined. To have them filled in your drawing, you need to set the **textfill** system variable to **ON** (textfill = 1).

- **Match Properties** (in the *Home* tab>Properties panel) enables you to copy the style from one text object to another in your drawing. It is also available in the *Text Editor* contextual tab.

Practice 7h

Estimated time for completion: 10 minutes

The color has been changed to black for printing clarity.

Creating and Using Text Styles

Practice Objective

- Create several new text styles.

In this practice, you will define several new text styles using the **Text Style** command, as shown in Figure 7–114.

The Standard Style | Hand lettering Style
Title Text Style | Dimensions Style

Figure 7–114

1. Open **AEC-Facilities1-A.dwg** from your practice files folder. It is an empty file.

2. Make the layer **Notes** active.

3. In the *Annotate* tab>Text panel, note that the active text style is **Standard.**

4. Switch to one of the layouts. Start the **Multiline Text** command. If the preview text (abc) is not visible with the cursor, zoom in until it displays. Place the text **The Standard Style** anywhere in the drawing.

5. In the Text Style list, select **Manage Text Styles....** Modify the Standard Style and change the *Font Name* to **romans**. Click **Apply** and **Close**. Note how the text you just entered has updated.

6. Open the Text Style dialog box again and click **New**.

7. Create a new style named **Title**. Set the *Font Name* to **Arial**, the *Font Style* to **Bold** and the *Width Factor* to **1.5**. Click **Apply** to save the changes.

8. Create another new text style named **Hand2**. For the *Font Name*, select **CityBlueprint**. Set the *Width Factor* to **1.5**. Click **Apply** to save the changes.

9. Create another new text style named **Dimensions**. For the *Font Name*, select **romans**. Set the *Width Factor* to **0.8**. Click **Apply** to save the changes and click **Close**.

10. Make each style current and then add text to the drawing using a text string to test the styles.

11. Set the current style to **Hand**. Erase all of the text and save the drawing.

7.11 Creating Dimension Styles

The dimension style controls all aspects of how your dimensions display (type and size of arrows, type of units displayed, text specifications, text placement, etc.). You might need to have several styles in a drawing to display different information, as shown in Figure 7–115. For example, in mechanical drawings you might have one style with decimal units that displays two decimal places of precision, another that displays three decimal places, and a third that displays both English and Metric units at the same time.

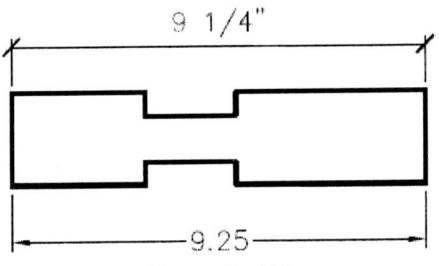

Figure 7–115

- You can set the current dimension style in the Dimension Style Control in the *Home* tab>Annotation panel or *Annotate* tab>Dimensions panel.

- There are two default styles: **Standard** and **Annotative**. You can create other styles as required.

How To: Create a Dimension Style

1. In the *Annotate* tab>Dimensions panel>Dimension Style list, select **Manage Dimension Styles...**.
2. Click **New...** in the Dimension Style Manager, as shown in Figure 7–116.

You can also open the dialog box by clicking the panel arrow in the *Annotate tab> Dimensions panel.*

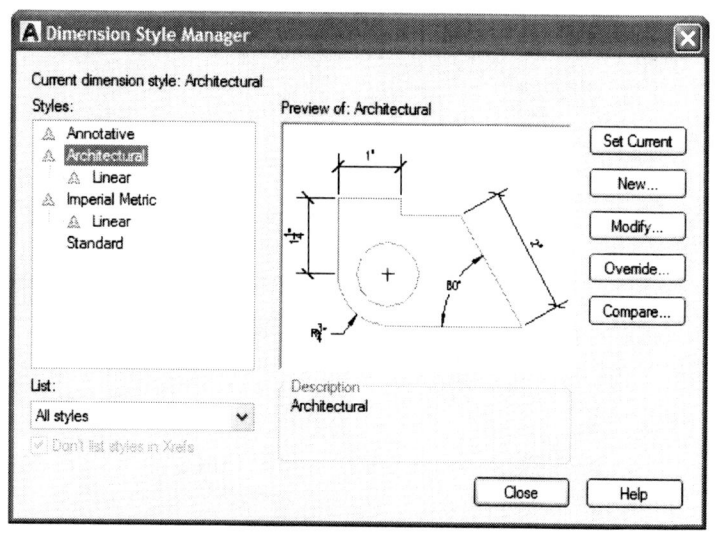

Figure 7–116

3. The Create New Dimension Style dialog box opens, as shown in Figure 7–117. In the Start With drop-down list, select a style to use as a template. In the *New Style Name* field, type a new style name and then select the **Annotative** option as required. Click **Continue**.

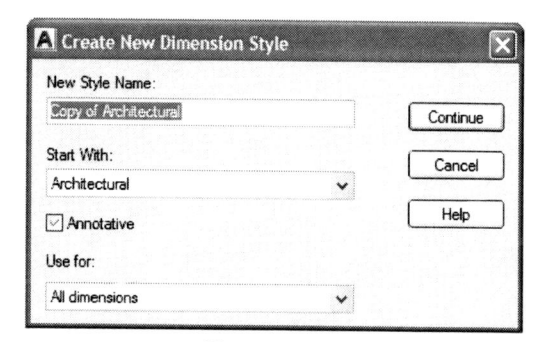

Figure 7–117

4. Modify the tabs as required and click **OK**.
5. If you want to make the new style current, double-click on its name in the *Styles* area or select it and click **Set Current**.
6. Click **Close**.

- All of the distances and sizes specified for the dimension style should be at their final plotted distance or size.

Modifying Dimension Styles

In the Dimension Sytle Manager, click **Modify** to open the Modify Dimension Style dialog box.

Dimension Style Lines Tab

The *Lines* tab controls the appearance of the dimension lines and extension lines, as shown in Figure 7–118.

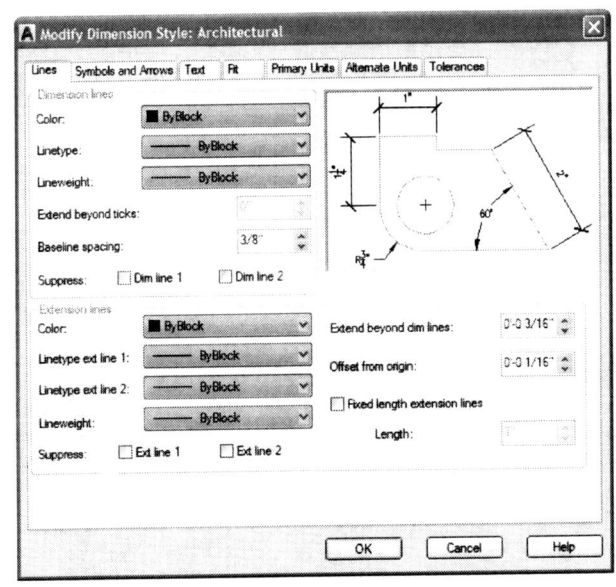

Figure 7–118

- *Color* and *Lineweight* are set to **ByBlock** by default. This is essentially the same as **ByLayer**. The dimension elements use the color and linetype of the current layer.

- *Extend beyond ticks* only applies if ticks are used rather than arrowheads.

- *Baseline spacing* is used for baseline dimensions that are applied with the **Baseline** or **Quick Dimension** commands.

- *Offset from origin* controls the size of the gap between the object and the start of the extension line.

- *Fixed length extension lines* controls how far the line reaches from the dimension line toward the dimensioned object.

Dimension Style Symbols and Arrows Tab

The *Symbols and Arrows* tab controls the size and style of the arrowheads on the dimension lines and leaders, and other symbols, such as Center marks (for circles and arcs) or the Arc length symbol, as shown in Figure 7–119.

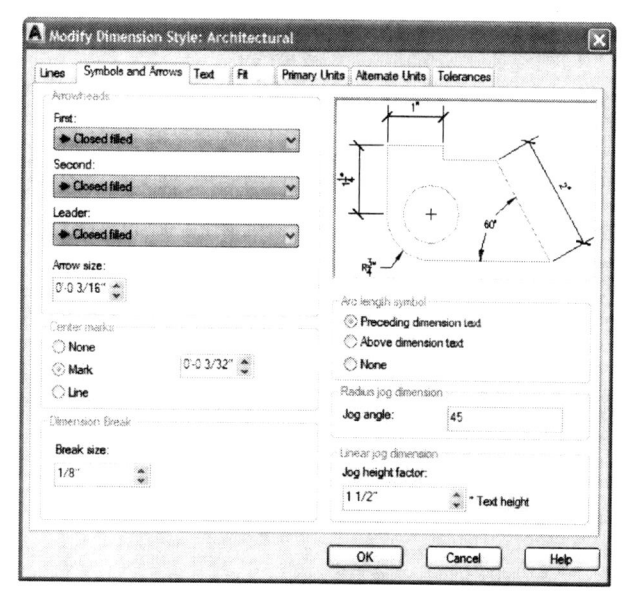

Figure 7–119

- The *Leader* (used for Radius, Diameter, and Angular dimensions) can have a different arrow style from the dimension lines.

- *Center Marks* are used with Radius and Diameter dimensions and the **Center Mark** command.

Dimension Style Text Tab

The *Text* tab controls the placement and appearance of the dimension text, as shown in Figure 7–120.

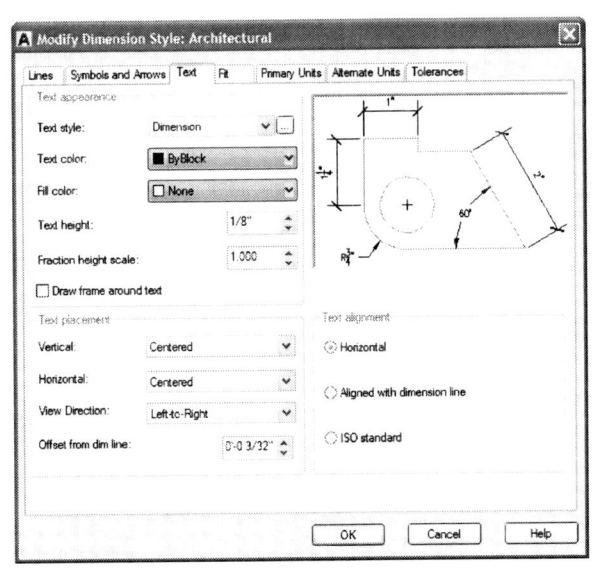

Figure 7–120

Do not set a height in text styles to be used for dimensioning. Use the dimension style to control the height.

- You can specify a text style in the Text style drop-down list. If you have not defined one, you can click ⋯ (Browse) to open the Text Style dialog box to create a new style. The text height should be set to the required plotted height.

- If you want the text to plot at a heavier weight than the rest of the dimensions (a standard drafting technique), set the text color to be a color that plots to a medium weight and leave the rest of the dimension elements with the *Text color* set to **ByBlock**. You can set the layer **Dimensions** to be a lightweight color.

- The *Fill* color can be set to **Background** or another color so that the text masks any objects behind it.

- *Offset from dim line* controls the size of the gap between the text and dimension lines. This applies when the text is centered on the line and above the line.

- *Text placement* can be set for **Vertical** and **Horizontal** dimensions.

- *View Direction* displays the dimension text **Left-to-Right** or **Right-to-Left**.

Dimension Style Fit Tab

The *Fit* tab controls the positions of arrows, text, leader lines, and the dimension line, as shown in Figure 7–121. It also controls the scale for dimension features.

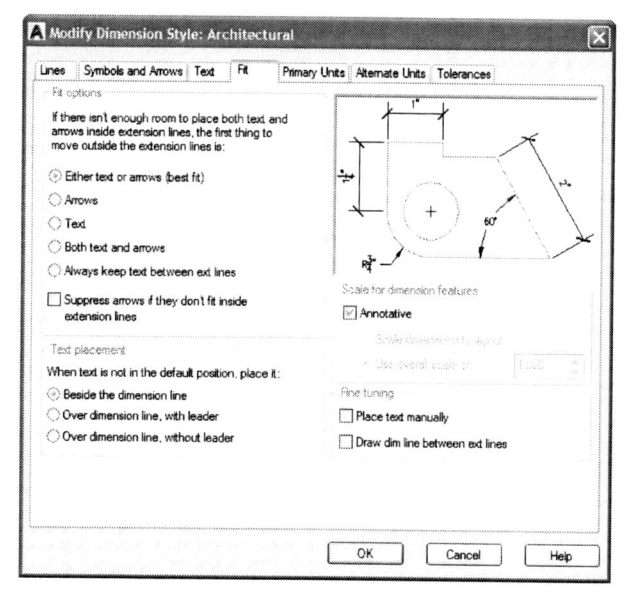

Figure 7–121

- When you set the *Scale for dimension features* to **Annotative**, the other options are grayed out. The dimensions are scaled according to the scale of the viewport through which they are inserted.

- If you are not using Annotative dimensions, you can use **Scale dimensions to layout** to display the objects in all viewports. You can also select **Use overall scale of** to dimension directly on the model when you are plotting from Model Space.

Dimension Style Primary Units Tab

The *Primary Units* tab controls the format of the primary units in the dimension text, as shown in Figure 7–122. This is independent of the type of units that are used in the drawing.

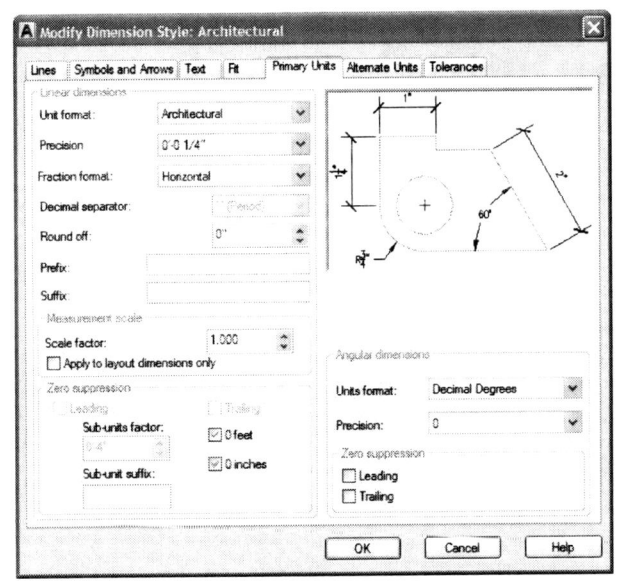

Figure 7–122

- You can set the required type of units for dimensioning, the number of decimal places, and other information to define the appearance of the text.

- A default *Prefix* and *Suffix* can be added in front or after all of the dimension values (for example, a suffix of mm for millimeters).

- The *Scale factor* multiplies the actual dimension value. For example, if the actual distance is 5 and the scale factor is 2, the value that displays in the dimension text is 10. If objects are drawn at full size, the scale should normally be set to 1.

- The *Sub-units factor* eliminates the leading zeros in dimension values by specifying that any measurement less than one primary unit be dimensioned in a smaller unit of measure. The *Sub-unit suffix* automatically appends a different dimension suffix to such dimensions.

Annotate Drawings

Dimension Style Alternate Units Tab

The *Alternate Units* tab is very similar to the *Primary Units* tab.

- *Multiplier for alt units* is the conversion factor between the units in which your drawing was created and the units you want to use for alternative dimensions. For example, if the Primary Units are decimal inches and the Alternate Units are millimeters, *Multiplier for alt units* should be **25.4** (1 inch = 25.4mm).

Dimension Style Tolerances Tab

The *Tolerances* tab is usually used in mechanical design to indicate the degree of precision required in manufacturing.

- *Method* determines how the tolerance is calculated and displayed. The options are **None**, **Symmetrical** (equal bilateral), **Deviation** (unequal bilateral), **Limits**, and **Basic** (places a box around the dimension and is used with Geometric Dimensioning & Tolerancing).

Creating Dimension Sub-Styles

You might need to use a slightly different style for a specific type of dimension. For example, you might want linear dimensions to use tick marks instead of arrows and to always be forced above the dimension line. You can create a style that uses arrows, and then create a sub-style that is only used for linear dimensions, as shown in Figure 7–123. When using that style, all of the dimensions that you place have arrows, except for the linear dimensions.

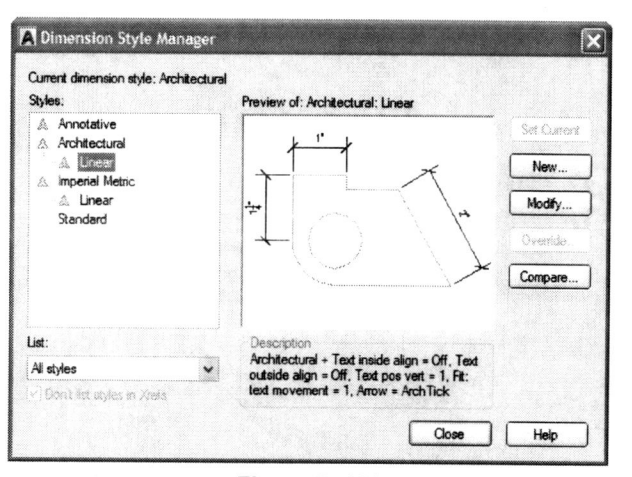

Figure 7–123

How To: Set Up a Dimension Sub-Style

1. Open the Dimension Style Manager.
2. Click **New...**.
3. In the Create New Dimension Style dialog box, in the Start With drop-down list select the style to use as a template.
4. In the Use for drop-down list, select a dimension type for the sub-style (linear, angular, etc.) that you are creating, as shown in Figure 7–124.

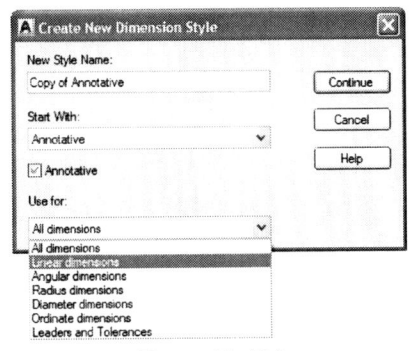

Figure 7–124

5. Click **Continue**.
6. In the New Dimension Style dialog box, define the sub-style as required with settings for lines, arrows, text, fit, etc.
7. When all of the settings have been adjusted, click **OK**. The new sub-style is listed in the Dimension Style Manager under the main style.

> **Hint: Modifying a Single Dimension**
>
> Select a dimension and use the Properties palette to modify the style of a single dimension without changing the style definition. In the Properties palette, all of the dimension style settings are listed. Each setting can be changed for the selected dimension.

Practice 7i

Estimated time for completion: 15 minutes

Dimension Styles (Mechanical)

Practice Objective

- Create dimension styles and apply them to dimensions.

In this practice, you will create two dimension styles and then apply dimensions with those styles, as shown in Figure 7–125 and Figure 7–126.

1. Open **Dim-I.dwg** from your practice files folder.

2. Create the two dimension styles (Tolerance and English_Metric) listed in the tables. *Start With* the **Standard** style, make each style **Annotative**, and use the default settings for options that are not specified.

	Tolerance	English_Metric
Lines tab		
Baseline spacing	0.38	0.5
Symbols and Arrows tab		
Arrowheads	Right angle	Closed Filled
Center marks	Mark	Line
Text tab		
Text style	Standard	Standard
Text color	ByBlock	Magenta
Text height	0.18	0.125
Vertical Placement	Centered	Above
Horizontal Placement	Centered	Centered
Text Alignment	Horizontal	Aligned with dimension line
Primary Units tab		
Unit format	Decimal	Architectural (horizontal fractions)
Precision	0.00	1/16
Alternate Units tab		
Alternate Units	None	Decimal, precision 0
		multiplier 25.4, suffix mm

© 2017, ASCENT - Center for Technical Knowledge®

Tolerances tab

Method	Limits	None
Upper Value	0.02	
Lower Value	0.03	
Scaling for height	0.75	

For English_Metric, include the following sub-styles:

	Angular	Diameter
Text tab		
Vertical text placement	Centered	Centered
Text alignment	Horizontal	Horizontal

3. Use the new dimension styles to dimension the objects shown in Figure 7–125 and Figure 7–126.

   - Set the layer **Dimensions** to be current.
   - A layout is prepared for each style. Use the **Add/Delete Scales** command to control which dimensions display in the appropriate viewport on each layout. The scale of the viewport in the **B-Sized Eng-Met** layout is 1:1 and the scale of the one in the **C-Sized Tol** layout is 2:1.

Tolerance

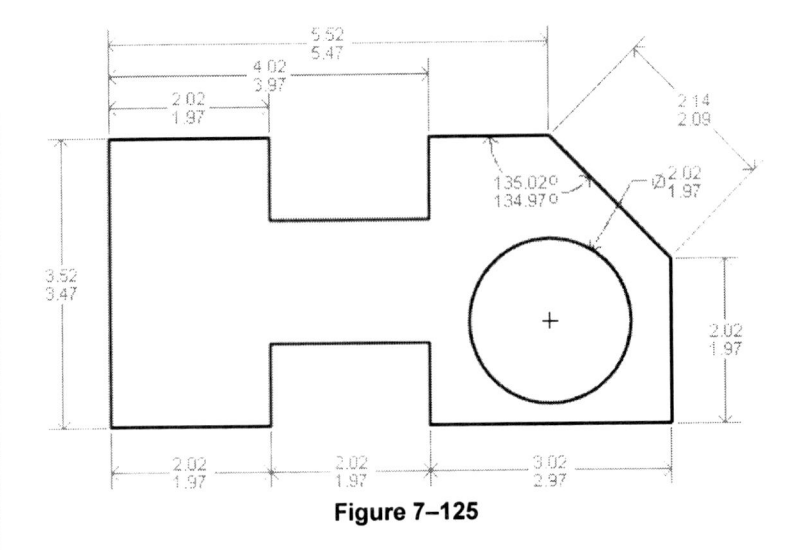

Figure 7–125

English_Metric

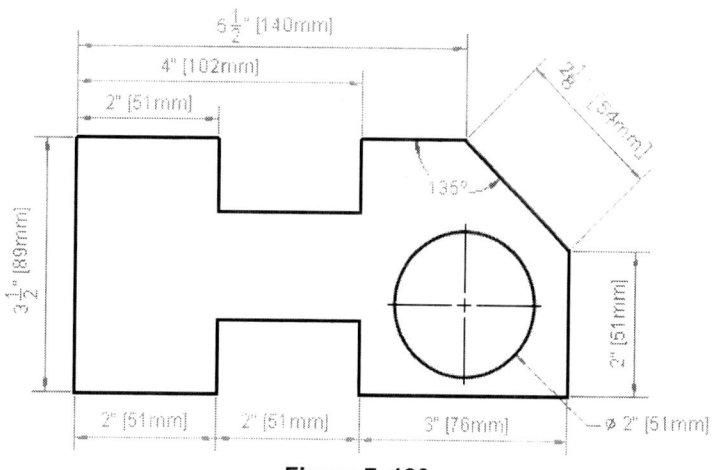

Figure 7–126

7.12 Creating Multileader Styles

Multileaders are used to point to objects in your drawing with text or symbols. Use the Multileader Style Manager to create styles that control the display options for different multileaders. The styles can be annotative or a specified scale, and have different arrowheads, text styles, colors, linetypes, etc., as shown in Figure 7–127. You can create styles for specific uses and then use the Multileader Style Manager to update them as required. This ensures accuracy throughout the drawing and makes it easy to modify multileaders.

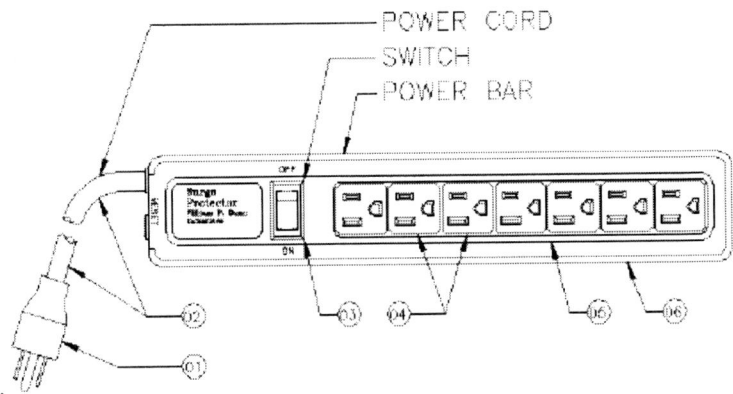

Figure 7–127

How To: Create a Multileader Style

1. In the *Annotate* tab>Leaders panel>Leader Style list, select **Manage Multileader Styles...**. The Multileader Style Manager opens, as shown in Figure 7–128.

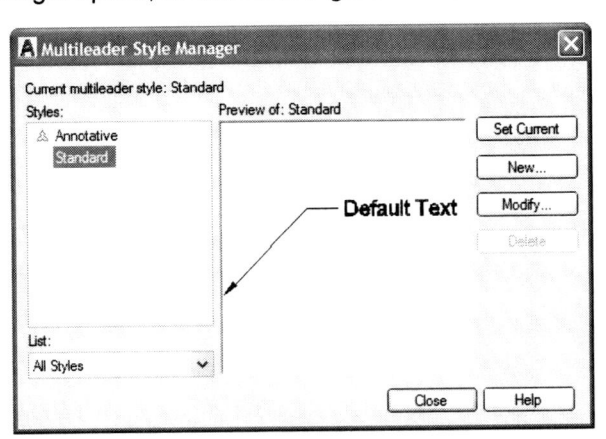

Figure 7–128

You can also open the dialog box by clicking the panel arrow in the *Annotate tab>Leaders panel*.

Annotate Drawings

2. Click **New...**
3. In the Create New Multileader Style dialog box, type a *New style name*, expand the Start with drop-down list and select a style, and select or clear the **Annotative** option, as shown in Figure 7–129.

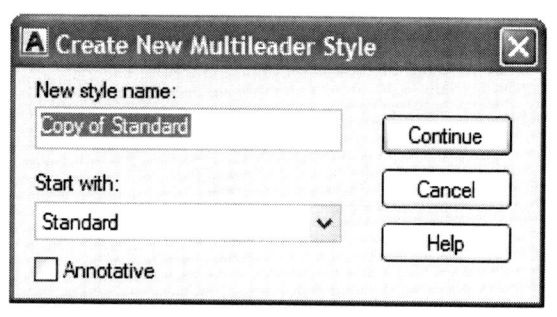

Figure 7–129

4. Click **Continue**. The Modify Multileader Style dialog box opens.
5. In the *Leader Format* tab, specify the leader's *Type* (**Straight**, **Spline**, or **None**), its formatting, the style and size of the Arrowhead, and the distance for the Leader break, as shown in Figure 7–130.

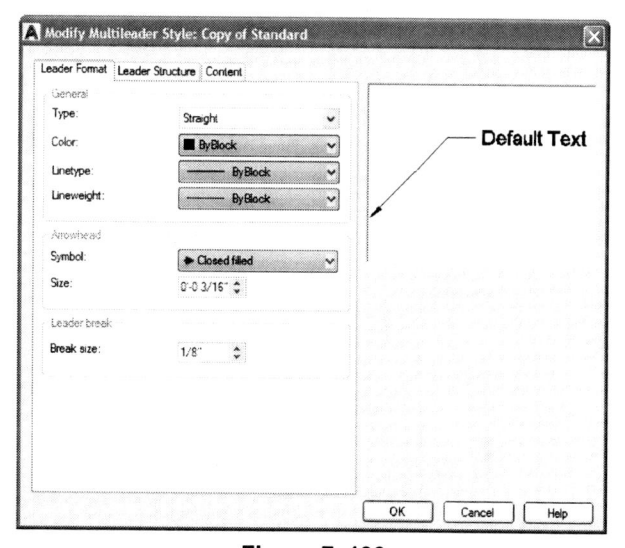

Figure 7–130

*If you are creating a spline leader style, you might need to clear the **Constraints** and **Landing Settings** options.*

6. In the *Leader Structure* tab, specify how you want the leader to work, as shown in Figure 7–131. For example, the default leader style has the *Maximum leader points* set to **2** and *Landing Settings* toggled on. Select **Annotative** if you are using the annotative scaling tools.

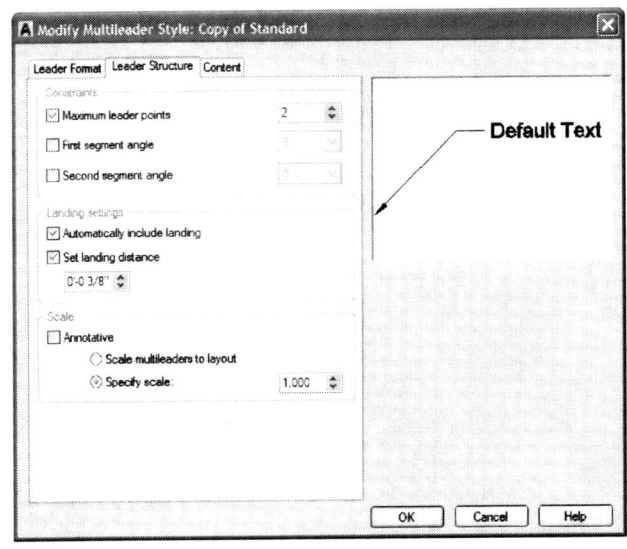

Figure 7–131

7. In the *Content* tab, you can specify whether you want the multileader content to be **Mtext**, **Block**, or **None**. Once you set the *Multileader type*, the rest of the options vary according to the selection. The **Mtext** option is shown in Figure 7–132.

*When you have selected text, you can set the attachment to be **Horizontal** or **Vertical**.*

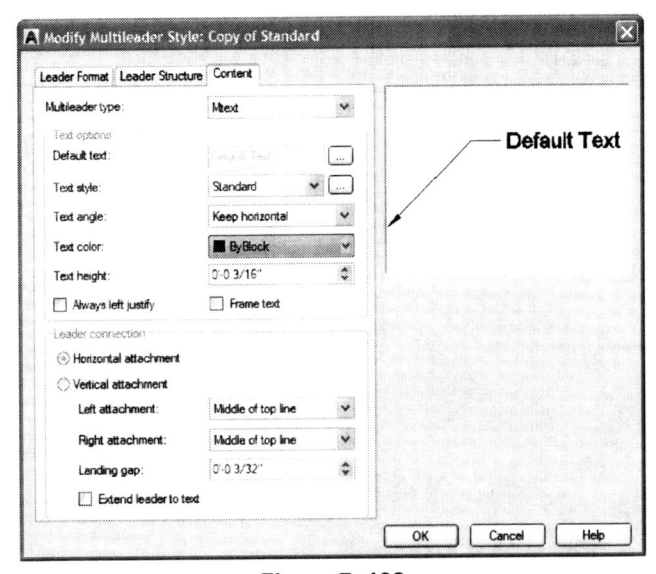

Figure 7–132

Annotate Drawings

8. When you use the **Block** *Multileader type*, you can select from a variety of preset blocks with attributes or use your own blocks, as shown in Figure 7–133.

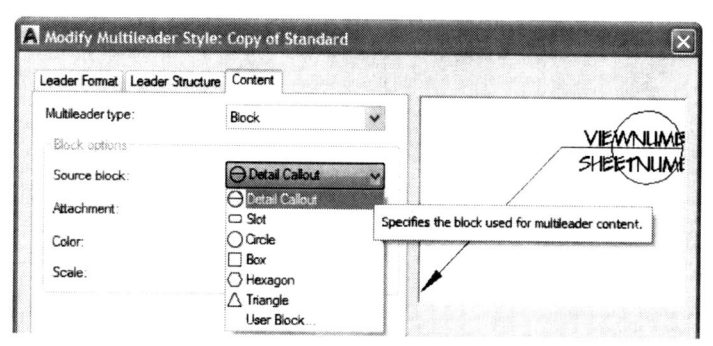

Figure 7–133

9. When you are satisfied with the style, click **OK**. In the Multileader Style Manager, select the new style and click **Set Current**.
10. Click **Close**.

- If you need to make a change to a style, open the Multileader Style Manager, select the style that you want to change, and click **Modify**.

- If you need to delete a style, open the Multileader Style Manager, select a style, and click **Delete**.

- You can also create style overrides for the Leader, Content, and Workflow by selecting **Options** in the **Multileader** command.

Practice 7j

Creating Multileader Styles

Practice Objective

- Create a multileader style.

In this practice, you will create a multileader style using a spline and a block, as shown in Figure 7–134.

Estimated time for completion: 10 minutes

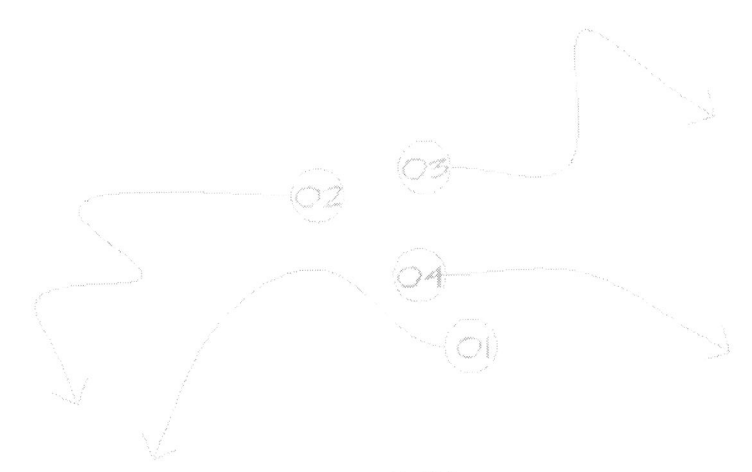

Figure 7–134

1. Open **AEC-Facilities3-A.dwg** from your practice files folder.

2. In the *Annotate* tab>Leaders panel, click .

3. In the Multileader Style Manager, click **New...**.

4. In the Create New Multileader Style dialog box, name the new multileader **Keynote**. Start with the **Standard** style and make it **Annotative**. Click **Continue**.

5. In the *Leader Format* tab, in the *General* area, set the *Type* to **Spline**. In the *Arrowhead* area, set the *Symbol* to **Oblique**.

6. In the *Leader Structure* tab, clear **Maximum leader points** (this enables you to make as many points on the spline as required).

7. In the *Content* tab, change the *Multileader type* to **Block**. In the *Block options* area, set the *Source block* to **Circle** and click **OK**.

8. In the Multileader Style Manager, select Keynote and click **Set Current**. Click **Close**.

9. Start the **Multileader** command to test the new multileader style by clicking several points to create a zig zag leader. Press <Enter> to stop selecting points along the spline.

10. In the Edit Attributes dialog box, enter a tag number for the keynote. Click **OK**.

11. Erase the leaders, switch back to Model Space, and save the drawing template.

7.13 Additional Annotative Scale Features

The Annotation Scale is connected to the Viewport Scale. Therefore, annotative objects, such as dimensions and text, display in viewports that have the same scale. You can add Annotation Scales to objects, enabling them to display in viewports of different scales. This ensures that all of the relevant information always displays at the correct scale and in the required viewports. For example, for the drawing shown in Figure 7–135, you might want the room names to display in each view, and to display different dimensions for each view.

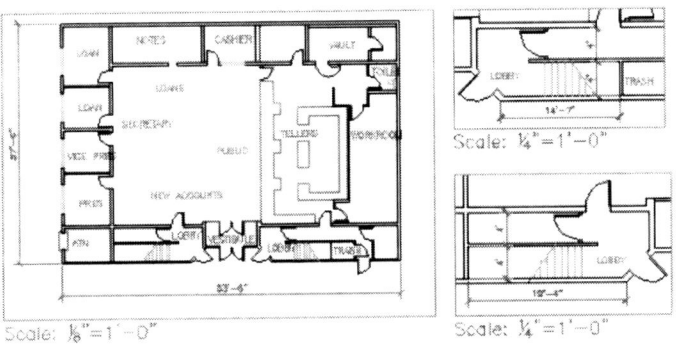

Figure 7–135

- When you change a Viewport Scale, the annotation objects displayed in the viewport change as well. The display of objects depends on what the annotation visibility is set to and whether or not the scale is automatically added to the object.

	Annotation Visibility: When toggled **Off**, only annotative objects with the current scale display. It is recommended that you use this option most of the time. It is what is plotted.
	Annotation Visibility: When toggled **On**, annotative objects for all of the scales display. Use when you need to add or remove an annotative object to the current scale.
	Automatically add scales to annotative objects when the annotation scale changes: When toggled **Off**, annotation scales are not automatically added to objects in the viewport.
	Automatically add scales to annotative objects when the annotation scale changes: When **On**, annotation objects in the drawing update to match the new annotation scale.

Annotate Drawings

- When you add a scale to an object, a scale representation is created. When you select an annotative object that has more than one scale, all of its scale representations display, as shown in Figure 7–136. There is no limit to the number of scales that can be added to an object, but too many scales can be confusing when you try to grip edit the object.

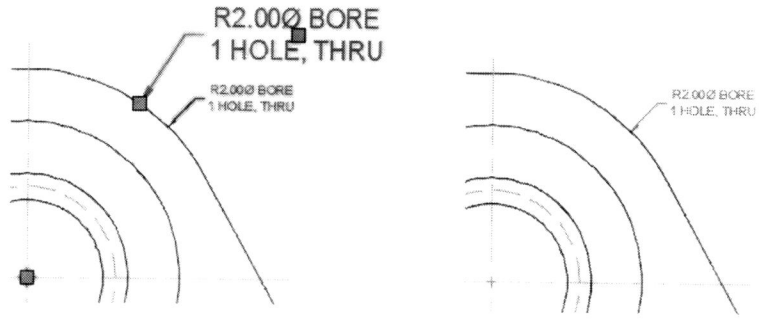

Figure 7–136

- If you modify the information contained in the annotation, it updates in all of the scale representations.

- You can grip edit each scale representation separately in its associated viewport so that it fits the location.

Modifying Annotative Object Scales

When you add annotative objects to a viewport, they automatically use the scale of the viewport. If you need to change the scale or move annotative objects out of a viewport, you can modify the scales associated with the objects or with the viewport, as shown in Figure 7–137.

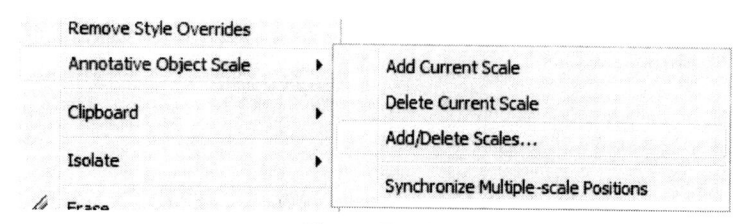

Figure 7–137

- These tools are available in the *Annotate* tab>Annotation Scaling panel or when you right-click on an annotative object.

- To display an annotative object in several viewports that use different scales, use **Add/Delete Scales** under **Annotative Object Scale** in the shortcut menu. This opens the Annotation Object Scale dialog box, where you can click **Add** and then add all the other annotative scales that are used in each viewport.

✗	If you do not want an annotative object to display in the current viewport, but do want it to be visible in a viewport at a different scale, **Delete** the current scale.
+△	If you want to include an annotative object in your viewport that is not displayed in the current viewport scale, toggle on **Annotation Visibility** in the Status Bar to display all of the scale representations of the objects. Then **Add** the current scale.
	If you want to add or delete multiple scales, click this icon in the Annotation Scaling panel to open the Annotation Object Scale dialog box.

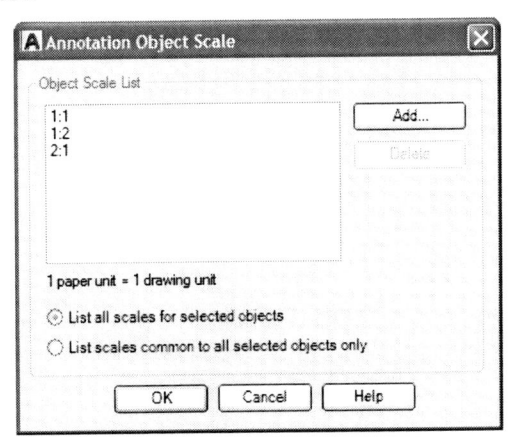

- You can change the locations of individual scale representations, but you might need to have them all return to one position. In the Annotation Scaling panel, click (Sync Scale Positions) to move all of the related representations to the same location as the selected item.

Practice 7k

Estimated time for completion: 15 minutes

Additional Annotative Scale Features

Practice Objectives

- Create annotative styles and annotative hatching.
- Control the visibility of annotation objects.

In this practice, you will specify annotative styles for text, dimensions, and multileaders. You will create annotative hatching using the Hatch command. You will then create viewports at different scales and add annotative objects to them, as shown in Figure 7–138.

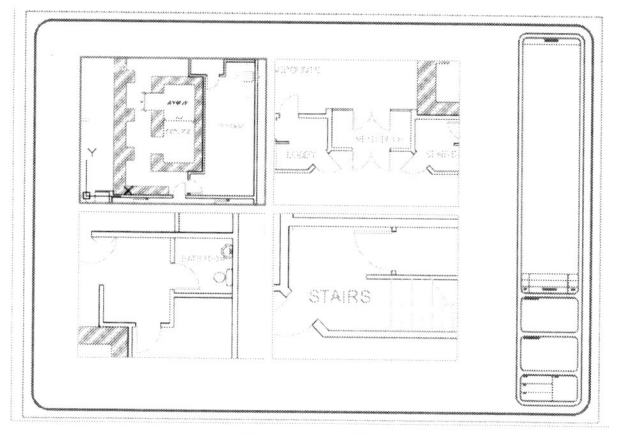

Figure 7–138

Task 1 - Define Annotative Text and Dimensions.

1. Open **Service-A.dwg** from your practice files folder.
2. In the *Annotate* tab, set the *Dimension style* to **Architectural** (an annotative style), as shown in Figure 7–139.
3. Set the *Text style* to **Hand** (an annotative style), as shown in Figure 7–139.
4. Set the *Multileader style* to **Annotative**, as shown in Figure 7–139.

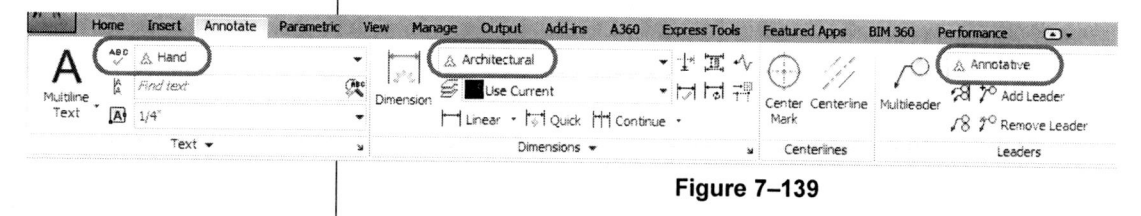

Figure 7–139

5. Switch to the **D-Sized** layout tab, which contains four viewports.

6. Select each viewport in Paper Space by clicking on the viewport border. Confirm the Viewport Scale in the Status Bar. They should be as follows: *Service*: **1/4"=1'-0"**, *Vestibule*: **3/8"=1'-0"**, *Bathroom*: **1/2"=1'-0"**, and *Stairs*: **3/4"=1'-0"**.

7. Click 🔒 (Lock/Unlock Viewport) to lock the Viewport Scales for each viewport.

8. Set the layer **Dimensions** to be current. Double-click in the viewport that displays the Service area and add the dimensions and text shown in Figure 7–140. They only display in the current viewport.

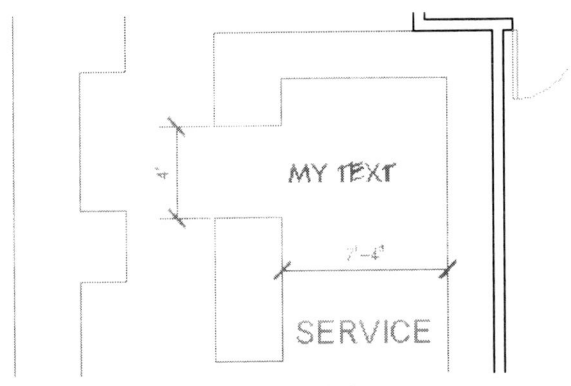

Figure 7–140

Task 2 - Define the annotative hatching.

1. Activate the viewport displaying the Service area, if it is not already active, and set the layer **Hatching** to be current.

2. Start the **Hatch** command.

3. In the *Hatch Creation* contextual tab>Options panel, click (Annotative).

4. Set the *Hatch Pattern* to **ANSI 31** and the *Hatch Pattern Scale* to **1**. Add hatching to the three counter areas inside the Service area viewport.

5. Close the Hatch Creation. The hatching only displays in the current viewport.

Annotate Drawings

Task 3 - Add annotative scales.

1. Select the hatch object that you just created.

2. Right-click on the selected hatching and select **Annotative Object Scale>Add/Delete Scales**. The Annotation Object Scale dialog box opens. The current Annotation Scale displays, which is **1/4"=1'-0"**.

3. Click **Add...** to add the other scales. The Add Scales to Object dialog box opens.

4. Select the *scales* **3/8"=1'-0"** and **1/2"=1"-0"**. Doing so enables the annotative hatch object to display in the Vestibule viewport and the Bathroom viewport.

5. Click **OK**. The scales display in the Annotation Object Scale dialog box.

6. Click **OK**. The annotation objects (hatches) now display in the Vestibule and Bathroom viewports.

Task 4 - Change the Annotation object display.

1. Switch to the Model tab and note how the annotative objects (text, dimensions, hatch) display.

2. Click (Annotation Visibility On) to toggle it off. Note that the annotative objects no longer display.

3. Save and close the drawing.

7.14 Annotation Scale Overview

The Annotation Scale features enable you to avoid creating multiple copies of the same annotation objects at different scales. This makes it easier to quickly dimension drawings that contain views at different scales. Using Annotation Scale, you can control which dimensions, text, etc., display in each scaled detail viewport, as shown in Figure 7–141.

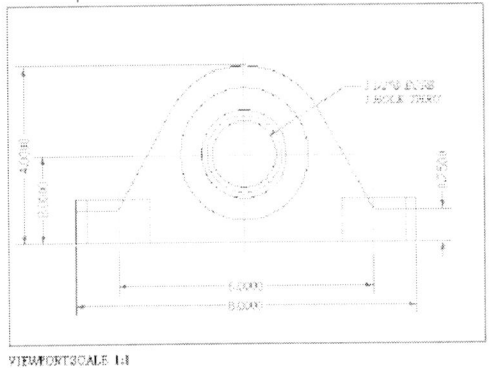

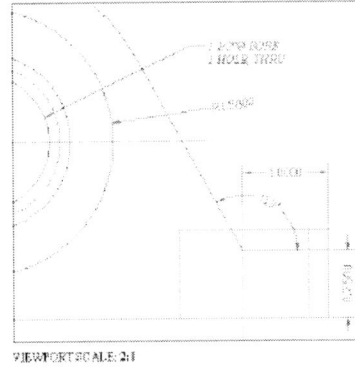

Figure 7–141

- Annotation objects include Single Line Text, Multiline Text, Text Styles, Dimensions, Dimension Styles, Multileaders, Multileader Styles, Geometric Tolerances, Blocks, Attributes, and Hatches.

> **Hint: Linetypes and Annotation Scale**
>
> Linetype spacing is controlled by the Annotation Scale through the **msltscale** system variable. This variable is set per drawing using templates.
>
> - When set to **1** (the default in the template files supplied with the AutoCAD® software), linetypes are automatically scaled to the annotation scale.
>
> - When set to **0**, they are not scaled to the annotation scale.

Annotate Drawings

Working with Annotative Styles

*The **Annotative** option is also available in the Hatch Editor contextual tab and the Properties palette for various objects, such as Tolerance.*

Annotative styles are set by selecting the **Annotative** option in the Dimension Style, Multileader Style, Block Definition, Attribute Definition, and Text Style dialog boxes, as shown in Figure 7–142.

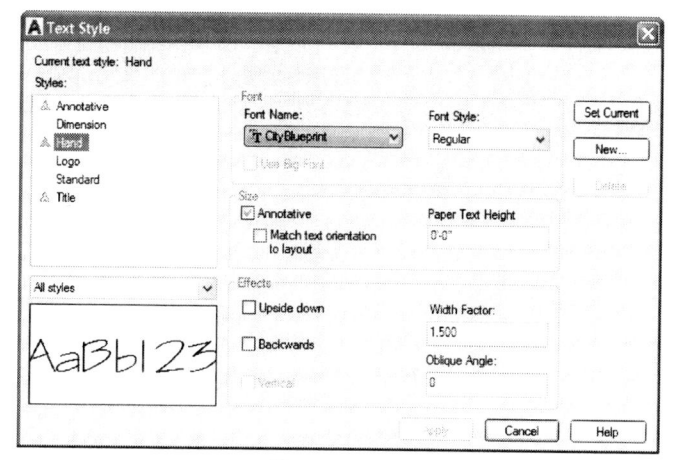

Figure 7–142

When set, you can identify an annotative style in one of the following ways:

- (Annotation) displays next to the style name in the Text Style dialog box and in the list of style names in the *Home* tab>Annotation panel, as shown in Figure 7–143.

The Text Style, Dimension Style, and Multileader Style are all set to be Annotative and display the Annotation icon.

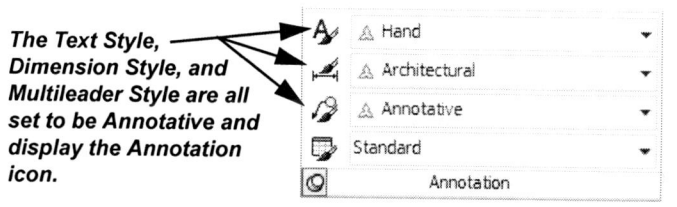

Figure 7–143

- (Annotation) also displays when you hover the cursor over an annotative object in the drawing window, as shown in Figure 7–144.

Annotation icon

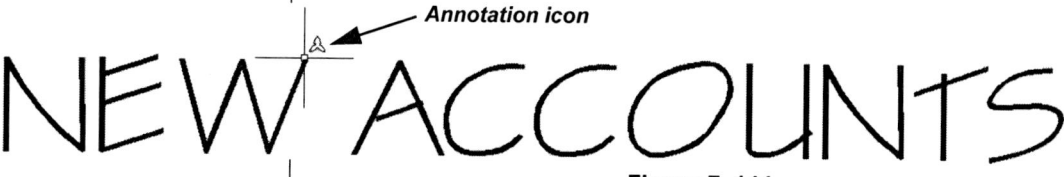

NEW ACCOUNTS

Figure 7–144

How To: Add Annotative Objects

1. In a layout, switch to Paper Space and set up the viewports as required.
2. Select a viewport by selecting its border.
3. In the Status Bar, click ▢ 1:2 ▼ (Viewport Scale) and select a scale in the list, as shown in Figure 7–145. The Annotation Scale automatically updates to match. Changing the Annotation Scale also changes the Viewport Scale.

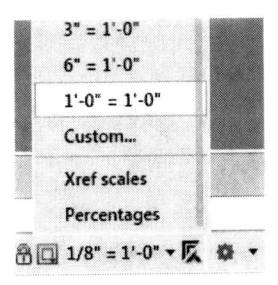

Figure 7–145

4. (Optional) Click 🔒 (Lock/Unlock Viewport) to lock the viewport so that the scale and location cannot change.

- You can quickly lock or unlock viewports using 🔒 (Lock/Unlock Viewport) in the Status Bar, as shown in Figure 7–146.

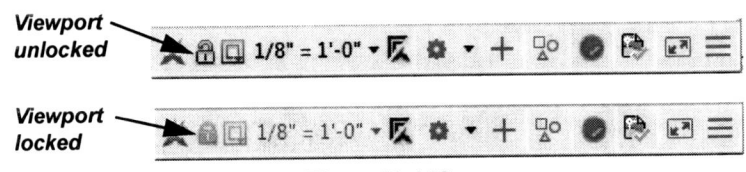

Viewport unlocked

Viewport locked

Figure 7–146

5. When you are ready to start adding annotative objects, activate one of the viewports.
6. Use annotative styles when creating the various annotation objects. They can be scaled to suit each viewport and do not display in viewports to which other annotation scales have been assigned.

- The annotative scale can also be set in the Properties of specific objects, such as text or dimensions, as shown in Figure 7–147.

Annotate Drawings

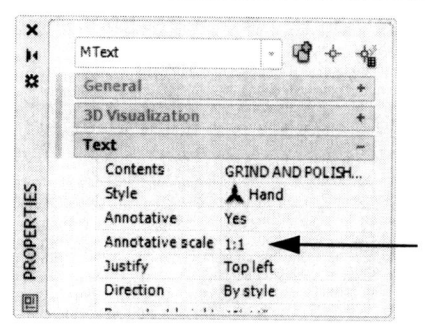

Figure 7–147

Hint: Changing Scale of Annotative Objects

In a viewport, when **Zoom** commands are used or the scale changes in the Viewports toolbar, the scale of the annotative objects is not modified. You must modify the Viewport Scale in the Status Bar for the annotative objects to change scale.

Viewing Annotative Objects at Different Scales

Annotation Scale is linked to the Viewport Scale, therefore, annotative objects (such as dimensions and text) display in layout viewports that have the same scale. If the Viewport Scale is changed, the annotative objects are not displayed. To ensure they remain displayed, add annotation scales to objects enabling them to be displayed in viewports of different scales. For example, you might want the room names to display in each view while the dimensions display in specific viewports, as shown in Figure 7–148.

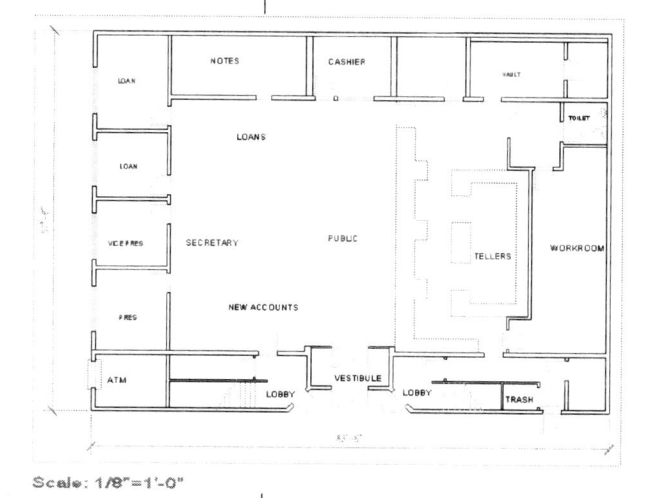

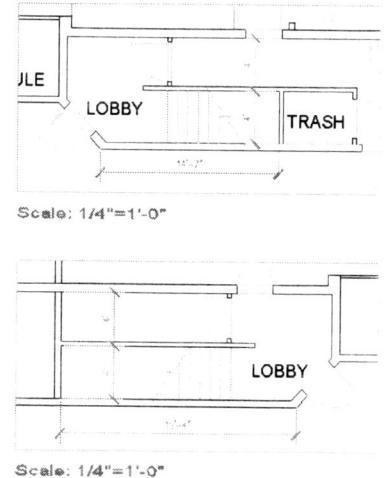

Figure 7–148

© 2017, ASCENT - Center for Technical Knowledge®

7–101

When a viewport's Viewport Scale is changed, the annotation objects displayed within it change as well. How the objects behave depends on how you set the annotation visibility and whether or not the scale is automatically added to the object.

Annotation Visibility: When toggled **Off**, only annotative objects with the current scale display. It is recommended that you use this option by default. It displays objects that are to be plotted.

Annotation Visibility: When toggled **On**, annotative objects for all of the scales display. Use when you need to add or remove an annotative object to the current scale.

Automatically add scales to annotative objects when the annotation scale changes: When toggled **Off**, annotation scales are not automatically added to objects in the viewport.

Automatically add scales to annotative objects when the annotation scale changes: When toggled **On**, any annotation objects in the drawing are updated to match the new annotation scale.

- When you add a scale to an object, a scale representation of that object is created.

- When you select an annotative object that has more than one scale, all of its scale representations display, as shown on the right in Figure 7–149. There is no limit to the number of scales that can be added to an object. However, too many scales can be confusing when you use grips to edit the object.

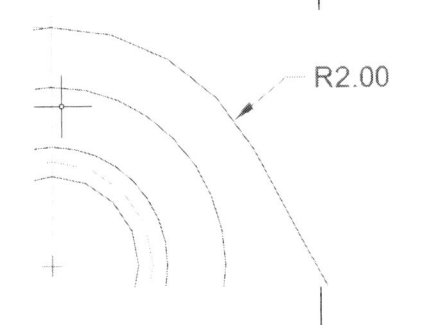

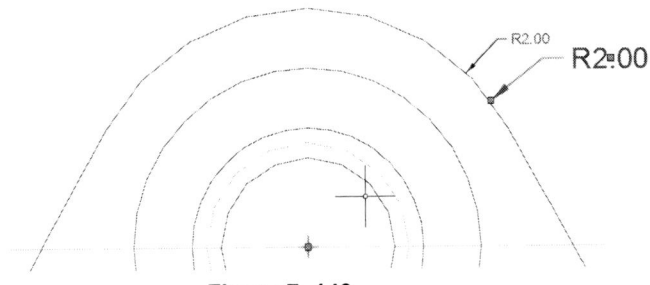

Figure 7–149

- If you modify the information contained in the annotation, all of the scale representations are updated.

- You can use grips to edit each scale representation separately in its associated viewport to suit the location.

Annotate Drawings

Annotation Scale and Model Space

You can annotate objects in Model Space by setting the Annotation Scale in the Status Bar. It is linked to the Viewport Scale and displays in viewports that use the same Annotation Scale, as shown in Figure 7–150.

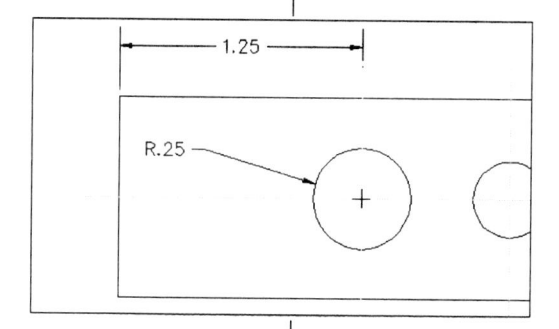

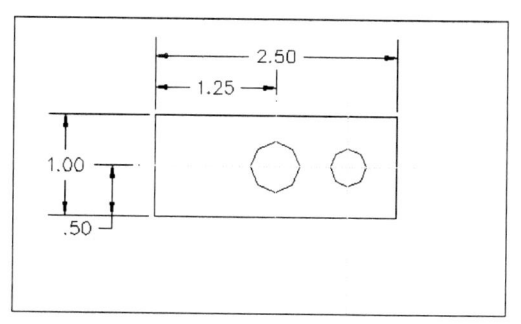

Figure 7–150

Modifying Annotative Object Scales

You can modify the scales associated with annotative objects or with the viewports.

- If you do not want an annotative object to display in the current viewport, but you do want it to be displayed in a viewport that is at a different scale, select the object, right-click, expand **Annotative Object Scale**, and select **Delete Current Scale**, as shown in Figure 7–151.

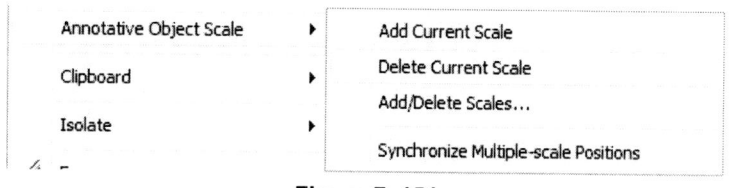

Figure 7–151

- If you want to display an annotative object that is not displayed in the current viewport scale, toggle on

  (Annotation Visibility On) in the Status Bar to display all of the scale representations of the objects. Right-click on the object that you want to include in your scale, expand **Annotative Object Scale** and select **Add Current Scale**.

- To add or delete multiple scales, right-click, expand **Annotative Object Scale** and select **Add/Delete Scales**. This enables you to display annotative object in several viewports that use different scales. The Annotation Object Scale dialog box opens, as shown in Figure 7–152.

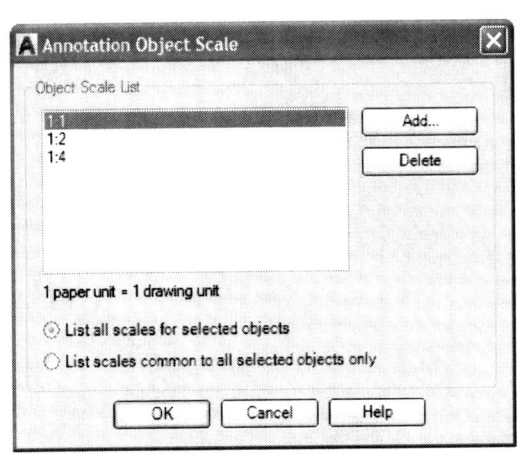

Figure 7–152

- You can change the locations of individual scale representations. If you need to return them to one position, right-click, expand **Annotative Object Scale**, and select **Synchronize Multiple-scale Positions** to move all of the related representations to the same location as the selected object.

Hint: Editing the Scale List

The Scale List is stored in each drawing file and is accessed using the Edit Drawing Scales dialog box, as shown in Figure 7–153. The list can vary from drawing to drawing. Therefore, if you want to use a standard scale list in each drawing you should create it in a template drawing.

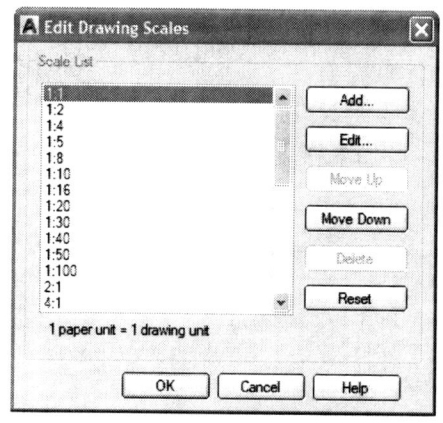

Figure 7–153

- To edit the Scale List, click 1:2 ▼ (Viewport Scale) in the Status Bar and select **Custom…** at the bottom of the list.

- You can also click (Scale List) in the *Annotate* tab> Annotation Scaling panel, as shown in Figure 7–154.

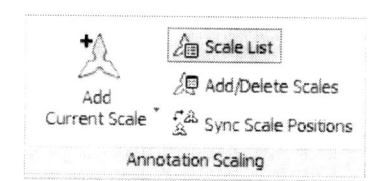

Figure 7–154

Practice 7I

Estimated time for completion: 15 minutes

Annotation Scale

Practice Objective

- Add annotative objects that are to be displayed in viewports that are set at a specific scale.

In this practice you will specify the annotative styles for text, dimensions, multileaders, and hatches. You will then add annotative objects at different scales to only be displayed in viewports with the same scale setting, as shown in Figure 7–155.

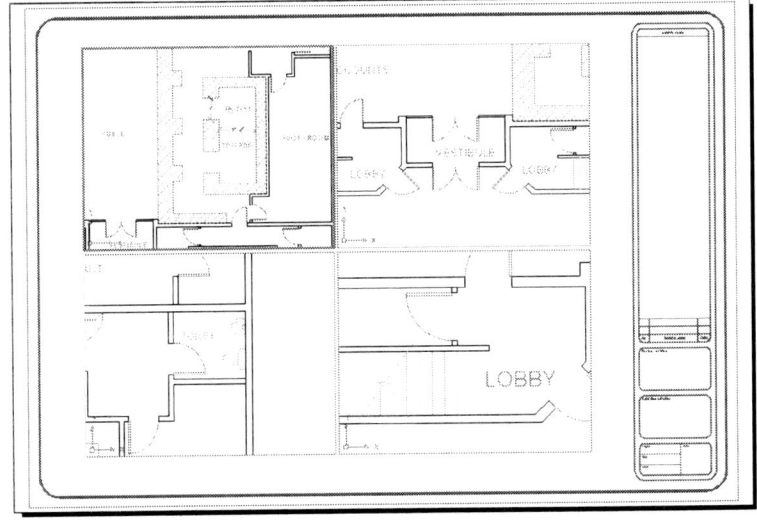

Figure 7–155

Task 1 - Annotative text and dimensions.

1. Open **Branch Bank-A.dwg** from your practice files folder.

2. In the *Home* tab>Annotation panel, set the *Text*, *Dimension*, and *Multileader Style(s)* to **Annotative**, as shown in Figure 7–156.

Annotate Drawings

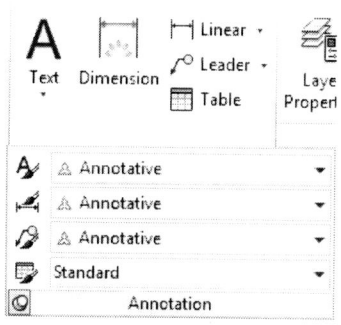

Figure 7–156

3. Switch to the **D-Sized** layout.

4. In Paper Space, select the border of the *Tellers* (top left viewport that displays the *Tellers* area) viewport. In the Status Bar, the Viewport Scale displays **1/4" = 1'-0"**. Press <Esc> to release the selected viewport.

5. Repeat the last step to verify that each viewport is displaying the correct Viewport Scale. The scales should be:
   - *Vestibule viewport:* **3/8"=1'-0"**
   - *Restroom viewport:* **1/2"=1'-0"**
   - *Lobby viewport:* **3/4"=1'-0"**

6. Select all four viewports. In the Status Bar, click (Lock/Unlock Viewport) to lock the viewports. Press <Esc> to release all selected viewports.

You can display the Layer Control in the Quick Access Toolbar for easy access.

7. Set the layer **Dimensions** to be current. Double-click inside the *Tellers* viewport to make it active. Add the text and dimensions, as shown in Figure 7–157. They only display in the current viewport.

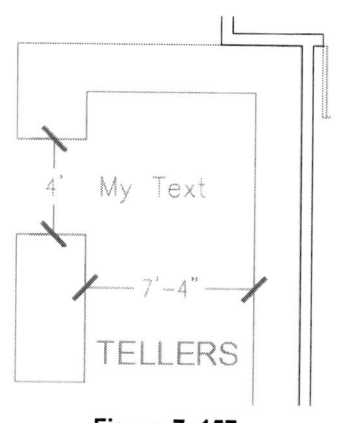

Figure 7–157

Task 2 - Set the annotative hatching.

1. Verify that the *Tellers* viewport is still active (or activate it) and set the layer **Hatching** to be current.

2. Verify that both Annotative options (and) are toggled off in the Status Bar.

3. Start the **Hatch** command.

4. In the *Hatch Creation* contextual tab>Options panel, click (Annotative).

5. In the Pattern panel, select **ANSI31**.

6. In the Properties panel, set the *Scale* to **1**.

7. Add hatching to the three counter areas inside the Tellers viewport.

8. In the Close panel, click (Close Hatch Creation).

9. In the *Vestibule* viewport, note that the counter area (top right corner) does not display the hatching. Since the hatching is annotative, it is only displayed in the *Tellers* viewport.

Task 3 - Add/delete scales.

1. Select the hatch object that you just created.

2. Right-click on the selected hatching, expand Annotative Object Scale and select **Add/Delete Scales**. The Annotation Object Scale dialog box opens. Only the **1/4" = 1'-0"** Annotation Scale displays.

3. Click **Add** to add a scale. The Add Scales to Object dialog box opens.

4. Select **3/8"=1'-0"**, which is the scale of the *Vestibule* viewport.

5. Click **OK**. The scale displays in the Annotation Object Scale dialog box.

6. Click **OK**. The hatching, which is an annotative object, now displays in the *Vestibule* viewport as well.

Task 4 - Set the annotation object display.

1. Switch to the *Model* tab and note how the annotative objects display.

2. In the Status Bar, click ![icon] (Annotation Visibility On) to toggle off the annotation object display.

3. Save and close the drawing.

7.15 Creating Tables

The **Table** command creates a unified table typically containing title and column headers with any number of rows/columns of data, as shown in Figure 7–158.

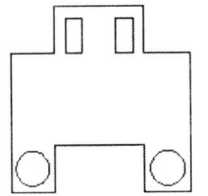

Figure 7–158

- You can create table styles that define custom standard properties. When you insert a table object, you add the values for each of the cells.

- You can also create tables to which you can add custom information by linking external Excel spreadsheet files, or by extracting AutoCAD object data and creating a table from the information.

- Tables can include calculations.

How To: Create an Empty Table

The **Table** command is used to create tables from scratch, and from links and data extractions.

1. In the *Annotate* tab>Tables panel or in the *Home* tab>Annotation panel, click ▦ (Table).
2. The Insert Table dialog box opens, as shown in Figure 7–159. In the Table style drop-down list, select the table style.

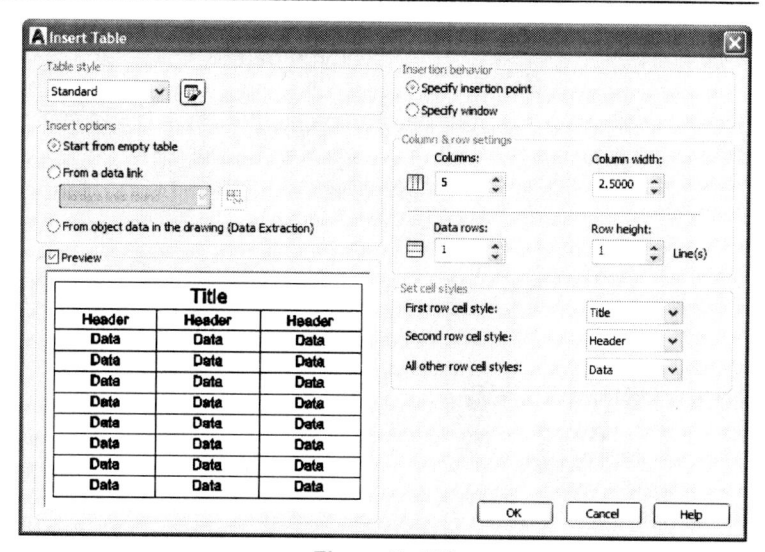

Figure 7–159

3. In the *Insert options* area, select **Start from empty table**.
4. In the *Insertion behavior* and *Column & row settings* areas, select the required options.
   - If you select the **Specify insertion point** option, you can set the number of columns and rows and their sizes.
   - If you select the **Specify window** option, you can set either the number of columns or the column width, and the number of rows or the row height (where the information not specified is automatically calculated by the size of the window).
5. In the *Set cell styles* area, select the required styles.
6. Click **OK** to place the table in the drawing.
7. Select a point in the drawing window to place the table or select two points to draw a window, depending on the option that you selected in the *Insertion behavior* area.
8. The *Text Editor* contextual tab opens and the title bar of the table is highlighted, as shown in Figure 7–160. Type the title.

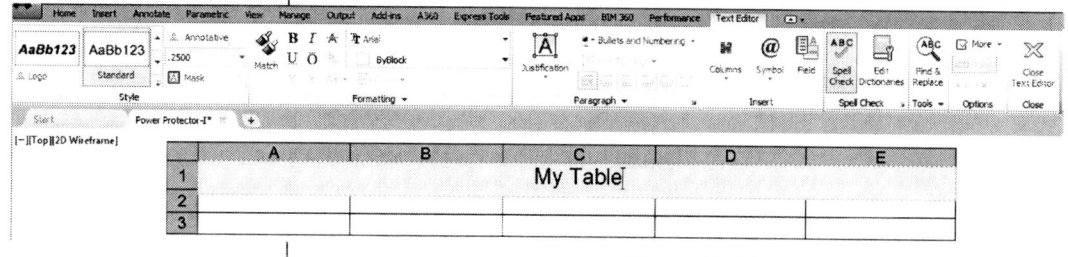

Figure 7–160

9. Press <Tab>. The first column and row highlight. Type the column heading or other information.
10. Continue to press <Tab> to move through the cells. You can also use the arrow keys on the keyboard to move from cell to cell. Press <Enter> to move down a row.
11. Click ✖ (Close Text Editor) to end the command.

- In the Insert Table dialog box, click 📝 (Launch the Table Style dialog) in the *Table style* area to create a table style.

Populating Table Cells

Table cells can contain plain text, blocks, and fields. The example shown in Figure 7–161 has blocks in the *Room #* column, fields that are linked to the area of polyline objects in the *Area* column, and the total area of the building using a formula next to the *Total Area* cell.

Occupancy Table			
Room #	Department	Area	Use
101	Marketing	452.0 SQ. FT.	Office
102	Marketing	463.2 SQ. FT.	Office
103	Sales	452.0 SQ. FT.	Office
104	Engineering	2712.8 SQ. FT.	Drafting Room
105	Engineering	463.9 SQ. FT.	Office
106	Engineering	466.9 SQ. FT.	Office
107	Engineering	463.9 SQ. FT.	Office
	Total Area:	5474.6876 SQ. FT.	

Figure 7–161

- Click once in a cell to open the *Table Cell* contextual tab. It contains a variety of tools for adding and modifying cells. The current cell is highlighted with a gold edge, as shown in Figure 7–162.

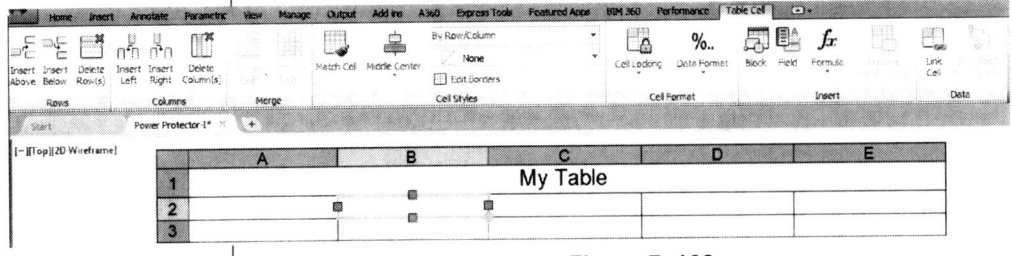

Figure 7–162

- Double-click in a cell to place the text and open the *Text Editor* contextual tab.

Annotate Drawings

Inserting Blocks, Fields, and Formulas

Table cells can include text, blocks, fields, and formulas. Tools for inserting them are located in the *Table Cell* contextual tab> Insert panel and in the shortcut menus.

Insert Block: Opens the Insert a Block in a Table Cell dialog box. Select the name of the block or browse for a file. Then set the properties and cell alignment. The **AutoFit** option scales the size of the block to fit the cell size.

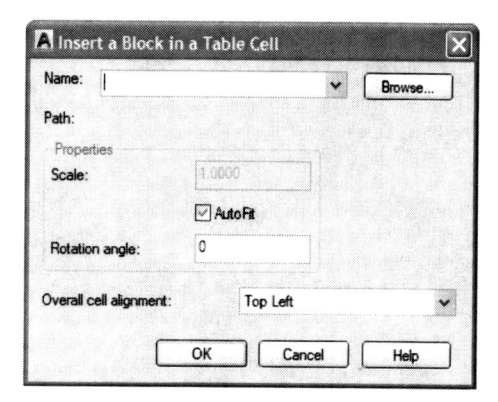

Insert Field: Adds a field selected in the Field dialog box into the cell. Hyperlinks are added using fields.

Insert Formula: Select **Sum**, **Average**, **Count**, **Cell**, or **Equation** to add a formula to the cell.

- To remove cell content, select the cell(s) and press <Delete>. You can also right-click and select **Delete All Contents**. This only deletes the selected cell(s).

- Tables are typically created in Paper Space. However, you sometimes need to access information in Model Space, such as the area of a hatch or polyline. When you are working with Object fields in a text object or table, you can select an object in a viewport even if the table is in Paper Space.

Calculations in Tables

You can make calculations directly in an AutoCAD table and the basic mathematical calculations are available, such as addition, subtraction, multiplication, division, and exponents, as well as **Sum** (as shown in Figure 7–163), **Average**, and **Count**. You can combine arithmetic functions, including parentheses, to create formulas.

	A	B	C	D
1		Replacement Costs		
2	Item #	Cost	Count	Total
3	AZ-408	255.45	12	3065.40
4	DG-411	18.29	22	402.38
5	DA-862	35.30	8	282.40
6			Grand Total:	=Sum(D3:D5)

Figure 7–163

- When the table is in edit mode, it displays letters for the columns and numbers for the rows. As in a standard spreadsheet, you specify a cell by its location, such as D3 (Column D, Row 3). When you finish editing, the table displays without this information.

- Cells used for calculations must only contain numeric information. The numeric information can be text or fields that have a numeric value (i.e., the area of a hatch or polyline).

Types of Calculations

The available types of calculations are described as follows.

Sum	Adds up numbers in the selected table cells.
Average	Computes the average of the numbers in the selected table cells. It adds up all of the numbers and divides the sum by the number of cells selected.
Count	Adds the number of selected cells, not the information in the cells. The cells must contain numerical information.
Cell	Repeats the information from a selected cell in the current cell. The selected cell can be in another table. The selected cell must have numerical information; otherwise, #### displays in the field.
Equation	Computes the entered equation. You can add (+), subtract (-), multiply (*), divide (/), and set exponents (^). You can also group items together in parentheses, such as =(B3 / B7) * 2. The calculation in parentheses is computed first. For example, =B3*B7.

Annotate Drawings

How To: Add Calculations to a Table

1. Create a table containing the numeric information that you want to calculate.
2. Click once in the cell in which you want the calculated value to be placed.
3. In the *Table Cell* contextual tab>Insert panel, expand f_x (Formula) and select the type of formula that you want to calculate, as shown on the left in Figure 7–164. Alternatively, right-click and select **Insert>Formula** and select the type of formula, as shown on the right in Figure 7–164.

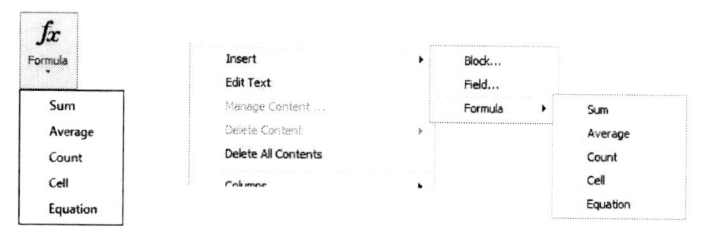

Figure 7–164

- **For Sum, Average, and Count:** Select two points for the corners of the table cell range. Click in the cells to be calculated when you select the points.

- **For Cell:** Click in another cell to place its value in the current cell. This can be a cell in another table.

- **For Equation:** Enter an equation using the cell coordinates, such as = B4 * C4.

- You can modify the equations created by any of the formulas. For example, you might select a cell range and want to add a cell or group of cells that are not in that range. In such a case, separate the new cell or range of cells by a comma, as follows.

=SUM (B3:E3)	Original formula
=SUM (B3:E3,C4)	Adding an additional cell
=SUM (B3:E3,C4:E4)	Adding a range of cells

- The calculated value in the cell is a formula field. It displays with a shaded background. You can edit the field to display the formula or change the formatting by double-clicking on the text.

Practice 7m Creating Tables

Estimated time for completion: 15 minutes

Practice Objective

- Create a table and add a formula.

In this practice, you will create a table that includes text, blocks, fields, and a hyperlink using the **Table** command. You will also add a formula summing up the values in one column using the **Formula** command.

1. Open **Occupancy-A.dwg** from your practice files folder.
2. Switch to the **Occupancy** layout.
3. Make the layer **0** current, and freeze all of the layers except **0**, **A-Area**, **A-Room-Symb**, and **Viewports**.
4. In the *Annotate* tab>Tables panel, start the **Table** command.
5. In the Insert Table dialog box, verify that the **Standard** table style and the **Specify insertion point** option are selected.
6. In the *Column & row settings* area, set the *Columns* to **4**, set the *Column width* to **2 1/2"**, and set the *Data rows* to **8**. Click **OK** and place the table in the drawing below the Floor Plan viewport.
7. Double-click inside the top row and type **Occupancy Table** for the title, as shown in Figure 7–165. Type the remaining titles for each of the column headings shown, using <Tab> to move to the next column.

	A	B	C	D
1	Occupancy Table			
2	Room #	Department	Area	Use

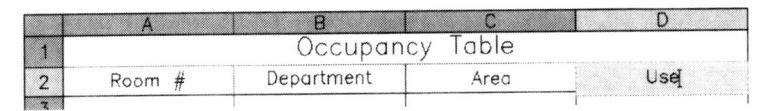

Figure 7–165

Annotate Drawings

Click once on a cell (until the individual cell is highlighted) to open the Table Cell contextual tab. The tools required are located in the Insert panel.

You might have to press <Esc> twice to select the next cell.

8. For the cells in each column, add the following information, as shown in Figure 7–166 (**Hint:** Use the Auto-Fill cells grip for similar content.)

Room #	Use (Block) to insert the block name **Room Number**. Set the *Overall cell alignment* to **Middle Center**. Toggle on **Auto-Fit**. Change the attribute to be the correct room number.
Department	Type the text shown in Figure 7–166 for the departments.
Area	Use (Field) to insert a field in each cell in the column (for the 7 rooms). In the Field dialog box, set the *Field category* to **Objects** and the *Field names* to **Object**. In the *Object type* area, click (Select object) and then select the magenta polyline around the corresponding room in the floor plan. In the *Property* area, select the **Area** property. Set the *Format* to **Architectural** and the *Precision* to **0.0**.
Use	Type the text shown in Figure 7–165 into each cell in the column.

9. In the bottom cell of the *Area* column, add a formula using **Sum** (select the cell, right-click, and select **Insert>Formula>Sum**). Using a window, select the room areas in that column as the range and then press <Enter>. The calculated sum displays in the last Area column, as shown in Figure 7–166.

Occupancy Table			
Room #	Department	Area	Use
101	Marketing	452.0 SQ. FT.	Office
102	Marketing	463.2 SQ. FT.	Office
103	Sales	452.0 SQ. FT.	Office
104	Engineering	2712.8 SQ. FT.	Drafting Room
105	Engineering	463.9 SQ. FT.	Office
106	Engineering	466.9 SQ. FT.	Office
107	Engineering	463.9 SQ. FT.	Office
	Total Area:	5474.6876 SQ. FT.	

Figure 7–166

10. Select the cell with the sum, right-click, and select **Insert> Edit Field**. Set the *Precision* to **0.0**.

11. Thaw all of the layers that you had previously frozen.

12. Save the drawing.

7.16 Modifying Tables

You can modify tables and table data in a variety of ways. Modifications can be made to individual cells, rows, columns, or to the entire table.

Modifying Cells, Rows, and Columns

When you select multiple cells, rows, or columns you can add and remove rows and columns, merge and unmerge cells, and modify cell properties. You can also modify an individual cell using grips.

- To select more than one cell, hold <Shift> or click and drag across the cells that you want to select.

- To select an entire row or column, select the corresponding letter or number that displays (gold) when a cell is selected with grips.

- You can also **Cut**, **Copy**, and **Paste** cell contents using the shortcut menu.

Cell Grips

The square grips around a cell change its height and width. If you modify the grips of a selected cell, it impacts all of the rows or columns in which it is located. The diamond shaped grip is used to click and drag to automatically fill the selected cells with the contents of the current cell. First select, and then right-click on the diamond grip to change the options, as shown in Figure 7–167.

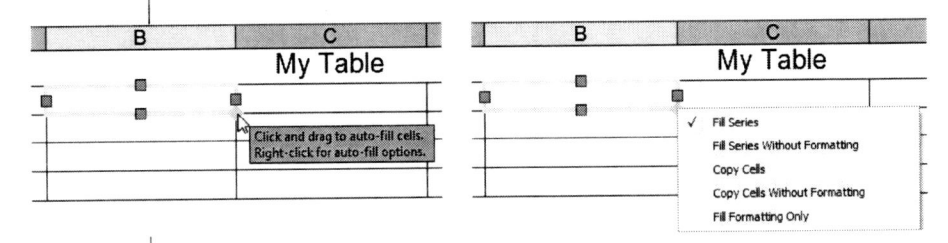

Figure 7–167

Modification Tools

With a cell selected, use the various tools available in the *Table Cell* contextual tab (as shown in Figure 7–168) to modify the tables.

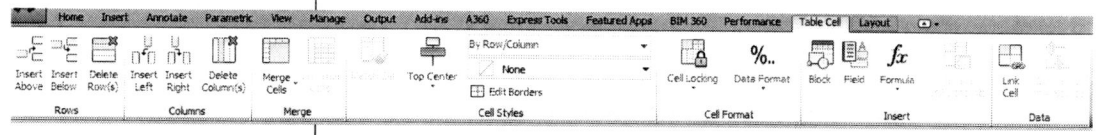

Figure 7–168

Adding and Removing Rows and Columns

	Insert Above: Inserts a row above the selected cell or row.
	Insert Below: Inserts a row below the selected cell or row.
	Delete Row(s): Deletes the selected row(s).
	Insert Left: Inserts a column to the left of the selected cell or column.
	Insert Right: Inserts a column to the right of the selected cell or column.
	Delete Column(s): Deletes the selected column(s).

Merging and Unmerging Cells

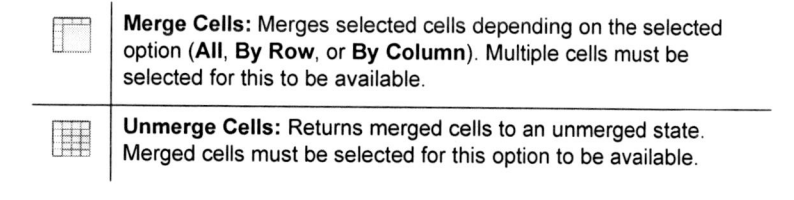

	Merge Cells: Merges selected cells depending on the selected option (**All**, **By Row**, or **By Column**). Multiple cells must be selected for this to be available.
	Unmerge Cells: Returns merged cells to an unmerged state. Merged cells must be selected for this option to be available.

Modifying Cell Properties

	Match Cell: Applies the properties of a selected cell to other cells, similar to the **Match Properties** command.
	Alignment: Applies the alignment selected from a list to the objects in the cell. You can align multiple cells at the same time. The current cell alignment icon might be displayed.
	Cell Styles: Changes the style of the cell to the one selected from the list.
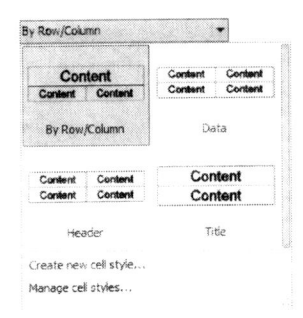	**Background Fill:** Changes the background color of the cell to the color selected from the list.
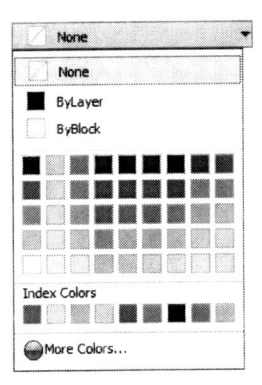	**Cell Locking:** Sets cells to be **Unlocked**, **Content Locked**, **Format Locked**, or **Content and Format Locked**.
	Data Format: Sets the data format of items in a cell. It is set to **General** by default. However, you can change the numerical data to **Angle**, **Currency**, **Data**, **Decimal Number**, **General**, **Percentage**, **Point**, **Text**, and **Whole Number**. If you need to customize the data format, right-click in the cell and select **Custom Table Cell Format** to open the Table Cell Format dialog box.
	Manage Cell Contents: Controls the location and flow of objects if there is more than one type of content in a cell, such as a block and text. This opens the Manage Cell Content dialog box.

Annotate Drawings

Edit Borders: Opens the Cell Border Properties dialog box, in which you can specify lineweights, linetypes, color, and border types for individual cells, rows, or columns. Toggle on **Lineweight** in the Status Bar, expanded Customization list to display the lineweights.

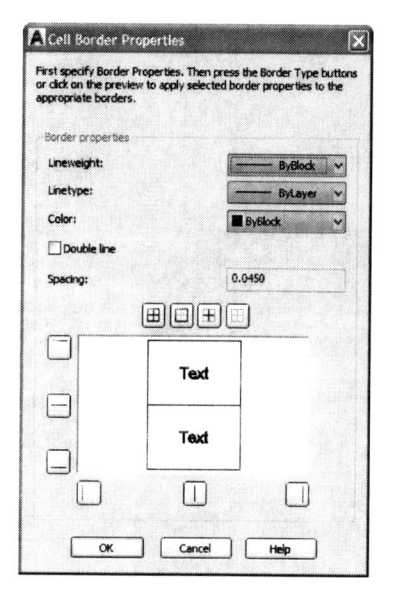

Modifying the Entire Table

When you select the entire table (click the edge of the table), as shown in Figure 7–169, you can use grips to modify its overall size, the width of columns, the height of rows, and to break the table into columns. You can also modify some of these options in the Properties palette or through the shortcut menu.

Figure 7–169

- Table-specific shortcut options include **Table Style**, **Size Columns Equally**, **Size Rows Equally**, **Remove All Property Overrides**, **Export**, and **Table Indicator Color**.

- **Table Indicator Color** is the color of the row numbers and column letters that display when the table is selected.

Table Grips

Tables can be extensively modified with grips, as shown in Figure 7–170. You can use them to adjust the width, height, and columns to fit the available space as required.

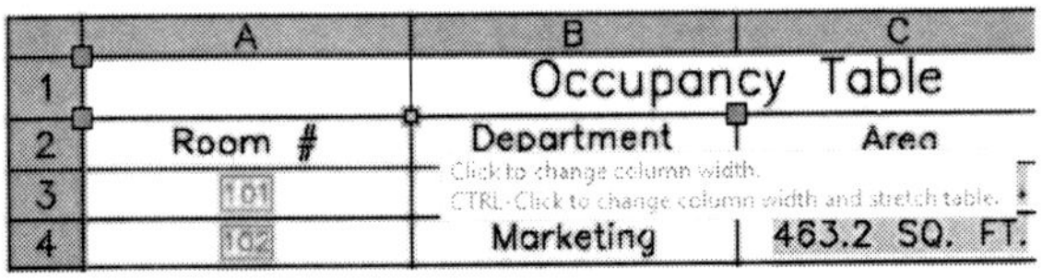

Figure 7–170

- **Column Width:** Controls the column width. Click the grip to change the width without changing the overall table width. The adjacent columns resize accordingly. Hold <Ctrl> to modify the overall width of the table. The upper left square grip moves the entire table.

- **Table Height:** Uniformly stretches the table height. The height of each row changes, including the title and headers. Rows are not added.

- **Table Width:** Uniformly stretches the table width. The width of each column changes. Columns are not added.

- **Table Height and Width:** Uniformly stretches both table height and width.

- **Table Breaking:** Activates table breaking, enabling you to control where the table is broken when it is in columns.

Breaking a Table

When a table is too long to fit on a sheet, you can break it and change its overall height. Click the grip (Table breaking) and drag it upwards until it reaches the required location in the table, as shown in Figure 7–171. The rest of the table is placed next to it in as many columns as required to contain all of the rows.

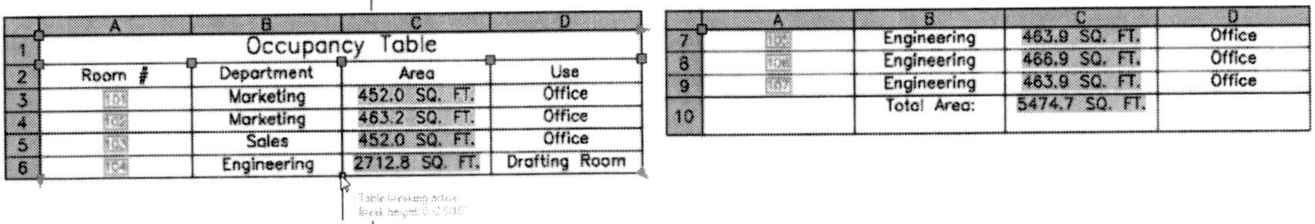

Figure 7–171

Practice 7n Modifying Tables

Practice Objective

- Modify the table using various modification tools.

Estimated time for completion: 10 minutes

In this practice, you will use grips to modify the width and height of rows and columns, add and merge rows to create a new header, insert rows, copy and paste information, use Auto-fill to add information to cells, and break the table into columns. The completed table is shown in Figure 7–172.

Figure 7–172

1. Open **Occupancy1-A.dwg** from your practice files folder.

2. Zoom into the *Table* area of the drawing.

3. Select the table to display the grips. Hold <Ctrl>, click and drag the square grip of the *Area* column to the right to increase the *Area* column width while also stretching the table, as shown in Figure 7–173. Click again to accept the stretch.

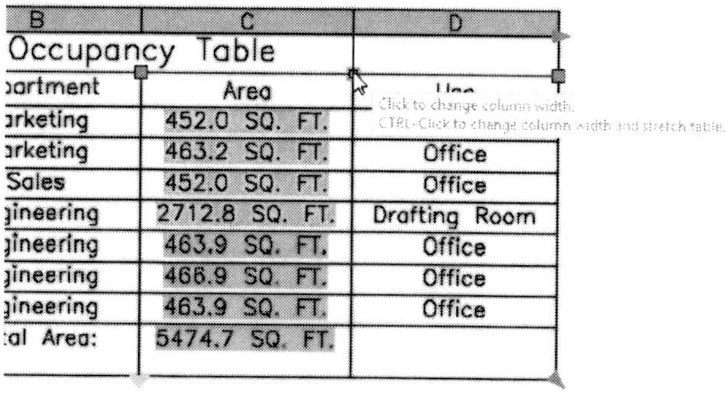

Figure 7–173

4. Click on the last row and use the bottom grip to make it the same height as the other rows.

5. Select the Row 2 of the table. In the *Table Cell* contextual tab>Rows panel, click (Insert Above) to place a row above Row 2. Fill in the first cell of the new row with the text **First Floor**.

6. Select the newly created Row 2. Right-click and select **Merge>By Row**.

7. With the row still selected, in the *Table Cell* contextual tab>Cell Styles panel, expand the Table Cell Styles list, and set the *style* to **Title**, as shown in Figure 7–174.

Figure 7–174

8. Select the bottom row. In the *Table Cell* contextual tab>Rows panel, click (Insert Below) eleven times (the last number displays row 22).

9. Select one of the cells containing a room number block. Right-click and select **Copy** to copy the cell to the clipboard.

10. Leave three open rows after the *Total Area* row and paste the block into the cell in the *Room #* column (Row 15).

11. Select the copied cell and click on the Auto-fill grip (cyan diamond) of the cell. Drag it to the Room # cell of Row 21, as shown in Figure 7–175. Click to copy the block to the next six cells below.

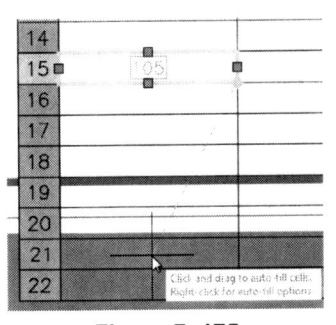

Figure 7–175

Annotate Drawings

12. Double-click on the first new block to open the Edit Block in a Table Cell dialog box. Click **OK**. In the Enter Attributes dialog box, change the *Room Number* to **201** and click **OK**.

13. Modify the rest of the room numbers.

14. Repeat the Copy and Auto-fill process for the *Department* and *Use* columns. Do not fill in the *Area* column at this time.

15. Select the entire table (use window selection) and break it under the *Total Area* row. Select ▼ (Table breaking) and then drag it near the right side of the existing table. Move the cursor down until all eleven rows display and click to break the table, as shown in Figure 7–176.

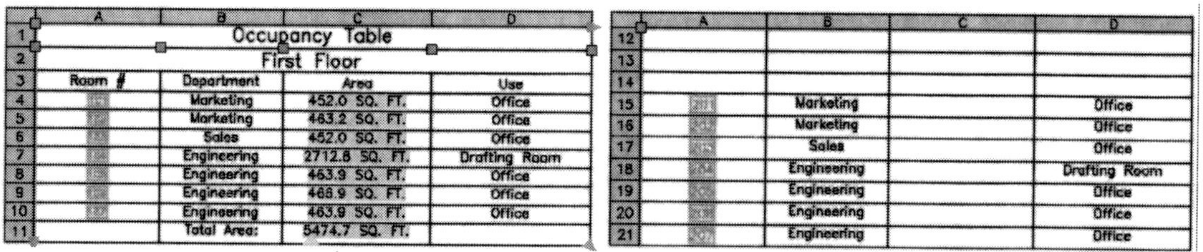

Figure 7–176

16. You can add and merge rows to specify an additional Title and Headers for the Second Floor, as shown in Figure 7–177. Set the Cell Styles, as required.

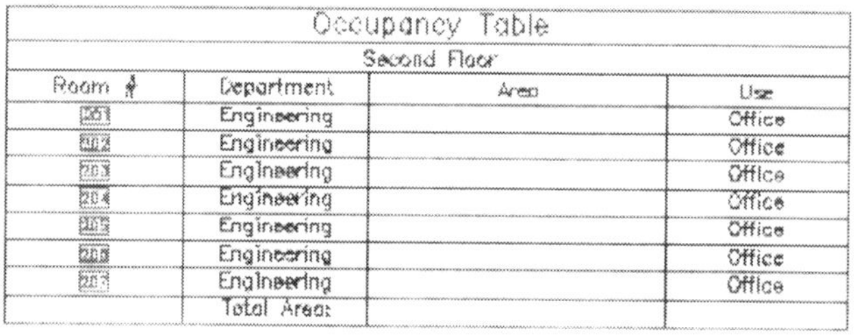

Figure 7–177

17. Save the drawing.

7.17 Working with Linked Tables

Many companies store information in spreadsheets that can be used in a drawing set. Instead of creating a table in the AutoCAD software and filling it in from scratch, you can create a table linked to an Excel spreadsheet. This can be done using the **Copy** and **Paste Special** from clipboard method or by linking to the table using the **Table** command. Figure 7–178 shows an Excel table that has been copied into the AutoCAD software.

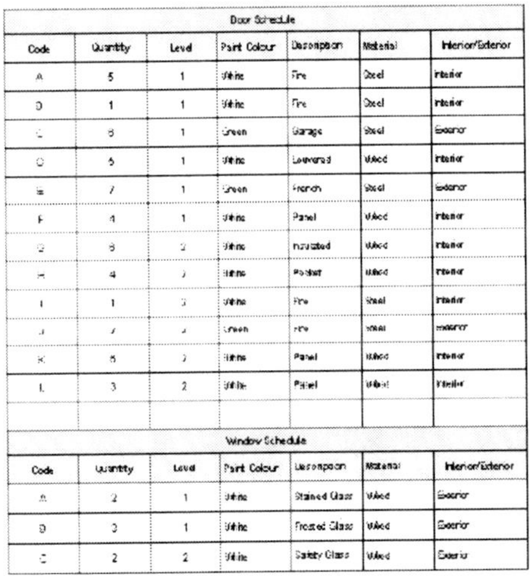

Door Schedule						
Code	Quantity	Level	Paint Colour	Description	Material	Interior/Exterior
A	5	1	White	Fire	Steel	Interior
B	1	1	White	Fire	Steel	Interior
C	8	1	Green	Garage	Steel	Exterior
D	5	1	White	Louvered	Wood	Interior
E	7	1	Green	French	Steel	Exterior
F	4	1	White	Panel	Wood	Interior
G	8	2	White	Insulated	Wood	Interior
H	4	2	White	Pocket	Wood	Interior
I	1	2	White	Fire	Steel	Interior
J	2	2	Green	Fire	Steel	Exterior
K	6	2	White	Panel	Wood	Interior
L	3	2	White	Panel	Wood	Interior
Window Schedule						
Code	Quantity	Level	Paint Colour	Description	Material	Interior/Exterior
A	2	1	White	Stained Glass	Wood	Exterior
B	3	1	White	Frosted Glass	Wood	Exterior
C	2	2	White	Safety Glass	Wood	Exterior

AutoCAD table

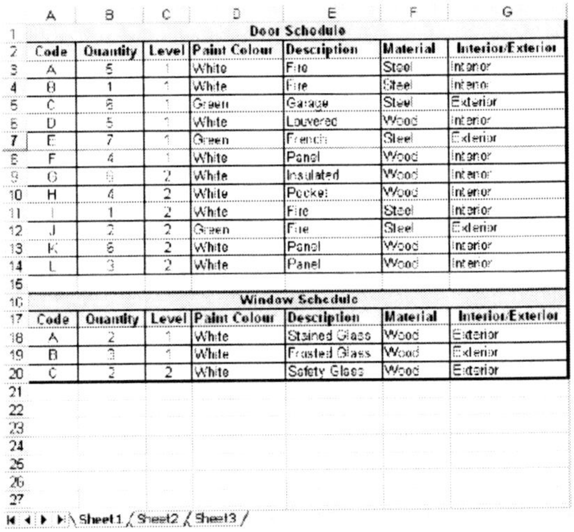

	A	B	C	D	E	F	G
1	Door Schedule						
2	Code	Quantity	Level	Paint Colour	Description	Material	Interior/Exterior
3	A	5	1	White	Fire	Steel	Interior
4	B	1	1	White	Fire	Steel	Interior
5	C	8	1	Green	Garage	Steel	Exterior
6	D	5	1	White	Louvered	Wood	Interior
7	E	7	1	Green	French	Steel	Exterior
8	F	4	1	White	Panel	Wood	Interior
9	G	8	2	White	Insulated	Wood	Interior
10	H	4	2	White	Pocket	Wood	Interior
11	I	1	2	White	Fire	Steel	Interior
12	J	2	2	Green	Fire	Steel	Exterior
13	K	6	2	White	Panel	Wood	Interior
14	L	3	2	White	Panel	Wood	Interior
15							
16	Window Schedule						
17	Code	Quantity	Level	Paint Colour	Description	Material	Interior/Exterior
18	A	2	1	White	Stained Glass	Wood	Exterior
19	B	3	1	White	Frosted Glass	Wood	Exterior
20	C	2	2	White	Safety Glass	Wood	Exterior
21							
22							
23							
24							
25							
26							
27							

Sheet1 / Sheet2 / Sheet3

Excel table

Figure 7–178

- The imported table uses the formatting from the Excel file.
- Any changes that you make to the linked Excel file can be updated in the AutoCAD table. You can also make changes in the AutoCAD table and save them back to the Excel file.

How To: Copy and Link a Spreadsheet to a Table

1. In Excel, select the cells that you want to include in the AutoCAD drawing and copy them to the clipboard.
2. In the AutoCAD software, in the *Home* tab>Clipboard panel, expand (Paste) and click (Paste Special).
3. In the Paste Special dialog box, select **Paste Link** and **AutoCAD Entities** as shown in Figure 7–179.

Annotate Drawings

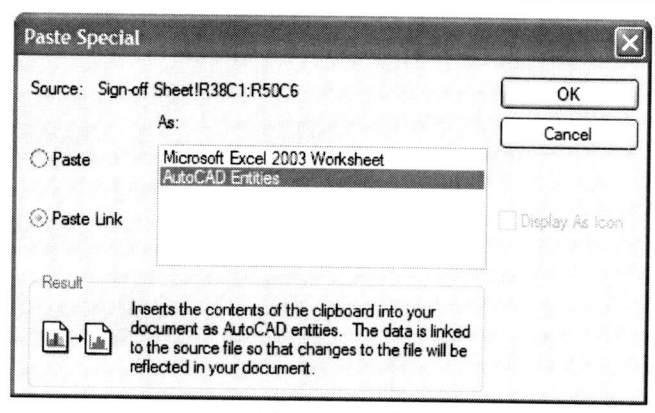

Figure 7–179

4. Click **OK**.
5. In the AutoCAD drawing, pick an insertion point for the table.

• If you use the **Paste** command rather than **Paste Special**, the table can still be updated in Excel but is not linked to the original file.

Table from a Data Link

The simplest way to link a table to an external file is to use **Cut** and **Paste**. Alternatively, you can use the **Table** command. The table can be linked to an entire Excel spreadsheet, a single cell, or a range of cells.

• You can have multiple data links in a drawing, all of which can be modified using the Data Link Manager.

How To: Create a Table from a Data Link

1. In the *Home* tab>Annotation panel or *Annotate* tab>Tables panel, click (Table) to start the **Table** command.
2. In the Insert Table dialog box, select the **From a data link** option, as shown in Figure 7–180.

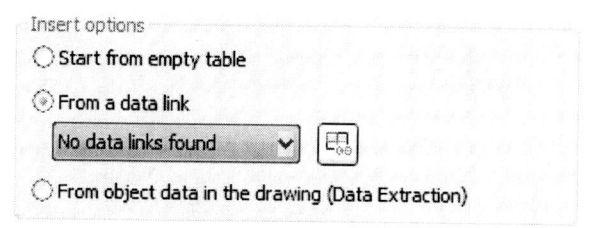

Figure 7–180

© 2017, ASCENT - Center for Technical Knowledge®   7–127

3. If you have an existing link, select it in the list and skip to Step 12.
4. If you want to create a new link, click ▦ (Launch the Data Link Manager dialog) to open the Select a Data Link dialog box.
5. In the Select a Data Link dialog box shown in Figure 7–181, select **Create a new Excel Data Link**.

Figure 7–181

6. In the Enter Data Link Name dialog box, type a name for the link and click **OK**.
7. In the New Excel Data Link dialog box, you can select a file in the list or click ⋯ (Browse) to browse for a file.
8. In the Save As dialog box, select a file and click **Open**.
9. In the New Excel Data Link dialog box, specify the Link options, as shown in Figure 7–182.

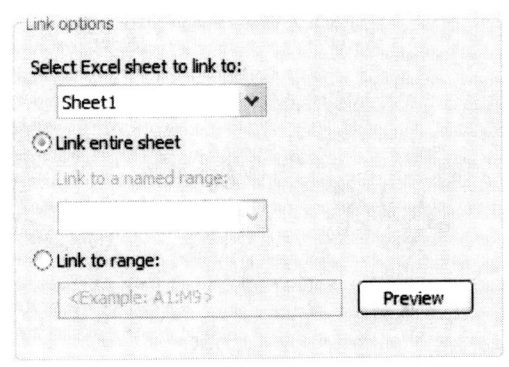

Figure 7–182

10. You can select a sheet (if there are several in the spreadsheet) and then link the entire sheet, a named range, or specify a range of cells.
11. When you have finished adding information to the table, click **OK**.
12. In the Select a Data Link dialog box, verify that the link you want to use is selected and click **OK**.
13. In the Insert Table dialog box, click **OK**.
14. Pick an insertion point on the sheet.

Annotate Drawings

- If you are specifying a range of cells and do not use the correct form, the Invalid Range alert box opens, as shown in Figure 7–183.

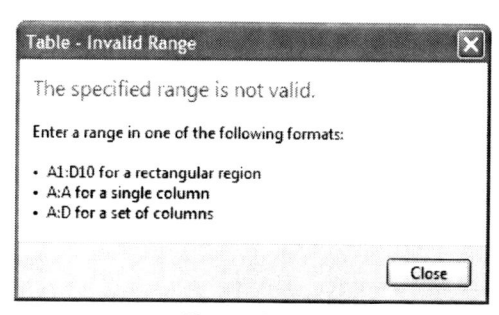

Figure 7–183

- Numbered ranges are functions in Excel that enable you to select a cell or range of cells and assign them a name. This name can be used in formulas and anywhere you would type a cell identifier or range of cells. It is a labeled shortcut to a set of data. By labeling a range of cells with a descriptive name, you can quickly identify the function or origin of the data contained in them.

> **Link Cell:** Displayed in the *Table Cell* contextual tab>Data panel when at least one cell is selected. Can be used to link individual cells or groups of cells to a cell(s) in a spreadsheet.

Using the Data Link Manager

If you know that you are going to link several files in your drawing, you can set them up using (Data Link Manager) before you start the **Table** command. You can then select the link from a list in the Insert Table dialog box, as shown in Figure 7–184. (Data Link Manager) is located in:

- The *Annotate* tab>Tables panel, and
- The *Insert* tab>Linking and Extraction panel.

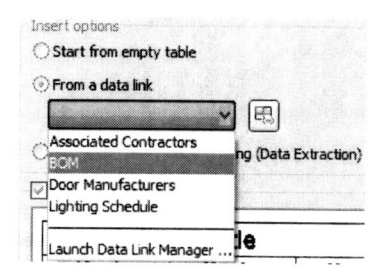

Figure 7–184

- To create a new Excel data link, in the Data Link Manager dialog box, select **Create a new Excel Data Link**, as shown in Figure 7–185.

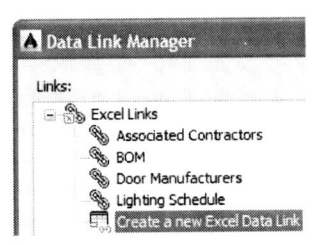

Figure 7–185

- Clear the **Preview** option to save time when working in the Data Link Manager.

- Expand the New or Modify Excel Data Link dialog box to display the extra options for modifying and creating data links, including cell content and formatting, as shown in Figure 7–186.

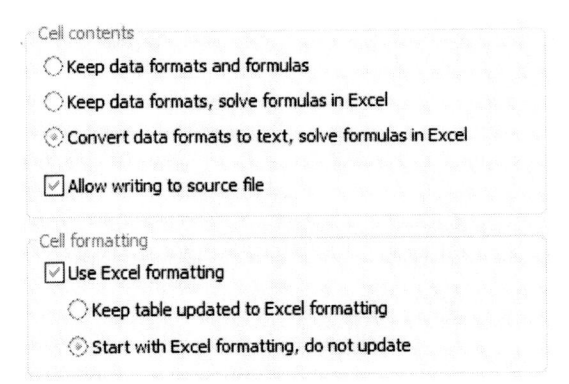

Figure 7–186

- Select **Allow writing to source file** to write modified data from the AutoCAD file to the source file.

Annotate Drawings

Updating Table Links

You can update table data in two directions in a linked table, in the current drawing.

- In the shortcut menu, use the **Update Table Data Links** option (shown in Figure 7–187) to update the AutoCAD table from the source. Use **Write Data Links to External Source** to write the AutoCAD data to the source (this only works if **Allow writing to source file** is selected in the *Cell contents* area, in the New or Modify Excel Data Link dialog box).

- In the *Annotate* tab>Tables panel or *Insert* tab>Linking & Extraction panel, you can also use (Download from Source) to update the linked table data from the external source file and (Upload to Source) to update the linked data in the external source file from the current AutoCAD table, as shown in Figure 7–188.

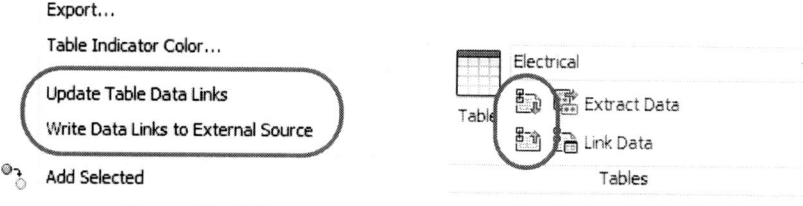

Figure 7–187

Figure 7–188

- The **Data Link Has Changed** bubble displays when the AutoCAD software detects that a linked file has been modified, as shown in Figure 7–189.

Figure 7–189

- In the Status Bar, right-click on (Data Link) as shown in Figure 7–190, and either open the Data Links dialog box or update all data links.

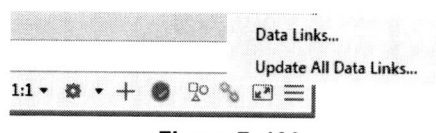

Figure 7–190

- Linked and locked tables display icons when they are selected and you move the cursor over them. If you hover the cursor, it displays information about the data link, as shown in Figure 7–191.

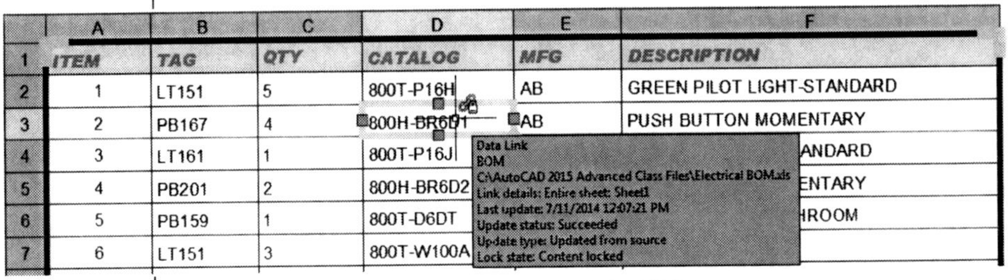

	A	B	C	D	E	F
1	ITEM	TAG	QTY	CATALOG	MFG	DESCRIPTION
2	1	LT151	5	800T-P16H	AB	GREEN PILOT LIGHT-STANDARD
3	2	PB167	4	800H-BR6D1	AB	PUSH BUTTON MOMENTARY
4	3	LT161	1	800T-P16J		ANDARD
5	4	PB201	2	800H-BR6D2		ENTARY
6	5	PB159	1	800T-D6DT		ROOM
7	6	LT151	3	800T-W100A		

Data Link
BOM
C:\AutoCAD 2015 Advanced Class Files\Electrical BOM.xls
Link details: Entire sheet: Sheet1
Last update: 7/11/2014 12:07:21 PM
Update status: Succeeded
Update type: Updated from source
Lock state: Content locked

Figure 7–191

- Linked cells are locked by default to protect them from accidental modification. Green corner brackets display when the table is selected, indicating their status. To edit a cell, select it, right-click, expand Locking and select **Unlocked**. When a cell is unlocked, it can be modified.

- You can add columns and rows to a linked AutoCAD table. They are not removed when the data is updated from the source file.

> **Download from source:** Available in the *Table Cell* contextual tab>Data panel when at least one cell is selected. Can be used to update the information in a linked file.

7.18 Creating Table Styles

Table styles define properties for table cell styles, such as text style and height, border properties, table direction, and cell margins. The standard templates in the AutoCAD software include a single predefined style named Standard. You can create custom styles as required in the Table Style dialog box, as shown in Figure 7–192.

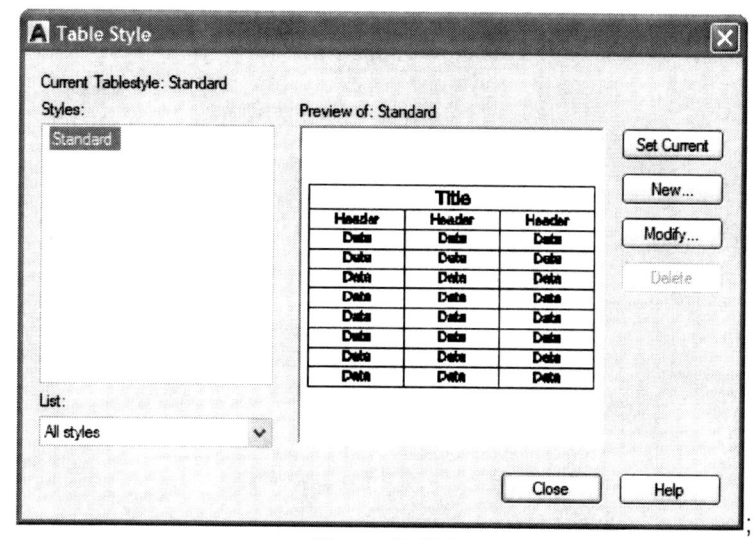

Figure 7–192

- The text style and size for each cell should be set in the table style, but you can also modify it in the *Text Editor* contextual tab as you enter the text.

- The number of rows and columns is specified when you insert the table. They are not defined in the style.

- Table styles do not include any values for the table cells.

How To: Create a Table Style

1. In the ribbon, *Home* tab>expanded Annotation panel click (Table Style) or in the *Annotate* tab>Tables panel, select the setting arrow.
2. Click **New**.

3. Type a name for the table style and select an existing style as the starting template, as shown in Figure 7–193.

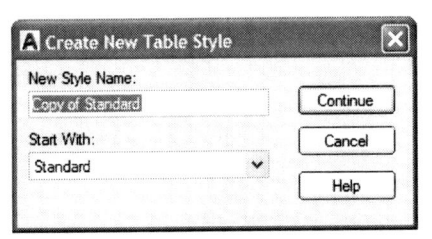

Figure 7–193

4. Click **Continue**.
5. In the New Table Style dialog box, you can select a table to use as a starting point in the *Starting table* area, and specify the table direction in the *General* area.
6. In the *Cell styles* area, select the cell style that you want to modify in the list or create a new style. The **Data**, **Header**, and **Title** options are included with the **Standard** style.
7. For each cell style, work through the tabs for *General*, *Text*, and *Borders*.
8. Click **OK** to return to the Table Style dialog box.
9. Select a style to be current and click **Set Current**.
10. Click **Close**.

Table Style Options

You can create a new table style and set the various options in the New Table Style dialog box, as shown in Figure 7–194.

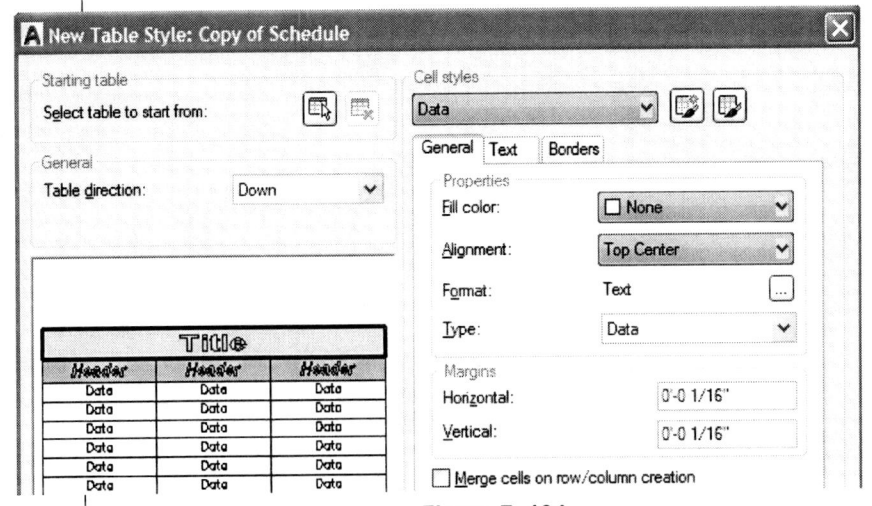

Figure 7–194

Annotate Drawings

The preview displays the default table style. If you would rather display the table you are working on, you can set it as the preview in the *Starting table* area in the New Table Style dialog box.

🗔	**Select a table to use as the starting table for this table style:** Sets the table you are working with to be displayed in the preview. Otherwise you can use the default style.
🗔	**Remove the starting table from this table style:** Sets the preview to display the default style or enables you to select a different table. An alert box opens to verify that you want to do this.

In the *General* area, the *Table direction* can be set to either **Up** or **Down**, as shown in Figure 7–195.

- **Down** locates the Title and Header rows at the top of the table.
- **Up** locates them at the bottom of the table.

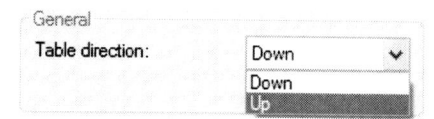

Figure 7–195

Cell Style Options

To modify the cell styles, you first select an existing cell style from the list, as shown in Figure 7–196. Then you work through the tabs to customize the cell style.

Figure 7–196

🗔	**Create a new Cell Style:** Opens the Create New Cell Style dialog box in which you can specify a new cell style name and select a starting style.
🗔	**Manage Cell Styles dialog:** Opens the Manage Cell Styles dialog box in which you can create new cell styles, and rename or delete existing ones.

General

In the *General* tab (shown in Figure 7–197), you can set properties, such as the *Fill color* and *Alignment* of objects in the cell. You can also specify the *Format* of the cell. The default is **General** but it can be set to **Decimal Number**, **Percentage**, **Text**, **Whole Number**, etc. The *Type* can be set to **Data** or **Label**. You can also set the **Margins** for the cell.

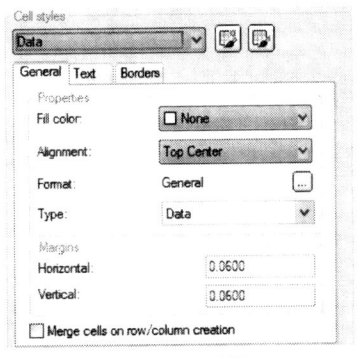

Figure 7–197

- New cells can be merged together automatically as you create columns and rows using the same cell style. For example, you might want all of the cells using the **Title** cell style to be merged together. By default, the *Standard* Table Style has the **Title** cell style set to merge, while the **Header** and **Data** cell styles are not.

Text

In the *Text* tab (shown in Figure 7–198), you can set the *Text style*, *Text height*, *Text color*, and *Text angle*.

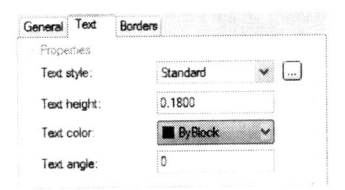

Figure 7–198

- The **Text angle** option forces the text to be at an angle. This rotates the text in the cell at the selected angle. In the example shown in Figure 7–199, the **Data** cell style is rotated at a 45 degree angle.

Figure 7–199

Borders

In the *Borders* tab (shown in Figure 7–200), you can control the visibility of the grid lines including **Lineweight**, **Linetype**, **Color**, and **Double line**, and where you want the borders to be placed around each cell of the style.

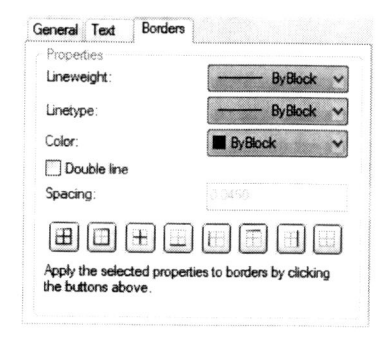

Figure 7–200

- When the **Double line** option is selected, you can enter a distance in the *Spacing* field to determine how far apart the double lines are going to be drawn.

Practice 7o

Working with Tables

Practice Objectives

- Add a table whose data is linked to an external spreadsheet file.
- Modify a table and update the data in the linked file.
- Create a new table style and apply it to an existing table.

Estimated time for completion: 20 minutes

In this practice you will create and update a table from an external link. You will also create and apply a table style and apply a cell style to individual cells. In the first two tasks you will create a table from an external link and then update it from the source and to the source. The completed drawing is shown in Figure 7–201.

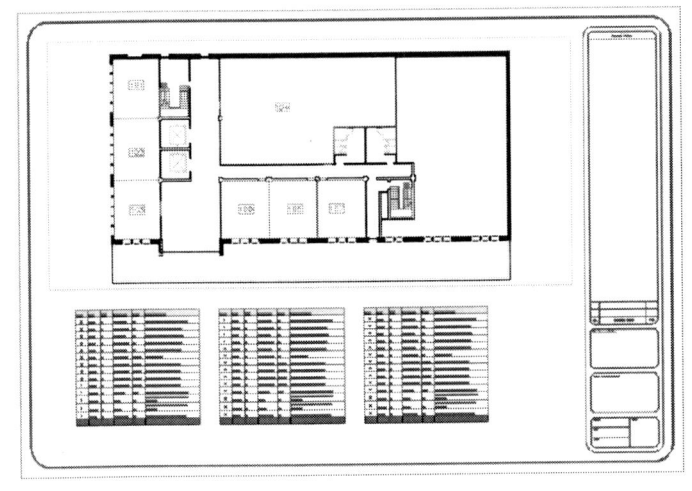

Figure 7–201

Task 1 - Create an externally linked table.

1. Open **Occupancy-Ad-A.dwg** from your practice files folder.

2. Switch to the **Electrical** layout.

3. In the *Home* tab>Annotation panel, click (Table) and set the *Table style* to **Electrical**.

4. In the *Insert options* area, select **From a data link** to create a table from an external source.

5. Click (Launch the Data Link Manager dialog) to open the Select a Data Link dialog box.

Annotate Drawings

6. Select **Create a new Excel Data Link**. The Enter Data Link Name dialog box opens.

7. Type **Bulbs and Wires** and click **OK**. The New Excel Data Link dialog box opens.

8. Click (Browse) to browse for a source file. The Save As dialog box opens.

9. Select **Electrical BOM.xls** in your practice files folder and click **Open**. The New Excel Data Link dialog box now displays additional options.

10. In the *Link options* area, ensure that **Link entire sheet** is selected, and then click **OK**.

11. In the Select a Data Link dialog box, click **OK**.

12. In the Insert Table dialog box, click **OK** and pick an insertion point below the viewport to locate the table in the drawing.

13. The table is too long to fit on the page. Use grips to break it into three columns.

14. Save the drawing.

Task 2 - Update the table and write data to the source.

To complete this part of the practice, you need to have a copy of Microsoft Excel on the workstation.

1. Open **Electrical BOM.xls** in Excel from your practice files folder.

2. Change several of the *QTY* (quantity) numbers.

3. Save and close the Excel file.

4. Switch back to the AutoCAD software. An information bubble opens (as shown in Figure 7–202) indicating that the external source has been modified.

Figure 7–202

5. In the information bubble, select **Update tables using the data link** to update the data in the table with the modified data from the Excel file. The changes that you have made display in the updated table.

6. Zoom in on the top of the AutoCAD table and select the cells E2 through E7. Right-click and select **Locking>Unlocked** (as shown in Figure 7–203) to unlock the cells.

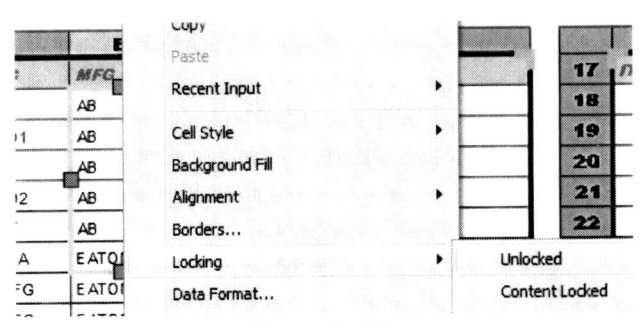

Figure 7–203

7. Change the *MFG name* in each of the cells to **SQD**.

8. In the *Insert* tab>Linking & Extraction panel, click (Upload to Source). Select the table and press <Enter>. All of the modifications in the AutoCAD table are written to the source file.

9. Open **Electrical BOM.xls** and note the changes to the cells.

10. Close the Excel file and save the drawing.

Task 3 - Create table styles.

In this task you will create a table style with several cell styles and apply it to an existing table. You will also select individual cells and apply a cell style to them. The completed table is shown in Figure 7–204.

Room #	Department	Area	Use
101	Marketing	452.0 SQ. FT.	Office
102	Marketing	463.2 SQ. FT.	Office
103	Sales	452.0 SQ. FT.	Office
104	Engineering	2712.8 SQ. FT.	Drafting Room
105	Engineering	463.9 SQ. FT.	Office
106	Engineering	466.9 SQ. FT.	Office
107	Engineering	463.9 SQ. FT.	Office
	Total Area:	5474.6876 SQ. FT.	

Occupancy Table — First Floor

Figure 7–204

1. Switch to the Occupancy layout.
2. In the ribbon, in the *Home* tab>expanded Annotation panel, click (Table Style).
3. In the Table Style dialog box, click **New** to create a new table style.
4. Name the new style **Schedule**, verify that the **Standard** table style is selected from the Start With drop-down list (as shown in Figure 7–205), and click **Continue**.

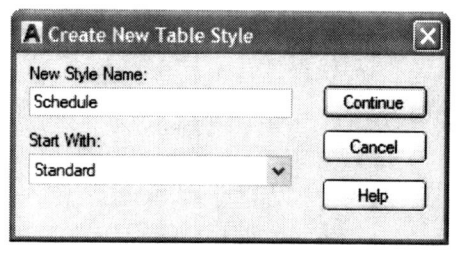

Figure 7–205

5. In the New Table Style dialog box, set the following:
   - In the Cell styles drop-down list, select **Title**.
   - In the *General* tab, set the *Fill color* to **Cyan**.
   - In the *Text* tab, set the *Text style* to **Title** and the *Text height* to **1/4"**.
   - In the *Borders* tab, set the *Lineweight* to **0.60mm** and click (Outside Borders).
6. Set the following:
   - In the Cell styles drop-down list, select **Header**.
   - In the *General* tab, set the *Fill color* to **Green**.
   - In the *Text* tab, set the *Text style* to **Logo**.
7. Set the following:
   - In the Cell styles drop-down list, select **Data**.
   - In the *Text* tab, set the *Text height* to **1/8"**.
8. In the Cell Styles drop down list, select **Create a new cell style** and name it **Areas** based on (Start With) the *Data* cell style. Click **Continue**.
9. With **Areas** selected, in the *General* tab, set the *Alignment* to **Middle Right**.

10. Click **OK**. In the Table Style dialog box, click **Close**.

11. In the *Occupancy* layout, select the table.

12. In the *Annotate* tab>Tables panel, select the new style **Schedule** (as shown in Figure 7–206) to apply it to the selected table.

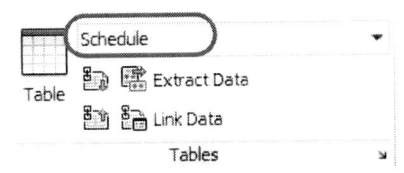

Figure 7–206

13. Use grips to modify the rows and columns as required to match the new layout of the table.

14. Select the cells under *Area*.

15. In the *Table Cell* contextual tab>Cell Styles panel, select **Areas** in the drop-down list to apply it to the selected cells. Note that the values are right justified, as shown in Figure 7–204.

16. Save the drawing.

Chapter 8

Layouts and Printing

This chapter includes instructional content to assist in your preparation for the following topic and objectives for the AutoCAD® Certified Professional exam.

Autodesk Certification Exam Objectives in this Chapter

Exam Topic	Exam Objective	Section(s)
Layouts and Printing	• Create layouts	• 8.1 to 8.4
	• Use viewports	• 8.5 to 8.6
	• Set printing and plotting options	• 8.7 to 8.10

8.1 Working in Layouts

When you first enter a layout, you are in a mode called Paper Space by default. You can identify this mode by the **Paper Space** icon displayed in the lower left corner of the screen and **Paper** displayed in the Status Bar, as shown in Figure 8–1.

- In Paper Space, you can add or edit the border and title block, add notes, and create or manipulate the viewports that display the model.

Paper Space icon

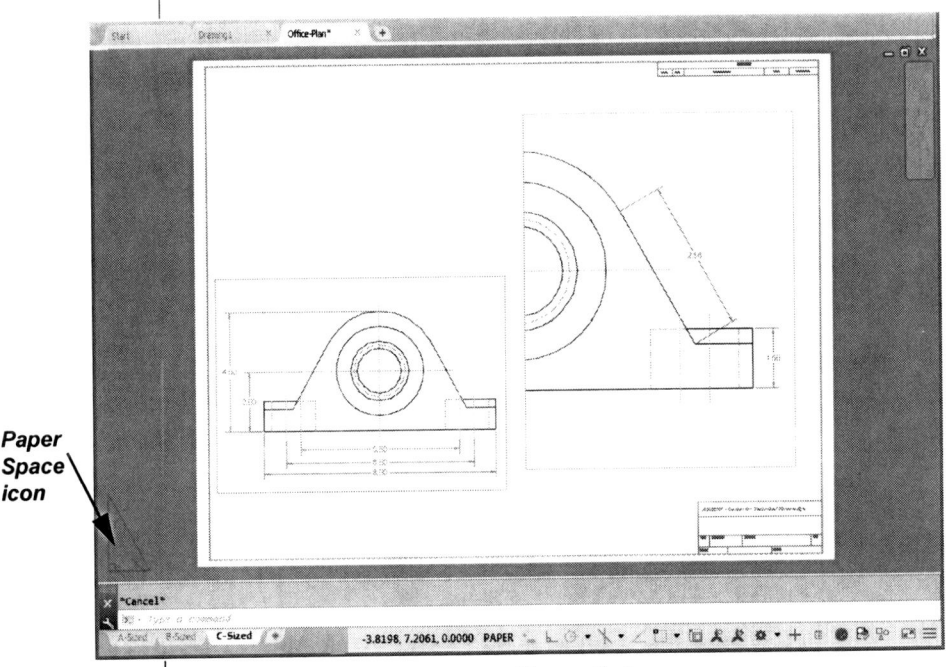

Figure 8–1

- Paper Space displays a graphic representation of the drawing sheet. A dashed boundary on the sheet represents the printable area (if a border is already inserted, it might hide the dashed boundary). The size of the layout reflects the actual sheet size specified in the layout settings. The model displays in one or more viewports in the layout.

Layouts and Printing

- When working in layouts, you can use any of the AutoCAD commands.

- If several layout tabs are available, you can hover the cursor over a tab to display a thumbnail view of the layout, as shown in Figure 8–2. Select a tab to make it active.

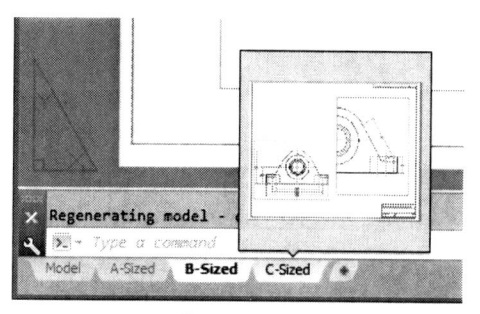

Figure 8–2

- If there are more layouts that cannot be accommodated in the Status Bar, a ⬇ displays. When repositioning layout tabs, you can drag layouts into positions that are currently hidden by the overflow menu. As a layout is dragged to the edge of the displayed layout tab, either on the left or right (as shown in Figure 8–3), tabs automatically scroll to show hidden layouts. This enables you to drop a layout to any location even if it is hidden.

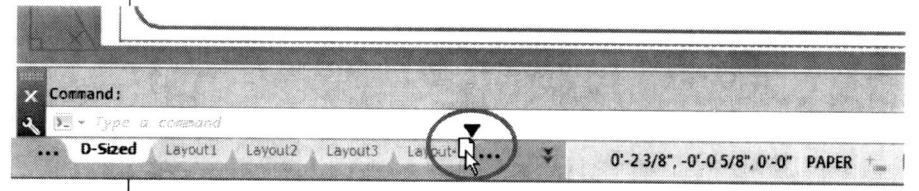

Figure 8–3

Switch Between Paper Space & Model Space

While making changes in a layout, you often switch between working on the sheet of paper and working on the model through the viewport to adjust the view.

Working Inside a Viewport (Model Space)

- When in a *Layout* tab, you can switch to Model Space by double-clicking inside a viewport. It makes that viewport the active work area. The active viewport displays with a thicker border (as shown in Figure 8–4), and the Status Bar displays **Model**.

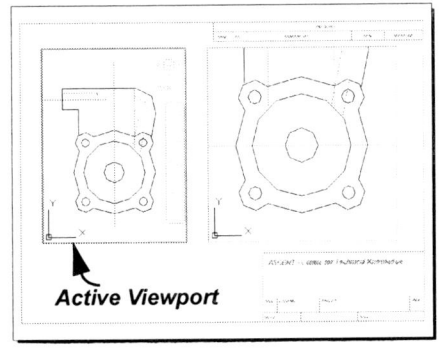

Figure 8–4

- Only one viewport can be active at a time. The active viewport displays the crosshair cursor. In other viewports and in the paper area, the cursor is an arrow. To make a different viewport active, click inside its border.

- In the active viewport, you can **Zoom** or **Pan** to display any part of the model.

- Any change you make to the model's objects through a viewport, such as moving or deleting them, is reflected in the model, the drawing, and all other viewports.

Returning to Paper Space

Double-click on the paper area of the layout to change from Model Space back to Paper Space, as shown in Figure 8–5. This makes the paper the active work area again. The **Paper Space** icon displays in the drawing window and the Status Bar displays **Paper**. The viewport border returns to its default thickness.

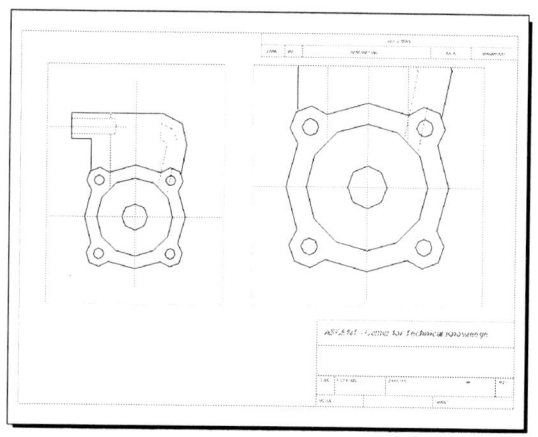

Figure 8–5

- If you double-click on the edge of the viewport, it opens the view in Model Space and fills the screen. This is called *maximizing* the viewport and makes it easier for you to modify the drawing. You can also click (Maximize Viewport) in the Status Bar to maximize the viewport and then click (Minimize Viewport) to return to Paper Space.

8.2 Creating Layouts

If you are working with large projects that contain many layouts, use the Sheet Sets Manager to coordinate the project.

When you are working with small projects, you need to have as many layouts in your drawing as the number of printed sheets required to describe the model. You can create new layouts from scratch (empty layouts), by copying existing layouts in your drawing, or create them from template files. You can then add viewports and other objects to the new layout.

How To: Copy and Rename a Layout

1. In the Status Bar, right-click on the layout tab that you want to copy and select **Move or Copy...**
2. In the Move or Copy dialog box, select the layout before which the copied layout is to be added. Alternatively, you can select the **(move to end)** option to add the copied layout as the last layout tab. Select the **Create a copy** option and click **OK**. The new layout is added before the selected layout or as the last layout, depending on the selected option, as shown in Figure 8–6.

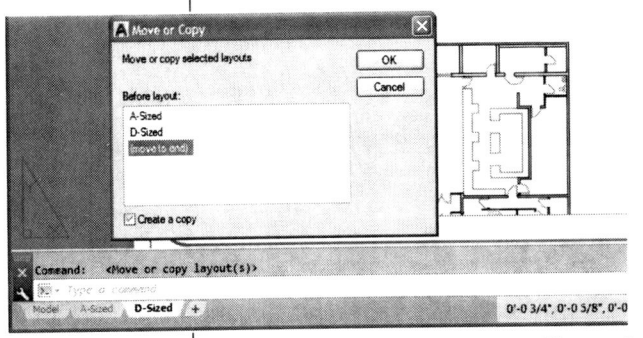

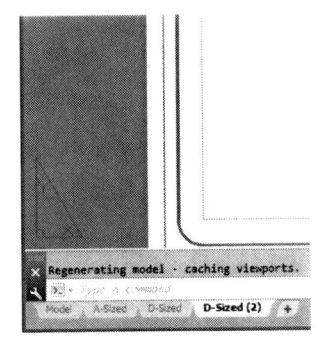

Figure 8–6

3. To rename the layout, double-click on the tab. It is highlighted in blue and you can type the new name, as shown in Figure 8–7. You can also right-click on the tab and select **Rename**.

Figure 8–7

- When you copy a layout, all of the related plotting information and any objects on the layout (such as titleblock, viewports, and notes) are copied as well.

Layouts and Printing

> **Hint: Best Practice for Layouts**
>
> The best way to create a new layout is to copy an existing one that includes all of the settings that you want to use. It is recommended that you have standard layouts containing company title blocks and page setups available in template files, so the parameters do not have to be recreated every time you are ready to set up a sheet.

How To: Create a Layout from a Template

You can also copy layouts from template files or other drawings.

1. In the *Layout* tab>Layout panel, expand (New) and click **From Template**. You can also right-click on a layout tab and select **From Template...**
2. In the Select Template From File dialog box, locate the template file you want to use and click **Open**.
3. In the Insert Layout(s) dialog box, select the layout you want to use, as shown in Figure 8–8.

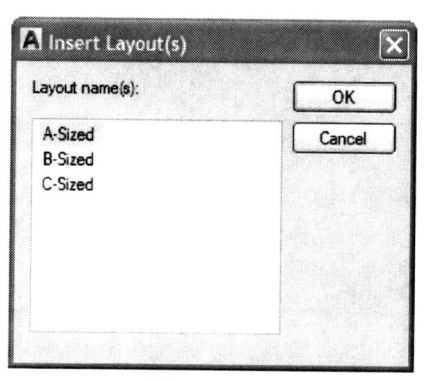

Figure 8–8

4. The new layout is added to the end of the row of tabs.

How To: Create a New Layout

Alternatively, use (New Layout) in the Layout tab>Layout panel. This prompts you to enter a new name or accept the Layout 1 name.

1. Click at the end of the *Layout* tabs to create a new layout. It creates a new layout with the name Layout 1 or the next available layout number.
2. Rename the layout (double-click or right-click and select **Rename**).

8.3 Creating and Using Named Views

If you are working on a large complex drawing, you might want to break it into views that you can readily access in both Model Space and in the Paper Space viewports.

The **View Manager** command (shown in Figure 8–9), stores areas of the drawing under specific names. For example, you can use named views to define a view of each quadrant in a map, or an area in a large mechanical assembly or architectural plan. These named views can easily be restored in the drawing area.

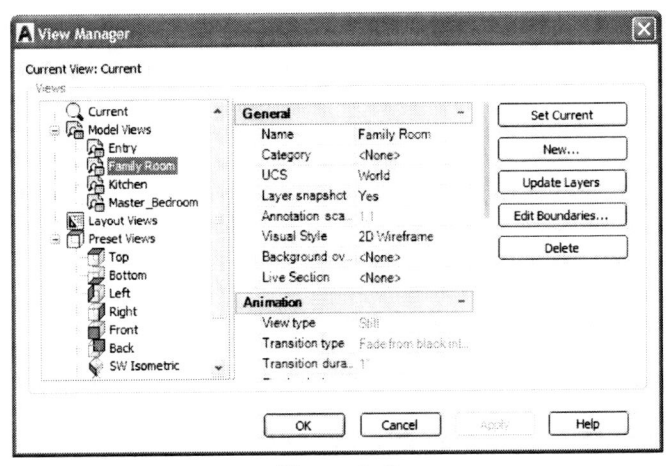

Figure 8–9

- In a large or complex drawing, named views provide a faster method of display control than the **Zoom** command.

- Once named views have been created, you can access them in the list in the *View* tab>Views panel as shown in Figure 8–10.

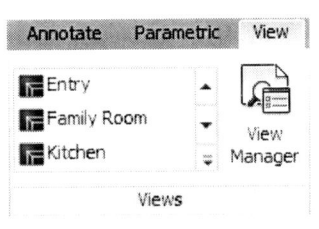

Figure 8–10

*The Views panel is not displayed by default. You need to right-click anywhere in the View tab and select **Show Panels>Views** to display the panel.*

Layouts and Printing

How To: Create a Named View

*In the AutoCAD LT® software, the **Shot Properties** and **ShowMotion** commands are not available. The **View Manager** command opens the New View dialog box.*

1. In the *View* tab>Views panel, click ⬚ (View Manager).
2. In the View Manager dialog box, click **New...**.
3. In the New View / Shot Properties dialog box, type a name in the *View name:* field, as shown in Figure 8–11.
4. The *View type* should be set to **Still**, as this option is typical for 2D views. The other *View type* options relate to 3D features.

*In the AutoCAD LT software, the New View dialog box contains the View Name field, and the Boundary and Settings areas. In the Settings area, only the **Save layer snapshot with view** option and UCS drop-down list are available.*

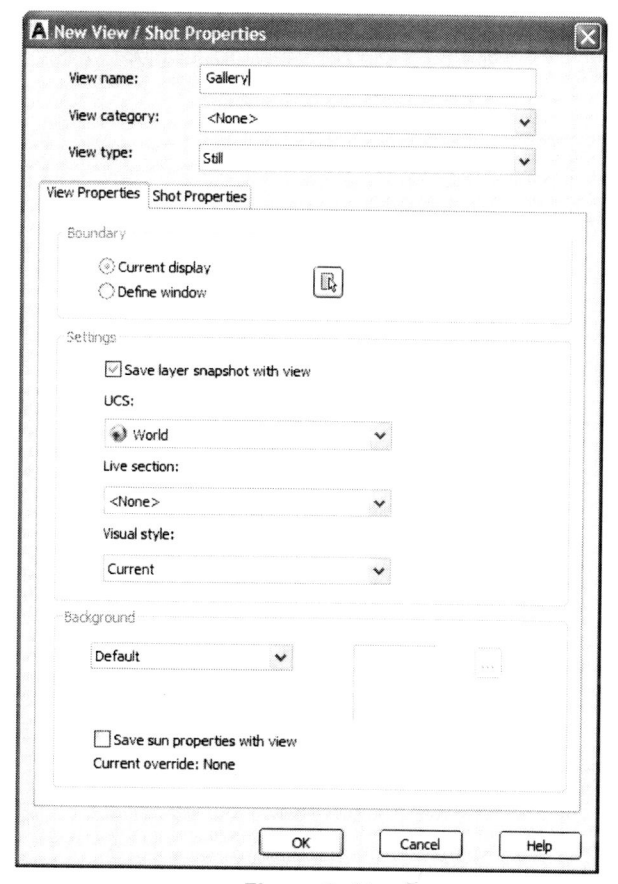

Figure 8–11

5. In the *Boundary* area, select the **Current display** option to save the current screen view, or select the **Define window** option to define a different view by clicking ⬚ (Define view window).
6. In the *Settings* area, select whether to save the layer snapshot with the view.
7. Click **OK** to create the view.

© 2017, ASCENT - Center for Technical Knowledge®

- The view can be defined to store the current layer settings (On/Off, Freeze/Thaw, etc.), so that these layers are automatically displayed when the view is restored.

- After a view has been defined, you can modify its boundaries by selecting it in the list and clicking **Edit Boundaries...**. The current view area is then highlighted. Select two points on screen to define a new area and press <Enter>.

- Views that store layer settings are marked **Yes** in the *Layer snapshot* under General in the View Manager dialog box. You can select a view in the list and click **Update Layers** to save the current layer settings with the view.

Layouts and Printing

8.4 Advanced Viewport Options

To be more efficient in the creation of layouts, you can use previously created Named Views of your model as the basis for Viewports in a layout. You can also modify the shape of existing viewports, as shown in Figure 8–12.

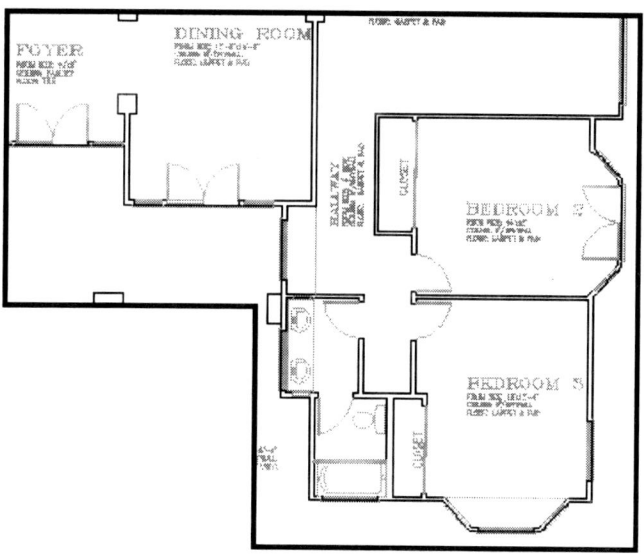

Figure 8–12

The Viewports dialog box enables you to select Named Views to use as the basis for new viewports in a layout. You can create single or multiple Named View Viewports at the same time.

Creating Viewports from Named Views

You are required to be in one of the layouts to display the Layout tab in the Ribbon.

How To: Use Named Views as Viewports

1. Verify that you are in an active layout.
2. Set the layer to which you want to add the viewports to be current.
3. In the *Layout* tab>Layout Viewports panel, click (Named).
4. In the Viewports dialog box, select the *New Viewports* tab.
5. In the *Standard viewports* area, select the standard viewport configuration that you want to use. If required, set the **Viewport Spacing**.

6. In the *Preview* area, select one of the Views as shown in Figure 8–13. The Preview View is highlighted.

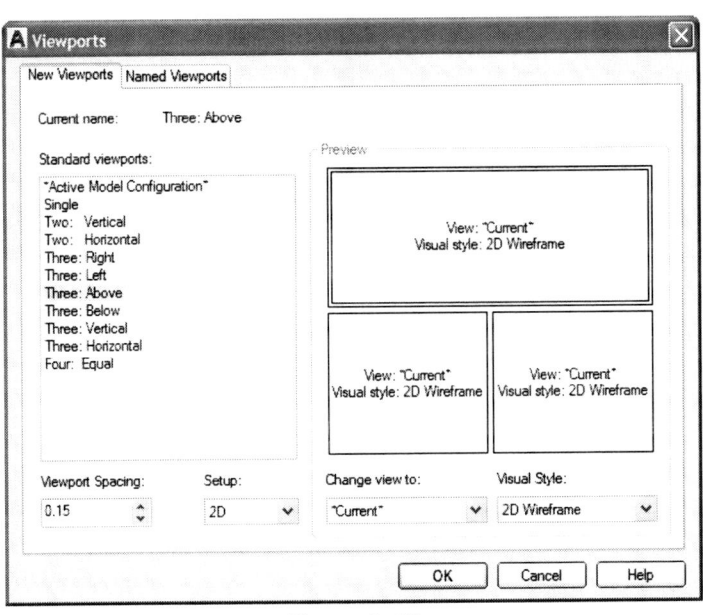

Figure 8–13

*By default, **2D** puts the current view in all of the viewports. **3D** puts standard 3D views (Top, Front, and SE Isometric) in the new viewports.*

7. In the Change view to drop-down list, select a Named View (if any have been saved), as shown in Figure 8–14, to display in that Viewport location.

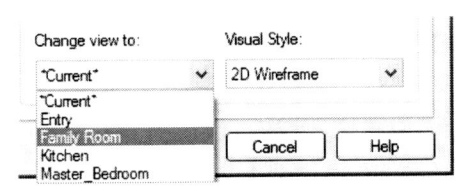

Figure 8–14

Layouts and Printing

8. The view name displays in the *Preview* area, as shown in Figure 8–15.

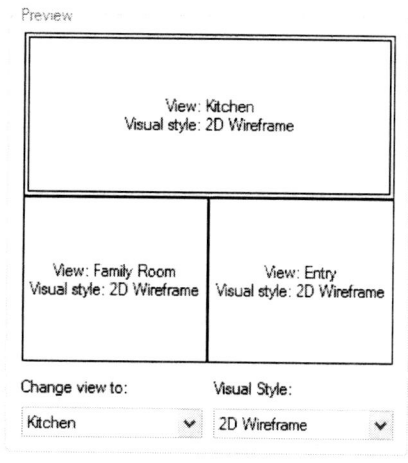

Figure 8–15

In the AutoCAD LT software, the Visual Styles drop-down list is not available.

9. The Visual Style can be preselected if you are working in 3D.
10. Click **OK** to continue.
11. If you are working in a layout, you are prompted to select two corners or to use fit to place all of the viewports on the sheet.

- The *Named Viewports* tab enables you to restore the saved configurations of Model Space viewports. However, the configuration of viewports in a layout cannot be saved.

- The Viewports dialog box works in both Model Space (for *tiled* viewports) and Paper Space or Layout mode (for *floating* viewports).

Hint: Model Space Viewports

Model Space can also be divided into viewports, but only for viewing. For example, if you have a very complex drawing you might need to display multiple close-up views at the same time as shown in Figure 8–16. The viewport that is currently active is highlighted with a blue border. You can drag the edges of the viewports to resize them.

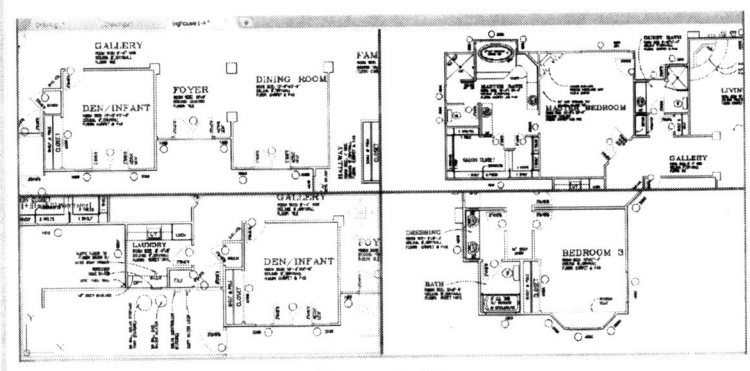

Figure 8–16

In Model Space, you can use **Named** in the *View* tab>Model Viewports panel to create a new viewport configuration.

However, it is easier to expand (Viewport Configuration) in the *View* tab>Model Viewports panel and select the required arrangement, as shown in Figure 8–17.

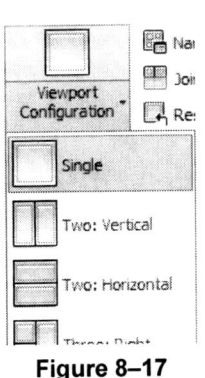

Figure 8–17

Clipping Viewports

You can remove any portions of a viewport that are not required, or make its shape fit better in the available layout space. This is most effective if you have already created the viewport with the correct scale and view of the drawing.

How To: Clip a Viewport

1. In the *Layout* tab>Layout Viewports panel, click ▢ (Clip).
2. Select the viewport that you want to clip.
3. Select a clipping object (which has already been created) or press <Enter> to draw a polygonal object, as shown in Figure 8–18.

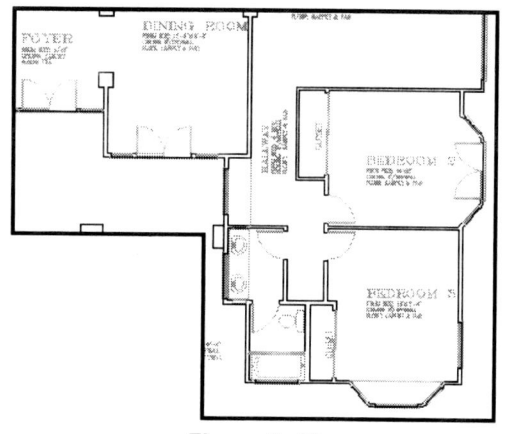

Figure 8–18

- Use the **Delete** option to remove the clipping boundary and restore the original viewport.

- If the clipping boundary extends outside the current viewport boundary, the viewport is extended in that direction.

- You can reclip a viewport without needing to delete the old clip boundary first.

- You can also change the shape of a polygonal viewport (without clipping) by using grips to stretch the vertices to new locations.

8.5 Creating Layout Viewports

You can create the required viewports in a layout using one of several viewport commands, or the Viewports dialog box. You can insert a single viewport, a standard configuration of multiple viewports, a polygonal viewport, or convert an object to a viewport. Each viewport in a layout can contain a different view of the model, displayed at any scale.

- Viewports should be placed on a layer that is used specifically for storing viewports. Toggling the layer off (or making it a non-plotting layer) hides the viewport border, but not the model objects inside the viewport.

- You can create multiple viewports in various shapes and sizes in a layout.

- You can create multiple viewports that overlap, but you should not place one completely inside another's boundaries.

Rectangular Viewports

How To: Create a New Rectangular Viewport

1. Verify that you are in a layout and in Paper Space.
2. Set the layer to which you want to add the viewports to be current.
3. In the *Layout* tab>Layout Viewports panel, expand the Viewports drop-down list and click ▢ (Rectangular).
4. Select the first corner of the viewport.
5. Select the opposite diagonal corner of the viewport.

- After starting the **Viewports, Rectangular** command, you can use the options at the Command Prompt to switch to the **Polygonal** or **Object** viewport creation by typing **P** for **Polygonal** or **O** for **Object**.

- Other options available at the start of the **Viewports, Rectangular** command are as follows:

ON/OFF	Toggle an existing viewport on or off.
Fit	Fits an entire rectangular viewport in the printable area of the layout sheet.
Shadeplot	Sets how viewports are plotted. Select from the **As Displayed**, **Wireframe**, **Hidden**, **Visual Styles**, and **Render Presets** options.

Layouts and Printing

Lock	Locks or unlocks a viewport's view and scale.
Restore	Restores the settings of a saved viewport.
Layer	Removes any layer overrides in the selected viewport and resets them to the global layer properties
2/3/4	Creates multiple preconfigured viewports.

Polygonal Viewports

How To: Create a New Polygonal Viewport

1. Verify that you are in a layout and in Paper Space.
2. Set the layer to which you want to add the viewports to be current.
3. In the *Layout* tab>Layout Viewports panel, expand the Viewports drop-down list and click (Polygonal).
4. Select a start point for the viewport.
5. Select the next point(s).
6. If you want to create an arc segment, select the **Arc** option in the <Down Arrow> menu or press <A>, and follow the prompts to create the arc. To switch back to straight line segments, select the **Line** option or press <L>.
7. Complete the command, using the **Close** option or by pressing <Enter>.

Object Viewports

How To: Convert an Object to a Viewport

1. Verify that you are in a layout and in Paper Space.
2. Set the layer to which you want to add the viewports to be current.
3. In the *Layout* tab>Layout Viewports panel, expand the Viewports drop-down list and click (Object).
4. Select a closed object to convert to a viewport.

Named Viewports

How To: Create a Viewport using the Viewports Dialog Box

1. Verify that you are in a layout and in Paper Space.
2. Set the layer to which you want to add the viewports to be current.
3. In the *Layout* tab>Layout Viewports panel, click (Named). The Viewports dialog box opens with the *Named Viewports* tab selected.

© 2017, ASCENT - Center for Technical Knowledge®   8–17

4. Switch to the *New Viewports* tab, as shown in Figure 8–19.

Figure 8–19

5. In the *Standard viewports* area, select the configuration you want to use. A preview of the arrangement displays in the *Preview* pane on the right, as shown in Figure 8–20.

In the AutoCAD LT® software, the Visual Style drop-down list is not available.

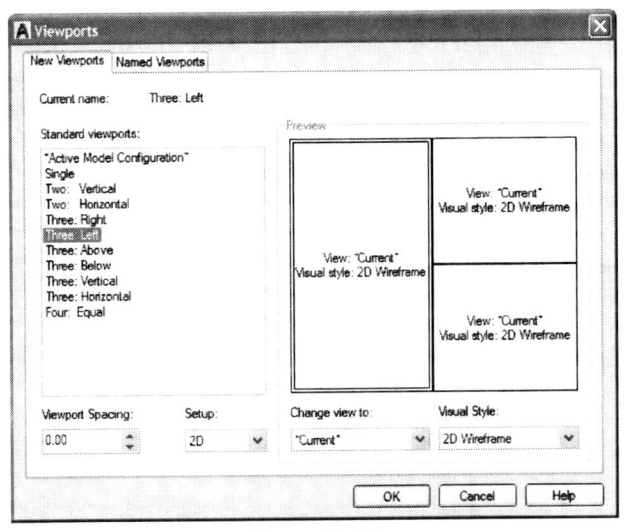

Figure 8–20

6. If you are creating multiple viewports, set the *Viewport Spacing*, which is the space or gap between viewports. The other options are primarily used in 3D drawings.
7. Click **OK**.
8. Select two corners to define the size and location of the viewport(s) in the layout.

Layouts and Printing

Modifying Viewports with Grips

You can move or resize the viewports using grips, as shown in Figure 8–21. You must be in Paper Space to modify a viewport.

Original viewport   *Modifying viewport with grips*   *Modified viewport*

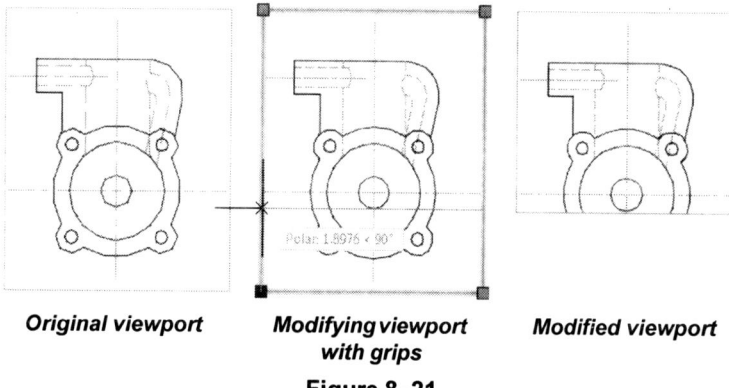

Figure 8–21

- You can also use the standard AutoCAD software editing tools, such as Copy, Move etc. to modify viewports.

- To remove a viewport, select the edge and erase the viewport. It is important that you select the viewport by its edge. The model objects are not affected when you erase or modify a viewport.

Scaling Viewports

You can scale the objects in a viewport to print at a specific scale factor relative to the paper. Select the edge of the viewport or make the viewport active to display the viewport tools in the Status Bar, as shown on the left in Figure 8–22. Expand

1:2 ▼ (Scale of the selected viewport) and select a scale, as shown on the right in Figure 8–22. The selected scale sets the size of the drawing relative to Paper Space and sets the Annotation Scale to match. This becomes critical when it is time to dimension and annotate the drawing.

Use the scroll bar in the list to display the required scale.

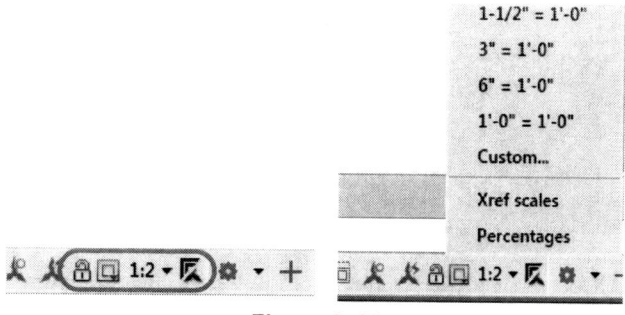

1-1/2" = 1'-0"
3" = 1'-0"
6" = 1'-0"
1'-0" = 1'-0"
Custom...
Xref scales
Percentages

Figure 8–22

© 2017, ASCENT - Center for Technical Knowledge®   8–19

- It is useful to activate the viewport and zoom in on the part of the drawing you want to display before setting the scale.

- Once you have set the scale, you can pan in the viewport without changing the scale. However, using the **Zoom** command modifies the scale.

- If the scale you want to use is not in the list, you can add a custom scale factor (e.g., **1:200** or **1"=6"**) by selecting **Custom...** in the Scale of the selected viewport list. In the Edit Drawing Scales dialog box, click **Add**, type a name for the scale, and enter the values for the *Paper units* and *Drawing units*. Click **OK** to add the custom scale to the scale list.

Locking the Viewport

When the viewport is displaying the correct view and scale, you should lock the display so that it is not changed by accident. When you try to **Zoom** or **Pan** in a locked viewport, the entire layout zooms or pans instead.

- To lock a viewport, select it and click (Lock/Unlock Viewport) in the Status Bar. To unlock a viewport, click (Lock/Unlock Viewport).

- You can also use the shortcut menu to lock and unlock viewports. In Paper Space, select the viewport border, right-click, and select **Display Locked>Yes or No**, as shown in Figure 8–23.

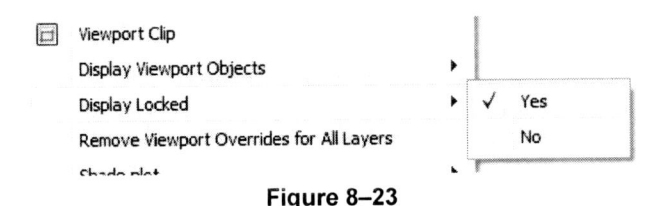

Figure 8–23

8.6 Layer Overrides in Viewports

When you are working in viewports, you might want to modify the layers that display in the various viewports, as shown in Figure 8–24. You can modify layers per viewport and change their color, linetype, lineweight, and plot style using the Layer Properties Manager. To create the viewport specific changes, you need to be working in a *Layout* tab.

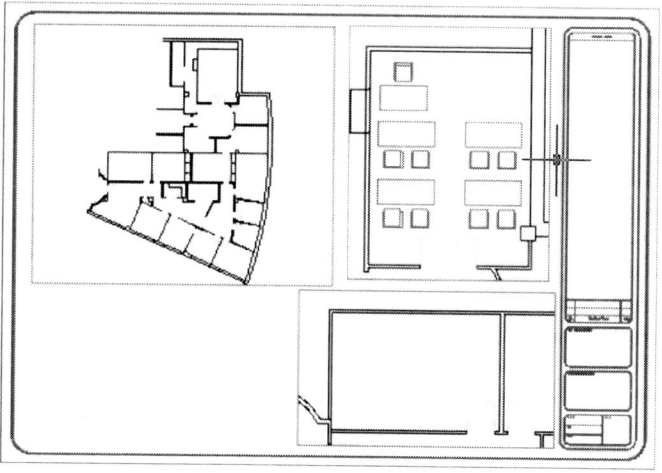

Figure 8–24

Overriding Layer Properties in Viewports

You can use the Layer Properties Manager to change layer properties (such as color, linetype, and lineweight) in a single viewport without the change being made in other viewports. The changes only affect the current viewport and not the model or other viewports, as shown in Figure 8–25.

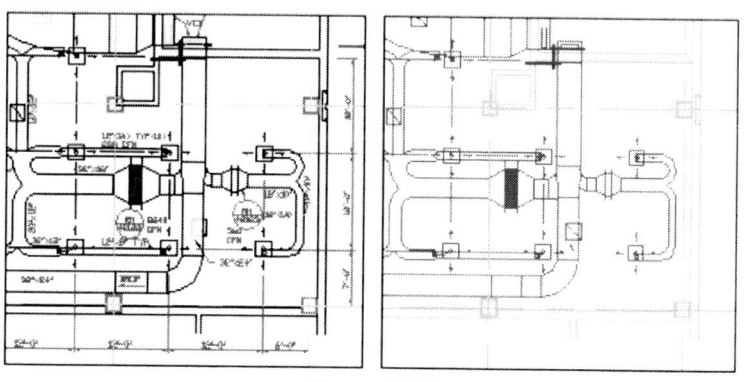

Figure 8–25

- Viewport specific settings include: **New VP Freeze**, **VP Freeze**, **VP Color**, **VP Linetype**, **VP Lineweight**, **VP Transparency**, and **VP Plot Style**. As the name specifies, the **VP Freeze** can be used to freeze/thaw a layer in only one viewport. Similarly, **VP Color** enables you to change the color of a layer in a single (current) viewport. The **New VP Freeze** tool can be used to freeze/thaw a layer in any subsequent viewport that you might create and does not affect the current viewport.

- To create these changes, you must be in a Layout tab and working through a viewport.

How To: Modify Layer Properties in a Viewport

1. In a *Layout* tab, double-click in a viewport to enter Model Space.
2. Open Layer Properties Manager and modify the viewport properties as required. They are highlighted as they are modified, making it easy to see the changes, as shown in Figure 8–26.

You might need to extend the Layer Properties Manager to display all the columns.

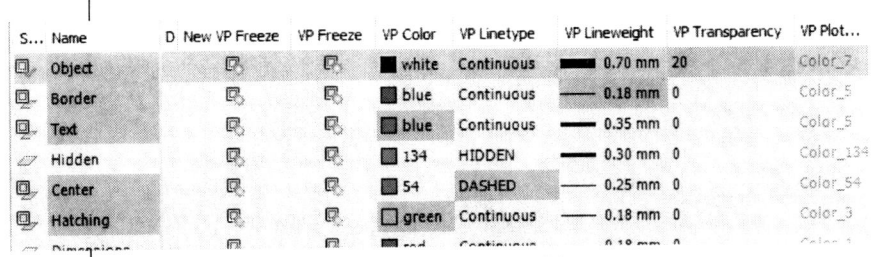

Figure 8–26

3. These changes are immediately and automatically reflected in the viewport.

- The layers also highlight in the Layer Control in the Layers panel as shown in Figure 8–27.

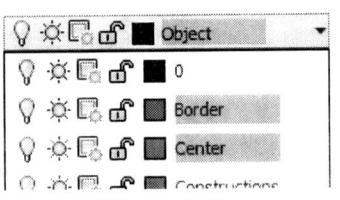

Figure 8–27

- The Viewport Overrides layer filter is automatically created when you use viewport overrides, as shown in Figure 8–28.

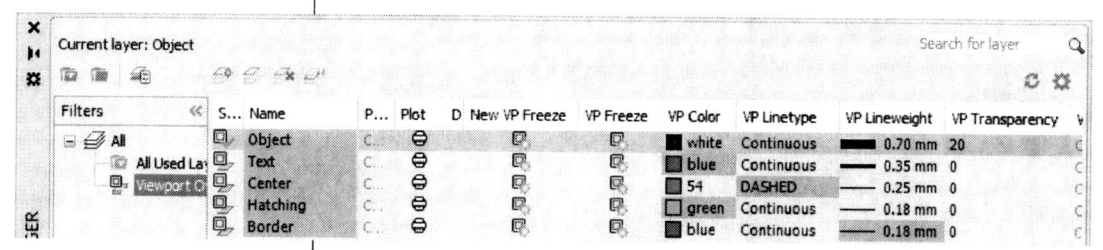

Figure 8–28

Freezing Layers in Viewports

If you freeze a layer or toggle it off using the standard tools, it becomes hidden in all of the viewports.

The **VP Freeze** tool is also available in the Layer Control for easily freezing a layer in a viewport. In the Layer Control, use ▢ (Freeze or Thaw in current viewport) to freeze/thaw a layer in only one viewport.

How To: Freeze a Layer in a Viewport

1. Make the viewport active in which you want to freeze the layer.
2. In the Layer Control, click ▢ (Freeze or thaw in current viewport) so that it displays ▢ for the required layer.
3. Repeat for any other layers that you want to freeze in the current viewport. If you use this tool when you are in a layout but not in a viewport, it freezes a layer in the layout without affecting other layouts. It does not affect the layer display in any viewports when used this way.

Practice 8a

Working With Layouts

Practice Objectives

- View Model Space and Paper Space in layouts.
- Create, update, modify, and delete viewports in a layout.

Estimated time for completion: 25 minutes

In this practice, you will note the differences between Model Space and Paper Space and switch between Model Space and Paper Space in a viewport in a layout. You will create, scale, and lock viewports in a layout. You will then create copies of the layout, rename the new layouts, and update them with different viewport information, such as the **Auditorium Wing** layout shown in Figure 8–29. You will also delete unused layouts.

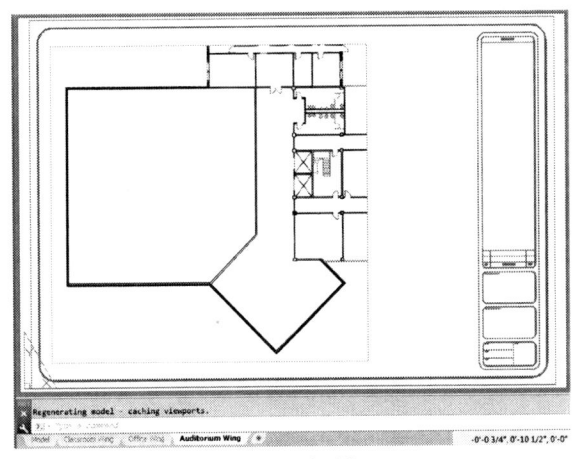

Figure 8–29

Task 1 - View Model Space and Paper Space in layouts.

In this task, you will note the differences between Model Space and Paper Space, and switch between Model Space and Paper Space in a viewport on a *Layout* tab.

1. Open **College Building-A.dwg** from your practice files folder. Note that **Model** displays in the Status Bar, indicating that the *Model* tab is active and that you are in Model Space.

2. Zoom in on one of the single doors. Ensure that Endpoint (Object Snap) is toggled on and use the **Measure> Distance** command to measure its opening. Note that it displays as 3' which is the *real-world* distance in Model Space.

Layouts and Printing

3. Select the *Sample* layout tab. You are now in Paper Space.

4. Zoom in on one of the open single doors and check the distance of the door (use Osnap). It displays the actual size of the door (3').

5. Toggle off ▢ ▼ (Object Snap) and check the distance again. It displays the approximate length of its printed size on the paper.

6. Toggle ▢ ▼ (Object Snap) back on.

7. Zoom out and measure the length of the border. It is drawn at the actual size required to fit on an A-sized sheet of paper.

8. Double-click inside the viewport (gray rectangle) to make it active.

9. **Zoom** and **Pan** so that only the Office Wing, near the top of the building displays, as shown in Figure 8–30.

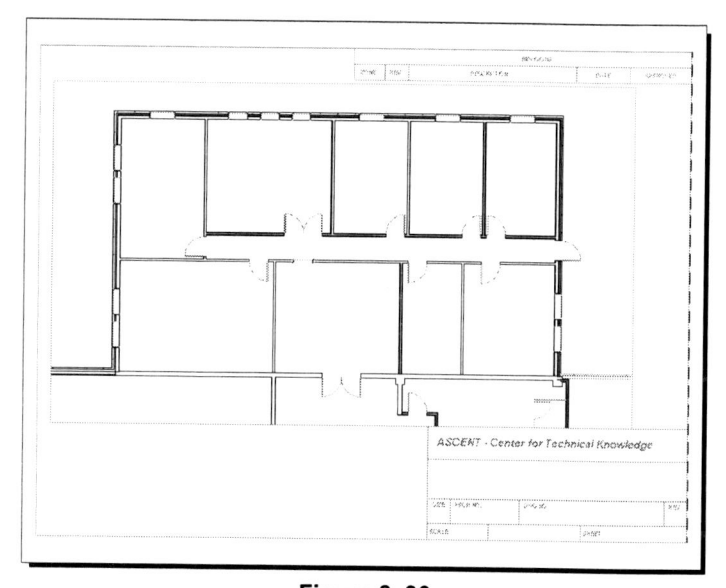

Figure 8–30

10. Save the drawing.

Task 2 - Work in a layout.

In this task, you will create, scale, and lock viewports in layout.

1. Switch to the **D-Sized** layout tab.

2. Make the layer **Viewports** current.

3. Delete the existing viewports in this *Layout* tab before beginning this step by selecting the gray rectangle and pressing <Delete>.

4. In the *Layout* tab>Layout Viewports panel, expand the Viewports drop-down list and click (Rectangular). Create three viewports arranged inside the border, similar to that shown in Figure 8–31. The entire drawing displays in each viewport.

Press <Enter> after creating each viewport to quickly repeat the command.

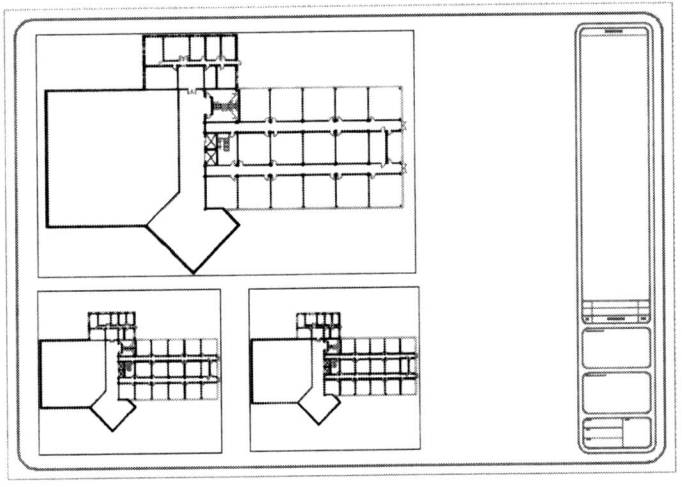

Figure 8–31

The active viewport has a thicker boundary edge.

5. Make the upper viewport active by double-clicking in it. **Zoom** and **Pan** until only the Classroom Wing (i.e., the right side rooms and staircase/elevator area) displays.

6. In the Status Bar, use the Viewport Scale Control list and select several different scales. Finish with a scale of **1/8"=1'-0"**, as shown in Figure 8–32.

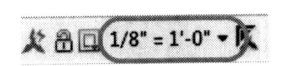

Figure 8–32

Layouts and Printing

If you Pan and Zoom before locking the viewport, the scale changes.

7. Switch to Paper Space by double-clicking in an empty area outside any viewport. Select the edge of the bigger (top) viewport and use grips to adjust the viewport size, such that all the required area is inside the viewport.

8. When you are satisfied with the way the viewport looks, select its edge and in the Status Bar, click 🔒 (Lock/Unlock Viewport) to lock the viewport.

Zoom in on two other separate areas of the building for the lower two viewports.

9. Repeat the process with the other two viewports.

10. Zoom into the elevators and stairs for the lower left viewport and then zoom into the toilets for the lower right viewport. Set their scales to **1/4"=1'-0"**, as shown in Figure 8–33. Use grips to adjust the sizes and then lock the viewports.

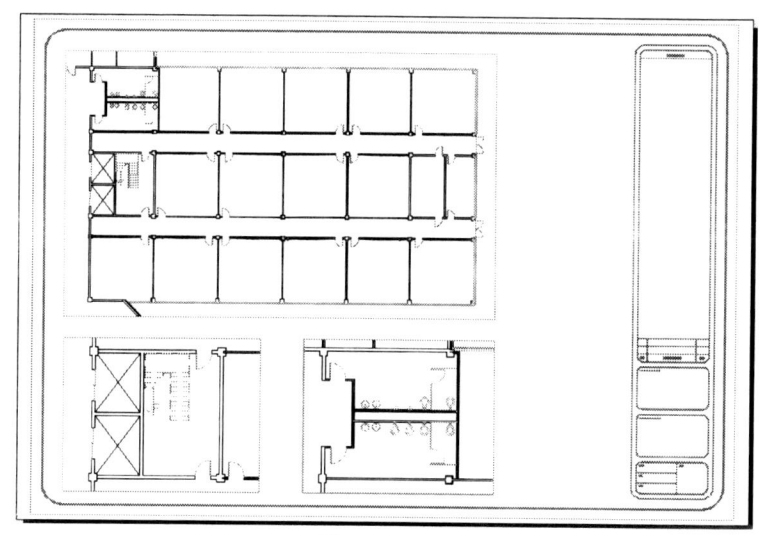

Figure 8–33

Task 3 - Copy and modify layouts.

In this task, you will create copies of the layout, rename the new layouts, update them with different viewport information, and delete unused layouts.

1. Make a copy of the **D-sized** layout by right-clicking on its tab name in the Status bar and selecting **Move or Copy...** In the dialog box, select **(move to end)** and **Create a copy**. Click **OK** to add a copy of the tab, named D-Sized (2) to the end of the row. Repeat the process to create one more layout.

2. Double-click on **D-Sized** tab name and type the name **Classroom Wing** to change it. Rename the other two layouts based on the **D-sized** layout as **Office Wing** and **Auditorium Wing**, as shown in Figure 8–34.

Figure 8–34

3. Select each of the new layouts and note that they contain the same information.

4. Open the **Office Wing** layout and delete the bottom two viewports.

5. Unlock the large viewport and change it so that it displays the **Office Wing** (top area of model) at a **1/4"=1'-0"** scale. Re-lock the viewport.

6. Open the **Auditorium Wing** layout and delete the bottom two viewports.

7. Unlock the large viewport and change the display so that it displays the **Auditorium** and **Entrance** at a **1/8"=1'-0"** scale. You might need to modify the size of the viewport so that the entire area displays. Re-lock the viewport.

8. Delete the **Sample** layout by right-clicking on the layout, selecting **Delete**, and then clicking **OK** in the confirmation dialog box.

9. Save the drawing.

Practice 8b

Estimated time for completion: 25 minutes

Viewports and Named Views

Practice Objectives

- Create and use named views.
- Modify an existing viewport and remove a viewport clip.
- Apply viewport overrides.

In this practice, you will create and use named views using the Viewport Manager and the **Viewports** command. You will set up multiple viewports based on Named Views. You will remove a viewport clip using the **Clip** command. You will also freeze layers in individual viewports and apply layer overrides to the color settings for layers in a viewport.

Task 1 - Create and use named views.

In this task you will create and restore views in a drawing.

1. Open **Office-M.dwg** from your practice files folder.

2. Zoom in on the stairway in the upper right corner, as shown in Figure 8–35.

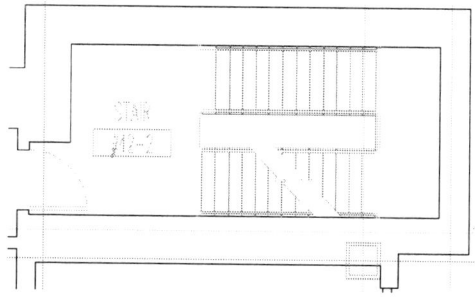

Figure 8–35

*In the View tab, if the Views panel is not displayed by default, you need to right-click anywhere in the View tab and select **Show Panels>Views**.*

*In the AutoCAD LT software, the **Named Views** command opens the New View dialog box.*

3. In the *View* tab>Views panel, click (View Manager). The View Manager dialog box opens.

4. Click **New...** to open the New View / Shot Properties dialog box.

5. In the *View name* field, type **Stairs** and verify that the **Save layer snapshot with view** option is selected.

6. Accept the other default settings and click **OK**. Click **OK** to close the View Manager dialog box.

7. Zoom to display the entire drawing, and toggle off the layer **HVAC**.

8. Open the View Manager dialog box again and click **New...**. Type **Elevators** for the view name.

9. Verify that the **Save layer snapshot with view** option is selected.

10. In the *Boundary* area, click (Define view window). The drawing area displays.

11. Use **Zoom** and **Pan** to display the two elevators in your drawing window. Select two corner points to define the view, as shown in Figure 8–36, and press <Enter> to return to the dialog box.

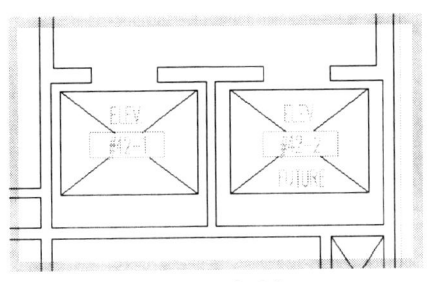

Figure 8–36

12. Click **OK** to complete the view creation. Click **OK** again to close the View Manager dialog box.

13. In the *View* tab>Views panel, use the View Control to select the view **Stairs,** as shown in Figure 8–37. The stairs area displays in the drawing window. Zoom out and note that the **HVAC** layer is toggled on (green HVAC components display).

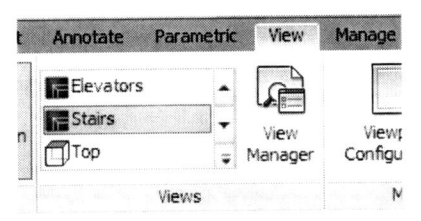

Figure 8–37

14. In the View Control, select the view **Elevators**. Zoom out and note that the layer **HVAC** is toggled off.

Layouts and Printing

Task 2 - Create multiple viewports from Named Views.

In this task you will create multiple viewports based on Named Views using the Viewports dialog box as shown in Figure 8–38.

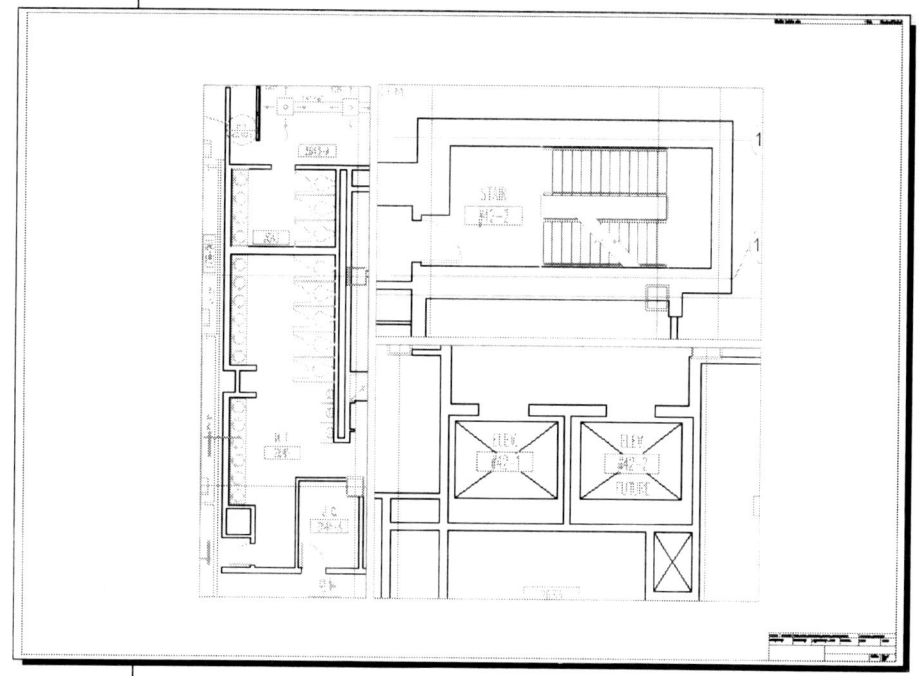

Figure 8–38

1. Switch to the **A-401 Detail Plans** layout and set the current layer to **Viewports**.

2. In the *Layout* tab>Layout Viewports panel, click (Named). In the Viewports dialog box, select the *New Viewports* tab. In the *Standard viewports* area, select **Three: Left**, and set the *Viewport Spacing* to **10** (distances in this drawing are in millimeters).

3. In the *Preview* area, click in the top right viewport. In the Change view to drop-down list, select **Stairs**. Click in the bottom right viewport and change the *View* to **Elevators**. Click **OK** to close the Viewports dialog box.

4. Select two corners to place the three viewports in the layout, as shown in Figure 8–38.

5. Activate the top right viewport, and in the Status Bar, scale it to **1:20**. It automatically scales the top right viewport to **1:20**.

6. Activate the viewport on the left scale it to **1:30** and pan inside it to display the restrooms located near the center left of the drawing. Use grips to make this viewport narrower to only display the restrooms, as shown in Figure 8–38.

7. Use grips to make the other 2 viewports wider. Move the three viewports as required to center them better in the layout.

Task 3 - Clip a viewport.

In this task you will clip an existing viewport using the **Polygonal** option.

1. Copy the existing layout by right-clicking on the tab and selecting **Move or Copy**. In the dialog box select **A-401 Detail Plans** and **Create a copy**. Click **OK**. The new layout is placed before **A-401 Detail Plans.** Rename the new layout as **A-201 1st Floor Plan**.

2. Switch to the **A-201 1st Floor Plan** layout. Delete the two viewports on the right side.

3. Use grips to resize the remaining viewport so that it fills most of the sheet. Display the entire floor plan at a *scale* of **1:50**. Pan to center the drawing in the viewport.

4. In the *Layout* tab>Layout Viewports panel, click ▢ (Clip).

5. Select the viewport, press <Enter> to select the **Polygonal** option. Starting from the lower left corner of the viewport, select points to define a clipping boundary that cuts out the bottom right portion of the view, as shown in Figure 8–39. Select the **Close** option to complete the polygon.

6. In Paper Space, draw a circle with a *radius* of **150** in the area cleared (right bottom corner area) by clipping the other viewport.

7. In the *Layout* tab>Layout Viewports panel, expand ▢ (Viewports, Rectangular) and click ▢ (Viewports, Object) and select the circle. Scale this *circular viewport* to **1:30** and pan in it to display one room of the plan, as shown in Figure 8–39.

Layouts and Printing

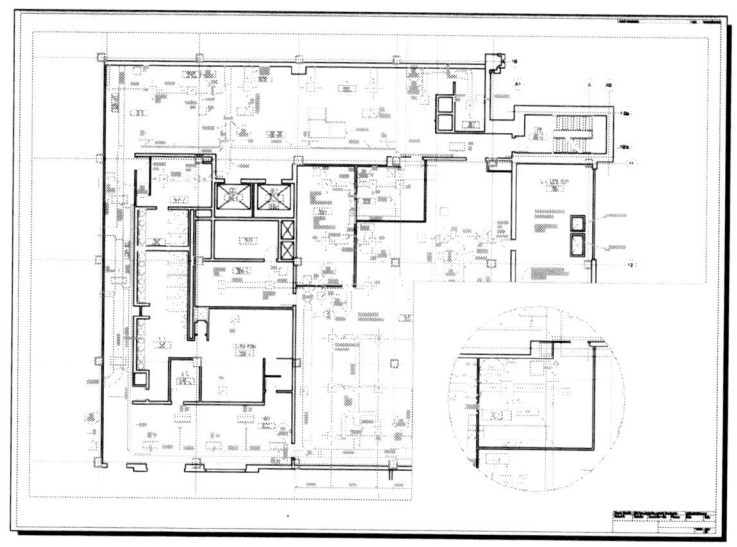

Figure 8–39

Task 4 - Remove viewport clip and apply viewport overrides.

In this task you will remove a viewport clip, freeze layers in individual viewports, and apply layer overrides to the color settings for layers in a viewport, as shown in Figure 8–40.

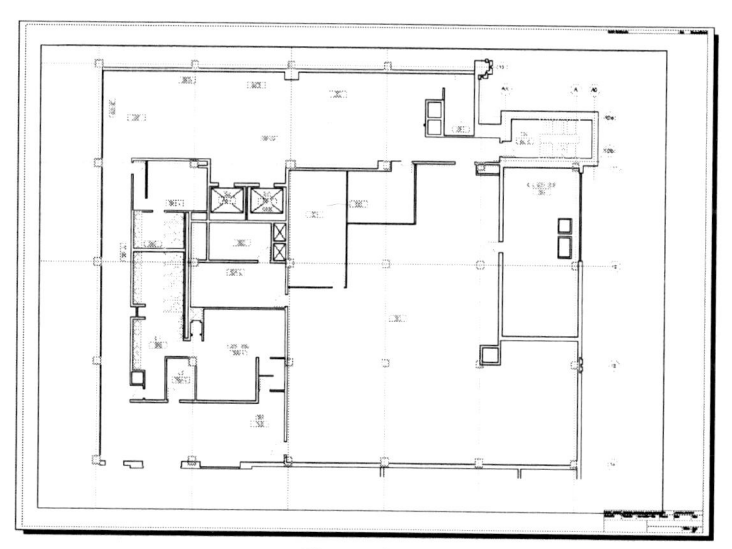

Figure 8–40

1. Copy the **A-201 1st Floor Plan** layout and rename it as **H-201 1st HVAC Floor Plan**.

2. Switch to the **H-201 1st HVAC Floor Plan** layout.

3. Delete the circular viewport.

4. Select the large clipped viewport. Start the **Clip Viewport** command. At the *Select clipping object* prompt, select the **Delete** option (as shown in Figure 8–41) to remove the clipping boundary. It becomes a rectangular area again.

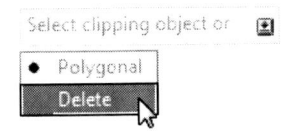

Figure 8–41

5. Activate the large viewport. Freeze the layer **HVAC** in this viewport, so that the HVAC components do not only display in this viewport.

6. Open the Layer Properties Manager and change the *VP Color* for the layer **Stair** to **Green**, as shown in Figure 8–42, so that the stairs are only green in this viewport.

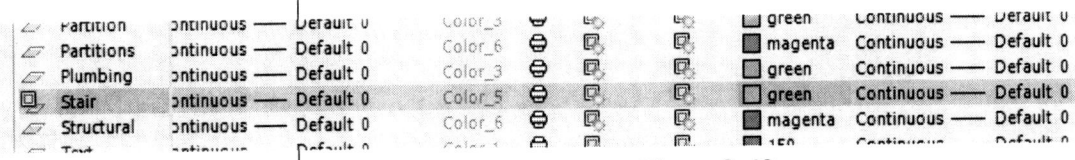

Figure 8–42

7. Switch to the **A-201 1st Floor Plan** layout. It should display differently from the **H-201 1st HVAC Floor Plan** layout. The **HVAC** layer should be visible and the stairs should be blue.

8. Save and close the drawing.

8.7 Printing Concepts

As you work on a drawing, it sometimes needs to be printed. For example, you can print a check plot while the drawing is in progress, and when the drawing is finished, you can print a full set of working drawings with dimensioning, text, and titleblocks, as shown in Figure 8–43. Depending on the size of your project, you can do all of these things from one or several drawing files.

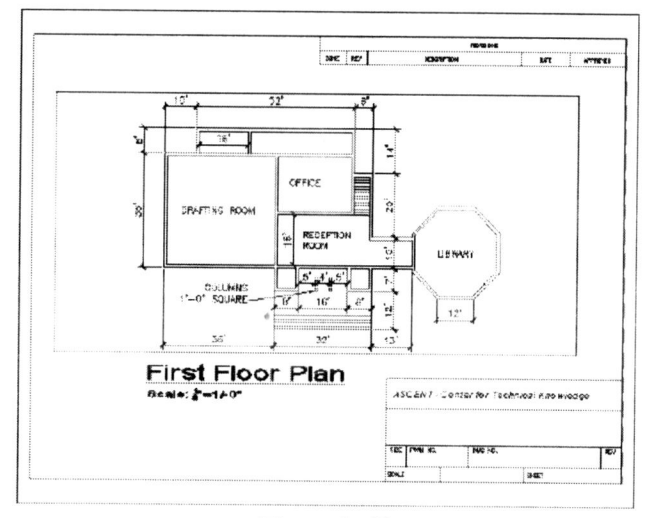

Figure 8–43

There are two methods of printing in the AutoCAD software:

- From *Model Space*.

- From *Paper Space Layouts*.

> **Hint: Printing vs. Plotting**
>
> Both of these terms are used to describe the process of getting an AutoCAD drawing onto a piece of paper. Most of what you do now is technically printing, but many people refer to large format printing as plotting because of the old plotters that were used before laser technology. Printing and plotting mean essentially the same thing today.

Model Space Printing

*When you print from Model Space, you set a scale in the **Plot** command. DO NOT scale the objects in the drawing.*

Everything you have done so far has been in AutoCAD *Model Space*. In Model Space, you draw the model full-size in its real-world units. You can print directly from Model Space for a quick *check plot* of all or part of the drawing, as shown in Figure 8–44.

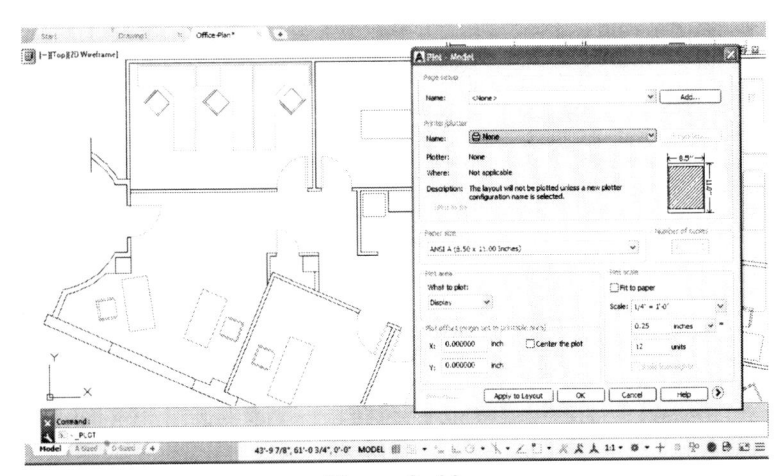

Figure 8–44

- You can set the scale in the **Plot** command to print the model at a precise scale factor, such as 1/4"=1'-0".

- If you need a border, titleblock, dimensions or other annotations to be printed at a specific size, these non-representational objects need to be scaled up to the scale of the drawing. This ensures that when the drawing is shrunk down to fit on the sheet of paper during the **Plot** command, their sizes are printed correctly.

- With Model Space printing you cannot easily print multiple views of the same drawing at different scales.

Paper Space Layout Printing

The primary way to print in the AutoCAD software is to use Paper Space Layouts. Think of the layout as a sheet of paper on which you can place snapshots of your model in *viewports*. These snapshots can be any size and at any scale, as shown in Figure 8–45. You can arrange, enlarge or crop them, as required.

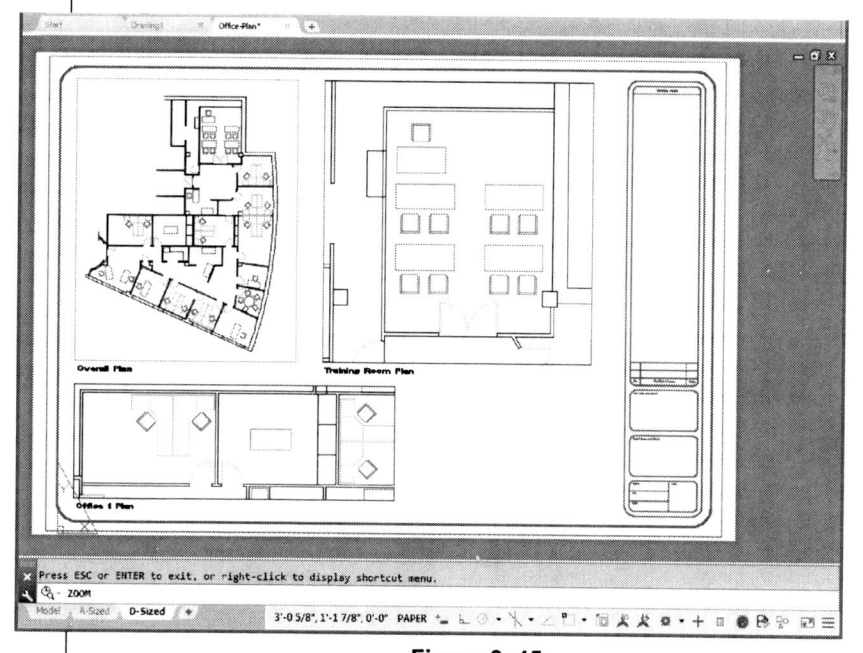

Figure 8–45

Using this method of printing separates the tasks of drawing into two stages:

1. In Model Space, all of the elements are drawn full scale (i.e., at their actual real-world size).
2. In Paper Space Layouts, all of the elements are drawn at the appropriate size for the sheet of paper and you add viewports to display the model.

- The border, titleblock, general notes, schedules, and titles are placed on the layout. They should be drawn at the actual size at which you want them to print on the sheet of paper. Most dimensions and text can be added through the viewport on the model. Their size is controlled by the scale of the viewport and the associated annotation scale.

Only one model can be displayed per drawing, but you can have multiple layouts. Each layout can have a different sheet size, scales, and plotter and these settings are stored in the layout.

8.8 Printing Layouts

When creating layouts in a drawing, each layout represents one sheet, as shown in Figure 8–46. By creating the layout, you define what should be printed. The layout is based on a paper size that is determined by the printer. If the layout is set up correctly, you can plot it without reviewing any additional information in the Plot dialog box.

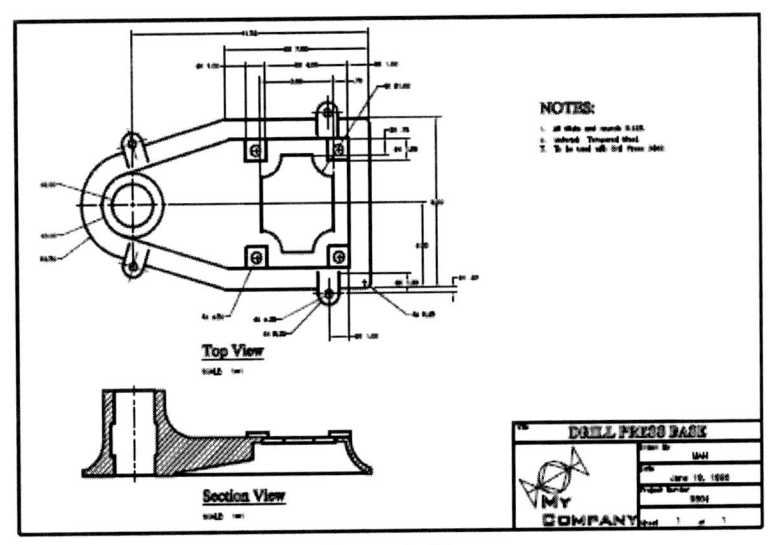

Figure 8–46

How To: Plot a Layout

1. Select the layout that you want to plot.
2. In the *Output* tab>Plot panel, click (Plot).
3. If everything is set up as required, in the Plot dialog box, click **OK**.

*You can also start the **Plot** command in the Status Bar by clicking (Plot), or in the Application Menu by selecting **Print**.*

Layouts and Printing

- If the drawing has multiple layouts, a Batch Plot notification dialog box opens where you can either use the **Try Batch Plot (Publish)** or select **Continue** to plot a single sheet, as shown in Figure 8–47.

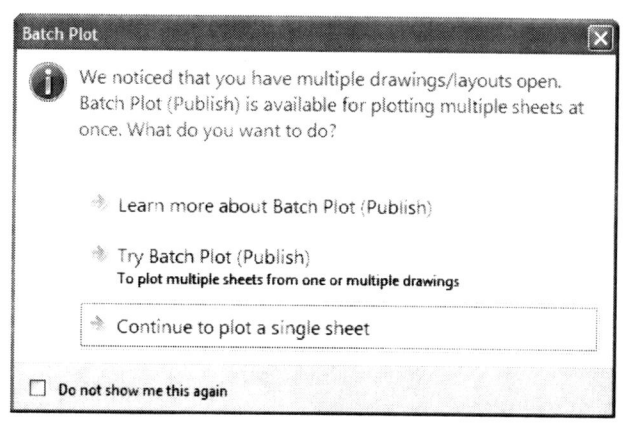

Figure 8–47

- If you are plotting to a DWF plotter or creating a PDF file (which creates a file rather than a paper plot), you are prompted for a name and location for the file in the Browse for Plot File or a Save PDF File As dialog boxes respectively.

- When the plot is finished, a balloon notification displays in the Status Bar, as shown in Figure 8–48. You can click on the link in the balloon to display details about the plot job.

Figure 8–48

Previewing the Plot

Previewing your plot can be helpful to ensure that you are plotting the correct objects before wasting paper and ink.

- You can access the preview in the *Output* tab>Plot panel by clicking (Preview), or in the Application Menu by selecting **Print>Plot Preview**.

- You can also click **Preview** in the Plot dialog box. This is useful when you are making changes in the dialog box and want to display the results before printing.

- In Preview mode, viewing tools, such as Pan and various Zoom options display instead of the ribbon. You can also right-click and select an option, as shown in Figure 8–49.

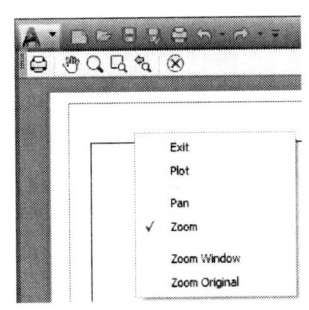

Figure 8–49

Layouts and Printing

8.9 Print and Plot Settings

While most of the options are typically set in a layout, you can adjust some additional options when plotting. For example, you might want to make a half-sized plot or just plot part of a layout or model so that you can check the design, as shown in Figure 8–50. You can make changes in the Plot dialog box without impacting the layout.

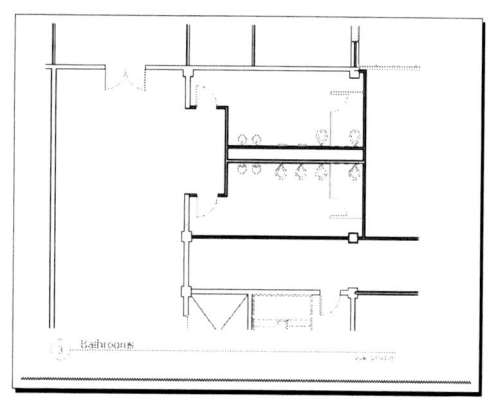

Figure 8–50

You can modify the plot settings in the Plot dialog box, as shown in Figure 8–51.

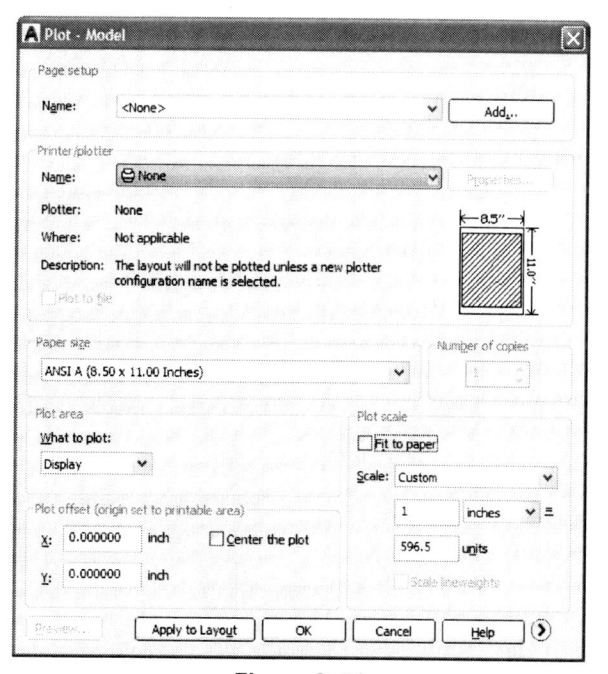

Figure 8–51

Printer/Plotter

- You need to select the plotter first because it determines the paper size.

- Depending on the type of plotter specified, the *Number of copies* area might be available, to set the number of copies to print, as shown in Figure 8–52. It is grayed out when you are using a DWF plotter and some options of PDF version because it plots to a file, rather than directly to paper.

Figure 8–52

What to Plot

The *Plot area* controls the part of the drawing that is plotted.

- The **Display** or **Window** options, as shown in Figure 8–53, can be used to plot part of a layout or model. While the **Display** option plots the objects that display on the screen, the **Window** option enables you to create a window around the area that you want to plot.

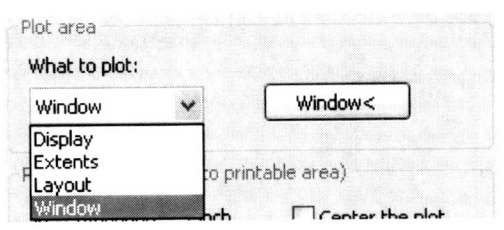

Figure 8–53

- The **Extents** option plots a view that includes every object in the drawing. It includes any objects that might be outside your main drawing. Note that with this option, the objects in the plot might be very small depending on how far apart they are in the drawing.

- The **Limits** option is only available in Model Space and plots an area that is defined by the limits that have been set in the drawing.

Layouts and Printing

Setting the Plot Scale

- While you typically print layouts at a 1:1 scale, you can print half-sized plots by selecting a *Scale* of **0.5=1.0**.

- The **Fit to paper** option, as shown in Figure 8–54, can be used when printing a check plot to a letter-sized plotter. Note that the drawing is not to scale when this option is selected.

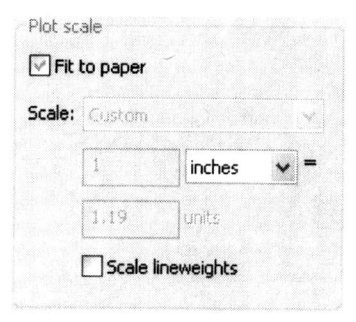

Figure 8–54

- You can also specify a *Scale* of **1/4"=1'-0"**. This is typically done if you are plotting from Model Space and want to have it to scale.

- The **Scale lineweights** option scales the lineweights in proportion to the plot scale. If not selected (the default), the lineweights plot at the line width size.

Plot Offset

- By default, the lower left corner of the plot area starts printing at the lower left corner of the page margin. You can move the plot area to the left or up from the lower left margin by specifying an X- or Y-offset, as shown in Figure 8–55.

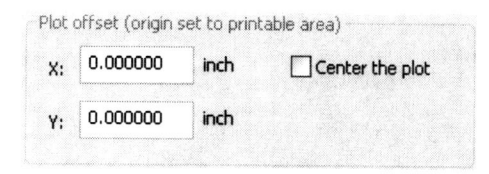

Figure 8–55

- The **Center the plot** option automatically calculates X- and Y-offsets so that the plot is centered on the paper.

*The **Center the plot** option is not available when the Plot area is set to **Layout** because the layout fills the printable area completely.*

More Options

If the dialog box displays in the compressed form, click ⊙ (More Options) in the lower right corner to display more options. Some of the options are shown in Figure 8–56.

Most of the options relate to advanced features.

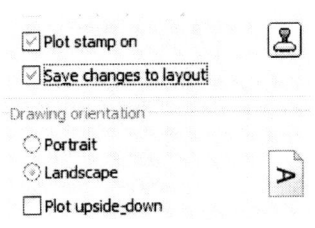

Figure 8–56

Plot stamp on	Adds a plot stamp with standard information, such as drawing name, date and time, etc. The (Plot Stamp Settings) icon becomes available when the **Plot Stamp On** is selected.
Save changes to layout	Automatically saves any changes you make to the plot settings with the layout, which become the new defaults when you plot the layout.

- **Apply to Layout** is similar to the **Save changes to layout** option, except that it only saves changes to the layout when you click the button, rather than automatically, all the time.

- You can also select the *Drawing orientation* options such as printing with **Portrait** or **Landscape** orientation.

Practice 8c

Estimated time for completion: 10 minutes

Printing Layouts and Check Plots

Practice Objectives

- Plot a layout to a file.
- Print a check plot from Model Space.

In this practice, you will plot a layout to a file and create a check plot, as shown in Figure 8–57.

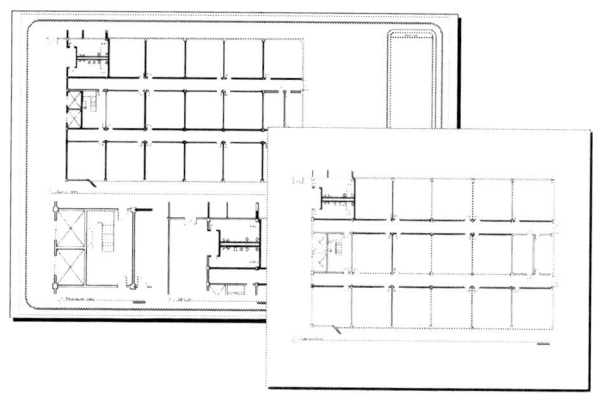

Figure 8–57

Task 1 - Print layouts.

In this task you will plot a layout to a file, as shown in Figure 8–58.

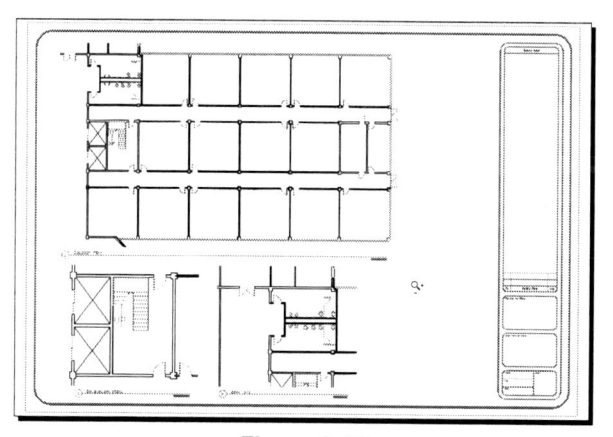

Figure 8–58

1. Open **College Building1-A.dwg** from your practice files folder.

2. Switch to the **Classroom Wing** layout tab and verify that you are in Paper Space.

3. In the *Output* tab>Plot panel, click 🖨 (Plot). If the Batch Plot confirmation dialog box opens, click **Continue to plot a single sheet**.

4. In the Plot dialog box, note that *Printer/plotter*, *Paper size*, and other options are all set according to the page setup for this layout. The layout is set to use the **DWF6 ePlot.pc3** plotter, which automatically plots to a file.

5. Click **Preview**. The viewing tools indicate that you are in **Zoom Realtime** mode. Zoom in a little, right-click, and select **Pan**.

6. After experimenting with panning and zooming, right-click and select **Zoom Original**. Right-click again and select **Exit** to return to the Plot dialog box.

7. Click **OK** to create the plot file. Accept the default filename and save it in your practice folder.

8. In the Status Bar, a balloon message displays when the plot is complete. Select **Click to view plot and publish details...** to display the plot details. Click **Close**.

Task 2 - Print check plots.

In this task you will create a check plot, as shown in Figure 8–59.

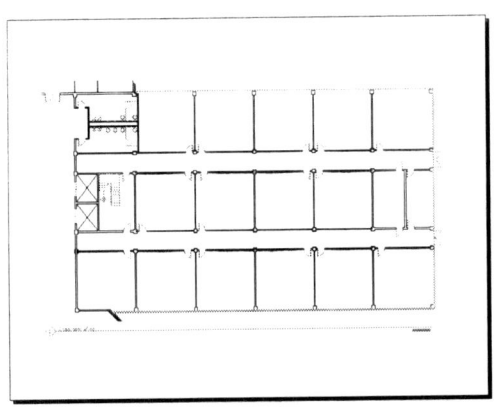

Figure 8–59

Layouts and Printing

1. Start the **Plot** command again. If the Batch Plot confirmation dialog box opens, click **Continue to plot a single sheet**.

2. Set the *Paper size* to **ANSI A (8.50 x 11.00 Inches)** and click **Preview**. Only a small portion of the entire plot displays, as shown in Figure 8–60. Right-click and select **Exit**.

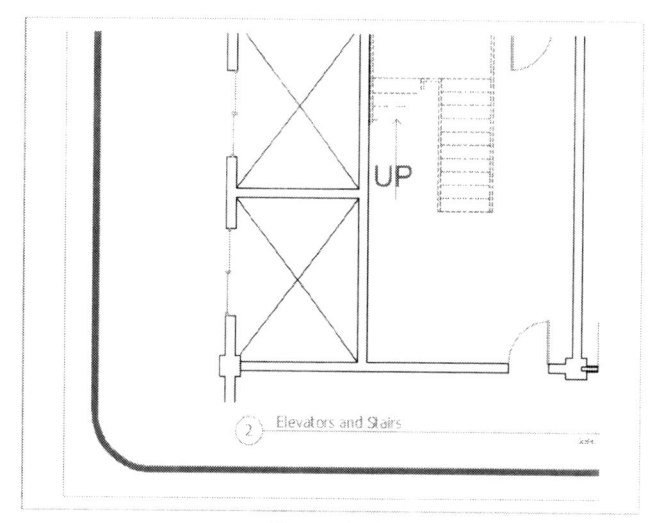

Figure 8–60

3. In the *Plot area*, expand the What to plot drop-down list and select **Window**, draw a window around the Elevators and Stairs viewport, and preview again. The selected viewport displays as it fits on an 8.5 x 11 sheet of paper at a 1/4"=1'0" scale. Exit the preview.

4. Click **Window<**, draw a window around the Classroom Wing viewport at the top of the layout, and preview the plot. A portion of the viewport displays. Exit the preview.

5. Set the *Plot Scale* to **Fit to paper** and the *Plot Offset* to **Center the plot**. Preview again. The whole viewport displays but is not to scale. Exit the preview.

6. Click **OK** to plot the drawing and name the file **Check Plot.dwf**.

7. Ensure that you are in the **Classroom Wing** layout tab. In the *Layout* tab>Plot panel, click **Preview**. The preview indicates that the entire layout is going to be plotted as was intended. The changes you just made to the **Plot** command did not change the layout information.

8. Exit the preview. Save and close the drawing.

8.10 Output For Electronic Review

You often need to share information in an AutoCAD drawing electronically with users who do not have the AutoCAD software or who only need to view (and not edit) the information. There are two main options for this: creating a DWF or DWFx file that can be viewed and marked up in the Autodesk Design Review 2013 software or creating a PDF file that can be viewed in Adobe Reader.

- Autodesk Design Review 2013 is a free program from Autodesk. It is the most current version of the software and can be downloaded from *http://usa.autodesk.com/design-review/*.

- Adobe Reader is a free third-party program and can be downloaded from *http://get.adobe.com/reader/*.

- You can create DWF, DWFx, and PDF files using the **Plot** command, **Batch Plot/Publish** command, or **Export DWF/DWFx/PDF** commands, as shown in Figure 8–61.

Figure 8–61

> **Hint: DWF vs DWFx**
>
> **DWF** (**Design Web Format**) is a compressed vector format that loads and displays faster than normal DWG files.
>
> **DWFx** can create multiple page DWF files with the **Batch Plot/Publish** command. It can also be opened in Microsoft's XPS Viewer (available with Windows 7 or as a free download). It enables you to open DWFx files in Internet Explorer without having any Autodesk products installed.

Plotting Electronic Files

Layouts can be set up to create DWF, DWFx, or PDF files, or you can specify the plotter type in the **Plot** command. Multiple PDF plotters are available. Each one sets the level of print quality.

How To: Plot to a DWF, DWFx, or PDF File

1. In the Quick Access Bar or in the *Output* tab>Plot panel, click (Plot).
   - If the software detects multiple drawings or layouts open, a Batch Plot dialog box displays. You can either use **Batch Plot** or plot a single sheet.
2. Select the appropriate plotter from the list, as shown in Figure 8–62:
   - **DWF6 ePlot.pc3** for DWF files
   - **DWFx ePlot (XPS Compatible).pc3** for DWFx files
   - Any of the **AutoCAD PDF** printers for PDF files

You can also access the Plot command in Application Menu>Print.

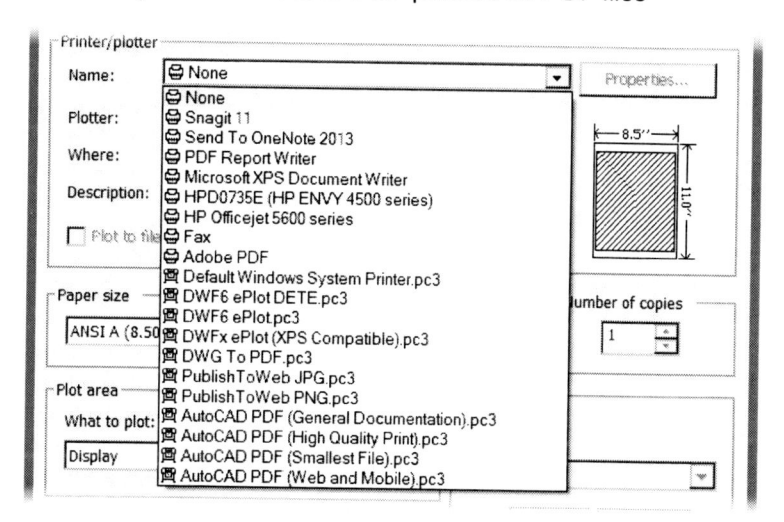

Figure 8–62

3. Click **OK** to plot the file.

- DWF, DWFx, and PDF files cannot be opened directly in the AutoCAD software, but can be accessed using DWF or PDF Overlays or the Markup Set Manager (for DWF).

- Normal DWF plots are in 2D. A separate command, **3DDWF**, enables you to create DWFs of 3D models, so that you can change the viewing angle in the DWF viewer.

Exporting DWF or PDF Files

Exporting to DWF, DWFx, or PDF is another way of creating electronic files to share with other companies or within your company. If you use the **Plot** command you can only plot one sheet at time, but using **Export** you can plot multisheet files to DWFx and PDF.

How To: Export Layouts to DWF, DWFx, or PDF

- If you want to create a multi-sheet DWFx or PDF, use <Ctrl> or <Shift> to select multiple layout tabs before you start the **Export** command.

1. In the ribbon, in the *Output* tab>Export to DWF/PDF panel, click the required **Export** command, (DWFx)/ (DWF)/ (PDF).
2. Review the information in the Save As dialog box, as shown in Figure 8–63.

You can also access the required Export command in Application Menu>Export.

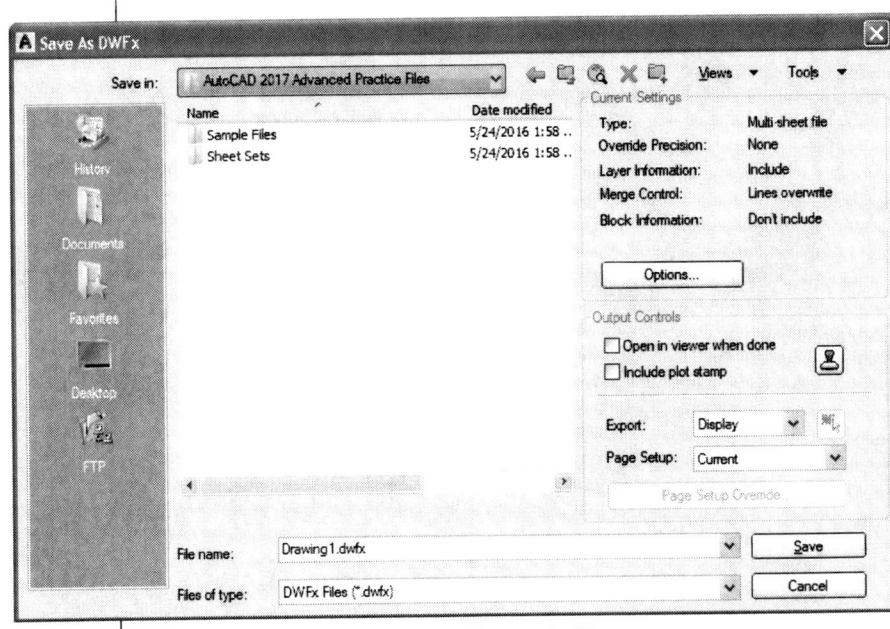

Figure 8–63

3. Click **Options** to modify any of the settings that need to be changed.
4. Select the required Output Controls.
   - If you selected the **Open in viewer when done** option, the associated viewer program opens, enabling you to view the exported file.
5. Specify whether you want to export the current layout or all of the layouts and the associated Page Setup.

Layouts and Printing

6. Assign the correct filename and location and click **Save**.

In the ribbon, in the *Output* tab>Export to DWF/PDF panel, you can set the following options:

- You can set up what to export (**Display**, **Extents**, and **Window** for the *Model* tab, and **Current Layout** or **All Layouts** for the layout tabs) and the page setup.

- Click (Preview) to display the proposed export.

- Click (Export to DWF Options) or (Export to PDF Options) to modify any of the options.

Export to PDF Options

When exporting drawing files to PDF files, you can control the quality of vectors, rasters, and merge control (enables lines to merge or overwrite each other), as shown in Figure 8–64. You can also include information about data, such as:

Layer information	Layer information can be included in PDF files.
Hyperlinks	Hyperlinks in the drawing file works inside the PDF file. This works for sheets that are linked and weblinks.
Bookmarks	Bookmarks are enabled. Each sheet and each sheet view becomes a bookmark in the PDF.
Fonts	TrueType fonts are embedded in the PDF file and do not have to be available in the PDF viewer. If this option is not selected, the PDF viewer uses substitute fonts. If you have a PDF file with shx fonts, they are converted to geometry and display as a comment in the PDF file. You can also convert all text to geometry during the export process.

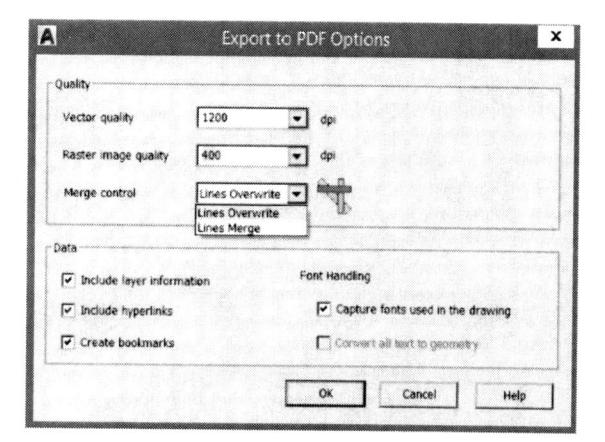

Figure 8–64

© 2017, ASCENT - Center for Technical Knowledge®

The AutoCAD PDF printers provide various print qualities. The table below lists the output settings for each PDF printer.

Printer/Plotter	Vector Quality	Raster Image Quality	Merge Control	Include Layer Info.	Include Hyperlinks	Create Bookmarks	Capture fonts used in the drawing
General Documentation	1200	400	Lines Overwrite	X	X	X	X
High Quality	2400	600	Lines Overwrite	X	X	X	X
Small Files	200	400	Lines Overwrite				
Web and Mobile	200	400	Lines Overwrite	X	X	X	X

Note: None of the default PDF printers *Convert all text to geometry*.

8.11 Publishing Drawing Sets

The **Batch Plot/Publish** command provides an easy way to create either electronic or paper drawing sets using the interface shown in Figure 8–65. With **Batch Plot/Publish** you can create multi-sheet and multi-drawing DWFx or PDF files that can be viewed using the Autodesk Design Review 2013 software or Adobe Reader. The same list of drawing sheets can also be plotted directly to paper.

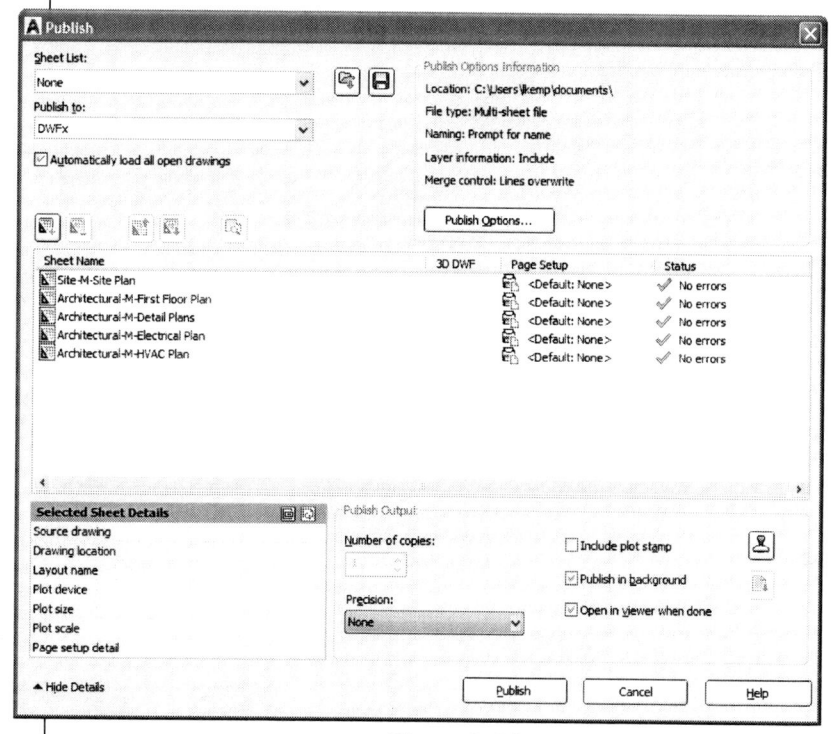

Figure 8–65

You can add layouts to the list for publishing from any drawing while controlling the order in which they are printed or presented. Once the list of sheets has been created, you can save it and easily reload it later to publish the same set of sheets again.

How To: Publish a Set of Drawings

1. Open a drawing containing multiple layouts that you want to publish.

2. In the ribbon, in the *Output* tab>Plot panel, click (Batch Plot).

3. In the Publish dialog box, a list of drawing sheets that were automatically created from the existing layouts in the drawing displays.

    - Click (Add Sheets) to include other drawings. Selecting a drawing file automatically imports all of its layouts.

    - Click (Remove Sheets) to remove any sheets that you do not want to include in the list.

    - Reorder the sheets as required using (Move Sheet Up) and (Move Sheet Down).

4. In the Publish to drop-down list, specify whether you are publishing to the plotters named in the page setup for each layout: a DWF, DWFx, or PDF file.
5. Click **Publish**.
6. You might be prompted to save the current list of sheets. Do so if you are planning to print the same group of layouts again. A DSD file is created.

- The publishing process takes place in the background, enabling you to continue with other projects. When it is finished, an alert balloon opens in the Status Bar, as shown in Figure 8–66. You can view the details to check for any errors or warnings.

Figure 8–66

- Click (Preview) to display the plot preview of the sheet that has been selected in the list.

- In the Publish Options dialog box you can specify the output, type of file (single or multi-sheet), prompt or default name for the multi-sheet file, security, and layer information.

- **Show Details** displays additional information about the selected sheet details, number of copies, plot stamp, publish in background, and viewer options. Click **Hide Details** to close the additional options.

How To: Work with Sheet Lists Files

1. In the ribbon, in the *Output* tab>Plot panel, click (Batch Plot).
2. In the Publish dialog box, click (Load Sheet List).
3. Select the DSD file that you want to load.
4. In the Load Sheet List dialog box (shown in Figure 8–67), select to either replace or append sheets to the current list.

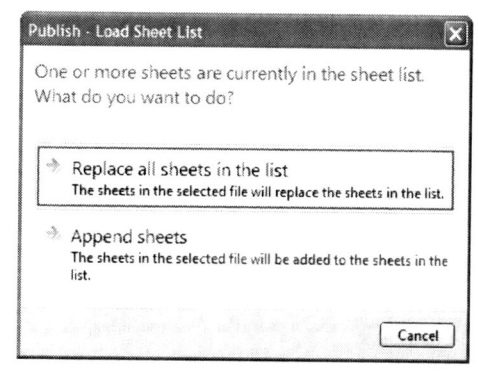

Figure 8–67

5. In the Publish dialog box, make any required changes and click **Publish**.

- You can change the default page setup in the list of page setups in the drawing. You can also import page setups from another drawing or template that contains named page setups. To change the page setup for a sheet, select its default setup in the list and then select from the drop-down list.

- The **Batch Plot** command automatically adds all of the open drawings to the Sheet list, including their Model tabs. This might create a problem when several drawings are open. An alert box opens and prompts you to change the names of the model sheets. To keep this from happening, clear the **Automatically load all open drawings** option.

Practice 8d

Reviewing and Publishing Drawing Sets

Practice Objectives

- Plot and export a single layout and multi-sheets to DWF and DWFx files, and view and mark them up in the Autodesk Design Review 2013 software.
- View DWF markups to revise its associated DWG file in the AutoCAD software using the Markup Set Manager.
- Set up a list of multiple layouts from multiple drawings to batch plot them.

Estimated time for completion: 15 minutes

This practice requires the Autodesk Design Review 2013 software to complete. You must install it before you start the practice.

In this practice you will plot a layout to a DWF file and open the file in the Autodesk Design Review 2013 software. You will also export a multi-sheet DWFx file, view it in the Autodesk Design Review 2013 software, and make several markups. Finally, you will import the DWFx file into the original drawing file using the Markup Set Manager and make a change based on the markup. You will then republish the DWFx and review the changes in the Autodesk Design Review 2013 software, as shown in Figure 8–68. Finally you will Batch Plot multiple drawings. If time permits, you can also export a PDF and view it in Adobe Reader.

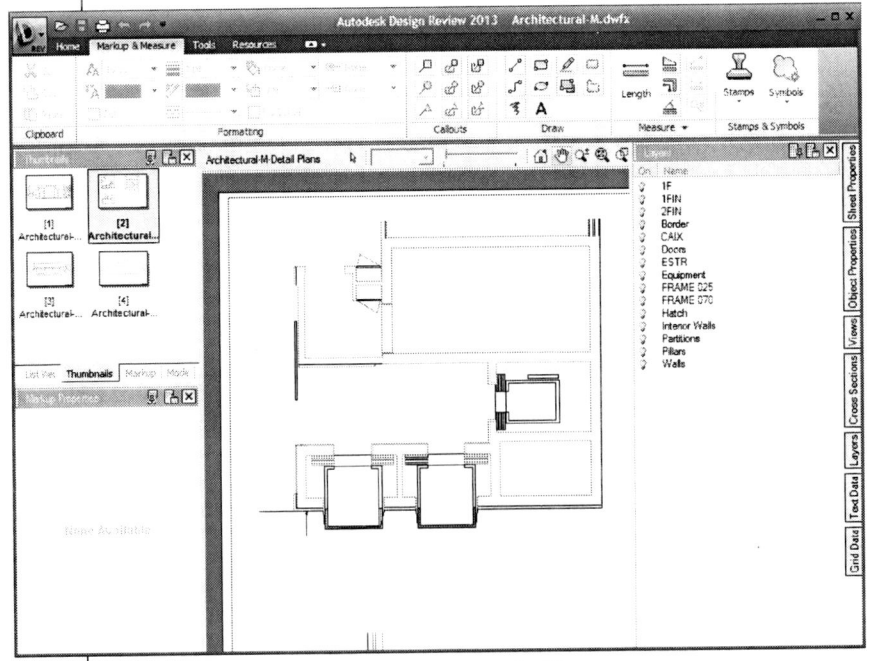

Figure 8–68

Layouts and Printing

Task 1 - Plot a DWF File.

1. Open **Architectural-M.dwg** from your practice files folder.

2. Switch to the **First Floor Plan** layout.

3. Start the **Plot** command. In the Batch Plot warning dialog box, click **Continue to plot a single sheet**.

4. In the Plot dialog box, verify that the *Printer/plotter* is set to **DWF6 ePlot.pc3**. (It was set in the page setup for the layout.)

5. Click **Properties** to open the Plotter Configuration Editor.

6. Select **Custom Properties** in the list. In the *Access Custom Dialog* area, click **Custom Properties**.

7. In the DWF6 ePlot Properties dialog box, in the *Additional Output Settings* area, select **Include layer information**, as shown in Figure 8–69. Click **OK** twice.

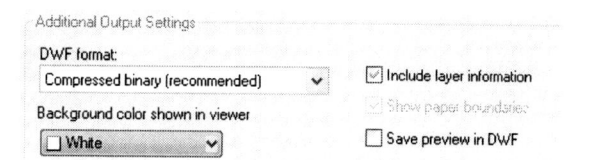

Figure 8–69

8. Click **OK** again to accept **Apply changes for the current plot only**.

9. The **Plot to file** option is on by default for this plotter. Set the *Plot Area* to **Layout**.

10. Click **OK** to create the plot. Save the DWF file in your practice files folder and name it **First Floor Plan.dwf**.

11. Close the *Plot and Publish Job Complete* balloon in the Status Bar.

12. In the Status Bar, right-click on (Plot/Publish Details) and select **View Plotted File...** to open it in the Autodesk Design Review 2013 software.

13. Pan and zoom to view the image.

14. Along the right side of the drawing window, expand the Layers palette. A list of layers should appear.

15. Close the Autodesk Design Review 2013 software.

The Autodesk Design Review 2013 software must already be installed.

Task 2 - Export a multi-sheet DWFx file.

1. Select all of the layout tabs by pressing <Ctrl> or <Shift> as you select each one.
2. Start the **Export DWFx** command.
3. In the Save as DWFx dialog box, browse to your practice files and click **Options**, as shown in Figure 8–70.

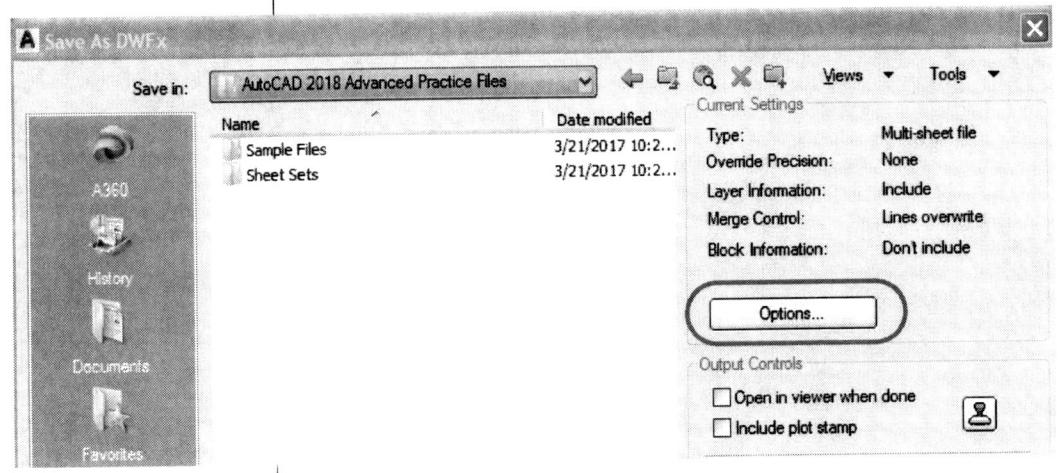

Figure 8–70

4. Verify that *Layer information* is set to **Include**, as shown in Figure 8–71. Click **OK**.

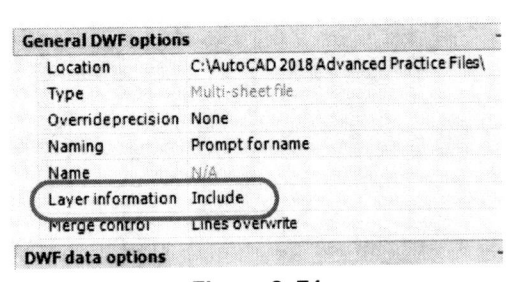

Figure 8–71

*Export is automatically set to **All layouts** because you selected more than one layout before starting the command.*

5. In the Save as DWFx dialog box, in the *Output Controls* area, select **Open in viewer when done**.
6. Verify that you are still in the practice files folder and use the drawing name as the filename. Click **Save**.

Layouts and Printing

7. the Autodesk Design Review 2013 software opens after the file is exported. You should see multiple thumbnails, one for each layout, and the list of layers (in the *Layers* tab), as shown in Figure 8–72.

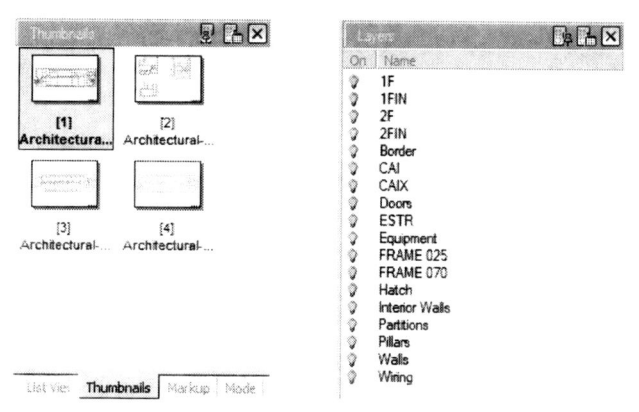

Figure 8–72

8. Open each of the thumbnails.

9. In the First Floor Plan layout, toggle off several layers to display the change. Toggle them back on.

Task 3 - Create a markup.

1. In the Autodesk Design Review 2013 software, in the ribbon, switch to the *Markup & Measure* tab.

2. In the Stamps & Symbols panel, expand (Stamps) and select **PRELIMINARY**. Place it near the top of the title block, as shown in Figure 8–73.

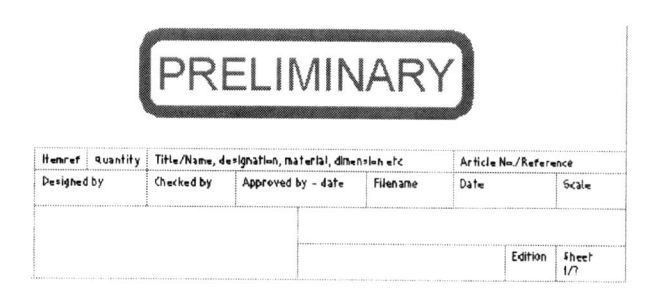

Figure 8–73

3. Zoom in to the middle of the First Floor Plan layout, where you see some long horizontal lines and small tick marks, as shown in Figure 8–74.

4. In the *Markup & Measure* tab>Draw panel, click (Polycloud) and add a revision cloud (click four points of the polygon) around some of the objects, as shown in Figure 8–74.

5. In the Draw panel, click **A** (Text Box), place a text box near the cloud, and type the words shown in Figure 8–74. Set the size of the text in the Formatting panel as required.

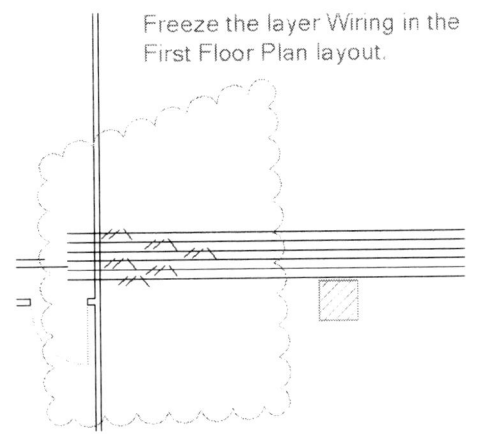

Figure 8–74

6. Save the DWFx file.

7. Close the Autodesk Design Review 2013 software.

Task 4 - Use the Markup Set Manager.

1. Select the First Floor Plan layout if you are not already in it.

2. In the *View* tab>Palettes panel, click (Markup Set Manager), if it is not already open.

3. In the Markup Set Manager, click **Open...**, as shown in Figure 8–75.

Layouts and Printing

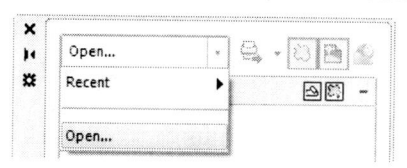

Figure 8–75

4. Select **Architectural-M.dwfx** from your practice files folder and click **Open**.

5. In the Markup Set Manager, expand the list of markups, as shown in Figure 8–76.

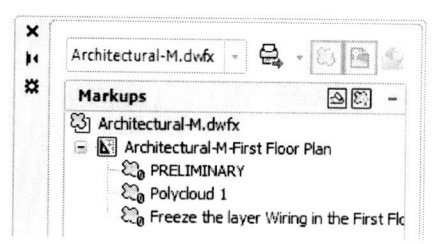

Figure 8–76

6. Double-click on one of the markups to display it in the drawing.

7. Zoom in on the revision cloud that is now displayed in the drawing.

8. Double-click inside the viewport to activate it.

9. In the *Home* tab>Layers panel, click (Freeze).

10. Select the horizontal lines or small tick marks to freeze the layer. Press <Enter> to end the command.

11. Zoom out to display the entire layout.

12. In the Markup Set Manager, select **Polycloud 1**.

13. In the *Details* area, change the *Markup status* to **Done**, as shown in Figure 8–77.

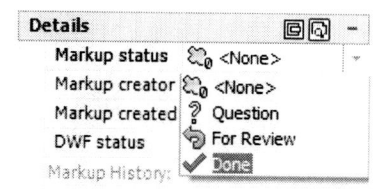

Figure 8–77

© 2017, ASCENT - Center for Technical Knowledge®

14. Repeat the process for the text **Freeze the layer Wiring...**.

15. Save the drawing.

16. In the Markup Set Manager, expand ![icon] (Republish Markup DWF) and select **Republish All Sheets**.

17. The Specify DWFx file dialog box should automatically list the associated DWFx file. Click **Select** and then click **Yes** to replace the existing file.

18. When the file has finished printing, open the Autodesk Design Review 2013 software. The changes are displayed and the markups are checked, as shown in Figure 8–78.

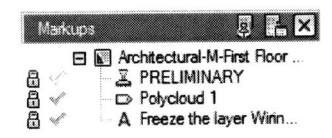

Figure 8–78

19. Close the Autodesk Design Review 2013 software.

20. Save and close the drawing.

Task 5 - Publish drawing sets.

In this task you will use the **Batch Plot** command to set up a list of drawing layouts using two different drawings, as shown in Figure 8–79, and to create a multi-sheet DWF file. You will also view the file in the Autodesk Design Review 2013 software.

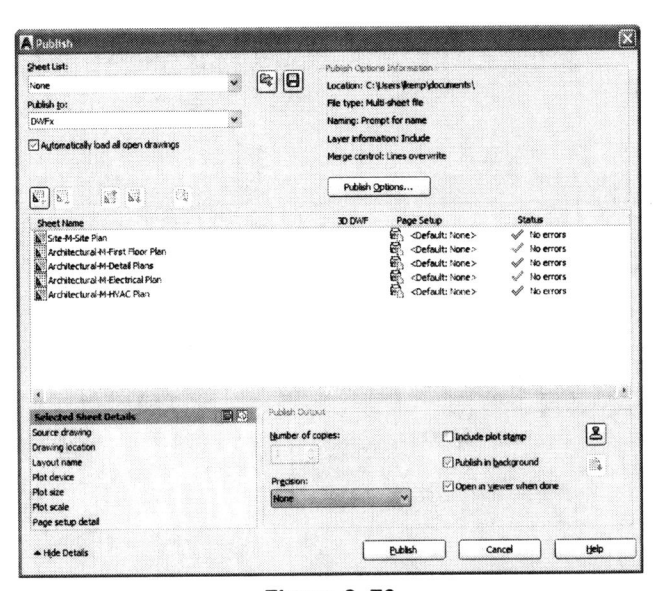

Figure 8–79

Layouts and Printing

1. Open **Architectural-M.dwg** from your practice files folder.
2. Save the drawing.
3. Start the **Batch Plot** command. The *Model* tab and several layouts are listed as sheets in the Publish dialog box.
4. Select the **Architectural-M-Model** sheet and click ![] (Remove Sheets) to remove it from the list.
5. To add a sheet, click ![] (Add Sheets) and select the file **Site-M.dwg** in the Practice Files folder. Two sheets from this drawing (the *Model* tab and one layout tab) are added to the list.
6. Remove the **Site-M-Model** sheet.
7. Select **Site-M-Site Plan**. Click ![] (Move Sheet Up) and move it to the top of the list, as shown in Figure 8–80.

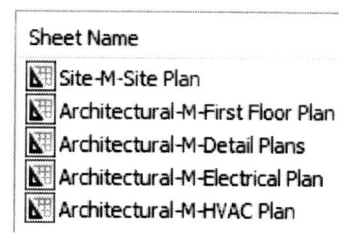

Sheet Name
Site-M-Site Plan
Architectural-M-First Floor Plan
Architectural-M-Detail Plans
Architectural-M-Electrical Plan
Architectural-M-HVAC Plan

Figure 8–80

8. In the Publish to drop-down list, select **DWFx**. (Publishing to DWFx creates individual files for each layout even if you have set multi-sheet files using **Publish Options....**)
9. Click ![] (Save Sheet List) and save the list in your practice files folder (**Architectural-M.dsd**). This makes it easy to publish the same set of sheets again.
10. Click **Publish**, type a new filename, and specify your practice files folder as the location of the file. Click **Select**.
11. If the Plot - Processing Background Job alert box opens, click **Close**. The job is then processed in the background and wait till the *Plot and Publish Job Complete* balloon displays indicating that the job is finished.

12. In the Status Bar, right-click on 🖨 (Publish Details) and select **View Plotted File...**.

13. In the Autodesk Design Review 2013 software, zoom and pan as required.

14. Close the Autodesk Design Review 2013 software.

15. Close the drawing file.

Appendix A

Review Questions

The following review questions are provided to help you to self-evaluate your understanding and retention of the topics presented in *AutoCAD® 2018: Review for Professional Certification*. They are not intended to represent the types of questions found in the AutoCAD Certified Professional exam.

Answers are provided at the end of each topic.

A.1 Draw Objects

1. When using the **Line** command, how do you exit the command once you have finished drawing line segments?
   a. Click the left mouse button.
   b. Double-click.
   c. Press <Enter>.
   d. Type **Done** in the Command Line.

2. When drawing a line using the **Line** command, you can specify its length, but not its angle.
   a. True
   b. False

3. Which of the following statements are true for Polar Tracking and Ortho mode? (Select all that apply.)
   a. With Polar Tracking on, a dotted tracking line displays when the cursor is at a specified angle location.
   b. Ortho Mode enables you to draw lines horizontally and vertically only.
   c. With Ortho Mode on, you can draw lines at specified preset angles.
   d. (Ortho Mode) and (Polar Tracking) can be used (toggled on) at the same time.

4. What is the best method to draw a perfectly horizontal line using the **Line** command?
   a. Drag the cursor horizontally until it looks horizontal.
   b. Toggle on Ortho Mode.
   c. Draw a line at any angle and then rotate it until it is horizontal.
   d. Follow the horizontal line of the grid.

Review Questions

5. How do you draw a rectangle using the **Rectangle** command?

    a. Draw individual lines and join them together to form a rectangle.

    b. Click and create three corners of the rectangle with the fourth corner being created automatically.

    c. Click to specify all the four corners of the rectangle.

    d. Click the first corner of the rectangle and then click the diagonally opposite corner.

6. Which one of the following is NOT a method for drawing circles with the **Circle** command?

    a. **Tan, Tan, Radius**

    b. **Center, Radius**

    c. **Tan, Tan, Point**

    d. **2 Points**

7. Which of the following is a valid method for constructing an arc in the AutoCAD software?

    a. **3 Points**

    b. **2 Points**

    c. **4 Points**

    d. **Center, Diameter**

8. Polygons are built from polylines and can be modified using the **Edit Polyline** command.

    a. True

    b. False

Answers: 1c, 2b, 3a,b, 4b, 5d, 6c, 7a, 8a

A.2 Draw with Accuracy

1. If you set the Polar Tracking increment angles to 30 degrees, you can track to 90 degrees, 120 degrees, and other multiples of 30 degrees.

    a. True
    b. False

2. Which settings in the Status Bar should be toggled on to use the Object Snap Tracking?

    a. Object Snap Tracking and Polar.
    b. Object Snap Tracking and Object Snap.
    c. Object Snap Tracking and Snap.
    d. Only Object Snap Tracking.

3. What does the Temporary Tracking Point enable you to do that Object Snap Tracking alone does not?

    a. Find a location based on two distances from another point.
    b. Draw circles, lines, and rectangles.
    c. Find a location based on the midpoints of two objects.
    d. Precisely pick a point without using an object snap.

4. How are points specified in the AutoCAD Cartesian workspace?

    a. X value x Y value
    b. Y value, X value
    c. X value, Y value
    d. X value - Y value

5. With Dynamic Input toggled off, after you pick the first corner for a rectangle, what are the typed coordinates that can be used to make it 20 units long and 8 units high?

    a. 20,8
    b. @8,20
    c. 8,20
    d. @20,8

6. What does @ represent in the AutoCAD software?

    a. Indicates that Object Snap is going to be used.

    b. Indicates that a temporary tracking point is going to be used.

    c. Indicates from the last point entered or picked.

    d. Used in place of 0.

Answers: 1a, 2b, 3a, 4c, 5d, 6c

A.3 Modify Objects

1. The **Move**, **Copy**, **Rotate**, and **Scale** commands use a base point, which is always the center or a midpoint of an object.

    a. True
    b. False

2. When selecting objects for a command, such as **Move** or **Copy**, how do you end the object selection?

    a. Press <Alt>.
    b. Press <Esc>.
    c. Press <Ctrl>.
    d. Press <Enter>.

3. How can you paste AutoCAD objects into a drawing at the same location as in the drawing from which they were copied?

    a. Select **Edit>Paste Special** in the Application Menu.
    b. Right-click and select **Paste to Original Coordinates**.
    c. Right-click and select **Paste as Block**.
    d. Select **Edit>Paste Special** in the Menu Browser.

4. What happens to the selected objects in the active **Rotate** command?

    a. The original objects fade to gray and the new objects maintain their original properties.
    b. The original objects maintain their original properties and the new objects fade to gray.
    c. The original objects are highlighted with a thicker line weight and the new objects fade to gray.
    d. The original objects maintain their original properties and the new objects are highlighted with a thicker line weight.

5. Which Scale Factor should you use to make an object half of its current size?

    a. -2.0
    b. 0.5
    c. 0.2
    d. -0.5

Review Questions

6. Which command would you use to array a number of trees around an irregularly-shaped pond?

    a. **Polar Array**
    b. **Path Array**
    c. **Spline Array**
    d. **Rectangular Array**

7. When you start the **Trim** command, what do you select first?

    a. The trimming distance.
    b. The objects to trim.
    c. The cutting edge(s).
    d. The base point.

8. Which of the following commands creates parallel objects of the selected objects?

    a. **Fillet**
    b. **Mirror**
    c. **Offset**
    d. **Extend**

9. What is the default mode of the hot grips of a circle?

    a. A quadrant hot grip stretches the circle whereas the center hot grip moves the circle.
    b. A quadrant hot grip moves the circle whereas the center hot grip stretches the circle.
    c. Both the quadrant hot grip and the center hot grip stretch/scale the circle.
    d. Both the quadrant hot grip and the center hot grip move the circle.

10. When selecting an object and then a grip, which of the following commands is started by default?

    a. **Stretch**
    b. **Copy**
    c. **Scale**
    d. **Move**

11. Which **Chamfer** option creates beveled edges at all of the vertices of a selected polyline?

   a. Angle
   b. Multiple
   c. Method
   d. Polyline

12. What do you need to set before you apply a fillet in your drawing?

   a. Distance
   b. Radius
   c. Angle
   d. Thickness

13. You can fillet two parallel lines to add an arc tangent to both lines.

   a. True
   b. False

Answers: 1b, 2d, 3b, 4a, 5b, 6b, 7c, 8c, 9a, 10a, 11d, 12b, 13a

A.4 Use Additional Drawing Techniques

1. Which of the following is NOT true for a polyline?
   a. The segments are all considered to be one object.
   b. It cannot include arcs.
   c. It can have varying widths in each segment.
   d. They can be open or closed.

2. Which command breaks a polyline into individual line and arc segments?
   a. **Break**
   b. **Explode**
   c. **Edit Polyline**
   d. **Snap**

3. Which command enables you to convert regular lines into a polyline?
   a. **Union**
   b. **Edit Polyline**
   c. **Join**
   d. **Make Polyline**

4. Polygons are built from polylines and can be modified using the **Edit Polyline** command.
   a. True
   b. False

5. A series of continuous line and/or arc segments that act as one unified object is a:
   a. Rectangle
   b. Construction Line
   c. Polyline
   d. Block

6. Which command enables you to create the more exact spline shape?
   a. **Spline** (within the **Edit Polyline** command)
   b. **Spline Fit**

7. In the *Hatch Creation* contextual tab, which tool do you use to specify an area of the drawing that you want to hatch?
   a. **Inherit Properties**
   b. **Island Detection**
   c. **Remove Islands**
   d. **Pick Points**

8. To hatch an area in a drawing, it must be...
   a. On the layer named **Hatch**.
   b. A closed area.
   c. A single polyline.
   d. Set to **Annotative**.

9. Increasing the *Hatch Angle* value creates an angled hatch pattern.
   a. True
   b. False

10. How do you find the area of a Hatch?
    a. Use the **Measure** command.
    b. Use the **Area** command.
    c. Select the hatch to display its area in the Properties palette.
    d. Use the **Distance** command.

11. What happens when an associative hatch is selected?
    a. Grips display at each of the boundary corners.
    b. Grips display at the midpoints of the boundary edges.
    c. Grips display at the centroid of the hatch and the midpoints of the boundary edges.
    d. A single grip displays at the centroid of the hatch.

12. Which option do you use to create new vertices on non-associative hatch boundaries?
    a. Remove vertex
    b. Convert to arc
    c. Add vertex
    d. New vertex

Answers: 1b, 2b, 3b, 4a, 5c, 6b, 7d, 8b, 9a, 10c, 11d, 12c

A.5 Organize Objects

1. One of the differences between List and the Properties palette is that with **List** you can only view the information, while with the Properties palette you can edit some of the information to modify the object.

    a. True
    b. False

2. When you select multiple objects, the Properties palette only displays which of the following?

    a. Their colors and layers.
    b. Their lineweights and linetypes.
    c. The properties that they have in common.
    d. Their X and Y values.

3. How do you move an existing object to a different layer?

    a. Recreate the object on the correct layer.
    b. Use the **Move** command.
    c. Change the current layer, select the object, and press <Enter>.
    d. Select the object and pick the required layer in the Layer Control.

4. After creating an object, how do you locate it on the same layer as another object in the drawing?

    a. Use **Match Layer**.
    b. Change the current layer.
    c. Use **Make Current (Layer)**.
    d. Redraw it on the correct layer.

5. When objects do not display on a specific layer and do not regenerated with the drawing, the layer is:

    a. Thawed
    b. Current
    c. Frozen
    d. Locked

6. What is the purpose of Layer States?
   a. To save a configuration of layers and layer properties.
   b. To control the objects on a layer.
   c. To control which layers are contained in a drawing.
   d. To change the names of layers in a drawing.

7. You cannot import layer states from drawing templates.
   a. True
   b. False

8. Objects on layers that are frozen stay displayed in the drawing but cannot be edited.
   a. True
   b. False

9. If you have finished drawing the walls in a floor plan drawing and want to display the objects, but do not want them to be erased or moved, what should you do?
   a. Lock the layer.
   b. Make a different layer current.
   c. Toggle the layer off.
   d. Freeze the layer.

10. What is a function of the **Layer Walk** command?
    a. Toggle the visibility of layers on and off by selecting them in the LayerWalk dialog box.
    b. Change the properties of a layer.
    c. Change the layer on which an object is located.
    d. Create new layers in the LayerWalk dialog box.

11. How do you remove columns that you do not want to display in the Layer Properties Manager?
    a. Select the column and press <Delete>.
    b. Right-click on the column and select **Delete**.
    c. Drag-and-drop the column out of the Layer Properties Manager.
    d. Right-click on the header and clear the checkmark next to the column name.

Answers: 1a, 2c, 3d, 4a, 5c, 6a, 7b, 8b, 9a, 10a, 11d

A.6 Reuse Existing Content

1. What are some advantages of using blocks? (Select all that apply.)
    a. Consistency of standard details and parts.
    b. Easier to select than separate objects.
    c. Can only be placed in the drawing where it was created.
    d. Reduced file size.

2. When inserting a block with the **Insert** command, which parameters must be specified?
    a. Insertion point, scale, and rotation angle.
    b. Angle, distance, and scale.
    c. Date and time.
    d. Insertion point, distance, and angle.

3. How can you insert another drawing into your current drawing file?
    a. Use the **Winsert** command.
    b. Use the **Make Block** command.
    c. Use the **Browse** button in the **Insert** command.
    d. You cannot insert a drawing into your current drawing file.

4. You can use Tool Palettes to insert blocks into the drawing by dragging and dropping.
    a. True
    b. False

5. What can you do using the DesignCenter?
    a. Return a layer to its previous state.
    b. Search for and drag and drop a block into your drawing.
    c. Create template files.
    d. Explode blocks into separate line segments.

6. Some dynamic blocks display the following modification grips:

    a. The grips are the same in every dynamic block.

    b. Explode, Move, and Align.

    c. Explode, List, and Scale.

    d. Flip, Rotate, and List.

7. When you define a block, you specify a base point. Which of the following are true about the base point?

    a. It is the handle that you use when inserting the block.

    b. It is always at 0,0.

    c. It is always at the center of the block.

    d. It is the point used to select the block objects.

8. Which command creates a separate drawing file from selected objects, that can be used in other drawings?

    a. **Make Block**

    b. **Wblock**

    c. **Purge**

    d. **Annotative Block**

9. If you change the definition of a block, what happens to any instances of that block that were already inserted in the drawing?

    a. They are automatically renamed.

    b. They are erased.

    c. They change to match the new definition.

    d. Nothing.

10. After adding blocks from a drawing to a Tool Palette, it does not matter if you move or delete the source drawing file.

    a. True

    b. False

11. Which of the following can you set in the Tool Properties for inserting a block?
    a. Offset
    b. Rotation
    c. Freeze
    d. Flip

12. If a layer that is specified in the Tool Properties of a block does not exist in the current drawing, what happens when you insert that block into that drawing?
    a. The block is inserted on layer 0.
    b. The block cannot be inserted into that drawing.
    c. You are prompted for a new name for the layer.
    d. The layer is automatically created in the drawing.

13. What type of object are attributes always associated with?
    a. Blocks
    b. Layers
    c. Text objects
    d. Any geometric objects

14. What are possible uses for attributes? (Select all that apply.)
    a. Tag labels on blocks.
    b. Store information, such as part numbers in drawing.
    c. Explode all of the blocks.
    d. Extract information from drawings for parts lists, inventory, etc.

15. What is the quickest way of editing attribute values in a block?
    a. Explode the block.
    b. Use **Edit Text**.
    c. Use the Block Attribute Manager.
    d. Double-click on the block.

16. Which Attribute Mode controls whether an attribute value normally displays in a drawing?
    a. Invisible
    b. Preset
    c. Constant
    d. Lock Position

17. When extracting attribute information from blocks, what can you write the data to?
    a. An AutoCAD table.
    b. A DWF file.
    c. A web page.
    d. Another block.

18. If you add an attribute to a block after it has been created, which command do you use to update the existing blocks in a drawing?
    a. **Update Block**
    b. **Synchronize Attributes**
    c. **Edit Attributes**
    d. **Data Extraction**

19. To create an attribute that cannot be modified when it is inserted with a block, set the Attribute Mode to...
    a. **Invisible**
    b. **Preset**
    c. **Verify**
    d. **Constant**

20. Which of the following describes how External References are different from blocks? An External Reference...
    a. Can contain one or many objects.
    b. Is a link to another file.
    c. Includes layers.
    d. Acts as one object in the drawing.

21. File types that can be used as Eternal References include: AutoCAD drawing files, raster image files, DWF underlay files, DGN underlay files, and PDF underlay files.

    a. True
    b. False

22. What happens when you open a drawing containing a referenced file that cannot be located by the software? (Select all that apply.)

    a. The References - Not Found Files dialog box opens.
    b. An exclamation mark (!) displays next to the drawing in the External References palette.
    c. It becomes a block.
    d. It is compressed to take up less memory.

23. Which of the following file formats cannot attach to an AutoCAD drawing as an external reference?

    a. .DWF
    b. .DOC
    c. .DWG
    d. .DGN

24. Drawing A is attached as a drawing reference file to host drawing B and both are then closed.
    Drawing A is then modified.
    Drawing B is opened and displays an image of drawing A. What happens to the image of drawing A when drawing B is opened?

    a. It displays a warning message.
    b. It does not change.
    c. It updates to display the changes.
    d. It displays as a blank image.

25. Which command or option enables you to bind one or more blocks, layers, linetypes, text styles, or dimension styles?

    a. **Reload**
    b. **Demand Load**
    c. **Bind**
    d. **Xbind**

Answers: 1a,b,d, 2a, 3c, 4a, 5b, 6d, 7a, 8b, 9c, 10b, 11b, 12d, 13a, 14a,b,d, 15d, 16a, 17a, 18b, 19d, 20b, 21a, 22a,b, 23b, 24c, 25d

A.7 Annotate Drawings

1. When creating Multiline text, you pick two points. What do those points determine?
   a. The text height.
   b. The text location and width of the lines.
   c. The rotation angle of the text.
   d. The thickness of the text.

2. Using the **Import Text** tool located in the *Text Editor* contextual tab>expanded Tools panel, the text that is imported does not include formatting.
   a. True
   b. False

3. What happens when you double-click on a text object?
   a. It opens the Properties palette.
   b. It opens the text for editing.
   c. It explodes the text.
   d. It updates the text to the current text style.

4. How do you add a text frame around a multiline text?
   a. By drawing a rectangle separately and adding it to the multiline text properties.
   b. Selecting **Outline** in the *Text Editor* contextual tab.
   c. Setting the *Text Frame* to **Yes** in the Properties palette.
   d. You cannot add a text frame to the multiline text.

5. When editing text, how do you change the justification of the multiline text object (left, right, centered, etc.)?
   a. Edit the Text Style.
   b. Click the ruler above the editing frame.
   c. You cannot change the justification after the text is created.
   d. Tools in the *Text Editor* contextual tab>Paragraph panel in the ribbon.

6. Which command would you use to display the length of a diagonal line so that the dimension line is parallel to the diagonal line (Aligned dimension)?
   a. **Dimension**
   b. **Quick Dimension**
   c. **Baseline Dimension**
   d. **Adjust Space**

7. Dimensions recalculate automatically when the objects they refer to are modified.
   a. True
   b. False

8. The **Center Mark** tool adds an associative center mark at the center of which objects? (Select all that apply.)
   a. Lines
   b. Polylines
   c. Circles
   d. Polygonal arcs

9. Which command would you use to create an arc length dimension from one end point of an arc to the other end point along the curve of the arc?
   a. **Dimension**
   b. **Quick Dimension**
   c. **Baseline Dimension**
   d. **Ordinate Dimension**

10. How would you move a dimension so that the dimension line is farther away from the object?
    a. Use the **Move** command.
    b. Use the **Baseline Dimension** command.
    c. Use grips to stretch the dimension.
    d. Use the **Dimension Update** command.

11. Which command do you use to clean up overlapping dimension lines?

    a. **Adjust Space**
    b. **Dimension Cleanup**
    c. **Dimension Break**
    d. **Jogged**

12. Which of the following statements is true regarding multileaders?

    a. The leader and text (or block) of a multileader are separate objects.
    b. The square grip at the end of the leader line moves the multileader.
    c. The square grip at the top left of the text moves the multileader.
    d. The arrow grip on the landing of the leader line changes the location to which the leader line is pointing.

13. To collect several multileaders together into one leader, the multileaders should have:

    a. Block content only.
    b. Text content only.
    c. String content only.
    d. Both block and text content.

14. What are dimension sub-styles used for?

    a. To override the dimension style settings for a particular type of dimension, such as angle or radius.
    b. To automatically dimension specific objects, such as rectangles and circles.
    c. To link dimensions to specific layers.
    d. To copy dimension styles between drawings.

15. You have a dimension style that uses decimal units and you want to change it to use fractional units. What do you do?

    a. Modify the *Alternate Units* in the dimension style.
    b. Modify the *Primary Units* in the dimension style.
    c. Edit the text of the dimension and change the value.
    d. Edit the *Fit* settings in the dimension style.

Review Questions

16. When creating a Text Style, Dimension Style, or Multileader Style, you want the size of the text and other objects to scale automatically according to the scale of the viewport in which they are used. In the related Style Manager, which of the following options would you set?

    a. **Text Size**
    b. **Alternate Units**
    c. **Scale Text**
    d. **Annotative**

17. If you want to display an annotative object in several viewports that use different scales, what should you do?

    a. Create separate layers for each viewport and put the objects on each layer.
    b. Create annotative styles (dimension, text, etc.) for each viewport.
    c. Use **Add/Delete Scales** to add the scales for each viewport.
    d. Lock each viewport.

18. What are the annotation scales linked to such that the annotative objects (e.g. dimensions and texts) display in the layout viewports that have the same scale?

    a. Dimension Style
    b. Text Style
    c. Linetype scale factor
    d. Viewport Scale

19. What object types can be contained in a table? (Select all that apply.)

    a. Text
    b. Blocks
    c. Fields
    d. Lines

20. When a table is selected, what does the square grip do?
    a. Breaks the link between the table and the Excel spreadsheet.
    b. Resizes the column width in the table.
    c. Uniformly stretches the table width.
    d. Uniformly stretches the table height.

21. You can create an AutoCAD table that is linked to data in an Excel spreadsheet.
    a. True
    b. False

22. How do you update a linked AutoCAD table from an external source file?
    a. **Create Table**
    b. **Link** Cell
    c. **Download from Source**
    d. **Upload from Source**

23. When you create a table, you can use a Data Link. To which type of file does the Data Link connect?
    a. Excel spreadsheet
    b. Google docs
    c. Word document
    d. Access database

24. Select the properties for which you can define a Table Style. (Select all that apply.)
    a. Number of rows and columns
    b. Cell margins
    c. Table direction
    d. Border properties

Review Questions

25. In the New Table Style dialog box, in the *General* area, which *Table direction* option locates the Title and Header rows at the top of the table?

    a. Up
    b. Down
    c. Top
    d. Bottom

    Answers: 1b, 2a, 3b, 4c, 5d, 6a, 7a, 8c,d, 9a, 10c, 11c, 12c, 13a, 14a, 15b, 16d, 17c, 18d, 19a,b,c, 20b, 21a, 22c, 23a, 24b,c,d, 25b

A.8 Layouts and Printing

1. Once you have scaled a viewport, how do you prevent the scale from being changed?
    a. Explode the viewport.
    b. Lock the viewport.
    c. Freeze all layers in the drawing.
    d. Lock the layer that the viewport is on.

2. When you copy a layout, which of the following is true of the new layout?
    a. Everything in the new layout matches the original layout.
    b. The new layout is always added at the end of all of the other layouts.
    c. The new layout is always empty and you need to setup the new layout.
    d. Only the title block is copied over from the original layout into the copied layout.

3. How can you modify the viewports? (Select all that apply.)
    a. Using grips.
    b. Using the Insert Layout dialog box.
    c. Using the standard AutoCAD editing commands, such as **Copy**, **Move** etc.
    d. You cannot modify the viewports once they are created.

4. Which of the following is true with respect to viewports in a layout?
    a. You cannot create multiple overlapping viewports.
    b. You can create multiple viewports only if they are of the same shape and size.
    c. You can create multiple viewports in various shapes and sizes.
    d. You can create only one viewport per layout.

Review Questions

5. What is the purpose of the View Manager?
   a. To create layouts using different areas of a drawing.
   b. To create a new block using selected objects.
   c. To create a new drawing file using selected objects.
   d. To store areas of a drawing under specified names.

6. It is possible to create a single or multiple Named View viewports at the same time.
   a. True
   b. False

7. What does the (Clip) command do?
   a. Fillets the corners of an existing viewport to make it circular.
   b. Removes the portions of a viewport that are not required.
   c. Joins multiple viewports to create a single one.
   d. Breaks a viewport to create multiple viewports.

8. How can you change the color of a layer in a single (current) viewport?
   a. In the Layer Properties Manager, change the *VP Color* property.
   b. In the Layer Properties Manager, change the *New VP Freeze* property.
   c. In the viewport, switch to Model space and change the color of the layer.
   d. Create a new layer and move the objects to the new layer.

9. With Model Space printing, it is very easy to print multiple views of the same drawing at different scales.
   a. True
   b. False

10. What does the dashed boundary on a layout represent?
    a. The printable area.
    b. The active viewport.
    c. The default viewport.
    d. The model space.

11. To plot a layout, what scale should you typically use in the *Plot Scale* area in the Plot dialog box?

    a. 1:1
    b. Custom
    c. Any standard scale
    d. Scale to fit

12. What is determined when you select the plotter first in the Plot-Model dialog box?

    a. Plot area
    b. Paper size
    c. Plot Scale
    d. Plot offset

13. When you plot from the *Model* tab, which *What to plot* option in the *Plot* area automatically plots all of the drawn objects?

    a. **Display**
    b. **Window**
    c. **Extents**
    d. **View**

14. Which of the following can you do using the preview of a plot?

    a. Modify objects in the drawing.
    b. Zoom or pan around the drawing.
    c. Only preview a portion of the entire drawing.
    d. Delete viewports from a layout.

15. In the Plot dialog box, which *What to plot* option do you set in the *Plot* area to plot the objects that are currently displayed in the drawing window?

    a. **Extents**
    b. **Window**
    c. **Layout**
    d. **Display**

Review Questions

16. What is a DWF file?
    a. A plot style table file.
    b. An AutoCAD system file that controls plot settings.
    c. A backup copy of a drawing file.
    d. A compressed file format for viewing drawings.

17. What information about data can be included when exporting drawing files to PDF files? (Select all that apply.)
    a. **Layer information**
    b. **Linetype information**
    c. **Fonts**
    d. **Hyperlinks**

18. Which tool can you use to plot several drawings at once to a DWF file, PDF file, or to paper?
    a. **Plotter Manager**
    b. **Export**
    c. **Plotter Wizard**
    d. **Batch Plot/Publish**

19. The **Batch Plot** command can add all the open drawings to the Sheet list, excluding their *Model* tabs.
    a. True
    b. False

Answers: 1b, 2a, 3a,c, 4c, 5d, 6a, 7b, 8a, 9b, 10a, 11a, 12b, 13c, 14b, 15d, 16d, 17a,c,d, 18d, 19b

Index

#
2018 Enhancements
    BIMobject **6-12**
    External References
        Change Path Type **6-86**
        Not Found Files **6-81**
        Path Type **6-85**
        Reloading Files **6-90**
        Select New Path **6-86**
    Quick Access Toolbar **5-32**
    Rubber-Band Line Color **3-5**

A
A360 Viewer **6-88**
Absolute Cartesian Coordinates **2-20**
Annotation Scale **7-67**, **7-98**
    Model Space **7-69**, **7-103**
    Model Text Height **7-67**
    Paper Space **7-67**
    Paper Text Height **7-67**
Annotation Styles **7-68**
Annotation Visibility **7-102**
Annotative Object Scale
    Add/Delete Scale **7-104**
    Modify **7-103**
Annotative Objects **7-103**
    Automatically Add Scales **7-102**
Annotative Scale
    Annotation Visibility **7-92**
    Automatically Add Scales **7-92**
    Modify **7-93**
Annotative Styles **7-99**
Arc **1-19**
Array
    Path **3-24**
    Polar **3-21**
    Rectangular **3-21**
Attributes **6-40**
    Associate with Blocks **6-54**
    Components **6-52**
    Define **6-51**
    Edit **6-43**
    Extract **6-65**
    Insert **6-40**
    Insertion Point **6-53**
    Manage **6-58**
    Modes **6-53**
    Synchronize **6-61**
    Text Settings **6-53**
    Update Blocks **6-60**
    Visibility **6-41**
Autodesk Seek **6-12**

B
Batch Plot/Publish **8-48**
BIMobject **6-12**
Blocks **6-2**
    Add from Tool Palettes **6-31**
    Annotative **6-21**
    Base Point **6-20**
    Create Block **6-19**
    Dynamic blocks **6-4**
    Editing **6-24**
    Exploding **6-26**
    Insert Command **6-6**
    Insert from DesignCenter **6-11**
    Insert from Tool Palettes **6-8**
    Layers **6-3**
    Manipulating **6-4**
    Object Snap **6-7**
    Tool Palettes **6-32**
    Wblock **6-22**
Break **3-34**
Break at Point **3-34**
ByLayer **5-33**

C
Cartesian Coordinates **2-18**
    Absolute **2-20**
    Angles **2-19**
    Relative **2-20**
Cell Style **7-135**
Center Mark **7-41**
Centerline **7-41**
Chamfer **3-57**

Circle **1-8**
Clipboard
    Copy **3-6**
    Cut **3-6**
    Paste **3-6**
Command
    Mirror **3-39**
    Polyline **4-2**
Coordinate Entry **2-20**
Coordinates
    Cartesian **2-18**
    Cartesian Angles **2-19**
Copy **3-4**
    Clipboard **3-6**
    Objects to New Layer **5-38**
Cut to Clipboard **3-6**

D

Data Extraction **6-65**
Data Link Manager **7-129**
DesignCenter **6-11**
Dimension **7-31**
    Adjust Space **7-53**
    Aligned **7-33**
    Angular **7-44**
    Arc Length **7-44**
    Baseline **7-35**
    Breaks **7-54**
    Center Marks **7-41**
    Centerlines **7-41**
    Command **7-32**
    Diameter **7-40**
    Edit Text **7-52**
    Grips **7-50**
    Jogged Linear **7-34**
    Jogged Radial **7-43**
    Linear **7-33**
    Oblique **7-34**
    Quick Dimension **7-36**
    Shortcut Menu **7-50**
    Spacing **7-53**
Dimension Style
    Alternate Units Tab **7-81**
    Annotative **7-74**
    Create **7-74**
    Modify **7-76**
    Standard **7-74**
    Sub-Styles **7-81**
    Tolerances Tab **7-81**
Drafting Settings
    Polar Tracking **2-2**
DWF **8-48**
DWFx **8-48**
Dynamic Blocks **6-4**
Dynamic Input **1-3**, **2-20**, **2-22**

E

Edit
    Hatch **4-23**
    Multiline Text **7-10**
    Polyline **4-4**
    Text **7-10**
Export
    DWF **8-50**
    Layouts **8-50**
    PDF **8-50**
Extend **3-34**
External References **6-80**
    Attachment **6-98**
    Binding **6-101**
    Clip Frames **6-92**
    Clipping **6-91**
    Demand Loading **6-103**
    Detach **6-89**
    DWF **6-96**
    Images **6-95**
    Modifying References **6-93**
    Open **6-88**
    Overlays **6-98**
    Palette **6-82**
    Properties **6-95**
    Reload **6-90**
    Underlays **6-95**
    Unload **6-89**
    Xbind **6-102**
    Xref Layers **6-99**
Extract Data **6-65**

F

Fillet **3-56**

G

Grips
    Changing the Base Point **3-48**
    Copying With **3-48**
    Dynamic Dimensions **3-45**
    Edit **3-47**
    Edit Dimensions **7-50**
    Hot **3-43**
    Multi-functional **3-44**
    Multileader **7-59**
    Options **3-44**
    Reference Option **3-49**
    Settings **3-50**
    Stretch Multiple **3-50**
    Text **7-10**

H

Hatch **4-13**
    Annotative **4-20**
    Apply with Hatch command **4-15**
    Apply with Tool Palettes **4-14**

Index

Area **4-22**
Associative **4-20**
Boundaries **4-25**
Edit Hatch **4-23**
Layer Override **4-19**
Options **4-20**
Origin **4-19**
Pattern **4-16**
Properties **4-16**
Type **4-17**

I
Insert block **6-6**
Isometric Snap **2-26**

J
Join **4-7**

L
Layer **5-31**, **5-44**
   ByLayer **5-33**
   Change Layers **5-14**
   Change to Current Layer **5-37**
   Copy Objects to New Layer **5-38**
   Current Layer **5-32**
   Filtering Layers **5-40**
   Freeze in New Viewports **5-62**
   Layer Delete **5-39**
   Layer Isolate **5-36**
   Layer Merge **5-39**
   Layer Previous **5-37**
   Layer Settings **5-60**
   Layer States **5-18**, **5-34**
   Layer Unisolate **5-37**
   Layer Walk **5-39**
   Linetypes **5-48**
   Lineweight **5-47**
   Load Linetypes **5-48**
   Modify **5-38**
   New VP Freeze **5-62**
   Overrides **5-62**
   Previous **5-19**
   Reconcile New Layers **5-61**
   Set Current Layer **5-32**
Layer Properties Manager **5-44**, **5-57**
   Columns **5-57**
   Reconcile **5-61**
Layer States **5-34**
   Create New **5-23**
   Edit **5-25**
   Import **5-26**
   Restore **5-24**
Layer States Manager **5-23**
Layouts **8-2**
   Model Space **8-4**
   Paper Space **8-4**
   Template **8-7**
   Viewports **8-4**
Line **1-2**
   Options **1-3**
Linetype Scale **5-48**

M
Match Properties **3-7**, **5-7**
Mirror **3-38**
Model Space **8-4**
   Print **8-36**
Modifying Viewports **8-19**
Move **3-2**
Multileader **7-57**
   Add Leader **7-60**
   Align **7-62**
   Collect **7-63**
   Modify **7-59**
Multileader Style **7-86**
   Create **7-86**
   Modify **7-86**
   Multileader type **7-88**
Multiline Text **7-2**
   Columns **7-24**
   Copy **7-4**
   Edit Text **7-10**
   Formatting **7-17**
   Grips **7-10**
   Import **7-4**
   Spell Checking **7-5**
Multiple Drawings
   Match Properties **3-7**

N
Named Views **8-9**
Nudge **3-3**

O
Object Snap **2-12**
   Tracking **2-6**
Object Snap Tracking **2-12**
Offset **3-39**
Ortho Mode **1-6**

P
Palettes
   Properties **5-3**
   Tool Palettes **6-8**
Paper Space **8-5**
   Print **8-37**
Paste from Clipboard **3-6**
Plot **8-35**, **8-38**
   DWF **8-49**
   DWFx **8-49**
   Electronic Files **8-49**
   Layouts **8-38**

PDF **8-49**
Plot Area **8-42**
Plot Offset **8-43**
Plot Scale **8-43**
Preview **8-40**
Polar Coordinates
    Relative **2-22**
Polar Tracking **1-4, 2-2**
Polygon **1-23**
Polyline
    Convert Line and Arc **4-6**
    Vertex **4-5**
    Width **4-4**
Print **8-35**
    Check Plot **8-41**
    Layouts **8-38**
    Model Space **8-36**
    Paper Space **8-37**
Properties
    Change Text **7-11**
    Match Properties **5-7**
    Modify Objects **5-4**
    Multiple Objects **5-6**
    Properties Palette **5-3**
    Quick Properties **5-2**
    Quick Select **5-8**
Properties Panel **5-33**
Publish
    Drawing Set **8-53**
    Sheet Lists Files **8-55**

Q
Quick Properties **5-2**
Quick Select **5-8**

R
Recognize SHX Text **6-87**
Rectangle **1-7**
Relative Cartesian Coordinates **2-20**
Relative Polar Coordinates **2-22**
Rotate **3-11**

S
Scale List **7-105**
Shortcut Menu
    Dimension **7-51**
    Editing Commands **3-5**
shx Fonts **8-51**
Spell Checking **7-5, 7-12**

T
Table **7-110**
    Calculations **7-114**
    Cell Locking **7-120**
    Cell Style **7-135**
    Cell Styles **7-120**
    Create **7-110**

Create from Data Link **7-127**
Create Style **7-133**
Data Format **7-120**
Data Link **7-127**
Data Link Manager **7-129**
Fill in Cells **7-112**
Grips **7-118, 7-122**
Insert Blocks **7-113**
Insert Fields **7-113**
Insert Formulas **7-113**
Link Spreadsheet **7-126**
Merge Cells **7-119**
Modify **7-118**
Style Options **7-134**
Updating Links **7-131**
Table Style **7-133**
Templates
    Layout **8-7**
Temporary Tracking Point **2-12**
Text
    Multiline Text (See Multiline Text)
    Style
        Annotative **7-70**
        Create **7-71**
        Standard **7-70**
        Style Effects **7-72**
Tool Palettes **6-8**
    Add Blocks **6-32**
    Creating **6-31**
    DesignCenter **6-33**
    Docking **6-9**
    Insert Blocks **6-8**
    Modify **6-34**
    New **6-31**
    Redefine Blocks **6-36**
    Tool Properties **6-34**
Tracking **2-12**
Trim **3-31**
    Select Objects **3-33**

U
User Coordinate System **2-24**

V
View **8-8**
    Create Named View **8-9**
View Manager **8-8**
Viewports **8-16**
    Clip Viewport **8-15**
    Create **8-16**
    Lock **8-20**
    Modify Layer Properties **8-22**
    Named Views **8-11**
    New **8-11**
    Override Layer Properties **8-21**
    Scaling **8-19**

W
Wblock **6-23**

X
X,Y Coordinates **2-18**
Xbind **6-102**
Xref (See External References)